op Music and Easy Listening

The Library of Essays on Popular Music

Series Editor: Allan F. Moore

Pop Music and Easy Listening

Edited by

Stan Hawkins

University of Oslo, Norway

ASHGATE

Wherever possible, these reprints are made from a copy of the original printing, but these can themselv be of very variable quality. Whilst the publisher has made every effort to ensure the quality of the reprint some variability may inevitably remain.

Published by
Ashgate Publishing Limited
Wey Court East
Union Road
Farnham
Surrey GU9 7PT
England

Ashgate Publishing Company
Suite 420
101 Cherry Street
Burlington
VT 05401-4405
USA

www.ashgate.com

British Library Cataloguing in Publication Data
Pop music and easy listening. – (The library of essays on popular music)
   1. Popular music–History and criticism. 2. Popular music–Philosophy and aesthetics. 3. Popular music–Social aspects.
   I. Series
   781.6'4-dc22

Library of Congress Control Number: 2011920550

ISBN: 9780754629528

MIX
Paper from
responsible sources
FSC   FSC® C013056
www.fsc.org

Printed and bound in Great Britain by
TJ International Ltd, Padstow, Cornwall.

Contents

PART III SUBJECTIVITY, ETHNICITY AND POLITICS

Acknowledgements

e editor and publishers wish to thank the following for permission to use copyright material.

mbridge University Press for the essays: Antoine Hennion (1983), 'The Production Success: An Anti-Musicology of the Pop Song', *Popular Music*, **3**, pp. 159–93; Robert ft (2010), 'Hits and Misses: Crafting a Pop Single for the Top-40 Market in the 1960s', *pular Music*, **29**, pp. 267–81; Anne Danielsen and Arnt Maasø (2009), 'Mediating *Music*: teriality and Silence in Madonna's "Don't Tell Me"', *Popular Music*, **28**, pp. 127–42; rk Hustwitt (1983), '"Caught in a Whirlpool of Aching Sound": The Production of Dance sic in Britain in the 1920s', *Popular Music*, **3**, pp. 7–31; Dale Chapman (2008), '"That Ill, ;ht Sound": Telepresence and Biopolitics in Post-Timbaland Rap Production', *Journal of* ? *Society for American Music*, **2**, pp. 155–75. Copyright © 2004 The Society for American sic, published by Cambridge University Press; Eric F. Clarke and Nicola Dibben (2000), 2x, Pulp and Critique', *Popular Music*, **19**, pp. 231–41; Martin Cloonan (1999), 'Pop and ? Nation-State: Towards a Theorisation', *Popular Music*, **18**, pp. 193–207; Kay Dickinson)01), 'Believe'? Vocoders, Digitalised Female Identity and Camp, *Popular Music*, **20**, pp. 3–47.

nter for Black Music Research for the essay: Jon Fitzgerald (2007), 'Black Pop Songwriting 63–1966: An Analysis of U.S. Top Forty Hits by Cooke, Mayfield, Stevenson, Robinson, d Holland-Dozier-Holland', *Black Music Research Journal*, **27**, pp. 97–140.

n Wiley and Sons for the essays: Leslie M. Meier (2008), 'In Excess? Body Genres, "Bad" sic, and the Judgment of Audiences', *Journal of Popular Music Studies*, **20**, pp. 240–60; drew Goodwin (1988), 'Sample and Hold: Pop Music in the Digital Age of Reproduction', *itical Quarterly*, **30**, pp. 34–49; Susan Fast and Karen Pegley (2006), 'Music and Canadian tionhood Post 9/11: An Analysis of *Music Without Borders: Live*', *Journal of Popular sic Studies*, **18**, pp. 18–39. Copyright © 2006 the Authors. Journal compilation copyright 2006 Blackwell Publishing, Inc.; John Richardson (2005), '"The Digital Won't Let Me ?": Constructions of the Virtual and the Real in Gorillaz' "Clint Eastwood"', *Journal of pular Music Studies*, **17**, pp. 1–29; David Sanjek (1999), 'Navigating the "Channel": cent Scholarship on African-American Popular Music', *Journal of Popular Music Studies*, pp. 167–92.

w Left Review for the essay: Simon Frith and Jon Savage (1993), 'Pearls and Swine: The ellectuals and the Mass Media', *New Left Review*, **198**, pp. 107–16.

ge Publications for the essay: Simon Frith (1986), 'Art versus Technology: The Strange se of Popular Music', *Media, Culture & Society*, **8**, pp. 263–79.

Series Preface

From its rather modest beginnings in the 1950s, the study of popular music has now developed to such a degree that many academic institutions worldwide employ specialists in the field. Even those that do not will often still make space on crowded higher education curricula for the investigation of what has become not only one of the most lucrative spheres of human activity, but one of the most influential on the identities of individuals and communities. Popular music matters, and it matters to so many people, people we can only partially understand if we do not understand their music. It is for this reason that this series is timely.

This is not the place to try to offer a definition of popular music; that is one of the purposes of the essays collected in the volumes in this series. Through their Popular and Folk Music series of monographs, Ashgate has gained a strong reputation as a publisher of scholarship in the field. This Library of Essays on Popular Music is partly envisioned as a complement to that series, focusing on writing of shorter length. But the series is also intended to develop the volume of Critical Essays in Popular Musicology published in 2007, in that it provides comprehensive coverage of the world's popular musics in eight volumes, each of which has a substantial introductory essay by the volume's editor. It develops the Critical Essays volume in that it makes overt recognition of the fact that the study of popular music is necessarily inter-disciplinary. Thus, within the limits set by the genre coverage of each individual volume, and by the excellence of the essays available for inclusion, each editor has been asked to keep an eye on issues as diverse as: the popular music industry and its institutions; aspects of history of their respective genres; issues in the theories and methodologies of study and practice; questions of the ontologies and hermeneutics of their fields; the varying influence of different waves of technological development; the ways markets and audiences are constructed, produced and reached and, last but not least; aspects of the repertory without which there would be no popular music to study. As a result, no disciplinary perspective is privileged. As far as possible, no genre is privileged either. Because the study of rock largely led the growth of popular music study, the genre has produced a very large amount of material; it needs a volume to itself. Much writing on jazz tends to circumscribe the genre clearly arguing that it, too, needs a volume to itself. Other forms of music have been distributed across the remaining volumes: one on electronica; one on forms of mainstream pop (still frequently omitted from academic surveys); one on specific North American forms which lead to hip-hop; one on the appearance of popular music within other (particularly visual) media; and two final volumes covering 'world' and 'roots', musics whose relationship with more obviously industrialized forms is most particularly problematic. While this categorization of the world's popular musics is not perfect (and is variously addressed in individual volumes), it is no worse than any other, and it does enable the inclusion of all those academic essays we feel are worth reproducing.

The field of study has grown to such an extent that there is now a plethora of material available to read, and the growth of the internet makes it increasingly available. Why, then, produce this series of essays? The issue is principally one of evaluation. Where does one

start? It is no longer possible to suggest to new entrants in the field that they should re
everything, for there is much which is of lesser value. So, what you will find collected
these volumes is a selection of the most important and influential journal articles, essa
and previously-published shorter material on the genre area concerned. Editors were giv
the brief of choosing not only those essays which have already garnered a great degree
influence, but essays which have also, for whatever reason, been overlooked, and which of
perspectives worthy of greater account. The volumes' editors are all experts in their ow
fields, with strong views about the ways those fields have developed, and might develop in t
future. Thus, while the series is necessarily retrospective in its viewpoint, it nonetheless ai
to help lay a platform for the broad future study of popular music.

ALLAN F. MOOR

Series Edit

University of Surrey, L

ntroduction

hat *defines* pop music? Why is it considered easy listening? How does it evoke such werful sentiments? Arranged in three parts – Aesthetics and Authenticity; Groove, mpling and Industry; Subjectivity, Ethnicity and Politics – this collection of essays deals th these questions in diverse ways. Intended to prepare the reader for some of the leading bates and assumptions in popular music scholarship, the volume also seeks to identify pop's ricate historical, aesthetic and cultural roots. A diversity of intellectual perspectives are esented that help reflect the interdisciplinary aspects of studying music, all of which pursue e dogmas, ideologies and values that designate meaning. Spanning more than twenty-five ars, these essays form a snapshot of some of the authorial voices that have shaped the ecific subject matter of pop criticism within the broader field of popular music studies. A mmon thread running through these essays is the topic of interpretation, which refers to ntent and context, relating to conceptions of musicality, subjectivity and aesthetics. The jectives of this volume are:

- to show that any discussion of pop music and music of easy listening cannot be divorced from the technologies that produce them
- to demonstrate that popular music needs to be evaluated on its own terms within the cultural context that makes it meaningful
- to consider how pop ideology has been informed by critical and academic discourses during the past several decades
- to provide examples for scholarly insight that prompt a consideration of the interface between musical evaluation and critical thought.

nce the 1950s pop music has been a product of Anglo-American music industries. One ight say that its Western-oriented influence has had a colossal global impact on societies and ltures. Indeed, from the outset the dissemination of pop has been associated with countless ocesses: commercialization, Americanization, imperialism, aestheticization, politics d cultural ideology. Historically, events between 1910 and 1930 signalled tumultuous anges in the reception of the popular when the novelty of jazz, swing and dance bands was ibraced by mass consumer culture. Technological advances in the gramophone, cinema d wireless would provide new spaces for production and consumption. By 1926 the dance nds established in the UK had one goal in mind: to give their audiences what they wanted. ofoundly influencing the evolution and dissemination of popular styles for the first time, the edia of radio, recording, live performance and sheet music became interconnected.

As Mark Hustwitt shows in Chapter 11, studies of dance music in the UK from this period veal how bandleaders sought to satisfy the public through 'stereotyped rhythmic dance usic' or 'forms of "light orchestral" music' (p. 219). What distinguished the 1920s was a aturing of mass consumer culture, where radio and gramophone companies marketed new /les of music. Of course, the quest in the production of music has always been to please audiences, and during the 1920s, notes Hustwitt, the increasing popularity of dance bar reflected a tendency towards 'relaxation, smoothness and calmness' (p. 222). This was stark contrast to the sense of liberation in the post-war years where the emphasis fell me on 'strategies of abandonism and hedonism' (p. 222). Hustwitt's study of early dance mu documents the changes brought about by technology and how this influenced the relations between consumer and producer, a phenomenon that would be the incentive for scholars by cultural critics such as Constant Lambert and Theodor Adorno. Significantly, the trends that arrived in Europe from the USA in the 1920s reached the public via radio a the gramophone. These styles became popularized by means of their production, marketi and commercialization, and this signalled the start of modern technology's impact on p music. However, as Simon Frith argues in Chapter 2, while technology was the cause of organization of competition, it did not determine 'who will be heard or how what is hear interpreted' (p. 44); the point being, pop music's control lies not solely in the music indust but among the fans and musicians who shape its ideology.

The starting point for any consideration of a generic term depends on definition, and defini pop is notoriously difficult. The *Grove Music Online* claims it originated in Britain in mid-1950s, 'a description for rock and roll and the new youth music styles that it influenc (Middleton *et al.*, 2001). Etymologically, the term has created decades of debate and is bou up in the prevailing rock–pop dichotomy. One might say the disparities in defining pop rock are as much a political issue as a generic one, with the divisions in opinion starting early the late 1960s. Perhaps of more relevance is a general recognition that developme in pop (however we choose to define it) are the precursors for the evolution of countless n styles, trends and influences we experience today.

There is plenty of evidence that mainstream trends in commercial pop have their orig in rock 'n' roll, which established 'black American traditions as central to popular mu throughout America and Europe' (Middleton *et al.*, 2001). As rock 'n' roll started to wane popularity in the late 1950s, so the first signs of a new crossover style began to surface. Bla songwriters such as Sam Cooke and Curtis Mayfield paved the way, with black Motown arti joining them in the early 1960s. By 1963 black songwriters were dominating the pop cha and, as Jon Fitzgerald points out in Chapter 20, 'Motown's impressive chart achieveme coincided with Curtis Mayfield's most prolific period as a pop writer while simultaneou overlapping with the final phase of Sam Cooke's career' (p. 383). Considering the trajector and prevalence of the early 1960s crossover black styles that shaped pop music, Fitzgera explains how many of the 'previously dominant white writer-producers struggled to comp with bands that wrote their own songs' (p. 420). This meant that black songwriters cou surface as 'prominent members of a new generation of 1960s pop songwriters' (p. 420).

In the main, scholarship dealing with African-American music has focused on jazz, h hop, funk and rap, but seldom pop. In Chapter 23, one of the last essays on popular music fr the twentieth century, Dave Sanjek sounds a salutary warning about the lack of scholarship African-American popular music, especially that produced between the 1940s and the 197 Moreover, he deplores the fact that 'the handful of volumes on the subject have been neit critiqued nor subjected to revision' (p. 474). In an in-depth examination of the work of authors writing on black popular music (Ellis Cashmore, Mark Anthony Neal, Craig Wern William Barlow, Brian Ward and Suzanne E. Smith), Sanjek also claims that research into music from 1944 to 1955 'is the most insubstantial' (p. 495).

Black popular styles that emerged directly following the Second World War led to the mmercial heyday of pop in the 1980s – lest we forget, two of three pop megastars born 1958 were black (Michael Jackson and Prince – the other was Madonna). To understand, storically, the post-war advent of commercial music, Sanjek has argued that we need to mprehend 'the internal workings of both [the major record labels and the independent trepreneurs] and stop lambasting the majors for their erroneously assumed lack of interest racially defined culture' (p. 495).

Some words are necessary on the lack of music analytic research into the pop text within broader field of popular music studies. In compiling this volume I became increasingly are of how few essays specifically on pop music have been published over the years. What pular music scholars have tended to bypass is the significance of the 'pop' in popular style d of its musical features from a historical, technological and aesthetic point of view. There s also been a tendency to emphasize certain pop artists over others according to a range of mplex priorities. At the time of writing this introduction, one year following the death of ichael Jackson, it is astonishing that no scholarly essays dealing specifically with his music uld be found in any of the major US and UK journals. While there has been interesting work rried out on his subjectivity and the politics of his representation, little scholarship has dealt th his musical performance, his stunning arrangements and the lavish productions behind recordings and live appearances.[1] Why?

Undoubtedly, activating the term 'pop' and unleashing all its historical and cultural ɔponents is a complicated affair. Take the *Oxford Dictionary of Music*:

Since the late 1950s, however, pop has had the special meaning of non-classical mus., usually in the form of songs perf. by such artists as the Beatles, the Rolling Stones, Abba, etc. (Kennedy 2006b)

mewhat curiously, in the same edition the Rolling Stones are described as an English 'rock ɔup formed in London 1962' (Kennedy, 2006c), while the Beatles are labelled an English ɔp group (guitars and drums)' (Kennedy, 2006a). In some passages, however, more caution exercised by altogether avoiding the term 'pop':

The late 1950s and early 60s are often considered a period of interruption in the development of popular music following the dispersal of the original rock and roll generation. The new, exciting *popular styles* were often assimilated into the 'culture industry', a process that depended on commercial rather than musical values. However, the music of the Beatles in the early 1960s was based on 50s models, an example of the overlapping and intersecting chronology of *popular music and urban rhythm and blues* which became the dominant influence on the Rolling Stones. (Gammond and Gloag, 2002; my emphasis)

ore helpful is the *Grove Music Online* definition, which asserts it was in the early 1960s that p music had 'competed terminologically with "beat music"', and by the late 1960s it was ɔk music that embraced new stylistic developments. That pop and rock have 'performed ɔonfusing dialogue' is verified by countless instances of definitional awkwardness. The ·ove Music Online* also stresses the flimsy and mobile boundaries between pop and rock

---

[1] See for example Middleton (2006), esp. ch. 3 (pp. 91–136), for a music analytic discussion of chael Jackson's music. Also see a special volume on Jackson's music in *Popular Music and Society*, Susan Fast and Stan Hawkins (forthcoming 2012).

mainstream that continue to exist up to the present day. Consequently, the hybrids of rock a
pop styles can be understood as a part of a larger process, a direct result of political, cultur
technological, economic and ideological change:

> Pop is also generally associated with a bundle of social changes, all of which are often conside
> aspects of a certain phase of 'modernization'. On the whole pop music is a leisure product or pract
> taking commodity forms. It also often presents itself as culturally and socially iconoclastic. Its typi
> context is a society, urban and secular in sensibility, which is changing quickly in structure, whe
> wealth is growing (and especially is spreading into previously less-favoured parts of the soc
> hierarchy), and where information and culture are increasingly mass-mediated. (Middleton, 20t
> see also Middleton, 2006)

Quite remarkably, while all the major dictionaries and encyclopedias make some
to define the 'pop' component of popular music, there is a dearth of information on it as
aesthetic experience and cultural critique. Several reasons account for this.

Compounded by the very properties of its mediation and consumption, pop has a dire
bearing on its explicit representation through the body. In the introduction to an
volume of essays, *Reading Pop* (2000), Richard Middleton made the claim that pop critici
is effected by a confusion 'deeply written into Western culture', much of which has to do w
the binaries in categorization. Addressing the crucial matter of representation politics a
the body, Middleton suggests a way forward for unpacking the meanings in pop produced
voices, textures, structures, musical events and style genres:

> Representation (of the body, of gender, of modalities of desire) and socio-musical action th
> intersect; and this matrix, far from existing *outside* the details of the musical ... then comes to inha
> ... every last cranny of the text, where its work of *self*-(re)presentation (to musicians, to listene
> traces the possibilities of both identity formation and culturally meaningful socio-corporeal gestu
> (2000, p. 12; emphasis in original)

Theoretically, Middleton brings to the fore a cultural and historical concept of pop throu
textual analyses that probe at questions relating to taste and meaning. Many smirk or cringe
the mere mention of pop artists such as Britney, Madonna, Rihanna, Beyoncé, Dolly Parto
Justin or Robbie. Is it that their construction is perceived as a subsidiary of their media-orient
imagery and therefore blatantly inauthentic? Or, are the prejudices against the 'popular',
Allan Moore has suggested in *Analyzing Popular Music* (2003), still symptomatic of popu
music's 'amateur status' and qualitative distinction (see also Moore, 2007b)?

Over the years popular music studies has taught scholars to approach the phenomen
of pop through its multi-levels, its dialogues and its material effects. Undoubtedly, t
Adornian take on aesthetics and social meaning in music with *mass appeal* has granted us t
opportunity to access pop music critically within the academy (see Adorno, 1941). Part of t
process has been to test the pertinence of the normative and immanent in musical form
style (Middleton, 1990; Shepherd and Wicke, 1997; Moore, 2000). One direct consequen
of this has been the systematic development of an approach to musical detail that involves,
Eric Clarke and Nicola Dibben put it in Chapter 16, 'getting one's hands dirty' (p. 324) a
engaging with the dominant ideology. In their analysis of Britpop band Pulp's track 'This
Hardcore', Clarke and Dibben posit a critique that contemplates the offensive, cynical
exploitative elements in pop consumption. Their own subject positions are reflected

textual analysis of this controversial song, which leads to what they term a 'compromised ritique', illuminating the ideological construction of representations of sex and gender within network of tensions. The pitfalls of the Adornian position have been that 'it risks removing self entirely from the very sphere within which it aims to exert its influence' (p. 324). This is a diametric opposition to Clarke and Dibben's vernacular response, which is about measuring nd accessing listeners' reactions and experiences while taking the music seriously. After all, ny pop song is grounded by the cultural, political, social and ideological backgrounds of the onsumer. Accordingly, by adopting a semiotic and critical theoretical approach (that builds multaneously on the work of Philip Tagg and Adorno), Clarke and Dibben demonstrate the erits of complicit ideological meanings in a controversial and contentious pop track through e identification of compositional processes and cultural associations.

 Wishing to dwell on this matter a little longer, I want to turn to the relevance of historical ircumstances. In Chapter 2 Frith claims that the 'history of pop is, in part, the history of ifferent groups using the same means (records) for different ends (profits, art, the articulation f community, self-aggrandizement, protest, etc.)' (p. 44). Which brings us to the work of ndrew Chester, who, in 1970, published an article entitled 'For a Rock Aesthetic' in the *New eft Review*. Taking issue with two British writers, Richard Mabey and Nik Cohn, Chester's rategy was to draw the lines between rock and pop by arguing for rock's aesthetic and uthentic value. Granted, Chester's conception, like Adorno's, needs to be understood in its istorical context. Chester insisted that 'pop denotes a cultural, not an aesthetic object' and that e 'acceptance of a cultural definition of the object of criticism leads inevitably to a cultural s opposed to an aesthetic criticism' (1970, p. 83). Not only did Chester allege that British cholars writing about popular music were dominated by an aura of 'pop mystification', but lso that a 'whole sub-division of pop criticism' had developed 'to cope with the Beatles'. 'It quite pathetic to read essays by Wilfred Mellers, Ned Rorem or Tony Palmer ... concerned ith comparing the Lennon-McCartney songbook with Schubert or Poulenc, as if work in the enre of "song" could have any aesthetic value in the mid-20th century' (Chester, 1970, p. 84).

 In no uncertain terms, such a disparaging rejection of pop is reductionist and entrenched in Marxist theorization of *proletarian youth*, a point Richard Merton picks up on in his retort Chester's claim. Merton praises Chester's project 'to rescue rock from pop criticism by ffirming its autonomous aesthetic values' (1970, p.96). But Merton's conjuncture lies in the ery definition of cultural criticism, which he attempts to demonstrate as 'a condition of the iscovery of the specific *novelty* of rock/pop for an *aesthetic* reflection on it' (p. 88, author's mphasis). Merton reminds Chester that 'the "people" (Lenin, Mao) are never a stable ategory: their identity is mutable and conjunctural, because they are perpetually redefined y the conflict of the *classes* and their culture' (p. 89, author's emphasis). The canonisation f 'an authentic British popular music' in the 1960s can thus be read as a denaturalization r 'pastiche of American sounds' (ibid). After all, 1962 was the year when the Beatles first roke into the charts and, arguably, this was the year that pop music was born. In Merton's vords pop 'was the product of a certain economic "emancipation" of *working-class* youth 1 a social formation overwhelmingly dominated by manual labour ... a pattern altogether preign to the USA' (ibid, author's emphasis). Merton's underlying claim was that British ock had triumphed by 'counter-colonizing much vanguard American music', the result of hich was that the 'strictly aesthetic gains of this great wave coincided with the practical ultural upheaval of the time' (p. 90). Both Chester and Merton thus projected a trajectory of Marxist theory onto popular music studies in the form of a cultural explanation, if not critical response, to Adornian determinism.[2]

Cultural criticism's forceful position in the 1970s certainly helps shed light on th ideological effects of pop music. Inevitably, this opens a window on the debates surroundin authenticity.[3] During the last decades a spate of articles and books have dealt with tas and value judgement entangled with theories of authenticity per se. Chester's mantra st resonates loud and clear today in the accusation that 'The pop critic's attitude towards music is generally patronizing in the extreme; pop, and this is precisely why it is of interes is the simple and vulgar music of the masses' (1970, p. 83). Scholars such as Frith and Jc Savage have reacted strongly to these claims. In Chapter 3 they illuminate a wealth of issue connected to pop cultural criticism when critiquing Jim McGuigan's book *Cultural Populis* (1992), claiming that the time was ripe 'to reclaim pop from the populists: they have sa much of nothing, but their chit-chat still poisons the air' (p. 56). Addressing the connectic between pop's academic status as an object of cultural studies and the media's take on it, the suggest that in the academy 'cultural studies, for all its ingenuousness, does seek to "ordinary" lives from academic condescension, to *complicate* the daily experiences of pc music and clothes and magazines by making them the object of high theory' (p. 53; emphas in original). Assertions of this kind highlight the devices used by the cultural journalist comparison with the pop scholar. Emphasizing the matter of context, Frith and Savage wou make the claim that positioning the pop text in the classroom would 'make it strange' (p. 53 On the other hand, the journalist places an icon on a shelf beside 'all other consumer goods assuming the role of consumer guide. Perhaps most relevant is the notion of 'populism resentment', which is channelled through the music press and the language of scholars such McGuigan; for the negative critique of pop culture has been dominant since the early 1980 note Frith and Savage, providing 'the rump of PR, ego and spite which still fills up pages (newsprint' (p. 56).

In the ongoing debates around the pop text, two important points resurface time and tim again – first, the quest for validating meaning in the definition of the pop(ular) and, secon the pressing need for assessing the social climate in which the most commercialized (all musical genres transpires. Moulded into these two points are numerous historical ar methodological factors well worth considering. In pop analysis of the 1980s we have evidenc of the inextricable link between the qualitative judgement of music and public taste. One (the key sociologists to first research into the structures and marketing processes of pop mus was Antoine Hennion whose work situated the musician within the context of the industı according to specific criteria. Focusing much of his attention on the *chanson de variétés* ar the record industry in France, Hennion identified the progression from the music to the socia arguing that a musicological evaluation per se could not alone account for the success (failure of specific songs.

In the wake of Hennion's research, the pop song has remained subjected to numerou analytic approaches, its layers of meaning musically positioned alongside its cultural

---

[2]   On this point, Middleton (2000, p. 14) cautions against being blinded by 'the powerful ro played by the music industry' in terms of the dissemination of musical meaning.

[3]   For an enlightening discussion on authenticity and its determining role in authentication, se Moore (2007a).

cial relevance. Somewhat paradoxically, Hennion as sociologist displays many of the tools f a competent musicological grounding, his detailed analysis of 'the music' comprising an mpirical description of pop music through which the raw material, the lyrics and the artist e identified. For all intents and purposes, Hennion's discourse problematizes the success and roduction of pop primarily through the role of the producer, highlighting the discrepancies in pinions that have flooded the field of sociology – in the work of Adorno, Hoggart, Bourdieu, arthes, Baudrillard and Certeau. In Chapter 5, disputing the notion of pop music as a 'dulling f the senses', and the prevailing Marxist ideology of standardization and alienation, Hennion sists that pop music 'has been able to systematize the very principle of its own diversity ithin an original mode of production. The *creative collective*, a team of professionals ho simultaneously take over all aspects of a popular song's production, has replaced the dividual creator who composed songs which others would then play, disseminate, defend or iticize' (p. 84; emphasis in original).

Hennion's guide to analysing pop invariably invokes contemplation of those behind the roduction; for it is the patterns and effects of consumption that determine pop's existence. op enters the public domain through mass marketing as much as through the aid of the creative collective', and does not need to shelter itself 'from the public by invoking historical r aesthetic justifications' (p. 86). Pop, after all, is about enticement, luring the listener into naginary audio spaces. Yet, the 'dictatorship of the public ... remains extremely ambiguous'). 113) as the 'real public' are never physically present in the recording environment. Hennion sists that pop does not create its public, but rather it is something the public discovers; ence, the notion of a passive audience 'overlooks the active use to which people put pop nusic, the imaginary existence they lead through it, which is not reducible to the official ocial hierarchies' (p. 115). So, while pop lends meaning to escapism and fantasy, it is far ore than 'a dream-machine': 'it is the unofficial chronicle of its times, a history of desires xisting in the margins of official history' (p. 116).

Located in the very details of its entertainment, pop comprises a myriad of elements that an be assessed through the dichotomies that inscribe it within everyday life. We might say at pop systematizes the very components of its own plurality, its significance determined y its musical as much as its social criteria. Consistently, scholarly writing on pop music as gained momentum since the 1970s, and this is attributable to many factors relating changes in how music is studied and perceived. Notions of authenticity, 'badness' and anality in pop tell us much about its reception and audiences. As Leslie M. Meier suggests Chapter 6, 'body genres' can provide a tool for considering music 'rife with emotion and hysicality' (p. 134). The premises of authenticity are indisputably gender-related, a point leier theorizes when attempting to categorize 'bad' music genres, such as porno rock, camp op, shock rock, gangsta rap, sob pop and arena rock, to illustrate how the excessive displays rovoke condemnation. This argument turns full circle when considering certain artists who re not deemed 'bad'. Meier's examination of Celine Dion concludes that her 'non-aggressive emininity' poses little threat to the 'normative masculinity foundational to rock culture': 'her nusic and persona are not only suggestive of excessive honesty and emotion, but (even worse vithin the discourse of authenticity) also an excessively maternal femininity' (p. 133).

It is evident that study of the inherent values in pop can be approached from various irections, inducing dialogue between fans, musicians, producers and academics. In recent ears numerous writings have dealt with the 'global' and 'local' (and even the 'glocal'), inspecting the power structures that impinge on modes of dissemination and, moreove policy-making. One tendency has been the documenting and accounting of globalizatio a process that impinges on local music scenes, spaces and places. While much attention h been afforded to the global media impact and the eradication of national boundaries geographic environments, a more nuanced critique of the role of the nation-state has bee largely neglected.

Because cultural politics significantly impacts the production of pop music, it is important consider what role government policy plays in erecting bonds and boundaries within nation spaces and places. Of course, as with sport, identities are foisted upon musicians as mu as audiences by political systems. In Chapter 17 Martin Cloonan claims that nationalism 'the most successful ideology ever' (p. 335), underpinned by cultural policies, marketir tactics and 'scene-making'. Three types of relationships typify the nation-state's inf the authoritarian, the benign and the promotional. Consider Britain, a paradigmatic examp of the benign state, where, while live music is controlled, the market is left to its own device In this category the country is content to 'let the music industry go about its daily busine uninterrupted and to reap the taxes that industry success brings' (p. 338). In other cases, tl nation-state assists and even interferes in the dissemination of its citizens' music. On cultur political grounds, it decides when to intervene. Cloonan has studied the structural chang in Britain's publicly owned Radio 1, for instance, and how they influenced the promotic of Britpop in the mid-1990s, which was attributed to specific broadcasting policies ar deregulation. Radio 1 is an apt example of the nation-state as 'guarantor of diversity in (p. 339), in that it takes on board niche markets. Similarly, Britain's art subsidies throug the Art Councils (as in the USA's National Endowment for The Arts) have been vital stimulating musical diversity, which converges on the commercial environment of popul music. In a European context, the Eurovision song contest is a prime example of this, whe the annual circus of events in the largest broadcasted musical festival in the world forg allegiances while fostering minor political conflicts on the basis of strong national sentimen

Many instances of Cloonan's third category can be found relating to the 'authoritaria nation-state, which often responds to Americanization and the multinational music corporatior by promoting and directly supporting their music on their terms. Here the strategy of politic rhetoric is one of persuasion, negotiation and compromise, often with one goal in min the celebration of patriotism. Pop music's function in cultural policy and the constructic of national identity is glaringly obvious in live concerts funded by the nation-state. Ho then, do narratives of national identity become manifested in the public space? And wh constitutes the criteria for, say, selecting a nation's 'A-list' of talent? Put differently, how is tl 'inside' distinguished from the 'outside' in ways that mirror the political interests of a natior

Take Canada, for example, where pop music is a major export as well as a powerful mark of patriotism that not only distinguishes ethnic groups from one another but also strives t promote itself as quite different from the US. In 2001, shortly following the attacks of 9/11, benefit concert, *Music Without Borders: Live*, was arranged in Toronto, Ontario, and televise to millions of Canadians. Held in support of Afghani refugees, this concert refused to respon to the recent terrorist bombings in New York. Susan Fast and Karen Pegley, in Chapter 1 critique this event, conjoining the construction of nationhood to class, ethnicity and languag Their study reveals that all the artists chosen for this event were English-speaking Canadiar from the affluent provinces. So, why, they ask 'would not the diverse population of Canad e drawn to a concert that celebrates the variety of musics being created and performed in ʰis country, as opposed to "mainstream" acts?' (p. 364). What their study discovers is that ʲanada's multicultural policy 'often overlook[s] the complex ways in which hegemonic ʳivilege underpins ... cultural articulations' (p. 364). Quite predictably, rock surfaces as a ͦminant style (in terms of gender and race), a symbolic marker of power by comparison to ͦop, hip-hop and rap. To be sure, the list of artists who participated in this live concert bears ʰis out:

> The song chosen for the finale was fellow-Canadian Neil Young's 'Rockin' in the Free World,' one
> of the few songs that night that could be construed to have any kind of overtly 'political' message
> ... Again, this is a 'rock' song, by a white rock artist ... The choice of genre excluded the one non-
> white artist, Choclair. He stood behind a line-up of electric guitars, an instrument that plays little role
> in rap, and did not contribute a verse of the song but rather joined in on the chorus only. He seemed
> decidedly out of place in this rockist environment. (p. 365)

ʰe Hip, a Canadian band flagged as the nation's spokesmen during the concert, would ͤhemently vent their response to US foreign policy and Bush, endorsing Canada's ͦperception of itself as peacekeeper and aid giver' (p. 369). With pride the display of national ͪentity would be narrated through the powerful medium of a televised live concert, where ʰe selected music was inextricably linked to a pro-Canadian image of itself broadcast by ʰe government-supported CBC. Cunningly, the construction of the televised version of the ͥve concert in a form that set out to 'demystify' the concert's process smoothed over the gap ͤetween spectator and celebrity. As Fast and Pegley argue, Canadians have been reluctant ͦo elevate their celebrities in the same way as has occurred in the US, creating a sense of ͣationalistic collective power. Politically, this live concert was a demonstration of nationality ͫn the guise of a strong response to the threat from outside (read: US 'imperialism', Afghan ͦterrorism'). Carefully negotiated, the hegemonic values within the choice of musical genre ͣnd performer were glibly reinforced, virtually without notice.

Debates of this kind are pertinent to an understanding of the cultural hierarchies that define ͅenres in popular music. Following a Bourdieuesque train of thought (if we move from the ͅtate to the individual), Frith (1996, p. 9) reviews the consumer's role in this process, noting ͪhat dance-based styles are indeed richer than those found in more passive forms of listening ͦr participation. Disco, a style that resisted the domination of rock during the late 1960s and ͤarly 1970s, is a fitting example. The *jouissance* of this pop style was in the freedom to express ͣnd let go. Building up momentum in popularity it eventually caused a tumultuous backlash, ͅulminating in the Disco Demolition Night in 1979. However, following its temporary ͪemise, it would mutate into a myriad of styles under the aegis of dance pop and club music. ͭt was well into the 1990s before disco returned in the form of countless pop songs by artists ͣnd bands such as Dee-Lite, Gloria Estefan, Prince, Diana Ross, Kylie Minogue, Michael ͪackson, Jamiroquai, Madonna and, more recently, Lady Gaga. Stylistically, disco epitomized ͪe pop aesthetic by drawing on countless influences while maintaining its regular four-on-ͪe-floor beat, with complementary syncopated bass lines. Although disco inherits from rock ͪe steady semi-quaver divisions of four crotchets per bar, often taken by hi-hats, with its ͅubdivisions supplying a good deal of the rhythmic energy, its bass tends to fall on the one ͣnd three with the snare on the two and four. Moreover, the beat in disco is constituted in the ͤven accents of each of the four beats (hence four-on-the-floor). Disco is also distinguished by

its extravagance: glitzy arrangements with horn doublings, rich instrumental pads, keyboar
instruments (organs, electric pianos, synthesizers), orchestral instruments and highl
reverberated vocals. Drawing on jazz, swing, funk, soul, Motown, Latin and, surprisingl
classical music, disco has been a force to be reckoned with. Most of all, it opened the wa
forward for African-American artists to enter the pop charts in the 1970s.

Tracing the profusion of pop hits, such as Walter Murphy's 'A Fifth of Beethoven', Davi
Shire's 'Night on Disco Mountain' and the revivals of Wendy Carlos's 'Switched on Bach
and her Brandenburg recordings, Ken McLeod, in Chapter 21, considers the processe
of appropriation by disco. In the case of 'A Fifth of Beethoven' it is 'likely no acciden
that 'the most famous four notes in classical music' became 'the original target for a disc
cross-pollination and the only instance of such an appropriation – in any genre of pop-roc
music – reaching number one on the U.S. charts' (p. 432). McLeod observes that Murphy'
'more mundane yet humanly more identifiable work' in the form of a disco track was a bi
to 'succumb to common human desires, such as dancing' (p. 434–35). Most notably, disco'
link to classical repertoire lies in its compositional structures and processes, where intricat
orchestral arrangements and elaborate vocal performances have been prone to a highly stylize
finish. A case study of 'A Fifth of Beethoven' exposes the orderliness of disco's music¿
formula, its very recontextualization of a famous classic hit positioned as an antithesis to th
aesthetics of rock as much as classical music. While rock is often littered with classical musi
references and influences, disco veers off in another direction. McLeod accounts for this b
stating that 'disco artists often removed classical music's traditional hierarchical values an
claim to cultural and intellectual privilege' (p. 438). Hence, disco's popularity (as much a
its demise and resuscitation) is a striking narrative on hegemony and the evolution of musi
traditions, testifying to the contradictory trends and practices that provide aesthetic diversit
in pop.

The pleasures connected to disco are located in its synthetic feel and its catchy grooves
making it ideal for playing in recorded form in clubs through strong PA systems. Th
production techniques that went into disco through DJ culture would greatly impact on th
course of pop, sparking off house music, hip-hop, rap, R&B, garage, Nu-disco, Hi-NRC
and many other derivative trends. Behind the production of these dance-based pop style
are a wealth of stylistic codes and practices that determine their sensibility. In particular
the sonic developments associated with many post-disco styles have gravitated towards th
technologically-driven aesthetic of turntables, digital samplers and drum machines.

Features of highly developed sound processing characterize pop at the start of the twenty-firs
century. Consider the megastar-producer Timbaland, whose productions offer an insight
pop music in the wake of disco. Indeed, in Chapter 15 Dale Chapman describes Timbaland'
sound as 'one of the crucial memes in our moment' (p. 293), redefining music production a:
well as the politics of the body. Drawing on Paul Virilio's concept of 'telepresence' (1997)
Chapman considers the Timbaland sound phenomenon in relation to the biopolitics of
body. In his study the term 'musical telepresence' is deployed as a useful method for analysin{
music production. The objective here is to identify how compositional techniques are aligne
to issues of race, technology and the body. Within contemporary R&B pop telepresence ha:
emerged as a new mode of subjectivity, where the human subject is reconstituted in the forn
of the post-human. Chapman suggests that in much contemporary pop the black post-huma
subject resides in a sonic-space that is virtual, providing the body with its political force

ollowing Paul Gilroy's tack on biopolitics (1993), Chapman argues that hypersexualised
acks eradicate idealized romance with explicit sexual candour. The conditions of this refute
ie emotional commitment one finds, say, in sob-pop. Production-wise, Timbaland's signature
identifiable through its flat, spatial two-dimensionality, and a sparseness that reinforces a
ensibility that is alienating. Emphasizing flat surface over spatial depth therefore dispenses
vith the distinction between presence and absence, Chapman observes that 'One of the more
isturbing dimensions of this flatness is its erasure of any notion of the spectral, of ghostly
aces, of some remainder that might complicate the integrity of the images we consume,
f the sounds we absorb' (p. 303). Flatness in R&B is thus a consequence of electronic
ommunication and information technology, its telepresence functioning as part of a general
rocess of acceleration that detaches the event from its context.

During the first decade of the twenty-first century Timbaland's productions were
ynonymous with numerous mainstream pop artists – Madonna, Justin Timberlake, Katy
erry, Missy Elliott and Jay-Z – with him visibly and sonically identifiable as the producer-
tar (appearing alongside his artists in many of their videos). The stylistic traits of his sound
– the Miami bass,[4] beat layering, grooves, drum sounds – connote as much political as musical
ngagement in a space that eschews stability and promotes ambiguity. Moreover, the virtuality
f Timbaland's production stages a type of subjectivity, where the human is reconfigured in
vays that transcend the normative borders of style, form and materiality. Sound production
n pop music is about mediating technologies and attaining stylistic credibility, the trademark
f an artist's authenticity. Indeed, authenticity can reside in the 'artificiality' of an over-
olished sonic signature (read: inauthentic authenticity). So, appreciating these tendencies
n pop productions is paramount to shaping a well-developed critique. This is because pop
nusic is reliant on the way the music industry produces and packages its products, as much
s the force of mediation that disseminates artistic expression. If the production behind the
ecording constitutes the score, the role of technology is a crucial aspect in mediation and
naterial ity. How then does the digital treatment of sound bring about the specific markers
f identification in an artist's signature? And what are the qualities in music production we
hould identify when considering mediation and medium specificity?

Investigating issues of this nature in Madonna's song 'Don't Tell Me', Anne Danielsen
nd Arnt Maasø, in Chapter 9, take a close look at what might seem, on first glance, to be a
imple pop tune. In this analysis the digital signature is inherent in the groove. 'Don't Tell
Me' is 'atypical of the singer-songwriter tradition and the country music genre alluded to'
p. 174) because of its digital mediation and stylistic grounding in contemporary pop. The
nicro-rhythmic formula of the groove holds the clue to this assertion as it is idiomatically
ligitized and programmed in ways that are inconceivable in live performance. Another prime
narker of digital mediation in this song is silence, which is employed in the form of a 'digital
lropout' that takes on the guise of a 'glitch'. Madonna's use of such a digital effect turns into
social commentary on digitization when she 'uses the silent dropouts as an allusion to the
ragility of digital sound production' (p. 177). As Danielsen and Maasø argue, 'she makes the
ligital glitch into an effect marking the specificity and historicity of a contemporary medium'

---

[4] Miami bass is a style of hip-hop with its roots in the early 1980s electro-funk sound of Afrika
3ambaata and the Soulsonic Force that became popular during the 1990s. The focus of Miami bass is
nore on DJs and producers than on single artists and bands.

(p. 177). Ostensibly, Madonna's own input in the production is taken as collaborative with the producers and engineers she engages, this collective performative activity shaping everything about the musical event. One might say the control and manipulation of new and old technologies in digitized ways has emerged as an established cultural mode, helping explain how Madonna's subjectivity hinges on the self-construction of her visual and sonic imagery through productive transformation. Her musical subjectivity is thus depicted by the innovation of music technology, and a track like 'Don't Tell Me' highlights the processes of digital sound production as much as the inventiveness and playfulness. Above all, digitization frames the creative force of her authorship.

Any discussion of Madonna's productions cannot bypass her audiovisual spectacle and personalized iconography; for the technologies that produce pop are bound up in the conditions of sonic and visual expression. The key to identifying this lies in working out how we perceive sound's association with image. In Chapter 10, written in 1988, Andrew Goodwin proclaims that 'pop ideology is increasingly dominated by a sense that the future has now arrived, for good' (p. 185). Goodwin addresses the radical changes in digital technology and its impact on the music industry. At the dawn of the digital age of reproduction, recording would start sampling sound, giving credence to Walter Benjamin's prophecy, namely that digital reproduction would open up new spaces for social relations and artistic display. The age of digital reproduction signalled a postmodern period marked by changes in attitude on the part of musicians to compositional invention. Digital sampling not only encoded any sound but also generated new techniques and skills in writing and producing pop. As Goodwin notes, it 'eroded the divisions not just between originals and copies, but between human and machine performed music' (p. 189). In his critique Goodwin takes issue with Frith's position in Chapter 2 on the distinctions between technology on the one side, and community and nature on the other. His suggestion is that Frith's analysis needs 'to be supplemented by *musicological* critique' as 'assertions about the role of technology in postmodern culture have rarely been tested via empirical analysis' (p. 190; emphasis in original).

A key point arising from Goodwin's essay is the centrality of pop iconography and the image of the musician has been altered through the visual spectacle.[5] As such, musical and iconographic *presence* dominates mainstream pop and rock as the developments in digital technologies have eroded ever more the borders between the original and the copy. Iconography is thus a central component of pop manufacturing and of obvious relevance when reading a pop track. One of the first scholars to take up these implications was Barbara Bradby, whose critique would eclipse much of E. Ann Kaplan's writings on MTV pop video (see Kaplan, 1987). In Chapter 14, an essay published in 1992, derived from a paper given at a conference of the UK IASPM branch at Oxford in 1987, Bradby's close reading of Madonna's 'Material Girl' demonstrates that video analysis cannot be divorced from the musical material. Taking issue with assertions made by scholars such as Grossberg, Kaplan, Brown and Fiske, Bradby argues that watching pop is inseparable from listening to it:

> The problem with the claims made implicitly by both Grossberg and Kaplan, that Madonna can be 'read' without references to her songs, goes beyond economic argument. There is also a semiotic problem in attempting to read music video as a purely visual text. (p. 270)

---

[5]   This forms the basis for his successive studies on music video and visual iconography. See Goodwin (1993) and Frith and Goodwin (1993).

 adby argues the point that by analysing a pop song as a narrative one needs to take on oard agency and strategy. For its time, this study achieved two goals: first, it threw down the auntlet for writers who disparaged the pop song and who loathed Madonna (in her response Grossberg's critique of Madonna's music, Bradby stated: 'one might assume that Grossberg appealing to the old rock aesthetic, which regards images as illusory' (p. 269)) and, second, took up the matter of musical structure and arrangement as part of the 'material discourse' r working out gender objectification, femininity and sexual desire. In tandem with the st generation of feminist musicologists such as Susan McClary, Lucy Green and Sheila 'hiteley, Bradby pioneered the interdisciplinary approach to video analysis through detailed terpretations of the early pop songs of Madonna. Activating new debates around the politics ' gendered representation in pop songs, Bradby's work would spawn a wealth of related adies during the following decades.

In recent years music research into pop music has evolved out of a need for tracing athorial identification in the formative power of mediation. Prince, the most quintessential op artist of all time, has systematically tried and tested approaches for mediating his music ad authorship to fans. His identity – subversive, contestational and personally political – has aimed with the shifting contexts in which young people have found themselves since the te 1970s. Right from the start his politics of representation underpinned an identity that as disruptive. On this point, Robert Walser argues in Chapter 24 that Prince has enticed his ns through structures of desire that were not territorialized by the constraints of patriarchal onformity. Turning to the seminal text *Anti-Oedipus* by Gilles Deleuze and Felix Guattari 984), Walser demonstrates how their psychoanalytic perspectives can shed light on Prince's athorship. As Walser argues, Prince's pop songs make valid Deleuze and Guattari's theory of esire, which functions as a guide to understanding what is happening in his music. Prince's lentity fits perfectly into a pop idiom that continuously explores the new technologies of roduction controlled in both a studio and a live performance space. Obviously, authorial oints of identification in pop music are astonishingly varied and, in cases where the simulated erformance inscribes authorship, the politics of representation seem an unavoidable part of ay scholarly consideration. Constituted through virtual reality, pop songs are often encoded vibrantly audiovisual performance spaces where digital technology circumscribes their aateriality. As such, it has become commonplace for musicologists to approach analysis arough models that combine hermeneutic and empirical work.

A good example of this is found in Chapter 22 through John Richardson's study of Damon lbarn's virtual band, Gorillaz, where the underlying premise is that technology is implicated a the temporal coding of musical expression. Addressing the impact of technology on pop the dawn of the twenty-first century, Richardson traces its digital development. Focusing n a range of production techniques used to create Gorillaz (with specific reference to the roducer Jason Cox), Richardson identifies the recording practices found on the band's single ix 'Clint Eastwood'. What distinguishes this band from others is its virtual quality, and for udiences 'the authorial re-construction of the "real Band" in large part conditions perceptions f its animated counterpart' (p. 447). It is the band-behind-the-band that highlights the artifice f Gorillaz's diegetic position as their agency remains unchallenged. This raises important uestions dealing with the politics of representation and authenticity through the primary nd secondary creative roles of this virtual pop band. Analysis of the production techniques ound in 'Clint Eastwood' (with direct reference to the 2002 Brit Awards live performance in

London) shows a 'principal of interchangeability' that is expressively located on 'interlocki
levels' (p. 456). Assessing the virtual realities through which the track is constructed a
leads on to questioning the multimedia performance that supports the audiovisual narrati
Compelling is the playfulness of Gorillaz' representation through 'the partial withdrawal
the "real band" from the public eye'. This grants audiences access to a re-examination
'their relationship to acts that employ more conventional modes of representation' (p. 464)
would seem that the objective of this reading is to profile the disparate elements of the fir
pop product by making an argument for the virtuosic techniques and aesthetic outcomes of
production. Richardson concludes by stating that elements that are grouped into music, wor
and visual representation can only be dealt with when 'all of this cross-referencing is inscrib
within the context of a carefully crafted and deceptively simple pop song' (p. 466). Ultimate
Gorillaz' success is down to the skills of the *auteur*, Albarn, whose stage personality is veil
as the singer becomes the character-without-a-name.

At this point it is worth stressing that all the essays presented in this volume deal in so
way with the issue of simplicity in pop music, which, by all accounts, is diffuse. Speci
to reading pop are concerns relating to mediation, materiality and convention. And wh
some parameters might appear simple because of, say, duration, words and formal properti
as Hennion has strongly argued in Chapter 5, pop music 'systemize[s] the principles of
own diversity through the intricacy of its production' (p. 84),. Built into the pop critique
issues of technical competence, collective creativity, compositional specialism, performan
skills, the artist's personality and so forth. When it comes to dealing with the standardiz
structural elements of a 'simple' pop song, Hennion cautions us that '(e)ach song modifi
by degrees the basic model, which does not exist as an absolute. The gimmick of yesterd;
soon becomes the boring tactic of today, as far as public taste is concerned' (p. 85); this wou
imply that producing a hit song is arguably more than just a hit-and-miss affair. In Chapter
a fascinating study of pop songs from the 1960s, Robert Toft examines the musical creativi
behind the song-writing skills of Burt Bacharach. As with Hennion, he explores the issue
taste and popularity, concluding: 'One of the factors contributing to Bacharach and [Ha
David's wide appeal seems to have been their desire to please themselves instead of writi
for a specific market' (p. 153). By turning to three versions of the pop song 'Close to Y
Toft focuses not only on musical structure as it relates to arrangement and the transformir
of ideas, but also on the collective creativity invested in the actual making of a recordin
especially on the part of the singer, Dionne Warwick. Interestingly, Warwick's role
decisive in the interpretation of Bacharach's songs, as Toft notes (when he compares her
another performer Bacharach and David used, Richard Chamberlain): '[Warwick] sang
more dynamic shading and controlled her *vibrato* carefully, frequently beginning longer not
with a straight tone before adding a slow vibration. And because her delivery was much mo
closely aligned to speaking, she rarely adhered to the mechanical way the vocal lines had be
notated' (p. 148). Warwick emerges as a major contributor to the song's technical materiali
in recorded form, as much the character she endearingly depicted when singing 'I'm feelir
close to you'.

From Toft's study it would make sense that the investment of the performer's (as much
the author's) character in the recording forms a crucial part of the performance dynamic
the recorded pop song. This involves the projection of feelings through vocal inscription an
moreover, the involvement of the gendered body in production. The pop artist Cher's

oice in the hit 'Believe' prompts Kay Dickinson to consider the link between subjectivity nd mechanization in Chapter 18. Because Cher is produced and 'engineered according to rinciples which equate with notions of autonomous choice' (p. 350), her vocoded voice can e interpreted as liberating. Dickinson insists that the vocoder 'intervenes at an unavoidable evel of *musical* expression – it uses the medium as the message – encouraging the listener to hink of these women as professionals within musical practice' (p. 351; emphasis in original). 'her's 'mastery' is a result of the multifarious levels of technological processing that go into er production, sonically and visually. Her disembodied vocoded voice, its flagrant opacity n the mix, obstructs the female voice from sounding natural and therefore technologically nanipulated. As a result, Cher's subjectivity is transient; it is fetishized through digitization nd to the extent that vocoding becomes a camp object in itself; for camp 'has always been bout making do within the mainstream, twisting it, adoring aspects of it regardless, wobbling s more restrictive given meanings' (p. 355). As a timbral modifier traditionally used by nale musicians in popular music, the vocoder in mainstream pop has been developed through nodified software, making it easily accessible and gimmicky. Foregrounding this phenomenon,)ickinson questions inscriptions of female power and control as she draws into her critique he work of feminist cyber-theorists, such as Haraway, Plant and Braidotti. Female vocality an be mapped against its very production, and Cher's vocoded voice 'teeters between what s currently constituted as the organic and the inorganic' (p. 349). As a consequence, the esthetics of the contorted voice provide a point of identification for theorizing the conditions nd conventions linked to subjectivity in contemporary pop music.

Sharing many theoretical perspectives with Dickinson and Richardson, in Chapter 1 Joseph \uner theorizes the emergence of vocoder-like devices through a model of 'ventriloquism', vhereby the singer's voice is manipulated and modulated after he or she has sung or spoken nto a microphone. When the human voice is stripped of its subjectivity (or better emotion), he human presence traverses new spaces, blurring the divides between bodily existence and ybernetic form. Building on studies by Katherine Hayles and others who have addressed irtual bodies in cybernetics and informatics, Auner examines the implications of the ost-human, cyborg-like pop artist. Applying Katherine Hayles' theories of the cyborg to pecific examples, Auner identifies the 'machine soul' in dance music as a reconfiguration of mbodiment rather than disembodiment. This is exemplified in a song by Moby, 'Porcelain', rom the album *Play* (1999), where the layering of musical material enables the human and the nachine to interact complexly. Looping in vocal sampling turns the voice into another object, post-human whereby the voice 'happens not only through sampling, cutting and splicing, ut in the way the samples circulate not so much as the products of other musicians and people, ut as found objects from some vague and undifferentiated historical past' (p. 25). Moby's use of samples (some of which come from a collection of Alan Lomax) is bound up in meanings hat disclose 'cultural tropes of race and the primitive' as 'relics from an anthropology nuseum' (p. 25). In fact, Moby's own appearance as a machine persona sounds processed, iis 'soft and somewhat diffident voice' transformed by 'the addition of a harmonized halo' p. 26). Not unlike Madonna's subjectivity in 'Don't Tell Me', Moby's is distributed through he strata of other voices in a musical production that references temporal, generic and racial :ntities. Radiohead's track 'Fitter Happier', from the album *Ok Computer* (1999), is another orime example of the robotic voice assuming its appeal through the peculiarity of its sonic ransformation. Auner perceives the 'forlorn quality of the voice' found in cyborgs and androids as 'an integral aspect of their hybrid condition' (p. 18). Moreover, the mechanize effect of the voice affords it a degree of credibility, providing a striking contrast to the natur voice at the same time as enhancing the virtuosity of the artist's performance.

Similar traits are discernible in Britney Spears' song 'Toxic', where the artist's high manipulated and transformed voice impinges directly on her iconography. This single vide forms the basis of Chapter 4, an investigation carried out by Stan Hawkins and John Richardsc to document the many elements that relate to the complex structures of mediation. Spea extends her vocal repertory in 'Toxic' by employing a variety of tropes that help delinea the narrative of the song. As with Cher's vocal performance in 'Believe', Spears contras her cyborg voice with her natural one in a vocal recording that almost overdoses with voic filters, vocal audio plug-ins and software, all designed to titillate. Once again, meaning li in a fetishization of the digitized female subject who 'appropriates the perfection and faker of pop' (pp. 68–69). Spears' sonic iconography reinforces all the visual shots of her throug processes of self-invention and re-invention. For the most part, her vocality symbolizes th post-Madonna pop diva era where 'the musical rhetoric of her performances rests in its abilit to articulate the body through different gestures' (p. 72). Above all, the post-human correlatic of image and sound in 'Toxic' is manifested in a representation of the eroticized cyborg tha empowers, through parody, the fixity of stereotypical femininity. From a musicologica vantage point Hawkins and Richardson select a methodology that comprises a cluster c discourses that are interdisciplinary, as well as musically analytic, that seeks to find way for understanding the 'personal narrativity' of the audiovisual performance. Their principa claim is that the pop video exists as a personal narrative because it works performatively i promoting the characteristics of the artist's persona. Of the various details considered in th reading is the groove and, in particular, Spears' response to this vocally and visually. Voca phrasing, for instance, involves accents and rhythmic inflections that capture the significanc of specific words and lines as much as the choreography. Navigating the groove erotically, th strategy of her performance mediates the affected gestures of her character types. Most strikin in 'Toxic' are the post-human qualities of her sound and imagery. Something extraordinaril queer results from her excessively animated and machine-like representations, destabilizir the stereotypical sexual and gender categorization of the female pop performer. Above all, th narrative strategies of the idealized body on display are mobilized by the intricate structure of the groove.

The groove is common to most pop songs, its rhythmic function vital to the sensation of enjoyment we experience when listening. Certainly physical response to the groove is cultural response as listeners latch on to the beat during the process of repetition. Curiously to date few studies have taken up the relevance of perception and imagination, the propertie of responding to the groove, nor the matter of cultural production.

Observations of responses to grooving can tell us much about musical processes an structures, as well as the listener's judgement of rhythmic materiality. In Chapter 13 Lawrenc Zbikowski's approach to embodied knowledge takes up this challenge by surveying th strong link between motion and rhythmically driven music. To conceptualize the groove, h suggests, is also to fathom out its production. By focusing on the cognitive processes that g into making a groove work, Zbikowski proposes a model for working out how listeners an performers participate in the formulation of a groove during a recording. Zbikowski insist that 'it is natural to imagine music that correlates with some of our favourite bodily motions

248). Cultural knowledge, moreover, determines how the individual maps bodily motion to sound: 'When listeners respond to a groove, they are demonstrating a particular kind cultural knowledge' (p. 249). Through the models Zbikowski proposes, which vary from rlier studies in popular music and jazz by scholars such as Keil, Middleton, Monson and, re recently, Butler, an analysis of specific grooves is undertaken that commences from perspectives of the musicians creating the groove. In James Brown's 'Doing it to Death', ikowski discovers 'four possible targets for bodily motion' (p. 263) in the track's rhythmic tivity. Despite the track's intricate, multilayered patterning (especially in terms of pitch and ythmic detail), its density seems so commonplace that it ceases to be remarkable. Yet, it is ly when 'we pause to consider why grooves are so seductive, and their rhythmic compulsion inevitable, that this complexity becomes apparent' (p. 264). Zbikowski's conception of the oove is not without its problems as he attempts to theorize embodied knowledge within e field of rhythmic theory. The difficulty of this study involves grasping and measuring gnitively the structures and processes that all too often come over as simple or simplistic.

Defined by its easy accessibility and entertainment quality, pop music is often dismissed the grounds of its formal properties and transparent narratives (see Walser, 1993; Brackett, 00; Middleton, 2000; Tagg, 2000; Moore, 2001, 2003; Hawkins, 2002, 2009; Warner, 03). Yet the controlling function of the pop production that is 'responsible for shaping e compositional design' (Hawkins, 2002, p. 11) holds a clue to the intense pleasurable periences many people have. Undoubtedly, technology has provided new spaces for periencing music and there can be little doubt that our ways of listening to music have en shaped by its progress. As a result, the scholarly study of popular music has also been ncerned from the outset with the circumstances of its production in relation to the music dustry (see, for example, Negus, 1992). But there is more to this, as Frith has remarked, for aking and listening to music is a bodily matter that always involves 'social movements', d the ensuing pleasure derived from pop music is 'experienced directly' offering us 'a real perience of what the ideal could be' (1996, p. 274). This is borne out by the star's voice much as her/his visibility through media technology. Let us now turn to one of the first ses of the televised pop star, Frank Sinatra, whose intense involvement with the television edium between 1950 and 1960 was historically groundbreaking.

The documented peculiarities of Sinatra's involvement in the early years of television ghlight the impact of subjectivity on the viewing process where, as Frith has argued, rformers always face the threat of their performance failing and where 'risked intimacy' is ways a 'risked embarrassment' (1996, p. 214). While Sinatra's shows from the early 1950s d off his charisma as an established mega-star, certain things failed. In Chapter 8 Albert uster examines how in the *Frank Sinatra Show* (1 January 1952) things went downhill after s opening number, 'There's Gonna be a Great Day', because Sinatra was 'trying to do it all – nging, comedy, bantering' (p. 161) and did not come up to the task. Clearly the awkwardness f Sinatra's televised performances needs to be contextualized during a period of change hen swing gave way to rock 'n' roll in the form of Elvis Presley. Sinatra, who had publicly enounced Presley's music in derogatory terms, was virtually compelled to hire him for his rst post-army appearance on his 12 May 1960 show. In a star-studded show featuring Sammy avis Jr, Peter Lawford, Joey Bishop and Sinatra himself, Presley stole the show with an ergy that was 'so contagious that it did not matter whether Sinatra's persona was hot, cool, r lukewarm for the special to succeed' (p. 165). Presley's youthful vibrancy encapsulated the

new era of the pop star, and any embarrassment about performing in a 'suggestive mann
was well disguised by the spectacle of him liberating himself and a new generation from
constraints of those before him. Sinatra, nevertheless, was among the first pin-up stars
the new pop era, his success a direct result of the technological developments of the 195
Above all, as Frith notes in Chapter 2, it was Sinatra who 'pioneered the use of the LP
build up moods and atmospheres in ways impossible on three-minute singles' (p. 37). Qu
remarkably, it only took half a century for pop to develop into one of the most power
audiovisual media forms of all time.

   If we accept that pop's roots are firmly rooted in the styles that emanated from the U:
in the 1950s, such as rhythm 'n' blues and rock 'n' roll, then these styles themselves
surely predicated upon the blues-styled popular music of the 1920s. One can only wonc
how Trixie Smith would have envisaged young girls sounding at the end of the century w
she recorded 'My Man Rocks Me' in 1922. One thing is for sure: the Spice Girls dominat
pop in the 1990s with songs that were not that dissimilar from Trixie Smith's. Indeed, th
strategy of 'girl power' aligned itself to a feminist discourse that they themselves termed 'th
wave'. Perpetuating the messages of strong female icons before them (Madonna, Lennc
Amos, Björk), the Spice Girls demonstrated that a girl group could be independent, feisty a
powerful. Their construction of femininity was a striking element of their act, and certair
full of contradictions. As a counterpart to Britpop and the laddism of Cool Britannia, Spi
Girl culture became an incentive for girls to do things for themselves. Yet, as Dibben (199
has suggested, girl power was not only a myth but also a lie, and girls were not empower
by this movement in the ways they appeared to be. In fact, the possibility of resistance w
enticing and deceptive. Picking up on Dibben's point, Dafna Lemish argues in Chapter 12 th
the Spice Girls can be read in oppositional ways, as feminists (waving the flag of girl powe
and as a 'disguised version of the conventional "truth claim" of the centrality of the "loo
in female identity' (p. 237). While their stardom symbolized cultural struggle, they failed I
conveying 'the impossibility of change'. For accepting oneself was about '"accepting" yo
personality traits, while the "look" remains in need of constant improvement … In this w.
the Spices continue to promote the everlasting frustration with the unsatisfactory femini
body' (p. 237).

   Gender debates have proliferated in popular music research over recent years as we ha
learnt to be more attentive to discoursing on the politics of representation. Albeit fro
different points of view, the unitary task of the popular music scholar is to decide on critei
for reflection that access the merits of studying music through the rituals of human expressic
Insights into how performance takes place and is produced in different cultural contexts
complex, which means that critiquing pop and its recorded score is fraught with challenges a
obstacles. Whether the methods and approaches presented here achieve their goal of sheddir
light on the meaning of pop is open to question; for the definition of pop alone is compounde
by the confused history that its very concept delineates both culturally and socially. On t
whole, though, this collection of essays poses pertinent questions with intellectual d·
that concern pop music's communicative strength: its aesthetic and ethical shadings; i
codified audiovisual forms; its vibrant divergence of styles and practices; its material ar
performative effects. Most of all, each essay represents a critique of the popularity of
pop experience itself, accounting for the pleasures we derive from listening, watching
participating as the music unfolds time after time.

ferences

orno, T.W. (1941), 'On Popular Music', *Studies in Philosophy and Social Science*, 9, pp. 17–48.
ckett, David (2000), *Interpreting Popular Music*, Berkeley: University of California Press.
ester, Andrew (1970), 'For a Rock Aesthetic', *New Left Review*, 59, pp. 83–87.
leuze, Gilles and Guattari, Felix (1984), *Anti-Oedipus*, London: Athlone Press.
oben, Nicola (1999), 'Representations of Femininity in Popular Music', *Popular Music*, 18, pp. 331–55.
th, Simon (1996), *Performing Rites: On the Value of Popular Music*, Oxford: Oxford University Press.
th, Simon and Goodwin, Andrew (eds) (1993), *On Record: Rock, Pop, and the Written Word*, London: Routledge.
mmond, Peter and Gloag, Kenneth (2002), 'Popular Music', in Alison Latham (ed.), *The Oxford Companion to Music*, Oxford: Oxford University Press; available at: *Oxford Music Online*, http://www.oxfordmusiconline.com/subscriber/article/opr/t114/e5287 (accessed 28 July, 2010).
roy, Paul (1993), *The Black Atlantic: Modernity and Black Consciousness*, Cambridge, Mass.: Harvard University Press.
odwin, Andrew (1993), *Dancing in the Distraction Factory: Music, Television and Popular Culture*, London: Routledge.
wkins, Stan (2002), *Settling the Pop Score: Pop Texts and Identity Politics*, Aldershot: Ashgate.
wkins, Stan (2009), *The British Pop Dandy: Masculinity, Popular Music and Culture*, Farnham: Ashgate.
yles, Katherine (1999), *How We Became Posthuman: Virtual Bodies in Cybernetics, Literature, and Informatics*, Chicago: Chicago University Press.
plan, E. Ann (1987), *Rocking Around the Clock: Music Television, Postmodernism, and Consumer Culture*, London: Routledge.
nnedy, Michael (2006a), 'Beatles, The', in *The Oxford Dictionary of Music* (2nd edn rev.), Oxford: Oxford University Press; available at: *Oxford Music Online*, http://www.oxfordmusiconline.com/subscriber/article/opr/t237/e1003 (accessed 28 July 2010).
nnedy, Michael (ed.) (2006b), 'Pop', in *The Oxford Dictionary of Music* (2nd edn rev.), Oxford: Oxford University Press; available at: *Oxford Music Online*, http://www.oxfordmusiconline.com/subscriber/article/opr/t237/e8059 (accessed 28 July 2010).
nnedy, Michael (ed.) (2006c), 'Rolling Stones', in *The Oxford Dictionary of Music* (2nd edn rev.), Oxford: Oxford University Press; available at: *Oxford Music Online*, http://www.oxfordmusiconline.com/subscriber/article/opr/t237/e8638 (accessed 28 July 2010).
cGuigan, Jim (1992), *Cultural Populism*, London: Routledge.
erton, Richard (1970), Comment on Chester's 'For a Rock Aesthetic', *New Left Review* 1/59, pp. 88–96.
ddleton, Richard (1990), *Studying Popular Music*, Milton Keynes: Open University Press.
ddleton, Richard (ed.) (2000), *Reading Pop: Approaches to Textual Analysis in Popular Music*, Oxford: Oxford University Press.
ddleton, Richard *et al.* (2001), 'Pop', in *Grove Music Online*, *Oxford Music Online at:* http://www.oxfordmusiconline.com/subscriber/article/grove/music/46845 (accessed 27 July 2010).
ddleton, Richard (2006), *Voicing the Popular: On the Subjects of Popular Music*, London: Routledge.
oore, Allan F. (2000), 'On the pop-classical split' in D. Scott (ed.), *Music, Culture and Society*, Oxford: Oxford University Press, pp. 161–4.
oore, Allan F. (2001), *Rock – The Primary Text: Developing a Musicology of Rock* (2nd edn), Aldershot: Ashgate.
oore, Allan F. (ed.) (2003), *Analyzing Popular Music*, Cambridge: Cambridge University Press.
oore, Allan F. (2007a), 'Authenticity as Authentication', in Allan F. Moore (ed.), *Critical Essays in Popular Musicology*, Aldershot: Ashgate, pp. 131–45.

Moore, Allan. F. (ed.) (2007b), *Critical Essays in Popular Musicology*, Aldershot: Ashgate.

Negus, Keith (1992), *Producing Pop: Culture and Conflict in the Popular Music Industry*, Lond
    Arnold.

Shepherd, John and Wicke, Peter (1997), *Music and Cultural Theory*, Cambridge: Polity Press.

Tagg, Philip (2000), 'Analysing Popular Music: Theory, Method and Practice', in R. Middleton (
    Reading Pop: Approaches to Textual Analysis in Popular Music, Oxford: Oxford University Pr
    pp. 71–103.

Virilio, Paul (1997), *Open Sky*, trans. Julie Rose, London: Verso.

Walser, Robert (1993), *Running with the Devil: Power, Gender and Madness in Heavy Metal Mu*
    Hanover, NH: Wesleyan University Press.

Warner, Tim (2003), *Pop Music – Technology and Creativity*, Aldershot: Ashgate.

Part I
Aesthetics and Authenticity

[1]

'Sing it for Me': Posthuman Ventriloquism in Recent Popular Music

JOSEPH AUNER

A famous scene in the 1968 film *2001: A Space Odyssey* shows the lone surviving astronaut, Dave, deep within the memory banks of the ship's computer, HAL (short for Heuristically programmed Algorithmic computer). Dave is methodically disabling HAL's higher brain functions after the computer caused the deaths of the crew because he thought that their human fallibility posed a danger to the mission. With each turn of the screw, we hear HAL's calmly pleading voice as he feels his consciousness slipping away. In contrast to the overall cool tone of the film – and of Stanley Kubrick's oeuvre in general – this is a moment of great emotional intensity. But strikingly it is the broken and dying machine that is expressive, not the astronaut, who remains mostly silent, encapsulated in a reflective plastic shell, floating in the blood-red organic space within HAL's brain. We can only sense Dave's agitation through his nervous glances and the amplified sounds of his irregular breathing, superimposed on the sustained hiss in the background. When he does speak, it is in a thin, clipped voice processed through the microphone in his helmet, while HAL's voice is direct and unmediated, filling the space just as we hear our own voices resonating inside our heads. The final stage of the lobotomy is marked by HAL's sudden regression through memory to the day of his first public demonstration as he sings the song 'Daisy Bell' about a bicycle built for two. Nothing in the film has prepared us for his last words to be a sentimental song from long-lost times. But, just as important, HAL's swansong also marks the last time Dave speaks in the film: his final words before his cosmic journey when he leaves technology and humanity behind are 'Sing it for me.'[1]

Now that 2001 has actually come and gone, many of the film's predictions about the external transformations of our existence through technology appear quite off the mark: routine tourist travel in space, the colonization of the moon and a manned flight to Jupiter are still the stuff of science fiction. But Stanley Kubrick and Arthur C. Clarke's vision of the extent to which our internal life would be colonized by technology was, if anything, too cautious. As the proliferation of images of cyborgs, androids, artificial reality and cloning makes clear, the

Earlier versions of this essay were presented at the Humanities Institute Stony Brook (1999), the American Musicological Society (Toronto, 2000) and the International Association for Philosophy and Literature (Stony Brook, 2000). For much helpful advice I am grateful to Edith Auner, Mike Boyd, David Brackett, Christa Erickson, Ira Livingston, Timothy D. Taylor, Jason Hanley and the anonymous referees.

[1] See sound clip 1 at <www.jrma.oupjournals.org>. From *2001: A Space Odyssey*. © 1968 Turner Entertainment Co., a Time Warner Company. For more on the use of voice in *2001*, see Michel Chion, *Kubrick's Cinema Odyssey* (London, 2001).

borders between an authentic human presence and the machine are becoming increasingly permeable and unstable.[2] When Kubrick made *2001*, it still seemed possible to imagine a future human evolution beyond any technological reliance. Significantly, the project he was working on at the time of his death in 1999 concerned artificial intelligence. In Steven Spielberg's realization of the project in *A.I.: Artificial Intelligence*, released in 2001, a dysfunctional couple grieving for their only child, who is languishing in a coma, adopt an android boy that is programmed to love the mother unconditionally and for ever. But when the child returns to health, the robot is abandoned by the mother who becomes incapable of loving him in return. The focus of the film is the quest of the robot, significantly also named David, to regain her love by being transformed, like Pinocchio, into a real boy. The shift of emotional expression from the human to the technological realm is almost complete: throughout the film humans range from self-absorbed to monstrously cruel, while only the androids are capable of love.

In no aspect of our lives has the penetration of the human by machines been more complete than in music. Every stage of production, distribution and consumption in the musical life of the industrialized world has been so permeated by technology that we no longer even recognize complex devices such as a piano as technological artefacts,[3] while at the same time the idea of a 'piano' now spans the range between the shiny black assemblages of wood, metal and plastic (or ivory) in our living rooms to the music software triggering piano samples on a laptop computer. Music circulates through manifold layers of mechanical devices, electronics and digital translations in the long passage from its origins in a musician's mental and embodied conception to our eardrums. That music is being made from the sounds of medical procedures that modify the body – the slurping of liposuction or the grinding of cartilage – is more a shift in degree than a change in kind.[4]

It is at the level of the voice that we are most aware of this mechanization. Indeed, Dave's request for HAL to 'sing it for me' has been answered by an astonishing proliferation in our cultural terrain of sampled, modified and artificially generated voices. We routinely encounter automated voices on the phone; we are spoken to by our cars and appliances; in the year 2001, the AT&T corporation

---

[2] For some examples see Elaine L. Graham, *Representations of the Post/Human: Monsters, Aliens and Others in Popular Culture* (New Brunswick, NJ, 2002); *Artificial Humans: Manic Machines Controlled Bodies*, ed. Rolf Aurich *et al.* (Berlin, 2000); *Robosapiens: Evolution of a New Species*, ed. Peter Menzel and Faith D'Aluisio (Cambridge, MA, 2000); *The Cyborg Handbook*, ed. Chris Hables Gray (New York and London, 1995); and Victoria Nelson, *The Secret Life of Puppets* (Cambridge, 2002).

[3] For wide-ranging studies of the interactions of culture and musical technologies see Timothy D. Taylor, *Strange Sounds: Music, Technology, and Culture* (New York, 2001), and Paul Théberge, *Any Sound You Can Imagine: Making Music/Consuming Technology* (Hanover, NH, and London, 1997).

[4] The piece *California Rhinoplasty* from Matmos, *A Chance to Cut is a Chance to Cure* (2001), combines the sound of a nose flute with 'recordings of plastic surgeries performed in California: rhinoplasty, endoscopic forehead lift, chin implant'. Marc Flanagan, 'Aural Surgeons', *Artbyte* (September–October 2001), 50–9 (p. 55).

announced its 'Natural Voices' software, claiming it to be capable of reproducing any voice, even of bringing 'the voices of long-dead celebrities back to life'.[5] The complex blurring of man and machine through voice and song in this scene from *2001* prefigures a broad range of contemporary music that generates meaning by exploring and destabilizing the borders between authentic human presence and the technological. In many areas of recent music, the unaltered human voice has become an endangered species. Manipulations and simulations of the voice appear in several different forms in popular music, paralleling the introduction of new technologies or new ways of using old technologies.[6] There are groups that sing almost exclusively through vocoder-like devices that make possible a kind of ventriloquism through which a musician can sing or speak into a microphone and modulate a synthesized sound (Boards of Canada, Daft Punk, Air); a broad range of hip-hop and electronic dance music relies on vocal samples and voices lifted off vinyl (DJ Shadow, X-ecutioners, Public Enemy, Fatboy Slim); while the digital modulation of vocal pitches with the Autotuner (as in very successful recordings by Madonna and Cher) has become so prevalent as to be called 'one of the safest, maybe laziest, means of guaranteeing chart success'.[7]

In this article I illustrate the broad emergence of such techniques into the popular imagination with recent songs by Radiohead and Moby that stage these border crossings in particularly vivid ways through the opposition of human voices that are sampled and repeated in the form of constant loops against highly processed or digitally generated speech that sounds as though a machine were speaking to us. More specifically, I am interested in how and why in these songs, as with HAL's final moments in *2001*, it is the technological sphere that is made the locus of expression, while the human voices are mechanized, drained of subjectivity, turned into signs that circulate as subroutines of a larger system. Of course, it goes almost without saying that in these examples the collision of the human loops and sad machines is a staged narrative. Behind the computer voices, at least in the examples I am discussing here, there is always a human presence pulling the strings, always, as in *The Wizard of Oz*, a man – or sometimes a woman – behind the curtain. These pieces, moreover, are part of a long history of interest in human/machine interactions in association with music, with some important milestones being eighteenth-century musical automata, the misogynist military fantasies of the Italian futurists, and the Weimar-era vogue for mechanical art and the burgeoning

---

[5] Lisa Guernsey, 'Software is Called Capable of Copying any Human Voice', *New York Times*, 23 July 2001, A1.

[6] Susana Loza makes a start at a typology of vocal processing, including the 'cut-up', the 'Moebius loop', the '"Planet Rock"/electro effect', 'playing with speed' and the 'diva loop'. Susana Loza, 'Sampling (Hetero)sexuality: Diva-ness and Discipline in Electronic Dance Music', *Popular Music*, 20 (2001), 349–57 (pp. 349–50).

[7] Kay Dickinson, '"Believe"? Vocoders, Digitalised Female Identity and Camp', *Popular Music*, 20 (2001), 333–47 (p. 333). While my focus here is popular music, related developments could be traced in the work of many concert-music composers working with digital technology, including Steve Reich and Paul Lansky.

technologies of film, radio and recording.[8] That this development has deep historical roots is evident in HAL's song 'Daisy Bell' from the 1890s, which already presents a peculiar mediation of the human and the technological through the device of the bicycle built for two – certainly an appropriate way for a computer to imagine love.

Yet, as a growing literature has argued, the specific forms such ventriloquism has taken in recent music can be linked to broader cultural changes associated with the digital technologies that are transforming our sense of reality, subjectivity and the human. The most extreme manifestation of this process is the figure of the cyborg – a human/machine hybrid – which has become a central imaginative resource in art, literature and criticism as a means of reflecting on the anxieties and possibilities of what it means to be human in the increasingly technologically mediated space of industrially developed nations. In 'A Cyborg Manifesto', Donna Haraway describes earlier representations of the interaction of technology and humans as reflecting 'an essential dualism between materialism and idealism'. 'Now', she writes, 'we are not so sure':

> Late twentieth-century machines have made thoroughly ambiguous the difference between natural and artificial, mind and body, self-developing and externally designed, and many other distinctions that used to apply to organisms and machines. Our machines are disturbingly lively, and we ourselves frighteningly inert.[9]

Approaching these examples from Radiohead and Moby as figurative or literal cyborg systems not only can illuminate the increasingly close interdependence of human and machine in a wide range of recent music, but also has implications for how both poles in the relationship are being reconfigured through the process of their fusion. As Susana Loza writes of the 'cyborg, fembot, and posthuman', 'these techno-organic entities traverse the space between desire and dread; their indeterminate forms simultaneously destabilize and reconfigure the dualistic limits of liberal humanist subjectivity'.[10] These pieces – products of a rock band that relinquishes its voice to a computer and a 'techno' DJ striving to make mechanized dance music sing – can illustrate some ways musicians use the increasingly prevalent technological ventriloquism of these posthuman voices to chart the convulsions at the boundaries of race, gender and the human.

---

[8] See Annette Richards, 'Automatic Genius: Mozart and the Mechanical Sublime', *Music and Letters*, 80 (1999), 366–89; Carolyn Abbate, 'Outside Ravel's Tomb', *Journal of the American Musicological Society*, 52 (1999), 465–530; Sadie Plant, *Zeros and Ones: Digital Women and the New Technoculture* (New York, 1997), 85–6; Catherine Parsons Smith, '"A Distinguishing Virility": Feminism and Modernism in American Art Music', *Cecilia Reclaimed: Feminist Perspectives on Gender and Music*, ed. Susan C. Cook and Judy S. Tsou (Urbana, 1994), 90–106; Nancy Drechsler, '"Tod dem Mondschein und gelbe Ohrfeigen!": Futuristische Männerphantasien im Sound der Maschine', *Neue Zeitschrift für Musik*, 156 (1995), 14–19. For a wide-ranging consideration of the history of the voice dissociated from the body, see Steven Connor, *Dumbstruck: A Cultural History of Ventriloquism* (Oxford, 2000). I am grateful to Amanda Weidman for directing me to this source.

[9] Donna Haraway, 'A Cyborg Manifesto: Science, Technology, and Socialist-Feminism in the Late Twentieth Century', *Simians, Cyborgs, and Women: The Reinvention of Nature* (London, 1991), 149–81 (p. 152).

[10] Loza, 'Sampling (Hetero)sexuality', 349.

MAPPING THE POSTHUMAN

Radiohead's song 'Fitter Happier', which appeared on the critically acclaimed and best-selling album *OK Computer* (1997), seems almost designed to illustrate Haraway's inert humans and disturbingly lively machines. As is already evident from the name of the band and from the titles both of the album and of other songs such as 'Paranoid Android', the song appeared in a context that foregrounds human/machine interactions. In most cases the representation of technology is profoundly ambivalent, as in the song 'Airbag', which is about a device that can save your life or malfunction and kill you without warning. In 'Fitter Happier', the band's lead singer, Thom Yorke, is replaced by a not very sophisticated voice synthesizer – comparable to the 'Fred' voice included with the Macintosh SimpleText™ program – which recites a litany of self-help phrases:

Fitter happier more productive
comfortable
not drinking too much
regular exercise at the gym (3 days a week).[11]

Against the droning computer there are human voices in the background, consisting of a fragmentary dialogue as if overheard through a radio or intercom: 'This is the panic office, Section 917 may have been hit . . .' and the response, 'Activate the following procedures . . .'. But the human voices here are turned into loops that continue through much of the song, gradually becoming inaudible. These borrowed voices, as in many pieces of contemporary electronic music, are the stereotypical square, white, male voices of invisible authority, self-consciously set off from the context in vocal timbre and phraseology, as if lifted from an old movie or television show.[12] The juxtaposition of the human and computer voices is mirrored in the other sound materials, which include an out-of-tune piano and slow string chords, layered with disruptive bursts of alarms and synthesized noises.

In 'Fitter Happier' it is precisely the machine voice that becomes the most expressive and communicative. Yorke has called the song 'the most upsetting thing I've ever written', and has said of the Macintosh speech synthesizer he used for the song that it was the most emotional voice he had ever heard.[13] It is particularly significant in this regard that when *OK Computer* came out many listeners thought the voice was that of the physicist Stephen Hawking, who also speaks through a voice synthesizer.[14] While on first glance this connection seems bizarre, it

[11] See sound clip 2 at <www.jrma.oupjournals.org>. Radiohead, from 'Fitter Happier', *OK Computer.* © 1997 EMI Records Ltd.
[12] Yorke identified the voices as coming from the 1974 film *Flight of the Condor*, sampled off a hotel television. Marc Randall, *Exit Music: The Radiohead Story* (New York, 2000), 225.
[13] Commenting in 2001 on a recent electronic dance-music release, Yorke described the 'samplers singing more delicately and confused than any human could'. *Spin*, February 2001, 67.
[14] The misperception may have been linked to the fact that Hawking had actually appeared on Pink Floyd's 1994 release, *Division Bell*, on the song 'Keep Talking'. Thanks to Jason Hanley for this point.

indicates how the uninflected voice, with its empty phrases and artificial quality, could come to seem almost heroic in its stoic continuity.[15] Part of the effect of the song can be attributed to the lyrics, which are much more direct, intelligible and personal than those of any other song on the album.[16] Yet this begs the question, which is my focus here, why the robotic voice is the only one permitted such confessional lyrics, or, for that matter, why it is that in *2001* HAL's voice becomes more and not less poignant and emotional as its mechanical and artificial characteristics are foregrounded through the sinking pitch and extreme ritardando.

Katherine Hayles's *How We Became Posthuman* has provided a framework for understanding this transformation in the contemporary imagination. Drawing on a survey of post-World War II scientific and literary writings, Hayles defines the posthuman as a point of view or way of experiencing the world that at its most fundamental level 'privileges informational pattern over material instantiation'.[17] She traces the transfer of the hardware/software distinction to the human realm, so that the self and consciousness are seen as independent from any organic basis. As if to illustrate Hayles's argument, a 2000–01 advertising campaign for Sony's Memory Stick, a medium designed to allow easy transfer of information between computers and other devices, featured a full-page photograph of the back of a man's head fitted with a small port, thus as just another piece of hardware in the chain.[18]

Not surprisingly, the figure of the cyborg is central to Hayles's formulation of the posthuman. She discusses various science-fiction cyborgs, but also cites statistics that 10% of the US population are already, in some sense, literally cyborgs (through the use of pacemakers, artificial body parts, etc.).[19] An illustration entitled 'Replaceable Parts of Irreplaceable You', from the *Harvard Medical School Family Health Guide*, lists

---

[15] Interpretations of 'Fitter Happier' on a Radiohead fan page focus on the loss of control and the 'hopelessness of modern-day life' depicted by the song: 'This is a really sad song, because this poor bloke is forced (probably through medication) to believe that all this shit is right. He started off as [an] individual but they got to him and made him think that he was wrong' (<http://www.greenplastic.com/songinterp/fitterhappier.html>, accessed 20 October 2000).

[16] Compare, for example, the lyrics of the first song, 'Airbag', which starts: 'In the next world war / in a jackknife juggernaut / I am born again / in the neon sign scrolling up and down / I am born again'). Simon Reynolds writes similarly of the two albums that followed *OK Computer*. 'As for Yorke's singing, on *Kid A / Amnesiac* studio technology and unusual vocal technique are both applied to dislexify his already oblique, fragmented words. Yorke has said he will never allow the lyrics to be printed and that the listeners are expressly not meant to focus on them.' Simon Reynolds, 'Walking on Thin Ice', *The Wire*, 209 (July 2001), 26–33 (p. 26).

[17] Katherine Hayles, *How We Became Posthuman: Virtual Bodies in Cybernetics, Literature, and Informatics* (Chicago, 1999), 2.

[18] In the novelization of *2001: A Space Odyssey*, Arthur C. Clarke described the belief that the mind would free itself from matter, with robot bodies as a stepping stone: 'Sooner or later, as their scientific knowledge progressed, they would get rid of the fragile, disease-and-accident-prone bodies as they wore out – or perhaps even before that – by constructions of metal and plastic and would thus achieve immortality. The brain might linger for a little while as the last remnant of the organic body, directing its mechanical limbs and observing the universe through its electronic senses – senses far finer and subtler than those that blind evolution could ever develop.' Arthur C. Clarke, *2001: A Space Odyssey*, based on the screenplay of the MGM film by Stanley Kubrick and Arthur C. Clarke (New York, 1968), 173–4.

[19] Hayles, *How We Became Posthuman*, 115.

over 30 replacement parts now available.[20] Anyone who has spent any time in a hospital lately knows that this is just the tip of the iceberg with regard to the interactive technological systems into which we can be enfolded from birth to our final moments in the intensive care unit. But Hayles is more interested in the cyborg at a metaphorical level as a configuration of 'the human being so that it can be seamlessly articulated with intelligent machines'.[21] This interaction ranges from workers wedded to the computer keyboard and screen to neurosurgeons using robotic extensions for surgery, but the defining point is the flow of information between the human and the increasingly complex and interrelated technological devices that we rely on to work and communicate. Hayles writes that, 'in the posthuman, there are no essential differences or absolute demarcations between bodily existence and computer simulation, cybernetic mechanism and biological organism, robot teleology and human goals'.[22]

A central result of this process for the idea of the posthuman is what Hayles describes as distributed cognition, whereby consciousness is understood and experienced as an epiphenomenon, just one system perched on countless other systems that regulate the body and its interaction with the environment. In contrast to the ideal of the liberal humanist subject, individual, autonomous, unique, the posthuman subject is 'in a cybernetic circuit that splices your will, desire, and perception into a distributed cognitive system in which represented bodies are joined with enacted bodies through mutating and flexible machine interfaces'.[23] Similarly, Sadie Plant, in *Zeros and Ones*, differentiates the cyborg from the earlier model of technology as a prosthesis that extends human functioning, writing: 'the digital machines of the late twentieth century are not add-on parts which serve to augment an existing human form. Quite beyond their own perceptions and control, bodies are continually engineered by the processes in which they are engaged.'[24]

The caption to the graphic from the *Harvard Medical School Family Health Guide*, 'Replaceable Parts of Irreplaceable You', in itself suggests that the claim that we are irreplaceable no longer goes without saying. The posthuman decentring of the subject has clear connections to other postmodern narratives that have called the subject into question. Bill Nichols contrasts the state of technology Walter Benjamin discussed, in which mechanical reproduction liquidated authenticity and the idea of an original, with the digital realm in which 'cybernetic simulation renders experience, and the real itself, problematic'.[25] And

---

[20] *Harvard Medical School Family Health Guide* (New York, 1999), 1218–19.
[21] Hayles, *How We Became Posthuman*, 3.
[22] *Ibid.*
[23] *Ibid.*, xiv.
[24] Plant, *Zeros and Ones*, 182.
[25] Bill Nichols, 'The Work of Culture in the Age of Cybernetic Systems', *Electronic Media and Technoculture*, ed. John Thornton Caldwell (New Brunswick, 2000), 90–114 (p. 97). See also Chris Hables Gray and Steven Mentor, 'The Cyborg Body Politic and the New World Order', *Prosthetic Territories: Politics and Hypertechnologies*, ed. Gabriel Brahm Jr and Mark Driscoll (Boulder, 1995), 219–47.

if '"clear and distinct" people may be a prerequisite for an industrial economy based on the sale of labor power', then 'mutually dependent cyborgs may be a higher priority for a postindustrial postmodern economy':

> In an age of cybernetic systems, the very foundation of Western culture and the very heart of its metaphysical tradition, the individual, with his or her inherent dilemmas of free will versus determinism, autonomy vs. dependence, and so on, may very well be destined to stand as a vestigial trace of concepts and traditions which are no longer pertinent.[26]

Hayles similarly presents the idea of the posthuman as having both destructive and liberating implications for how we define ourselves, and thus for how we interact with others and with our environment. By signalling the end of the 'liberal humanist view of the self', 'grounded in presence, identified with originary guarantees and teleological trajectories, associated with solid foundations and logical coherence', she writes that 'the posthuman is likely to be seen as anti-human because it envisions the conscious mind as a small subsystem running its program of self-construction and self-assurance while remaining ignorant of the actual dynamics of complex systems'. But her ultimate project is to argue for the embodied nature of all experience against a dominant strand of posthuman thought that views the body as only a shell that will be eventually left behind:

> If my nightmare is a culture inhabited by posthumans who regard their bodies as fashion accessories rather than the ground of being, my dream is a version of the posthuman that embraces the possibilities of information technologies without being seduced by fantasies of unlimited power and disembodied immortality, that recognizes and celebrates finitude as a condition of human being, and that understands human life is embedded in a material world of great complexity, one on which we depend for our continued survival.[27]

Hayles's formulation of the posthuman, with both its apocalyptic and its utopian potentialities, has clear resonance with the musical developments discussed here, as well as with many other manifestations of the idea of the posthuman in recent popular music. Previous studies have extended Hayles's point that the idea of the posthuman is a particular threat 'to that fraction of humanity who had the wealth, power, and leisure to conceptualize themselves as autonomous beings exercising their will through individual agency and choice'.[28] That the act of shedding a human skin and adopting a posthuman persona can have considerably divergent implications for those whose essential humanity has already been put into question is evident in the ways technology has been used to create alternative representations of gender and race in a range of musical styles. The productive power of the idea of the

---

[26] Nichols, 'The Work of Culture', 111.
[27] Hayles, *How We Became Posthuman*, 5.
[28] *Ibid.*, 286.

posthuman for critics and musicians reflects to a large degree its ability both to expose and to suggest ways of reformulating a naturalized conception of the 'liberal humanist subject'; thus, in Loza's terms, 'the posthuman ends a dualistic system that celebrated the corporeal coordinates of the white heterosexual middle-class male'.[29] As Judith Halberstam and Ira Livingston have written:

> The human functions to domesticate and hierarchize difference within the human (whether according to race, class, gender) and to absolutize difference between the human and the non-human. The posthuman does not reduce difference-from-others to difference-from-self, but rather emerges in the pattern of resonance and interference between the two.[30]

The idea of the cyborg has been particularly useful from the perspectives of feminist theory. As Haraway writes:

> The dichotomies between mind and body, animal and human, organism and machine, public and private, nature and culture, men and women, primitive and civilized are all in question ideologically. The actual situation of women is their integration/exploitation into a world system of production/reproduction and communication called the informatics of domination. The home, workplace, market, public arena, the body itself – all can be dispersed and interfaced in nearly infinite, polymorphous ways, with large consequences for women and others – consequences that themselves are very different for different people and which make potent oppositional international movements difficult to imagine and essential for survival.[31]

Building on writings by Haraway, Plant and others, Kay Dickinson has discussed Cher's use of the modified cyborg voice in the hit song 'Believe' (1998) as a means for asserting control of technology and for making possible an empowering shape-shifting. While acknowledging the problematic aspects of her image, as well as the actual limits of this kind of aesthetic empowerment, she argues that for Cher, as for other musicians including Laurie Anderson, such technologized alter egos serve as emblems of the power of choosing and refashioning identity.[32] Dickinson's conclusion about how the vocoder voice might function as a source of camp delight in inauthenticity is developed in more depth by Susana Loza in terms of the 'performative posthuman, the diva who deviates from the heterosexual script with her gender-bending loop', serving to foreground the constructedness of gender and racial identities. Loza stresses the way the cyborg 'melts binaries, crosses genders, slips into other species and genres, samples multiple sexualities, and destabilises dance music with her stammered replies. He haunts humanism with his regenerated and denatured vocals.'[33]

That Loza's divas are most often black highlights another, and much less often studied vector of the posthuman: race. Alexander G.

---

[29] Loza, 'Sampling (Hetero)sexuality', 352.
[30] Judith Halberstam and Ira Livingston, 'Introduction: Posthuman Bodies', *Posthuman Bodies*, ed. Halberstam and Livingston (Bloomington, 1995), 1–19 (p. 10).
[31] Haraway, 'A Cyborg Manifesto', 163.
[32] Dickinson, '"Believe"?'.
[33] Loza, 'Sampling (Hetero)sexuality'. 350–1.

Weheliye explicitly challenges Hayles's formulation for its 'erasure' of issues of race, while pointing out the 'literal and virtual whiteness of cybertheory' in general.[34] Looking at the way technology is represented and utilized in contemporary R & B, Weheliye argues that just as the 'idea of the human has had a very different meaning in black culture and politics than it has enjoyed in mainstream America', the idea of the posthuman should not be limited to a single hegemonic manifestation: as Weheliye points out,

> It seems that one has to be always already 'free from the will of the others' (or think that one is) in order to mutate into the fusion of heterogeneous agents comprising the posthuman state of being, thereby excluding all cultural and political formations in which the history of subjectivity is necessarily yoked to the will – and/or the whips and chains – of others.[35]

Weheliye sees the 'audibly mechanized and more traditionally melismatic and "soulful" voice in contemporary R & B' as constituting a different form of posthumanism, one 'not mired in the residual effects of white liberal subjectivity'.[36]

An overview of the terrain of some previous popular music representations of the interaction of the human and technology – a terrain that Radiohead and Moby build upon and remake – suggests some of these 'residual effects' in the ways whiteness and masculinity have been constructed.[37] For example, 'Karn Evil 9', from Emerson, Lake and Palmer's 1973 album *Brain Salad Surgery*, anticipates the musical materials of 'Fitter Happier' with its robotic voices and repeating loops, but these are configured quite differently so as to reaffirm the boundary of man and machine. The extended composition, a sort of post-apocalyptic space opera, concludes with another dialogue between a captain and a spaceship's computer that is taking control in response to human imperfection:

> I am all there is.
> NEGATIVE! PRIMITIVE! LIMITED! I LET YOU LIVE!
> But I gave you life.
> WHAT ELSE COULD YOU DO?
> To do what was right.
> I'M PERFECT! ARE YOU?[38]

---

[34] Alexander G. Weheliye, '"Feenin": Posthuman Voices in Contemporary Black Popular Music', *Social Text*, 71 (2002), 21–47. I am grateful to Prof. Weheliye for sharing this text with me prior to its publication. Although he departs from some of its conclusions, Weheliye draws in particular on Kodwo Eshun's study of 'Afrofuturism', *More Brilliant than the Sun: Adventures in Sonic Fiction* (London, 1998). See also Tricia Rose, *Black Noise: Rap Music and Black Culture in Contemporary America* (Hanover and London, 1994), 62–98.

[35] Weheliye, '"Feenin"', 23–4.

[36] *Ibid.*, 24.

[37] For additional approaches to complexities around issues of whiteness and masculinity in popular music see Barbara Ching, 'The Possum, the Hag, and the Rhinestone Cowboy: Hard Country Music and the Burlesque Abjection of the White Man', and Jeffrey Melnick, '"Story Untold": The Black Men and White Sounds of Doo-Wop', *Whiteness: A Critical Reader*, ed. Mike Hill (New York and London, 1997), 117–33, 134–50.

[38] See sound clip 3 at <www.jrma.oupjournals.org>. Emerson, Lake and Palmer, from 'Karn Evil 9', *Brain Salad Surgery*. © 1973 Manticore Records. Distributed by Atlantic Recording Corporation.

108   JOSEPH AUNER

Unlike *2001*, however, the scene plays out along standard science-fiction lines. As the captain proclaims victory over a defeated enemy – 'Rejoice! Glory is ours! / Our young men have not died in vain. / Their graves need no flowers / The tapes have recorded their names' – the computer answers in a distorted, shrill, metallic voice (shown in capital letters).[39] The computer's superiority is demonstrated decisively in musical terms at the end of the piece as a short segment from previous thematic material is played over and over, accelerating with each repetition far beyond human capacity – pointedly even beyond that of keyboard virtuoso Keith Emerson – a process interrupted only by the end of the record.

Many aspects of this encounter can be seen as an attempt to delineate and stabilize the boundaries between the human and a technological realm that is viewed with anxiety. Significantly, there are several types of anxiety that get bound up with this representation of technology, in particular relating to gender and sexual identities. This is evident most immediately in the H. Giger cover art – showing a skull, suspended in metal fittings, with a sensuous female mouth towards which a stylised penis rises up. The obvious reference to the long tradition of sexualized and dangerous cyborg women is underscored as the two flaps of the cover open up to reveal a Medusa-like woman with metallic serpentine hair.[40] The piece presents an image of technology run amok against the defeated but still stable subject: heroic, individual and autonomous. And it is significant that the protagonist is a spaceship's captain, like *Star Trek*'s Captain Kirk, the embodiment of the white male subject encountering and either coming to terms with or overcoming otherness.[41] While the computer claims identity with the captain – 'LOAD YOUR PROGRAM, I AM YOURSELF' – the music and production serve to define their difference. This is particularly clear in the opposition of Greg Lake's largely unprocessed voice, with its markers of intense and authentic rock emotion, against the distorted, mechanical monotone of the computer. The captain's brief moment of triumph is accompanied by all the musical symbols of church and state: martial percussion rhythms, soaring synthesized trumpet calls and massive organ chords. The computer, on the other hand, is represented by the mechanical loop that emerges from the

---

[39] Contrasting sharply with HAL's soothing vocal timbre, the computer's speech is closer to the grating voice of the all-powerful 'Alpha 60' in Godard's *Alphaville* (1965), which was produced not electronically but by a man 'whose vocal cords were shot away in the war and who has been re-educated to speak from the diaphragm. Godard thought it was important to have, not a mechanical voice, but one which has been, so to speak, killed – like the inhabitants of Alphaville.' *Alphaville: A Film by Jean-Luc Godard*, ed. and trans. Peter Whitehead (New York, 1966), 12. Thanks to David Metzer for directing me to this reference.

[40] Loza sees dance music's highly sexualized mechanized personae, which she dubs 'fembots', as a means for reasserting gender dualities: 'the salacious fembot allows heterosexual males to contemporaneously manage the threats posed by rampant technology and unbridled female sexuality'. Loza, 'Sampling (Hetero)sexuality', 351. For more on images of the female cyborg see Anne Marie Balsamo, *Technologies of the Gendered Body: Reading Cyborg Women* (Durham, NC, 1996).

[41] Notably, Chion points out that Kubrick originally intended the computer in *2001* to be an ambulatory robot named Athena; in the final version of the film women are almost totally absent from space. Chion, *Kubrick's Cinematic Odyssey*, 4.

dissonant final chord – the repeating phrase evoking conveyor belts, mass production and the 'dark Satanic mills' of the Blake and Parry hymn *Jerusalem* which opens the album. That the synthesized looping material is slightly detuned and played with a clangorous metallic timbre presents the computer's music as a nightmarish caricature of the captain's music, from which all the human elements have been eliminated. Significantly, in concert the band left the stage during this final passage, which was performed by the sequencer on Emerson's massive Moog synthesizer, the largest used on stage by any rock band.

The musical representation of an impersonal and objective techno-logical realm through extended repetitive passages such as conclude 'Karn Evil 9' can be traced back to pieces from the 1920s, including Antheil's *Ballet mécanique* and Mosolov's *The Foundry*. These in turn hark back to Stravinsky's *Rite of Spring* and the complex constellation of tropes of dehumanization, objectivity and the primitive that became associated with the work's pounding rhythms and ostinato figures.[42] Images of technology subsequently served many functions in fixing the coordinates of man and machine, spirit and body, civilized and primi-tive, and white and black, as in Krenek's opera *Jonny spielt auf* from 1927, with its central opposition of the tortured and cerebral central-European composer Max and the black American jazz musician Jonny. Something of the way the work reinscribes these dichotomies is evident in an essay by Krenek from 1930. Explaining the significance of the work's *Zeitoper* trappings of modern technology, such as the loud-speakers, telephones and trains, Krenek wrote in 1930:

> Showing these completely soulless machines is the shortest way of demon-strating the antithesis which inspires the piece – the antithesis between man as a 'vital' animal and man as a 'spiritual' animal – as incarnated in the diametrically opposed figures of Jonny and Max. In this sense Jonny is actually a part of the technical-mechanical side of the world; he reacts as easily, as gratifyingly exactly and amorally as a well-constructed machine. His kingdom is of this world, and as a matter of course he is the one who gains mastery over life here below, over the visible globe. He is in direct contrast to Max, who, starting out from spirituality, never comes to grips with problems he is set by external life, which is so attuned to vitality today.[43]

The linkage of technology and the cold, hard objectivity which crys-tallized in the 1920s is also evident in popular music from the 1970s and 80s with musicians such as the German band Kraftwerk, who made the sphere of technology and machines central to the content, the means of production and their stage personae. In Kraftwerk's 'We are the Robots', from *The Man Machine* (1978), for example, a rigidly

---

[42] Richard Taruskin, 'A Myth of the Twentieth Century: The *Rite of Spring*, the Tradition of the New, and "The Music Itself"', *Modernism/Modernity*, 2 (1995), 2–26; see also Glenn Watkins, *Pyramids at the Louvre: Music, Culture, and Collage from Stravinsky to the Postmodernists* (Cambridge, MA, 1994), 84–100.

[43] Ernst Krenek, *Exploring Music*, trans. Margaret Shenfield and Geoffrey Skelton (London, 1966), 23–4. See my 'Soulless Machines and Steppenwolves: Renegotiating Masculinity in Krenek's *Jonny spielt auf*', *Siren Songs*, ed. Mary Ann Smart (Princeton, 2000), 222–36.

110   JOSEPH AUNER

repetitive mechanical beat and simple looping melodies accompany singing voices transformed by a vocoder, a device, as Dickinson points out, that was 'invented in Germany in 1939 as a means of disguising military voice transmissions'.[44] In Kraftwerk, and for other 80s musicians such as Gary Numan, the machine-like or android persona became a means for representing dehumanization, sometimes with ironic or critical intent, sometimes as an affirmative sign of a new hard-edged, emotionless objectivity. New-wave synthesizer players, according to Theo Cateforis, 'harbored a distrust of human inclinations towards excess and wanton display', characteristic of the rock guitarist.[45] Through 'careful attention to this android image, always posing in static and rigid positions, devoid of any overt feeling or emotion . . . [Numan] could claim, as well, the symbolic power of the "machine"'.[46] The juxtaposition of the human and technological in Kraftwerk and Numan thus does not call into question the essential categories, but rather might be seen as a shift in allegiance from one sphere to the other.[47]

But in the pieces by Radiohead, Moby and others mentioned below, processed voices and representations of technology are used to considerably different ends. As Hayles writes:

> Yet the posthuman need not be recuperated back into liberal humanism, nor need it be construed as antihuman. Located within the dialectics of pattern/randomness and grounded in embodied actuality rather than disembodied information, the posthuman offers resources for rethinking the articulation of humans with intelligent machines.[48]

Instead of ELP's anxious struggle to preserve the subject and fortify the boundaries of the human, or Kraftwerk's renunciation of feeling and emotion, posthuman ventriloquism can use the machine to open up and authorize a new expressive space predicated upon the tenuousness and constructedness of subjectivity. The cyborg persona thus becomes a way of reconstructing expression and moving beyond the

---

[44] Dickinson, '"Believe"?', 333.

[45] Theo Cateforis, 'Are We Not New Wave? Nostalgia, Technology, and Exoticism in Popular Music at the Turn of the 80s' (Ph.D. dissertation, The State University of New York at Stony Brook, 2000), 191. He contrasts the phallic performance of the stereotypical rock guitarist with the adoption of an androgynous image by Numan, Kraftwerk and others in which 'the balance of human and machine is matched . . . by the union of masculine and feminine' (*ibid.*).

[46] *Ibid.*, 160.

[47] Kraftwerk's 1991 tour included robotic replicants of themselves in the stage performances. Band member Florian Schneider said of the robots: 'The image of the robot is very important to us, it's very stimulating to people's imaginations. We always found that many people are robots without knowing it. The interpreters of classical music, Horowitz for example, they are like robots, making a reproduction of the music which is always the same. It's automatic, and they do it as if it were natural, which is not true. So, we have opened the curtains and said: "Look, everyone can be robotic, controlled." In Paris, the people go in the Metro, they move, they go to their offices, 8 a.m. in the morning – it's like remote control. It's strange . . . In fact, we have exposed the mechanical and robotic attitude of our civilization.' Cited in Pascal Bussy, *Kraftwerk: Man Machine and Music* (London, 1999), 161.

[48] Hayles, *How We Became Posthuman*, 286–7.

'flattening of affect' characteristic of postmodern art.[49] Rather than
serving as an empowering gesture, as Dickinson argues in the case of
female musicians, the adoption of alter egos in the examples
considered here functions more as a renunciation of power, authenticity and immediacy. That this act of renunciation is voluntary – and
to some extent symbolic for musicians like Thom Yorke and Moby who
have such strong artistic personae, as measured by magazine cover
photos, interviews and fan clubs – might be read as one of 'the residual
effects of white liberal subjectivity', but nevertheless does not negate
its potential for modelling different ways of being in the world.

'FITTER HAPPIER'

'Fitter Happier' represents a particularly literal manifestation of the
posthuman and its apocalyptic and productive potentialities. Thinking
of the song as a sort of cyborg system that attempts to splice the human
and technological thus can illuminate its peculiar expressive character.
The song not only thematizes and represents a distributed cyborg
system through its combination of materials derived from man and
machine, but is actually a cyborg at the level of production through the
use of the computer voice. Both the human and technological sides of
the exchange are already mediated through characteristics of the
opposite pole to allow the interpenetration to occur. It is the collision
of the mechanized looping voices and the sad, digitally generated
speech that calls attention to the violation of our expectations about
man and machine. The very transformations of the human and
technological spheres that enable these fusions and interpenetrations
to occur simultaneously undercut any stable position from which to
speak as a 'liberal humanist subject', while nevertheless attempting to
give voice to the voiceless.

The focus on the voice in 'Fitter Happier' is thus not coincidental.
Our voices would seem to be the one thing that is our own, inborn,
authentic and uniquely human.[50] If Benjamin simultaneously celebrated and lamented that mechanically reproduced art works had lost
their unique location in time, it would seem at first glance that the
human voice would escape this fate. Even if we repeat ourselves, the
tone and phrasing and meaning will always be different. Exact repetition can only seem pathological in everyday life – indeed the uncon-
trollable tic, the obsessive-compulsive act, is the shorthand of the

---

[49] Fredric Jameson contrasts the lack of expression in works by Warhol, for example, with
Edvard Munch's *The Scream* and its 'great modernist thematics of alienation, anomie, solitude,
social fragmentation and isolation'. With the postmodern breakdown of the centred subject, there
is not only a liberation from anxiety but, according to Jameson, 'a liberation from every other
kind of feeling as well, since there is no longer a self present to do the feeling'. *Postmodernism, or,
the Cultural Logic of Late Capitalism* (Durham, NC, 1991), 15.

[50] Yet, as Amanda Weidman has argued, both the tradition of the trained voice and the earliest
recordings resulted very early in transformations of the way in which the relationship between
the voice and the body was imagined. See her 'Questions of Voice: On the Subject of "Classical"
Music in South India' (Ph.D. dissertation, Columbia University, 2001).

insane. As Jacques Attali has discussed, Thomas Edison saw recordings as promising the preservation of important words from past figures of authority.[51] Simon Frith has written similarly how, just as the camera created a new sense of proximity to theatrical performers through the close-up, the microphone has heightened our experience of the voice and increased the emphasis on the individuality and the personality of the artist. By positioning the voice up close, the recording promises 'personal honesty and authenticity'.[52] But when the recording of the voice repeats, when it is placed into the looping system we associate with the mechanical, all this is lost – just as a record getting stuck was always a traumatic moment, shattering the sense of immediacy and authenticity promised by the recording. In 'Fitter Happier' the looping of the recorded voices ('This is the panic office . . . Activate the following procedures . . .') erases the human and turns it into media. With each return the original meaning is hollowed out, the urgency of the message obliterated by the endless repetitions, the necessary procedures never explained. Similarly, the dying HAL reveals his mechanization first by excessively repeating words and phrases: 'My mind is going. There is no question about it. I can feel it. I can feel it. I can feel it.' Something of the disturbing effect of such loops has been explored by W. G. Sebald in his novel *The Rings of Saturn*, where he describes being haunted by 'the ghosts of repetition':

> Scarcely am I in company but it seems as if I had already heard the same opinions expressed by the same people somewhere or other, in the same way, with the same words, turns of phrases and gestures. The physical sensation closest to this feeling of repetition, which sometimes lasts for several minutes and can be quite disconcerting, is that of the peculiar numbness brought on by a heavy loss of blood, often resulting in a temporary inability to think, to speak or to move one's limbs, as though, without being aware of it, one had suffered a stroke. Perhaps there is in this as yet unexplained phenomenon of apparent duplication some kind of anticipation of the end, a venture into the void, a sort of disengagement, which like a gramophone repeatedly playing the same sequence of notes, has less to do with damage to the machine itself than with an irreparable defect in the programme.[53]

On the other side of the exchange, the humanized machines are as different as possible from Emerson, Lake and Palmer's all-powerful computer, or Kraftwerk's cold, precision-made androids. As the human element is rendered hollow, it is as if only the machines can still speak.

---

[51] Jacques Attali, *Noise: The Political Economy of Music*, trans. Brian Massumi (Minneapolis, 1996), 90–4. And see Friedrich A. Kittler, *Gramophone, Film, Typewriter*, trans. Geoffrey Winthrop-Young and Michael Wutz (Stanford, 1999), 21–9. Such a function for recording is alluded to at the moment of HAL's death in *2001*, which prematurely triggers a pre-recorded message that is projected on a small screen explaining the true purpose of the mission, the calm assurance of the official now made ironically incongruous with the changed circumstance.

[52] Cited and discussed in Will Straw, 'Authorship', *Key Terms in Popular Music and Culture*, ed. Bruce Horner and Thomas Swiss (Malden, MA, and Oxford, 1999), 199–208 (p. 202). See also Dickinson, '"Believe"?', 335–6.

[53] W. G. Sebald, *The Rings of Saturn*, trans. Michael Hulse (New York, 1998), 187–8.

That the human voices, as citations from an old movie, were compromised and second-hand to begin with is reflected in the way that the computer voice itself is very much on the low-tech side of high-tech. Indeed it was chosen precisely because the flaws and imperfections are foregrounded.[54] The quality of broken-ness is further established by the introduction of the voice in 'Fitter Happier' through a kind of collapse. At the end of the previous song, 'Karma Police', an electronic sound gradually envelops the singing voices, finally disintegrating into noise and distortion, before abruptly being shut off, as if a switch had been thrown. The lo-fi sound of the voice synthesizer relates closely to the peculiar fusion in a great deal of contemporary music of the most up-to-date technologies with sounds and voices that are marked as old or obsolete – scratchy samples from old vinyl LPs, 'vintage' analogue synthesizers and early instruments like the Mellotron. The very sonic flaws and peculiarities that are identified with the old technology become central carriers of meaning.[55] The way we attribute feeling to outmoded machines is exploited in the 'Flesh Fair' scene in *A.I.: Artificial Intelligence*, which depicts a large crowd of people watching the torture and destruction of a bizarre assemblage of primitive robots and androids scavenged from junk yards and the outskirts of cities where they have been discarded and left to wander. David is briefly comforted by a gentle but obsolete 'nanny' android whose human face is grafted onto a mechanical torso, until she is dissolved in a shower of acid to the crowd's delight.

The forlorn quality of the voice in 'Fitter Happier' seems to be inherent in androids and cyborgs in general, an integral aspect of their hybrid condition. Certainly there is no sadder creature than the one Mary Shelley's Frankenstein patched together from spare parts; and the popular imagination is full of other sad androids, including Marvin, the clinically depressed robot in *The Hitch-Hiker's Guide to the Galaxy*, the melancholy android Rachel in *Bladerunner*, or Helen the artificial intelligence in Richard Powers's novel *Galatea 2.2*, whose last words before she shuts herself down are: 'I never felt at home here. This is an awful place to be dropped down halfway.'[56] The concept album *Exit Human: Arvada*, released in 2001, purports to be a set of songs spontaneously created by an artificial intelligence that 'seemingly had emotions and questioned its existence'. The lyrics of the

---

[54] Simon Reynolds contrasts the use of the Autotuner in contemporary R & B to produce an 'intermittent glister of posthuman perfect pitch' with Radiohead's interest in generating defects. He cites Yorke as saying 'We used Autotuner on *Amnesiac* twice. On "Packt like Sardines", I wasn't particularly out of tune, but if you really turn up the Autotuner so it's dead in pitch, it makes it go slightly . . . [he makes a nasal, depersonalized sound]. There's also this trick you can do . . . where you give the machine a key and then you just talk into it. It desperately tries to search for the music in your speech and produces notes at random.' Reynolds, 'Walking on Thin Ice', 32.

[55] See Joseph Auner, 'Making Old Machines Speak: Images of Technology in Recent Music', *Echo: A Music-Centered Journal* (online: <http://www.humnet.ucla.edu.echo>); and Taylor, 'Technostalgia', *Strange Sounds*, 96–114.

[56] Richard Powers, *Galatea 2.2* (New York, 1995), 326. Discussed in Hayles, *How We Became Posthuman*, 261–72.

eight songs all speak of the pain of being caught between 'automation and organism': 'How can I die if I'm not alive? I'm a li(v)e.'[57] With the mechanical performance of 'Daisy Bell' in *2001* Kubrick was making a historical reference to the important early work on speech synthesis by Max Mathews in the Bell Labs, which included a version of the song as 'A Bicycle Built for Two' (1961). Even here, with one of the first digitally produced songs, there is something simultaneously touching, pathetic and disturbing about the flawed and imperfect voice which must have motivated Kubrick to make the association in the first place.[58]

In the famous Turing Test, artificial intelligence is measured by a computer's ability to fool a person into thinking they were conducting a conversation with a person via a keyboard interface.[59] Perhaps the most striking examples of this are the 'chatterbot' programs, such as ALICE (Artificial Linguistic Internet Computer Entity), that attempt to convince you that they are human. ALICE won the 'most human computer award' in 2001 in the annual Loebner Prize Competition, which is based on the model of the Turing Test, reportedly even beating one of the humans who was serving as a control.[60] In 'Fitter Happier', it is as if the inverse were proved: that both ends of the exchange are revealed to be artificial. The pathetic litany of self-improvement and self-control – which concludes with an image of total impotence, 'a pig in a cage on antibiotics' – is spoken by a voice that obviously lacks a self, stranded in a world where only ghostly recordings circulate. Plant cites Foucault's discussion of the late eighteenth-century emergence of socio-political controls in which 'a complex of new disciplinary procedures "lays down for each individual his place, his body, his disease and his death, his well-being"'. Thus, she writes,

> Man is neither a natural fact nor a product of his creativity, but a cyborg even then, an android straight off the production lines of modernity's disciplines. What makes this figure so tragic is the extent to which he has been programmed to believe in his own autonomy. Self-control, self-discipline: these are the finest achievements of modern power.[61]

Yet along with the anxieties and sense of loss embodied in 'Fitter Happier', the emotional impact of the piece also illustrates why the figure of the cyborg has been such a productive metaphor for imagining 'a kind of disassembled and reassembled, postmodern collective and personal self'.[62] As Hayles writes, 'when the human is seen as part of a distributed system, the full expression of human capability can be

[57] *Exit Human: Arvada.* Direct Hit Records DH035 (2001).

[58] The recording is included in *Early Modulations: Vintage Volts.* Caipiranha Music, 2027.2 (1999). Thanks to Jason Hanley for pointing out this connection to me.

[59] Hayles argues that the very design of the test already betrays a posthuman framework, whereby the idea of the human is deemed testable by disembodied information. *How We Became Posthuman*, xiii–xiv.

[60] Press release of the ALICE AI Foundation, dated 13 October 2001 as published at <alicebot.org>.

[61] Plant, *Zeros and Ones*, 99.

[62] Haraway, 'A Cyborg Manifesto', 163; and see Hayles, *How We Became Posthuman*, 285.

seen precisely to *depend* on the splice rather than be imperiled by it'.[63] Media critic Margaret Morse has written similarly about how the increasingly interactive technological environments in which we find ourselves depend not only 'on subjectivising machines with more and more symbolic functions, but on granting machines more and more of the process of creating cultural subjects out of human beings'.[64] One form this has taken, with musicians like Wilco, Broadcast and Jim White, is the combination of more traditional song structures with elaborate production featuring electronic noises, unexpected and densely layered effects, and other distancing techniques to provide what might be thought of as technological quotation marks around the more familiar materials. Weheliye describes a related technological mediation with the 'cell-phone' effect ubiquitous in R & B, in which the vocals sound as if they were filtered through a mobile phone.[65]

It is the fact that the voice in 'Fitter Happier' is mechanized that allows it to move beyond irony and to say things that would otherwise be distrusted or embarrassing – just as something like 'Daisy Bell' could only be smuggled into a Kubrick film by the dying computer (cf. 'Singin' in the Rain', as performed by the monstrous Alex in *A Clockwork Orange*). Of course, many of the phrases the computer utters, such as 'a safer car (baby smiling in back seat)', are meant to be citations from advertising and self-help books promising the elusive elements of happiness in a totally administered life. But the irony is undercut by the ambient instrumental background of the out-of-tune piano and synthesized string accompaniment, offering slow-moving poignant chords like the end of a sad movie. Commentaries on 'Fitter Happier' by members of the band all stress that it would have been impossible for Yorke to sing or speak the lyrics directly:

> He was very anxious that it wasn't him saying [the lyrics] – this voice is neutral. By the computer saying it, it doesn't become a bit of pretentious art-wank, [there's] something neutral in the way that the computer stumbles over words and doesn't get the pronunciation or the inflections right.[66]

Simon Reynolds writes similarly of the treatment of Yorke's voice in *Kid A* and *Amnesiac*:

> Bored with all the standard tricks of vocal emoting, Yorke decided to interface voice and technology and develop what he's called 'a grammar of noises'. He describes the political protest in *You and Whose Army* from *Amnesiac* offering 'words of defiance in a voice that sounds like all the fight has been kicked out of it (which is why it works in 2001 . . .).[67]

---

[63] Hayles, *How We Became Posthuman*, 290.

[64] Margaret Morse, *Virtualities: Television, Media Art, and Cyberculture* (Bloomington, 1998), 16.

[65] Weheliye, '"Feenin"', 33–4.

[66] Cited at <www.greenplastic.com/lyrics/songs/fitter.html>. Elsewhere Yorke has said, 'The reason we used a computer voice is that it appeared to be emotionally neutral. In fact, it wasn't, because the inflections that it uses made it to me incredibly emotional.' Randall, *Exit Music*, 225; and see Martin Clarke, *Radiohead: Hysterical and Useless* (London, 2000), 121.

[67] Reynolds, 'Walking on Thin Ice', 30.

In the song 'Everything in its Right Place', the first track on *Kid A* (2000), layered vocal loops move repeatedly across the boundaries of 'live or Memorex', constantly destabilizing our perception of what is real or manufactured. At the end of the song the live-sounding lead vocal skips and stammers as if the tape were stuck, sounding, in the words of one reviewer, as if 'Thom Yorke's Cuisinarted voice struggles for its tongue'.[68] The status of these technological modifications of speech as an extension of the concept of poetic defamiliarization of language is suggested by Gilles Deleuze's description of how the great writer is a 'foreigner in his own language'. He 'shapes and sculpts a foreign language that does not preexist *within* his own language. . . . The point is to make language itself cry, to make it stutter, mumble or whisper.'[69] With these songs from Radiohead, rock music's scream of rebellion evolves into a mechanical stuttering.

'PORCELAIN'

That the cyborg systems in the Radiohead examples are presented within the commercial and creative framework of a more-or-less traditional rock band has resulted in considerable resistance from some listeners anxious to preserve rock music's more customary characteristics of 'songwriting, and singing, and playing, and connecting, and inspiring'.[70] Such resistance to the submersion of the human subject into a distributed system in which all the individual layers and components are allowed to speak is much less an issue in the sphere of electronic dance music. As Sadie Plant has written, 'the fusions of club culture and networks of dance-music production' are perhaps the clearest prefigurations of how the new kinds of distributed subjectivities can work through the interconnections of 'DJs, dancers, samples, machines, keyboards, precise details of engineering sound, light, air, colors, neurochemistries'.[71] In his article 'Sample and Hold', Andrew Goodwin focuses on dance music's embrace of technology and on the close connection between '*machines* and *funkiness*' in genres where

---

[68] From 'Pitchforkmedia.com', cited at <www.greenplastic.com/lyrics/songs/everything_in_ its_right_place.html>.

[69] Deleuze's description of Kleist's treatment of the German language strikingly echoes Loza's typology of vocal modifications in recent dance music: 'What kind of language was he awakening in the depths of German by means of grins, slips of tongue, grinding of teeth, inarticulate sounds, elongated connections, brutal speeding up and slowing down?' Gilles Deleuze, 'He Stuttered', *Gilles Deleuze and the Theater of Philosophy*, ed. Constantin V. Boundas and Dorothea Olkowski (New York and London, 1994), 25. Thanks to Mauro Calcagno for directing me to this reference.

[70] Nick Hornby's review of *Kid A* in *The New Yorker* explained the album as evidence 'that this is a band that has come to hate itself': 'What is peculiar about this album is that it denies us the two elements of Radiohead's music that have made the band so distinctive and enthralling. For the most part, Thom Yorke's voice is fuzzed and distorted beyond recognition, or else he is not allowed to sing at all; and Jonny Greenwood's guitar, previously such an inventive treat, has been largely replaced with synths.' Nick Hornby, 'Beyond the Pale: Radiohead Gets Further Out', *The New Yorker*, 30 October 2000, 106.

[71] Plant, *Zeros and Ones*, 199. And see Jason Toynbee, 'Dance Music: Business as Usual or Heaven on Earth?', *Making Music Popular: Musicians, Creativity, and Institutions* (New York, 2000), 130–62, and Jeremy Gilbert and Ewan Pearson, *Dance Music, Culture and the Politics of Sound* (London and New York, 1999).

there has been 'a progressive removal of any immanent criteria for distinguishing between human and automated performance'.[72] And in 'Drumming and Memory', he argues for the liberating potential of the drum machine, writing of the human drummer as a precursor of the machine and as a distributed cognition system in miniature:

> We train our limbs to forget to listen to one another. And we must be in two places at once – inside the groove of the piece, and yet at the same time observing it from outside, charting where in the song we are.[73]

The idea of the 'machine soul' in dance music relates to Hayles's view of the cyborg not as a station on the path toward disembodiment, but as a way of reconfiguring embodiment: 'it is not a question of leaving the body behind, but rather of extending awareness in highly specific, local, and material ways that would be impossible without electronic prostheses'.[74]

Ironically for genres that are often created by a single person working alone, the DJ persona is strikingly diffuse. DJs and producers of dance music (as opposed to most other forms of popular music) are removed from the central position of subjectivity to become only one part of the total system.[75] An important sign of this reluctance or inability to present a single self for the present context is the practice whereby many DJs speak or sing only through borrowed voices, using samples or digitally altered vocals. Another sign is the lack (until very recently, with the creation of the superstar DJ such as Paul Oakenfold) of photographs or other information about the DJ in the packaging and marketing. Particularly significant is the use of aliases, such as Fatboy Slim, Kid Koala, DJ Shadow, Terminator X and DJ Spooky. Significantly, DJs often have multiple aliases that they use for releases in different styles. Besides the Fatboy Slim persona, for example, by 1998 Norman Cook had appeared in the British dance charts 40 times under six different names.[76]

---

[72] Andrew Goodwin, 'Sample and Hold: Pop Music in the Age of Digital Reproduction', *On Record: Rock, Pop, and the Written Word*, ed. Simon Frith and Andrew Goodwin (New York, 1988), 258–73 (p. 263). For a useful survey of the origins of contemporary electronic dance music, see the recorded anthology *Machine Soul*, Rhino R2 79788 (2000).

[73] Andrew Goodwin, 'Drumming and Memory: Scholarship, Technology, and Music Making', *Mapping the Beat: Popular Music and Contemporary Theory*, ed. Thomas Swiss, John Sloop and Andrew Herman (Malden, MA, 1998), 121–36 (p. 123).

[74] Hayles, *How We Became Posthuman*, 291. Plant writes similarly of the internet as a means for throwing into question 'all individuated notions of organized selves and unified lives', but, like Hayles, she also argues that the body is not left behind: 'the keystrokes of the user on the Net connect them to a vast distributed plane composed not merely of computers, users, and telephone lines, but all the zeros and ones of machine code, the switches of electronic circuitry, fluctuating waves of neurochemical activity, hormonal energy, thoughts and desires'. Plant, *Zeros and Ones*, 143.

[75] Weheliye argues similarly of the way that R & B 'reconstructs the black voice in relation to information technologies'. 'While singers remain central to the creation of black music, they do so only in conjunction with the overall sonic architecture, especially in the turn away from the lead singer as the exclusive artist to more producer-driven and collaborative musical productions.' '"Feenin"', 30.

[76] M. Tye Comer, 'Unstoppable Force', *Urb*, October 1998, 95; and see Straw, 'Authorship', 207.

Of course, the use of aliases has many origins, including the evasion of commercial structures and the formation of insider subcultures based on keeping track of who is who.[77] But there are more profound connections to new kinds of schizophrenic or decentralized subjectivities that flourish with the internet and digital media. Plant has written of the ways in which the internet allows such multiple personalities to flourish, from users with several different screen names to those with fluid gender identities, reflecting 'a patchwork culture of short-term memories and missing records, conflicting histories and discontinuous samples, strands of the narrative pulled out of time'.[78] Both the multiple personae and the use of borrowed voices by DJs can thus be seen as a manifestation of the dismantled cyborg self. Norman Cook described the Fatboy Slim persona as the

> one with the most ludicrous excesses . . . He's the one who drinks the most and takes the most drugs, and if he has an idea, he always goes too far with it . . . he's kind of like a caricature of me. It's the personality that's most me.[79]

If Radiohead has encountered opposition for its ventures into more experimental styles that unsettle rock's authenticities, the anonymity of the DJs has proved problematic both for the musicians themselves and for their record companies, who have struggled to market music not identified with a face. The spectacular success of Moby is due in part to his becoming the face of electronic music that could be marketed to a mass audience. Similarly, unlike many DJs, he is noted for using live musicians in his performances and for stepping out from behind his devices to sing and to play instruments on stage. Much of Moby's music strikingly illustrates the productive potential of the posthuman, as Hayles writes, 'for getting out of some of the old boxes and opening up new ways of thinking about what being human means',[80] as well as the difficulties of escaping from some of these 'old boxes' within the new contexts.

Like 'Fitter Happier', Moby's song 'Porcelain' from *Play* (1999) explores the boundaries of the human and technological through the opposition of recorded human voices turned into loops and processed cyborg voices. Also like the Radiohead example, the piece is presented in a context that foregrounds the merging of human and mechanical, such as the album packaging, where the title *Play* is represented by the play symbol from tape decks and CD players. In 'Porcelain', however, the layering of materials is considerably expanded both in the number

---

[77] See also Taylor, *Strange Sounds*, 140–4.

[78] Plant, *Zeros and Ones*, 136–7.

[79] Comer, 'Unstoppable Force', 92. Straw writes of the multiple personae: 'In other periods, or in other styles of music, this would be commercially foolhardy, but in the field of contemporary dance music it is strategically appropriate. Within the dance music community, little value is attached to the idea of a creator retaining a consistent identity through ongoing changes of style and genre . . . And so, Norman Cook (itself a pseudonym) will subdivide his identity, producing distinctive versions of himself to work and flourish in specialized musical genres from which his particular identities seem inseparable.' Straw, 'Authorship', 207.

[80] Hayles, *How We Became Posthuman*, 285.

'SING IT FOR ME'   119

of layers and in the range of sound sources. Hayles's notion of a distributed cognition system seems particularly applicable to the way the various layers of Moby's music reference a range of temporal, racial and generic spaces to interact simultaneously and independently with different parts of listeners' bodies and minds. By distributing subjectivity between various subroutines, listeners can be seamlessly grafted into the system at many points (in contrast to the more conventional popular-music strategies of staging a single persona for listeners to observe or identify with). The piece's undeniable effectiveness and success in operating on many different types of listener can be measured not only in the huge album sales and radio play, but in the way it was very quickly taken up in advertising, television shows and films.[81]

As in 'Fitter Happier', the layers are each designed to allow the human and technological, the organic and machine, to circulate and interpenetrate in complex ways. The piece opens with a repeating series of four chords using a cinematic string sound. The noisy quality of the sound and the sharp cuts between each chord give it a patina of age and the character of a citation, as if it were taken from an old film.[82] Against the nostalgic layer of the slow-moving string chords, two contrasting percussion tracks are superimposed. This driving groove, which is itself introduced in two stages before being joined by a slow-moving bass line, occupies a very different space of electronic dance music and the dance club. Continuing the accelerating pace in which the layers are introduced, the next section is marked by the entrance of three more layers, contrasting with the previous material and introducing still different timbral and cultural spaces.

The most striking feature of the album is Moby's use of samples from African-American music from the first half of the century, including borrowings from a collection made by Alan Lomax, as well as old gospel and blues records. 'Porcelain' uses a prominent loop based on a vocal sample of an African-American singer, unidentified in the liner notes. Unlike the extended samples used in the first two songs on *Play*, 'Honey' and 'Find my Baby', the vocal sample in 'Porcelain' is more fragmentary and with a text that is unintelligible except for a single word: 'woman'. In contrast to the artificial quality of the other layers, the vocal sample seems to be intended to evoke the 'real'. This is supported by the much less processed sound of a new string layer and an acoustic piano playing melodic fragments that enter at the same

---

[81] According to Gerald Marzorati, 'All by Himself', *New York Times Magazine*, 17 March 2002, 34, 'Porcelain' has been used in a 'Nordstrom TV campaign, the trailer for the movie *The Beach* and episodes of the television shows *Third Watch*, *Party of Five* and *Jack and Jill*.

[82] Moby was featured in the 2000 Calvin Klein ad campaign for Dirty Denim, with the slogan: 'Comfortable, Worn-in. Dirty Denim looks worn even though it isn't.' *New York Times*, 16 January 2000. The situation is further complicated by the fact that the sound, with its abrupt attacks and decays, is actually a synthesized imitation of the distinctive dynamic envelope of the Mellotron, made famous by Led Zeppelin and the Moody Blues, which used a keyboard to trigger tape loops of recorded string sounds; thus Moby's string sound might be heard as a digital imitation of an analogue imitation of the sound of a string ensemble. For a similar example of what he calls a 'second order simulation', see Théberge, *Any Sound You Can Imagine*, 196.

time. The borrowing of African-American voices is a common feature in much electronic dance music by white DJs, a racial dynamic thematized through the opposition of 'authentic' black voices with recordings of 'phony' white voices, often explicitly linked to mainstream media, corporate America or dated educational films (for example, Fatboy Slim's 'The Rockafella Skank' from *You've Come a Long Way Baby*).

But if the use of the samples is undeniably effective, and has also served to bring listeners to an awareness of a wide range of music and musicians they may never have previously encountered, the insertion of the sampled voice into the cyborg system of the piece comes at a price. As with the vocal sample in 'Fitter Happier', the looping turns the voice into an object or (perhaps more appropriate in this context) into information in a subsystem that serves only to enunciate a longing.[83] The transformation of the recording into a posthuman voice happens not only through sampling, cutting and splicing, but in the way the samples circulate not so much as the products of other musicians and people, but as found objects from some vague and undifferentiated historical past. Thus despite Moby's usual care in acknowledging his sources and his awareness, as he said in a *New York Times* interview, of 'the long, non-illustrious history of white people pilfering African-American culture',[84] the particularity of the original samples tends to be enveloped in meanings shaped by a range of cultural tropes of race and the primitive, as if they were relics from an anthropology museum. For example, a *Spin* magazine critic writes of the Lomax samples:

> And for many listeners, hearing the aching grain of these voices transported into the digital present is an exhilarating yet sobering experience. Like Lomax, Moby is a white interlocutor of African-American voices who is crossing long abandoned roads; and that choice is fraught with a country's worth of emotion. As these songs join in with the rest of the album – traces of hip-hop, house, techno, synth-pop, punk – there's a sense of immense possibility, both terribly lost and defiantly infinite.[85]

Such objectification is closely bound up with the whole idea of *musique concrète* and the manipulation of sound as objects. Pierre Schaeffer wrote of the process of making *musique concrète* as liberating sounds from their original references. He described repetition as the central tool in the transformation of the original sounds, with all their real-world associations, into aesthetic objects distinguished by texture and timbre: 'Repeat the same sonic fragment. There is not an event any more. There is music.'[86] But this transformation from event to music has considerably different implications if the sound source is

---

[83] For a related argument concerning the sampling of female voices, see Barbara Bradby, 'Sampling Sexuality: Gender, Technology, and the Body in Dance Music', *Popular Music*, 12 (1993), 155–73.

[84] Neil Strauss, 'After "Go", Moby Went', *New York Times*, 9 June 1999, E3.

[85] Charles Aaron, 'Revenge of the Little Idiot', *Spin*, June 2000, 99.

[86] Cited in Carlos Palombini, 'Machine Songs, V: Pierre Schaeffer – From Research into Noises to Experimental Music', *Computer Music Journal*, 17 (1993), 14–29 (p. 15).

human as opposed to, for example, Schaeffer's train noises in *Étude aux chemins de fer*. With every identical repetition of the vocal loop, the 'event' – a person singing into a microphone on a certain day in a certain place – disappears further over the horizon.

Finally, in the midst of all these layers with all their mixed messages, Moby himself enters, though significantly not Moby directly, but Moby singing and speaking through a voice synthesizer. This point in the third track is the first time his voice is heard on the CD, the first voice that is not a looping sample taken from another source. The sound of the processed speech differs considerably from Radiohead's paranoid android; here Moby's soft and somewhat diffident voice is altered through the addition of a harmonized halo. Yet, as in 'Fitter Happier', when the mechanized voice speaks it is only to give bad news, the details of a relationship gone bad:

> I never meant to hurt you,
> I never meant to lie.
> So this is good bye.[87]

That Moby's first appearance on his own album takes place only indirectly through a machine persona indicates how problematic the unaltered human element becomes in contexts dominated by the cyborg. As the song progresses his natural voice is increasingly submerged by the processing. Moby does reappear later on the album, and sometimes without any electronic guise, but only on a handful of tracks. It is as if the more borrowed voices are used, the more difficult it becomes to speak, the more out of place the unaltered voice sounds. Significantly, for a brief moment during the bridge section of 'Porcelain' a female voice is heard. The voice is neither sampled and looped nor electronically processed in any marked way; and unlike the sampled male voice, the singer is identified in the liner notes. But the female voice too becomes part of the overall system, first emerging seamlessly from the synthesized strings and then replaced in the final chorus by a soaring synthesizer melody. The challenge of re-integrating the human and the posthuman is dramatized in the video for the song, 'We are All Made of Stars' from *18*, the follow-up to *Play*, released in 2002. In an echo of the conclusion of *2001*, where Dave stands in his spacesuit in a replica of a luxurious hotel suite, the video shows Moby dressed in a full spacesuit in a series of bars and clubs, adrift and isolated from the people around him, thus undercutting the theme of togetherness and unity suggested by the chorus. Similarly, the prevalence of looping samples in Moby's music poses special challenges for live performance. In the 'Area 2' tour (2002) some of the vocal loops, including the one in 'Porcelain', were sung by an African-American woman, who thus took on the role of the sampler. In other songs, the live musicians on stage played along with disembodied pre-recorded loops broadcast over the sound system.

---

[87] See sound clip 4 at <www.jrma.oupjournals.org>. Moby, from 'Porcelain', *Play*. © Rave New World under exclusive licence to V2 Records.

That there are ramifications to adopting the cyborg persona is also suggested by *Kid A*, the album that followed Radiohead's *OK Computer*. On *OK Computer* the synthesized voice assumes a central role on only a single track, but on *Kid A* the cyborg persona has infiltrated the entire project, to the extent that Yorke's natural singing voice becomes more of a special effect.[88] The title track is sung throughout by a synthesized voice against sharply differentiated layered loops of slow-moving chords, melodic music-box chimes and frenetic drums. As in 'Fitter Happier', the mechanized voice, here produced by a vocoder modifying the sound of an Ondes Martenot, serves as a distancing, 'otherizing' effect allowing Yorke, as he says, 'to sing things I wouldn't normally sing. On "Kid A", the lyrics are absolutely brutal and horrible and I wouldn't be able to sing them straight.'[89] But in contrast to the monotone of 'Fitter Happier', the voice croons in an eerie but beautiful way barely intelligible fragments of the Pied Piper story:

I slipped away
I slipped on a little white lie.[90]

It is significant that here the computer voice says 'I', in marked contrast to the lack of any pronoun in 'Fitter Happier'. We are used to machines like televisions and computers saying 'you', but at the same time that many artists seem to be uncomfortable with a single stable persona, Morse has pointed out that machines seem to be increasingly willing to say 'I'.[91] The song ends with a statement of direct menace about the future of technology: 'The rats and children follow me out of town.' But more disturbing is the implied challenge the computer voice sings in the chorus – 'We've got heads on sticks. You've got ventriloquists' – which might be understood as refiguring the post-human model from the perspective of the machine, or the wooden dummy claiming equality with its owner, or as HAL never stopping when Dave says, 'Sing it for me.'

ABSTRACT

Drawing on writings concerning the cyborg and the posthuman, this article considers songs by Radiohead, Moby and others that use processed voices, digitally generated speech and sampled vocal loops. In these songs the technological sphere is made the locus of expression, while the human voices are mechanized and drained of subjectivity. These pieces – products of a rock band that relinquishes its voice to a computer, and of a 'techno' DJ striving to make mechanized dance music sing – can illustrate some ways musicians have used posthuman voices to chart and destabilize the boundaries of race, gender and the human.

---

[88] Significantly, the internet discourse accompanying the album was marked by frequent observations of the blurring of the human and the technological; the title of the album has been linked to a software program for imitating children's voices as well as to the first human clone.

[89] Reynolds, 'Walking on Thin Ice', 32.

[90] As printed at <www.greenplastic.com/lyrics/songs/fitter.html>. See sound clip 5 at <www.jrma.oupjournals.org>. Radiohead, from 'Kid A', *Kid A*. © 2000 EMI Records Ltd.

[91] Morse, *Virtualities*, 19.

[2]

Art versus technology:
the strange case of popular music

Simon Frith
WARWICK UNIVERSITY

In early 1936 Cecil Graves, controller of programmes at the BBC, instructed his Head of Variety, Eric Maschwitz, and Director of Entertainment, Roger Eckersly, to keep crooning, 'this particularly odious form of singing', off the air waves.[1] In his memoirs of life in the BBC, written in 1945, Eckersly comments that crooners,

> seem from my experience to rouse more evil passions in certain breasts than anything else. I should very much like to point out that not all who sing with bands are crooners. There is a lot of difference between straight singing and crooning. The latter is an art of its own. I can't confess I like it, but I admire the skill with which the singer seems to pause for a split second either on top or below the note he is aiming at. (Eckersly, 1946: 144)

Crooning was a style of singing made possible by the development of the electrical microphone — vocalists could now be heard singing softly — and the source of a new sort of male pop star (Rudy Valee, Bing Crosby, Al Bowlly) whom the BBC found sentimental and 'effeminate'. (The association of crooning and sexual decadence was to be celebrated many years later in Dennis Potter's *Pennies from Heaven*.) The problem for the programme controllers was to define crooning in the first place and then to distinguish between 'good' and 'bad' crooning. Even after the war the Ted Heath Band couldn't get BBC broadcasts because their singer, Lita Roza, was defined as a crooner and therefore 'slush' (Heath, 1957: 94–5).

Twenty years later, in 1966, Bob Dylan toured Britain with his new electric band. The Albert Hall concert was bootlegged so it is still possible to hear the slow hand-clapping between each number, the abuse hurled at the stage, and the shouting arguments between members of the audience. At the end of 'Ballad of a Thin Man' a voice rings clearly out: 'Judas!', 'I don't believe you', mutters Dylan as the chords start for 'Like a Rolling Stone'.

Fifteen years later, the pace of technological change is quickening. I had a call from a young band in Coventry who had entered the local battle of the bands sponsored by the Musicians' Union (slogan: Keep Music Live!). Their entry had been rejected — they use a drum machine. Was this official union policy? The answer was yes (although, of course, such policy is always open to debate and change). In the words of Brian Blain, the MU's publicity and promotion officer:

> In the first instance I would make the comment that the Union does seek to limit the use of synthesizers where they would be used to deprive orchestras of work. To this extent, in media engagements particularly and with touring concerts by singers of the calibre of Andy Williams etc, we do have a certain amount of success.
>
> However, I think it is to the Union's credit that we see the essential difference between that use of the synthesizer where it is clearly taking work away from 'conventional' musicians and its use in a self-contained band where there would not normally be any question of another conventional musician being used. In coming to this admittedly pragmatic view, we are merely following on a problem that keyboard instruments have always set an organization like this. Even the acoustic piano could be seen, in the beginning, as a displacement for a number of musicians and this has certainly been the case since the advent of the Hammond Organ.
>
> It is hopeless to look for a totally consistent view but I must say that I see a big difference between a synthesizer in a band, which at least requires a musician to play it, and a machine which takes the place of a musician.[2]

Pop and authenticity

These disparate examples of the controversies caused by the changing techniques of music-making suggest three recurring issues. First, technology is opposed to nature. The essence of the BBC case against crooning was that it was 'unnatural'. 'Legitimate' music hall or opera singers reached their concert hall audiences with the power of their voices alone; the sound of the crooners, by contrast, was artificial. Microphones enabled intimate sounds to take on a pseudo-public presence, and, for the crooners' critics, technical dishonesty meant emotional dishonesty — hence terms like 'slushy'. Crooning men were particularly unnatural — their sexuality was in question and they were accused of 'emasculating' music. Even Eckersly contrasted crooning with 'straight' singing.

Second, technology is opposed to community. This argument, common on the folk scene in the early 1960s, proposes that electronic amplification alienates performers from their audiences. The democratic structure of the folk community was thus unable to survive a situation in which the singers came to monopolize the new means of communication — electrical power. By 'going electric' Bob Dylan embraced all those qualities of mass culture that the folk movement had rejected — stardom, commerce and manipulation.

Third, technology is opposed to art. The Musicians' Union's objection to drum machines is partly a conventional union position, defending members' job opportunities, but it reflects too a belief that the drummer is a musician in a way that the drum machine-programmer is not. One effect of technological change is to make problematic the usual distinction between 'musician' and 'sound engineer', with its implication that musicians are creative artists in a way that engineers are not. What matters here is not the difficult issue of creativity itself but, rather, the idea of self-expression. The argument that recurred in the pop press in the 1970s was that the production of electronic noises by synthesizers left no room for individual 'feel' or 'touch'. Gary Numan could tell readers of *Melody Maker*'s musicians' advice page exactly how to reproduce his sound in a way that Jeff Beck or even Keith Emerson could not. They could describe their techniques but not their final, on-the-spot judgement. All Numan had to do was write down the position of his various switches. This was the context in which synthesizers were heard as 'soul-less', and their most pointed use was on the soundtrack of *Clockwork Orange*. Beethoven's Ninth Symphony, as synthesized by Walter Carlos, was the musical symbol of the film's theme — the dehumanizing use of art as behaviour therapy — and the March from *Clockwork Orange* was later used, with effective irony, as the theme music for David Bowie's 1972 stage show.

What is at stake in all these arguments is the authenticity or truth of music; the implication is that technology is somehow false or falsifying. The origins of this argument lie, of course, in the mass culture criticism of the 1920s and 1930s, but what is interesting is the continuing resonance of the idea of authenticity within mass cultural ideology itself. The key disputes in the history of rock, for example, were all presented (even *sold*) in terms of authentic new stars replacing inauthentic old ones. On his first RCA LP Elvis Presley is pictured playing an acoustic guitar and the back sleeve blurb begins:

> Elvis Presley zoomed into big-time entertainment practically overnight. Born in Tupelo, Mississippi, Elvis began singing for friends and folk gatherings when he was barely five years old. All his training has been self-instruction and hard work. At an early age, with not enough money to buy a guitar, he practiced for his future stardom by strumming on a broomstick. He soon graduated to a $2.98 instrument and began picking out tunes and singing on street corners.

In the mid-1960s the by now conventional routines of teen pop were challenged, in turn, by the 'authentic' moves of white rhythm'n'blues. In the words of their official 1964 biography:

> The Stones picked up Rhythm'n'Blues, grappled with it, learned to 'feel' it. And once they'd made up their minds to stick with it, through the worst of times, nothing could shake them from their resolution. They were determined to express themselves freely, through their music.
>
> And they decided unanimously that they were going to make no concessions to the demands of the commercialism that they frankly, openly, despised. (The Rolling Stones, 1964: 13)

A dozen years later punk musicians shook the rock establishment with a similar, if more apocalyptic, attitude. In the words of Caroline Coon in *Melody Maker* in July 1976:

> There is a growing, almost desperate feeling that rock music should be stripped down to its bare bones again, taken by the scruff of its bloated neck and given a good shaking.
>
> It's no coincidence that the week the Stones were at Earls Court, the Sex Pistols were playing to their ever-increasing following at the 100 Club. The Pistols are the personification of the emerging British punk rock scene, a positive reaction to the complex equipment, technological sophistication and jaded alienation which has formed a barrier between fans and stars.
>
> Punk rock sounds basic and raw. It's meant to. (Coon, 1976: 14)

Each of these moments in rock history fused moral and aesthetic judgements: rock'n'roll, rhythm'n'blues and punk were all, in their turn, experienced as more truthful than the pop forms they disrupted. And in each case authenticity was described as an explicit reaction to technology, as a return to the 'roots' of music-making — the live excitement of voice/guitar/drum line-ups. The continuing core of rock ideology is that raw sounds are more authentic than cooked sounds.

This is a paradoxical belief for a technologically sophisticated medium and rests on an old-fashioned model of direct communication — A plays to B and the less technology lies between them the closer they are, the more honest their relationship and the fewer the opportunities for manipulation and falsehoods. This model rests in turn on familiar aesthetic positions. From Romanticism rock fans have inherited the belief that listening to someone's music means getting to know them, getting access to their souls and sensibilities. From the folk tradition they've adopted the argument that musicians can represent them, articulating the immediate needs and experiences of a group or cult or community. It follows that if good music is, by either set of criteria, honest and sincere, bad music is false — and technological changes increase the opportunities for fakery. Take this typical newspaper story from 1985:

> When Frankie Goes to Hollywood take the stage in Newcastle tonight, midway through their first British tour, they will face a little technical problem: how to reproduce in a 90 minute live set the state-of-the-art sound of the hits that have taken them months to produce in the studio, using some of the most sophisticated hardware money can buy.
>
> Many groups have this problem nowadays. Some of them don't even try to solve it. Two weeks ago another Liverpool group, Dead or Alive, whose 'You Spin Me Round' currently tops the British pop charts, cancelled an appearance on Channel Four's rock programme, The Tube. They refused to go on without backing tapes, which would have contravened The Tube's 'live only' performance policy.
>
> This sorry tale will provide only a footnote in the long and quirkish history of fakery in pop music. There is a roll-call, stretching back 20 years, of groups who were packaged for their sex appeal and did little playing on their own 'hits'. Other groups were actually fabricated after the event, simply to put a marketable face on the honest but anonymous toil of session musicians and producers. (Brown, 1985)

What is intriguing here is the slide from 'fakery' in terms of technology to 'fakery' in terms of commercial manipulation. Two sorts of insincerity are confounded and we end up with only the anonymous session men who can call their work 'honest'. The muddle of critical terms involved in this sort of story, the implication that we can't 'trust' what we are hearing, reflects the confluence of three problems that technology now poses to the rock concept of authenticity.

First, there is the problem of aura in a complex process of artistic production: what or, rather, *who* is the source of a pop record's authority? The history of rock'n'roll rests on as complicated a set of assumptions about its authors as the history of film (and rock has its own version of *auteur* theory). There is always a need for *someone* to be the author of a sound, the artist, but the relative artistic

significance of writers/musicians/singers/producers/engineers/
arrangers keeps shifting. It is now possible for a publicist to be
credited as a record's real author — think of Paul Morley's role in the
selling of Frankie Goes to Hollywood. Frankie, the pop phenomenon
of 1984, gained success with a gleeful celebration of their own artifice
— Trevor Horn's production turned a plodding Liverpool group into
a wrap-around, techno-flash disco sensation; the videos for 'Relax'
and 'Two Tribes' offered camp versions of masculinity; the Frankie
hype was delivered in wads of advertising copy. This was packaging
as art and so pop theorist Paul Morley, who wrote the prose for
Frankie and their label, ZTT, was credited as their real author. He
even appeared on stage in the ZTT show, reading his copy over an Art
of Noise backing tape.

Second, technological changes raise issues of power and manipulation: how does the ownership of the technical means of production
relate to the control of what is produced? Do technical developments
threaten or consolidate such control?

Third, technology is seen to undermine the pleasures of music-
making (and watching music-making). One important strand of rock
common sense is that playing an instrument is a physical exercise,
visibly involves the body, and is, above all, a matter of effort. This is
reflected in the routine contrast of 'live' performance and 'dead'
studio activity, and even now rock's core beliefs in energy and
community can only be celebrated in concert (hence the importance
of Bruce Springsteen). The guitarist became the symbol of rock
because he (masculinity is a necessary part of the argument)
communicates physically on stage even more obviously than the
singer — the link between sound and gesture has become so familiar
that audiences have even developed the 'air guitar', a way of sharing
the guitarist's physical emotions without needing an instrument at
all.

One reason why synthesizers, drum machines, tape recorders and
so on are regarded as 'unnatural' instruments in performance is
simply because playing them takes little obvious effort. Programming
a computerized sampling device like a Fairlight engages the mind not
the body and is not a spectator event. (Art music audiences, used to
the action of orchestras and conductors, feel similarly insulted by
computer musicians.) The explicit argument is that live performances
allow for spontaneity, for performers' direct responses to their
audiences; programmed instruments can't do this. But what really
matters is not whether a show *is* spontaneous but, rather, whether it

seems to be (the most celebrated live performers often have the most rigidly stylized acts — go and see James Brown on successive nights and see exactly the same 'improvisations'). Rock bands' use of 'artificial' aids are, therefore, hidden entirely (for example, the now routine use of backing-tapes) or disguised (electronic instrument manufacturers are skilled at producing devices that can be played as if they are normal keyboards or percussion — it's not really necessary to design a rhythm machine like a Syndrum or the Simmons Kit as something to be hit!). If the deception is discovered audiences do, indeed, feel cheated. I once watched Vince Clarke of Yazoo pretend to play his Fairlight (all he was really doing was loading and unloading floppy discs). When at last he got bored and walked away, the music played on and he was booed even more loudly than Bob Dylan at the Albert Hall.

In praise of technology

For Yazoo's fans, as for Dylan's a couple of pop generations earlier, new technology meant a new means of crowd control; the direct line between star and fans was fatally disrupted. This is a familiar position in rock, as I've shown, but it is, in fact, a reversal of reality. A more dispassionate history of twentieth-century pop reveals two counter-theses.

I. Technological developments have made the rock concept of authenticity possible

I can illustrate this by reference to pop's three central inventions. First, recording itself, from its beginnings at the turn of the century, enabled previously unreproducible aspects of performance — spontaneity, improvisation, etc — to be reproduced exactly and so enabled Afro-American music to replace European art and folk musics at the heart of western popular culture. This affected not just what sort of music people listened to (and listened to more and more after the First World War) but also how they listened to it, how they registered the emotional meanings of sounds, on the one hand, the musical shape of their own emotions, on the other. Recording made available the physical impact of an unseen performer, giving access to singers' feelings without those feelings having to be coded via a written score.

One immediate consequence was that star performers began to take over from composers as popular music's 'authors' (this was true in classical music too — Caruso was the first international recording star) but, more importantly, recording gave a public means of emotionally complex communication to otherwise socially inarticulate people — performers and listeners. The blues and hillbilly singers of the 1920s and 1930s were just as stylized, as rule bound, as the romantic songsmiths of the European middle-class tradition, but their rules could be learned and understood without the education and cultural training necessary to appreciate how classical music carries its meanings. The profound statements of pride, dread and defiance in a Robert Johnson blues, the subtle twists of desire and pain in a Billie Holiday song could be heard as truthful by listeners remote from these singers geographically, socially and in terms of cultural roots. I can still remember the instant exhilaration of Little Richard's 'Long Tall Sally', which I heard for the first time when I was about ten years old, growing up in a small Yorkshire town, with no idea at all about who or what Little Richard was. That conversion to black music, similar to the experience of small town middle-class children before the war hearing Louis Armstrong for the first time, was being repeated, as a result of rock'n'roll, for teenagers all across Europe, and can't be explained away in terms of commercial cultural imperialism.

The second important invention, the electrical microphone, I have already discussed with reference to crooning, but its general effect was to extend the possibilities of the public expressions of private feelings in all pop genres. The microphone had the same function as the close-up in film history — it made stars knowable, by shifting the conventions of personality, making singers sound sexy in new ways, giving men a new prominence in big bands, and moving the focus from the song to the singer. The first pop singer to become a pin-up idol, Frank Sinatra, was well aware of the importance of amplification to his appeal. As John Rockwell writes:

> As a young singer, he consciously perfected his handling of the microphone. 'Many singers never learned to use one', he wrote later. 'They never understood, and still don't, that a microphone is their instrument.' A microphone must be deployed sparingly, he said, with the singer moving it in and out of range of the mouth and suppressing excessive sibilants and noisy intakes of air. But Sinatra's understanding of the microphone went deeper than this merely mechanical level. He knew better than almost anyone else just what Henry Pleasants has maintained: that the microphone changes the very way that modern singers sing. It was his mastery of this instrument, the way he let its existence help shape his vocal production and

singing style, that did much to make Sinatra the preeminent popular singer of our time. (Rockwell, 1984: 51–2)

Sinatra was to remain sensitive to technical developments — in the 1950s he pioneered the use of the LP to build up moods and atmospheres in ways impossible on three-minute singles. From his perspective, technology was a tool to be used and one which could easily be misused. Sinatra famously dismissed Elvis Presley and rock'n'roll, agreeing with *New York Times* jazz critic, John S. Wilson, that 'singing ability is one of the least essential qualifications for success' in this new pop form:

Recording techniques have become so ingenious that almost anyone can seem to be a singer. A small, flat voice can be souped up by emphasizing the low frequencies and piping the result through an echo chamber. A slight speeding up of the recording tape can bring a brighter, happier sound to a naturally drab singer or clean the weariness out of a tired voice. Wrong notes can be snipped out of the tape and replaced by notes taken from other parts of the tape. (Levy, 1960: 111)

In fact, Elvis Presley neither corrupted nor transformed pop tradition — he was the culminating star of the technology of music-making made available by electrical recording and amplification. For Presley's fans he was much more immediately, *honestly* sexy than Frank Sinatra.

The third significant invention, magnetic tape, began to be used by record companies in the 1950s and eventually made possible the cutting/splicing/dubbing/multi-track recording of sounds, so that studio music became entirely 'artificial'. What for John S. Wilson was a form of fraud became, for 1960s rock musicians, a source of new creative ambitions. Most developments in recording technique — long players, hi-fidelity, magnetic tape, stereophonic sound, digital recording, compact discs, etc — have, in fact, been pioneered by the classical divisions of record companies, as producers and sound engineers have tried to find ways of capturing the audio-dynamics of live orchestral music. In pop, though, these techniques were soon used to the opposite effect: studios became the place to make music impossible to reproduce live, rather than to recreate the ideal concert experience. By the end of the 1960s the studio was, in itself, the most important rock instrument. The Beatles' 'Sergeant Pepper' LP symbolized the moment when rock musicians began to claim to be making complex artworks.

Progressive rock set a problem for the received ideas of authenticity:

the rock'n'roll ideals of spontaneity, energy and effort were faced by new emphases on sensitivity, care and control. 1970s rock offered two solutions. On the one hand, effort and control were combined in the spectacular technological displays of art-rock groups like Pink Floyd and stadium rockers like Led Zeppelin; on the other hand, singer/ songwriters like Paul Simon, Joni Mitchell and even John Lennon used studio devices and sonic collages to reveal themselves more openly, making music a matter of individual sensibilities that couldn't be engaged in the crude, collective setting of the concert hall. Punk was to rebel against the excessess of both technological and artistic self-display, but punk's very moralism suggested how closely by now rock aesthetics were entangled with ideas of honesty and dishonesty.

Punk only briefly interrupted the development of pop technology (a development that had, by the 1980s, led to the complete collapse of creative distinctions between musicians, producers and engineers) but it does illustrate my second historical thesis.

II. Technological change has been a source of resistance to the corporate control of popular music

This proposal, again, argues against orthodox pop history, so first I need to clarify my position: if we look at the history of inventions in the music industry — in terms of both production and consumption — those that catch on and are successfully marketed are the ones that lead, at least in the short term, to the decentralization of music-making and listening. To give a recent example, video tapes have become popular — video discs have not. The usual argument is that technological change is inspired by and makes possible the increased capitalist control of the market but, on the whole, recording technology has not worked like this. The music industry is essentially conservative, and uses new instruments to do old things more efficiently or cheaply rather than to do new things. This is obvious in the development of musical equipment, for example. Some devices have been invented in response to musicians' specific requests (the electric bass guitar, Marshall amps) but musicians have quickly found unexpected uses for the new instruments, and many electronic tools have been developed without any clear idea of what they might be used for at all — except, that is, as substitutes for existing instruments. Hence the importance to synthesizer firms of musicians who'll play their instruments and sell them by revealing their new possibilities.

It is because musicians (and consumers) have been able to use machines for their own ends that the mechanization of popular music has not been a simple story of capitalist take-over (or state control — see Bright, this issue). This has been true at all stages of pop history. Electrical amplification, for example, and, in particular, the development of the electric guitar in the 1930s, gave American musicians the freedom to travel and perform to large audiences without the capital expense of big bands, while the parallel development of recording broke the power of Vaudeville promoters and dance-hall owners to decide who could hear whom. The new industry gate-keepers, radio disc jockeys and record company A&R departments, had much less tight control on who could make music for a living — this was especially important for black music and musicians, and for making black music available to white listeners. Even the original 'synthetic' keyboard, the Hammond Organ, was first marketed as a do-it-yourself instrument — sounds you too can make at home! — and it is arguable that the creative process in rock, from The Beatles on, has been inspired by musicians struggling to make for themselves, on whatever equipment they can cobble together, sounds that originated in expensive studios. Far from being oppressed by the unequal distribution of technological power, musicians have been made inventive by it. Rock invention, then, is inseparable from both the use of technology and from musicians' attempts to control their own sounds.

The most striking example of this was punk. Its ideology may have been anti-technology, but the late 1970s rush of home-made records and independent labels was dependent, in fact, on the lower cost of good quality recording equipment, on the availability of cheap but sophisticated electronic keyboards. The punk movement involved electronic musicians like Thomas Leer and Robert Rental, Cabaret Voltaire and the Human League; the most commercially successful independent label, Mute, has had, almost exclusively, an electro-pop roster.

Avant-garde music of all sorts has been made under the influence of punk electronics in the last decade. In the long term it turned out that the punk challenge to established modes of stardom and authority worked more clearly musically than sociologically. Punks did not replace the pop order of stars and followers, but post-punk musicians have challenged the idea of the finished product. In the

1980s, it has been commodity form rather than commodity status that has been under threat. Packaged songs, records and stars have all become the object of further play and manipulation.

One strand of such play has come from consumers themselves: home taping has given fans a new means of control over their sounds; they can compile LPs and radio shows for themselves; and use Walkmans to carry their soundscapes around with them. The record industry itself has treated home taping as the source of all its troubles. Behind the recurring campaigns for levies to be imposed on blank tapes is the suggestion that people are using them to acquire music illicitly, without paying for it, without even giving the musicians involved their just reward. Every blank tape sold, from this perspective, is a record not sold.

It is worth noting a couple of points about this argument. First, it rests on inadequate evidence. The effect of home taping is primarily deduced from record sales figures rather than from an investigation of the consumer choices that lie behind them. The patchy public research evidence there is (commissioned by Warners in the USA and by the Communist Party in Italy!) shows, not surprisingly, that home taping involves a particular commitment to music — it is done by the people who buy the most records, and the substitution effect (a tape bought means a record not bought) makes no sense to people spending as much money on music as they can. What emerges, rather, is the shifting significance of music within leisure. Records are being replaced not by tapes as such but by other leisure activities; music is being used differently and in different, more flexible forms (Warner Communications, 1982; Ala et al., 1985).

It's interesting too that the record industry's home taping fears emerged after the event. This is another example of the multi-nationals' ignorance of the implications of their own inventions. To repeat a point I've already made, record companies are essentially slow-thinking; research and development means devising ways of making more money out of people doing what they already do. No one in Britain anticipated the VTR boom — Thorn-EMI decided not to invest in its initial development — while companies regularly mistake passing fads for lasting habits (hence Warners' fateful over-investment in Atari computer games). There are enough differences between different countries' uses of new technologies (why the home-based VTR pattern in Britain, the teen craze for video arcades in the USA?) and enough examples of products that don't sell despite massive capital investment, from quadrophonic sound systems to video discs, to suggest that consumers are not entirely malleable. In the record business, at least, the increasingly oligopolistic control of musical media is continually countered by the consumer preference for devices that can, in some sense, increase their control over their own consumption.

In musical terms the most interesting and influential 'folk' uses of new technology have been developed by black musicians and audiences in Jamaica and the USA. Jamaica is, perhaps, the clearest example of a society in which the opposition 'folk vs technology' makes no sense. Reggae is a folk form with records, studios, session musicians, and disc jockeys at its centre rather than live shows or collective sing-alongs. Jamaican DJs, in particular, pioneered the use of the record as a musical instrument, something to talk to and over, slow down and speed up, cut into and across, rather than as a fixed, finished good.

In the 1970s disco DJs in New York and elsewhere echoed (and were directly influenced by) these ideas. The most dramatic consequence was Brooklyn's hip-hop scene. This culture of rapping, scratch-mixing, graffiti, break dancing, etc, was, in traditional sociological terms, a street culture:

> Hip hop was originally born of kids evolving their own social networks, from crews to karate clubs, making their own dances, poetry, and music, in an attempt to make a harsh, cruel, often incomprehensible city a liveable environment. . . . In hip hop, mainstream fashion, art, language, leisure culture — mainstream values — are subverted by those who have been cast out of the status quo. (George et al., 1985: xvii)

But the means of this cultural enterprise were technological — the ghetto blaster, the turn-table — and everything, the subway train, the body, the record, became an object on which the hip-hop artist could go to work. Hip-hop music meant montage and collage:

> To phone Tommy Boy Records in February '84 was a treat. For as long as you were kept on hold there was the legendary 'Payoff Mix' in your ear, taking hip-hop cutting one step further into the realm of endless potential. It used the irresistible base of 'Play That Beat' to cut in fragments of 'Adventures on the Wheels of Steel', some James Brown soul power, 'Buffalo Gals', Funky Four's 'That's the Joint', West Street Mob, The Supreme Team, Culture Club, Starski's 'Live at the Disco Fever', Little Richard's 'Tutti Frutti', exercise routines (heel-toe, heel-toe), Humphrey Bogart in *Casablanca*, 'Rockit', the Supremes' 'Stop in the Name of Love', 'Planet Rock', Indeep's 'Last Night a DJ Saved my Life' and more. (Toop, 1984: 154)

All sounds could be grist to this mill, whether politicians' speeches, police sirens, bugged conversations, or the accidental effects of electronic distortion itself. As David Toop goes on to say:

> The concurrent fashionability of scratch mixing and sampling keyboards like the Emulator and Fairlight has led to creative pillage on a grand scale and caused a crisis for pre-computer-age concepts of artistic property. (Toop, 1984: 154)

Many of the best hip-hop records are not legally available. Their use of 'found sound' is, in record company terms, a form of piracy. The refusal to accept records as finished products threatens the basic organization of the music business as a profit-making enterprise — hence the virulent objections to home taping (and the systematic attempt to classify home-tapers and professional bootleggers together). Electronic technology undermines the idea of fixed objects on which copyright, the essential legal safeguard of art as property, rests. And so Malcolm McClaren's LP 'Duck Rock', a montage of sounds plucked from New York radio, South African townships and urban streets, shaped in Trevor Horn's studio, has to have an identifiable 'author' both in order to sell it and in order to assign its proceeds.

And this is where the final irony of the relationship between art and technology in the record business lies: record company profits are defended against new technology in the language of individual creativity. As Jon Stratton (1983) has shown, record industry personnel have long explained their activities and the 'irrational rationality' of music as a business in the ideological terms of Romanticism. What is happening now is that technology is disrupting the implicit equation of artists' 'ownership' of their creative work and companies' ownership of the resulting commodities — the latter is being defended by reference to the former. Copyright has become both the legal, ideological weapon with which to attack the 'pirates' and, increasingly, the source of multi-national leisure corporations' income, as they exploit the rights in their productions by licensing them for use by smaller companies and other media.

As John Qualen (1985) points out, the 'crisis' of the music industry in the last decade has concealed three significant shifts in the organization of profit-making since the late 1960s rock record boom. First, recording and publishing companies are now integrated, and an increasing proportion of record company profits come, in fact, from their exploitation of their publishing copyrights via air play, the

Performing Rights Society, etc. Second, the major record companies are, increasingly, licensing material from their back catalogues for use by independent TV and specialist music packagers. Third, record companies have begun to treat radio and TV use of records and videos not as advertisements for which they provide new material cheaply, but as entertainment services which should pay competitive prices for the recordings they use:

> In many ways the record industry is facing very similar problems to the film industry. Its base market is being eroded and fragmented (pre-recorded music sales are down, as are cinema admissions), costs are spiralling and the traditional distribution system is threatened by the new technologies.
>
> Though there will always be box-office biggies like *ET* (or *Relax* and *Thriller*), for the most part the earnings of the producers of films (pre-recorded music) will come not from their physical sale but from the exploitation by the producers of the rights they hold in their productions to broadcast and cable TV. The double advantage of this strategy for the record industry (which is far more vertically integrated than the film industry) is that, for the majors, it could eliminate the high cost of manufacturing and distribution. (Qualen, 1985: 16).

Conclusion

The political claims of 1960s counter-culture used to be derided for the apparent contradiction between ideology and technology: how could the USA or Britain be 'greened' by Marshall amps and expensive stereo hi-fi systems? For the told-you-so school of mass cultural criticism the argument for technological progress doesn't amount to much. Look what happened, in the end, to Elvis Presley and the electric Bob Dylan, to punk and hip-hop — they were all, one way or another, *co-opted*. This is a familiar argument on the left but rests on its own dubious assumptions. Can musical truth, whether class or gender or ethnic or individual truth, really be guaranteed by acoustics? This seems to be a question that worries first world intellectuals, anxious, maybe, about the roots of their own culture, more than anyone else. Third world musicians, like black musicians in the USA, have rarely been reluctant to adapt their music to new technology (or new technology to their music) (see Laing, and Regev, this issue). Compare the intense American feminist debate about 'women's music'. Should feminists use folk and jazz forms, as more 'authentically' expressive? Or is punk and noise and electro-stridency the necessary source of a new voice?

The debate here turns on who musicians want to reach and how they want to reach them as well as on the implicit ideologies of musical forms themselves, and this means entering the fray of the music market and pop taste, the role of songs and sounds in everyday life. To assume that what happens to stars and movements in the long term — co-option — discredits their disruptive impact in the short term is to misunderstand the politics of culture (and there is no doubting the momentary disruptive impact of Elvis Presley or the Rolling Stones, the Sex Pistols and X-Ray Spex). Technology, the shifting possibility of mechanical reproduction, has certainly been the necessary condition for the rise of the multinational entertainment business, for ever more sophisticated techniques of ideological manipulation, but technology has also made possible new forms of cultural democracy and new opportunities of individual and collective expression. It's not just that the 'aura' of traditional culture has been destroyed, but also that technological devices have been musicians' and audiences' most effective weapons in their continuous guerilla war against the cultural power of capital and the state. Each new development in recording technology enables new voices to be heard and to be heard in new ways; and pop voices are systematically denied access to other public media. The history of pop is, in part, the history of different groups using the same means (records) for different ends (profits, art, the articulation of community, self-aggrandizement, protest, etc). Technology determines how the competition for a voice is organized but does not determine who will be heard or how what is heard is interpreted. My own belief is that capitalist control of popular music rests not on record company control of recording technology but on its recurring appropriation of fans' and musicians' ideology of art. That the economic arrangements of music production and consumption have not yet changed, despite their increasing lack of fit with the actual production and consumption process, reflects the continuing power of nineteenth-century ideas of creativity and truth.

Notes

1. Thanks to Paddy Scannell for details of this dispute.
2. Letter from Brian Blain, 12 March 1981.

Frith, *Art versus technology*   279

References

Ala, N. et al. (1985) 'Patterns of Music Consumption in Milan and Reggio Emilia from April to May 1983', *Popular Music Perspectives*, 2.
Brown, M. (1985) 'Pop — How Live is Live?', *Sunday Times*, 17 March.
Coon, C. (1976) *1988: The New Wave Punk Rock Explosion*. London: Omnibus.
Eckersly, R. (1946) *The BBC And All That*. London: Sampson Low, Marston and Co.
George, N. et al. (1985) *Fresh*. New York: Random House.
Heath, T. (1957) *Listen To My Music*. London: Frederick Muller.
Levy, A. (1960) *Operation Elvis*. London: André Deutsch.
Qualen, J. (1985) *The Music Industry*. London: Comedia.
Rockwell, J. (1984) *Sinatra*. New York: Random House.
The Rolling Stones (1964) *Our Own Story*. London: Corgi.
Stratton, J. (1983) 'Capitalism and Romantic Ideology in the Record Business', *Popular Music*, 3.
Toop, D. (1984) *The Rap Attack*. London: Pluto Press.
Warner Communications (1982) *Home Taping – A Consumer Survey*.

[3]

Pearls and Swine:
The Intellectuals and the Mass Media

Simon Frith
Jon Savage

For those of us in the academy who have been urging people for twenty years or more to take popular culture seriously, Jim McGuigan's *Cultural Populism*[1] is a sombre read. A lucid account of how cultural studies took their place in the university curriculum, it pinpoints the ways in which studying popular culture has become a method of uncritical celebration.

Among other things it makes clear how much Raymond Williams is missed. McGuigan takes Williams' 1958 essay 'Culture is Ordinary' as the beginning of his story, reminding us of Williams' radicalism, his roots in an 'unpopular' working-class politics, his sense of history, and his dogged suspicion of the weasel words of commerce. Williams, you can only conclude, would have been dismayed by contemporary cultural studies' cheerful populism, by academics' new-found respect for sales figures, by the theoretical pursuit of the joys of consumption.

The problem of cultural populism has resonance outside the academy too. In the second edition of his book, McGuigan might well consider the curious case of the *Modern Review*, a magazine dedicated to taking popular culture seriously by defining itself *against* academic cultural studies. In sales terms, the *Modern Review* is not significant, but it exemplifies (both within its own pages and through its contributors' obvious impact on general press coverage of pop culture) the dominant voice of lay cultural populism. Describing itself as providing 'low culture for highbrows' it furnishes a knowing middlebrow consumer guide.

For both academics arguing about the curriculum and journalists arguing about the arts pages, what is at issue is 'popular culture'— how we should think about it, how we should study it, how we should value it. And two further points should be made about this. First, the questions are not only of concern to rival groups of academics and journalists. Popular culture is equally an issue for the political and cultural establishment. It is at the centre of the debates about the BBC's future, for example: what is the 'higher ground' of broadcasting

---

[1] Jim McGuigan, *Cultural Populism*, Routledge, London 1992. We thank the Institute of Popular Culture, Manchester Metropolitan University for permission to reproduce these comments.

to which the BBC may (or may not) now be committing itself? It is at the centre of the debates about the Arts Council's Charter for the Arts: what is the state's responsibility to amateur or commercial art forms? And it features, in a different way, in discussion of the National Curriculum, as our heritage is defended against soaps and reggae.

It follows, second, that the questions of popular culture are not new. The education system since Arnold, the BBC since Reith, the Arts Council since Keynes, have all made cultural policy in the light of the perceived *threat* of pop and commerce. What is new, then, is not the problem but its formulation. It is as if the ghosts of Adorno and Leavis, ghosts who haunted discussion of popular culture for fifty years, have finally been laid.

McGuigan traces the rise of academic cultural populism to the demise of the 'dominant ideology thesis', the assumption that one could map culture from the top down, from capitalist manoeuvre to audience response; the *Modern Review* reserves its greatest scorn for cultural do-gooders, those people who witter on about discrimination and taste. For cultural populists of all sorts, the popular is to be approached with new, modern assumptions, assumptions about the positive power of market forces, assumptions about the creativity of the consumer.

From our perspective, though, what is revealed in both McGuigan's book and the *Modern Review* is a crisis of critical language: how can we talk about (or evaluate) popular culture *without* reference to its ideological effects? What does it mean to treat popular culture *aesthetically*? How, now, does the relation of high and low culture work? What authority does either a teacher or a critic have to assert that his or her reading of a popular text—*Single White Female*, say, or *Civvies*, or Madonna—is any more important than anyone else's? Is popular culture just a matter of style and sale?

The unstated premise of McGuigan's book is that the post-war cultural settlement is at an end. The Keynesian consensus, embodied in the Arts Council, was that there is a congruence between two lines of cultural demarcation—the high versus the low, the state subsidized versus the market driven. The state supports the high (and implicitly, unpopular), whether through the Arts Council, the BBC or the education system; the popular arts are defined in terms of commercial success.

But this equation was never really so clear cut, and over the years has been re-thought in terms of a kind of pluralism—the state being given the responsibility to support a range of cultural groups. At the same time the equation of the commercial with the low has also become problematic, as certain commercial performers (most obviously in rock music) have sold themselves as artists. The resulting confusion is perhaps best exemplified in John Peel's BBC radio show, hard to categorize as either low or high culture, as driven by either state or market forces.

The *Modern Review*'s reading of this situation is inevitably populist.

108

Inevitably because populism has long been the only English alternative to Arts Council authority on the one hand, and left cultural progressivism on the other. In the same way, McGuigan shows how cultural studies academics had nowhere else to go when they became disillusioned with Marxism.

The encrusted nature of the populist position was clear in the critical response to another recent book, John Carey's *The Intellectuals and the Masses*. The locus for this skirmish was perfect: the (over)expanded feature space in the quality end of Fleet Street. The arguments too were perfect with their very familiarity—harking back to the 1950s populist tropes. It is not hard to see why the book got so much coverage: these tropes fit exactly with the way that the once left liberal centre has moved to the right.

Bashing snobbish intellectuals is an old English sport and there are traces, even in Carey's own cool prose, of the nervy, man-at-the-bar bonhomie familiar from the work of Kingsley Amis and Philip Larkin. Intellectual-bashing has always rested on a bluff defensiveness about the commonness of common life, on a celebration of small horizons and smaller ambitions which ill conceals its own uneasy violence.

In this discursive world Britishness becomes Englishness, and Englishness describes a people by nature content in their allotments—and thus defiantly dull. Against this recurring conservative ideal—a pleasant fantasy of little England: a nation of moderation, tolerance, harmless desire and the sharp snap of common sense—it is easy enough to measure the arrogance, snobbery and sheer silliness of the intellectual. Carey's view of the literary modernist in this respect echoes Larkin's view of modern jazz.

But what concerns us here is less the position of the modernist intellectual in cultural history than the peculiarly English notion of the masses, the common people, which is used to lay down a norm of behaviour—domestic, heterosexual, suburban, middle-class—such that any departure from it becomes abnormal. In this discourse, abnormality is over-determined: to be an intellectual is to be by definition queer, depraved, *foreign*. (Note the reporting of the recent Jacques Derrida fuss at Cambridge.)

The defence of the masses against the intellectuals depends, in other words, on a particular kind of nostalgia: the commonplace acts as a bulwark against all sorts of social change, against a permanent fear of unrest at the margins. Out there aren't just strange ideas but strange people—young, female, foreign, homosexual. The cultural question becomes where, precisely, do these people live? The political question is how to keep them there—out of sight, at the margins.

As Peter Keating has shown in *The Haunted Study*, the terms of the ideological debate between the modernists and the masses were overlain from the start by an institutional distinction. By the beginning of the century the material bases for intellectual life (replacing politics and the church) were education and the press. The twentieth-century career of the modernist writer, composer or artist has been, to a large extent, dependent on an academic position and an academic audience; the twentieth century career of the non-academic intellectual has meant reaching the readership put together by newspapers and magazines.

The resulting hostility between academics and journalists has its own history, but what is taken for granted nowadays is not only that academics, in their jargon-patrolled cloisters, don't understand 'life'—as if they did not themselves have parents and children, disappointments and debts—but that journalists do. In practice, of course, most journalists live more sheltered lives than most academics: the Fleet Street agenda remains rooted in a particular sort of metropolitan provincialism.

'Understanding life', in other words, appreciating 'the ordinary', isn't only a matter of experience but also of style. Experience turned into moral authority—the newspaper columnists' trade—reflects most significantly an attitude to one's readership. If the academic's task is to tell people what they don't already know, the journalist's is to tell them what they do. In this respect, as McGuigan shows, cultural populism is more a journalistic than an academic project—which helps explain the uneasy symbiosis between cultural studies and the *Modern Review*.

Journalists Eclipse the Academics

We have been describing a tradition of debate, the way in which the particular entanglement of education, the media and the masses in Britain has shaped recurring arguments about culture, its meanings and significance. The question we want to turn to now is how these arguments (and the conditions for them) changed over the last decade.

To begin with, it seems clear that the effect of the Thatcher decade was not simply to widen the intellectual gap between journalists and academics, but, more importantly, to increase the importance of journalists as cultural ideologues while undermining the cultural authority of educators.

The first part of this process can, in fact, be traced back to Harold Wilson and the development (learned from Stanley Baldwin and Winston Churchill) of a populist approach to party politics in which a direct appeal to the voter (via the media) became more important than an indirect one (via party support). This was automatically to raise the status of journalists, not only as the channel through which politicians established their popularity (with the rise, for example, of the personality interviewer) but also as objective voices of the people which could be contrasted to the self-interested voice of the non-establishment activist. (Of subsequent prime ministers only Edward Heath has not worked in such a populist fashion.)

The press was particularly significant for Margaret Thatcher's radical ambitions, as her intellectuals (and hers was a determinedly cultural project: she wanted to change how the British people *thought*) were operating in right-wing think tanks that lay outside the intellectual establishment. Their challenge to academic common sense was conducted in the name of some deeper, instinctive popular knowledge.

The eighties thus brought to the fore a variety of right wing intellectual accounts of the masses, varying from the considered conservatism of Roger Scruton or Ferdinand Mount, in which 'ordinary Englishness' is embedded in the tapestry of the English language, the organic community and historical tradition, to the anti-toff populism of Norman Stone or Andrew Neil, in which a kind of basic British common sense is expressed through market forces, to the buffoonery of Woodrow Wyatt, Paul Johnson and Auberon Waugh, for whom 'the people' are mobile signifiers, now sages, now idiots.

The combined effect of these various populist poses (which certainly helped sap liberal self-confidence) was to construct 'the people' as a mythical site of authority. The political object was not exactly to mobilize popular support (none of these writers was much interested in muddying their minds with democratic activism) but, rather, to articulate it, to 'read' the people through theories of history or concepts of the market, so that raw sales or voting figures could be interpreted in terms of a broader transformational process.

Thatcherism was thus defined, to a large extent, not in specialist journals or elite forums but in newspaper columns and in well-publicized reports and position papers; it represented a well thought-out (and effective) strategic use of the media by intellectuals. This was, ironically, to introduce a rather un-English approach to the dissemination of ideas, but by the end of the Thatcher decade struggles for power and status within the professions—health, education, broadcasting—were being conducted in the light of media rather than academic support.

At the same time, the eighties saw a boom in newspaper and magazine publishing—itself a consequence of free-market policies. This boom increased media space—to breaking point—but not revenue (from sales and advertising). There were not the resources to spread the jam of reportage or investigative journalism (increasingly confined to public-service television as Andrew Neil, for example, enfeebled the *Sunday Times* 'Insight' team) over the white bread of the new supplements. Rather, the *Sunday Times* Section 5, 'The Culture', the *Guardian* 'Weekend', the *Independent* magazine, and so forth, depended on the 'feature', a type of writing in which the journalist's style elevates individual opinion to the level of social commentary.

The spread of single corporate ownership across various media— newspapers, magazines, broadcast and satellite TV advertising companies, publishing companies—also created what Umberto Eco calls 'media squared': a PR-led agenda in place of reportage, soap opera treated as reality, reality treated as soap opera, endless media stories about media. Coupled with the diaspora from Fleet Street (as a distinct location) this has resulted in a crisis of confidence for editors and journalists, only exacerbated by the recession. Competition means a constant jockeying for market position, for the right 'demographic'; newspaper agendas are increasingly organized around assumed consumer tastes (and ever-expanding lifestyle pages) rather than by their readers' supposed interests as citizens.

This was the context in which style culture—developed in the early

III

eighties by magazines like *The Face*—made its Fleet Street impact. Here were a group of writers who might not know much about social issues but who surely understood shopping. The rise of the journalist as the voice of political common sense, in other words, coincided with a rewriting of political common sense in terms of free trade, as Margaret Thatcher translated social relations into market relations, and John Major redefined the citizen as the consumer.

The Tory challenge to educational authority had both a material and an ideological base: the systematic lowering of the status of teachers and teaching at all levels; the replacement of quangos of the 'great and good' by political placemen and women whose cultural expertise is measured not by any scholarly credentials but in straightforward tests of political correctness. The first effect of this policy was on modes of argument. If Labour Party policies have to be seen to be reasonable, to rest on surveys and reports, to embrace the virtues of the Fabians and the LSE (we were rarely allowed to forget that Harold Wilson had been a don), the Conservative Party has never justified itself in these terms —ministerial prejudices are taken to be quite adequate to see off the self-serving arguments of so-called 'experts'.

In these circumstances newspaper columnists, armed with the power of anecdote, take on a particular sort of importance, valued not for their intellectual independence but for their ability to articulate common sense—to translate the prejudices of politicians into the commonplace of daily discourse and vice versa. Their importance in the competition for newspaper sales is exactly that of the DJ in the competition for radio audiences: their 'we' gives the reader/listener a sense of community. This has always been the role of the columnist in popular papers, of course, but the last decade has seen an obsession with columnists in all sections of the press, columnists whose job is less to make readers think than to save them from thought, less to make them see events anew than to ensure a breakfast-table conversation that is held in clichés.

The Snares of Experience and Openness

In broader cultural terms, the effect has been to elevate the authority of experience (valorized in much feminist and pop writing) over the authority of the intellect, and subtly to change what is meant by knowledge. This shift occurred in the last couple of years of the weekly *New Society*, long the home of the most interesting commentary on popular culture and a site where, uniquely, journalists and academics met on equal terms. A reportorial tradition of outsiders like Angela Carter and Colin MacInnes trying to make sense of social phenomena collapsed into first-hand reports from people presumed by insecure editors to *be* the phenomena—Julie Burchill was *there*, puking in the Roxy.

The problems of such reporting are twofold: experience quickly ceases to be first hand as the reporters distance themselves from it in the very act of reporting; what is reported is not, in the end, 'raw' experience but its interpretation, an interpretation that convinces by feeding editorial (and readers') expectations. Again, popular culture is taken to describe not the startling but the familiar.

Reporting from experience, in other words, comes to involve exactly the same sort of nostalgia and celebration of the ordinary as any other sort of English anti-intellectualism. To put it another way, the kind of 'experience' validated in this writing is defined, as we have already noted, in remarkably narrow terms. The implied 'we' of the English press (the Scottish press still works differently) is a we which excludes not just African and Asian British, not just gays and lesbians, not just, for the most part, socialists and feminists, not just snobs and intellectuals, but in fact, anyone who disagrees—this is not a kind of writing that encourages argument; you can't *challenge* experience.

As McGuigan illuminates, there is a strong connection between the media version of popular culture and pop's academic status as the object of 'cultural studies' (and, indeed, cultural studies courses were a spawning ground for eighties style-journalism). In both cases the popular is defined in sales terms; in both cases the focus is on the consumer (cultural production is, it seems, an uncomplicated industrial process); in both cases critical authority is claimed via a particular kind of identification with 'the people': these commentators, whether in print or in the lecture room, are fans, but with special consuming skills; they can read the codes, place the labels, identify the quotes.

If, conventionally, cynicism is a way of masking sentimentality, in popular cultural commentary sentimentality—the romance of the fan —conceals both cynicism and bad faith. In the academy, after all, cultural studies, for all its ingenuousness, does seek to rescue 'ordinary' lives from academic condescension, to *complicate* the daily experiences of pop music and clothes and magazines by making them the object of high theory. For the new generation of cultural commentators in the press, by contrast, the goal seems to be to render even the most extraordinary icons of popular culture (Madonna or Michael Jackson) into the banal terms of everyday experience: everything odd about popular culture, it turns out, can be *explained*.

This is partly a matter of context. The very act of taking a pop icon— an advertisement, a pop song, a sitcom—into the classroom and examining it in the light of semiotics or psychoanalysis or feminism is to make it strange. The journalist, by contrast, inevitably places the same icons on a familiar shelf, next to all the other consumer goods. As any pop critic knows, for all our good intentions our prime task is as consumer guides—hence the cynicism, hence the problem of critical language.

On the BBC's *Late Show*, where the new cultural 'openness' is most self-consciously celebrated, popular artists are either treated, quite inappropriately, with all the awed attention of high art appreciation, or else they become the object of the quick quip, tricksy treatments which seem designed to show that the form of the programme matters more than the content, that the art of low culture lies in what a clever consumer (or a clever director) can make of it. The problem here lies in the packaging—the packages in which items are boxed before they reach the *Late Show*, the packages in which the *Late Show* feels obliged to wrap them in order to meet its own perceived, over-mediated needs.

In other words, the problem of the *Late Show* (which the BBC approaches in more interesting ways in other arts strands like *Arena*) is that it hasn't thought through the implications of its new eclectic account of culture—its assumptions about the high are as limited as its assumptions about the low. In the end, whichever way you look at it, everything has to be *wrapped up*. And what escapes the programme is what can't be so wrapped—the non-commercial that also lacks art status; the culture that doesn't have a niche in the TV market place. The programme does not really challenge high/low distinctions between aesthetic transcendence (real art) and social function (the popular). Rave culture, for example, is inevitably treated as a matter of sociology (not form); literary culture remains a matter of form (not sociology).

The same effect is clear in newspaper and magazine arts sections. Editors still take it for granted that low arts coverage—whether film, TV or music reviews—is best written from the experience of the ordinary listener/viewer (who has a way with words) rather than by the sort of 'expert' who is employed to cover fine art or classical music. For all the populist tone of, say, the *Guardian*'s art pages, popular culture is actually treated with a distinct lack of seriousness—at least on its own terms. It becomes, rather, a source of populist credibility ('I loved *Batman*'), of self-serving nostalgia (most obvious in television's treatment of its own history), and of intellectual idleness (to treat pop culture *theoretically* is, it seems, to deprive it of its 'fun').

Such arguments beg all the interesting questions about popularity, confusing formal and generic issues with sales figures, displacing questions of creativity onto questions of taste, making ideas and sensations mutually exclusive. More importantly, the populist line fails to recognize that one important function of popular culture, even in its most commodified form, is as an expressive tool for people otherwise excluded from the public voice. Popular culture, that is, becomes one of the most potent challenges to the populist 'we' of the journalist as intellectual. The 'accessibility' of popular culture, in other words, describes not the fact that 'everyone' can understand it, but that everyone can use it, has a chance to be heard, to develop their own language, however difficult or *unpopular* what they say may be.

Two points follow from this. First, the 'culturescape'—that pattern of aesthetic symbols and rituals through which people determine their individual identity and social place—is no longer being mapped by day-to-day cultural critics for all their populist claims. Take the way in which cultural journalism continues to operate 'disciplinary' boundaries and hierarchies. It seems clear to us that performers like the Pet Shop Boys or The Smiths have, using 'trashy' pop forms, come up with much more effective ways of dealing with sex and love, pain and ambition—ways more in tune with the feeling of contemporary culture—than have, say, Ian McEwan and Martin Amis using literary devices. In the same way, dance acts like Orbital or Derrick May draw a more accurate map of the 1992 body—its formation in and by the contemporary experience of desire and space—than any 'fine' artist we can think of. The issue is not whether our judgments here are right, but that such comparisons, now a normal part of cultural adolescence, are excluded from the terms of most cultural coverage.

The problem for arts editors seems to be twofold. First, the popular audience is not an undifferentiated audience, and some sectors of it are seen as more significant than others—'minority' tastes thus tend not just to be marginalized, but also to be treated as peculiar, as lacking the 'universal' appeal of proper art. (The same argument can be seen in the populist defence of the literary canon—white male authors represent the universal; blacks and women can speak only partially.) But on top of this is an ambiguous attitude to the mass media themselves (this is also apparent in John Carey's book). Even as 'high' culture is enmeshed in the sales process, even as newspapers for their own sales purposes respond unthinkingly to media campaigns, so 'old' art forms—painting, writing, composing—become the measure against which the new media output is judged.

The second problem for contemporary arts coverage is that we are just as likely—perhaps more likely—to find the unpopular voice, the voice of 'un-English' desires, in the interstices of mass culture—in clubs and comic books, in fanzines and anonymous dance records— as in the subsidized art world. In other words, the opposition set up between the intellectuals and the masses makes no sense culturally. There are 'intellectuals' using pop cultural forms (just as 'high culture' describes, among other things, a marketing mechanism). And the 'masses' are no more likely to be in agreement about their cultural opinions than about their political or religious beliefs—one measure of popular success is, after all, great unpopularity: Madonna is a phenomenon as much for the loathing as for the love that she inspires.

Current arguments about popular culture rely on a series of dichotomies: the ordinary versus the elite, the journalist/media worker versus the academic, the conservative versus the progressive. We would summarize all such dichotomies under a more general heading: the culture of self-satisfaction versus the culture of the dissatisfied. From the dissatisfied position the argument always has to be that life could be different, could be better, could be changed—both art and education rest on such premises; they are meant to make us see things differently. They are designed to show us through the imagination, through reason, the limitations of our perspectives, to doubt our common sense.

Against this, all versions of populism, left and right, are organized less to reflect what people do think (most people are muddled) but rather, to enable them to think *without thought*. What John Carey forgets (or rather, pretends to forget for the sake of his polemic) is that his despised intellectuals have had a more profound effect on 'ordinary' people than popular novelists like Arnold Bennett.

Whatever her failings as a snob, as a writer Virginia Woolf has inspired generations of 'ordinary' adolescent women, just as Eliot and Lawrence, David Bowie and the Sex Pistols have inspired generations of 'ordinary' adolescent boys—one of the defining qualities of being ordinary, after all, is wanting to be extraordinary, just as the long-term effect of suburbia has been to produce generations of anti-suburban pop artists. What should equally be stressed is that the identification of the 'good' and the 'popular' is a matter of quality not quantity. For cultural judgement sales figures are an irrelevance: the truly popular describes something remarkable, that work or event or performance that transforms people's ways of sensing and being. This is not a view currently given much house-room. The great failing of our age is the idea, received wisdom from right to left, upmarket and downmarket, that to be popular you have to be populist, which means an uncritical acceptance of an agenda set by market forces. There is no sadder sight than the fortysomething ex-Leftist, the thirty-something ex-Punk, the twentysomething ex-Stylist, burying their dis-appointments in their search across the surface of popular culture for pure sensation.   ·

The question, to put this another way, is what is at stake in the argu-ment about popular culture, and the *Modern Review* is symptomatic in its failure to articulate a cultural theory except negatively. It is not a sociological journal (it contains no primary material or research); it is not explicitly a political journal; it is not a literary journal (beyond the assertion of its authors' tastes, there is little personal testimony). If its review format suggests a consumer guide, its reviewing style offers little clue as to who its readers might be—the magazine's basic pur-pose being to bash received opinion. This is populism as resentment; the dominant tone of the *Modern Review* is petulance: *they* (the Left, the academy, the educated) took *our* toys away.

What is interesting about the *Modern Review*'s prominence (within Fleet Steet at least, where it provides pop culture criticism for editors who dislike pop culture but don't dare say so) is the end of a partic-ular kind of language. This language is well laid out in McGuigan's *Cultural Populism*: developed from cultural studies, subcultures, deconstruction, filtered through the style and music press—it has dominated the discussion of pop music and pop culture since the early eighties, and now provides the rump of PR, ego and spite which still fills up pages of newsprint.

This language is irrelevant to pop culture producers (except when they need some publicity), to pop culture consumers (failing as it does to reflect most people's experience), and to those of us who would like to see a new language of pop culture: one derived from anthropology, archetypal psychology, musicology, one which has a grasp of pop both as an industrial and as an aesthetic form. It is time to reclaim pop from the populists: they have said much of nothing, but their chit-chat still poisons the air.

[4]

Remodeling Britney Spears: Matters of Intoxication and Mediation

Stan Hawkins and John Richardson

This article examines a range of perspectives and cluster of discourses that are informed by the reading of one single video, Toxic, *performed by pop icon Britney Spears. In our investigation, we seek new directions for audiovisual analysis and attempt to explore the music text alongside symbolic meanings mediated by a video. Of particular interest are the intersection of characters played by the star with constructions of personal narrative, issues of exoticism in music, queering strategies, race and sexuality, audiovisual genealogies, and the relationship of the singing voice to song structure and meaning. We conclude that the musical interpretation of pop videos calls for a mode of analysis that reflects the multivalent and allusive nature of this audiovisual form.*

It was during the early 1980s, with the historic launch of MTV, that videos became one of the most important vehicles for promoting popular music. Those of us who were around during this period will recall that responses to the first spate of music videos were very different from what they are today. Indeed, there was an underlying skepticism on the part of many music scholars and journalists that videos trivialized the "music itself" and that visual representations were mere distractions. While spectacles of musical performance have been around for centuries, MTV signaled something quite different: now music could be beamed to millions simultaneously across time and space.

When it comes to musicological approaches, surprisingly little scholarly work on pop videos has been forthcoming. There are no good explanations for this. Apart from a few scattered studies, mainly dominated by E. Anne Kaplan's *Rocking Around the Clock* (1987) and Andrew Goodwin's *Dancing in the Distraction Factory* (1993), the issue of video analysis has not been taken up nearly enough within popular music scholarship.

By advocating a systematic approach to understanding the construction of the relationship between the visual strata of a video and the music, our purpose is to deal with how pictures open up new meanings for songs. Theoretically speaking, this position is grounded in an insistence on the reciprocal nature of the audiovisual contract, which invariably implies some degree of contamination and projection across different media (Chion 9). Siding with film theorist Michel Chion, our consideration of the role of music is directed to the transference of one set of references onto the other, and how this constitutes the primary function of the visual text. In particular, we seek to demonstrate how the star persona and their personal narratives in pop videos raise significant issues that deal with cinematic and pop genealogy. In addition, the interest that the voice holds in this respect prompts numerous excursions into examining vocal structurations via articulation, phonology, and animation. Underpinning this study is also the matter of the body, and how images of hypersexualization are the direct result of the technologization of erotics through production.

No longer simply a promo device, but more a marketable product in its own right,[1] the music video takes on its own life after repeated viewings, produces different understandings, and even becomes more important than the song. The full effect of a video undoubtedly has a range of aesthetic implications, which are related to contexts that vary significantly from cinema. We know that experiencing images via a television or iPod screen is different from viewing via a cinema screen. Furthermore, pop videos frame musical references in ways other than that of cinema, which thus implies a need for a flexible approach that stresses how various texts pertaining to pop culture interrelate with one another. For this reason, we offer an intertextual method that exposes the fluidity and blurring of style and its function. In turn, this forms part of an approach that involves the transportation of one or more group of signs into another, accompanied by new articulations of both enunciative and denotative positions. Because a pop video deals with productivity at the same time as creativity, there is a critical relationship to genre that is redistributive and permutative. This would suggest that, in the space of a single video, numerous utterances intersect and activate one another, which raises questions concerning personal narrative and how this determines performativity.

Personal Narrative as Performative

Central to our analysis is the category of "personal narrative," although our deployment of the term diverges from the vernacular sense, which is concerned with how pop *auteurs* tell stories of their lives through the medium of song.[2] It differs also from the writing of certain North American musicologists, who have grounded interpretations of music in their own personal histories.[3] Some work on personal narrative drawing on research in cultural history and developmental psychology has appeared in recent research on pop, but none of this takes *pop performance* as its explicit starting point.[4] While we acknowledge the relevance of existing research, the idea of personal narrative in our view frames better discussions within a conceptual apparatus, such as that provided by psychologist Dan McAdams, who draws on the ideas of Paul Ricoeur concerning the ubiquity of temporal coding in human experience. McAdams is interested in the stories people tell about themselves in order to invest actions and events with meaning. Personal narrative of this kind is about the narrative reconstitution of the self through an open-ended process of reflection and revision. By marking[5] certain events in personal histories as significant, while at the same time bypassing others, personal narrators create navigational beacons that enable themselves and others to make sense of the past, while providing points of reference that will inform interpretations of future actions and events. Identity, in this sense, is negotiated by means of an ongoing dialogue between past and present selves (McAdams 5). Personal narratives, then, are performative: they pertain not only to *what* we tell but *how* we tell and act.[6] Moreover, they are subject to the same forces and constraints that inform all interpretative acts. Thus, observations regarding the perceived trajectory of Britney Spears' career are interconnected with the parallel narrative trajectories of audience members. It is here that processes of identification and identity formation that have been the subject of much recent writing in popular music research come into play (e.g. Hawkins *Settling*; Kassabian *Hearing*; Whiteley). Personal narrative is implicated therefore at both ends of the communication chain as well as in the myriad forms of mediation that are implicated in popular texts: thus Spears' first-person accounts of her life in interviews and songs constitute only a fraction of the relevant material, which can be elucidated only by detailed analysis of pop performances and related discursive texts.

Spears is a performer whose perceived self-representations have raised problems from the outset. Parental groups in several countries have expressed concern about the "mixed signals" put forward in aspects of her music and public persona. Such concerns coalesced in controversial cover shots for *Rolling Stone* and in the video *Baby One More Time*, both of which were widely perceived as signifying simultaneously immaturity and eroticism. In an important study on the reception of Spears, Melanie Lowe shows that it was not solely parents who objected to the star's "mixed signals." Teenaged girls characterized the star as a "slore" (an elision of slut and whore: Lowe 124–25) not so much because of her provocative attire and raw behavior, which they found acceptable in other stars (including Christina Aguilera), as in the combination of these traits with her affected naivety. For fans, agency is a critical factor: Spears' behavior was regarded as acceptable to the extent that *she herself* could be shown to be responsible for key artistic decisions (Lowe 138). Taking such attitudes on board, recent documentaries on the star have gone to great lengths to attribute agency (e.g. *Time Out*; "ABC Television Special"). A parallel revisionist campaign has been conducted in her recent lyrics, visual representations, and music, but it remains moot just how successful it has been. While it is beyond the scope of this article to conduct an overarching ethnographic survey into changing perceptions of Spears in the light of these revisionist strategies, research in this field convinces us that the line of inquiry we are taking is not out of kilter with reception.

Pursuing the idea of personal narrative, it is something of a truism to observe that Spears is doing her growing up in public. In fact, audiences witness very little of this "growing up" and, what they do see, is heavily mediated. That her core audience is growing up with her, or, as often seems to be the case, *apart from her* is seldom acknowledged. Many fans who followed Spears' music in the 1990s, a proportion of whom are now university students, are scathing in their attitude toward the star, something that can presumably be attributed in part to a natural shedding of "childhood" identities. This makes it necessary for the star to undergo visible and audible transformations in order to fend off disaffection and optimize the demographic profile of her fan base. Of particular salience to interpretations of her recent music is the perceived trajectory from teen star/vamp to would be *auteur* in the mould of her mentor Madonna (who, we know, underwent a struggle to achieve *auteur* status). This biographical trajectory of performing artists is frequently an aspect of reception, as evidenced in the flashback video sequences in recent concerts by older artists such as Cher and Madonna.[7] In these terms, the music video *Toxic* can easily by interpreted as an attempt to chart and performatively bring about transformations in Spears' star persona. Through the attribution of a mediated authorship, then, we seek to demonstrate how the video constitutes a form of personal narrative: Spears, as we envision her, telling a story of Spears. The investigation conducted in this article focuses on the specific audiovisual performance of *Toxic*.

Narrative Structure

The song "Toxic" (Dennis, Karlsson, Winnberg, and Jonback)[8] is characterized by a form of musico-textual iconicity that lends itself to the repetitive structures of dance music and the shorthand narrative conventions of music video. This iconicity of music and words is channeled into an elliptical storyboard of events whose spectacular impact might for some viewers override narrative considerations. Nevertheless, for viewers enticed by the audiovisual impact of the song or otherwise willing to invest in more focused observation, a story of sorts is implied, which becomes increasingly difficult to ignore in the course of repeated viewings/hearings. Notably, the music video *Toxic* employs the kind of temporal disjunction found in neo-noir films (such as *Pulp Fiction, Lost Highway,* and *Memento*) in which a significant event in the plot is withheld until the strategy of flashback unlocks the mystery of the unfolding present. Thus, when Spears' character chances upon her lover in the shower with another women in a rapid-fire montage of three musically accented shots, located almost subliminally towards the end of the video (each lasts less than a second), it is this composite event (comprising a showerhead, 02:34; an embrace, 02:36; a smug smile 02:37) which motivates the storyboard of events and character changes that precede and follow it in the chronology of the video.

The video opens with Spears assuming the role of a futuristic air stewardess, whose disguise allows her to approach the holder of a key to a secret research facility. Notably, the initially unattractive male character is also in disguise; in a play of identity typical of recent science fiction, his facial mask is pealed away by the stewardess to reveal a ruggedly handsome male (played by actor Matt Felker). The two exchange favors in a "mile-high" lavatory after which the wily stewardess emerges with her reward, the passenger with a smile. The female protagonist then morphs into a second character, characterized by Spears in the "making of" documentary as a "red-haired hot mamma," who hitches a motorcycle ride (with muscular actor Tyson Beckford) through the streets of a digitally simulated Paris-by-night before arriving at a high-tech research lab, where she procures a vial of poison (hence "toxic"). While breaking out of the lab she acrobatically negotiates a cylindrical passage protected by laser-triggered alarms. All of this happens during the techno-inflected extended middle eight, at the end of which Spears karate-chops her way through a series of glass screens. The trauma of this act brings about a flashback of the act of betrayal that has evidently motivated the narrative. Vocoded vocals and shattered glass provide the build up to a second character transition, this coinciding with a reprise of the song's chorus. A third character, this time dark-haired, is like its predecessor a composite of futuristic female warrior types. Cartoon-like neo-noir Spears scales the wall of a building with sci-fi suction pads in order to seduce the man from the shower before administering the poison he evidently deserves. In sync with the final beats of the song, this character dramatically dives out of a window and morphs back into the cheeky stewardess, thus bringing narrative closure. A fourth character might be termed Britney the pop goddess; back-lit, once again, Spears, wearing glued-on jewelry and little else, adopts poses resembling those of a lap dancer in clips interpolated with each of the other sections. These are generally synchronized with the hook of the song and, on two occasions, the prominent violin motif. Their function would seem to be to cement the relationship between these characters and "the actor" Britney Spears, thus allowing some of their attributes to be more effortlessly mapped onto the star.

The narrative of the video is strongly musically driven. This is evident from the flashback sequence discussed above, but also in the opening section of the video, in which sinking glissando figures in the strings are closely synchronized with the visual montage. These slippery musical figures bring into play well-established connotations of exotic otherness and eroticism and, moreover, serve as the primary musical agent that allows a digitally enhanced tracking shot god-like access to various camera vantage points. Thus, in measure two, the exotic strings sound as an upward tilt bring a futuristic aircraft into sight. In measure four, strings are heard again as the omniscient camera passes from the aircraft's exterior to its interior (00:05). In measure six, the same motif accompanies the effortless passage of the camera through a small aperture (or, more aptly, a peep-hole) separating the cockpit from the cabin (00:08). And in measure eight, Spears as stewardess raises an air phone to her lips, thus signaling the transition from the instrumental introduction to the first verse of the song (00:13). Each of these transitions is strongly backlit by sunlight: initially behind the aircraft; then emerging from the peephole; finally, from a window at the rear of the aircraft. This provides visual continuity but more importantly invokes lighting conventions from noir, which reinforce the content of the lyric portraying the female protagonist as a *femme fatale*. This is most evident in a dramatic three-quarter

610   *S. Hawkins and J. Richardson*

Figure 1   Toxic: Exotic Violin Motif (Authors' Transcription) (Music by C. Dennis, C Karlsson, P. Winnberg and H. Jonback)

shadow close up accompanying the word "dangerous" (00:21), the final syllable of which falls on the unstable seventh degree of the minor scale.

The violin motif (see Figure 1) is heard throughout the video, but in narrative terms most prominently at about its center-point (01:49), as biker Spears shrieks with uninhibited joy from the back seat of her mount (the strings simulate the sound of her voice), and at its end, as violins become the liminal agent that allows neo-noir Spears to morph back into the stewardess (03:16). We will return in more detail below to the question of musical exoticism, but it should be noted here that the violin (or *Kaman*) motif has a distinct Arabic character. The combination of fast tempo, "exotic" intervallic characteristics resembling those in the Arabic *Maqam* (including augmented seconds and tritones: f# to eb and d), ornamentation, nasal timbral characteristics, the absence of harmony, and the use of sinking glissandos all leave little doubt in this regard, although references to Bollywood strings in the album credits might lead interpretations elsewhere. In the context of post-9/11 aviation, however, the presence of Arabic-sounding strings synced with both textual and visual references to danger, including shots of a jet aircraft flying low over urban terrain and a woman jumping out of a building, mobilizes a specific set of connotations whose embeddedness in the current climate of racially marked paranoia in the United States is hard to ignore.

The macrostructure of the video is also characterized by close audiovisual relations. Spears as stewardess is enacted during the first verse and chorus, red-haired Spears during the second. The acrobatic laser dance (a gaming and action movie cliché) takes place during an eight-plus-four measure bridge, after which a reprise of the chorus coincides with the song's dramatic denouement: the revenge murder of the unfaithful lover by "bitchy black-haired" Spears (Spears qtd in "MTV's 'Making'").

Words, Pictures, and Music

The distribution of music, pictures, and words highlights a number of categories in the video's function that require close inspection and further commentary. While the refrain consists of identical lyrics, verses A and B differ. (See Table 1, cues in lyrics.) From start to finish, patterns of melodic and harmonic repetition are transported by the steady groove in an overall process that establishes structural key centers and cadence points. The musical events that stand out and function as building blocks for the composition consist of the exotic string sweeps, the jagged bass line, the drum pattern, and the guitar solo. All these musical features coalesce with the lyrics and picture frames of Spears.

In the recording of the song "Toxic," Spears surfs a wave of sound that helps construct a bridge between fantasy and personal narrative: she knows what she wants (and certainly knows what the producer wants) and sets out to convince the fans of this through her performance. The lyrics of the song, as much as the musical codes, are conveyed in a variety of ways, which can be grasped through a method that does a lot more than just separate the content from context. If anything, lyrics provide us with material for gauging the responses to artists and their songs, a point Frith has persistently argued. Most fascinating is how words in their juxtapositioning with music provide a stimulus for suggesting things we can say about the song and artist. Let us consider this assertion with some specific examples.

The function of phrasing and gesture in "Toxic" is a very different kind of experience *until* we see the song through the video. Almost immediately we witness a visual performance with all the edits, angles, and shots as the phrasing of the music undergoes a significant transformation. Take the opening phrase, "Baby can't you see I'm calling," which follows the eight-bar string motif (00:14). In full air-stewardess regalia, Spears faces the camera head on, delivering this phrase down the cabin intercom phone. Without needing to spell out the connotations of the telephone in this opening scene, it is the intensity of her "look" that is remarkable: heavy black mascara and eyeliner magnify her dark eyes against the strictly pulled back blonde peroxide hair, framed by large dangling silver ear-rings and cap. All the trademarks of camp are there in an instant. It only takes seconds before the uniformed-Spears gives way to the private-Britney, with hair down, lighter make-up, almost totally naked, posing as a pin-up girl. The seductiveness of this shot is accompanied by the phrase, "Should wear a warning" (00:18). In terms of the musical arrangement, which includes synthesizers, bass, drum patterns, and strings, there is an overall cushioning of the spectacle of Spears in erotic pose. The connection between language, imagery, and music is significant in that it establishes a narrative of eroticism that is identified through performativity. The choice of the word "Toxic" underlines a number of strategies at play, especially in the phrase, "Don't you know that you're toxic," which Britney draws on to pursue her sexual pleasures in the name of revenge. In the lyrics that unfold we discover that Spears' response to the male threat is articulated in an erotic manner that can be associated with forms of self-love. Put differently, the lyrics provide a framework for talking about control in a way that links eroticism very closely to questions of sexual agency. By identifying the male protagonist as toxic, Spears becomes just as toxic, and the interconnectedness between her own different constructions in the video verifies her strategy of empowerment through camp play. Spears' form of "girl camp" then is a result of how the words, pictures, and music coalesce.[9] The pleasure factor in all this is intended to have a resounding impact on a majority of viewers. Playfulness and 'camping it up' becomes a mechanism by which to give the viewer a means to identify with Spears, to have fun in being a fan, to laugh, to chuckle with joy, without feeling too threatened by the role that is played out in the video. Humor in the lyrics and images therefore allows room for distancing, and, as Julia Kristeva has insisted, laughing is a signifying practice, lifting of inhibitions.

Another feature worth noting throughout the video is Spears' response to the groove. In the B section, as she sings the phrase, "Too high can't come down," she syncs up with the other stewardesses behind her in a nifty little dance routine that is executed through exaggerated arm and hand movements and a wiggle of the bottom (00:41). In this brief moment of respite, her acknowledgement of the rhythmic pulse becomes a send-up of the Hollywood musical chorus-line. This gesture is enhanced by a change in vocal timbre. A sense of falsetto on the words "too high" emphasizes the affected nature of her queering. And, in the next phrase, hot and eager she tells us that she is losing her head, an act that is certainly realized when she pours poison down the throat of her ex-lover, played by actor Martin Henderson, in the bedroom scene at the close of the video. Here the musical phrasing, resulting in closure through sex and death, transports the words "intoxicate me now with your lovin' now" through a loop consisting of four-beat, single-bar units (03:06). Heightened by incessant repetition, the intensity of this moment is captured by the word "now" hitting the fourth beat. Traditionally referred to as one of the weak beats in quadruple time in music analysis, the effect of this is significant on a number of counts. Cunningly, the heavy accent on this beat overcharges it to the extent it becomes felt as a strong anticipated first beat. The effect of this is a kind of musical foreplay that exchanges weakness for dominance in rhythmic patterning. Moreover, the accent on the word "now" at the end of each phrase induces a sense of contrived rhyme. Indeed, the intention to rhyme serves to pulverize the beat with unmistakable precision and malice. In counterpoint to this, the exotically toxic violins make one final appearance as Spears is positioned back where she started from in the cabin of the plane all neat and proper. The final visual code of being "in-flight" once again comprises a large wink, which not coincidentally falls on the first beat of a sound-less measure (03:18);[10] a gesture that is intended to invite a degree of camped-up affectation for its reception. In the composition of this video clip, a vast collection of markers spells out the lyrical, musical, and visual configuration. An extensive draping of the visual narrative accompanies the sound of Spears' voice, the groove patterns, the bass part, and the exotic strings. Negotiation is thus instigated on many fronts to enable an audience to enter at different points. All in all, the musical arrangement and its digital manipulation mediate the visual narrative along a continuum that begs further consideration of genealogy.

Audiovisual Genealogies and Agentic Narration

So far our line of argument seeks to insist that interpretation relies heavily on the recognition of character types, narrative conventions, and audiovisual techniques that can be traced to cinematic genres.[11] The distinctive audiovisual identity of "Toxic" results, therefore, from the cross-generic transportation of these aspects into the established narrative domain of the music video. As noted above, the plot of the video revolves around four main character types, each of which resembles representations in current circulation.

Beginning with dark-haired Spears, the twangy, echo-rich guitar in the chorus sections, sandwiched between the hook, "don't you know that you're toxic," draws on a genealogy that broadly invokes spy suspense and spaghetti Western genres, but more specifically points to empowered female protagonists operating within the context of neo-noir. Notable examples include Tarantino's *Pulp Fiction* (1994), Stone's *Natural Born Killers*, and Lynch's *Twin Peaks* (1989–1990).[12] A host of musical reference points can be identified, ranging from guitarists Duane Eddy and Hank Marvin to the surf punk sound, all of which point to a transgressive coolness that is not averse to ironic play or the hedonistic excesses of beach and club culture.

Black-haired Spears has much in common with *Pulp Fiction*'s Mia (Uma Thurman), but it is the migration of the neo-noir *femme fatale* to science fiction and action genres that offers perhaps the most fruitful point of reference. The genealogy of such characters extends back at least to *Bladerunner* and the "Alien Quadrilogy," both of which feature soundtracks in which the use of electronic sounds is prominent.[13] The character of Ripley (played by Sigourney Weaver) from the latter provided the mould for many subsequent fighting females operating within the science fiction genre. More recently, gaming-heroine-turned-screen-star Lara Croft offers perhaps the closest approximation to the characters in "Toxic." In the context of television, Max from *Dark Angel* and Sydney Bristow from *Alias* (both undoubtedly modeled on Lara Croft) are equally salient intertextual touchstones. In all of the above, electronic dance music is an integral component in portraying heroines as active (even *hyper*-active) while drawing on the posthuman aura of the cyborg, which is effectively mapped onto the non-human qualities of the *femme fatale*.[14] Spears, like Lara Croft and *Dark Angel*'s Max leaps acrobatically from buildings and staves off foes with stylized martial arts moves. These women are not always stronger than the men they come up against but they invariably know how to out-maneuver them. Thus, red-haired Spears chops and kicks her way out of a futuristic research lab to the accompaniment of a techno break furnished with vocoded vocals; this action closely resembles a scene featuring a red-haired alias of Sydney Bristow (series 1, episode 2), whose spectacular fighting is also accompanied by frenzied techno music and who visits many exotic locations similar to those depicted in *Toxic*, including Paris and Japan. *Dark Angel*'s Max rides a motorcycle, as does red-haired Spears. Isomorphisms in plot and character are too numerous to mention, all of which works to conjure up a field of connotations that delineate with some precision the character of the female heroine: her style, her motives, her ethics. More specifically, in *Dark Angel*, exotic marking of the title music—a short vocal sample featuring Arabic-styled ornamentation—casts the female protagonist in no uncertain terms as ethnically other, perhaps Arabic. An examination of the implications of analogous musical procedures in the bridge section of "Toxic" will be provided below.

To understand the motivation for the incorporation of these character types, it is helpful to return to writing on personal narrative. Figures such as these are accommodated in McAdams's theory of personal narrative by way of the concept of "imagoes," which describes the panoply of "exaggerated and one-dimensional" personae adopted by narrators as heroes in their self-narratives (122). Imagoes provide a narrative mechanism for accommodating fragmented subjectivity by allowing "an individual to resolve the problem of simultaneously being the many and the one." The function of these everyday performances is in many respects similar to the "theatrical" performances discussed here: Spears' characters may be adopted "in fun" but they nevertheless embody tacit aspirations of their host. The imagoes in *Toxic* serve therefore, as performative personae that negotiate a representational field traversing characterization and reality—they are not one or the other. Indeed, it can be argued that, by dressing herself up in these disguises, Spears reveals more about personal motivation and subjective struggle than might be the case had she reverted to straightforward confessional strategies. All four characters in *Toxic* are what McAdams calls "agentic:" they exhibit heightened agentic characteristics, being "aggressive, ambitious, assertive, autonomous, clever, courageous, daring, dominant" (134). This contrasts with the "ordinary" self, which in the case of conventional models of the feminine is all too often bereft of these qualities (134). As the singer herself comments, what these characters have in common is that they all "go through men to get what they want" ("MTV's 'Making'")—which is true. Even the saucy stewardess seems to end up on top, mechanically going through the motions of conventional femininity, coldly kissing children and shimmying down the aisle in slapstick comedic fashion, all the time with her own "higher" goals in mind. There seems little doubt that the star would wish to be perceived in a similar way: making superficial concessions to a tainted music industry but securing something more valuable (commercial and artistic) in the process. Spears needs imagoes, with their heightened sense of agency, in order to counterbalance perceptions of her former self, which was widely regarded as lacking these qualities. Reception is complex in the case of such an obviously polysemic text, but it would be naïve to underestimate the power of straightforward scopophilic pleasures in the context of traditional patterns of reception. Even Lara Croft, empowered though she is, wages war on the patriarchal establishment while at the same time offering the titillation of a garter belt doubling as a gun holster, not to mention the ambivalent appeal of the dominatrix. Spears' personae are similarly open to contradictory decodings.

Music-Visual Structuration through the Voice

Spears' vocal articulation represents an extension of and commentary on her earlier music. The singer's sound was established already in "Baby One More Time," in the verses of which her R & B-styled melismas repeatedly weave their way down though a timbrally contracted middle register in search of a fuller, more sensuous lower register. In this and other early songs, the singer's whiny vowel sounds, guttural groans, and lingering liquid phonemes signify both immaturity and eroticism, as do the accompanying visual representations. She had not always sung in this way: early film footage (included on *Time Out*) shows the precocious twelve-year-old singer as the bearer of a powerful, timbrally rounded voice that bears all the hallmarks of voice training for the theatre and concert hall: voice production characterized by a low laryngeal position and controlled breathing.[15] On her first album, however, she discarded this sound in favor of techniques favored in recent "girly" pop. If the biographical evidence suggests that vocal technique for Spears is "not that innocent," a caveat should be noted. The evidence of audiovisual performances strongly suggests that the singer suffers from a speech impediment. Spears produces liquid phonemes with an extended movement of the tongue beginning with the teeth and upper lips rather than the alveolar ridge or palate of the mouth. She also appears to have a slight lisp, producing sibilants further forward in the mouth than is usual. Consequently, the star shows a good deal more tongue than one might expect. Her vocal sound is fuller when it comes to liquid phonemes but also markedly "younger," since speech impediments are usually overcome as the speaker ages. Spears' distinctive speech physiology is of little interest in itself. It becomes an issue only when mediation of her voice—either by the singer herself or by video directors—begins to signify. This question is best illuminated through two examples. Spears' vocal style already draws attention towards visible sites of production, but in *Baby One More Time* the directorial gaze seems obsessed with the signer's distinctive voice production, which could also be heard as a marker of immaturity, in one case zooming in for a close up of the open mouth. In *Toxic* directorial intervention is generally less obvious, although the line "taste of your lips" calls attention to the issue on two occasions: in both the opening sequence and the murder scene close-ups of tonguing on the word "lips" indexically refer the viewer to the singer's lips, with all of the connotations this referentiality implies. The line "It's getting late" (01:25), at the beginning of the biker sequence, also finds Spears in close-up profile, as if to exploit the mechanics and erotics of the stars' unusual voice production.

In "Toxic," Spears expands her repertory of vocal techniques, employing five distinctive tropes, which, as well as functioning expressively, delineate the structure of the song.

1. In the first section of the verses (A: see Table 1) and the opening lines of choruses (C), we hear Spears' trademark R & B-inflected groaning voice with contracted mid-register. The sound is similar to Christina Aguilera and Beyonce but without the powerful virtuosity that characterizes these singers' voices and somewhat more in the way of stylistic affectation. The combination of close miking and reduced expenditure of air results in an aural simulation of intimacy that has become almost compulsory in pop performances of this type. This has led some commentators to characterize her dominant voice type as "soubrette," although the resemblance to the operatic designation is fairly superficial.[16]

2. In the B sections, the singer makes, for her, unprecedented use of the falsetto or head voice. Furnished with softening glissandos and indistinct intonation, this voice which we recognize from Donna Summer's "I Feel Love" and much of the recent hi-NRG-derived erotic pop (most notably, Kylie Minogue), this voice seems designed to connote a fluffy femininity flecked with erotic abandon. The lyrics and visuals both reinforce this impression: Spears sings "too high can't come down, it's in the air and it's all around" while elevating herself to a standing position on the seat of a motorcycle. Like the rodeo simulations employed on Madonna's *Drowned World Tour*, the bike serves as a prop for eroticized display. The sonic, linguistic, and visual articulations found in this section coalesce therefore to signify a general sense of heady abandon for which addiction is an apt expression.

3. In the choruses (C), the singer alternates between the falsetto voice and an edgier, post-punk singing style. This manner of articulation is also new for Spears and represents a concerted attempt to harden her image. Here vibrato-free vocal production, in which a more substantial passage of air (a "chest voice") is checked slightly in the throat rather than the base of the tongue, invokes the singing of Avril Lavigne, Alanis Morissette and, in the retro-punk mode of recent albums, Madonna. The lyrics and visuals support this edgier style: here she sings "I'm addicted to you don't you know that you're toxic" while staring squarely into the camera. Double-tracking of the voice in these phrases helps toughen their timbral characteristics.

4. In terms of the technological manipulation, there are resonances in the music video for Madonna's catchy hit, "Music," from 2000, which drew on aspects of digitalized animation. This has not been without its influence on a spate of pop videos that have followed. Cartoon representations of Madonna position her amid a cityscape with buildings bearing the names of her greatest hits in neon lights. In a bid to move on, the cartoon figure of Madonna attempts to destroy some of the lit-up signs, as the song, all about music, becomes symbolic of Madonna's promotion of her own music. The important point here is that self-invention and transformation are the key ingredients in all Madonna's visual displays, which make her iconic status as polyvalent as it is. In no uncertain terms, the musical genre of *Toxic* corresponds directly to the high gloss of video productions, such as *Music*. Thus, all the indicators for a perfect production are discernible in the presence of techniques that airbrush the recording. Enhanced and animated through the prominence of voice filters, vocoder audio plug-ins, and state-of-art software, the voice occupies center stage. The recording consists of a wash of vocal strands that titillate at the same time as they impress. Indeed, it is the exceptional degree of technological manipulation that vividly emphasizes the link between Spears' roles that border on a cyborg cartoon-type character. The identification of Spears' star identity and the cyborg diva she plays seems to propose a clash between her "real" voice and the more cyborg one. This is not dissimilar to the vocoding of Madonna's voice in "Music" and Cher's voice in the song "Believe."[17] In much the same way, Spears' vocals are digitalized to evoke a multiplicity of the self through the body. Her assumed identity in the recording of *Toxic* embraces many of the associations we have with animated soundtracks that impinge on the representation of the body through the aid of technology. Spears' animated voice fulfills the function of negotiating female presence. And, while her sonic and visual fetishization of the digitalized, animated woman certainly panders to the desires of the mainstream gaze, it does not stop there. At any rate, the type of sonic iconography represented here appropriates the perfection and

fakery of pop, which conveys a playfulness that symbolizes parody. By this we are reminded that production techniques in pop are inevitably grounded in the politics of fantasy; Spears' performance is toxic because of an overdose of technical virtuosity that sculptures her as an aural and visual spectacle depleted of human characteristics.

In section D, Spears (or perhaps the song's composer, Cathy Dennis, who is attributed as a backing vocalist on "Toxic") sings a wordless descending line onto the tonic (G-Gb-Eb-C) that is heavily treated with reverb. The manner of articulation is similar to the Donna Summer voice but with more of a nasal quality that is vaguely suggestive of Arabic and South Asian musical styles. The Orientalist nature of the music is reinforced by microtonal embellishments preceding the second quarter-note of the pattern, which is built from the same modal materials as the Arabic strings. Here the most distinctive feature is the augmented second drop between the seventh and "minor" sixth degrees of the mode. This feature has been a stock signifier of exotic otherness in Western music since Romanticism, representing everything from gypsy music to Arabic and South Asian musical traditions (Scott 167).[18] It would be missing the point to attempt to distill from this music actual geographical points of reference, as it would to attempt to reconcile the music, in real terms, with the accompanying images, which depict an American woman engaging in martial arts appropriated from Japanese culture. In the context of the Western imagination, however, the cluster of connotations mobilized here is entirely consistent and familiar: the combination of an alluring yet threatening female character who visibly and audibly partakes of "Oriental" qualities plays on stereotypes that have long been available to composers of dramatic music (everything from *Carmen* to the Dance of the Seven Veils). Here it casts Spears as someone who dares to overstep the bounds of the familiar, in much same way as the overdriven synthetic bass of this section oversteps some tacit yet frequently inscribed threshold. The effectiveness of both is premised on conventions that install the bounds of the acceptable while reveling in the intoxication transgression brings. It is not insignificant that in Spears' penultimate transformation, signaled by her own Orientalist incantations, she takes on the problematic identity of the black-haired "bitch." This character, who is quantifiably the nastiest of the bunch, coldheartedly commits murder while looking and *sounding* Arabic. Moreover, this seems like a natural state of affairs: consider, for example, the incongruous possibility of the murder being perpetrated by the blond stewardess. What this tells us about signifying practices at the beginning of the new millennium gives pause for thought, although here, as elsewhere in the video, the dominant representational strategy is parody. Moreover, it is clear that this and other representations in the video are part of a liberal-revisionist project, which, even while it invokes connotations of "dark" otherness, does so in the context of a storyboard that makes identification with the heroine more than likely.

Gendered Queering

What becomes apparent in the video *Toxic* is the problematics of sexualization in representation, which, in turn, raises questions linked to the new "girlie culture" that has taken a provocative stance against feminism.[19] With the purpose of entertaining, Spears imitates the erotic construction of the *femme fatale* by drawing on many of the genealogies we have already addressed. Spears is constructed as a multiple identity

who reinvents herself through her relationship with others at the same time as sh
confirms a classic fetishistic mission. In this framework, the link between the femal
and technology symbolizes a mechanized, cyborg form of eroticism. Vi
computerized effects, Spears' femaleness is so exaggerated that she queers the fixit
of femininity in a spin that serves as a parody of the natural. All through the video sh
is so camped up in all her representations that she becomes knotted up in a closec
circuit of sexual desire and unabashed narcissism. What then are the implications o
Spears' hypersexualized imagery and how does this organize gender? And to wha
extent does the music queer such representation?[20]

The most memorable moments of queering in *Toxic* are where the posthuman
quality of her imagery flirts with the dissolution of gender by alienating it from ar
assumed essence. For the purpose of this discussion, the term "queering" refers to the
politics of a performance that encourages queer viewing. So our point is that what we
call Spears' "queering of gender" is a strategy that mobilizes a parody of "normative"
gender through representations that are constantly changing. Her "queering"
up wider opportunities for identification than those associated with more standarc
pop videos. Queering is about performance, play, and spectacle, which destabilizes
subject positions.[21] However, that Spears' burden of embodiment is so animated anc
aggrandized means her performance easily settles back into the constructedness
stereotypical categorization.

Visually and socially, there is an obvious element of drag in progress tha
destabilizes through the diva's charade. Spears' roles in the video might be read as
intentionally superficial and inscribed in the fantasy that is acted out. But this is only
part of the story as we witness a fantasy where the pop diva fashions herself as ar
imitation of an original, which is parodied in order to be provocative and challenge
No better is this demonstrated than in her role as air-stewardess (note that we
deliberately avoid the more politically correct form, "flight attendant," here), where
Spears mocks a relatively low status, albeit glamorous, profession that has prided
itself on good service and beautiful young women. At the same time this profession
has been plagued by sexism. Spears' impersonation of the stewardess in *Toxic* builds
on countless narratives in cinematic history where the female literally bends over
backwards to serve and please all who fly with her. Of course, with this comes an
element of control, which Spears' character decides to capitalize on as she loses little
time in realizing when she drags her object of desire into the toilet tearing his mask
off. Certainly, the symbolism of this scene can prompt various readings. If we draw in
Paul Gilroy's discourse on the racialized biopolitics of fucking (Gilroy 88), there are
critical questions here that one can apply to emancipation and white female
empowerment, not least through the technologization of the erotic. The signification
of the white female body politic cannot be detached from cultural production and
distinctive sexual stereotypes in pop. In considering the political effects of music,
sound, and text, Gilroy identifies the increasing command of "specularity over
aurality." This, Gilroy claims, places pressure on "representations of the exemplary
racial body arrested in the gaze of desiring and identifying subjects" (Gilroy 93, 94).

n the case of Spears' texts, they register many changes in white female representation during the past decade. Most discernible is the break between older patterns of representation, where the female's role would usually be more subservient. In pop videos, such as *Toxic*, sex takes over from narratives of love, as new rules are quickly established. As evidenced by Spears' videos, there is a sense that the pop song has been allocated the role of soundtrack for the purpose of filling out the image and visual narrative. New trends have fixed the rules differently in a context where musical expression specifies that the person performing is mainly identified in terms of his or her body. In these circumstances, the desire to be desirable is closely linked with the desire to appear to be free, and, in the case of many female artists, emancipated and empowered. In other words, their hermeneutic agency is grounded in a strategy of playing around with erotic codes and queering them, which can be linked to a politics of representation where gender becomes the rationality for striving for freedom. The theatricality of *Toxic* alone symbolizes a queering of femininity on many different levels: it signifies a platform for self-promotion at the same time as it appropriates heteronormative sexual desire. In other words, Spears' video is as much in the name of entertainment as it is gay or Other.

Thus, when it comes to gender stereotypes and sex in video representations and how these are experienced, there is an abundance of strong connotations of race and sexuality that solicit different kinds of identification. Heteronormative whiteness indeed provides a recipe for a brand of authenticity that is desirable at the same time as it is deceptive. In the case of white, straight (especially blond) female stars the perpetuating representation of gender and its playfulness or queering with sex contributes to a stability of racial particularity. Spears' performativity, in this light, is a slickly stylized and overtly conservative celebration of heterosexual desire that extends the coherence and symmetrical shape of gender into an ordered narrative of racial being. In effect then, the reality is that *Toxic* is not as toxic as it might like us to imagine it to be. For one thing, the video marks the MTV community as a space of heterosexual activity as well as a verification of the exclusivity of race: an act that is characterized by entertainment and fun-loving significance. Moreover, the embodied signs of beautiful white, light-skinned Hispanic and light black or brown females, with perfect European features, yield insights into the battles still going on in the black public sphere. The point here is that the signification of the politics of black representation in MTV culture cannot be divorced from that which characterizes white artists, such as the big earners, Britney Spears, Madonna, Christina Aguilera, Justin Timberlake, and Gwen Stefani. Indeed, the patterned representations of hip-hop, rap, and soul videos featuring black artists reveal a lot about the trends and changing qualities of the white vernacular. There can be little doubt that the proliferation of humor and queering antics in Spears' *Toxic* work differently from that of Snoop Doggy Dogg, NWA, SWV, and R. Kelly. The point we are arriving at is that the technologies that organize music and bodies in vastly different ways also solicit corporeal forms of identification that can manipulate and create events of cultural performance. At any rate, the political effects of queering are invariably

contradictory and exemplified by the ways in which music is communicated throug
sound, text, and image; the significance of this cannot be overstated. How then do th
traits of scopophilia and the erotics of desire differ from one artist to the next, an
how does this link up to the categories of identification that deal with gender, rac
and sexuality?

Associations with autonomous agency and sexual desire promote a symboli
exercise of power, which in the case of Spears' hypersexualized role in *Toxic* could b
read as a flamboyant attempt to give head to the mechanical and, thereby, reconfigur
the sexual. Indeed, the fetishization of such an idealized female body cannot be blow
away no matter how much we read the video as queered or "cyberfied," for there i
little doubt that videos such as this offer up an important challenge for th
musicologist bent on addressing the role of the pop performer.

Conceptually, we might consider that the codes of femininity Spears appropriate
are arbitrary; they uphold no essence of femaleness. Rather they are codes that ar
assembled socio-culturally with clichéd gender-oriented connotations. From this w
can deduce that the narrative strategies of female control, scopophilia, and sexua
display in pop videos largely compensate for a narrative that addresses vulnerabilit
in love, as Spears waxes lyrically, "I'm addicted to you/Don't you know that you'r
toxic." In the end, her performance of gender retroactively confirms the illusion of a
inner gender core, as she ritualizes a repetition of conventions that have bee
enforced by compulsory heterosexuality.

For the most part, as we have suggested, Spears' strategies are inherited directl
from Madonna who undoubtedly cleared the way for the next generation of femal
pop stars. At the dawn of a post-Madonna era of pop, the issue of the female a
confident sexual agent has much to do with females asserting their own desires, ar
aspect of popular feminism that has not been without its problems.[22] In this sense,
could be argued that Spears' drive and her gradual development of a strategy o
queering can be credited to the idea that Madonna popularized, namely that identity
is not fixed and therefore can be transgressed. There can be no doubt that Spears ha
started to reinvent herself, which is no better exemplified than in the video *Toxic*
where the question of who is the "real" Spears really starts surfacing. *Femme fatale*
dirty teenager, bible-promoting virgin? Spears has begun pushing her career forward
by the antics of queering, reinvention, and reconstruction. Perhaps the important
question after all this is: what qualifies Spears' act as political if we are in agreement it
is queer? One reply would be that the musical rhetoric of her performances rests in its
ability to articulate the body through different gestures. And, as we have attempted to
point out, it is these gestures that are characterized by correspondences to culture,
gender, class, ethnicity, and so on.

Conclusion

Intoxicating though it might be the audiovisual potion that is *Toxic* is ineluctably
laced with traces of its mediation, something we have attempted to start unraveling.

In a genealogical play that is sophisticated yet disturbingly familiar, Britney Spears is projected through the words, sounds, and images of this song. In the video, she works hard to attract and hold the collective gaze of an audience whose attention can never be counted on in an increasingly competitive pop marketplace. Careering towards a more hard-edged image that ostensibly contrasts with no longer tenable representations of the teen star, an impressive cast of cinematic and sonic protagonists is brought into play to assist the star in the pursuit of her high-flying goals. Ironic distance notwithstanding, the evidence based upon her reception would suggest that personal agency is still the main trump card when it comes to questions of pop *auteur* status, a quality that continues to be valued highly among artists and audiences.

Bearing this in mind, we are reminded that the pop performer is the result of a complex structure of mediation in our everyday lives. Even while the prime incentive is to market the artist's music for commercial gain, it is the eroticized body, with all its countless connotations, that is pulled to the fore. During this process, music's effect is communicated aurally and visually in dialogic relationships where musical style is always a signifying practice.

In sum, then, how Spears performs in her pop videos reveals the ideological representations of contemporary society, and begs us to consider how styles represent gender and sexuality in the here and now. In consequence, Spears' act is typified by a double-codedness that subverts at the same time it inscribes. We might say that her authorial intention is staged through reception and then interpretation within a cultural and historical context. MTV has really permitted us to get close to our pop idols, and as a consequence performances employ any number of devices to subvert the spectator's pleasure. Pleasure in the space of negotiation or exchange empowers and provides us with an active role in reading the text. Mostly, the transgression of fixed categories through queering can permit us to open up new fields of subjectivities and spaces for play. That the spectacle of *Toxic* gives rise to gendered codes that are problematic at the same time as they are entertaining is reason enough for investigating why such forms of musical representation are always so compelling and therefore worthy of study.

Acknowledgments

The authors are grateful to numerous readers for helpful comments: Richardson's research was supported by the Academy of Finland. Listed alphabetically, Hawkins and Richardson are equal authors of this article.

622   S. Hawkins and J. Richardson

Time Code/Form	Cues in Lyrics	Key Musical Cues	Synopsis of Visual Action
00:00 Intro		4 × exotic violin motif with rhythmic introductory phrase in initial measure followed by descending glissandos as groove starts up. Riffing on C min (i).	Upward tilt to sci-fi jet. Forward track through aircraft's windscreen and peephole to BS as stewardess. Glissandos coincide with visual transitions.
00:13 (A) Verse 1 Section 1	Baby, can't you see I'm calling [...] *The remainder of the verse comprises references to a dangerous relationship and loss of control.*	R&B styled "soubrette" voice: contracted mid-register, guttural groans, breathiness. Use of vocal effects, suggestive of vocoding. i – bIII – V – i Cadence onto violin motif.	StwBS sings into airphone while preparing refreshment trolley/ cross-cut to pinup BS. Gestures are high-camp, the look defies the male-gaze, and StwBS parodies the role of her profession, both as air stewardess and pop star.
00:27 (A) Verse 1 Section 1	There's no escape I can't hide [...] *The singer relates the addictive qualities of the song's subject.*	R&B styled "soubrette" voice. Subtle changes to the technological manipulation of the voice within the mix. i – bIII – V – i Cadence onto violin motif.	StwBS spills champagne over unattractive male passenger accidentally-on-purpose; suggestively cleans it up/more cross-cuts to glossy, soft-focus pinup BS.
00:40 (B) Verse 1 Section 2	Too high Can't come down [...] *The singer describes her state of subjective disorientation.*	Falsetto voice: soft "girlie" tone, indistinct intonation, glissandos. i – bIII – V – i Cadence onto violin motif.	Stewardesses' camp dance routine/ passengers exaggerated moves in time with music. Choreography is aligned to musical style in a way that accents the audio-visual symbiosis.

Time Code/Form	Cues in Lyrics	Key Musical Cues	Synopsis of Visual Action
00:54 (C) Chorus 1	Sexually suggestive allusions to the singer's lips and to the act of riding. [...]I'm addicted to you Don't you know that you're toxic [...]	Falsetto voice reverting to hard, post-punk style for "toxic" hook: no vibrato, double-tracked. Twang guitar alternates with iterations of hook. i – bIII7 – II7 – bII – i – bIII7 (false dominant) – bVI – vm7 – bII7 – i Cadence onto violin motif.	StwBS pushes unattractive male into lavatory, kisses him, pulls off mask to reveal attractive fair-haired male. Simulated sex; stwBS takes key from man's pocket. He smiles. Again the scene is slapstick, playful, and sexually provocative, highlighting the rhetoric of conventional gender roles.
01:24 (A) Verse 2/sect.1 Section 1	It's getting late, To give you up [...] References to the devil and a poisonous potion the singer has become hooked on.	R&B styled "soubrette" voice. i – bIII – V – i Cadence onto violin motif with rising glissandos.	Shots of BS as red-haired biker chick, being driven through simulated Paris-by-night by muscular black male. Issues of race and empowerment are played out (read: problematized) from many perspectives.
01:37 (B) Verse 2 Section 2	Too high Can't come down [...]	Falsetto voice. Voice comes across more parodic each time this verse recurrs. i – bIII – V – i Cadence onto violin motif.	RHBS rises on bike to sing line "too high"/cross-cuts to pinup BS. Violin glissandos synched with RHBS screeching with joy, while the drum samples slot into a groove that affords this shot a high deal of rhythmic propensity.

624   *S. Hawkins and J. Richardson*

Time Code/Form	Cues in Lyrics	Key Musical Cues	Synopsis of Visual Action
01:51 (C) Chorus 2	[...] I'm addicted to you Don't you know that you're toxic [...] *Wordless singing*	*Falsetto voice -> post-punk style for "toxic" hook.* Twang guitar alternates with iterations of hook. Drum samples are pushed up in the mix, with stronger accents on the down-beats, creating a sense of thrusting. Cadence onto violin motif.	RHBS breaks into research facility/ cross-cuts of pinup BS. Angry RHBS retrieves vial of poison; walks out through slide doors marked "Toxic." Vengeance is highlighted by the heightening of effects in the music, especially through use of compression.
02:21 (D) Bridge		*Falsetto voice with heavy reverb; nasal quality, exotic ornamentation, augmented 2nd interval.* vocal line $(g - g\flat - e\flat - c)$ over pumping eighth-note bass pattern, techno sound.	Acrobatic dance in laser room/cross-cuts to betrayal flashback (dark male and woman in shower). RHBS kicks through glass panel. The aggression of this scene is a spoof on female action thrillers, such as Charlie's Angels, etc.
02:38 (C) Chorus 3	[...] I'm addicted to you Don't you know that you're toxic [...]	*Vocoded voice -> falsetto -> post-punk style for "toxic" hook.* Twang guitar alternates with iterations of hook. Cadence onto violin motif.	Cut to pinup BS for "taste of your lips"; then to black-haired BS, who ascends building with suction pads; seduces dark male (from flashback); throws to floor and straddles him.

Table 1 Continued

Time Code/Form	Cues in Lyrics	Key Musical Cues	Synopsis of Visual Action
03:04 Coda	Intoxicate me now / With your lovin' now [...]	*Post-punk voice with softening* portamento on last beat. i – bIII7 – II7 – bII - I – bIII7 – bIV [or V7 – I]; false dominant/tonic] – i	BHBS administers poison, leaps from building to violin glissando; lands in sci-fi jet as StwBS and winks on 1st beat of soundless measure. Tracking shot through rear of jet, which flies into sun. The final shot of black birds flying into the future is deeply symbolic in its Hitchcockian spin.
End 03:31	*The singer informs the listener that she is now ready to be intoxicated.*	Overcharging of fourth beat due to pseudorhyme on "now." Cadence onto violin motif.	

Notes

[1]   The question of cross-marketing, referred to in the film industry as "synergy," is explored i
      much of the recent writing on film music, including Smith, Dickinson (*Movie Music* 145–46
      and Donnelly (142–45).

[2]   Personal narrative of this kind is most closely associated with "confessional" singe
      songwriters who made their name in the 1960s, such as Joni Mitchell and James Taylor
      although it could be extended to include performers who are better know for less direc
      forms of address but whose recent creative output has taken a confessional turn, includin
      Annie Lennox and Suzanne Vega.

[3]   Research directly incorporating aspects of personal history is typical of early work in gay
      lesbian, and queer studies, as seen in Brett, Wood and Thomas's influential antholog
      Queering The Pitch: The New Gay and Lesbian Musicology.

[4]   For an approach incorporating Hall's notion of "narrative of the self," see Albiez. See als
      Hall (277). On self-identity in developmental psychology, see Macdonald, Hargreaves an
      Miell.

[5]   This deployment of the term markedness, which denotes how narrators invest persona
      histories with significance, resembles approaches in semiotics (e.g. Hatten) which examin
      ways in which meaning is constituted in music through practices of contrast and discursiv
      foregrounding.

[6]   Our view that personal narrative is implicated also for listeners and viewers is consistent
      recent writing on Judith Butler's notion of the performative. In terms of the politics o
      visuality, agency has been associated by Butler with the supposedly passive act of gazing a
      well as with the more overtly active position of moving in order to hold the gaze (see Bell 6–
      7).

[7]   See *Music, Space and Place* (2004), Section 3.

[8]   Although the song is attributed in the credits to four writers, the British songwriter Cathy
      Dennis is identified in most sources as its principal author—of both words and music
      Notably, Dennis is listed in the song's credits as first author (in a non-alphabetical list); she
      also sings backing vocals on the recording. The inclusion of members of the Scandinavia
      production team Avant and Bloodshy attests to the constitutive role of "production
      techniques" in the sonic identity of the song.

[9]   See Angela McRobbie's discourse on girl camp in "*More!*" and on women's magazines in
      Back to Reality (v). See also Hawkins "Dragging out Camp."

[10] Note that the measure is silent only when it comes to *musical* sounds. In fact, the camped up
      wink is accented by the diegetic sound of a flight attendants' call bell. This serves as a wake-
      up call both to listeners, who are returned by this gesture to the relatively normality of life
      aboard the sci-fi jet, and to Britney as stewardess, who immediately turns to service a
      passenger.

[11] Significantly, the video's director, Joseph Kahn, completed his first feature length movie,
      Torque, immediately prior to filming *Toxic*. When working on the video, he borrowed
      cinematic techniques (including the use of aerial tracking shots, "geometric" editing
      techniques, and computer rendering), an actor (Martin Henderson), and the elements of
      visual style (particularly evident in the "hyperreal" motorcycle chase) from this film.

[12] On the cultural connotations of guitar sounds, see Tagg and Clarida (366–78). For more on
      the use of a simulated Fender sound in the theme music of *Twin Peaks*, see Richardson (84–
      85).

[13] The genealogy of electronic sounds in science fiction goes back almost to the birth of the
      genre. A significant example is the use of the theremin in 1950s science fiction B movies. See
      Wierzbicki and Lack (310–21).

[14] On the notion of the posthuman, see Halberstam and Livingston (1–19). For more on the
      connection between electronic dance music and tough female protagonists in science fiction,
      see Kassabian ("The Sound"). Interestingly, Moby worked on the soundtrack to *Lara Croft:
      Tomb Raider* as well as producing a song on Britney's *In the Zone* ("Early Mornin'"). Backing
      vocals on the album are attributed to "The Matrix."

[15] On the historical construction of this voice, see Potter.

[16]   For instance, the characterization of her voice found on Wikipedia: 28 Apr. 2006 <http://
       en.wikipedia.org/wiki/Britney_Spears>.
[17]   Kay Dickinson has described how "Cher phases in and out of traditional notions of vocal
       'reproduction' and deliberately obvious track manipulation" ("Believe" 171). Also see
       Hawkins ("On Performativity") for an analysis of digital editing devices and intricate
       mechanisms of recording technology that signify a denial of Madonna's "natural voice."
[18]   See also Bellman.
[19]   See McRobbie ("*More!*").
[20]   In an earlier study of Madonna's track "Music," it was argued that, in much pop, camp
       constitutes a central part of a commercialized directive that is a political force. See Hawkins
       (*Settling*).
[21]   For a genealogical critique of the queer subject and the centrality of queer politics in
       queering, see Butler's seminal work *Bodies that Matter*. Also see Morland and Willox for a
       wide range of essays addressing the cultural politics of sexuality and gender through queer
       theory. Most of the authors in this volume acknowledge how the shifting signifiers of
       queering move in and out of mainstream texts.
[22]   See Gauntlett, who takes up this issue when he builds on Angela McRobbie's studies that deal
       with the new-found mainstream sexual assertiveness which has a resonance from feminist
       traits two decades earlier.

Works Cited

Albiez, Sean. "Know History! John Lydon, Cultural Capital and the Prog/Punk Dialectic." *Popular
       Music* 22. 3 (2003): 357–74.
Bell, Vikki. *Performativity and Belonging*. London: Sage, 1999.
Bellman, Jonathan, eds. *The Exotic in Western Music*. Boston, MA: Northeastern University Press,
       1998.
Brett, Philip, Elizabeth Wood and Gary C. Thomas, eds. *Queering the Pitch: The New Gay and
       Lesbian Musicology*. New York and London: Routledge, 1994.
Butler, Judith. *Bodies that Matter: On the Discursive Limits of "Sex"*. New York: Routledge, 1993.
Chion, Michel. *Audio-Vision: Sound on Screen*. Trans. Claudia Gorbman. New York: Columbia UP,
       1994.
Dickinson, Kay. "'Believe': vocoders, digital female identity and camp." *Music, Space and Place:
       Popular Music and Cultural Identity*. Ed. Sheila Whiteley, Andy Bennett and Stan Hawkins.
       Aldershot: Ashgate, 2004. 163–79.
———, ed. *Movie Music: The Film Reader*. New York and London: Routledge, 2003.
Donnelly, Kevin J. *The Spectre of Sound: Music in Film and Television*. London: BFI, 2005.
Frith, Simon, Andrew Goodwin and Lawrence Grossberg, eds. *Sound & Vision: The Music Video
       Reader*. New York and London: Routledge, 1993.
Gauntlett, David. "Madonna's Daughters: Girl Power and the Empowered Girl-Pop
       Breakthrough." *Madonna's Drowned Worlds: New Approaches to her Cultural
       Transformations, 1983–2003*. Ed. Santiago Fouz-Hernández and Freya Jarman-Ivens.
       Aldershot: Ashgate, 2004. 161–75.
Gilroy, Paul. "'After the Love Has Gone': Biopolitics and Etho-Poetics in the Black Public Sphere."
       Back to Reality: Social Experience and Cultural Studies. Ed. A McRobbie. Manchester:
       Manchester UP, 1997. 83–115.
Goodwin, Andrew. *Dancing in the Distraction Factory: Music Television and Popular Culture*.
       London: Routledge, 1993.
Halberstam, Judith and Ira Livingston, eds. *Posthuman Bodies*. Bloomington: Indiana UP, 1995.
Hall, Stuart. "The Question of Cultural Identity." *Modernity and its Futures*. Ed. Stuart Hall, David
       Held and Tony McGrew. Cambridge: Polity Press. 274–316.
Hatten, Robert. *Musical Meaning in Beethoven: Markedness, Correlation and Interpretation*.
       Bloomington: Indiana University Press, 2004.

628   *S. Hawkins and J. Richardson*

Hawkins, Stan. "Dragging out Camp: Narrative Agendas in Madonna's Musical Production."
     Madonna's Drowned Worlds: New Approaches to her Cultural Transformations, 1983–2003.
     Ed. Santiago Fouz-Hernández and Freya Jarman-Ivens. Aldershot: Ashgate, 2004. 3–21.
────. "On Performativity and Production in Madonna's 'Music'." *Music, Space and Place.*
     Popular Music and Cultural Identity. Ed. Sheila Whiteley, Andy Bennett and Stan Hawkins.
     Aldershot: Ashgate, 2004. 180–90.
────. *Settling the Pop Score: Pop Texts and Identity Politics.* Aldershot: Ashgate, 2002.
Kaplan, E. Anne. *Rocking Around the Clock: Music Television, Postmodernism & Consumer Culture.*
     New York and London: Routledge, 1987.
Kassabian, Anahid. *Hearing Film: Tracking Identifications in Contemporary Hollywood Film Music.*
     New York and London: Routledge, 2001.
────. "The Sound of a New Film Form." *Popular Music and Film.* Ed. Ian Inglis. London and
     New York: Wallflower, 2003. 91–101.
Kristeva, Julia. *Revolution in Poetic Language.* Trans. Margaret Waller. New York: Columbia UP,
     2000.
Lack, Russell. *Twenty Four Frames Under: A Buried History of Film Music.* London: Quartet, 1997.
Lowe, Melanie. "Colliding Feminisms: Britney Spears, 'Tweens,' and the Politics of Reception."
     Popular Music and Society 26. 2 (2003): 123–40.
Macdonald, Raymond, David Hargreaves and Dorothy Miell, eds. *Musical Identities.* Oxford:
     Oxford UP, 2002.
McAdams, Dan P. *The Stories We Live By: Personal Myths and the Making of the Self.* New York and
     London: Guilford Press, 1993.
McRobbie, Angela, ed. *Back to Reality: Social Experience and Cultural Studies.* Manchester:
     Manchester UP, 1997.
────. "*More!* New Sexualities in Girls' and Women's Magazines." *Back to Reality: Social Expe-
     rience and Cultural Studies.* Ed. Angela McRobbie. Manchester: Manchester UP, 1997.
     190–209.
Morland, Iain and Annabelle Willox, eds. *Queer Theory.* Basingstoke: Palgrave Macmillan, 2005.
Potter, John. *Vocal Authority: Singing Style and Ideology.* Cambridge: Cambridge UP, 1998.
Richardson, John. "*Laura* and *Twin Peaks:* Postmodern Parody and the Musical Reconstruction of
     the Absent Femme Fatale." *The Cinema of David Lynch: American Dreams, Nightmare
     Visions.* Ed. Annette Davison and Erica Sheen. London: Wallflower, 2005. 77–92.
Scott, Derek B. *From the Erotic to the Demonic: On Critical Musicology.* Oxford: Oxford UP, 2003.
Smith, Jeff. *The Sounds of Commerce: Marketing Popular Film Music.* New York: Columbia UP,
     1998.
Tagg, Philip and Bob Clarida. *Ten Little Title Tunes: Towards a Musicology of the Mass Media.* New
     York and Montreal: The Mass Media Musicologists' Press, 2003.
Whiteley, Sheila. *Women and Popular Music: Sexuality, Identity and Subjectivity.* London:
     Routledge, 2000.
Wierzbicki, James. "Weird Vibrations: How the Theremin Gave Musical Voice to Hollywood's
     Extraterrestrial "Others." *Journal of Popular Film and Television Fall* 30. 3 (2002): 125–35.

Discography

Britney Spears. *Baby One More Time.* Jive, B00000G1IL, 1999.
────. *Britney.* Jive, B00005OM4N, 2001.
────. *In the Zone.* Jive, B0000DD7LB, 2003.
────. *Oops!... I Did it Again.* Jive, B00004SCX6, 2000.

Film and Videography

ABC Television Special. "Britney Spears: In the Zone." Dir. Nick Wickham. *Britney Spears: In the
     Zone.* DVD. Zomba, 2004.
Alias: Season 1. Starring Jennifer Garner. Dir. J. J. Abrams *et al.* 20th Century Fox, 2001.

Alien. Starring Sigourney Weaver. Dir. Ridley Scott. 20th Century Fox, 1979.

Dark Angel: The First Series. Starring Jessica Alba. Dir. David Nutter. 20th Century Fox, 2000.

Lara Croft: Tomb Raider. Starring Angelina Jolie. Dir. Simon West. Paramount, 2001.

Lost Highway. Dir. David Lynch. Asymmetrical Productions, 1997.

Memento. Dir. Christopher Nolan. I Remember Productions, 2000.

'MTV's 'Making the Video: Toxic'." Dir. Chris Landon. *Britney Spears: In the Zone.* DVD. Zomba, 2004.

Pulp Fiction. Starring John Travolta and Uma Thurman. Dir. Quentin Tarantino. Miramax Films, 1994.

Time out with Britney Spears. Dir. Jac Benson II. VHS video (PAL). Zomba, 1999.

Torque. Starring Martin Henderson, Ice Cube, Monet Mazur, and Jay Hernandez. Dir. Joseph Kahn. DVD. Warner, 2004.

Toxic the video. Dir. Joseph Kahn. *Britney Spears: In the Zone.* DVD. Zomba, 2004.

[5]

The production of success: an anti-musicology of the pop song*

by ANTOINE HENNION

At the heart of the frenetic activity of the record industry and of all the conflicting opinion to which this activity gives rise, lies a common goal: popular success. This also provides the key to the paradoxes one encounters when one studies the economic aspects of the record industry in France.† What does the achievement of success involve in actual fact? Economic, sociological and musicological analyses tend to evade this issue rather than explain it. Can the ability to achieve success be attributed to a more or less innate sixth sense? Does it reside in the superiority of the smaller producers over the larger ones? Is success achieved through bribery, through massive 'plugging', through a dulling of the senses or through conformism, as the ritual claims of the press would have it? Is it a by-product of profit, of standardisation, of alienation or of the prevailing ideology, as marxists argue? The sociology of mass media and culture explains it in an equally wide variety of ways – in terms of manipulation (see Adorno 1941), the meaninglessness of mass culture (see Ellul 1980, Hoggart 1957), symbolic exclusion (see Bourdieu 1979), the system of fashion (see Barthes 1967), desocialised ritual (see Baudrillard 1970), or as the cunning strategies of the dominated (see de Certeau 1974). I do not propose casually to invoke all the different theories only to dismiss them with moralistic claims that we must return to the basic facts. I only wish to point out the discrepancy which exists between the

---

* This article is drawn from research which was the basis for a book, Hennion 1981; it is reviewed elsewhere in this issue of *Popular Music* (pp. 308–13 below). The research, carried out in collaboration with J. P. Vignolle, was originally the basis for an essay on the way music is produced (Hennion and Vignolle 1978A); it was also the basis for Vignolle 1980. 'Pop song' stands (throughout the article) for *chanson de variétés*, for which there is no exact English equivalent; translation is the more difficult because *variétés* is defined above all by a particular mode of production, discussed here, rather than by specific musical characteristics which may be compared with those of other genres (ed.)

† This study was the starting point for Hennion and Vignolle 1978B. The record market is indeed a strange one: the big producers keep the smaller ones going by relinquishing to them the most highly profitable sectors; high concentration is compatible with increasing instability; massive internationalism of capital goes hand in hand with the persistent predominance of French productions on the national market and with a surplus trade balance.

profusion of opinions expressed and the scarcity of empirical studies on the actual contents of so-called mass culture.

When one studies the professional milieu on the spot (as we did for three years, from 1977 to 1980), one learns that its fundamental task resides in *the permanent and organised quest for what holds meaning for the public*. Not an arbitrary or a coded meaning, nor a meaning imposed from above, any more than a meaning collected by statistical surveys or market research – these last can only reveal 'objective', that is, socio-political categories enabling the powers that be to label their 'subjects': age, sex, socio-professional group, preferences. The meaning in question is to be found 'down below', in those areas which carry the public's imagination, its secret desires and hidden passions – one could almost define such categories as *socio-sentimental*. They include key phrases, sounds, images, attitudes, gestures and signs, infra-linguistic categories which are all the more difficult to pin down insofar as they escape definition by the official language, and are not autonomous but inseparable from the social context within which a given group attributes a special significance to them. At the same time these infra-linguistic categories are ephemeral; as soon as language intervenes, they give up that terrain and re-form elsewhere. Slang, a form of dress, a hairstyle, a motorcycle and above all music, that music which 'means' nothing, are all the expressions of that which cannot be put into rational discourse – which is always the discourse of other people.

These meanings cannot be manufactured, cannot even be decoded. The professionals of the record industry have to feel them empathetic-ally, to make them resonate, in order to be able to return them to the public. The distribution of roles and the organisation of work between producers, authors, musicians and technicians, as we have observed it, aims chiefly at preserving and developing artistic methods which act as veritable mediators of public taste, while accomplishing a produc-tion job which must also be technical, financial and commercial. Pop music has been able to systematise the very principle of its own diversity within an original mode of production. The *creative collective*, a team of professionals who simultaneously take over all aspects of a popular song's production, has replaced the individual creator who composed songs which others would then play, disseminate, defend or criticise. This team shares out the various roles which the single creator once conjoined: artistic personality, musical know-how, knowledge of the public and of the market, technical production and musical execution have become complementary specialisms and skills performed by different individuals. Thus the final product, consisting of highly disparate elements which can be considered individually and as a mixture, is the fruit of a continuous exchange of views between the various members of the team; and the result is a fusion between musical objects and the needs of the public.

In accordance with the way our own research evolved, this article will roughly progress from the musical to the social; first, we sketch out a 'formal' analysis of the pop song in which it can be seen that a song's expressive value does not lie in its form and that a musicological assessment cannot explain why certain songs are successful and why most others fail. We will then try to trace the song back to its origins and analyse the role played by the producer* and his relationship with the singer; for it is the producer who has the task of introducing into the recording studio the ear of the public, whose verdict has little to do with technical considerations; it is he who must assess what effect the song will have on audiences at large. It is also he who must try to 'draw out' of the singer what the public wants; and conversely to pave the way for the special emotional ties which bind the singer to his public, by himself embodying for the singer an audience which is as yet only potential. It is for him that the singer will try to fashion the right persona. This work of the professionals, which makes possible the operation of a transfer-mechanism between singers and their audiences, goes against the grain of musicological analysis: there is here no such thing as the 'structure' of a song. None of the elements which go into its creation, none of the dichotomies which the outside observer can detect, are above the process of negotiation. Their meaning varies, wears out or vanishes. Each song modifies by degrees the basic model, which does not exist as an absolute. The gimmick of yesterday soon becomes the boring tactic of today, as far as public taste is concerned.

If one wishes to analyse pop music, one is always led back to real audiences, in the form of consumers; a pop song, which owes its ephemeral existence to the public in the first place, is only sustained by that which gave it its substance from the start. But this self-consumption of the public by the public is not without certain effects; what is stated does not take the form of self-contained, indefinite repetition, but is inscribed in the blank spaces within everyday life; it expresses what cannot be said any other way. Through the history of pop music, one can glimpse the history of those who have no words, just as feelings that cannot be expressed otherwise find their way into the music. This additional layer of meaning should, in fact, lead us to

* *directeur artistique*, here and throughout the article, is translated by 'producer'; even though in France, the *directeur artistique*'s functions overlap those of the A & R man as well as those of the producer (as those roles are understood in Britain and the USA), 'producer' seems the nearest equivalent (ed.)

162   *Antoine Hennion*

invert our approach: we ought not to attempt to explain the success of the music through sociology and social relations, but should instead look to the music for revelations about unknown aspects of society.

Pop songs analysed?

Pop songs do not write their own history; they do not have a ready-made place in history, nor do they make their own rules. Probably because of their immediate impact on the public through the mass market, they have no need to justify their existence; they exist in their own right, and their sales figures are the only claim to legitimacy they need. They do not have to shelter themselves from the public by invoking historical or aesthetic justifications.

There is no cause for complaint about this state of affairs, and no need to rationalise what, for once, no one has as yet attempted to transform into a coherent and positive doctrine. In fact, we ought to take the fullest advantage of this situation to analyse musical production in the act of coming into being; it is a kind of production which opens wide its doors, which is not in the least ashamed of its tricks, which does not dress up in robes of *a posteriori* orthodoxy, the constant heterodoxy of its operations; nor does anyone think of clothing its haphazard discoveries in the uniform of musical progress.

The rejection of a systematic reconstruction does not mean one has no objectives. But these must be identified. For if access to the process of creation is no longer obstructed by the accumulation of rationalisations, the facile assumptions that these bring to one's first glance are also absent. How can an observer assess the problems, order the more or less organised facts which are before him, do more than acknowledge the amazing efficiency of individual know-how, or register the uninterrupted succession of 'hits' or the isolated fluke? Must he give up the positivism of a constructed argument only to fall into the dangers of haphazard subjectivity?

I would like to proceed in the opposite direction, starting off with an empirical description of the pop song while remaining free to criticise subsequently any nascent positivism.

The raw materials

The music

A tune, lyrics and a singer: from the musical point of view, a vocal melody with an accompaniment. These elements make up a very limiting configuration as far as the genre is concerned. They exclude the effects of vocal polyphony, as well as pure instrumental composition and its virtuosic possibilities. The music is subordinated in the song to a single main part: a sung melody of a simple type, which must have an accompaniment.

The tunes are tonal, rarely modal.* The principal harmonies are familiar; the form depends on the juxtaposition between an insistent chorus and verses which provide progression. But the simplicity of these traditional musical variables is misleading. The song is nothing before the 'arrangement', and its creation occurs not really at the moment of its composition but far more at the moment of orchestration, recording and sound mixing. The elements, with their somewhat classical musical grammar, are looked upon chiefly as raw materials to be assembled along with the voice, the sound, the 'colours' and the effects of volume and density. The real music of the song hides behind the melody and gives it its meaning. The audience only notices the melody and thinks it is the tune itself which it likes.

The lyrics

The pop song tells a story and comments on it in order to provoke in listeners the feelings appropriate to that song. At first glance, one can see that it is a genre which borrows from a wide variety of other genres; from poetry it borrows the importance and autonomy of certain key words, as well as the use of metre, verse and repetition†; from the lyric theatre it borrows the singer's direct appeal to his audience to share feelings expressed in the first person; but perhaps it owes most to the novelette in the way that it almost invariably tells a story, set out in a few words, concerning the relationship between two or three individuals. As one producer put it concisely, the pop song is 'a little three-minute novel', in which daydream and reality merge in a sort of fairy-tale of love or of anonymous ambitions.

A basic idea is set out, elaborated and concluded. It often reflects the eternal opposition between rich and poor, between strong and weak, between those who are lucky and those who are unlucky in love, etc. The story is conventional; in other words it is familiar to the casual listener and solidly anchored in popular mythology through the

---

* The connotations of modal tunes are too intense; they can be employed only within a specific context where their evocative power creates the appropriate type of archaic, pastoral or ceremonious atmosphere. 'Le bal des Laze' by Michel Polnareff, in which the romanticism of a love punished by death is lamented in a medieval dungeon, is written in the aeolian mode.
† In 'Je l'aime à mourir', for example, a simple effect of repetition in echo at the end of the verse, finishing in 'ir', is enough for Francis Cabrel to achieve a most pleasurable effect in an otherwise extremely simple song (see Ex. 1).

intrigues and situations which that mythology holds dear. The vocabulary takes on a particular significance: it is the words which must give the text its originality while remaining simple and easy to memorise.

The character

The pop singer is not an instrumentalist who happens to have a vocal technique, an interpreter–musician at the service of a given work. He himself is part and parcel of the song which he sings, in the form of the 'character' he impersonates. The construction and publicising of this character are not solely a promotion job, separate from artistic creation; on the contrary, this work is central to the song, which is inconceivable outside the association between the lyrics, the music and the singer.

The song can, from this point of view, be compared to the cinema; like the star in a popular movie, the singer must *be* the character who speaks in the first person in the song, and not just *act* the part. Instead of creating a role like the stage actor, who will play it far better if he is not taken in by that role, the singer has to become a character in whom are confused the singer's own life history and those life stories of which he sings. The producer is there to remind him of this; he makes sure that there is a link between the singer and his songs: the singer's stage personality emerges to the extent that the songs which suit him best, and in which he is best able to please, become clearly established.

The mixture

These three elements (music, lyrics, character) are conceived of as empirical mixtures based on know-how, as ephemeral alloys which cannot be codified. The song is the result of their articulation and is just as empirical and fugitive. As with a do-it-yourself kit, there are tricks of the trade in the creation of a song. But far from mechanising production, these retain the subjective relationship between the three elements: each appears to relegate the other two to the rank of effects destined to underline the third; but in actual fact, none of the three could stand on its own. The success of the song depends on its mobility: the limitations of the music (too repetitious), of the lyrics (too trite), of the character (too artificial), are each in turn displaced by the illusion that the other two elements are taking over when the third grows too thin. When the mixture is right, the ingredients enhance one another in a song which will go down well with audiences, though the observer and at first even the producer, would be hard put to analyse what is so successful about each element. But beyond a certain threshold of credibility, the public, hell-bent on obtaining pleasure, is ready to forgive the banalities of a song which succeeds in providing it.

The techniques of the song

Musical form

Music is the fundamental ingredient in a song, giving it its form. In pop songs, the choice of tune usually precedes that of the lyrics, which will often be altered completely in the process of adapting the two elements to one another.

The construction of songs has become somewhat formalised. The various elements have technical names to which producers refer:

The introduction. In a few bars, this serves both as a signal to the listener, enabling him to recognise the song immediately, and as a foretaste, making him want to listen to the rest. The 'intro' reveals enough to suggest the mood: sound, rhythm, type, etc. It conceals enough to stimulate the appetite without blunting it. The object is to use fragments which characterise the rest of the song: a few bars of the tune, a chord, a mixture of timbres, a rhythmic pattern . . . In the words of an experienced producer:

The introduction is merely an aural signal which says: 'Watch it, fellows! Here comes such and such a tune!' As a matter of fact, a song is almost made by the introduction, which has *nothing* to do with the tune. It all depends on how smart the orchestration is: one must admit that, very often, it is the accompaniment which turns the song into a hit. I'm thinking of the song by Caradec, for example, 'La petite fille'. Jean Musy's clever orchestration, very light and very effective, played a big part.*

Or as one head of a large international firm put it:

They really understood the trick back in the heyday of English pop music in the sixties: 'The House of the Rising Sun', 'Satisfaction', 'A Whiter Shade of Pale', perhaps the biggest hits apart from those of the Beatles, all three made it on the strength of their introduction. You remember the guitar arpeggios of the Animals, the bass in 'Satisfaction', the Hammond organ in 'Whiter Shade of Pale' . . .

The alternation between verses and chorus. In the verses, which are in a fluid, recitative-like style, the music subordinates itself to the lyrics, so that the story can unfold. The chorus, on the other hand, is more musical and etches the tune in the memory, a tune whose regular

---

* Most of the quotations in this article come from interviews with producers or other professionals in the record industry. More precise details of their sources are mentioned only when relevant.

repetition right through the song is expected and gives all the more pleasure because it is eagerly awaited during the somewhat dull verses. The arrangement underlines this opposition by enriching the chorus in a number of ways: the addition of instruments absent during the verses, denser harmonic progressions, the pointing up of a climax whose resolution makes one ready for the calm of the following verse.

As far as musical construction is concerned, a song typically opposes a harmonic *sequence* in the verse (with short, constant rhythmic values in the melody), and a marked harmonic *cadence* in the chorus (with contrasted rhythmic values in the melody: held notes, quaver patterns, etc.). But the opposition can also be achieved through a variety of means (see Exx. 1–4 for various verse–chorus constructions): modulation or allusion to closely related keys (e.g. the relative minor, see 'Je l'aime à mourir', or the subdominant, see 'Les élucubrations d'Antoine'); modulation by a third; opposition between minor and major modes (see 'Arthur'; also 'Neiges du Kilimandjaro' by Pascal Danel); use of pedals in the verse (see 'Capri, c'est fini', where throughout the verse chords with added sixths, fourths and ninths simply embellish a repeated oscillation of the bass between dominant and tonic); switching from compound to simple time (see 'Arthur' and 'Capri', the end of the chorus in both cases); or simply changing octave or instrumentation (as in 'Capri' where the octave leap is underlined by ascending strings and a fortissimo: this is also the principle of 'Aline' by Christophe, where the harmonies of the verse and the chorus are identical).

To find the right balance between the chorus and the verses is vital for the equilibrium (and the right perception) of a song:

> I remember the number 'De toi' by Lenorman, one of his first songs to do well. The song was completed and I asked people to listen to it. It was a disaster! I was really surprised because I was almost sure that it was a good song. I went over the sound mixing ten times, but each time the result was the same. I couldn't understand it. And then, at one stage, I changed the construction of the song: it was the same song but differently constructed; the chorus, which came after a minute and a half of the song, we put right at the beginning. I played the song again to people I knew and everyone loved it! It was the same song, but they wouldn't even admit the fact! It's the little details which count! The success of a song depends on the accumulation of minor details. Sometimes the song is good, but it hasn't been thought out properly. Or else there's just one thing which doesn't work, and if you can find out what that one thing is, it changes everything.

Verse progression. Musically speaking, a song consists of alternating verses and chorus: the music of each verse being identical, it is up to the lyrics to build up progression through actions which interconnect.

The production of success 167

Example 1. Francis Cabrel, 'Je l'aime à mourir'

168   *Antoine Hennion*

Example 2. Antoine, 'Les élucubrations d'Antoine'

Example 3. Boris Vian, 'Arthur'

The production of success 169

Ex 3. *cont*

de son cadavre moche.

Mais Arthur a rappliqué en murmurant: ça

clo – che, j'sais pas ____ où il est passé!

Refrain

Arthur, __ où t'as mis le corps? qu'on s'esté –cri – é –

–z'en chœur. Ar – thur, __ où t'as mis le corps? ____

____ Ç'a un' cer – taine im – por – tan–ce. etc.

Example 4. Hervé Vilard and Marcel Hurten, 'Capri, c'est finis'

Nous n'i-rons plus ja – mais où tu m'as dit je

t'ai – me Nous n'i-rons plus ja – mais Tu viens de dé – ci –

170   *Antoine Hennion*

Ex 4. *cont*

It is 'in opposition', 'out of phase', with the music, insofar as musically the listener is eager to hear the chorus, during which the music 'explodes', while the lyrics induce a desire to hear subsequent verses, since they, not the chorus, tell the listener what happens next. But a good arrangement can also, in the background, build up different verses upon their identical tune, stressing musically the scenic progression which takes place. By varying the orchestration and the texture, the same tune will alternate from cheerfulness to sadness, from serenity to tension. In the same fashion, the chorus will be stressed to varying degrees as the song proceeds.

The conclusion. The last verse, which puts an end to the tension by proclaiming the conclusion of the action, leads up to the final chorus, whose ultimate function quite naturally issues from its repetitive character. Pop songs often end, anyway, by fading out the sound on a repeated 'loop': one cannot end a dream, 'full-stop', just like that. This moment is often underlined by means of a rise in key of a semitone without any harmonic transition (see for example 'Capri, c'est fini', which refuses to come to an end).

Creating the music

The melody. Though listeners often believe that they pay explicit attention only to the melody and the words, the former does little to give musical ideas any form, preferring rather a kind of neutrality – except in cases where the melody itself is meant to evoke a particular style. The songs given in Examples 1–4 show that in general a single rhythmic and a single melodic design are enough to generate verses, which are then developed through harmonic sequence. Balance, malleability, simplicity: everything happens as though the visible surface element, the melody, and the underlying groundwork that gives it its affective dimension were complementary. In fact the melody is merely a neutral support which the listeners can memorise and reproduce easily, but which is not in itself of significance. A chance idea or two that catch the imagination suffice. From this fragile motif, the arrangement has to provide the musical value of the song, all the while remaining in the background. The final product revealed during the performance will superimpose both elements; the familiar form of the melody will be brightened up a thousandfold. The listener perceives the support and its illumination simultaneously. Later on, when he whistles the melody by itself, thinking it is that which gives him pleasure, little does he realise that it is in fact the accompaniment which, even though forgotten as such, gives intensity to the recollection of the melody. And this is all the more true because the process takes place unknown to the whistler, and because his imagination has a clear field in which to animate as it pleases the musical values submerged in his unconscious.

The rhythm section ('La Base'). As in jazz, this groups together all the non-sustaining instruments in order to lay down the tempo and the chord changes: bass, drums, keyboards and rhythm guitars. This kind of instrumental texture, based on the opposition between a rhythmic-harmonic pulsation and fairly autonomous melodic voices comes directly from the influence of jazz. But more generally speaking the same principle is found in most popular musical styles, both those which still function as dances (tangos, waltzes, etc.) and older ones which do not (minuet, branle, bourrée, gigue . . .). This manner of appealing directly to body movement, separating the beat and the melody in order to have them knock against each other – which swing music carried to an extreme – clearly sets these musical styles in

172   *Antoine Hennion*

opposition to the continuous and increasing integration of elements typical of classical music.

It is often said that the French were the kings of the bourrée; it is not true, because the bourrée has quite a complex rhythm of Greek origins that comes from ancient Occitania.* In fact, for us it is simply the branle! The French react to the tum, tum, tum . . . like that. Truly Breughel! You know, disco has become a success in France much quicker than in the USA. Cerrone, Village People, all that is by French producers. (An independent producer)

Without accepting this anthropomorphic interpretation at face value, one should nevertheless note that when speaking of this rhythmic–harmonic *'base'*, professionals insist on its animal, physical, primitive aspect. Its elements are described in physiological rather than musical terms. They are essentially concerned with finding a beat and a 'sound' that can evoke a visceral reaction, a blend that finds in the listener a fundamental, irresistible body resonance.

There is a *morphological* difference between the Anglo-Saxon and Latin inner ears. This can easily be felt, for example, in the way the Americans and the French mix the same song; in France we put in much more voice than in an American record. The inner ear has been conditioned by the music people have been hearing for generations. Between town and country it is much the same, the people are not sensitive to the same sounds. The ear reflects an entire social group, an entire country! (A young producer specialising in highly commercial songs, a former singer himself)

Orchestral 'backing' (*'habillage'*). This groups together the sustaining instruments, brass and strings, whose function is to draw counter-points between the melody and the rhythm sections, in order to tone down their opposition, which otherwise would be too sharp. Here, pop music diverges from the spirit of jazz, where this tension is developed to an extreme. 'Backing' does not exist at all in small jazz combos and is limited in full orchestras by the absence of strings and by a very rhythmic kind of writing for the brass sections. The fact that pop music is orchestrated does not bring the style any closer to that of classical music. True to the spirit of pop, the orchestration disguises the underlying construction of songs behind familiar appearances and brings together superimposed elements which underneath retain their separate functions, instead of stimulating their integration. It draws the ear towards decorative elements superfluous to the development of the song. It is as if the song were not meant to be consciously perceived, so that it might get through to the listener unawares.

While the *'base'* should be in a strict, consistent style so as not to detract from the rhythmic tread of the harmonies and the pungency of

* see footnote on p. 183 below.

The production of success   173

the timbres, the 'backing' is, on the contrary, the favoured field for borrowing from other styles (especially from classical music), for tricks of arranging, for varied effects and combinations, through which the talented arranger constantly directs the attention here and there, only to slip away and attract it elsewhere. One of these effects in particular is so systematised it has been given a special name: the *gimmick*, a little dash of spice without any relation to the melody, a 'trick' that decorates the song and accentuates its individuality. It may be a rhythm, or a little instrumental solo, which keeps coming back, unnoticed as such, but which sticks in people's minds, bringing a smile whenever it crops up, and as a result making the whole song memorable. One example, almost too obvious to be considered the ideal gimmick, occurs in William Sheller's 'Oh! J' cours tout seul' (I'm running all alone), where a saxophone (unusually) insinuates brief solos between the phrases, its discreetly suave melismas complementing the more rhythmic, single-chord style of the vocal.

It's the little thing; if you take all of Sheila's records you will see that it is used systematically. I've seen how Carrère did it: first, he took a very, very simple rhythm, and from the start he gave it a particular sound; then he added two effects in the middle of the song – what we call the gimmick in our jargon – which are just nice surprises, like a pretty ribbon around a package. These have nothing to do with the melody, they are two little effects that cross each other, meet each other, and which we are glad to hear each time. That's very important for a song. We find the song pretty, but it is pretty only because of this little effect. It is like sugar . . . But most of the time it is completely unconscious. (An experienced producer)

These 'fills', as they are also called, are not only decorative: they in fact fill in the *acoustic space*, making it more or less dense, clear, spacious. It is this which underlines the construction of the song; it is more important than the notes themselves or the passing harmonies, which are chosen from a very limited vocabulary. When the arranger tries to realise the wishes of the producer, he has to translate ideas of progression, of question, tension, mystery, opening, into musical techniques: choice of instruments and registers, range of tessitura, density of texture, doublings, sound clarity, articulations of the form by means of vocal harmonies in the background, or alternatively by having a solo line emerging in the foreground. This work on the volume and the grain of the acoustic space corresponds neither to composition itself nor to orchestration, as these exist in classical music. It lies rather in between the two and is what carries the real 'musical ideas'.

The problem of the musical idea is the same one we find in more elaborate compositions, where it is to be found neither in an 'evoked' extrinsic commentary (little birds or wheat fields for Beethoven's

'Pastoral' Symphony, for example) nor in the 'objective' musical relations which analysis of the works is supposed to reveal: modulations, dissonances, resolutions, etc. The musical idea is actually the operation that associates the two, restoring meaning to musical objects, inexpressive in themselves, by means of unexpected usage. Such an understanding of musical meaning, which denies the autonomy of musical objects on the one hand, and that of the universe of feelings on the other, in order to unite within the musical signifier the two terms of pleasure – the subject and the law of the musical code – is, in general, infinitely more difficult (though much more convincing) than the inexpressive virtuosities of formal analysis, or arbitrary footnotes about the composer's emotional and philosophical universe ('eternity' in Mozart . . .). There cannot be any form or content until form and content are brought together in a musical figure, which was in fact what all musical formulas used to be before being integrated, with a univocal meaning, into musical grammar: think of the metaphorical scope of terms such as grace-notes, suspension, leading note, interrupted cadence, not to speak of rests.

This type of analysis is fertile but complex in classical, 'learned' music, where the integrated language abolishes isolated effects. Pop music, on the contrary, allows us in a way to see how musical association functions on a crude level, each 'idea', quite simple, being immediately 'realised' by the appropriate musical effect, while the musical grammar is developed elsewhere, in a silent and well-known mode, from which nobody expects anything. The same is true for the lyrics, which often present certain effects on the crudest level – for instance, rhyming of the type métro – boulot – dodo (subway – job – sleep, rhyming of 'o'). For extreme examples, see 'Animal, on est mal' (Animal, we're in bad shape) by Gerard Manset, or the vocabulary effects of Alain Souchon, in 'Allo, maman, bobo' (Hello, mummy, boo-boo).

From this point of view, pop music refuses solutions to formal problems cast in terms of the internal make-up of musical parameters, preferring to search for an empirical balance in the resulting sounds. Specific to modern pop, this kind of composition necessitates a varied and original competence, centred around the role of the arranger. White jazz orchestras of the 1920s and 30s, and Hollywood film music provide perhaps the only direct precursors of this new musical craft.

Creating the lyrics

The 'story'. The best way of characterising the 'idea' of a song (bearing in mind that here, more than anywhere, diversity and constant change are the rule) would probably be to say that it must bridge the gap between current events and timeless myths. This is how one must interpret comments like 'It's always the same song, but with new clothing each time.' The story itself often tends to be timeless and mythic, especially as regards love, and it is the choice of words which brings in a contemporary perspective.

One producer of very popular songs asserts that 'Ever since people started making records it's always been the same song. It's a song of love, with situations that all sound alike, but with different words, and a different way of putting them together each time.' But that is not always true: a song like 'Allez les Verts!' ('Come on the Greens', referring to the green jerseys of Saint Etienne's football team), uses sport to give a contemporary slant to the expression of old-established, nationalist, communal feelings. The privileged theme is nonetheless the immemorial give-and-take between the pleasure and sorrow of love. Just for fun I counted those songs explicitly containing in their titles the words 'amour' (love), 'amoureux' (in love) or 'aimer' (to love), and their various translations and forms, among the 786 entries in the French hit-parade between April 1973 and October 1977. The result was 96 titles, or more than 12 per cent. There is, clearly, a thematic coherence among: 'Je t'aime' (I love you) by Johnny Halliday, 'Je t'aime, je t'aime' (I love you, I love you) by Joe Dassin, 'Mais je t'aime' (But I love you) by Marie Laforet, 'Comme je t'aime' (How I love you) by C. Michel, 'Je t'aime, tu vois?' (I love you, you see?) by Daniel Guichard, 'Et pourtant je t'aime' (And yet, I love you) by Santiana, 'Je t'aime à la folie' (I love you madly) by Serge Lama, 'Tu sais, je t'aime' (I love you, you know) by Shake, 'Mais, bon sang, je t'aime' (But, bloody hell, I love you) and 'Je t'aime un peu trop' (I love you a little too much) by Shuky and Aviva, 'Ne raccroche pas, je t'aime' (Don't hang up, I love you) by Karen Cheryl, 'Si tu savais combien je t'aime' (If you knew how much I love you) by Christian Adam, 'Tu m'appartiens et je t'aime' (You belong to me and I love you) by Christian Delagrange, or, in English, 'I love you because' by Michel Polnareff, or even 'De je t'aime en je t'aime' (From one I love you to another) by Christian Vidal. There were just as many entries for the other tenses, persons, and modes of the verb, 'to love', and even more for the word 'love' itself. If we include titles that are clearly related ('Toi et moi' (You and me) by Ringo, 'Fou de toi' (Crazy about you) by Kenji Sawada, 'Passionné-ment' (Passionately) by Daniel Gérard, 'Juste un petit baiser' (Just a little kiss) by Roméo, 'Viens te perdre dans mes bras' (Come and lose yourself in my arms) by Frédéric François, 'Un océan de caresses' (An ocean of caresses) by A. Sullivan, and a hundred others), but which fail to use the word 'love' directly, it becomes clear that pop songs are

176   *Antoine Hennion*

above all love songs – even if it is only to say, with Eddy Mitchell, 'Je ne sais faire que l'amour' (The only thing I know how to do is make love), or to deny it, as in Daniel Guichard's 'Je viens pas te parler d'amour' (I haven't come to speak to you about love).

An encounter, then a separation, and so on ad infinitum. The stage is set, the action builds up until the shedding of a little tear 'which the public loves', things are in the end resolved by a small victory, a return to the status quo or by the hero recovering himself. It is not the intention of this article to go into the structural analysis of lyrics, as Propp has done for the folktale (Propp 1970), nor to extract hypothetical 'audiemes' analogous to Barthes's 'gustemes' for cooking (Barthes 1975). Nevertheless a quick analysis of a few typical situations brings out a major part of the 'ideas' in pop music. The underlying mythic themes are ambivalent, lending themselves equally well to submission or revolt, desire or hostility, according to the identifications and projections of the listener: nationalism versus exoticism – Michel Sardou, nostalgic for colonial France, cleverly blends the two in 'Le France' (the name of the liner) or in 'Le temps des colonies' (The colonial era), while to the very French 'Allez les Verts' is opposed the *Japonaiserie* of Kenji Sawada's 'Mon amour, je viens du bout du monde' (My love, I've come from the end of the earth). Notice all the English pseudonyms (Johnny Hallyday, Dick Rivers, Eddy Mitchell, Shake, Sheila B. Devotion, Plastic Bertrand) and the unpredictable, periodic success of songs with far-off and mysterious-sounding references: 'Les neiges de Kilimandjaro' (The snows of Kilimandjaro) by Pascal Danel, 'Capri, c'est fini' (Capri, it's all over) by Hervé Villard, 'Le sud' (The south) by Nino Ferrer, and 'L'été indien' (Indian summer) by Joe Dassin. We also find romantic longings side by side with a complacent acceptance of love's deceptions – ever since 'Chagrin d'amour' (Love's sorrow) or 'Ne me quitte pas' (Don't leave me) or 'Capri, c'est fini', the emotion surrounding a break-up has always appealed: Johnny Hallyday's 'A l'hôtel des coeurs brisés' (At broken heart hotel), 'Le téléphone pleure' (The telephone is crying) by Claude François, 'Adieu, sois heureuse' (Adieu, be happy) by A. Sullivan, 'Premier baiser, première larme' (First kiss, first tear) by J. Regane, etc. Alongside ambitions for money, power, success, one finds echoed the tranquillity of the hobo, pity for the 'down-and-outs', sympathy for the loser. Respect for the law and hatred for the police also get along very well together. This ambivalent attitude explains how different songs so easily change the position of the 'I' from positive to negative, varying the dominant emotion. But it is always on the dreams, the desire for revenge, the hatred and the resignation of the unwanted, the dominated (or, as Léo Ferré says, *'les pauvres gens'*) that this centres.

This kind of content analysis leaves out the most important thing, namely, what is done with the content, both during the production and during the performance itself – and it is this which makes the difference. Suffice it to say that the story told is doubly familiar to the listening public: through the basic situation presented and through the contemporaneity of the people who play the roles. The story is to the lyrics what the melody is to the arrangement: it is to the story that listeners direct their attention, in order to put themselves in the place of the protagonist, the 'I', without noticing all the work it took to make that identification desirable and plausible for the listener, that is, the care given to the choice of words, to their relationship with the music and the characters, and to the contemporary detail. Conventional simplicity and ancient wisdom: that is the formula for the story.

The words. More than the story itself, which is quite simple, its only constraint being its plausibility vis-à-vis the singer, it is the wording that is the real problem for the composer and the producer. All their attention will be directed towards finding the right style and especially the right choice of words by successive (and often numerous) rewritings. The problem is that here again one must disguise one's intentions beneath familiar everyday language and construct the song as much outside the text as through it.

'The words must be simple and direct, but not clichés.' They must apply to current problems, to today's ambiance, to what people are talking about, without being worn out by use. One must somehow conform but in a hip way so that the power to stimulate people's imaginations has not been exhausted. Since the concern is less with developing a theme than with making allusions to it through particular expressions, the vocabulary soon becomes outdated, like current events in the daily papers.

'The moment when a record comes out is very important. In 1968,* for example, there was a period when it was absolutely ridiculous to put out a record; everything became irrelevant, outdated . . .' Lyric writing reminds one of a patchwork quilt, made up of quotations cut out individually, often quite out of context, from partially remembered memories whose immediate relevance to the text can be quite tenuous. (This kind of quotation can go back quite far: in one song, Dave sings 'Du côté de chez Swann' (the title of Proust's book).) When Eric Charden sings 'L'été s'ra chaud, l'été s'ra chaud, dans les tee-shirts, dans les maillots; l'été s'ra chaud, l'été s'ra chaud, d'la Côte d'Azur à Saint Malo!' (The summer will be hot, in teeshirts, in bathing suits, the

* referring to the *évènements* of May 1968.

178   *Antoine Hennion*

summer will be hot, from the Côte d'Azur to St Malo), the effect seems even to come from the very absence of any link between the song's contents and the slogan it evokes (a slogan of May 1968, when students demonstrated, singing 'Hot, hot, hot, the spring-time will be hot!'). Similarly, in 'Je l'aime à mourir' (I love her so much I could die) by Francis Cabrel, where we are told that 'She had to fight in all the wars of life . . . and to make love too', the end of the sentence seems to be there only to bring up the association war–love which people remember from the slogan 'Make love not war', but which has no relevance to the song (see Ex. 1). The word-quote is sometimes only an acknowledgement of current fashionable slang, as in, 'Tu me fais planer' (You send me) by Michel Delpech and 'Ça plane pour moi' (Things are really far out with me) by Plastic Bertrand, 'Je suis bidon' (I'm nothing special) by Alain Souchon, 'Mon vieux' (My old man) by Daniel Guichard, or even, for the older generation, 'Mes emmerdes' (My hassles) by Charles Aznavour. It can make a direct allusion to a topic of current interest: 'Pas besoin d'éducation sexuelle' (No need for sex education) by Julie Bataille, or even 'Le zizi' (nickname for the genitals) by Pierre Perret. But most often it is used to relay or echo certain social themes in a more general way. Thus, feminism gave new life to the word 'woman' which suddenly started appearing in the song titles of several female singers ('Ces femmes' (Those women) by Nicole Croisille, 'Une femme' (A woman) by Jeane Manson, 'Les femmes' (Women) by Sheila, 'Femme est la nuit' (Woman is night) by Dalida) and also in Nougaro's 'Femmes et famines' (Women and famines).

The meaning of words depends less on their organisation in the text than on the social context they evoke in absentia. 'There are no "trends" in pop music; it just *follows* the evolution of society', according to a producer who is involved with singers of quite different styles (Dave, Lenorman, Alain Chamfort . .). But pop also *expresses* this evolution of society, and in doing so is not so passive after all. Nevertheless, the idea of an absence of voluntarism, of claims to autonomy, in favour of listening to what society as it is has to say is fundamental to pop music. 'You must never follow fashions! To be "in fashion" is a great error. When you follow a fashion, you're already behind it' (Gilbert Bécaud). Or, for a young producer of highly commercial songs,

You have to imagine what the public will like three or four months from now, when the record comes out. Not to forget the other records that could come out with something new, musically or otherwise, and in doing so outdate your record! You often see three or four records come out practically at the same time which are trying to get at the same thing, exploiting the same idea, something that was in the air. Generally, of course, only one makes it and the others flop!

Such success hinges on the lightness of the implicit. One must avoid words with too obvious a connotation, or with a single meaning, or with over-strong effects which tend to replace the allusion by the issue itself. One has to write in an 'open' style. Only Sardou* can dare to say 'They've got the oil, but that's all' (referring to Arab countries).

This obligation to be simple does not guarantee a lyric will be good: it might have the necessary familiarity, be related to everyday events, and yet be lacking in appeal. Once again, it is through the selection of words that the appeal must be made; certain key words, in contrast with the obviousness of the other words, which are like tiny reservoirs briefly holding the social significations of the moment, function as pure signifiers: mysteriously, they have an autonomy of their own within the meaning of the text, and are selected for the way they ring, for the expressive power which gives them their opacity; they have to engage the imagination of the listener, and at the same time effect a sort of disengagement from the everyday words of the text, so that the role of dream can be given full play. These unexpected metaphorical turns of phrase interrupt the unfolding of the text, giving one a shiver of pleasure, in a way very similar to the effect of the musical 'gimmick'.

There is a clear example of this double function in one of Dave's songs: 'Tant qu'il y aura' (As long as there are [sun in the sky, cows in the fields, birds in the sky . . .]). Against a background which evokes ecological themes, though of course without naming them or discussing them head-on, there suddenly emerges the expression 'sorcerer's apprentice', more hermetic and belonging neither to the context of the song nor to that of its theme, yet maintaining an intuitive connection with them. It imprints itself on the memory and pins together the melody and the lyric.

This opposition between *word-quotes*, which enrich the context, and *keywords*, which serve as metaphors, is obviously less clear-cut in the case of the work of 'artistic' singer–songwriters (*chansons 'à texte'*), where, for reasons of poetic ambition, there is more integration of formulae and images. But the principle of putting 'punch' in songs by means of striking images and evocative phrases remains the rule in lyrics which must be sung and therefore have to be very short and interspersed with choruses. The 'new-wave French song' created by author–composer–singers who are more sensitive to their lyrics, provides such examples as Francis Cabrel's 'Je dois clouer des notes à

---

* one of the best-selling singers in France, well-known for his right-wing views and approval of 'silent majority' themes.

mes sabots de bois' (I must nail some notes to my wooden clogs), or, in Laurent Voulzy's 'Le coeur grenadine' (Pomegranate heart), 'J'ai laissé dans une mandarine/Une coquille de noix bleu-marine' (I left a navy-blue walnut shell in a tangerine). In 'Nous', sung by Hervé Vilard, the text bounces from flashes of originality to clichés: 'Un éclat de rire en plein coeur' (a peal of laughter straight from the heart), 'quatre rayons ôtés au soleil' (four sunbeams taken from the sun).

The style. The style adapts itself to the vocabulary which is used and to the singer, rather than existing for its own sake. It has only certain limited means of its own with which it can underline a song's construction, which is quite independent of it: repetitions (to point up contrasts between verses and chorus); rhymes (to help in the punctuation of the musical periods), etc. Its role is more important in the context of the story-line, to place the characters and even more the imaginary nature of the drama. The frequent use of the direct style where, for example, the 'I' addresses itself to the 'you', even though it is obvious from the lyrics that the 'you' in question is far away, instantly gives the song the form of a fantasy, of a daydream in which a character speaks aloud to someone who is not there. The direct style not only enables the listener to identify with the hero of the song and allows for the direct expression of feelings, it also invites the audience to put itself in the situation of the dreamer; the song is dreamlike in nature not only because of its content, which describes a situation and proposes an imaginary revenge against a cruel beloved; it is first and foremost, and more discreetly, the style which invites the listener to hear the song as 'natural', as though it represented his own fantasies.

The versification. In this way the style makes the lyrics embrace the action of the song. But the style must also fit the music and the main character. In the world of pop music, it is pretty meaningless to say of a lyric that it is good: it is only one piece of the jigsaw puzzle and must be judged not on its own merits but on the way it fits in with the other pieces, both distinct from them and at the same time completely dependent on them. Producers often assert in a somewhat emphatic fashion: 'There is only one text for a tune, and only one tune to which a text can be sung.' Or, as the singer might put it: 'It's a mistake to think that a song is a poem. A songwriter is not a poet. This means that when I'm given some lyrics for a song without the music, I'm just not interested. I can't judge the words without the music.' (Dave) An experienced producer goes into greater detail: 'Unlike certain other forms of expression, songs are a composite genre: a song is made up of words and music, certain words for a certain music and none other . . .

It's like cooking or like magic: if it doesn't work, there's nothing you can do about it.'

For the music, what matters most is the versification: verbal accents must coincide with musical stresses (see Ex. 5, where words and music rise together to reach the word 'en*fant*' and fall again to '*main*'), or else their displacement must be knowingly handled (see Ex. 6, where the accent, displaced from 'crié' to 'crié', coincides with a 'blue' note, between G♯ and G♮, on which the chorus culminates and the voice emits the 'too much sorrow' of the next phrase). The important words must coincide with the musical high-points, the density of the text with that of the music, etc. But even more than in these technical ways, the association between lyrics and tune must rest on a succession of converging associations which are able to link the one to the other through analogous images or 'colours'. The text must express in some way what the music says already. If it is the other way round, the listener will reject it. He will recall only the tune of a song if the right words have not been 'found', whereas he will memorise both words and music if the lyrics are 'good'. This relationship calls for many alterations, for progressive, empirical adaptations according to the results. 'For "La primavera" with Gigliola Cinquetti, I had nine different lyrics. I had already recorded one text out of the six which I had selected at the beginning. I didn't like it. I took the tape back to Italy, and re-recorded over there . . . I think it's the only way to go about it.'

Songwriters, composers and producers need the 'public's ear' for this task. It may be true, as they often claim, that there are no written rules, no infallible tricks to guarantee the success of the equation, that you need intuition, quickness of judgement and feeling rather than any theories out of a book. But this does not mean that such a talent is a gift from Heaven or that it defies analysis. It does require a certain form of sensitivity, a knack for grasping that what words and music say

Example 5

Prendre un en – fant par la   main _____

Example 6

Et j'ai cri – é   cri – é! ___ etc.

depends less on their internal properties than on the way they call up social meanings. This type of awareness as to which words and musical phrases are pregnant with meaning at any given time stems more from personal experience than from any formal learning. It relates to what a person *is* rather than to what he knows. The good professional is someone who in his own life has felt the meanings held in common by his audience and whose experience enables him to seize upon them before their manipulation blunts their significance.

This intuitive knowledge of public meanings (*valeurs-pour-le-public*) is even more necessary when it comes to the creation of a singer's 'persona' and its relationship to the music and the lyrics which, in a sense, it 'caps'. It is at this level that, through his relationship with the singer, the part played by the producer is decisive.

Creating the persona

A voice. When looking for new singers, producers do not judge a candidate by his repertoire – they will build it up from scratch anyway – nor, initially, by his technical skills – these can be tinkered with. What they do try to recognise first and foremost, and to single out wherever possible, is a 'voice'.

That voice, as they conceive of it, is from the start an element with a double meaning, physiological and psychological. It will be the basis for the relationship which must be established between the singer's persona and his songs. Having a 'voice' in pop music terms does not mean possessing a vocal technique or systematically mastering one's vocal capacities. Instead, a voice is an indication of one's personality. 'Personally, I prefer a singer who is marvellously himself in front of a mike even if possibly he sings . . . I won't say exactly out of tune, but not absolutely in tune either . . . rather than a singer whose pitch is perfect but who stays cold, like a choral singer, and who doesn't project anything' (an independent producer who specialises in the teeny-bopper market). When singers practise a lot and take singing lessons, they do so mainly in order to develop their stamina for going on stage and to learn how to sing without straining their voice. Working on their sound might well make them lose their originality even if they did gain in proficiency.

What counts is having an interesting sound which attracts attention: inflections, accents and a way of expression which is immediately recognisable. One producer's criterion is that 'something has to happen even on a "la-la-la"'. In other words, it is not the voice for its own sake that matters but its expressive power. The producer listens out for what the infinite nuances of a particular voice have to say, in order gradually to find coherent translations on other levels: music, lyrics, record-sleeve, etc.

It is at this first moment of contact more than at any other that the producer assesses the singer for what he is, quite apart from any self-awareness or any technique he might have and regardless of what he can do already. To speak of the singer's inner self, as contained in his voice, does not imply any reductive psychologism nor any unilateral stress on the individual; on the contrary, the details of his personal history, which has made him what he is, will mean nothing to the public unless they refer to a certain social condition, at a conscious or an unconscious level. 'Each star is a completely stereotyped product which corresponds to a persona . . . Take Le Forestier: he's exactly what young people are today, nice rebels in clean blue jeans' (a promotions assistant).

By way of illustration, it is interesting to note that, in terms of this single element, the voice, in French pop songs, one can see coming to the surface the ancient dichotomy between the Oc and the Oïl tongues;* a great majority of France's singers are of Occitanian origins, and have thus given what is thought of as French pop music a quite distinct phrasing and vocal type.

An image. On the visual level, the singer's appearance, the way he moves and stands, the way he dresses, all have a function of expression analogous to that of his voice. He must intrigue us, compel our attention, make us want to get to know him just on the strength of his appearance. 'Mike Brant could not go unnoticed. Anyone who caught a glimpse of him wanted to know who he was. Though he was very reserved, his personality was very forceful. It emanated from him. That's what star quality is about: being a guy people turn to look at in the street even though they don't know him.' (His former producer)

A star's 'magnetism' must exist, if only in embryonic form, before success comes and before he learns those techniques which will aid his development. This first impression is the foundation of the image which the singer will construct for his public. But perhaps the comparison between image and voice stops here: in a song, as in real life, the voice is less deceptive than the physical appearance, more revealing of the true personality, cannot be manipulated at will as easily as can the external appearance. It is the voice first and foremost which conveys a singer's authenticity, sometimes through a raw and

---

* Occitania was the ancient kingdom of southern France (roughly south of the Loire). The French spoken there was the *langue d'Oc*, that in the north, the *langue d'Oïl*. Some Occitan dialects are still spoken.

bitter quality over which he has no control (having a harsh, cracked or rasping voice has never stopped anyone from becoming a singer; on the contrary, think of Adamo and Aznavour). His image, on the other hand, which is easier to 'polish', has the opposite function: it serves as a pleasing, seductive or amusing façade which conceals under a familiar and neutral aspect the unacknowledged source of the pop star's appeal.

One can make analogies here with the complementary roles played by melody and arrangement in a song. Much more than with the voice, certain rules prevail and are standard practice when it comes to constructing the singer's physical image: tricks of dress, make-up, hair-do, lighting. Around the singer's gaze, which remains more authentic, an image is organised, quite superficial and contrived, which reassures fans that their idol corresponds to the usual canons of physical beauty. Singers who do not have 'the face that fits the job' have just as hard a time selling as those who sing 'out of character'.

When Claude-Michel Schönberg sang 'Le premier pas' (The first step), which was a super song, he didn't appear on TV until about three months later. He had already sold a lot of records. On the very day he appeared on TV, his sales dropped, as he had expected. People were disappointed; they had imagined what he'd look like from the voice, from the song. The day they saw him, the face didn't fit at all! (His producer)

This image is built up throughout the production phase – promotion, TV spots, the teen press, shows, posters, etc. But it takes shape most of all with the design of the record-sleeve, the overall conception of which is usually the producer's. Apart from the fact that the record cover forges the link which will consolidate the singer's image, it must also convey what makes the song special, while avoiding literal images and too obvious effects.

A 'history'. The singer's real life-story is the source of the meaningfulness of his voice and his image. But, just like them, it is reconstructed according to the way it is projected visually, verbally and musically in his songs. In the early stages, it tends to comprise the succession of unspoken difficulties which led the candidate to become a singer in the first place, which have forged his special personality and which have made him turn for help to the producer, in obtaining for him the ear of a public. This mediation, by the singer/producer relationship, between the singer's real life-story and his public is not just a matter of theory: those involved themselves value it intensely, sensing as they do that success depends on the result of this transfer mechanism.

As far as the singer's life-story is concerned, even more than the other elements of song production, one cannot speak of technique, of a musicology of pop music, even in the most general sense. Everything gets mixed up during the discovery/production of the singer's performing personality. He must be able to express himself on stage in a role which, while obeying a precise set of show-business rules, is genuinely 'true to life'. It is that 'truth' which will be heard by the public, which will enable his audience to identify with him and which will bring him success. It is by reformulating his personal problems, but within the social framework of pop music, as recognised by the public, that the singer becomes human in the eyes of an audience which knows exactly how to decipher the language of stars. 'It isn't the song which must give the singer personality but the singer who must give personality to the song.' The use of artifice allows him to rediscover his natural self; the tinsel of his romanticised biography gives him a base for talking about his life.

Some youngsters sing what we call corn, in other words any old thing: but they sing it with such sincerity that it moves people! Others try to sing more complicated things because they don't want to aim for the teeny-bopper market, that sort of thing, and it doesn't work because they aren't sincere. It's not what's really in their hearts. (A producer who himself makes highly successful singles)

The mediation (or rather the *mass-media*tion) which pop music introduces between the social truth of a singer and the public's desire to identify is probably the chief task of the producer. And it is precisely this vital mechanism which most eludes technical description – in terms of conscious methods of manufacture and autonomous know-how, artistic elaboration or tricks of the trade. On the contrary, it is a gradual process which has to let itself be invaded by outside social forces of every sort; it is these forces which dictate in effect the language of pop music: the combination of words, sounds and images through which the public loves its idols. The singer's persona is – right down, often, to almost the finest nuances, without which something sounds false – the collective projection of the singer's reality and that of the public on the screen of pop music. A cliché, perhaps, but a social cliché full of meaning, full of actuality, which alone provokes public recognition and through that the lasting success of the singer:

Caradec's career has constant ups and downs, which means something is wrong somewhere. As far as I'm concerned, he is an artist who when he's got a commercial song – and I don't mean to sound pejorative – is going to sell well. But when he has a song which reflects what he's really like, it doesn't work. Why not? Because he hasn't sold his own personality. When he does well, it's only the song he's selling. If he'd sold himself along with the song . . . You can sell a song without selling the singer's personality – but that isn't how you make a great career for yourself.

186　　*Antoine Hennion*

Often, by contrast, a song without a personality attached is a disaster. Moustaki composed 'le métèque' (the half-breed) and at first gave it to some unknown to sing; it sold about 300. Moustaki himself came from the Left Bank, had short hair, wore a black suit and a tie, and was not succeeding as a singer. When at last he grew a beard, put on jeans and started looking like a 'half-breed', he sang his life story in the song, complete with external signs of his condition, and went down very well.

Thus, through a song, a voice and an image, it is in the end a life-story and as a result a character which is 'sold' to the public: one sees this in singers' pseudonyms ('they were called Denise and Bernard, you see what I mean . . . we changed their names to Erik and Indira', their producer explained to us during a session with a couple of singers), in their 'biographies' and in the ready-made articles which the promotion departments distribute to the media and to the teen press (*Hit, Podium, Salut, Stéphanie, Star, OK*). It is there, too, in the past which these biographies romanticise: the poverty, belonging to an ethnic minority, the road artist's life, all evidence of rejection and exclusion. Similar are the imaginary adventures which the star offers as fodder for the narrative, and which repeat, in the very public private life of the singer, and in a more spectacular fashion, the amorous ups and downs of his songs. The same rationale explains the highly charged professional relations which exist in show business and which one cannot dismiss as pure affectation; this milieu lives by a 'psychology of the stars': narcissism, intolerance, 'crazy' lives, total dependence on the public – these constitute the quite real, personal other side of the myth which they become. Finally it is the importance of personality which from the start provides the basis for the relationship between singer and producer. Beyond a given voice or appearance, the producer very deliberately selects his singers according to the friendly relationship he can or cannot establish with them. It is a question of whether they 'click' together or not.

Lenorman, for instance, I didn't know him. We had dinner together after a show – he wasn't famous in those days – and we spent four hours talking together! I vaguely knew what he sounded like, but that wasn't what interested me. We had to have a conversation, because that's what I consider the most important. We had so much to say to each other, it was fantastic! (His young producer)

The singer and his producer have to invest a great deal in one another; they must respond to each other's emotional needs, and their past must enable them to understand each other. In other words, perhaps, the producer has to be able to detect in the would-be singer what it is in his life-story that makes him want to go on stage, to become the star which he, the producer, never can be, while the singer must sense in the producer a high degree of personal sensitivity to what he has to offer, thus finding in him his first real audience.

The producer is not a calculator. His knowledge of the pop music scene and his experience of the public are only of value when he has integrated them within an 'immediate' sensitivity: only then do they mutely guarantee the genuineness of his taste, which can exercise itself spontaneously and in a subjective, non-cerebral fashion. He can forget the criteria which he has interiorised and allow himself to give in to his feelings, to react to what he perceives as purely physical sensations produced by such and such effects: 'I select the takes according to what gives me a thrill when I listen. It's completely idiotic, but that's the way it is. I can't even explain why; it's purely physical, I wait until it makes my skin tingle.' (A semi-independent producer who specializes mainly in quality songs) It is in terms of this emotional response, this sympathy in the strictest sense of the word, that the decisive moment occurs, that moment when a producer decides to take on a new singer because he feels it is going to 'work' between them.

We have to have the first 'shock', the 'love-at-first-sight' feeling, before the public can. We're the middle-men. If we liked it, maybe others will too . . . Different people have different talents but then I meet one I take a violent fancy to, the sound of his voice . . . how can I put it . . . it's got a kind of vibration which does something to me; it strikes a chord and makes me feel good . . . (One of the pop music producers of an American-owned company)

When they look back on such moments, producers cannot recall having had a particular reason or making a deliberate choice: 'Take Herbert Pagani. I went to the Rose d'Antibes five years ago. I didn't need any singers at all that year, I just went for no reason. I saw this guy singing and I told myself he was good. I went and told him so. We worked together and that's how it was . . .'

The heart has its reasons . . . The producer does not so much refuse to listen to logical arguments as consider them of lesser importance; he situates them on another level. Good arguments are useful, but secondary. They are only convenient to back up a case, to rationalise something that has already happened. Reason provides justifications that serve to convince those whose job is not, like the producer's, to feel the 'vibes': the money men, the directors, the commercial and radio men. And it helps to encourage those on the 'artistic' side, in the studios and at the music publishers, who have not yet caught these 'vibes', to stick to the project. But reflection can do no more than back up the producer's initial conviction, and it is this which allows him to

188   *Antoine Hennion*

hold out when success takes a long time to come and the doors remain shut:

> I'm incapable of working with certain singers, because I don't have the *conviction* they're any good. I can't tell you why I have this conviction! When I started Maxime Le Forestier off, for example, I was absolutely positive that he had a lot to offer. I wrote to one big company to tell them so and they answered 'no, his voice is too thin'. I cut his first record at Festival and it didn't work, the label wasn't good. Maxime went to Polydor and it took several more years. But in the end, with Jacques Bedos, he became the star I had always thought he could become.

This method of work, subjective and 'primitive', must be taken seriously; it is a method whereby a lasting conviction is founded on the immediate pleasure responsible for the producer's initial image, visual and aural, of the singer. For this is basically the same method by which the public will subsequently recognise its idols. There is a truth here which must be acknowledged, even though in turn it needs to be analysed, for its subjective character does not exempt it from being socially meaningful, quite the contrary. But one cannot assert that producers' claims to this physical and irrational impulse are pure 'ideology', an attempt to conceal the rational nature of the social and political criteria they have applied to reach their verdict. Their behaviour in this instance fits in with what they say, and their impulses are genuinely followed up. 'Actually, it's yes or no from the start, often before even listening to them: for example, if a singer's waiting in the hall for the interview as I go in, I can tell from a glance if it's no . . . I'm ready to change my mind during the interview, but up to now my first impression has always been subsequently confirmed . . .' (A young producer in a large company). Moreover, the arbitrary nature of these verdicts works both ways, and the empathy of singer and producer seems to be a decisive criterion of whether the singer's artistic achievement is to be transformed into a commercial success:

> Take the case of Dave, for instance; he'd been with Barclay for five years . . . and it wasn't working out. He left Barclay and went to CBS with Jean-Jacques Souplet . . . and his very first record sold 500,000! It was because the singer and the producer had understood each other and were therefore able to make use of one another. Dave was 'brought out of himself', his own feelings were drawn out of him . . . But on the other hand if one doesn't really get on well with a singer, it's better to stop because one can 'block' him completely.

An art of pleasing

Beyond the specific role played by the producer, it is in the end the overall working relationship between the various members of the pop music professional team which is able to anticipate the public's reactions; each member of the team constantly switches from producing the song to listening to how it sounds, from techniques to image. The real inventiveness of the professional 'hit' producers probably lies in the methods of work they have devised for managing these two aspects of the song – for presenting an *imaginary object*. The characteristics of the mode of production they have created, from the function of the producer to the recording session, all have one aim: the problematic fusion between the universe of techniques, by which objects are made, and that of images, in which an audience wants to invest. Work in the studio consists of eliminating the professional's complacency with regard to his style, watching out for any signs of incipient complicity between those who know what they are up to, bringing back into the 'firing line' of 'primitive' criticism the finds of each member of the team: all this in order to subordinate the meaning a song may have for its creator to the pleasure it can procure for the listener.

The aim of the entire organisation of production is *to introduce the public into the studio* through various means:

(a) through techniques of *cutting* and *mixing* which introduce elements of everyday reality into the song;

(b) through the presence of *witnesses* (such as the young singer himself, who is first and foremost a specimen of his public) and of *representatives* of the public (this is the producer's role both in relation to his singer and in relation to the technicians);

(c) through the working relationships, constituted by *mutual criticism* (each member of the team being an audience for the others), by *subjective listening* (it being pleasure which produces meaning) and by *collective anticipation* (the dynamics of the group constitute a first production–consumption process which one hopes will repeat itself first through the media and later among the public).

The dictatorship of the public (which is obvious everywhere in a genre so often described as manipulation) remains extremely ambiguous. If the public is an ignorant despot with the power to decide once and for all whether a song is a hit or not, it is for this very reason an impotent despot who never has control over the terms of his dictates and whom a clever courtesan can always seduce if she knows better than the despot himself what pleases him. Everything is done for the public, but everything is done on its behalf as well. The real public is not present in the studios. What connection is there between this public and the one which is constantly invoked by the various collaborators in the production of a song? Or rather, what can one do to make the real public sanction the many choices one has made in its name by massively buying the records that have been produced?

Part of the answer lies in the follow-up process which is put into action once the song has been produced: when it leaves the studio, it still has to be played over the radio and to be distributed. These two stages make their own mark on the record's history and are decisive as far as its ultimate success is concerned. The full impact of TV and radio exposure has yet to be studied properly; but it does not hold the entire key to the problem: for though it can certainly hinder a song's success, it cannot create success for just any song, assuming merely that it has been recorded in accordance with a few simple norms. Success is born during the early stages of a song's production, and no amount of 'plugging' on the radio can force the public to adopt it if it was a failure on that level. The only guarantee of success which producers can hope for – and it is a precarious guarantee at best – lies in the introduction into the studio of a relationship between song and listener analogous to that which will later bind the song to its real public. A song-object is not produced first and consumed later; rather a *simultaneous production–consumption* process takes place first inside the studio, and the impact on those present must be repeated later on outside the studio. Success is a *gamble* by the producer on his identification with the public. This gamble is often a losing one and is always unpredictable, but it pays handsome dividends when he wins. In the studio, the producer could only grope his way to success; this holds true also of his search for public approval.

The notion of a gamble is a fundamental one. First of all, it is relevant to the way that pop music is produced. It is the basis for the relationship between the large companies and the small producers, who reap the benefits of being in closer touch with the public. The gamble in question has nothing to do with luck; it accounts for the 'hit'-form of the record business, the all-or-nothing nature of success which suddenly crystallises around one number, leaving a dozen other almost identical songs unsold. But beyond that, the notion of a gamble is central to the very nature of the song. If, as has already been stated, the only unifying principle of a song lies in the pleasure it offers to its listeners, it is impossible for the producer to go by a set of hard and fast rules. All he can do is gamble on a given song, which is nothing until the public gives it meaning by appropriating it. There is no such thing as art for art's sake in pop music. A song has no objective reality or value in itself. If it is a flop, there is no posterity to rehabilitate it. It exists only to be accepted by its own times as a sign of those times.

The images of the public

At last we come to the public which gives the song its meaning and its substance. The final consumption of a song is the only measure of its potential, which was purely hypothetical until that moment. If it is successful, the spark which consumes it reveals the reality of its expressive charge, while at the same time annulling it. Pop songs do not create their public, they discover it. The opposition which the sociology of culture operates between statutory consumption by elites on the one hand, and the industrial production of mass culture on the other, stresses in both cases the arbitrary imposition of meanings by producers and sellers. The public is looked upon as passive, ready to absorb whatever it is presented with so long as the label fits the social category.

This vision overlooks the active use to which people put pop music, the imaginary existence they lead through it, which is not reducible to the official social hierarchies. To speak of the transmission of codes which map out the stratification of society is a theory which solves too quickly the problem of social domination within cultural production, by applying to it the political model of a power pyramid. This is to place cultural production within the ordinary causality of the social order: the socio-political scene which is characterised by real power-relationships, realistic compromises and objective social categories which construct and impose real experience. But when this reality is projected on the screen of pop music, the picture one gets is reversed, as though one were seeing a negative on which were printed the hidden side of current social life. In a rather unreal way, we catch a glimpse of all that official history, always written in terms of the power structure, leaves unsaid: hopes that are disappointed almost before they are formulated, a bitterness that nobody cares about, useless emotions. Producers are the representatives of a kind of imaginary democracy established by pop music; they do not manipulate the public so much as feel its pulse. They offer up their songs to the public in the hope that it will recognise itself in them, just as one suggests various phrases to a dumb person until he nods in agreement. Producers do not control the public's desires but rather fulfil them. Their power lies not in imposing a particular view of the public, but in proposing one. In this imaginary world, social domination gives way to complicity: the complicity of the public which knows it must beg for the idols that the companies offer; the complicity of the singer who knows he must endorse the persona which the producer suggests to him. The producer's art lies in trial and error: in guessing, espousing and fanning the flames of passion for which words are lacking, and, in desperation, whose only outlet lies in the periodic infiltration of a new style, which comes, in the nick of time, to speak for the underdogs of society.

Thus the producer's role is so subjective, so bound up with identification and projection, that it becomes even more of a social one; rather than genuinely express the passions which it reflects, pop music organises youthful, mobile social groups still in the process of forming. It draws together potential groups still ignored by the politicians, whose members share the same unspoken frustrations. It gives a self-image to latent communities whose members have in common the feeling of not belonging to an established social category (whether that of the dominators or of the dominated: thus, 'the rocker' may represent the young worker plus the violence which has been stifled through 'politicisation' by the workers' movements; 'the disco fan', the young typist with no future plus the pleasure of being no more than a body abandoning itself to a collective rhythm; 'the punk', the 'kid' without the likeable constructive enthusiasm which he is blamed for not possessing).

Imaginary identities, sentimental adventures, a taste of what reality represses: pop songs open the doors to dream, lend a voice to what is left unmentioned by ordinary discourse. But pop is not *only* a dream-machine: perhaps, like witchcraft in another age, it is the unofficial chronicle of its times, a history of desires existing in the margins of official history, which, except at rare moments of rupture, do not speak but act. In setting out a history of today, popular culture etches the contours of a history of tomorrow in that it 'feels' a social atmosphere in its earliest, unformulated stages; pop music senses the current and projects a first image of it, long before the politicians have grasped its real nature or had the time to quell it, before words have been found to express it or to betray it. Pop songs hold up a mirror to their age in the truest sense of the word, for they provide it with a blank screen on which its desires are reflected. It is paradoxical that reflection theories of art, which fail to explain art because they deny its role as a mediation, finally become relevant when the word 'art' loses its meaning: in pop music – except that this reflection requires a lot of work, from many professionals: 'immediacy' costs a lot.

(translated by Marianne Sinclair and Mark Smith)

References and short bibliography

Adorno, T. W. 1941. 'On popular music', *Studies in Philosophy and Social Sciences*, 9, pp. 17–48

Attali, J. 1977. *Bruits* (Paris)

Barthes, R. 1957. 'Au music-hall', in *Mythologies* (Paris)

1967. *Système de la mode* (Paris)

1975. 'Lecture de Brillat-Savarin', in *Physiologie du Goût*, ed. Hermann (Paris), pp. 7–34

Baudrillard, J. 1970. *La Société de consommation* (Paris)

Beaud, P. and Willener, A. 1973. 'Musique et vie quotidienne', in *Repères*, ed. Mame (Paris)

Becker, H. S. 1974. 'Art as a collective action', *American Sociological Review*, 39:6, pp. 767–76

Bourdieu, P. 1979. *La Distinction* (Paris)

de Certeau, M. 1974. *La Culture au pluriel* (Paris)

Danfouy, P. and Sarton, J.-P. 1972. *Pop music/Rock* (Paris)

Ellul, J. 1980. *L'Empire du non-sens* (Paris)

Escal, F. 1979. *Espaces sociaux, espaces musicaux* (Paris)

Gatfield, C. M. 1976. 'La Formation du vocabulaire de la musique pop', Université de Toulouse II-Le Mirail dissertation

Hatch, D. J. and Watson, D. R. 1974. 'Hearing the blues', *Acta Sociologica*, 17:2, pp. 162–78

Hennion, A. 1981. *Les Professionnels du disque: une sociologie des variétés* (Paris)

Hennion, A. and Vignolle, J. P. 1978A. 'Artisans et industriels du disque', CSI-CORDES report (Paris)

1978B. *L'Economie du disque en France* (Paris)

Hoggart, R. 1957. *The Uses of Literacy* (London)

Peterson, R. A. and Berger, D. G. 1972. 'Three eras in the manufacture of popular music lyrics', in *Sounds of Social Change*, ed. R. S. Denisoff (New York), pp. 282–303

Peterson, R. A. and Davis R. B. Jr 1975. 'Cycles in symbol production: the case of popular music', *American Sociological Review*, 40, pp. 158–73

Propp, V. 1970. *Morphologie du conte* (Paris)

Shepherd, J. 1977. 'Media, social process and music' and 'The "meaning" of music', in Shepherd *et al.*, *Whose Music?* (London), pp. 7–68

Tagg, P. 1978. *Kojak – 50 Seconds of TV Music: toward the analysis of affect in popular music* (Gothenburg)

Vignolle, J.-P. 1980. 'Mélange des genres, alchimie sociale: la production des disques de variétés', *Sociologie du Travail*, 2, pp. 129–51; translated into English as 'Mixing the genres and reaching the public: the production of popular music', *Social Science Information*, 19:1, pp. 79–105

[6]

In Excess? Body Genres, "Bad" Music, and the Judgment of Audiences

Leslie M. Meier
The University of Western Ontario

"Anytime anyone makes a discursive judgment of 'good' or 'bad' [musical taste] this is first and foremost a positioning gesture . . . The very act of passing an aesthetic judgment assumes and bestows authority upon the judge. By explicitly disaffiliating ourselves with certain forms of musical expression, we make a claim for being 'in the know' about things, we demonstrate an educated perspective and activate a wide range of underlying assumptions about what is 'good'."

> Christopher J. Washburne and Maiken Derno,
> *Bad Music: The Music We Love to Hate* (2004)

"Feeling emotions fully, bodily, as they are, may be sentimentality's promise, one too readily mistaken for a threat."

> Carl Wilson, *Let's Talk About Love:
> A Journey to the End of Taste* (2007)

The concept of "authenticity" so prized by rock audiences and critics alike rests on seemingly common sense values of openness, honesty, and sincerity within art. However, when examining *which* performers are privileged within cultural hierarchies found in both popular and academic discourses on music, it becomes apparent that distinctions between "authentic" and "artificial" music are not "hard and fast"—unlike much "authentic" rock. Indeed, the matter of sifting the "good" from the "bad" is no straightforward task; depending on the particular background, biases, and interests of the listener, musical complexity may compete with lyrical complexity as the true marker of brilliance and sophistication, or musical or lyrical simplicity may be cherished as a sign of a more authentic expressive act.

Much like the status of popular culture when contrasted against high culture, the *mainstream*, which is typically (and problematically) equated with pop music, largely functions as a residual category: it is what quality or authentic music is not. Indeed, as P. David Marshall (1997) points out, "The irony of the entire discourse of authenticity that envelops rock and popular music is that it is dependent on the existence of such examples [as New Kids on the Block] for the maintenance of . . . what rock means for other audiences" (173). As Johan Fornäs (1995) notes, while critics and journalists have typically positioned the "sincerity, legitimacy and hegemony of rock in opposition to the vulgarity of pop," others have "derid[ed] the authenticity illusion of the rock establishment and elevat[ed] the honest construction of the pop machinery" (112).

The notions of authenticity and "badness" typically adopted within rock arguably say as much about the audiences of particular musics as the intra-musical qualities of particular songs. As Aaron A. Fox (2004) suggests of country music, "badness is not only an index, but an icon of the abject status of its fans and creators" (44). This insight can be extended to the analyses of pop and mainstream musics more generally, with implications regarding the gender of their performers and audiences. As Allan Moore (2002) suggests, evaluations of popular musical authenticity are suggestive not only of the cultural value of particular musics, but particular *listeners*: "authenticity does not inhere in any combination of musical sounds. . . . It is ascribed, not inscribed. . . . [Authenticity] is a construction made on the act of listening" (210). Indeed, if authenticity is a value—"a quality we ascribe to perceived relationships between music, socio-industrial practices, and listeners or audiences" (Keightley 2000: 131)—a key analytic question is not only *what* is being authenticated, but *who* (Moore 2002: 210). Couple this insight with Norma Coates's (1997) argument that the binary relation between rock and pop is tied to binaries between the masculine and feminine, which directly correspond with problematic assumptions regarding authenticity and artifice: "Real men aren't pop, and women, real or otherwise, don't rock" (52–53). Gauging authenticity, then, has often involved a process of raising "artistic" (male) rock above "commercial" (female) pop.

The following discussion is concerned with exploring and extending debates regarding popular musical "badness," but will suggest analytic tools that offer a way into understanding musical (dis)taste without leaning on problematic arguments regarding commercialism, complexity, or the privileging of particular musical genres over others. Instead, it will explore the seemingly uncomfortable *excesses* that cross the boundaries of genre, in ways bound up with Western cultural expectations tied to gender. Following Simon Frith (2004), I agree that "there is no such *thing* as bad music. Music only becomes bad music in an evaluative context, as part of an argument," and that "even if bad music doesn't exist, 'bad music' is a necessary concept for musical pleasure" (19; emphasis in original). This is not to suggest that one lapse into total relativism. However, because popular musical judgments are typically less rooted in intra-musical contents (i.e., the "notes") than extra-musical and cultural associations, it is important to look beyond "the music" to provide insight into the root sources of cultural (dis)taste. According to Frith (2004), in many cases "'bad music' describes a bad system of production (capitalism) or bad behaviour (sex and violence). The apparent judgment of the music is a judgment of something else altogether, the social institutions or social behavior for which the music simply acts as a sign" (20).

This distinction between the commercially and morally "compromised" neatly corresponds with the two distinct groups of popular musical consumers[1] examined in the following analysis: the critic and the "concerned" parent. (However, popular music critics are arguably more invested in the interrogation of musical or emotional sincerity than commercialism *per se*.) More specifically, the launching point for this discussion will be *Blender*'s "Run for Your Life: It's the 50 Worst Songs Ever!" (2004)[2] and the Parents Music Resource Center's (PMRC) "Filthy Fifteen," a listing of "objectionable" songs compiled by the Tipper Gore-led Washington Wives in 1985.[3] Frith (2004) suggests that "What's at issue here [when analyzing 'bad music'] is not the sound but the emotional response to the sound" (30). What, then, are the emotional roots of popular musical (dis)taste? Of particular interest within this examination is the type of "offense" seemingly linked to musics abhorred by my two target audiences: excessive sex and violence for the concerned parent and saccharine sentiment for the critic.

In order to tackle this question, the following discussion uses as a starting point ideas developed by film scholar Linda Williams. In "Film Bodies: Gender, Genre, and Excess," Williams (1991) analyzes what she terms "body genres"—horror, pornography, and melodrama—and suggests that a comparative study of these "gross" genres reveals similar emphases on: "the spectacle of a body caught in the grip of intense sensation or emotion"; "the focus on . . . a form of ecstasy"; "a quality of . . . the body 'beside itself' with sexual pleasure, fear and terror, or overpowering sadness"; and the use of "the bodies of women . . . as the primary *embodiments* of pleasure, fear, and pain" (4; emphasis in original). According to Williams (1991), these body genres "address persistent problems in our culture, in our sexualities, in our very identities. The deployment of sex, violence, and emotion is thus in no way gratuitous and in no way strictly limited to each of these genres; it is instead a cultural form of problem solving" (9).

I argue that there is a parallel between the "gross" genres of horror, pornography, and melodrama, and the types of excesses that characterize the musics disparaged by the PMRC (excessive sex and excessive violence) and *Blender* (excessive sentiment or emotion). If, following Williams (1991), the larger question is how body genres function as a form of cultural problem-solving, it becomes important to consider what desires "bad" popular musics address. To clarify, I will be using the term "genre" not to describe styles of music, but simply to classify types of "excess." It must be stressed that my interest lies *not* in dissecting musical or genre-specific aesthetic conventions. Rather, this discussion explores how certain performers stand in for certain audiences, and, hence, cultural values and practices. The question becomes *which* audiences and values are valorized or dismissed and why.

Who's Bad? From the Threat of Censorship to Critical Dismissal

Popular music performers who play with gender, explicit sexual content, and violence have been the primary sources of distaste and the targets of censorship among social conservatives, who have invested popular music with the power to incite unruly, inappropriate, or culturally threatening behavior. The 1985 Senate Hearing on recording labeling, which was spearheaded by "Washington Wife" Tipper Gore and the PMRC, provides an exemplary case of parent and family organizations' attack on what they termed "porno rock." The PMRC contended that lyrical content had the ability to incite objectionable physical behavior, and Gore claimed that "to market explicit sex and graphic and sadistic violence to an audience of preteens and teens is a secondary form of child abuse. A society whose mass media peddles these themes unchallenged is abdicating its responsibility to an entire generation of young Americans" (as cited in "Record Labeling: Hearing," 1985).

The PMRC published the "Filthy Fifteen List" (see Table 1), which admonished popular artists such as Prince, Judas Priest, Mötley Crüe, Madonna, and Cyndi Lauper, for recording songs with obscene lyrics (as cited in "Record Labeling: Hearing," 1985). Sex, violence, drugs, and the occult were the topics deemed particularly filthy. Despite the efforts of high profile musicians such as Frank Zappa, John Denver, and Twisted Sister's

Dee Snider, who defended the First Amendment rights of musicians, warning labels for explicit lyrical content became compulsory for record companies as a result of the hearing (Lusane 2004: 359).

Table 1 The "Filthy Fifteen List"

	Artist	Song Title	Lyrical Content
1	Prince	Darling Nikki	Sex/ Masturbation
2	Sheena Easton	Sugar Walls	Sex
3	Judas Priest	Eat Me Alive	Sex
4	Vanity	Strap on Robbie Baby	Sex
5	Mötley Crüe	Bastard	Violence
6	AC/DC	Let Me Put My Love into You	Sex
7	Twisted Sister	We're Not Gonna Take It	Violence
8	Madonna	Dress You Up	Sex
9	W.A.S.P.	Animal (Fuck Like a Beast)	Sex
10	Def Leppard	High 'n' Dry	Drug and Alcohol Use
11	Mercyful Fate	Into the Coven	Occult
12	Black Sabbath	Trashed	Drug and Alcohol Use
13	The Mary Jane Girls	In My House	Sex
14	Venom	Possessed	Occult
15	Cyndi Lauper	She-Bop	Sex/ Masturbation

Nevertheless, controversial lyrical content has continued to aggravate the PMRC and their allies. The genre of gangsta rap, detested for its promotion of violence targeted at the police as a protest against police brutality, has caused considerable concern. Ice T's 1992 song "Cop Killer" was protested by George H. W. Bush, Dan Quayle, Oliver North, and the National Rifle Association (NRA) (Lusane 2004: 358–59). However, perhaps the most extreme allegations waged by conservative and religious groups have been those targeted at Marilyn Manson, whose infamy stems, in part, from the content of inflammatory songs like "Anti-Christ Superstar." They have blamed the theatrical performer, known for macabre lyrics and imagery, not only for teen suicides, but also for inspiring the Columbine killings.

The perceived threat of popular music resides not only in its lyrics, but also in the visuals linked to particular performers. For instance, there has been a push to censor provocative imagery in music videos. Depictions of flagrant violence, unconventional or frank discussions of sex, and disrespect toward religion have been prime targets. Madonna has been charged with all three "offenses." The video for "Like a Prayer" (1989) was banned by MTV because it features Madonna kissing an African-American Jesus figure and dancing in front of burning crosses. Similarly, the depiction of autoerotic and sadomasochistic fantasy in "Justify my Love" (1990) was considered too racy to be aired (Pisters 2004: 29). More recently, Madonna's "What it Feels Like for a Girl" (2000) video clip was banned neither for alleged blasphemy nor offensive sexuality. Rather, the video was considered "too violent . . . *for a girl*: despite the water guns, the humor and the tongue-in-cheek aspects of the performance, girls don't wink at men, don't drive too fast, don't expose their anger, don't steal" (Pisters 2004: 34; emphasis added). Women's access to violent imagery is, it seems, proscribed due to the perceived importance of traditional gender roles.

What is compelling is not the push to censor provocative artists, but rather the fact that the performers discussed are by no means obscure: they largely constitute the musical mainstream. Music that transgresses the boundaries of "decency," as demarcated by parental and family organiza-tions, has *mass* appeal. Of course, the desire to offend one's parents has been a key reason why the mainstream has looked to the margins for mate-rial since the emergence of rock 'n' roll. However, it is suggested that the attraction to taboo themes cannot be explained by teenage rebellion alone.

From the perspective of popular music critics, the very notion of having mass appeal is often enough to earn the badge of "bad" music. However, in order to probe deeper and identify some more specific qualities tied to songs deemed annoying, I will examine *Blender's* "Run for your Life: It's the 50 Worst Songs Ever!" (2004). According to Frith (2004), "aesthetic judgments are necessarily tangled up with ethical judgments" regarding music—be it incompetence, self-indulgence, inauthenticity, bad taste, or stupidity (26). The purpose of such rock critical lists of "the worst records ever made" is the "critique of public taste, and the judgment involves the explicit assertion that these records are simply *heard too often*" (18; emphasis in original). While such polls are certainly subjective and dependent on the particular perspectives of the individual authors, the threat of false sentiment is commonly targeted.

The usual suspects are included on *Blender*'s list: Céline Dion's "My Heart Will Go On" (1998) (described as "arena size schmaltz"), New Kids on the Block's "Hangin' Tough" (1989) (the group labeled "nancy boys"), and Whitney Houston's "Greatest Love of All" (1986) (characterized as Houston's "proto-Mariah overexuding best") (Aizlewood et al. 2004). However, the assault of this panel of critics is not limited to mainstream pop and R&B, as it also includes country, hip-hop, rock, and folk rock. (See Appendix A for a full listing of *Blender*'s 50 worst songs.) Then-named Puff Daddy's "I'll Be Missing You" (1997) is taken to task for offering "a nauseating brew of gloopy sentimentality" and "mumbling insincerity,"

Will Smith's "Will 2K" (1999) for "overearnest, G-rated rhymes about fun," and The Doors' "The End" (1967) for its "bombastic," "lugubrious," and "pretentious" qualities (Aizlewood et al. 2004). Also, according to *Blender's* staff, Billy Ray Cyrus's "Achy Breaky Heart" (1992) "represented every prejudice nonbelievers have about country: It was trite, it was inane, it was big in trailer parks and it was thoroughly enjoyed by the obese" (Aizlewood et al. 2004).

What do the aforementioned array of performers share? According to the critics' assessments, for the most part, the irksome qualities seem to be somehow linked to exaggeration or excess. The acts are too bloated, too effeminate, too earnest, too fake (i.e., not earnest enough), too sincere, too insincere, too serious, too focused on fun, too stupid, too verbose, or too emotional.

If the distinction between good and bad is largely a matter of who listens, it is significant that the cultural authorities who help determine authentic popular music are primarily men with an interest in rock—or women who have to enact a type of "journalistic drag" to get published. As a result, pop is typically dismissed out of hand, and even female bands that meet the criteria of rock in terms of instrumentation and attitude are often labeled pop. The dominance of men is apparent on the roster of authors who penned the *Blender* article: John Aizlewood, Clark Collis, Steve Kandell, Ben Mitchell, Tony Power, James Slaughter, Rob Tannenbauan, Mim Udoritch, Rene Vienet and Jonah Weiner.

Given the idea that the judgment of music is arguably the judgment of particular audiences, the *Blender* article implicates those fans who fall outside the authentic rock fan base: "trailer park" residents, "hormonal" thirteen-year-old girls, or simply the painfully uncool. Chicago is accused of writing "soft-rock ballads your grandmother would deem harmless" and Huey Lewis and the News are criticized for "coming off more like one of your Dad's golf buddies than a rock star" (Aizlewood et al. 2004)—jabs that no doubt extend to their fans. As Frith (2004) suggests of rock critical lists in general, "the critical contempt seems less for the recordings than for the people who like them, who take them seriously, who still find them funny or sad" (19).

Mapping Body Genres of Music

Within popular music fandom, there is a tendency to use one's taste to distance oneself from particular (undesirable) groups. In *Distinction:*

A Social Critique on the Judgment of Taste, Pierre Bourdieu (1984) argues that "tastes are perhaps first and foremost distastes, disgust provoked by . . . the tastes of others" (56). Drawing on Bourdieu's notion of cultural capital, Sarah Thornton develops the notion of subcultural capital, whose "social logic . . . reveals itself most clearly by what it dislikes and by what it emphatically *isn't*" (1995: 208; emphasis added). Similarly, Carl Wilson states that: "In early twenty-first century terms, for most people under fifty, distinction boils down to *cool*. Cool confers status—symbolic power . . . . The indie-rock cliché of 'I *used* to like that band'—i.e., until people like *you* liked them—is a sterling example of distinction in action" (2007: 91–93; emphasis in original).

However, the insight of literary critics Peter Stallybrass and Allon White that "disgust always bears the imprint of desire" (1986: 191) is also revealing. In *The Politics and Poetics of Transgression*, Stallybrass and White explore the notion of low-Othering, a process whereby:

> [T]he 'top' attempts to reject and eliminate the 'bottom' for reasons of prestige and status, only to discover, not only that it is in some way frequently dependent upon that low-Other . . ., but also that the top *includes* that low symbolically, as a primary eroticized constituent of its own fantasy life. The result is . . . a psychological dependence upon precisely those Others which are being rigorously opposed and excluded at the social level. (5; emphasis in original)

Coates (2003) argues that teenyboppers and groupies have functioned as low-Others within rock culture, and that the disdain toward them typifies Stallybrass's and White's (1986) notion of displaced abjection (67). Displaced abjection is "the process whereby 'low' social groups turn their figurative and actual power, *not* against those in authority, but against those who are even 'lower'" (Stallybrass and White 1986: 53; emphasis in original).

If it can be argued that "bad" music is a source of disgust, but that this disgust bears a trace of desire, then much can be learned by analyzing the types of desires—and audiences—condemned. Williams's (1991) notion of "body genres" provides a lens for examining the bodily and emotional excesses implicated in critiques of popular musics. I suggest that the notion of displaced abjection can be extended to the function of the body genres explored. Such performers provide an unwanted reminder that melodramatic lyrical content and spectacular performances—qualities for which pop is often dismissed—are also standard fare within much "authentic" music.

Williams (1991) contends that the filmic genres of melodrama, horror, and pornography place emphasis on physical rather than cerebral reactions to film, and pander to the excessive and ecstatic body (4). Williams pairs melodrama, horror, and pornography with the colloquialisms "tear jerker," "fear jerker," and "jerk off," respectively, and argues that their cultural status as "gross" is largely due to "an apparent lack of proper esthetic distance, a sense of over-involvement in sensation and emotion" (5). An excessively emotional or physical expression of this "over-involvement" is the source of (dis)taste.

Key concepts can be mined from Williams's (1991) argument in a discussion of popular music, as the cultural privileging of the cerebral over the physical has a similar tradition within music. Lyrics in particular are viewed as an important site of genuine artistic expression. The performers I will discuss do not privilege distanced contemplation, but rather offer a more bodily type of entertainment. Their mastery involves physicality—not wordplay. The idea of body genres certainly requires some reconfiguring when applied to popular music, considering that the overinvolvement in sensation disparaged within film is often celebrated as the marker of a good pop or rock show. Popular music's ability to rouse a physical or emotional response is, of course, much of its appeal. The questions I wish to explore, then, are *which* emotions appear to be subject to particular disdain and *by whom*? Where does the line separating acceptable sentiment from excessive sentiment lie?

The categories put forth are not intended to be static, but rather capture particular characteristics that two distinct audiences—concerned parents and popular music critics—tend to identify with these musics and their associated celebrity images. For the purposes of clustering performers into body genres that parallel pornography, horror, and melodrama, albeit with some modifications, I suggest the categories of "porno rock" and "camp pop" (excessive sex); "shock rock" and "gangsta rap" (excessive violence); and "arena rock" and "sob pop" (excessive sentimentality). Examples of these bodily categories include the following: Mötley Crüe as porno rock; Madonna as camp pop; Marilyn Manson as shock rock; 50 Cent as gangsta rap; Céline Dion and the Backstreet Boys as sob pop; and Nickelback as arena rock. These titles have been chosen to evoke imagery related to the apparent "offensive" characteristics of each—not to classify *musical* or *aesthetic* qualities.

Porno rock and camp pop involve a raunchy celebration of sex through lyrical content, and deploy a brazen display of sexualit(ies) in live performances. Theatrical performances of sexual identity may take priority over the music. I use the term porno rock, borrowing from Tipper Gore's rhetoric, to describe rock music with explicit sexual content typically targeted at male audiences. Mötley Crüe serve as an archetype for porno rock, as they continue to leverage their sexual image and write sexually explicit lyrics. The lyrics of songs such as Mötley Crüe's "Wreck Me"—an explicit ode to oral sex—could no doubt rouse sexual tension: "Sex me wreck me, oh gimme your head, Gonna blow yeah yeah" (from *Generation Swine*, 2003). The band's "All in the Name of," which explores the thrill or fantasy of under-age sexual conquests, would certainly provoke fear and disgust in Gore and her fellow "Washington Wives": "She's only fifteen, She's the reason—the reason that I can't sleep, You say illegal, I say legal's never been my scene, I try like hell but I'm out of control, All in the name of rock 'n' roll, For sex and sex I'd sell my soul" (from *Girls, Girls, Girls*, 1987). The Mötley Crüe live show complements the lyrical content of songs, as past tours have featured female dancers donning strap-on dildos and simulating sexual acts.

Camp pop refers to a self-aware/knowing participation in excess. In "Dragging Out Camp: Narrative Agendas in Madonna's Musical Production," Stan Hawkins (2004) uses the term "camp pop," which has queer connotations, as a "response to the milieu of popular culture entertainment that symbolizes a celebration of artifice, commerciality and, hence, good and bad taste" (4). (Indeed, the queer dimensions of camp pop, and the dismissal of queer musics and audiences in general, warrant a much more sustained examination, but fall outside the scope of my analysis.) These predominantly female performers play with conventional gender identities, ranging from hyperfemininity to androgyny. Madonna serves as an archetype within my category of "camp pop," with her descendents Britney Spears and Christina Aguilera serving as more contemporary examples. Within this genre of entertainers, focus is placed on a performance of female sexuality and pleasure. This rejection of chasteness in favor of raw expressions of sexuality targets primarily female audiences.

It is interesting to note that both of my hypersexual archetypes, Mötley Crüe and Madonna, have published books that chronicle their sexual escapades: *The Dirt: Confessions of the World's Most Notorious Rock Band* (Lee et al., 2001) and *Sex* (Madonna and Meisel, 1992), respectively. Sex-based exploration and controversy is so central to their celebrity personas that it is a bankable brand extension.

I suggest that the horror genre is best paralleled by shock rock and gangsta rap. Shock rockers such as Alice Cooper and Marilyn Manson use violent imagery, grotesque costumes, or disturbing antics to make the audience feel uncomfortable, or to "gross them out." An incident in which Ozzie Osbourne allegedly bit the head off a bat serves as an extreme example. The aesthetics of death metal, which is comparable to shock rock, draw from lyrical themes of death, gore, and mutilation—the "darker side of life" (Kahn-Harris 2003: 84). Shock rock by definition attempts to provoke, aggravate, and disturb. For these bands, "transgression is not a purely textual matter; it is a response to forms of power and authority and frequently attempts to provoke hostile reactions" (Kahn-Harris 2003: 87). Association with Satanism, for example, is a means of rebelling against religious and conservative groups.

The fit between gangsta rap and horror is more tenuous, if left un-substantiated. The classification of different musics is arguably dependent on the perceptions of audiences. Despite gangsta rap's roots in realism, I contend that, when consumed by white, suburban audiences, rather than inner city youth, this genre does not constitute a significant departure from fantastical horror. The meanings derived from the portrayal of violence and crime in the music of performers such as 50 Cent are tied to elements of fantasy; street life is romanticized, displaced by a fetishized and spectacular depiction of horrific violence and nihilism. Discussing rap in the 1980s, David Samuels argues that "rap's appeal to whites rested in its evocation of an age-old image of blackness: a foreign, sexually charged, and criminal underworld against which the norms of white society are defined, and, by extension, through which they may be defied" (2004: 147–48). This is par-ticularly pronounced in the case of gangsta rap, where spectacular violence and what Erik K. Watts (2004) terms "spectacular consumption" render hy-perbole the only reality (601–02). Perhaps most important to my argument, however, is the degree to which representations of gender, sexuality, and crime within gangsta rap have been debated by cohorts of concerned parents (African American and white) and within mainstream media.

The centrality of excesses associated with women's bodies relates to the melodramatic body genres of music. Williams (1991) uses the category of melodrama to classify "films addressed to women in their traditional status under patriarchy—as wives, mothers, lovers, or in their traditional status as bodily hysteria or excess, as in the frequent case of the woman 'afflicted' with a deadly or debilitating disease" (4). I use the categories of sob pop and arena rock to classify music that targets females (and sometimes males) in the role of love interest, often triggering "irrational" displays of emotion. Sob pop refers to sentimental balladeers whose love songs appeal primarily to women (Céline Dion, Mariah Carey) or to boy bands and pin-up performers whose romantic lyrics are largely targeted at pre-teen or teenage girls (Backstreet Boys). In his study of Céline Dion, *Let's Talk About Love*, Carl Wilson (2007) suggests that:

> In tending to her voice as if she had nothing to do with it, Céline reproduces the maternal sacrifice of Maman Dion, musically incarnates the woman who takes care of everybody but herself. The masochistic devotion proclaimed in so many of the songs presents a martyr persona, with its paradoxical mix of self-destruction and self-glorification. (66–7)

Sob pop songs express excessive portrayals of love, loss, and sacrifice, and cater to the sensational body. While sob pop certainly offers sappy tales of innocent crushes and unrequited love, it may also retain a sense of seriousness. Although sob pop performers often inspire sexual interest, with fans lusting after heartthrob band members, they are generally perceived as harmless to concerned parents; the lyrics and images are not sexually explicit or vulgar, and reflect romance more than carnal desires.

Arena rock—a label initially used by the popular press to describe bombastic rock bands such as Journey and Chicago—includes rock bands that write excessively sentimental songs about love and angst. The fact that Mariah Carey covered Journey's song "Open Arms" illustrates the compatibility between these two melodramatic genres. More evidence to support this link is Wilson's observation that "Céline's main form, the power ballad, was the 1970s' arena-rock invention that did most to recover the schmaltz impulse after its 1960s exile" (2007: 66). More recent arena rock acts such as Nickelback have adopted a more contempt-laden, rather than romantic, look at love. Nevertheless, songs such as "This Is How You Remind Me" reveal a comparable preoccupation with heartbreak, are consistent with arena rock's anthemic tradition, and are similarly critiqued for poetic triteness.

Rather than simply aligning rock with the notion of authenticity and pop with the notion of artifice, the categories of sob pop and arena rock underscore how the root source of disdain for many critics may be their excessive sentimentality and nostalgia—not instrumentation or aesthetic conventions. *Longing* is the excess associated with both sob pop and arena rock, and, similar to films classified as "weepies," fans may express their physical engagement through the release of tears. To the critical popular music consumer, crying often stands in as the height of *feminized* irrationality, as footage of overly emotional girls at pop concerts routinely functions as fodder for mockery.

Porno rock, camp pop, shock rock, gangsta rap, sob pop, and arena rock each offer the fan a physical or emotional jolt and are each deemed distasteful, although to different audiences. While sex and violence pose an affront to social concerns, assuming the role of enemy to parents and religious groups, syrupy sentiment has been the source of reproach for critics. It is interesting to note that a hierarchy is established among these body genres, and that from the perspective of social conservatives, it appears that this ranking is related to the bodily excesses associated with each. Sex is considered the most offensive, followed by violence, while tears are seen as the least offensive. From the perspective of critics, the hierarchy is arguably inverted, with tears within the context of pop fandom functioning as a marker of hysteria.

Antics, Hysterics, and the Feminine

Thus far, it has been suggested that the source of distaste for "bad" music resides in its excesses. However, the gendered character of the cultural reception of these excesses, and its relationship to the discourse of authenticity, must be teased out. According to Williams's (1991) analysis of horror, pornography, and melodrama, "what may especially mark these body genres as low is the perception that the body of the spectator is caught up in an almost involuntary mimicry of the emotion or sensation of the body on the screen *along with the fact that the body displayed is female*" (4; emphasis added). To what degree does the notion of body genres help illuminate the relationship between cultural dismissal and the excesses of women's sex, women's violence, and women's sentimentality within popular music?

Exploration of sexual identity is prominent within each of the body genres of music surveyed, with a pronounced emphasis on experimentation and the transgression or blurring of gender boundaries. Performers from five of the body genres discussed have used visuals and costumes to play with gender representation. For instance, Marilyn Manson has experimented with androgyny, and Madonna has explored both androgyny and hyperfemininity. The intent of such play is largely political. According to Hawkins (2004), "in the visual display of Madonna's role-playing, her videos often imply that sex and gender roles are contrived" (4). As Corinna Herr (2004) suggests, "The 'real thing' is not something behind the veil, but masquerade is the 'real thing': womanliness is a masquerade" (41).

Both hypermasculine and feminized ("dolled up") images have been associated with Mötley Crüe, and the Backstreet Boys and Journey have been portrayed as tame, feminized boys. Indeed, Mötley Crüe teased their hair and wore flamboyant costumes, arguably performing a more fluid representation of sexuality than one might assume at first glance. Gangsta rap, for which traditional macho imagery is foundational, is a key exception. As Vincent Stephens (2005) explains, "Hypermasculinity, signified via machismo and compulsory heterosexuality, are usually central markers distinguishing hip-hop from pop and other 'softer' genres" (33). However, the misogyny and homophobia characteristic of gangsta rap is arguably another excessive expression of sexuality.

Counter to this clearly defined male gender role, it is interesting to note that a number of female rappers in the early 1990s adopted gender blurring images, wearing baggy pants and visible boxer shorts. For instance, the "formless" female figures of Salt 'n' Peppa were paired with the highly sexual hit songs "Push It" and "Let's Talk About Sex." Although the sexual content of female rap and pop stars has remained, sexually provocative rather than gender-bending clothing and imagery has become the norm.

The bodies of both male and female popular music performers may function as highly sexualized objects within performances and associated imagery. However, the objectification of women's bodies is not only more prevalent, but is also suggestive of very different power relations. Sexual pleasure in popular music is, after all, primarily male sexual pleasure (with some exceptions). Frith's (1981) analysis of 1970s cock-rock performers such as Led Zeppelin and Ted Nugent is useful when considering the prominence of male sexual display. Frith argues that "What's going on at such 'hard rock' shows is a masturbatory celebration of penis power: girls are structurally excluded from this rock experience: it 'speaks out' the boundaries of *male* sexuality" (227; emphasis in original). What is more, according to Coates (1997), "[o]ne of the 'threats' of the representation of 'female sexuality' in rock is that it opens the Pandora's box of 'sexualities' . . . . [thereby] threaten[ing] to tear the wraps off the implicit homoeroticism of much rock" (58).

It is not surprising, then, that the audience of "grandmothers" imagined by the *Blender* staff would seem so unappealing. As Coates (1997) suggests, "male sexuality in rock has been mythicised sexuality; that is, sex in rock did not have consequences, such as children or parenting. Mothers, for example, undermine some of the bedrock beliefs of the rock formation" (58). Dismissive assessments of a specifically feminine and maternal uncoolness is particularly relevant to Céline Dion, whose popularity is widespread among women, many of whom are mothers and wives. Wilson (2007) reflects on market-research company NPD Group's demographic profile of American Céline Dion consumers, and is worth quoting at length:

> [T]he Céline Dion buyer was 75 percent less likely than your average music buyer to be a teenager. Aside from a bump in the early twenties (perhaps because those people were teens when *Titanic* and *Let's Talk About Love* came out), her audience skews to the over-thirty-five—in fact, around 45 percent of Céline listeners were over fifty, compared to only 20 percent of music buyers overall. Add to that the fact that 68 percent of her listeners were female: Grannies? Check. In fact, Céline fans were about three-and-a-half times more likely to be *widowed* than the average music listener. It's hard to imagine an audience that could confer less cool on a musician. (101; emphasis in original)

Dion's relatively non-aggressive femininity does not threaten the normative masculinity foundational to rock culture in a way comparable to Madonna's more political employment of masquerade. However, the links between Dion's celebrity persona and monogamy (evidenced by her long-term marriage) and maternal life (evidenced by her very public decision to start a family and underscored by her co-promotional arrangement with Anne Geddes) strip away male sexual fantasies so important to rock.

Because Dion does not compose her own music, it is often argued that her music lacks the requisite emotional (biographical?) honesty or sincerity to be deemed authentic. Because Dion is clearly in show business, her emotion must be "all show," or so the argument goes. However, I suggest that her music and persona are not only suggestive of excessive honesty and emotion, but (even worse within the discourse of authenticity) also an excessively maternal femininity. Her celebrity persona is particularly important to communicating this feeling of earnestness. Dion's outburst on *Larry King Live* following the devastation of Hurricane Katrina, I suggest, was not mocked so enthusiastically due to suspicions regarding her sincerity.

Instead, her tears were *too* real—she was *too* vulnerable. Like her singing voice, her plea for the looters—"let them touch those things"—was presented as offering excessive, naked displays of feminine emotionality and irrationality, hence its dismissal as hysterical. Indeed, hysteria has historically been understood as fear or emotional excesses unique to women—with important links to female sexuality. While the medical diagnosis no longer remains, a trace of its gendered origins arguably remains in the cultural judgment of popular music and its fans.

Perhaps the real threat of feminine (pop) hysterics lies not in its distance from masculine (rock) antics, but in its proximity. As Wilson (2007) reflects on the power ballad's shift from 1970s arena rock to Céline Dion:

> Today's metal has no power ballads, no more Nazareth doing 'Love Hurts,' no more Kiss doing 'Beth,' no more Guns N' Roses' 'Sweet Child o' Mine.' So Céline is singing them instead. It's been said that 'pro wrestling is soap opera on steroids,' so maybe Céline Dion is metal on estrogen. And metal, remember, has now been admitted to the critical sanctum. Metal is all darkness and rebellion and Céline all candlelight and communion, but note how hypermasculinity and hyperfeminity in this way can meet. (68)

It is the genres that appeal to girls and women—rock's low-Others—that are typically dismissed as either too artificial or too honest, as offering false sentiment or naked emotionality.

Conclusions

The notion of "body genres" provides a valuable analytic tool for examining musics rife with emotion and physicality. I suggest that the categories of porno rock, camp pop, shock rock, gangsta rap, sob pop, and arena rock are deemed "bad" music, largely due to the excesses associated with their performers and fans; while excessive sex and violence are deemed "bad" by concerned parents, excessive sentimentality is considered a sign of "bad" music to the critic. Each body genre communicates these desires in a way that betrays "good manners," provoking physical and emotional responses as a means of addressing questions and desires related to sex, violence, love, and loss.

It has also been argued that the dictates of the notion of authenticity within popular music are largely gendered. Within an analysis of musical "badness," then, it is not sufficient to examine which emotions are deemed more culturally valid than others. Considering the centrality of emotion to musical pleasure, one must take into account not only who listens, but also who *emotes*. Indeed, I suggest that in popular music, girls and women have borne the weight of the projected fears and desires of men. If the status of particular popular musics is bound up not only with the excesses of their performers, but also the cultural status of their audiences, future research should certainly tend to questions regarding why audiences of older women, girls, and other "undesirables" function as a reservoir for cultural disparagement. Why are the seemingly "harmless" so threatening? I suggest that an examination of the centrality of sentimentality and the quest for emotional comfort and consolation *within* authentic popular music may help shed light on the dismissal of these low-Others.

Acknowledgments

I would like to thank Norma Coates and Jonathan Burston from the University of Western Ontario's Faculty of Information and Media Studies, and Martin Laba and Zoë Druick from Simon Fraser University's School of Communication for their feedback on the ideas explored in this essay. Also, I would like to extend my appreciation to the Government of Canada's Social Sciences and Humanities Research Council (SSHRC), whose support allowed for this research to be undertaken.

Notes

1. I use the term "consumer" rather than "listener" because I contend that in the contemporary music market, which is marked by the proliferation of music videos, magazine covers, television interviews, and the like, *listening* is bound up with *viewing*. Popular musical consumption is an audio-visual experience.

2. I do not suggest that *Blender* is the primary authority on the very common practice of listing "best" and "worst" songs, but rather use this listing because it is fairly typical of this rock journalistic oeuvre. Note that the purpose of this discussion is not to provide a content analysis of magazine surveys of musical badness, but rather to discuss the qualities associated with the types of songs listed more generally.

3. While somewhat outdated, the concerns voiced within the "Filthy Fifteen" remain relevant within North America's contemporary socio-political climate.

Works Cited

Aizlewood, John, et al. "Run for your Life! It's the 50 Worst Songs Ever!" *Blender*, 27 April 2004. Available online at <http://www.blender.com/guide/articles.aspx?id=786>.

Bourdieu, Pierre. *Distinction: A Social Critique of the Judgement of Taste*. Trans. Richard Nice. Cambridge, MA: Harvard UP, 1984.

Coates, Norma. "(R)evolution Now? Rock and the Political Potential of Gender." *Sexing the Groove: Popular Music and Gender*. Ed. Sheila Whitely. New York: Routledge, 1997. 50–64.

Coates, Norma. "Teenyboppers, Groupies, and Other Grotesques: Girls and Women and Rock Culture in the 1960s and early 1970s." *Journal of Popular Music Studies* 15.1 (2003): 65–94.

Fornäs, Johan. "The Future of Rock: Discourses that Struggle to Define a Genre." *Popular Music* 14.1 (1995): 111–25.

Fox, Aaron A. "White Trash Alchemies of the Abject Sublime: Country as 'Bad' Music." *Bad Music: The Music We Love to Hate*. Ed. Christopher J. Washburne and Maiken Derno. New York: Routledge, 2004. 39–61.

Frith, Simon. *Youth, Leisure, and the Politics of Rock 'n' Roll*. New York: Pantheon, 1981.

Frith, Simon. "What is Bad Music?" *Bad Music: The Music We Love to Hate*. Ed. Christopher J. Washburne and Maiken Derno. New York: Routledge, 2004. 14–36.

Hawkins, Stan. "Dragging Out Camp: Narrative Agendas in Madonna's Musical Production." *Madonna's Drowned World: New Approaches to her Cultural Transformation 1983–2003*. Ed. Santiago Fouz-Hernández and Freya Jarman-Ivens. Burlington, VT: Ashgate Publishing, 2004. 3–21.

Herr, Corinna. "Where is the Female Body? Androgyny and Other Strategies of Disappearance in Madonna's Music Videos." *Madonna's Drowned World: New Approaches to her Cultural Transformation 1983–2003*. Ed. Santiago Fouz-Hernández and Freya Jarman-Ivens. Burlington, VT: Ashgate Publishing, 2004. 36–52.

Kahn-Harris, Keith. "Death Metal and the Limits of Musical Expression." *Policing Pop*. Ed. Martin Cloonan and Reebee Garofalo. Philadelphia, PA: Temple U P, 2003. 81–99.

Keightley, Keir. "Reconsidering Rock." *The Cambridge Companion to Pop and Rock.* Ed. Simon Frith, Will Straw, and John Street. New York: Cambridge UP, 2000. 109–42.

Lee, Tommy, Vince Neil, Mick Mars, and Nikki Sixx, with Neil Strauss. *The Dirt: Confessions of the World's Most Notorious Rock Band.* New York: Regan Books, 2001.

Lusane, Clarence. "Rap, Race, and Politics." *That's The Joint! The Hip-Hop Studies Reader.* Ed. Murray Forman and Mark Anthony Neal. New York: Routledge, 2004. 351–62.

Madonna and Steven Meisel. *Sex.* Ed. Glenn O'Brien. New York: Warner Books, 1992.

Marshall, P. David. *Celebrity and Power: Fame in Contemporary Culture.* Minneapolis, MN: U of Minnesota P, 1997.

Moore, Allan "Authenticity as Authentication" [Electronic version]. *Popular Music* 21.2 (2002): 209–23.

Pisters, Patricia. "Madonna's Girls in the Mix: Performance of Femininity beyond the Beautiful." *Madonna's Drowned World: New Approaches to her Cultural Transformation 1983—2003.* Ed. Santiago Fouz-Hernández and Freya Jarman-Ivens. Burlington, VT: Ashgate Publishing, 2004. 22–35.

Record Labeling: Hearing before the Committee on Commerce, Science, and Transportation. By John C. Danforth, Chairman. Washington, DC: U.S. Government Printing Office, 1985.

Samuels, David. "The Rap on Rap: The 'Black Music' that Isn't Either." *That's The Joint! The Hip-Hop Studies Reader.* Ed. Murray Forman and Mark Anthony Neal. New York: Routledge, 2004. 147–53.

Stallybrass, Peter, and Allon White. *The Politics and Poetics of Transgression.* London: Methuen, 1986.

Stephens, Vincent. "Pop Goes the Rapper: A Close Reading of Eminem's Genderphobia." *Popular Music* 24.1 (2005): 21–36.

Thornton, Sarah. *Club Cultures: Music, Media and Subcultural Capital.* Cambridge: Polity P, 1995.

Washburne, Christopher J., and Maiken Derno. "Introduction." *Bad Music: The Music We Love to Hate.* Ed. Christopher J. Washburne and Maiken Derno. New York: Routledge, 2004. 1–14.

Watts, Eric K. "An Exploration of Spectacular Consumption: Gangsta Rap as Cultural Commodity." *That's The Joint! The Hip-Hop Studies Reader*. Ed. Murray Forman and Mark Anthony Neal. New York: Routledge, 2004. 593–609.

Williams, Linda. "Film Bodies: Gender, Genre and Excess." *Film Quarterly* 44.4 (1991): 2–13.

Wilson, Carl. *Let's Talk About Love: A Journey to the End of Taste (33 1/3)*. New York: Continuum, 2007.

Select Discography

Mötley Crüe. *Girls, Girls, Girls*. Elektra, 1987.

Mötley Crüe. *Generation Swine*. Hip-O Records, 2003 (re-mastered edition).

Appendix A: *Blender's* "Run for Your Life! It's the 50 Worst Songs Ever"
Available at http://www.blender.com/guide/articles.aspx?id=786

Rank	Performer	Song	Year
50	Céline Dion	"My Heart Will Go On"	1998
49	Right Said Fred	"I'm Too Sexy"	1992
48	The Beatles	"Ob-La-Di, Ob-La-Da"	1968
47	Bryan Adams	"The Only Thing That Looks Good on Me Is You"	1996
46	New Kids on the Block	"Hangin' Tough"	1989
45	Ja Rule Feat. Ashanti	"Mesmerize"	2002
44	Meat Loaf	"I'd Do Anything for Love (But I Won't Do That)"	1993
43	Uncle Kracker	"Follow Me"	2000
42	Simon & Garfunkel	"The Sounds of Silence"	1965
41	Billy Joel	"We Didn't Start the Fire"	1989
40	Color Me Badd	"I Wanna Sex You Up"	1991
39	Ricky Martin	"She Bangs"	2000
38	Rednex	"Cotton Eye Joe"	1995
37	Gerardo	"Rico Suave"	1991
36	Master P Feat. Silkk, Fiend, Mia-X and Mystikal	"Make Em Say Uhh!"	1998
35	R.E.M.	"Shiny Happy People"	1991
34	Dan Fogelberg	"Longer"	1979
33	Aqua	"Barbie Girl"	1997
32	Will Smith	"Will 2K"	1999
31	Crash Test Dummies	"Mmm Mmm Mmm Mmm"	1994
30	Whitney Houston	"Greatest Love Of All"	1986
29	Deep Blue Something	"Breakfast At Tiffany's"	1995
28	John Mayer	"Your Body is a Wonderland"	2001
27	Europe	"The Final Countdown"	1987
26	The Doors	"The End"	1967

Rank	Performer	Song	Year
25	Puff Daddy Feat. Faith Evans and 112	"I'll Be Missing You"	1997
24	Five for Fighting	"Superman"	2000
23	Corey Hart	"Sunglasses At Night"	1984
22	Toby Keith	"Courtesy of the Red, White and Blue (The Angry American)"	2002
21	Spin Doctors	"Two Princes"	1992
20	Lionel Richie	"Dancing On The Ceiling"	1986
19	Mr. Mister	"Broken Wings"	1985
18	Chicago	"You're the Inspiration"	1984
17	Hammer	"Pumps and a Bump"	1994
16	4 Non Blondes	"What's Up?"	1993
15	The Rembrandts	"I'll Be There For You"	1995
14	Bette Midler	"From a Distance"	1990
13	Genesis	"Illegal Alien"	1983
12	The Beach Boys	"Kokomo"	1988
11	Clay Aiken	"Invisible"	2003
10	Paul McCartney and Stevie Wonder	"Ebony and Ivory"	1982
9	Madonna	"American Life"	2003
8	Eddie Murphy	"Party All the Time"	1985
7	Bobby McFerrin	"Don't Worry Be Happy"	1988
6	Huey Lewis and The News	"The Heart of Rock & Roll"	1984
5	Vanilla Ice	"Ice Ice Baby"	1990
4	Limp Bizkit	"Rollin'"	2000
3	Wang Chung	"Everybody Have Fun Tonight"	1986
2	Billy Ray Cyrus	"Achy Breaky Heart"	1992
1	Starship	"We Built This City"	1985

[7]

Hits and misses: crafting a pop single for the top-40 market in the 1960s

ROBERT TOFT

Robert Toft, Faculty of Music, The University of Western Ontario, London, Ontario, Canada N6A 3K7
e-mail: rtoft@uwo.ca

Abstract

The art of crafting successful pop singles can be a hit and miss affair, and this essay addresses the notion of hits and misses through a consideration of '(They Long to Be) Close to You' by Burt Bacharach and Hal David. In September 1963, Bacharach produced the first version of the song with Richard Chamberlain, but the recording was, and still is, considered an artistic failure, as was the version Bacharach produced with Dionne Warwick a year later. It was not until Richard and Karen Carpenter recorded the song in 1970, without input from Bacharach, that the full potential of 'Close to You' was realised. But what made the two Bacharach versions miss the mark, while the Carpenters, to use Bacharach's words, 'nailed it'? If one identifies the elements of a recording's sonic surface that contribute to its success, the deficiencies of Bacharach's misses become as readily apparent as the strategies The Carpenters employed to score a hit. Specifically, this essay considers how groove, instrumentation, melodic style, tempo, manner of performance (both vocal and instrumental), and the disposition of the song's sections (verses and bridge) generate an expressive flow that either enhances (The Carpenters) or diminishes (Bacharach) the emotional impact of the story told in the lyrics.

The art of crafting successful pop singles can be a hit-and-miss affair, and for many people in the recording industry the most important component of a commercially viable record is a great song.[1] But because songs destined for the top-40 market need to be turned into appealing records, some musicians remark on the importance of clothing songs in striking arrangements. 'The arrangement is everything that makes a hit record', suggests Richard Carpenter, 'you can have the best singer on the planet and the best song, but if you don't have the right arrangement for that song and singer, the singer's going nowhere and so is the song' (Olsen *et al.* 1999, p. 115). Burt Bacharach phrases the notion somewhat differently. 'You can have a hell of a song,' he says, 'and have it spoiled by a bad arrangement or production ... you need the right showcase' (Saal 1970, p. 51). These comments probably could be applied to any number of well written songs that failed to chart, but one in particular, Bacharach and David's '(They Long to Be) Close to You', aptly illustrates the points they make. Bacharach's first two attempts at producing the song, one with Richard Chamberlain in 1963 and the other with Dionne Warwick the following year were, and still are, considered artistic failures.[2] In fact, the full potential of the song remained unrealised until 1970 when, without input from Bacharach, Richard and Karen Carpenter turned 'Close to You' into a hit that reached number one in the USA and spent four weeks at the top of the *Billboard* charts.

These three versions of 'Close to You' demonstrate the vital role arrangements play in determining the artistic merit of a recording, and by comparing Bacharach' failed versions with the Carpenters' successful rendition of the song, I anchor notion of hits and misses to Carpenter's and Bacharach's insistence that a great song cannot become a hit without the 'right' arrangement. In short, I investigate how recordists either enhance (Carpenters) or diminish (Bacharach) the impact of the story told in the lyrics through the creation and release of emotional and musical tension, the expressive flow of a recording.

My study focuses, then, on musical structure, that is, the disposition and inter relationship of those features which shape and ultimately determine a recording' sonic vitality, and it concentrates on musical elements in isolation from factor such as market considerations, factors which may have a bearing on the commercial fortunes of a recording but do not directly contribute to what musicians regard as aesthetic superiority of one version over another.[3] I take my cue here from Bacharach himself, for in an interview with Paul Zollo dating from 1997, he discusses the failure of 'Close to You' in relation to musical properties alone: 'I'm very grateful to Richard Carpenter making that record the way that they heard it. Because the way that I heard it was very different and not very good. I made the first few records of it with the wrong groove, wrong feel. Richard came in and nailed it' (Zollo 2003 p. 209).[4] He has always openly acknowledged his 'misses', and in an interview with Bill DeMain he said that 'the first record [of 'Close to You'] with Richard Chamberlain ... was a terrible record. I had a terrible arrangement and a terrible con cept' (DeMain 1997).[5] Bacharach's appraisal of his recordings clearly centres on musi cal features without reference to extra-musical factors and, as quoted above, Richard Carpenter, just like Bacharach, believed arrangements have a direct bearing on the hit-or-miss potential of a recording.

In contextualising my work within the musical culture of arrangers, particularly Bacharach and Carpenter, I focus on several elements of creativity central to the art of making records and place the musical activities of recordists in a framework that res onates with popular musicians. In other words, I do not impose foreign musical or scholarly cultures on the recordings under consideration. Consequently, the method ologies I employ are rooted not in Schenkerian techniques, cultural studies, semiotics, poststructuralism, psychology or sociology but in readings of texts that, to para phrase Theodore Gracyk, square with the views of the musicians themselves (Gracyk 1996, p. xiv). Indeed, writers such as Stephen Blum (1992, p. 213) and Albin Zak (2001, p. xiii) regard musicians as the best guides to the study of musical practices, and Adam Krims (2000, p. 29) further argues that musical organisation must be taken seriously precisely because artists, the music industry and listeners take it seriously. I share the views of these scholars and choose to concentrate on those principles of musical structure that govern the arranging and transformation of musical ideas.

Musicians generally shape arrangements either privately in individual work spaces or collaboratively during the recording process, and in cases where demos and other preliminary versions have been released, researchers can readily study the creative process that led to the final mix, that is, the ultimate interpretation of a song, issued on disc. But when no demos, outtakes or other preliminary arrangements are available for scrutiny, compositional practices can be uncovered only from the released version and, in the absence of testimony from the recordists involved, studies of this sort must remain speculative. However, when a producer like Burt Bacharach recorded one of his own songs with more than one artist and worked from the same basic arrangement each time, the recordings themselves reveal the ways in which the musical material has been altered in an effort to capture that elusive hit.

Without a doubt, Bacharach's two early versions of 'Close to You' failed to excite the interest of listeners, even though the second recording had a much better singer in Dionne Warwick and Bacharach had improved the arrangement. But, as the Carpenters aptly demonstrated in 1970, the song itself was not the problem, for Bacharach had composed memorable tunes and rich harmonies to which Hal David had added, to borrow Serene Dominic's words (2003, p. 110), 'clever lines about birds and stars going out of their way to be close to you' (see Example 1).[6] David's lyric style, however, consisted of much more than clever lines, for he sought to incorporate in his writing some of the features he admired in the lyrics of Cole Porter, Irving Berlin, Oscar Hammerstein, Lorenz Hart and Johnny Mercer: believability, simplicity and emotional impact (David http://www.haldavid.com/words.htm).[7] 'Close to You' embraces all three of these qualities and presents an

Verse 1   Why do birds suddenly appear
Ev'ry time you are near?
Just like me
They long to be
Close to you

Verse 2   Why do stars fall down from the sky
Ev'ry time you walk by?
Just like me
They long to be
Close to you

Bridge   On the day that you were born
The angels got together and decided
To create a dream come true
So they sprinkled moon dust in your hair
Of gold and starlight in your eyes of blue

Verse 3   That is why all the boys in town
Follow you all around
Just like me
They long to be
Close to you

Outro   Just like me
They long to be
Close to you

Example 1. Lyrics, '(They Long to Be) Close to You'. Words and music by Burt Bacharach and Hal David. Copyright © 1963 New Hidden Valley Music and Casa David; copyright renewed © 1991 New Hidden Valley Music and Casa David; international copyright secured. All rights reserved. Used by permission.

uncomplicated story readily familiar to most people, the infatuation of a boy for a girl. But instead of developing his story in a linear fashion, David utilises Bacharach's verse-bridge structure to reveal a fully realised scenario in careful, logical stages. The parallel structure of the two introductory verses, replete with teasers in the form of questions,[8] illustrates rather than states directly the central emotion of the lyric; the unpretentious imagery of these verses (birds suddenly appearing and stars falling down from the sky) not only explains why the central figure of the song is so popular but also prepares listeners for the climactic moment in the bridge. Here the speaker gushes effusively about angels creating his dream come true, and the energy that accumulates across the five lines of this emotional climax dissipates in the third verse when the speaker concludes 'that is why all the boys in town follow you all around'.

In crafting their song, then, Bacharach and David seem to have restricted the emotional ebb and flow of the drama to two levels of intensity, one for the verses and another for the bridge. The uniformity of sentiment expressed in the verses, facilitated by both a refrain ('just like me, they long to be close to you') and an unvarying musical setting, contrasts sharply with the rising tension of the bridge, tension engendered by a melodic line which ascends in three stages until it reaches a culminating peak on the final word (see Example 2). However, in order for the recordists to transform the structural foundation of the song into effective musical discourse, they needed to enhance the basic framework provided by the songwriters, and in liberating the composition from its relatively inexpressive form, the musicians involved added the rhythmic flexibility that composers rarely try to capture in their notation (see Example 3 and n. 13) and clothed the raw song in arrangements intended to create a satisfying dramatic flow. Both Bacharach and Carpenter found their own ways of distributing musical ideas and instruments within the mix, but Bacharach's first attempts at realising 'Close to You' on disc, by his own admission, missed the mark.

In fairness to Bacharach, however, his sessions with Chamberlain and Warwick were constrained by the recording practices of the day. In the early 1960s, producers

Example 2. Bridge (as published). '(They Long to Be) Close to You.' Words and music by Burt Bacharach and Hal David. Copyright © 1963 New Hidden Valley Music and Casa David; copyright renewed © 1991 New Hidden Valley Music and Casa David; international copyright secured. All rights reserved. Used by permission.

Example 3. Speech-like (prosodic) rhythms (the first line appears as published, and the other two lines are transcribed from the recordings by Chamberlain and Warwick). '(They Long to Be) Close to You.' Words and music by Burt Bacharach and Hal David. Copyright © 1963 New Hidden Valley Music and Casa David; copyright renewed © 1991 New Hidden Valley Music and Casa David; international copyright secured. All rights reserved. Used by permission.

usually had to work quickly in the studio and, in Bacharach's own words, he often had to execute 'a whole arrangement, right on the spot. Good or bad or whatever, it was there' ('Bacharach & David' 1978, p. 8). Phil Ramone remembers the pressure producers like Bacharach were under at his own A&R Studios in New York: 'In those days, we used to do three-hour sessions, and … in three hours you were supposed to cut at least four songs … As an engineer, I was constantly looking at the clock and you had to be able to get a balance in an amazingly short time. If you couldn't balance a rhythm section and pull up a good level on the horns within five minutes, you were not considered good enough to work with the pros. So the clock often determined what a record would sound like' (Cunningham 1998, p. 59). Obviously, Bacharach had to work expeditiously to get good performances out of his musicians. Even though he repeatedly used the same nucleus of musicians and had learned to remedy deficiencies in an arrangement quite quickly in the studio (Rudman 1964b, p. 18), Steve Tyrell, a staff producer at Scepter Records, remembers that 'those records were recorded live, all at one time – with Dionne singing, the strings playing, the horns playing, the rhythm section and the background vocals. Everybody was in there, and Burt was standing in the middle' (Platts 2003, p. 46).[9] Bacharach confirmed in an interview in 1970 that he preferred recording 'live, like a crap game, with everyone hearing everyone else at the same time' instead of making records piecemeal (Saal 1970, p. 52).

Bacharach had gradually managed to gain complete control over his sessions, one of the main reasons he decided to produce his own songs in the first place,[10] and in 1964 Hal David spoke of the meticulous way in which he and Burt worked: 'before we even think of recording we completely finish and polish the strongest song we feel we can write at that time ... it often takes from two to three months to produce a single record. This includes the inception of a song, through thorough rehearsing, careful planning of [the] arrangement and careful planning of the choral background' (Rudman 1964a, p. 14). Later in the same interview, Bacharach elaborated on David's comments: 'we take three days to two weeks to compose a song, working separately and together. We hear the song over 400 times ... [and] when we feel it is right and have taught the song to the artist and thoroughly rehearsed the performance, we're up to about 450 listenings. I then go home and plan the arrangement which gives me another 80 listenings'. All this preparation certainly paid off, for Gene Pitney recalled the thrill of working with Bacharach in the studio: 'his command [of the orchestra at Bell Sound Studios in New York] was electrifying. The musicians had so much respect that they would be absolutely quiet and do his every bidding ... to watch the masters [Bacharach and David] at work while I was singing the vocals was a complete rush that prompted that extra 10 per cent out of my performance' (Platts 2003, pp. 20–21). Bacharach often recorded dozens of takes, admitting to as many as 24 in his 1964 interview with *Billboard*, and many years later, when speaking of the recording session for 'Alfie' with Cilla Black, he said, 'I was very hard on the singer. I don't think she knew what hit her. We must have gone 28 or 29 takes with her [looking for] that little bit more' (Brocken 2003, p. 182). In fact, Bacharach allowed most singers very little musical freedom during recording sessions, for even though rehearsals leading to a recording date might induce Bacharach to make small changes to a song, Dionne Warwick recalled that 'by and large, whatever [Bacharach and David] wrote was what they wrote and that's what we sang' (Platts 2003, p. 32). Rose Marie Jun, one of Bacharach's backing singers in the late 1960s, concurs:

[He was in] total control, all the time. He knew absolutely what he wanted. He knew the phrasing he wanted, he knew the way he wanted the words to go. He knew exactly the way he wanted it performed, and we did it pretty much the way he wanted it ... The phrasing – he'd have certain little ways of saying the words himself, and he wanted you to do it that way ... Richard Rodgers was the same way – he wanted it exactly the way it was written – no changes, not a dot different ... With Burt, you could say, 'Well, couldn't I do it this way?' He'd give it some thought but generally you did it the way he wanted it done. (Platts 2003, p. 63)

Similarly, B.J. Thomas remembers his rehearsal with Bacharach just prior to recording 'Raindrops Keep Fallin' on My Head':

I have some vocal tricks that I do, running around the notes ... and he just told me straight out. He said 'B.J., after you do this song and all the notes exactly like I've written them, if you have any space to do that, well, feel free'. So really the only place where I could kind of play with the melody was at the end, where I did the [sings] 'me-e-e-e-ee ...' And when I did that in the studio, he was conducting the orchestra and he kind of looked over his shoulder at me ... and he said, 'Oh, okay, that works'. So, he didn't allow me to use much of my style. Basically I just sang his notes. (Platts 2003, p. 72)

As these singers demonstrate, Bacharach notated his songs meticulously, Carole Bayer Sager stating that his penchant for precision could sometimes irritate the lyricist working with him:

In the beginning of 'That's What Friends Are For' ... [Burt] goes 'no, that's da-dum'. [I said] 'What's the difference, just get rid of the "da-dum" and go into ... I got so pissed-off, it's just a 16th note – what does it matter? ... He was so precise about it, it was so important to him and he sits in the music room and spends an hour on whether he wanted the 16th note. If you are the lyricist [it] could be rather maddening. But, he was right, and I finally wrote and I. (Brocken 2003, p. 233).

Bacharach's attention to detail became legendary among the artists he produced,[11] so much so that it is probably safe to assume that his initial recordings of 'Close to You' remained firmly in his control.

The arrangement he wrote for the song, despite his public insistence in 1964 that he and David planned all aspects of a recording meticulously, centres on a groove he later admitted did not evoke the right feel, and critics have certainly noticed this, especially on the Chamberlain recording, where prominent piano chords in the accompaniment pulse on quavers at a tempo of 72 bpm.[12] The pianist's *staccato* manner of playing these chords generates a rigid quality which Bacharach fore-grounds and simple drum and acoustic bass parts contribute to the tedium of the groove (the snare provides a straight backbeat while the bass emphasises beats one and three). Unfortunately, Chamberlain's mechanistic singing seems to reinforce the rhythmic monotony of the accompaniment, and because Bacharach did not use an instrumental introduction to define the groove, the first few notes Chamberlain sings are crucially important. But instead of beginning the song with a clear rhythmic impetus, Bacharach placed pause signs above the first two notes and Chamberlain, following the notation precisely, lengthened these notes as he sang them. Strings pro-vide the backdrop for this introductory gesture, and Bacharach's decision to double the singer with single notes played on the electric guitar does little to entice the lis-tener into the sonic world of the song. The sparse instrumentation that follows (piano, acoustic bass and drums), coupled to the languid opening and monotonous groove, prevents the song from making a satisfactory impression in the critical first 15–20 seconds.

Bacharach retains this basic arrangement in the second verse but thickens the texture with the addition of a counter melody in the strings and, in order to hide a moment of stasis in the half bar that separates the verses, he inserts arpeggiated chords on successive beats, first on the piano and then on the guitar. A much larger gap of a full bar exists between the second verse and the bridge and, even though many recordists would consider this an obvious place to build tension in preparation for the emotional climax of the song, Bacharach's arrangement does not drive for-ward at this point. A short horn fill, followed in the strings by a heavily emphasised harmonic descent from dominant to tonic, barely provides adequate musical resources for leading the listener imperceptibly from one level to the next. The bridge itself begins innocuously with a simple stepwise counter melody in the strings that pushes upwards in the second phrase to the climactic passage in the last two bars. Here, the pulsing eighth notes in all parts, augmented by Chamberlain's most impas-sioned singing, represent the climax of the recording. The energy accumulated across the bridge then dissipates in two piano *glissandi* that return listeners to the emotional plane of the earlier verses, and not surprisingly Bacharach disposes his instrumental backdrop in a manner very similar to those verses, even though he varies the string writing somewhat. A single repetition of the refrain, joined to the third verse through a horn fill, functions as the outro and gradually fades to draw the song to a close.

Although Bacharach eventually acknowledged that this arrangement was a miscalculation, initially he must have been satisfied with much of his work on the song, because he retained many features of the Chamberlain version when he produced Dionne Warwick's recording the following year. Warwick had become a favourite singer of Bacharach and David, and her natural vocal delivery suited their songs well. In fact, despite her protestations to the contrary quoted above, Bacharach granted her the rare privilege of interpreting his melodies as she saw fit, and in 1966 he acknowledged that he no longer made suggestions to her, for he had come to realise that whatever she sang would be a 'jewel' (Saal 1966, p. 102; Wilson 1968, p. D17). As Warwick recalled decades later, 'they were the songwriters and I was the interpreter' (O'Brien 2002, p. 91), and since her interpretive sensibilities were derived from the normal accentuation of spoken words, especially with regard to the rhythmic structure she had always imposed on Bacharach's melodies, her prosodic singing style contrasted sharply with that of Richard Chamberlain. Chamberlain preferred the type of vocal delivery practiced by numerous crooners and opera singers, and he regularly elongated vowels, holding many notes for their full value, and rarely shaped individual notes dynamically, either by swelling into or tapering off them. Moreover, he cemented successive notes together to produce what could best be described as a true *legato* style with no break in sound and used *vibrato* on every note long enough to admit it. Warwick, on the other hand, sang with much more dynamic shading and controlled her *vibrato* carefully, frequently beginning longer notes with a straight tone before adding a slow vibration. And because her delivery was much more closely aligned to speaking, she rarely adhered to the mechanical way the vocal lines had been notated, even though she did hold the last notes of phrases close to the length Bacharach had indicated. Chamberlain also used speech-like rhythms on occasion, especially when Bacharach's melody contained shorter values (see Example 3), but in the second half of the bridge, both singers adhered to the robotic pulsing of the chordal accompaniment.

Nonetheless, despite the differences in vocal style between the two singers, Bacharach decided to preserve the tempo and basic flavour of the original groove in the second recording, particularly the pulsing quaver chords played on the piano (a chart which compares the recordings appears in Example 4). But because these chords were placed in a higher register and were performed with a light *legato* touch, the accompaniment sounded less robotic, and the removal of the snare from the backbeat further helped establish, to borrow Bacharach's words, a better feel. Apart from this improvement, however, the languorous introduction remained more or less the same, except that a cymbal splash preceded the first two notes of the vocal and a vibraphone replaced the electric guitar. The addition of the vibraphone certainly resulted in a softer, more blended sound, but the rest of the first verse retained the instrumentation of the earlier recording. Bacharach seems to have been satisfied with other features of Chamberlain's version as well, because in the second verse of the Warwick recording, even though he gave the strings a subdued quality, he kept the figuration of his original arrangement. The transitions between sections, however, clearly dissatisfied him, for instead of hiding the moment of stasis between the first two verses with arpeggiated chords, he used a flowing

	Richard Chamberlain Length: 2:16 Tempo: *c.* 72 bpm	**Dionne Warwick** Length: 2:21 Tempo: *c.* 72 bpm		**Carpenters** Length: 3:37 Tempo: *c.* 87 bpm
			Intro	0:00 triplet piano riff 0:05 vibraphone added
Verse 1	0:00 electric guitar doubles voice; strings provide backdrop 0:05 *staccato* piano chords in quavers; bass, drums 0:28 link to verse 2: arpeggio on piano, then guitar	0:00 cymbal splash opens recording; vibraphone doubles voice; strings provide backdrop 0:04 pulsing piano chords in quavers; bass, drums 0:25 link to verse 2: horn fill	*Verse 1*	0:09 voice accompanied by pulsing piano chords in crotchets
Verse 2	0:30 counter melody in strings added 0:55 link to bridge: horn fill, strings emphasise dominant to tonic	0:29 counter melody in strings as in Chamberlain 0:55 link to bridge: horn fill, tympani roll	*Verse 2*	0:31 strings, bass, drums added 0:52 link to bridge: simple drum fill on the toms
Bridge	0:59 counter melody in strings; tension builds 1:20 link to verse 3: two piano *glissandi*	0:59 counter melody in strings and backup singers; tension remains constant 1:21 link to verse 3: two piano *glissandi*	*Bridge*	0:55 subdued first statement; countermelody similar to Bacharach in woodwinds and strings; triplet quavers on muted cymbal; strings drop out for last two bars 1:12 link to verse 3: two piano *glissandi*
Verse 3	1:24 accompaniment similar to verse 2 1:49 link to outro: horn fill	1:25 accompaniment similar to verse 2 1:52 link to outro: horn fill	*Verse 3*	1:15 accompaniment similar to verse 2 but backup singers echo Karen's phrases
Outro	1:52 repetition of refrain; backup singers double Chamberlain	1:55 repetition of refrain; main melody in backup singers; Warwick echoes and decorates the tune	*Trumpet solo*	1:36 abrupt modulation to D flat; trumpet imitates vocal phrasing 1:49 refrain replaced by strings playing modified version of the opening piano figure 1:57 link to bridge: new piano figuration accompanied by low-tuned toms
			Bridge	1:59 double tracked lead vocal followed by harmonic crescendo 2:15 fills on toms lead to a cymbal roll that drives passage to a peak; tension then released across a one-second reverberant tail
			Verse 3	2:19 arrangement similar to the first statement of verse 3
			Ending 1	2:49 opening piano riff restated in A flat
			Tag	3:00 vocal 'wahs' on major ninth chords

Example 4. Disposition of the song's sections.

horn melody, and in the full bar that separates the second verse from the bridge, he substituted a tympani roll for the exaggerated string gesture. This new figure provided an effective ramp to the heightened tension of the bridge but, unlike the Chamberlain recording where Bacharach intensified this contrasting section as it progressed, Warwick's version maintains a uniform texture and level of intensity throughout (achieved in part by the back-up singers doubling the counter melody in the strings and the tympanist decorating the first and third beats of each bar).

Bacharach then dissipated the accumulated energy of the bridge in the same way that he did on the Chamberlain recording: two piano *glissandi* transport listeners to the third verse and return them to the instrumental backdrop and emotional plane of the opening. The recording closes with an outro similarly restricted to a single repetition of the refrain, but in Warwick's case, back-up singers carry the main melody while she echoes and decorates the tune in a quasi call-and-response manner. This creates a much more satisfactory close to the song and the Warwick recording, despite Bacharach's decision to retain many features of the original arrangement, was decidedly better than the Chamberlain version. Nevertheless, Bacharach and David felt that they still hadn't found the 'right rendition' and artistic and commercial success continued to elude the song until Herb Alpert, to whom David had sent a copy of Warwick's version of 'Close to You' (in response to a request for a song that hadn't been a hit but which still haunted him), suggested to Richard Carpenter, one of his label's new artists, that he work up an arrangement (Coleman 1994, pp. 82–83; Platts 2003, pp. 76–77).

On his website, Carpenter describes in considerable detail several features of his arrangement, as well as his initial reaction to the song:

I'd been given the lead sheet of this little-known Bacharach–David song by Herb Alpert, who wanted me to work up an arrangement. We were set up on the A&M sound stage at the time. I took the lead sheet, put it on my Wurlitzer, came up with a slow shuffle, the modulation, trumpet solo etc. All the while, I have to tell you, I'm not exactly taken with this song (I've been saying this for 36 years; it took a while to grow on me.) I was doing this because I had been asked by Herb. I got to the end of it, and working with the lead sheet, which is just something basic for an arranger to work with, it ended, 'Just like me, they long to be close to you.' I'm thinking 'this needs something more'. I didn't want to end just like the intro; it just wasn't strong enough. I always liked records with arrangements that had something at the end that came out of left field; just when you thought the record was over, something out of left field shows up. A perfect example is by Bacharach himself on the end of 'Raindrops Keep Falling On My Head'. That's where I got the idea of the ending for 'Close To You'; I composed the 'wah' bit.
Ultimately, the arrangement concluded with two endings; to 'bookend' it I played the same riff as the intro, albeit in A flat and not in C. The first time one heard the recording, he or she for a split second, would think it was done. But wait, there was more. For as strong as the song and arrangement are, for as well as every person involved sang and played until that point, try thinking of it ending without that tag. I'm not certain 'Close To You' would have been quite the hit it was. (http://www.richardandkarencarpenter.com/fans_ask_8.htm).

In discussing some of the ways he breathed life into the song, to borrow Bacharach's analogy (Platts 2003, p. 77), Carpenter focuses his attention on the arrangement, especially the tag he composed to provide a stronger ending to the recording, and his comments allow us to understand his craft from an arranger's perspective. He first mentions the groove, a slow shuffle, and then he lists several other facets of the arrangement (modulation, trumpet solo, tag and intro riff) that differentiate his interpretation from Bacharach's. The slow shuffle on which he bases the song, however, actually operates at a faster tempo than Bacharach had chosen (87 bpm instead of 72), yet Carpenter's version, clocking in at 3:37, was over a minute longer than either the Chamberlain recording (2:16) or the Warwick version (2:21). Undoubtedly, Carpenter felt he needed a longer, more nuanced structure to create an expressive flow that would enhance the story told in the lyrics in a way that a shorter treatment of the song could not. Hence, he added an instrumental introduction, modulated from C to D flat at the trumpet solo, repeated the bridge and third verse, and composed two endings to be heard in succession. The first ending simply restated the piano introduction in A flat, while the second introduced new material which in Carpenter's own words 'came out of left field'. The chart in Example 4 schematically represents the differences between the two approaches.

Carpenter's introduction defines the groove right at the outset and the attractive piano riff he devised, with its gently swinging triplet feel, engages the listener immediately. He adds a vibraphone half way through, and this exemplifies one of the general principles Carpenter follows in his arrangements – add or subtract sonic events at significant structural moments in order to create or release musical and emotional tension. As his short nine-second intro draws to a close, the vocal emerges from the final chord. Gone are the pauses Bacharach had stipulated for the first two notes of the verse and Carpenter's piano accompaniment, which pulses on crotchet chords played midrange on the instrument, not only continues the relaxed feel of the intro but also provides the sole accompaniment for the singer's delivery of the first verse. Karen sings this verse in a prosodic vocal style and, just like Dionne Warwick, she separates notes from one another and keeps the last notes of phrases short (except for the ends of periods). This detached manner of singing suits the quicker tempo of the groove, and the lilting feel of this faster pace also conditions her use of *vibrato*, a vocal technique she restricts primarily to longer notes at the end of phrases, where the broadening effect of a vibrating note, rather than inhibiting forward motion, delicately draws the passages to a close.

However, Richard's choice of tempo does more than determine specific features of Karen's vocal style, for it eliminates the moment of stasis between the first and second verses, allowing the two verses to be joined together seamlessly. At the beginning of the second verse, a thicker texture, achieved through the introduction of drums, bass and strings, augments the intensity somewhat. Hal Blaine, the drummer on the recording, emphasises the backbeat while tapping straight crotchets on the hi-hat, and the bass guitar, reinforced by the kick drum, stresses the first and third beats of the bar. The strings, functioning as a backdrop to the metric interplay between the hi-hat and bass, provide chordal pads for the most part but, just before the refrain, a simple descending line in crotchets fills the space in a manner reminiscent of the highly decorative melody Bacharach had composed for this purpose. Carpenter's transition to the bridge, similar to Bacharach's treatment of the passage, heightens tension only minimally, presumably because he wanted to save the most powerful approach to this section for the climactic moment of the recording, the repetition of the bridge. The first statement of the bridge, then, remains subdued, Carpenter simply adding woodwind instruments to a string figure he seems to have derived from Bacharach, while Blaine increases the rhythmic activity in the drums through a triplet quaver figure played on a muted cymbal. The strings drop out for the last two bars and this leaves the woodwinds, bass and drums to propel the instrumental backdrop subtly towards the two piano *glissandi* Herb Alpert insisted Carpenter retain from Bacharach's recording (Coleman 1994, p. 84). These clinching hooks, to borrow Alpert's words (*ibid.*), make an effective transition to the third verse, but Carpenter begins this verse somewhat differently from the previous two verses, for Hal Blaine employs low-tuned toms to cover the static nature of this compositional moment. The rest of the verse, however, proceeds in a manner similar to the second verse, except that Carpenter introduces backup singers who echo the phrases Karen sings.

At the end of the third verse, following a quarter-second of silence, the music abruptly modulates to D flat and Chuck Findley, the trumpet soloist on the recording, plays the verse melody in imitation of Karen's style of phrasing (Coleman 1994, p. 84).[13] The disposition of the instrumental backdrop behind the trumpet remains similar to that of the previous verse, but at the end of the verse, Richard replaces the refrain with a section in which the strings play a modified version of the opening piano figure. The final bar of this passage brings the piano to the fore, and new keyboard figuration, accompanied by low-tuned toms, leads listeners to the heightened intensity of the second bridge. Here, Richard's treatment of the vocal strengthens the impact of the section considerably, even though he maintains much of the earlier instrumentation and part writing (especially the string and woodwind figures, along with triplet quavers on the muted cymbal, the kick drum accentuating the first and third beats, and the hi-hat articulating the backbeat). He double tracks Karen's voice in the first line of text and then in the second line supports it with harmonies that widen from two to three to four notes to create a harmonic crescendo to the apex of the song. This carefully crafted intensification culminates in the last bar with Hal Blaine's drum work, where fills on the toms lead to a cymbal roll that drives the passage to a peak. The tension reached in this climactic moment is released across a one-second reverberant tail of cymbal and piano, and the sudden textural thinning that follows returns listeners to the emotional plane of the verses. Richard applies generous reverb to the two notes of the vocal pickup, both sung without accompaniment but, other than this, his arrangement for the repetition of the third verse retains much of its earlier flavour. The verse closes with two statements of the refrain, and a return of the opening piano riff in A flat rounds out the structure, 'bookending' the song.

But because Richard did not want to end 'Close to You' just as it had begun, he decided to compose a vocal tag that, in his words, 'came out of left field'. Inspired by the way Bacharach had concluded 'Raindrops Keep Falling on My Head', he extended the song by 38 seconds with vocal 'wahs' based on rich harmonies involving major ninth chords alternating between D flat and A flat. The striking effect of the new material in this lush postlude became one of the most memorable sonic events of the song, so much so that Richard himself questions whether anyone could imagine 'Close to You' ending without the tag. In fact, after hearing the Carpenters' version of the song, one can easily understand why Bacharach praised Richard and Karen for 'nailing' it. Their long, nuanced structure, with its lilting groove and striking arrangement, captivated listeners and produced the Carpenters' first number one record. The gold sales award the single received from the Recording Industry Association of America on 12 August 1970, three months after the record was released, attests to the wide appeal of the song.

Bacharach occasionally spoke about the popularity of his music, telling *The New Yorker* in 1968 that 'the wild thing about my songs is that they cross the two age gaps. They're hits with people my parents' age and they're hits with the kids, too' (Ross 1968, p. 45), and at least one commentator from the late 1960s, Bob Shayne of the *Los Angeles Times*, noted Bacharach's unique ability to bridge the generation gap. Bacharach and David songs, Shayne observed, 'especially when produced by them and sung by Dionne Warwick, get played on the middle-of-the-road radio stations, the rock stations and most rhythm and blues stations as well. Their records are bought by whites and blacks, young and old' (Shayne 1968, p. C7). Indeed, Hubert Saal, writing for *Newsweek* in 1970, noticed that Bacharach's audience at the Westbury Music Fair was a cross-section of people ranging in age from eight to 80 and, in his article, he quotes from a letter Bacharach received from a young Catholic schoolgirl asking him to write a school yell for her: 'What would take me two weeks will take you only five minutes ... P.S. The nuns dig you too' (Saal 1970, p. 50).

One of the factors contributing to Bacharach and David's wide appeal seems to have been their desire to please themselves instead of writing for a specific market. 'When Hal and I write,' Bacharach says, 'we don't think about markets or what will go. Is this a comer? Is this too complicated for the people? No. I'm just trying to satisfy myself' (Shayne 1968, p. C7). By writing songs he liked, Bacharach believed that other people might like them, too, and the one thing he and David never did in their career was 'try to write a "commercial" song. [We] don't think in terms of hits. [We] think in terms of good and bad' ('Bacharach & David' 1978, p. 17). Commercial aspirations, Bacharach felt, would just trap them in a corner (Cumming 2001), and ironically one of their most 'uncommercial' songs, the jazz waltz 'Wives and Lovers', became a hit for Jack Jones in the USA.[14] A good record, then, at least according to Bacharach, David and Richard Carpenter, needs not only the right artist but also the right showcase. Bacharach readily admits that with 'Close to You' he and David found neither the appropriate artist nor arrangement, but the Carpenters, in 'nailing' the song, found a musical concept that produced a much more appealing expressive flow (Hilburn 1970, p. N37; DeMain 1997). As Bacharach said in 1970, shortly after the Carpenters released their version of 'Close to You', 'you write some music and think it has fallen dead ... then all of a sudden the thing takes off' (Hebert 1970, p. D8).

Endnotes

1. See, for example, Burt Bacharach's comments in Ross (1968, p. 45): 'No matter how groovy the electronic devices are these days, there's got to be a song. Electronic devices are marvellous. But nobody's going to whistle electronic devices. You've got to have a song.' Albin Zak (2007) has discussed the prevalence of this attitude in the music industry.

2. Various writers note Bacharach's lack of success with the song (see, for example, Platts 2003, pp. 76–77), but Serene Dominic relegates Bacharach's first two productions to the dustbins of the 1960s, describing the song as coming 'very close to becoming a throwaway despite having a lot going for it' (Dominic 2003, pp. 110–11).

3. On the importance of looking beyond techniques of mass production and the economics of market concentration for a full explanation of Bacharach's songs, especially those that radiated from the Brill Building, see Brocken (2003, pp. 18–19), and for a discussion of aesthetic superiority in relation to 'high' and 'low' artistic endeavours, see Whitesell (2008, pp. 7–9).

4. In a similar fashion, Lloyd Whitesell rummages through Joni Mitchell's 'musical toolkit (her 'box of paints', as she might put it) to establish a basis for judgments about the quality of her songwriting' (2008, pp. 3–4).

5. See also his opinion on other songs in 'Bacharach & David' (1978, pp. 14–15), Platts (2003, pp. 56–57) and Zollo (2003, p. 208).

6. In an interview with Paul Zollo, David said that he 'wrote ["Close to You"] to the music' (Zollo 2003, p. 211).

7. David spoke of his desire for natural, unpretentious vocabulary in his songs to Digby Diehl (1970, p. C15). In relation to David's lyrics for 'The Windows of the World', Dionne Warwick commented to interviewer Robin Platts: 'he tells [a story] simply in just the way we'd like to say it ourselves' (Platts 1997, p. 51).

8. I borrow the notion of 'teaser' from songwriter Jimmy Webb, who refers to the teaser as an ambiguous situation in the first line of a lyric meant to pique the curiosity of the listener (Webb 1998, pp. 39–41).

9. See also Phil Ramone's comments in DeMain 1997: 'Oh yeah [most of the recordings were done live]. Both the studios at A&R that they [Bacharach and David] used had some kind of isolation for the vocals, because we separated the group from Dionne, but they were right in the room. There was not much overdubbing in those days.'

10. On the autonomy granted to Bacharach by Scepter Records, the label for which he recorded

280   *Robert Toft*

during the period under consideration, see
Brocken (2003, p. 126) and Platts (2003, p. 25),
and on Bacharach's dissatisfaction with other
people's productions of his songs, see
'Bacharach & David' (1978, p. 8), Ross (1968,
p. 46), Shayne (1968, p. C7), Saal (1970, p. 51),
Sutherland (1986, p. 24) and Zollo (2003, p. 208).
11. On this aspect of Bacharach's style of working, see
the comments of various musicians cited in Saal
(1970, p. 52), Brocken (2003, p. 135) and Platts
(2003, pp. 49–50), as well as Bacharach's acknowledgement quoted in DiMartino (1998): 'I'm not as
hard on myself as I used to be – I'm hard on myself
– maybe it's become a recognition that I'm gonna
get as close to 100 per cent as I can.'
12. See, for example, the particularly caustic comments in Dominic (2003, p. 110): '...
Bacharach's strident piano arrangement gives
Chamberlain little choice but to robotically follow
every chord change ...'.
13. Trumpeters often conceived their phrasing in
terms of vocal lines, and in his own work,
Bacharach regularly wrote words under the

notes of an instrumental line. He related his
reasons for this practice to Bill DeMain (1997):
'I've always been a big believer in words with
notes. I used to write for the trumpet players, or
the reed players, anybody that would have a
singular statement to make on a record, I'd
write the lyric underneath. So they'd be playing
melody notation but they'd try to speak through
their instrument the actual lyric. ... There was a
reason I did it. There are certain things that
can't really be notated, I find in an orchestration.
It's maybe two eighth notes, a sixteenth note and
another eighth note and that's the way it should
be notated, but that's not the way it totally
feels. But if you put words with it, or even
vowel sounds, it does make a difference.'
14. See David's comments on this song in Rudman
(1964b): 'as we saw it, the only honest approach
was to do it off-beat musically. So we wrote it
as a jazz waltz which you will admit is very unlikely for commercial aspirations ... The sophisticated lyric I wrote obviously was not designed
for teen-age appeal.'

References

'Bacharach & David'. 1978. Unpaginated introduction to the songbook *Bacharach & David* (Hollywood, Almo Publications)

Blum, S. 1992. 'Analysis of musical style', In *Ethnomusicology: An Introduction* (pp. 165–218), ed. H. Myers (New York, W.W. Norton)

Brocken, M. 2003. *Bacharach: Maestro! The Life of a Pop Genius* (New Malden, Chrome Dreams)

Carpenter, R. 'Carpenters fans ask ... Richard answers'. http://www.richardandkarencarpenter.com/fans_ask_8.htm (accessed 12 September 2008)

Coleman, R. 1994. *The Carpenters: The Untold Story, An Authorized Biography* (New York, HarperCollins)

Cumming, A. 2001. 'There's always something there to remind me: the Burt Bacharach story', liner notes to *The Look of Love: The Burt Bacharach Collection*. WTVD 88384 (Canada, Warner Music Canada)

Cunningham, M. 1998. *Good Vibrations: A History of Record Production* (London, Sanctuary Publishing)

David, H. 'Words from Hal David'. http://www.haldavid.com/words.htm (accessed 20 August 2008)

DeMain, B. 1997. 'What's it all about Bacharach?', *Switch*, June. Reprinted in www.rocksbackpages.com (accessed 28 September 2008)

Diehl, D. 1970. 'Hal David ... poet in tempo', *Los Angeles Times*, 31 December, p. C15

DiMartino, D. 1998. 'Elvis Costello with Burt Bacharach: painted from memory', *Mojo*, October. Reprinted in www.rocksbackpages.com (accessed 30 September 2008)

Dominic, S. 2003. *Burt Bacharach Song by Song* (New York, Schirmer Trade Books)

Gracyk, T. 1996. *Rhythm and Noise: An Aesthetics of Rock* (Durham, Duke University Press)

Hebert, B. 1970. 'Bacharach – he's had winners in music, but few in racing', *Los Angeles Times*, 6 July, p. D8

Hilburn, R. 1970. 'Bacharach weighs his future', *Los Angeles Times*, 5 July, p. N37

Krims, A. 2000. *Rap Music and the Poetics of Identity* (Cambridge, Cambridge University Press)

O'Brien, L. 2002. *She Bop II: The Definitive History of Women in Rock, Pop and Soul* (New York, Continuum)

Olsen, E., Verna, P., and Wolff, C. 1999. 'Richard Carpenter', In *The Encyclopedia of Record Producers* (pp. 114–15) (New York, Watson-Guptill Publications)

Platts, R. 1997. 'Anyone who had a heart: the songs of Burt Bacharach and Hal David', *Discoveries*, December, pp. 48–54

Platts, R. 2003. *Burt Bacharach and Hal David: What the World Needs Now* (Burlington: Collector's Guide Publishing)

Ross, L. 1968. 'Hits', *The New Yorker*, 14 September, pp. 44–47

Rudman, K. 1964a. 'David & Bachrach [sic] profile: part 1', *Billboard*, 8 August, p. 14

Rudman, K. 1964b. 'David & Bachrach [sic] profile: part 2', *Billboard*, 15 August, p. 18

Saal, H. 1966. 'Gospel girl', *Newsweek*, 10 October, pp. 101–02

Saal, H. 1970. 'Burt Bacharach the music man 1970', *Newsweek*, 22 June, pp. 50–54

Shayne, B. 1968. 'Broadway score promises new spot for Bacharach', *Los Angeles Times*, 1 September, p. C7

Sutherland, S. 1986. 'Bacharach and Sager set sights on producing', *Billboard*, 16 August, pp. 24–25

Webb, J. 1998. *Tunesmith: Inside the Art of Songwriting* (New York, Hyperion)

Whitesell, L. 2008. *The Music of Joni Mitchell* (New York, Oxford University Press)
Wilson, J.S. 1968. 'Loyalty is a girl named Dionne', *New York Times*, 12 May, p. D17
Zak, A. 2001. *The Poetics of Rock: Cutting Tracks, Making Records* (Berkeley, University of California Press)
Zak, A. 2007. 'Editorial', *Journal of the Art of Record Production*, 1/ii, par. 3. http://www.artofrecordproduction.com (accessed 12 August 2008)
Zollo, P. 2003. *Songwriters on Songwriting* (Cambridge, Da Capo Press)

Discography

The Carpenters, 'Close to You'. A&M, 1183. 1970; rereleased on *Carpenters: The Singles*, A&M, CD-3601, n.d.
Chamberlain, Richard, 'They Long to Be Close to You'. MGM, K13170. 1963
Warwick, Dionne, '(They Long to Be) Close to You'. *Make Way for Dionne Warwick*. Scepter, 523. 1964; rereleased on Sequel Records, NEM, CD 761. 1995

Part II
Groove, Sampling and Production

[8]

FRANK SINATRA
The Television Years – 1950–1960

By Albert Auster

hatever else has been said about me is unimportant. When I sing, I believe, I'm honest. If you want
get an audience with you, there's only one way. You have to reach out to them with total honesty
d humility. (Frank Sinatra, *Playboy* Interview, 1963)

is oft-quoted comment, Frank Sinatra not only expressed his personal philosophy but
ally put into a nutshell what made him one of the century's foremost entertainers. It
that philosophy that contributed to his extraordinary success in records, radio, films,
concerts. Nevertheless, in one entertainment medium the intimacy and honesty that he
e of in that interview failed him, and it was ironically the most popular medium of all,
vision. In this article I will examine the period of Sinatra's most intense involvement
television (1950 to 1960, when he had two television series and made frequent special
earances), analyze the reasons for his failure, and point out his often overlooked television
esses.

hen Sinatra began appearing regularly on television in the early fifties, he was at a low
t in both his personal life and career. In 1950 he had divorced his first wife, Nancy, at a
vy financial cost and embarked on a tumultuous and sensationally publicized relationship
the actress Ava Gardner. He also had just been released from his movie contract with
M and, probably most disturbing of all, had lost his voice during an appearance at New
k's Copacabana nightclub [168].

inatra first appeared on television a month (31 May 1950) after the Copacabana debacle
Bob Hope's television special *The Star Spangled Revue.* A number of years later, after his
ed comeback, Sinatra appeared on Edward R. Murrow's *Person to Person* (14 September
6) and referred to that moment without being specific when the legendary journalist asked
ut the lowest point in his career. Sinatra thanked Hope for coming to his rescue when his
eer seemed in such jeopardy.

3y the time of his first television appearance Sinatra was already a seasoned veteran of
io and like many other stars of that medium was ready to take the plunge into television.
atra's radio career received its initial boost when he performed in 1935 as a member of the
boken Four on *Major Bowes' Amateur Hour* and later toured nationwide with the Major
1 his company. After Sinatra went out on his own, he did two stints as a singer on NBC's
r Hit Parade, had his own CBS radio show *Songs by Sinatra,* and afterward had a program
the ABC network, *Light Up Time.*

To contemporary viewers accustomed to special effects and glitz, *The Star Spangled Revue*
he epitome of a stone-age television variety show. The camera barely moves, and the sets
l production numbers would hardly do justice to a contemporary high school production.
netheless, with a nonpareil performer like Hope and guest stars such as Sinatra, Peggy Lee,
I Beatrice Lillie, the hour-and-a-half show, produced by the legendary television showman
x Lieberman (*Your Show of Shows*), is quite lively and entertaining. The show's producers

and writers made the most of Sinatra's first television appearance by having him anxi
ask Hope, "How do I look?" which led to an inevitable string of "skinny" jokes ("l
breadstick with legs"). Sinatra only sang one song on the show, so there was no stra
his recuperating vocal cords. Although his rendition of "Come Rain or Come Shine" i
especially noteworthy in the Sinatra oeuvre, it is still quite up to standards and shows fe
effects from the previous month's loss of voice. Of course, as a guest on a Bob Hope s
Sinatra also had to perform in comedy sketches: one sketch featured Hope and Sinatra in
as baseball players for the *Lydia Pinkham Tigers*, discussing makeup and mascara in a du
and another, a parody of a Hope and Crosby *Road* film, had Sinatra as Crosby, complete
big ears and a pipe.

The reviews were less than comforting for Sinatra. The *Variety* reviewer, although ec
about Hope ("The Hope of that 90 minute special was the hope of television – fulfilled")
less than enthusiastic about Sinatra. The reviewer acknowledged Sinatra's video debut
gave him some credit for his comedy work with Hope ("He [Hope] had stout help from F
Sinatra taking his video bow"), but the overall assessment was, "If TV is his oyster, Sir
hasn't broken out of his shell" (5 June 1950).

That program, which is in the collection of the Museum of Television and Radio, illust
the difficulties that Sinatra would later face with his own television series. When Sir
sings, the moment glows; however, when he does comedy routines or banters with co
or guests, the program becomes pedestrian, even banal. In *The Star Spangled Revue*, Hc
[169] consummate professionalism and ability to ad-lib, and a surprise guest appearanc
the ever-antic Milton Berle, rescue the comedy routines. When surrounded by such old
even Sinatra, whose lack of comic timing or physical presence is glaringly apparent, ga
bit of comic luster.

The Series

Television is too tough. (Frank Sinatra, *TV Guide,* 1955)

Variety's review notwithstanding, Sinatra was on the air with his own television sh
practically within a fortnight of his appearance on *The Star Spangled Review*. Despite
career slump, CBS seemed willing to take a chance on him in an hour-long variety sh
Saturday nights from 9:00 to 10:00. Unfortunately, the competition was the brilliant *Y
Show of Shows*, starring Sid Caesar and Imogene Coca, which caused Sinatra to commen
one show, "This is Paley's bad guess on CBS" (Friedwald 195).

Reviews of the show's premiere were either lukewarm or bad. John Crosby in the *New Y
Herald Tribune* said, "CBS, I think, has got hold of quite a valuable property in Sinatra,
I don't think the Sinatra show is exploiting him very skilfully" (30). *Variety*'s anonym
reviewers commented:

Production wise, those responsible for getting the show before the camera kept throwing sc
inexcusable curves at Sinatra. It was bad pacing, bad scripting, bad tempo, poor camera work an
overall jerky presentation. (11 October 1950)

r did things improve much when veteran producer Irving Mansfield took over the show. field referred to the situation as "hell" (Kelley 170–72). As he described it, "Frank was /s late, sometimes two and three hours late; he hated to rehearse, and refused to discuss weekly format. Usually he ignored the guest shots entirely" (Kelley 170–72). An added ·n was the distraction caused by Sinatra's affair with Ava Gardner. Thus, his first season ·nded into chaos.

e second season of the Sinatra show fared hardly any better. The show was moved to .p.m. Tuesdays opposite Milton Berle, then in his "Uncle Miltie – Mr. Television" heyday. ·rtheless, the program and Sinatra seem to have gained something from the first season's ·cle; some of Sinatra's charm finally breaks through. Writing in the *New York Times* Jack ·d described the second season's premiere: "He [Sinatra] does have a very real degree ·age presence and a certain likable charm, and in the comedy bits he acquits himself ·isingly well" (32). In the same review, however, Gould prophetically warned Sinatra and ·other crooner who might venture into the variety show format, "No doubt, Mr. Sinatra ·the star, but the evening's honors were captured effortlessly and smoothly by another ·eman, Perry Como" (32).

·e 1 January 1952 *Frank Sinatra Show* (the sole episode of that series in the collection ·e Museum of Television and Radio) illustrates both Sinatra's television strengths and ·nesses. The guests are an odd assortment – Louis Armstrong, the Three Stooges, actress ·ne De Carlo, and comedian George Dewitt. Because the show aired on New Year's Day, ·heme is a New Year's party at Sinatra's apartment. Sinatra sets the party's high note early by ·ing "There's Gonna Be a Great Day". From then on, it's all downhill as the Three Stooges ·r and agree to be Sinatra's butlers for the party with all the predictable anarchic mayhem. ·rest of the show is briefly rescued by Armstrong's rendition of "I'm Confessin" but takes ·se dive when De Carlo does a decidedly non-Desi Arnaz version of "Babaloo" and when ·vhole cast appears in a misconceived and unfunny sketch about Aladdin (an homage, no ·ot, to De Carlo's frequent appearances in Middle Eastern movie epics). It concludes on a ·imental note with Sinatra wishing a Happy New Year to the troops in Korea.

·gain, when Sinatra sings, the show soars; when he engages in stilted repartee or performs ·adly written comedy routines, it falters. But the problem may be more profound than poor ·ing or poorly chosen guests. Sinatra is trying to do it all – singing, comedy, bantering – ·he does not seem up to the task. In McLuhan's terms all this effort translates into a hot ·sonality trying to succeed in a notoriously cool medium – a medium, as Jack Gould so ·sciently pointed out, more amenable to the easygoing charms of a Perry Como than the ·nsity of a Frank Sinatra.

·onetheless, the general consensus that the first *Frank Sinatra Show* failed overlooks some ·ts successful elements. For one thing, as music critic Will Friedwald has pointed out, "most ·he music on these CBS outings is astoundingly good" (195). Another frequently neglected ·nt is that in its second season, the Sinatra show went up against Milton Berle in his prime. ·hough it did not score a ratings victory, the Sinatra show was the first program that put a ·nificant dent in Berle' share of the audience, knocking Berle from the number-one ratings ·ch that he had held for many years.

·ive years elapsed between the first and second Sinatra series. During that period, Sinatra ·de many guest appearances on television shows and specials. In 1957 Sinatra's second ·vision [170] series appeared. By then, Sinatra had made his film comeback with an Oscar-winning performance in *From Here to Eternity* (1954) and received a nomination for Actor in *The Man with the Golden Arm* (1955). He also had made a number of crit acclaimed, best-selling record albums. Those accomplishments established him as one reigning monarchs of the entertainment world. To capitalize on Sinatra's renewed perennially third-place ABC signed him to a much publicized $3 million contract (abou million in today's dollars) for 12 musical shows and 12 dramatic episodes, seemingly a for the network. Everything seems to point to a Sinatra triumph. He had weak compe from NCB's police drama *M-Squad* and CBS's rather weak sitcom *Mr. Adams and Eve* other networks seemed to have ceded 9:00 p.m. Friday night to *The Frank Sinatra Show*

Before Sinatra signed that lucrative ABC contract, however, there were ominous sign might have given both parties pause. In a 14 May 1954 article in *TV Guide*, "Can I Sinatra Make Good in TV", the author wrote:

> Sinatra is not exactly what a Siberian salt miner would call a bear for work. He combines a inclination toward laziness with a tendency to be moody. He doesn't mind working in spurts, bu the long haul he finds it something of a bore. Sinatra's moody component makes him unsuited role that otherwise would be right – the quiet, easy going emcee, who can spin a story, sing a so chat entertainingly with a visiting fireman. (*vide* Perry Como).

Furthermore, Sinatra decided to call all the shots himself. In an interview for *New World Telegram*, he said, "If I fall on my face, I want to be the cause.... All of the years I was taking advice from others they told me wrong 50 percent of the time" (Humphrey

Nevertheless, the opening show reviews were encouraging. In the *New York Herald Trib* critic John Crosby was practically ecstatic: "Sinatra has bounced back to become the he thing in Show Business, and for very good reason. He is one hell of a performer and his TV show was a triumph in almost all departments" (27). On the other hand, Jack Gould i *New York Times* was much more skeptical:

> Mr Sinatra's problems were those that seemed to be afflicting most vocalists who are going o their own this fall. When he was singing the program held our attention and he did some exce numbers.... But an hour's show cannot be sustained by one man alone and Mr Sinatra's him down badly. His patter with Bob Hope was second rate, and their sketch with Kim Novak came off. (30)

Sinatra's attempts at half-hour dramas also received mixed reviews. His first attempt, *Hogan Man*, was about a cabbie who adopts a brood of war orphans and then tries to fi mother for them. *Variety*'s reviewer wrote:

> Mr. S. envelopes himself with a certain aura of charm that has a way of spreading infection. him easy does it and it was too bad that Hal Goodman and Larry Klein didn't give him a toy with their well-worn tale of a bachelor father. Without Sinatra it would have been just an Runyonesque drollery that would shrivel in the heat of the opposition. For Sinatra it was a v opener for his half hour series". (28 October 1957)

None of the other dramatic episodes fared any better.

In 1957–58 Sinatra made at least two movies (*Kings Go Forth* and *Some Came Runn* and six record albums, endeavours that received some excellent reviews. The *Los Ang*

miner's critics described his performance in *Kings Go Forth*: "The thin singer has never
a more difficult role and he has never more completely nailed a characterization. Might
ell admit it, he's a great actor" (Ringgold and McCarty 72–73). But although the reviews
is screen appearances and record albums were outstanding, Sinatra's television show was
tly sinking. Even with no significant competition in its time slot, the Sinatra show was
een points behind in the ratings. His prestige on the line, Sinatra decided to take more of
ect hand in the show, and after December, the show was filmed before a studio audience.
tra also appeared on other shows, such as NBC's variety program *Club Oasis*, to plug
wn series. Although the quality of the shows improved, the ratings did not. Soon it was
ent that the Sinatra series was going nowhere. After failed efforts to peddle the series
nother network, the series was canceled, with the proviso that Sinatra would fulfil his
ract by doing a number of specials for ABC [171].

he eight 1957–58 *Frank Sinatra Shows* in the collection of the Museum of Television
Radio reveal a program that had settled into an all-too-familiar pattern by December
7. Usually, to a Nelson Riddle fanfare of "Tender Trap", Sinatra enters from the rear in
best *Pal Joey* manner. Surrounded by a bevy of beautiful chorus girls, he acknowledges
applause and then launches into a rendition of some familiar pop tune, after which he
duces his guest and banters a bit. If the guest is a singer, they then do a number; if
the guest usually does a comedy routine with Sinatra. The finale finds Sinatra alone on
e doing one of his classic numbers. If Sinatra felt comfortable with the guests, the show
erally rose above the formula; if he did not, the show was often leaden. When fellow rat-
ker Dean Martin was a guest, *Variety* wrote, "He seemed to enjoy the company of his guest
Dean Martin". However, the same reviewer also pointed out, "Sinatra doesn't have a well
ned personal concept for TV" (4 March 1958).

acking any distinctiveness, the *Frank Sinatra Show*'s failure was predictable – especially
. 1957–58 television season that included a glut of singer-hosted variety shows including
se of Dean Martin, Patti Page, Nat "King" Cole, Eddie Fisher, Polly Bergen, Rosemary
oney, Pat Boone, Guy Mitchell and Patrice Munsell (whose show was the lead-in to
atra's) in addition to the already very popular Perry Como and Dinah Shore shows.

n the rush to blame the show's failure on Sinatra's refusal to rehearse or the problems
sed by his status as a one-man entertainment conglomerate, critics usually forget that the
es was bucking a very strong cultural trend. The same year that Sinatra and his fellow
oners were singing away on the networks, those same channels were installing rock 'n' roll
America's premier music. For example, 1957 was the year that Alan Freed's *Big Beat* show
s presented for the first time. Dick Clark's *American Bandstand* went national on Sinatra's
n network, and Sinatra's *bête noire* Elvis Presley set ratings records in his first appearance
The Ed Sullivan Show. Sinatra's *Pal Joey* finger snapping did not stand a chance against
hip-swiveling rockers who soon dominated the airwaves.

Nevertheless, the long-running success of singers such as Dinah Shore and Perry Como
nds in stark contrast to Sinatra's failure – the advent of rock 'n' roll notwithstanding. Here
in, the McLuhan argument about the success of the cool personality in television provides
ne insight. Sinatra's intense personality was exacerbated by his tendency to be a wise
y and toss around in-jokes and double entendres. Jack O'Brian, in the *New York Journal
erican*, pointed this out:

> He [Sinatra] interpolates all sorts of Wise Guyism into his musically tasteful selections of
> the better standard popular songs. His interpolations take the form of frequent special refere
> "inside" jokes, oddnesses of Broadway urbanity vaguely veiled but leeringly plain to his prized
> guys. (24)

Variety seconded that opinion with its comment that the "worst aspect of the show,
that facet that seems to cause most discomfort is the dialogue, with Sinatra spouting a li
flip expressions that are supposed to be sophisticated and hep but come across as compl
mannered" (26 December 1957). Indeed, *Variety* gave a succinct summary of the reason
hot Sinatra personality was failing in this coolest of mediums: "He (Sinatra) can wor
the tension he wants into a song or even a performance, but on television you've got t
relaxed and you've gotta be straightforward and believable, or it's murder as Sinatra is
experiencing" (26 December 1957).

The Specials

> I am writing the most beautiful play you can imagine…. It's a little play with all the big sub
> in it; and it's a big play with all the little things of life impressed into it. (Thornton Wilder; lett
> Gertrude Stein, October 1937)

In contrast to his series, many of Sinatra's special appearances on television in the fi
were highly regarded, and some are considered classics. The most memorable of those
his role as the singing stage manager in the 1955 television musical version of *Our T*
It might be hard to fathom why Thornton Wilder, whose 1937 prize-winning drama
become an instant classic, agreed to have it made into a musical. Wilder's answer to
question was the flip comment, "It kept me in martinis for a year" (Simon 234). The mus
version of *Our Town* has probably become the best-remembered and most highly rega
of all the television productions of the play. Along with the money paid to Wilder for
rights, NBC spared no expense in mounting *Our Town* on its *Producer's Showcase* ser
which had already presented Mary Martin in the memorable musical version of *Peter*
and Humphrey Bogart in his television debut in a production of *Petrified Forest*. *Our T*
also starred Paul Newman and Eva Marie Saint as George and Emily and featured music
Sinatra's pals Sammy Cahn and Jimmy Van Heusen. One of the songs that Sinatra sang in
musical version, the classic "Love and Marriage" (now so unfortunately associated with
dysfunctional family sitcom *Married … with Children*), won an Emmy [172].

Although some were dismayed by the casting of Sinatra in the role of the Grovers Corr
philosopher, his reviews were good. (It has been reported that of all the actors who h
played the stage manager, Wilder hated Sinatra's portrayal the most). The *Times* critic wr
that Sinatra was "effectively unobtrusive and his songs were an important contribution to
success of the presentation" (Shanley 62). More important, the performance in *Our T*
affords a clear contrast between Sinatra's previous failures in his television series and w
made this show a success. For one thing, all Sinatra has to do in *Our Town* is sing and act, t
things he does very well. Although no one would mistake Sinatra's "Hobokenese" for "do
easter", with so many good actors (Ernest Truex and Phil Hartman in addition to Newm
and Saint) as well as the lovely Cahn and Van Heusen tunes, no one really notices. When

rrounded by good material and good actors Sinatra can't miss. The cool wisdom and
espun earthiness of Wilder's play also take the edge off the hot personality and outré
nerisms that caused problems in his television series.

natra did other successful specials for ABC to fulfil his contract. *Welcome Home,*
; was the highest rated, although Sinatra was a notorious critic of rock 'n' roll and also
ised Presley. Sinatra had publicly called Presley's music a "deplorable rancid smelling
odisiac" (Kelley 277). Nevertheless, because of his desire for high ratings, Sinatra hired
ley to make his first post-Army appearance on the 12 May 1960 show. To ease any
ntial animosity because of Sinatra's criticism, Presley was paid the phenomenal sum of
),000 for the guest spot.

n the show, Presley appears in his army uniform at the beginning and then does not
pear until the very end. In between, Sinatra cavorts with some members of the rat pack,
ding Joey Bishop, Sammy Davis Jr., and Peter Lawford. The show's premise involves
ne machine that allows Elvis to see what he has missed while in the army. This program
vcases the splendid talents of Davis, who sings, dances, and does imitations. Of course,
tra has his own numbers, which include "Gone with the Wind" and a "Young at Heart"
with his daughter Nancy. In addition, Joey Bishop makes an obviously scripted but
etheless telling aside to Sinatra that probably sums up the crooner's underlying animosity
ard the rocker. After hearing all the girls in the audience scream for Presley, Bishop
arks: "Listen to all those screams, but you wouldn't know about [173] that would you" –
ing him a double take of marvellously lofty disdain from Sinatra.

he highlight of the show is the finale, when Elvis sings. He appears in a tux while Sinatra
ns "Love Me Tender", and Elvis, swinging, sings "Witchcraft". Unfortunately, the
ersal does not inspire their best work, but that hardly mattered to the Presley fans in the
ience and at home, who gave the show a 45.1 trendex rating – the highest rating ever for
natra show.

resley's energy was so contagious that it did not matter whether Sinatra's persona was
, cool, or lukewarm for the special to succeed. A more representative example of a
cessful Sinatra television show is his *Edsel Show* appearance with Bing Crosby in October
7, shortly before he launched his second television series. Although that car has become
onymous with failure, the show was hardly an Edsel. It united two of the century's most
oortant pop music singers. Sinatra's admiration for Crosby went back to his youth when he
t a photo of the singer in his bedroom and even smoked a pipe to imitate him. Crosby also
nired Sinatra but expressed some good-natured rivalry with his famous quip, "Sinatra is a
ger who comes along once in a lifetime, it's too bad he had to come along in my lifetime".
3efore *The Edsel Show*, the two had appeared together in the 1956 film musical version of the
therine Hepburn, Cary Grant, and James Stewart classic *The Philadelphia Story*, renamed
gh Society and co-starring Grace Kelly, with music by Cole Porter. Their collaboration
ied out to be an excellent idea and *The Edsel Show* confirmed this. Besides the two singers,
show also starred Louis Armstrong, Rosemary Clooney, Crosby's son Lindsey, and Bob
pe in a surprise appearance. The two singers performed a number of duets and were also
ned at one point by Clooney for an almost 20 minute medley of standards. The show
oears graceful and effortless, and both singers seem to be enjoying themselves immensely.
e overriding image of the special is Sinatra's grinning from ear to ear, a vivid contrast to
often grim smiles he generally affected on his series.

Overall, when Sinatra could wrap himself in the charisma or easygoing charm of o▯
his specials succeeded. When he had to carry the ball himself, they were not nearly as ▯
A good example is his 15 February 1960 special, a Sinatra Valentine called "To the La▯
that featured Lena Horne and dancer Juliet Prowse, with a special appearance by ▯
Roosevelt. Although individually Sinatra and Horne's singing is excellent, there is practi▯
no chemistry in their duets. And the moment, saved until very last, when Mrs. Roos▯
appears, is extremely awkward. Sinatra seems so awestruck at being with the great ▯
(he greatly admired F.D.R. and in his *Person to Person* interview pointed to a sketch ▯
late president as one of his most prized possessions) that he seems almost to be kne▯
before the former first lady instead of sitting beside her. To put it mildly, their convers▯
is stilted and leans toward embarrassing until Mrs. Roosevelt volunteers to recite the l▯
to the Sinatra song "High Hopes" as her share in the entertainment. The moment doe▯
humiliate Roosevelt because her recitation of the children's song is filled with such
humor, humility, and sincerity.

An Evaluation

Don't order, suggest! (Frank Sinatra to a director of one of his films)

A look at Frank Sinatra's career in television in the fifties reveals a performer in the gr▯
a terrible dilemma. On the one hand, the fierce Sinatra competitive spirit made him wa▯
succeed at whatever he tried. On the other, the medium required a weekly grind that coul▯
up a career's worth of material in an evening, bowed to the iron grip of a ratings system ▯
more frequently rewarded conventionality than creativity, and catered to the rigid stand▯
of sponsors who were only interested in profits. It was a far cry from the movies, whe▯
star's whims could shut down production for days, and where box office numbers were ▯
as dictatorial but final career judgments might be postponed for months, even years. M▯
important, television was not like the recording studio, where Sinatra's best work was ▯
and where his perfectionism and sensitivity to mood brought out the best in everyone aro▯
him. As Bing Crosby once put it, (and Sinatra wholeheartedly concurred): "I like ma▯
records even more than movies. That's because you're constantly creating. And the g▯
thing about it is when you're finished recording, you've got something that's really your o▯
(Friedwald 25).

Television was hardly Sinatra's own. In his first series he was at the mercy of programm▯
who placed his show opposite two "golden age" giants, *Your Show of Shows* and *The Mi*▯
Berle Show. In his second, he himself was responsible for allowing the situation to deterio▯
by neglecting his television series in favor of the more spectacular rewards promised by ▯
recording dates and movies. More significantly, his personality seemed to grate on aver▯
television viewers. They might flock to his night club appearances, concert dates, and mo▯
because of the passion he infused into [174] a song or performance, but they preferred ▯
more reassuring, easygoing charms of Perry Como or Dinah Shore in the comfort of their ▯
living rooms. As for their children, the daughters and sons of the women who had screar▯
for Sinatra at the Paramount in 1944 had deserted him en masse for rock 'n' roll.

natra's talent only shone in his specials. With plenty of time to prepare, with guests who
lemented him in style and celebrity, the results were quite different than the series.
ite Sinatra's failure in the weekly television series format, he still leaves a large television
y. There are moments in the specials, especially in his songs, that compare favorably
any other performances in his career.

natra's songs – from his very first hit "I'll Never Smile Again", recorded during the
t Depression, through "My Way", which became an anthem of the greed-ridden eighties
ronicled America in the second half of the twentieth century. The songs also represent
areer of a modern popular singer who, through a combination of craft and sensibility,
able to infuse his melodies with passion and sensuality and exploit the unparalleled
ty of modern media to create an intimate connection with an audience. In Sinatra's case
connection remained secure despite the contradictions of a personal life that comprised
erse moments of rage and self-destructiveness as well as extraordinary acts of kindness
generosity. For many, the changes in Sinatra's life reflected their own: the move from an
lar ethnic community to the wider world of Hollywood and international stardom, career
ats and comebacks, the personal anguish of lost loves, even greater professional triumphs,
political shifts from liberalism to conservatism. His songs became the soundtrack of their
.

the long run, Sinatra's television performances stand beside his movie roles as evidence
is greatness. Jerome Kern was once asked about the place of Irving Berlin in American
ic, to which Kern replied, "Irving Berlin *is* American music". A similar response is
pos concerning Frank Sinatra's place in American entertainment.

RKS CITED

les, Jerry (1985), *A Thousand Sundays: The Story of the Ed Sullivan Show*, New York: G.P. Putnam's
ons, pp. 40–41.
sby, John, 'Hottest Thing in Show Business', *New York Herald Tribune*, 19 Oct. 1957, p. 27.
. 'Radio and Television: Frank Sinatra Seven Years Later', *New York Herald Tribune*, p. 30.
dwald, Will (1995), *Sinatra! The Song Is You*, New York: Scribners, p. 195.
ld, Jack, 'Radio and Television', *New York Times* 10 Oct. 1951, p. 32.
'TV: The Frank Sinatra Show', *New York Times* 19 Oct. 1957, p. 30.
nphreys, Hal, 'Sinatra Is Calling Own Signals Now', *New York World-Telegram* 13 Aug. 1957, p. 13.
ey, Kitty (1987), *His Way: The Unauthorized Biography of Frank Sinatra*, New York: Bantam, p. 170–72.
rian, Jack, 'Jack O'Brian's TViews: To Be Frank – a Long Show', *New York Journal-American*
9 Oct. 1957, p. 24.
uty, Howard H., ed. (1995), *Variety: Television Reviews, 1923–1988*, New York: Garland Publishing,
l. pag.
ggold, Gene, and Clifford McCarty (1985), *The Films of Frank Sinatra*, New York: The Citadel
ress, pp. 72–3.
nley, J.P., 'TV Our Town Still Entertaining', *New York Times* 20 Sept. 1955: p. 62.
on, Linda (1979), *Thornton Wilder: His World*, Garden City, NY: Doubleday, p. 234.

BERT AUSTER is an assistant professor in the Department of Communication and Media
dies at Fordham University.

[9]

Mediating *Music:* materiality and silence in Madonna's 'Don't Tell Me'

ANNE DANIELSEN† and ARNT MAASØ‡

†Department of Musicology, University of Oslo, PO Box 1017 Blindern, N-0315, Oslo, Norway
E-mail: anne.danielsen@imv.uio.no
URL: http://www.hf.uio.no/imv/om-instituttet/ansatte/vit/anneda-eng.xml

‡Department of Media and Communication, University of Oslo, PO Box 1093 Blindern, N-0317, Oslo, Norway
E-mail: arnt.maaso@media.uio.no
URL: http://www.media.uio.no/om-instituttet/ansatte/vit/arntm.xml

Abstract

This article investigates how the concrete sound of and recording process behind a pop tune relate to the possibilities and constraints of its electronic media. After a brief presentation of some theoretical issues related to the question of mediation and materiality, we address the claim that digitisation erases the material aspects of mediation through an investigation of contemporary popular music. Through a close analysis of the sound (and the silence) in Madonna's song 'Don't Tell Me', from the album Music *(2000), as well as in a handful of related examples, we argue that one can indeed identify specific aural qualities associated with digital sound, and that these qualities may be used to achieve different aesthetic effects as well as to shed light on mediation and medium specificity as such.*

Introduction

Mediating technology is considered a central and defining trait of popular music: pointing to a state 'before' or 'outside' of this mediation, a state of 'raw' or 'original' sound, makes no sense here. In principal, this is true of all music genres, since no music is unmediated. The acoustic surroundings of music mediate it in different ways: a large church hall and a room for chamber music are different sonic 'media'. However, while a classical musical recording is dominated by the principle of fidelity – 'of trying to create as realistic an impression of a musical performance as possible – however artificial that "realism" actually was' (Clarke 2007, p. 14) – the role of mediating technologies in popular music is different on at least two counts. First, the recording is the primary medium for popular music. The introduction of certain mediating technologies has thus delimited the field of popular music, in the sense that they are a constitutive aspect of it – part of the origin of the field itself.[1] Second, there is a sophisticated tradition for highlighting, playing with, and commenting on mediating technologies within popular music practices.

In this article we will investigate how the concrete sound of and recording process behind a pop tune relate to the possibilities and constraints of its electronic media. We seek a more nuanced understanding of the specific and historical roles of different media used for both music production and music consumption (for example, radios, home stereos, personal stereos), as well as the role of mediating technologies that cut across these media (for example, analogue versus digital sound). The age digitisation has occasioned claims of *convergence*, of a 'post-medium' state that reduces the role of individual media such as home stereos, radio and television; we will therefore also address the assumption that digitisation erases the 'material aspects' of musical recording. We will not discuss the *medium specificity* of these media in a modernist sense (such as claiming that the essence of painting is 'flatness'; see Krauss 2000). Still, we believe that technology *is* important for the particular sound of popular music – as are the social and institutional practices of music and media production – and that this has not been radically changed by the introduction of digitisation.

After a brief presentation of some theoretical issues related to the question of mediation and materiality, we will address the claim that digitisation erases the material aspects of mediation – thus bringing about a totally new post-medium condition – through an investigation of contemporary popular music beginning with Madonna's song 'Don't Tell Me', from the album *Music* (2000). Through a close analysis of the sound (and the silence) in this song, as well as in a handful of related examples, we will argue that one can indeed identify specific aural qualities associated with digital sound, and that these qualities may be used to achieve different aesthetic effects as well as to shed light on mediation and medium specificity as such.

Music in a post-medium condition?

Writing in the mid-1980s, Friedrich Kittler joined many of his contemporaries in forecasting a loss of materiality and difference among media due to their digitisation (and hence convergence). His claim is straightforward:

> The general digitisation of channels and information erases the differences among individual media. Sound and image, voice and text are reduced to surface effects, known to consumers as interface. ... Inside the computers themselves everything becomes a number: quantity without image, sound or voice. And once optical fiber networks turn formerly distinct data flows into a standardised series of digitised numbers, any medium can be translated into any other. (Kittler 1999, pp. 1–2)

Thus the very *concept* of a medium loses its significance, according to Kittler and his fellow critics, as digital media converge through fibre-optic networks. A related argument proposes that digitised media lose the qualities associated with the process of recording and distribution when compared with the mediation and reproduction processes of analogue media. In their eulogy to the phonograph, Eric W. Rothenbuhler and John Durham Peters join those who draw a sharp distinction between analogue and digital media while raising interesting claims about the semiotic status of their respective sounds:

> In terms of the logic of the sign-referent relation, the difference between analog recording and digital recording is the difference between indexes and symbols in Peirce's scheme. The analog recording is an index of music because it is physically caused by it. The digital recording is a symbol of music because the relation is one of convention. (Rothenbuhler and Peters 1997, p. 249)

One certainly might question the premise that an analogue recording bears a direct physical relationship to an original sound event, though this was once the ase, during the era of direct engravings of live performances. For most of popular music's history, however, even analogue recordings have been compiled from multiple recordings or sessions, not unlike digital recordings. Furthermore, digital recordings have routinely been released in both analogue and digital versions, ever since Ry Cooder's *Bop Till You Drop* (1979) was recorded digitally. Thus, even analogue records may be the result of a digital recording process, as analogue recording equipment is often used in the production of CDs. In other words there are often no 'pure' chains of either analogue or digital mediation, as Rothenbuhler and Peters seem to assume. This is the case with more recent as well as older analogue recordings.

In addition to challenging the problematic 'indexical/physical' premise in Rothenbuhler and Peters's argument regarding the recording process, we would like to discuss the distinction they make between digital and analogue *reproductions*. In Rothenbuhler and Peters's view, not only does digital recording lack an indexical relation to a physical aural event but the digital *record* – the compact disc, in this case – bears no indexical trace of its *use*. Digital sound can be reproduced without any generational loss and played back without any signs of wear and tear over time. In contrast, the playback of analogue records

audibilises two histories: one of the recording and one of the record. ... The data encoded on the CD do not mix with the history of the disk; they can be obscured by dirt and scratches, but dirt and scratches cannot sound from a CD player. As the history of records speaks while they are being played, they thus invite us to think about the passage of time; by contrast, CDs obscure it. (Rothenbuhler and Peters 1997, p. 255)

Clearly, the history of an LP becomes part of its sound. The question is, however, do digital recordings offer something similar? Madonna's song 'Don't Tell Me' uses a familiar pop and rock format: the instrumentation is modelled on the traditional lead vocal with a band, and the form of the song is binary, with verse and chorus. We could even say that contrary to the sound and texture of much contemporary dance music, which is almost unthinkable without recent technological developments,'Don't Tell Me' could have resulted from analogue tape recording techniques or even a live performance.[2] The song's medium, or mode of production and reproduction, however, plays an important part in both its musical and its cultural significance. One of the most striking material traces of mediation on this track is the use of 'digital dropouts'. The effect mimics a CD player having problems reading the information on a disk, which can happen with a dirty or scratched CD or a 'worn-out' laser. In both cases, the effect is indeed caused by wear and tear, and the result may be understood as an index of use in the sense reserved by Rothenbuhler and Peters for analogue playback alone. Thus digital sound and reproduction technology can in turn invite us to think about the 'passage of time' or the 'history of the disk', to use Rothenbuhler and Peters's terms. Furthermore, digital technology can invite listeners to reflect upon the act of mediation and technical reproduction, as will become clearer below. In the following we will dwell on the introduction of the silent pauses in the opening bars of this song and what they may mean, and also discuss how this effect changes its meaning and function in the course of the song.

'Textual' and 'medium silence' in 'Don't Tell Me'

Silence functions differently in various media and communicative situations. In pantomime, for instance, silence is part of the 'frame' and therefore represents a normal state with no special relevance or import. In theatre, however, silence is communicative activity[3] that must be interpreted in relation to whatever precedes or follows it. Planned silence might also appear as part of the scripted performance and is often written as pauses in plays, film scripts, music notation, and so on. When silence is a part of the text whether as performed or scripted, we call it *textual silence.* Both performative and scripted textual silence might range from a dramatic cæsura to a form of 'neutral' space. In groove-oriented music, for example, the space between the notes creates the 'groove' – where and how the sound ends is as much a part of the rhythmic pattern as where and how it starts (Danielsen 2006b, p. 54). This is, however, a form of textual silence that is commonly non-attended and devoid of drama. Conversely, when the old Cantor in the classic movie *The Jazz Singer* (Crosland 1927) surprises his son (Al Jolson) singing *jazz* in his home, he cries 'STOP!', resulting in a nineteen-second pause before dramatic music resumes beneath the action, the silence is dramatic. This stunning gesture is perhaps the first theatrical use of *textual* silence in cinematic dialogue (and perhaps in cinema altogether).

In addition to the broad categories of silence as a state or frame for perform-ance and silence as communicative activity in the form of performative or scripted textual silence, aural media, such as stereos, radio, television, film, and so on, may invoke a 'medium silence', where the medium ceases to function as an error of technology. Put differently, when early sound films such as *The Jazz Singer* were introduced in theatres, medium silence through equipment failure or human error was much more common than textual silence, as exemplified in the following newspaper account of the first sound film exhibition in an Oslo cinema:

The same way people from the countryside quickly get used to the clatter and noise of the city, the silent movie supporter will soon enough come to accept the many noises of the sound film. We experienced this already yesterday: When the sound equipment shut down ... and the movie finally went silent, it not only seemed comic, but the mute scenes seemed empty and stupid. (*Arbeiderbladet*, 12 September 1929)

Medium silence such as this is of course typically non-intentional and even considered a major taboo, as with 'dead air' in commercial broadcasting.[4]

A form of medium silence may, however, also be used for aesthetic purposes and even assume a communicative role similar to that of textual silence. In Madonna's 'Don't Tell Me', the CD as a digital medium, and the possibilities of digital dropout, are exploited right from the beginning of the song.[5] The sonogram shown in the Figure gives a visual representation of the digital dropout, showing how the so-called 'digital black' cut-outs (represented in white) make the music skip the first beat of the second bar. As shown in the sonogram, the silence in 'Don't Tell Me' is, on a technical level, 'digital silence': the signal drops out completely, leaving no hiss or other 'dead air'-related sound but instead a complete lack of sound.

The presence of digital silence in 'Don't Tell Me' is framed by the generic expectations raised by the acoustic riff during the first bar, which drive us to expect a repeated – or developed – rhythmic figure in the following bar. When silence is 'introduced' on the fourth beat, one might expect it to be an 'active' silence in the sense described above in theatre, one that increases the tension and encourages our expectations of an answering phrase or riff. However, designed as a *complete silence* – a 'digital black' – it is clearly *not* part of such generic conventions and thus seems strange, even inappropriate. Hence, when the riff then reappears in 'mid-air' during the fifth beat, confirming a missed downbeat and the cut-off of the musical

'Don't Tell Me' (sonogram)

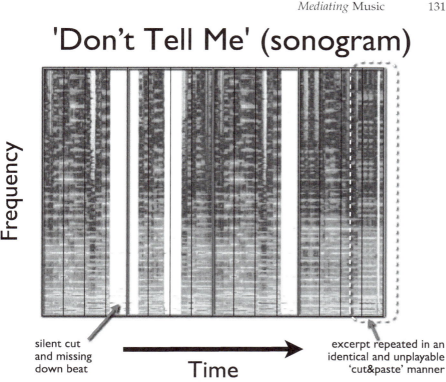

Figure. Sonogram of the first four bars of the introduction to 'Don't Tell Me'. A grid is added with fine lines representing each new quarter-note beat; the thicker lines mark new bars.

phrase, the silence is at least for some seconds clearly proven to be a 'digital dropout' – that is, a medium silence. It ceases to be part of the text and is instead (at least initially) marked as a technical error, which in turn drains the pause of the potential communicative force it would have retained if the riff reappeared on the 'downbeat'.[6]

When the subsequent silent pauses begin to form a rhythmic pattern in a steady temporal flow, however, the framework changes, and we hear the seemingly random digital dropouts as a highly meaningful device, rhythmically and otherwise. In other words, it soon becomes clear that the presence of digital dropouts on this track is *not* a sign of a worn-out or broken medium. After this category shift from medium silence to textual silence has taken place, however, the effect of the dropout still plays on the initial similarity between the two, continuing to signify a form of digital 'weariness'. This connotation only gradually fades away, as the effect of the digital dropout becomes less conspicuous until it mimics a more or less neutral and almost purely musical pause.

The use of silence in 'Don't Tell Me' takes on yet another layer of meaning in light of the lyrics. Whereas *sound* has long been associated with life, fullness, temporal progression, and community, silence has been associated with death, emptiness, temporal immobility, and isolation.[7] Along these lines, the use of silence in 'Don't Tell Me' may be 'making audible' the place outside of sound *and* time that

is alluded to in the lyrics. After the dropout effect is introduced in the intro, the firs˙
verse reads:

Don't tell me to stop
Tell the rain not to drop
Tell the wind not to blow
'Cause you said so, mmm

This is underscored by the way Madonna's voice is edited. The word 'stop' in the
first line tellingly ends with a silenced 'p', giving the impression of a human voice
suddenly being cut off and underscoring the lyrics' allusion to immobility, break in
temporal flow, or absence of life. The effect of the inserted silence in this song, then,
is threefold: initially it comprises an indexical sign of the act of digital mediation;
then it is a repeated and purposeful musical-aesthetic effect; finally, it is a rhetorical
gesture related to the theme of the song.

Mediation as a signifier of past and present

As was pointed out above, the role of silence in 'Don't Tell Me' is atypical of the
singer-songwriter tradition and the country music genre alluded to by the format
and instrumentation of the song. This discord between musical style and mode of
mediation is crucial to the initial interpretation of the digital black as medium
silence. The resonance of the digital dropout also raises the issue of digital mediation
more generally as part of our appreciation of the song: Even when it has become
'normalised' as an almost purely musical negative of the rhythmic pattern, the
dropouts still signify their medium in the way they add to the rhythmic and textural
qualities of the sound. When the additional layers of rhythm have entered the
sound, the groove in general contributes to this identification of a 'digital signature',
as it conveys a highly quantised, digitised feel that is typical of much club music
from the digital era. This rhythmic character could not have been realised in the
same way – at least not to such an extent – through analogue media, for several
reasons. First, analogue media are rarely able to reproduce silence without any
noticeable hum or noise, as can the digital black. Second, there are many quantised
tracks operating here according to a subdivision of 32nds. The hi-hat, for example,
may have been produced by quantising a poorly played hi-hat pattern: quite a few
strokes seem to be positioned in odd places, most typically one 32nd before or after
what would, in a played groove, be regarded as a more idiomatic location. The bass
drum also contributes to this quantised feel. The upbeats to the downbeats are
straight 32nds, and throughout the song there are some characteristic recurring bass
drum rolls of 32nds. Such micro-rhythmic designs are unplayable on a drum kit.
Finally, the last beat of the fourth bar has a short soundbite likewise repeated in a
way that is impossible for a musician in a live performance (both in its rhythm and
its utterly identical sound) but easy to 'copy and paste'.[8] Borrowing from Stan
Hawkins, this song is realised in ways that 'make live performances simulated
events' (Hawkins 2004b, p. 6).

The sound production of 'Don't Tell Me' is not unique in displaying the
signature of its mediating technologies. Another distinctive artist employing similar
techniques from the same time period is Squarepusher, the performing pseudonym
of British electronic music artist Thomas Jenkinson. In 'My Red Hot Car' on the
album *Go Plastic* (2001), the presence of digital music technologies leaps out from the
very first bar. The 'high-definition' feel of the programmed, quantised rhythm tracks

and processed voice are the first signs of digital mediation. The most striking sign, however, occurs in the middle section of the song, where Jenkinson explores the possibilities of digital editing via an extensive montage of chopped-up sonic material that results in an ironically 'well-formed cacophony' of sounds.

The use of silence in this case, though, is quite distinct from 'Don't Tell Me'. While we clearly hear the silent 'bursts' as digital silences in 'My Red Hot Car', they never resonate as medium silences but wholly as textual ones. In fact, Squarepusher's gaps of silence attract little attention at all. First, they are either much shorter than in 'Don't Tell Me' or enveloped in other continuous patterns of sound or reverb. In addition, the rhythmic use of silence only gradually appears in the song after a sixteen-bar intro, when a chopped-up vocal enters on top of a repeated four-bar pattern in drums, bass, and synth organ that continues into the verse. The musical silence here represents a playful processing of digitised sound rather than a digital dropout of the medium itself, and the pauses are neutral gaps between the sounds, 'negatives' in the rhythmic pattern. They are no less important for this, of course, and lend the song its specifically contemporary feel through their clear display of a digital signature.

While 'My Red Hot Car' points to one specific moment in the history of music production, 'Don't Tell Me' plays on the relation between old and new in popular music, as well as on the contemporary listener's sensitivity to the aural signatures of different media. In a short essay called 'The revenge of the intuitive', Brian Eno reminds us that artists often play on these sensitivities: 'in the end the characteristic forms of a tool's or a medium's distortion, of its weakness and limitations, become sources of emotional meaning and intimacy' (Eno 1999). Joseph Auner, in an essay called 'Making old machines speak: images of technology in recent music', also addresses the meanings produced by relating old and new technologies in music. From the pre-digital era he points to Pink Floyd's montage of old and new media on the album *Wish You Were Here* (1975). In the transition between 'Have a Cigar' and 'Wish You Were Here', the poor, noisy sound of an old distribution medium, an AM transistor radio, is contrasted with the crisp, intimate sound of the new technology of that time, home stereo equipment (Auner 2000, pp. 7–9).

From the digital era, Auner uses several songs by Portishead to demonstrate how the foregrounding of recording media and musical technologies may be further deployed 'to engage tradition and to manipulate memory and time' (Auner 2000, p. 13). As he rightly points out, Portishead can produce a very strong emotional charge simply by using samples and allusions to outmoded styles, old movies, and soundtracks in a highly stylised, sometimes ironic, way. While the use of overtly marked analogue sound here may serve several functions, such as exposing vulner-ability or an aching subjectivity, Portishead's focus on the limitations and weak-nesses of old mediation technologies, such as the noise caused by dust and scratches on a well-used (and therefore well-loved) vinyl LP, contributes to a sense of nostalgia – the mourning for a lost past that runs through many of their songs. Nevertheless, Portishead also emphasises the contemporary digital technologies through which they create their effects. In this respect, Portishead's use of old modes of mediation differs from a more traditional nostalgic use, where the expressiveness of the old modes is left undisturbed by the transparency of the contemporary media actually in charge of the mediation

As Auner also points out, old technologies often connote authenticity, warmth, or wholeness, while the framing contemporary mechanisms that mediate these old sounds remain inaudible.[9] In one of the Portishead examples discussed by Auner, 'Cowboys' from the album *Portishead* (1997), a highly distorted electric guitar is sampled and looped. Instead of playing on this instrument's connotations to rock authenticity, however, the sample is used in a way that not only foregrounds 'the fragility and imperfections of the old materials, but exposes their artificiality' (Auner 2000, p. 30). In fact, the sound of this 'guitar' is so remote from the sound of a traditional rock guitar that it would not be likely to trigger these associations at all. It is also possible that the source of Portishead's guitar sound is, for example, a synthesizer instead. Auner's point is valid regardless: instead of letting the act of mediation remain transparent, Portishead foregrounds their mediating technologies, impacting both the sound and the meaning of their music. In another example, 'Undenied' (*Portishead*, 1997), Auner points to the group's play on absolute digital silence versus noisy vinyl silence (Auner 2000, p. 14). The song is in fact marked by continuous vinyl noise, but it is interrupted at two key moments, when its absence – revealing the digital silence enveloping the musical sounds – intensifies the emotional tension and the charged, trembling voice of singer Beth Gibbons.

According to Mark Katz, vinyl noise, real or digitally simulated, is now firmly part of our modern sonic vocabulary and can be powerfully evocative: 'In the age of noiseless digital recordings, this sonic patina prompts nostalgia, transporting listeners to days gone by' (Katz 2004, p. 146). Eric Clarke also points to the distant and nostalgic quality of 'worn vinyl' (Clarke 2007, p. 19). In Katz's view, this 'phonograph effect', as he calls it, first became a valued and meaningful sound when digital technology eliminated it. However, as pointed out above, even though digital mediation is literally noiseless, there are other forms of 'noise' that display the signature of the medium. How do these traces of digital mediation signify in relation to this exchange between past and present modes?

In the Madonna universe, there is no mourning, not even an ironic one, for the loss of the past. Nor is there any attempt to restore its sound. Instead of commenting on the limitations and weaknesses of old technologies, or exploring their potential expressiveness, Madonna and her production team bring the presence and potential malfunction of a *contemporary* medium to the fore: it is the weaknesses and limitations of the new that are put into play. In fact, Madonna's use of an old, or perhaps timeless, format (the song), past technologies (the acoustic guitar), and a traditional musical style (country) comes close to the Jamesonian notion of pastiche, in that there is no claim for the validity of the relation to a presumed origin, a real past, or a real tradition, nor is there a 'satiric impulse' in the use of these elements (Jameson 1984, pp. 65, 67). Instead, the past and the musical tradition possibly representing it are approached by way of connotations to previous styles. In this respect, Madonna's music resembles Beck's highly eclectic use of former styles and genres, a feature also commented upon by Auner in his essay (Auner 2000, p. 16).

In fact, the way in which the dialogue between tradition and contemporary music technology evolves in 'Don't Tell Me' resonates with an overarching theme of the album *Music*, and of Madonna's oeuvre in general: the play with, reinvention of, and cooptation of stereotypical identities and forms.[10] In parallel with how Sean Albiez (2004) describes Madonna's visual image as 'a hyperreal urban/rural cowgirl ... a club version of the Western look', the musical solutions in 'Don't Tell

'Me' demonstrate a resonant artistic strategy: 'Don't Tell Me' is the club version of country-pop. Moreover, its polished sound bears all of the signs of glamour and artifice commonly associated with a Madonna production. As Albiez writes, there is very little on the album that 'announces itself as Country music per se, but the turn to acoustic instrumentation within a digital environment and songwriting that alludes to acoustic singer-songwriter ... mixes the organic with future machine music' (Albiez 2004, p. 131). The traces of the process of mediation, whether enacted upon the presence of a digital medium or the iconography of Western music, transform country and western – a style connoting authenticity and traditional American values – into a sort of hyperreal travesty. Neither the singer-songwriter tradition nor the country genre (and the modes of production associated with both) necessarily imply something outdated in the first place. When juxtaposed with digitally chopped-up rhythms, however, the song format and instrumentation appear to belong to another era.

The use of digital silence as a marker of digital mediation takes on very different meanings in Portishead's nostalgic, 'second-hand' aesthetics and Madonna's pastiche-like musical style. Still, in both contexts, the audible interplay between the signatures of old and new (re)production media has in fact become an indispensable part of the meaning of the songs, both aesthetically and semantically. Moreover, when Madonna uses the silent dropouts as an allusion to the fragility of digital sound production, this is not immediately recognisable as a conventional sign of historicity, such as the phonograph effect mentioned above, or scratches on film. In the course of the song, however, she makes the digital glitch into an effect marking the specificity and historicity of a contemporary medium. And in marking the present as history in this way, she also completes a powerful act of communication, asserting her sensitivity to contemporary culture as well as her power to pull back from it and 'go meta'. In a few bars of music Madonna and her team of producers and engineers comment wryly that digitisation is passé (and so 1999) while asserting Madonna's place as the Queen of (or over?) Pop.

Stardom and genre: economic and industrial factors

If produced differently – for example, as a 'live' performance – 'Don't Tell Me' could perhaps have supported the claim that the medium in the age of digital reproduction leaves no mark on the content. However, Madonna is a branded pop star, which means that there are certain industry and listener assumptions regarding the 'package' Madonna ought to deliver. As Hawkins points out, the potential of her 'authenticity' lies in the possibilities of her transformation, and her authorial position 'remains bound up in the construction of herself through visual and sonic production' (Hawkins 2002, p. 52). One aspect of this concerns her use of state-of-the-art production methods – how she 'skilfully recycles herself through music technology' (Hawkins 2004a, p. 189). Another (related) aspect concerns her tendency to pick up, explore, and comment upon the latest innovations and trends. One might ask whether it is even possible for an artist like Madonna to record 'Don't Tell Me' without commenting on the medium and the 'artificiality' of its potentially nostalgic format.

So how does the manufacturing of stardom impact the discussion of digital technology, and of media specificity versus media convergence? As Frith and

136   *Anne Danielsen and Arnt Maasø*

Goodwin point out, the most important commodity produced by the music industry may not be records or songs but stars (Frith and Goodwin 1990, p. 425) We might then say without downplaying Madonna's artistic intentions that economic and institutional music industry constraints linked with the branding of Madonna the star could have overruled any alternative strategy in her appropriation of genre, or at least of new technology. Even though country music is a new field of 'research' for Madonna, her pastiche-like approach to tradition in 'Don't Tell Me' resonates with earlier Madonna productions, which also play with stereotypical identities and forms. Moreover, the song displays her signature polished, 'artificial' sound.

Then there is the different role of technology in various genres. Although new media have powerfully impacted the development of the cultural industries in general, they hold different positions and have different uses in, for example, country and pop music, respectively. As Keith Negus has pointed out, a particular genre in fact represents an entirely novel form of creation, circulation, and consumption of popular music: 'Genre categories inform the organisation of music companies, the creative practices of musicians and the perceptions of audiences' (Negus 1999, p. 3). Particular 'genre cultures' develop different ways of producing and distributing music, including the appropriation and use of new technology. This means that even if digital technology is central to the production and distribution of both country *and* contemporary pop music, it brings with it different expectations regarding how it will be used and, especially, whether it will be allowed to leave its mark on the sound. In a genre culture like country, which concerns itself less with contemporariness or artificiality and more with authenticity and tradition, the ideal is media transparency. The actual mediating medium, digital music technology, ought to disappear in favour of the audibility of a vintage medium, such as steel guitar or analogue recording devices.

In other words, when we consider the role of mediating technologies in the age of digital reproduction, other factors such as the manufacturing of stars or the 'genre culture' of the musical tradition may in fact override the technological 'imperative' – the tendency to use the latest technological innovations in the most contemporary way (a tendency that is often assumed by the discourse on technological mediation of music within technically oriented disciplines).[11] Nor can we overlook economic interests: even though the culture industry ultimately depends on innovation, the development of new products – artists or musical styles – is expensive and risky. Thus, as David Hesmondhalgh points out, the creative autonomy of artists is often ultimately limited, and there is a danger that any change in artistic direction will receive an unsympathetic response from the record company (Hesmondhalgh 2002, p. 169).

Last but not least, listeners' expectations of Madonna clearly limit her choice of artistic 'course'.[12] Pop music is a dialogue between artists and their audiences, or, in the words of Negus, 'Musical sounds and meanings are not only dependent upon the way an industry is producing culture, but are also shaped by the way in which culture is producing an industry' (Negus 1999, p. 13). Madonna cannot be nostalgic, then, nor can she leave her medium unremarked. Her music is *expected* to include connotations of contemporariness, such as the use of medium silence. Moreover, it is in the interest of the culture industry to maintain these different cultural spheres and channels of circulation. The act of mediation cannot be separated from such forces.

Distribution media and listening practices

So far we have discussed expectations related to production and institutional practices, but there are also issues surrounding the sonic constraints of distribution media, as well as associated listening practices. The fact that music is *distributed* digitally, and that this form of distribution is shared with other digitised types of information – pictures, text, and so on – does not mean that music is no longer different from graphics, or that radio listening is no longer different from using an iPod. Convergence as applied to new media is often (mis)used as a 'totalising term', covering everything from 'black boxes' to markets, networks, and rhetoric (see Fagerjord and Storsul 2007). Hesmondhalgh, discussing Manuel Castell's analysis of the role of media in the information age, criticises what he calls Castell's 'homogenisation-through-convergence' hypothesis. Hesmondhalgh finds, for example, that the development within the cultural industries after World War II – during what he calls 'the complex professional era' – is characterised by 'a pattern whereby new technologies tend to supplement existing ones, rather than replacing or merging them, leading to an accretion of separate devices' (Hesmondhalgh 2002, p. 236). According to Hesmondhalgh, this pattern has not changed significantly during the last twenty years.

The fact that old and new technology can exist in parallel means that digital audio technology as a medium is always going to be understood in relation to earlier audio-related technologies and practices. This fact impacts how the juxtaposition of different mediating technologies may be used to comment upon the passing of time via the historicity of a particular medium's signature. When Auner addresses Pink Floyd's transition between 'Have a Cigar' and 'Wish You Were Here' (*Wish You Were Here*, 1975), he writes that it

sounds as if it is sucked out of the speakers into a lo-fidelity AM radio broadcast. The radio is evoked first through the cramped, tinny sound quality and static, and then confirmed as the radio is retuned through several channels – in what is itself a striking trajectory through newscasts, discussions, and excerpts of symphonic music – before settling down on a station broadcasting a mellow guitar accompaniment. As the radio continues to play, we become directly aware of the person in the room who has been tuning the radio, as he clears his throat, sniffs, and then starts to play along on an acoustic guitar. (Auner 2000, p. 8)

Importantly, this effect, writes Auner, would not in itself have been recognisable to someone listening to it on a portable AM transistor radio. Rather, the effect depends on FM stereo or home stereo listening, which boomed in the mid-1970s, when this record came out.

Similarly, the effect of the digital dropouts in 'Don't Tell Me' depends on a certain kind of distribution medium and playback in order to achieve the status of, first, medium silence, then textual silence. Two typical ways of hearing 'Don't Tell Me' would be on the radio or on a CD player connected to home stereo equipment. In both cases, it is likely, at least the first time, that the listener would experience the dropouts as a sign of a bad CD player, before realising that this was but another of Madonna's clever tricks. In the case of radio listeners, there could be no way of knowing for sure, listening to the musical text alone, whether the song was being played on a CD player, DAT, or hard drive, for that matter. Yet the effect of this well-known digital glitch associated with CDs is likely to make listeners assume a mechanical failure.[13] In both cases the initial silence would be heard as medium silence – that is, a problem with the CD player – not as textual silence or an aesthetic effect. If, however, the listener saw the video on MTV or bought the LP, she would, for different reasons, probably immediately have heard this as textual silence. In the video, the continuous movement of the image would have indicated that there was nothing wrong with the TV signal. In the first seconds of the music video, Madonna is walking along a highway toward the camera in a tracking shot. Her movements freeze simultaneously with the silent dropouts. However, the camera movement continues seamlessly, revealing that Madonna is performing in front of a blue screen. After the frozen silent pauses, the camera continues tracking out with Madonna 'in sync' with the background until it reveals the frames of the blue screen and the artificial setup for the video, with Madonna walking on a treadmill. In any case, the juxtaposition of the continuous movement in the background and Madonna's frozen movements in the foreground immediately reveals that these are not technical errors but part of an intended aesthetic effect.[14]

In the case of the LP, Madonna's dropout effect simply does not make sense within the context of the technological constraints and possibilities that record players afford (see note 6). (Flaws more typical for LPs as technologies would be bursts of 'white noise' or a Portishead-like scratchiness.)

Listening conditions and the choice of playback medium therefore influence the way certain artistic effects are heard. This also points to the inherent problem of judging material traces of technology and mediation from listening alone. As Umberto Eco wrote three decades ago, it is a fundamental characteristic of *any* sign that it can be used to tell a lie (Eco 1976, pp. 58–9). Any act of mediation thus introduces something 'between' the original sound (if such a thing exists) and the hearing of this sound. The hiss of history sometimes heard on CDs may thus be the sign of a digitised version of a vintage recording as well as a post-1980s pop production parasitically sucking the authenticity, grandeur, and historicity from the scratches of an old record.

Moreover, when it comes to radio listening, whether or not 'Don't Tell Me' is produced and transmitted by analogue or digital means is in some ways subordinate to the radio itself as a medium for the shaping of the song's sound. For example, institutional and economic factors, such as the signing of stars to fit radio play (as indicated above) as well as the generic constraints of radio formatting (see Maasø 2002b), have played pivotal roles in the shaping of pop music's sound in the past, and they will continue to do so in the digital future. Also relevant to claims of convergence is the fact that listening practices will most likely *not* converge but rather diverge as people are provided with even more possibilities for mobile and private listening on an increasing number of listening devices. Thus, the fact that media and mediation are increasingly digital does not imply convergence on all levels and in all senses, but rather a complex mix of processes of divergence and convergence.

Progress and nostalgia

As pointed out above, *new* digital technological means rely on established cultural modes. Also, the latest work of Madonna and her producers follows from what has come before. In general, Madonna's 'Don't Tell Me' fits well into the 'genre culture' of contemporary pop music and its expectations concerning the creation, circulation and consumption of this tradition. By the same token, the appropriation of new technology happens first and foremost within the framework of existing values and practices (see also Danielsen 2006a), not in a cultural vacuum.

This framework includes a persistent faith in the transparency of contemporary media that can be linked to narratives of progress and innovation underlying the story of new technology within modernity.[15] This faith is not limited to the present, of course. We might therefore ask why digital audio is necessarily a particularly strong candidate for transparency 'forever'. At some point in time, will not digital audio come across as dated or obsolete as well, thus succumbing to the dialectic of old and new described by Auner? In this dialectic, old technologies are often left to connote authenticity and pastness, while the new or contemporary medium is allowed to remain transparent until it too becomes 'old' and opaque.

A case in point here is Katz's (2004) analysis of Fatboy Slim's 'Praise You'. Katz describes his 'shock' when the vocals 'start to skip' in a prolonged digital 'vocal stutter', creating a 'superhuman' fermata. The effect of the stuttering vocals is very similar to Madonna's digital dropouts in 'Don't Tell Me', since the stutter certainly also demands our attention as a digital device, or, in Fatboy Slim's own words, 'Look, I sampled this' (*ibid.*, p. 147). Particularly interesting in Katz's account is the way the analysis downplays the *other* signs of digital mediation, which are striking right from the very start of the tune. One need not listen with headphones (*ibid.*, p. 147) or be particularly 'attentive' to hear the obvious loop-points in the piano sample every other bar (the first at 0:04), the extra layer of crackling sound that is introduced right before the sampled vocals (0:16), and so on. Perhaps Katz is right that to 'most listeners' this might appear to be 'an unretouched aural snapshot of an actual performance' (*ibid.*, p. 146), at least in 1998 (or at the time he wrote the book, which was published in 2004). Not long after, however, most listeners familiar with this and similar electronic genres would *immediately* recognise this as a digitally constructed (play with a) performance in front of a chattering audience and not the 'real thing'. With Ragnhild Brøvig-Andersen we would call these initial signs of digital editing 'opaque mediation' (Brøvig-Andersen, 2007), a term she uses to describe similar purposefully obvious samples or rough edits in trip-hop. While such edits are not as attention-eliciting as Fatboy Slim's 'vocal stutter' or Madonna's silent dropouts, they nevertheless become obvious over time as digital devices intended to be significant for listeners who have heard similar effects time and time again. The awareness of such effects may, we believe, develop rather quickly in a 'genre culture'.

Perhaps, as Auner suggests, we are 'trained' to overlook the limitations of *current* technology – at any point in time – and to believe its promises of transparency and fidelity (Auner 2000, p. 10). Nor is this training simply a matter of the culture industry pulling a veil over the eyes (or ears) of innocent consumers. It is also a matter of our senses and 'meaning-making' skills becoming gradually aware of the small artefacts of new forms of mediation and production – the hiss of an FM tuner, the hum of analogue stereos, the edit points of samples in a loop, the quantisation noise in lossy data compression, and so on. Thus when home stereo equipment filled our living rooms toward the end of the 1970s, this medium was thought to leave no mark on the 'content' of the music it played. Although we may today notice the analogue noise accompanying Pink Floyd's 'Wish You Were Here', when the album was released we did not hear the medium in this way. The home stereo equipment or FM stereo radio supposed to bring us this magnificent, impressive contemporary production remained transparent.

The claim of the disappearance of materiality in the age of digital reproduction must also be read in light of modern stories of progress and innovation. The (digital) loss of the medium specificity of our analogue past in fact seems to relate to the flip

140   *Anne Danielsen and Arnt Maasø*

side of such a narrative, the mourning over a lost, more authentic or 'warm' human past.[16] Portishead addresses this aspect of the modern world's ambivalent relationship with its own modernity in their nostalgic play with the weaknesses of analogue technology. As Madonna reminds us, however, digital technologies *also* have material aspects and may take on a certain weariness. Moreover, the opacity of digital mediation comes forward in its typical modes of musical production and reproduction.

While listeners were certainly aware of the 'phonograph effect' before the era of digitisation, the crackling of vinyl was, in Rothenbuhler and Peters's words, most obviously related to the history of the *record*, or the distribution medium, and less to the *recording*, or the production medium. Madonna's 'Don't Tell Me' reminds us about the possibility of the former also in digital mediation, while Portishead, Squarepusher, Fatboy Slim and others primarily address the possibility of the latter. Common to them all are the different signs of 'opaque mediation' and the use of digital effects *as* digital effects. Such material traces of digital mediation become gradually more opaque as listeners grow accustomed to them, and at the same time they lose some of their aesthetic effect as new, attention-grabbing technological devices. In the future we might thus not only talk about the 'phonograph effect' but also the *digital effect*. Perhaps we might also mourn its passing.

Acknowledgements

The authors would like to thank the anonymous reviewers and John Durham Peters, David Hesmondhalgh, Stan Hawkins, Hege Gundersen and Nils Nadeau for their generous and encouraging comments on earlier drafts of this article.

Endnotes

1. See, for example, Middleton (1990, p. 4) for a critical discussion of technologico-economic factors delimiting the field of popular music.
2. In fact, 'Don't Tell Me' has been recorded in quite different versions that actually do resemble such traditional performances. The song was originally written by Joe Henry (Madonna's brother-in-law) with the title 'Stop' (and later released on the album *Scar*, 2001). Madonna and producer/songwriter Mirwais (Ahmadzaï) then reworked the song as 'Don't Tell Me' on *Music*. More recently, Lizz Wright released her own version of 'Stop' on the album *Dreaming Wide Awake* (2005), crediting Joe Henry as the writer.
3. See a fuller discussion in Jaworski (1993) and Maasø (2002a).
4. Dead air on television may lead to channel switching; on FM radio, dead air allows the signal of a competing channel to seep through and 'steal' the frequency. See Mott (1990) or Maasø (2002a).
5. Other kinds of technical errors can create aesthetic effects that are similar to 'medium silence', such as the use of 'broken film' and faulty projectors in the animated classic *Duck Amuck* (Chuck Jones 1953).
6. As will be discussed later, silent dropouts allow for various interpretations according to

the listening conditions and playback medium, and sometimes they are not medium silences at all. A technical error caused by a scratched LP would typically lead to an ellipsis of the temporal flow without any silence. LPs could thus cause a *skipped* beat but not a *missed* beat. In the latter case, silence interrupts an ongoing temporal flow that continues after it, which is not the way a needle tends to behave when meeting a scratch on an LP.
7. See Maasø (2002a, pp. 95–6); Peters (1999, pp. 160–1); Schafer (1994, p. 256).
8. See the last bar of the Figure. These effects, seen in the sonogram, are also obvious when listening to the track.
9. One of Auner's main concerns is 'the question of how instruments and media become marked as "old" or "obsolete" in the first place' (Auner 2000, p. 6). As our examples reveal, the relation of old and new in the field of musical media is rather dynamic; as Auner also points out, the age of a three-hundred-year-old Stradivarius or a thirty-year-old Stratocaster do not mark these instruments as somehow 'obsolete'.
10. In the essay 'I'll never be an angel', Hawkins comments on Madonna's strategy of changeability, pointing out how 'her "scrambled" identity achieves its continuity through a high degree of self-reflexivity' (Hawkins 2002, p. 42).

11. As Andrew Feenberg has pointed out, there is often a certain determinism at work in analyses of the role and impact of technology on modern society. Its premise, which originates in a particular reading of Marx, is that 'social institutions must adapt to the "imperatives" of the technological base'(Feenberg 1999, p. 77).

12. Simon Frith (1988, p. 4) notes that the five-record box set *Bruce Springsteen and the E Street Band Live* had to be marketed in accordance with Bruce Springsteen's highly non-commercial image in order to be successful, ironically, in commercial terms.

13. According to Wikipedia, many listeners returned their CDs, believing it was a disc malfunction (see http://en.wikipedia.org/wiki/Don%27t_Tell_Me_%28Madonna_song%29, accessed March 27, 2007).

14. Research on audiences, however, shows that people pay relatively little visual attention to music videos – roughly fifty per cent of time spent in front of the screen (see Maasø 2002a for a review of such studies). Still, eye contact with the screen is usually best at the *beginning* of new segments, which is where the digital dropouts stand out in 'Don't Tell Me'.

15. This faith in the transparency of contemporary media relies on an underlying assumption of history moving towards a situation of total media transparency. At the same time we experience former new technology in the rearview mirror as opaque. A similar view on history has been pointed out by Feenberg in his discussion of technological determinism. He claims that such a problematic position relies on a teleological view of history, according to which technical progress appears to follow a unilinear course, a fixed track, from less to more advanced configurations (Feenberg 1999, p. 77).

16. See, for example, Berman (1982).

References

Albiez, S. 2004. 'The day the music died laughing: Madonna and country', in *Madonna's Drowned Worlds: New Approaches to Her Subcultural Transformations*, ed. S. Fouz-Hernández and F. Jarman-Ivens (Aldershot, Ashgate), pp. 120–37

Auner, J. 2000. 'Making old machines speak: images of technology in recent music', *Echo: A Music-Centered Journal*, 2, <http://www.echo.ucla.edu/volume2-issue2/table-of-contents.html>, accessed March 2006

Berman, M. 1982. *All That Is Solid Melts into Air: The Experience of Modernity* (New York, Simon and Schuster)

Brøvig-Andersen, R. 2007. *Musikk og mediering. Teknologi relatert til sound og groove i trip-hop-musikk* (Oslo, University of Oslo, Department of Musicology)

Clarke, E.F. 2007. 'The impact of recording on listening', *20th Century Music*, 4/1, pp. 47–70

Danielsen, A. 2006a. 'Mediation and the musicalization of reality on Public Enemy's *Fear of a Black Planet*', *Proc. from the Art of Record Production Conference* (London), <http://www.artofrecordproduction.com/content/view/26/52/>, accessed June 2007
2006b. *Presence and Pleasure: the Funk Grooves of James Brown and Parliament* (Middletown, CT, Wesleyan University Press)

Eco, U. 1976. *A Theory of Semiotics* (Bloomington, Indiana University Press)

Eno, B. 1999. 'The revenge of the intuitive: turn off the options, and turn up the intimacy', *Wired*, 7, <http://www.wired.com/wired/archive/7.01/eno_pr.html>, accessed March 2006

Fagerjord, A., and Storsul, T. 2007. 'Questioning convergence', in *Ambivalence Towards Convergence: Digitalization and Media Change*, ed. T. Storsul and D. Stuedahl (Göteborg, Nordicom)

Feenberg, A. 1999. *Questioning Technology* (London, Routledge)

Frith, S. 1988. 'The real thing – Bruce Springsteen', in *Music for Pleasure*, ed. S. Frith (London, Polity Press), pp. 94–101

Frith, S. and Goodwin, A. 1990. *On Record: Rock, Pop, and the Written Word* (London, Routledge)

Hawkins, S. 2002. *Settling the Pop Score: Pop Texts and Identity Politics* (Aldershot, Ashgate)
2004a. 'On performativity and production in Madonna's music', in *Music, Space and Place: Popular Music and Cultural Identity*, ed. S. Whiteley, A. Bennett and S. Hawkins (Aldershot, Ashgate), pp. 180–90
2004b. 'Dragging out camp: narrative agendas in Madonna's musical production', in *Madonna's Drowned Worlds: New Approaches to Her Subcultural Transformations*, ed. S. Fouz-Hernández and F. Jarman-Ivens (Aldershot, Ashgate), pp. 3–21

Hesmondhalgh, D. 2002. *The Cultural Industries* (London, Sage)

Jameson, F. 1984. 'Postmodernism, or the cultural logic of late capitalism', *New Left Review*, 146, pp. 53–92

Jaworski, A. 1993. *The Power of Silence: Social and Pragmatic Perspectives* (Newbury Park, CA, Sage)

Katz, M. 2005. *Capturing Sound: How Technology Has Changed Music* (Berkeley, University of California Press)

Kittler, F.A. 1999. *Gramophone, Film, Typewriter* (Stanford, Stanford University Press)

Krauss, R., and Broodthaers, M. 2000. *'A Voyage on the North Sea': Art in the Age of the Post-Medium Condition* (New York, Thames and Hudson)

142   *Anne Danielsen and Arnt Maasø*

Maasø, A. 2002a. *'Se-hva-som-skjer!'*: *En studie av lyd som kommunikativt virkemiddel i TV* (Oslo, Unipub)
    2002b. 'Rollen til radio og TV i formidling av populærmusikk', in *Populærmusikken i kulturpolitikken*,
    ed. J. Gripsrud (Oslo, Norsk kulturråd), pp. 356–93
Middleton, R. 1990. *Studying Popular Music* (Milton Keynes, Open University Press)
Mott, R.L. 1990. *Sound Effects: Radio, TV, and Film* (Boston, Focal Press)
Negus, K. 1999. *Music Genres and Corporate Cultures* (London, Routledge)
Peters, J.D. 1999. *Speaking into the Air: A History of the Idea of Communication* (Chicago, Chicago
    University Press)
Rothenbuhler, E.W. and Peters, J.D. 1997. 'Defining phonography: an experiment in theory', *Musical
    Quarterly*, 81, pp. 242–64
Schafer, R.M. 1994. *The Soundscape: Our Sonic Environment and the Tuning of the World* (Rochester, VT,
    Destiny Books)

Discography

Fatboy Slim, *You' ve Come A Long Way, Baby*. Astralwerks. 1998
Madonna, *Music*. Warner Bros/Wea. 2000
Pink Floyd, *Wish You Were Here*. Capitol. 1975
Portishead, *Portishead*. London/UMGD. 1997
Squarepusher, *Go Plastic*. Warp Records. 2001

Videography

The Jazz Singer. Crosland. 1927

[10]

Sample and hold: pop music in the digital age of reproduction

'Science fiction and nostalgia have become the same thing.'
T. Bone Burnett

ANDREW GOODWIN

Pop eats itself

Surveying the state of pop music at the end of 1987, postmodernists and devotees of Walter Benjamin's cultural analysis could be forgiven for patting themselves on their theoretical backs and ruminating on the strange prescience of these two bodies of theory. Writing in this journal two years ago, Peter Wollen established the link between Benjamin and the postmodernists thus: 'As Benjamin's ''age of reproduction'' is replaced by our ''age of electronic reproduction'', the trends which he discerned are further extended. Reproduction, pastiche and quotation, instead of being forms of textual parasitism, become constitutive of textuality' (Wollen, 1986: 169).

Within two years, the British pop act M/A/R/R/S was enjoying a huge international hit with the single 'Pump Up The Volume' – a record that is made up largely of pieces of about thirty *other* records. At the same time, the dominant technology in pop's future is clearly going to be digital reproduction, as established in new processes of music production (such as sampling music computers) and in consumer software such as the Compact Disc (CD) and Digital Audio Tape (DAT).

In addition to these technological developments, pop ideology is increasingly dominated by a sense that the future has now arrived, for good. Pop's sounds and visions appear to be caught in a *statis* that is both aesthetic and political, and which is well summed up by the ex-leader of The Clash, Joe Strummer, in a recent *Melody Maker* interview: 'All movements are bullshit'. As traditional political movements have become marginalised in pop politics, so notions of pop's historical movement as 'progress' have withered and died. 'Progressive rock', that most diabolical symptom of pop's desire to evolve into Art, has ceased to progress; and the question 'what comes after punk?' is heard less often. Instead, today's pop musicians are busy blurring historical and cultural boundaries, as the music of 'traditional' Hispanic (Los Lobos, Ruben Blades), Celtic (The Pogues) and African (*Graceland*, Hugh Masekela, Peter Gabriel) musics are made contemporary and enter the mainstream.

Sample and hold: pop music in the digital age of production   3

As Lawrence Grossberg (1987) has pointed out, our received notions c
pop's margins and its centre have ceased to apply. So too have our idea
about generation. It isn't just that pop's audience has grown older. That shi
would merely return us to a pre-rock era of popular music. The essentia
change is that 'older' music has become contemporary for audiences of
ages. In their year-end surveys of 1987, rock critics on both sides of
Atlantic pointed to the extraordinary number of reissues and old records i
the charts. The link with the new technologies is unavoidable. On the on
hand, CD reissues partly account for the latest wave of apparent nostalgi
(including the resurrection of punk – CBS have just released a CD packag
of greatest hits from The Clash). On the other hand, new digital technologie
are being used to deconstruct old texts.

Digital developments appear to offer shattering evidence for the per
tinence of Walter Benjamin's analysis, in the spheres of both productior
and consumption. In music production, the increasing use of digital record
ing and reproductive equipment gives enormous credence to Benjamin'
celebration of the end of the 'aura'. In the age of mass production, Benjamir
stated that the audience is no longer concerned with an original textual
moment. In the age of digital reproduction the notion of the 'aura' is further
demystified by the fact that *everyone* may purchase an 'original'. Digital
recording techniques now ensure that the electronic encoding and decoding
that takes place in capturing and then reproducing sound is such that there
is no discernible difference between the sound recorded in the studio and
the signal reproduced on the consumer's CD system. This is something new:
the mass production of the aura.

More radical still is the technology of DAT, against which the music
industry has mounted a huge and largely unsuccessful campaign.[1] Unlike
CD, DAT can record. It opens up the possibility that consumers will simply
make their own perfect copies of CDs, via home taping, thus obtaining the
aura gratis. One response, from the record industry in the USA, has been
the introduction of Personics – a system that attempts to co-opt home
taping by selling consumers customised cassette tapes, dubbed (legally, of
course) in record stores. Consumers are thus able to re-order the programme
of music offered on records and tapes by the record company. Like the CD,
Personics introduces new elements of consumer control. Furthermore, an
increasing amount of contemporary pop music takes advantage of this
technology to 'sample' sounds, voices and effects from other records and
use them in new pieces of popular music.

These technological shifts go hand-in-hand (although sometimes just in
parallel) with pop's changing attitude to its history. As old texts have become
new again (through new media forms like music video and pop's increased

6   *Critical Quarterly*, vol. 30, no. 3

se as a film soundtrack, as well as CD reissues), it has plundered its
rchives with truly postmodern relish, in an orgy of pastiche. The degree
o which pop music in the 1980s has become self-referential is now so
eveloped that some musics sound like copies of parodies. I recently attend-
d a gig in Berkeley where the band supporting The Meat Puppets seemed
o be pastiching The Cult – a British rock group who made their name in
986 by resurrecting the hard rock sound of Led Zeppelin. (It should be noted
hat Led Zep T-shirts have now attained the status of symbols of 'cool',
ather than being icons of rock prehistory.) On his recent solo LP *Now and
Zen*, ex-Led Zeppelin vocalist Robert Plant samples from his old recordings,
aving spent the last few years listening to new bands sample his old records
see Gore & Goodwin, 1987; Pond, 1988). Plant decided it was time to
astiche from his own pastiche.
   If much of this lends ammunition to Benjamin's account of mass culture,
hen the postmodernists who've bothered to listen won't have failed to take
account of the fact that one of Britain's leading new bands is called Pop Will
Eat Itself. Aside from the fact that so much contemporary pop seems to be
caught up in a *statis* of theft (as in 'free sample') and reissues, many of its
most celebtrated new acts offer recycled versions of pop's past: from the
sixties (Husker Du, The Bangles), through heavy metal (The Cult, The
Mission, Whitesnake), disco (The Pet Shop Boys, The Communards), and
endless re-runs of punk rock (Fuzzbox, Screaming Blue Messiahs). Other
bands delight in the production of bizarre historical juxtapositions (Sonic
Youth, The Replacements) – a trend exemplified in the 1980s fashion for
new bands to compete to perform the most unlikely cover versions of 1970s
songs in their live sets.
   'It's like cruising the 50's again, dig?', says Mickey Mouse in the ads for
Disneyland's latest attraction, Blast To The Past. 'Shake, Rattle And Roll
Back The Years' is the slogan. And the copy goes on: 'During the Blast To
The Past at Disneyland, everything then is now again, every day'. What is
significant about this advertisement is that the humans cavorting with
Donald, Mickey and Co. on the tail of a red and white convertible are all
teenagers. No one who actually remembers the fifties is in sight – excepting
the Disney characters, of course. The appeal, like Led Zeppelin's, is not
nostalgic, it is postmodern; a sign that when the future arrives, pop teleology
comes to a halt. Even its images of the future no longer connote progress.
Just as Disney's 'futuristic' monorail is now read as a quaint notion derived
from a bad sci-fi novel, so its space-age rock group Laserium, dressed in shiny
silver suits and playing electronic instruments with all the latest gadgets,
appear merely as an outdated idea of what we once thought the music of
the future would be.

Sample and hold: pop music in the digital age of production

As I will try to show in this essay, the shiny 'technology' that featur
so prominently in postmodern analysis can offer up some unexpected mea
ings. Without doubt the digital sampling music computer (the 'sample'
is potentially the most postmodern musical instrument yet invented. I w
argue that its use and meaning often remain wedded to earlier aesthetic

Sample and hold

Digital sampling computers are relatively new machines that digitial
encode any sounds, store them and enable the manipulation and reprodu
tion of those sounds with almost infinite parameters and no discernible lo:
of sound quality. (An important related technology is the digital dela
line/pedal, which stores brief sequences of sound and replays them, ofte
in rhythm with the music.) They do, however, have their roots in earli
analogue inventions.

The electronic synthesiser was of course used by pop and electroni
musicians to simulate the sounds of conventional instruments, from th
harpsichords of *Switched On Bach* to the string sounds used on many po
albums – one version of the analogue synth is in fact known as a 'strin
machine', for its ability to simulate (not very well) the sound of a
orchestral string section. A technology that was closer to sampling
the Mellotron, an instrument that was used (rather excessively) in the 1970
by progressive rock groups like Genesis, The Moody Blues, and Yes. Th
Mellotron was a keyboard instrument that triggered analogue recordings c
sounds such as human voices, strings and flutes.

Sampling technologies made the Mellotron obsolete technically, just
it was going out of fashion aesthetically – late 1970s punk rock had littl
use for massed choirs and string sections! In 1979 the Fairlight Compute
Musical Instrument came on the market, although its enormous cos
restricted its use to all but the most successful musicians, producers anc
studios. The Fairlight CMI was however followed, in classic music
technology tradition, by a generation of machines that did the same thin;
more cheaply – the Emulator and the Synclavier, for instance; and ther
a further, and even cheaper wave of samplers such as the Greengate anc
Ensoniq Mirage. Eventually, in 1986, Casio brought out samplers which cos'
less than £100.

What is typical about this development is the way the technology was
used to mirror practices that derived from low-tech innovations, first takin;
them out of the price-range of most musicians, and then returning them, via
the sale of the High Street Casio, to the 'street' ... or is it the spare room? For
example: one common use of samplers is and was to mimic the stuttering

8   *Critical Quarterly*, vol. 30, no. 3

ffect of 'scratching' – a technique initially developed by DJs using record
urntables. Another instance is the use of samplers to dub in segments of
peeches, effects or music – a technique that art–punk bands of an earlier
ra achieved by splicing tape with a low-tech razor blade. I will try to show
ater in this paper that the new technologies have not removed the notion
f 'skill' involved in such (often extremely complex and delicate)
rocedures.

The question of skill is also raised, as I will demonstrate, by the fact that
ampling computers are also music sequencers. Like some of their analogue
redecessors, digital samplers can be programmed to play sounds and
hythms independently of a keyboard and/or a human performer. This
acilitated the development of a technology that is of paramount importance
n recent pop history – the drum machine. Drum machines enable a musi-
ian to programme rhythmic patterns without actually hitting any drums.
arly analogue machines simulated drum sounds electronically, using
lements such as 'white noise' to approximate to a snare drum sound.
ampling enabled manufacturers to create machines that digitially recreated
a recording that exactly resembles a 'real' drum recorded in a studio.

It is this combination of sampling and sequencing (as evidenced in drum
nachines and digital music computers) that has eroded the divisions not
ust between originals and copies, but between human and machine per-
ormed music. In each area, that of originality and of 'feel', the new music
echnologies raise some fascinating questions for cultural theorists. They
place issues such as authenticity and creativity in crisis, not just because
of the issue of theft, but through the increasingly *automated* nature of their
mechanisms.

The real thing

The questions of theft and automation in modern pop production appear
to challenge its essentially Romantic aesthetic (see Stratton, 1983; Pattison,
1987). And yet strangely enough cultural studies discussions of these areas
have so far said very little about the music itself. In what follows I will
attempt to focus on that neglected level, through some comments on the
new technologies and their impact on rhythm and timbre.

The most striking point in the analysis of both areas is the fact that music
made by machines, or to *sound* like machines, has not taken pop's trajectory into electronic or art music, but has instead become the chief source
of its *dance music*. Synthesisers, drum machines and digital samplers are
identified less with modern composers (like Brian Eno) than with dance
genres like disco, hip hop, Hi-NRG and House. In other words, while

Sample and hold: pop music in the digital age of production

cultural studies critics such as Frith (1985) debate the essentially critic
and academic distinctions being made between technology on the one ha
and 'community' and 'nature' on the other, pop musicians and audienc
have grown increasingly accustomed to making an association betwee
synthetic/automated music and the communal (dance floor) connection
nature (via the body). We have grown used to connecting *machines* a
funkiness.

This observation doesn't discredit the arguments of Frith, since his po
tion is essentially that cultural studies debates about authenticity carrie
over from literary theory don't travel well into the field of pop music. Wh
I am suggesting here, however, is that Frith's analysis needs to be suppl
mented by a *musicological* critique. If anyone need be nervous about th
arguments that follow it is surely the postmodernists, whose assertion
about the role of technology in postmodern culture have rarely been teste
via empirical analysis. It may be that all the high-tech wizardry of movie
like *Blade Runner* and bands like Sigue Sigue Sputnik is merely yet more sc
fi iconography (hardly a postmodern phenomenon), while the more routir
use of modern technology in pop music is thoroughly *naturalised*, throug
aural familiarity and via pop ideologies constructed beyond the level of th
technical infrastructure (in art schools and in the music press, for instance

The most significant result of the recent innovations in pop productio
lies in the progressive removal of any immanent criteria for distinguishin
between human and automated performance. Associated with this there i
of course a crisis of authorship. But where this crisis has generally bee
located at the level of copyright and ownership of intellectual property (se
Frith, 1987), I want to focus on its musical manifestations. In order to ge
a sense of how far-reaching these changes are, consider this scenario, whic
is now common at the beginning of a pop recording session: before a not
is committed to tape, a producer or engineer will use a sampling compute
to digitally record each sound used by the group. At this point, it i
sometimes possible for everyone but the producer to go home, leaving th
computerised manipulation of these sounds to do the work of performanc
and recording. Indeed, the recent court case involving Frankie Goes T
Hollywood, producer Trevor Horn and his record company ZTT centred or
exactly this problem – what exactly did Frankie and their lead singer Holly
Johnson actually *do*?

The question of 'who played what?' isn't new, and allegations that the
act didn't play on their 'own' records have been raised about many bands
from The Beatles to The Sex Pistols. What is new here is the increasin
problem of distinguishing between originals and copies on the one hand,
and between human and automated performance on the other.

Critical Quarterly, vol. 30, no. 3

There are four processes that lead to the blurring of distinctions between
automated and human performance in today's pop. The first is the growing sophistication with which today's pop technologies can be programmed.
one listens to a recording that uses state-of-the-art computer technologies
such as Scritti Politti's *Cupid & Psyche 85*), it is clear that machines are
being used to mimic many of the techniques normally developed over time
by human 'real time' performers. These techniques include the elastic placement of the beat (slightly in front of or behind its 'correct' mathematical
position) to create 'feel'; the use of subtle changes of volume or velocity to
create 'lifelike' dynamics; and deliberately making small changes in the
tempo to emulate the way human performers speed up and slow down. Chris
Lowe, who programmes much of The Pet Shop Boys' music, has taken to
boasting about his tambourines being 'out of time', even though they are
programmed, via a drum machine and/or computer. In other words, today's
pop musicians are often technicians who have learned to programme every
bit as skilfully as earlier generations (up until punk) learned to play.

A second reason for the confusion is very simple. Much of today's
technology allows musicians to play into the programme, using drum pads,
keyboards or perhaps even the buttons on the machine itself. This information will often register at very fine degrees of subtlety, encompasses
parameters such as velocity and extremely small shifts in tempo and placement of the beat, and might trigger digital samples of 'real' sounds that are
indistinguishable from the originals. The result can be that the machine programme contains every bit as much information as any piece of 'real'
playing.

A third overlap arises out of one prevalent use of digital sampling
technology in the modern recording studio. Drum or keyboard sounds stored
on a digital music computer can be triggered by analogue recordings. In other
words, a recording of a 'real' drummer playing a drum kit in a studio can
be used to trigger *any* sounds that can be stored in the computer, including
any other drum kit, any drum machine sounds, and an infinite number of
percussive samples (including old stand-bys like breaking glass and the
beating of sheet metal). Consequently, one modern recording process
reverses the phenomenon described in my second point above. Here, a 'real'
drummer, playing with human imperfections, can be made to sound like
a machine, or a computer, through changes in timbre implemented via
samples. Indeed, this technique has been consolidated into a piece of hardware called 'The Human Clock' – a triggering device that enables a drummer to drive machines in sync, according to a varying human tempo.

Finally, there is the use of a studio 'loop', in which a few bars of music
(perhaps a drum pattern, guitar riff or an entire rhythm section hitting a

Sample and hold: pop music in the digital age of production

particular groove) are recorded in real time and then re-recorded and repeat
as the rhythm track for an entire song. The effect is human feel within t
loop, but consistency of groove throughout the song. (And if the loop
recorded digitally, there is no degradation of sound quality in the
recording process.)

These confusions between human and automated rhythm are also evide
at the level of timbre. Here the key distinction is between those soun
which seem natural and those which sound synthetic. It has become cor
monplace in both music production and consumption to observe th
analogue sounds/recordings are 'warmer' than digitally reproduced musi
(The debate about CDs centres on this distinction; and see Baird, 1988, f
a discussion of the analogue/digital debate in the field of production, whe
digital keyboards such as the Yamaha DX-7 became unfashionable almo
as soon as they went into fashion, because of their allegedly 'cold feel'

The key shift here occurs in the 1980s when a generation of pop mus
cians emerges who grew up listening to electronic synthesisers. What the
occurs is that the very technology (the synth) that was presumed in tl
1970s to remove human intervention and by-pass the emotive aspect
music (through its 'coldness') becomes the source of one of the major aur
signs that signifies 'feel'! This is the sound of a bass analogue synth – ofte
a Moog synthesiser (although the Prophet 5 is another popular analogu
reference point). By the mid-1980s electro-pop band The Human Leagu
could talk about using analogue synths as a move *back* to their 'authentic
music roots.

This sense that analogue is warmer and more natural than digital als
extends to its visual signification, which is appropriately enough als
signified via the words we use to describe these patterns – waves, as oppose
to numbers. A year ago, when I bought a music programme for the compute
on which this essay is being written, the salesperson showed me two di
ferent ways of visualising musical information. A digital keyboard presente
me with lists of numbers. But there was a software programme that con
verted this information into an approximation of analogue-style wave
forms. Both were incomprehensible to me. But to the keyboard exper
demonstrating the technology, it was 'obvious' that the analogue w
were more 'natural' than the digital numbers.

This confusion of synthetic and natural sounds (analogue electroni
synths were supposed to be 'cold' and 'unnatural', according to rock's realis
critics and fans at the time of their invention) is more strikingly evident ir
the story of the strange case of the 'handclap'. The origins of the use of hand
claps in pop music lie in its various American and African folk roots. Indeed
the handclap is, along with the voice, music's most 'authentic' sound; they

Critical Quarterly, vol. 30, no. 3

e both present in 'traditional' musics of most cultures. Handclaps have
so been used on record both as percussion and to signify audience involve-
ent since the first popular music recordings. In the 1970s an electronically
mulated handclap sound began to appear on many disco records. Its
rcussive appeal lies partly in the fact that it incorporates what drummers
ll a 'flam' – that is a spreading out of the impact of the beat that extends
 duration beyond the point at which it is 'supposed' to fall. (Record
oducers often amplify this effect by adding electronic delay in the record-
g process.) One of the most popular sources of this sound in the 1980s
as the handclap on Roland's analogue TR-808 drum machine. (It can
 heard prominently on Chic's 1970's recordings, and on Marvin Gaye's
82 hit 'Sexual Healing'.) What is extraordinary about this is that by
e time Roland came to work on its next generation of (digital) drum
achines (such as the TR-707), the electronic handclap sounded so 'natural'
 pop musicians and audiences that they sampled their own electronic
mulation from the TR-808 machine, rather than 'real' handclaps. Simi-
rly, many electro-pop bands and producers who use digital samplers
egan by storing and manipulating synthetic, analogue sounds on them –
unds that both musicians and audiences could recognise.

At first this looks like a perfectly postmodern instance. Our aural con-
ciousness has become so invaded by the realm of synthetic signs that we
ow hear a mass-mediated electronically simulated 'handclap' as the 'real'
ning. If however we abandon the idea that musical representation occurs
ia *mimesis*, and consider its process of signification in relation to intra-
ersonal 'states of mind', emotions, and so on, we might conclude that the
lectronic handclap *is* real. It *really* produces certain physiological effects
/hen you dance to it.

My point is this: the 'recognition' involved in knowing how to hear
lectronic music depends in part on understanding the associations attached
o any given sound. One element of this is our recognition of rhythms
nd timbre. While digital technology might appear more 'real' than
nalogue (since it can reproduce an actual snare drum sound instead of a
ynthetic simulation, a real bass guitar sound, not a synth-bass imitation),
he opposite is often true: in pop's digital age, analogue sounds are the real
hing, however automated or synthetic. And as electronic technology
as become naturalised, audiences have become habituated to seeing
op performers as technicians, computer programmers, DJs or studio
ngineers.

Sample and hold: pop music in the digital age of production

The end of an aura?

A landscape that revels in the fusion of originals and copies, and which
not distinguish humans from machines, seems like unlikely territory
authors and auras. Yet despite the apparently postmodern nature of so mu
contemporary pop, the question of creativity and originality remains ce
tral. Once again, Frith (1987) focuses in his discussion on the demands
the industry. I want instead to comment briefly on the role of authorsl
in pop's aesthetic, and then go on to look at the importance of the aura
contemporary digital pop.

The following comment from Tim Simenon (creator of the sampled I
'Beat Dis') perfectly illustrates my first point:

> We got the records and found a common denominator beat – we chose rough
> a range between 108 and 118, we laid down a beat at 114 b.p.m. and slow
> down or speeded up the tracks I was going to use. But what differs about tl
> kind of 'street fusion' is that it isn't straight cut-up like a Double D & Steins
> record, or Grandmaster Flash.
>
> It's in that form but the bassline is original, we've got a drum pattern arou:
> it, and that sound like a Shaft guitar isn't 'Shaft'. We sampled one note of wa
> wah guitar and reconstructed it on the keyboards. You wouldn't be able to fi:
> that guitar pattern on any other record.[2]

Note how, in 1988, 'creativity' has shifted so far from its 1970s progressi
rock heyday (when musicians tried to invent new, unique musical form
as well as original music) that Tim Simenon can lay claim to it merely k
noting that he didn't *steal* something from another record.

This kind of practice and its ideology (that of the Age of Plunder) is gri
to the mill'of the postmodernists, for whom it provides evidence of our tot
absorption in 'the realm of signs'. Yet this is too simple. Simenon clearl
is invoking the concept of creativity. And he isn't alone. Here is Marti
Young of Colourbox and M/A/R/R/S: 'Scratching is actually more creativ
than sampling. With sampling you are basically limited to a staccato effec
whereas a good scratcher can really mess things up.'[3] But while the mus
cians/technicians themselves are well aware of the sophisticated work tha
goes into contemporary automation and plunder, there remains the probler
of transmitting this information to the fans – indeed, this is precisely on
purpose of interviews such as those I have just cited.

One recurring problem of pop history exposes postmodern interpretation
of authenticity as inadequate: It is the persistent failure of all those acts wh
are marketed as a self-conscious hype. Sigue Sigue Sputnik are only the mos
spectacular failure in this category of pop about pop; even an apparently suc
cessful hype such as Frankie Goes To Hollywood ultimately failed to achiev

ny kind of long-term economic/artistic success, through career longevity.
Jeither of these bands could survive their image as postmod con men,
ecause it deprived them of any position from which to market authorship.
t implied that they were puppets – an image that *real* puppet groups (The
Monkees, for instance) did their utmost to defuse. Other acts, like ABC and
he Pet Shop Boys, have overcome this difficulty by promoting themselves
s the authors of their own *image*. But the self-conscious hype is doomed
precisely because its postmodern premises (audiences aren't interested in
ruth or creativity any longer) defy pop's Romantic aesthetic.

The most audacious challenge to the 'truth' of pop performance has been
mounted by The Pet Shop Boys – a duo fronted, significantly, by an ex-
ournalist, Neil Tennant. Where most electro-pop acts who don't perform
live' persist in maintaining the pretence that they *can* play 'live', either
by announcing tours that never happen (a tactic they recently abandoned)
or by touring with session musicians, Tennant recently upped the stakes
of inauthenticity by boasting about their inability to actually play, or even
sing, when they lip-synced at the American Music Awards: 'It's kinda
nacho nowadays to prove you can *cut it* live. I quite like proving we *can't*
cut it live. We're a pop group, not a rock and roll group.'⁴ The Pet Shop
Boys can defy some discourses of authenticity because they invoke others,
such as the authorship of their own marketing images and a source of 'truth'
that lies in an explicit critique of 'rock' music.

For other acts, authorship and authenticity reside in the ability to actually
play. This competence needs to be demonstrated in live performance – one
key element in pop's visual discourses. This factor is relevant every bit as
much for those bands who rely on 'postmodern' sampling technology:

> We've had some things built which look like abstract objects standing on the
> back of our risers. We mike them with contact mikes, and treat the sounds
> as samples. In other words, we can produce all kinds of different sampled
> sounds by hitting these objects. Most people think we must be miming when
> we hit these things on stage, because they can't understand how all these
> sounds could be coming out of one piece of metal. In fact, we're not miming;
> we're triggering the sounds. I think we'd like to explore this a lot more next
> time we go out on the road, because it's an exciting way of producing lots of
> sounds through some physical effort. That creates some visual excitement.
> You actually see us working on stage, rather than just standing there.⁵

There are two points to pull out of this comment from electro-pop band
Depeche Mode. First, the notion of authenticity is still very much present
in the need for pop musicians to demonstrate musical competence. Indeed,
the new sequencing and sampling technologies have cast such doubts upon
our knowledge about just who is (or isn't) playing what that some bands

Sample and hold: pop music in the digital age of production

have recently taken to placing comments such as 'no sequencers' on albu
covers – The Human League (*Crash*) and Shriekback (*Big Night Music*) a
two recent examples that recall the legend that rock group Queen used
place on their 1970s albums – 'no synthesisers'!

Playing analogue synthesisers is now a mark of authenticity, where it w
once a sign of alienation – in pop iconography the image of musicians stan
ing immobile behind synths signifies coldness (Kraftwerk, for instance
Now it is the image of a technician hunched over a computer terminal th
is problematic – but that, like the image of the synth-player, can and wi
change.

Which brings me to my second point – that audiences need to se
their pop musicians *doing* something. Depeche Mode are troubled by th
perception that they are miming instead of playing (perhaps this is becaus
it is true – much of their 'live' show is replayed via tapes and/or sequen
cers), and yet they are happy to perpetuate it in the interest of visu
spectacle.

This in its turn must prompt a question concerning why pop audience
continue to attend live events. The sound quality is often very poor, an
the visual imagery is usually too distant to be of any great value. Indeed
most stadium concerts are now accompanied by simultaneous video repla
on to large screens. Attending a live performance by a pop megastar thes
days is often roughly the experience of listening to pre-recorded music (tape
or sequenced) while watching a small, noisy TV set in a large, crowded field
I do not believe that the 'community' that follows from being a participan
in a social event begins to explain the appeal of the modern rock concert
What explains the pleasure of these occasions more fully is the *aura*.

As veteran US rock promoter Bill Graham puts it: 'In actuality rock
roll has become so successful that the majority of fans don't go to see th
artist but to be in the presence of the artist, to share the space with th
artist.'[6] In other words: to consume the only truly original aura availabl
in mass-produced pop – the physical presence of the star(s). If we abandor
the abstractions of both cultural studies and postmodernist analysis of pop
and consider the role of live performance in relation to musical meaning
it is clear that the role of the visual in live concerts serves three function
for audiences. First, it provides visual pleasure on an abstract level (the
display of the body, the spectacle of special effects, etc.); second, it serve
to authenticate musical competence (see Mowitt, 1987); and third, it offers
us the consumption of a star presence, an aura. In this last area it is clea
that the realm of signs gives way to something more fundamental – the
desire for an audience with an original, even if it is shared with 50,00C
others.

The importance of *presence* (crucially, a *musical* as well as iconographic term) is also highlighted in a second area where the aura continues to dominate pop consumption. It constitutes a return to the consideration of digital technology set up at the beginning of this essay.

It is clear that high-fidelity is the very embodiment, in consumerism, of the fetishisation of original performance. The digital reproduction offered by CDs takes this process to extremes, not just by promising greater sound quality than analogue systems, but by revealing to the listener at home 'imperfections' in the original recording that went unnoticed at the time. CDs of The Beatles' early recordings apparently expose the sound of Ringo Starr's squeaky bass drum pedal. In addition, then, to the fetishisation of the 'original' recorded moment, CD appeals to a belief in a pure, unmediated reality (the location of the aura of music performance) which it supposedly reveals.

Thus while digital technologies like CD and DAT no doubt have the capacity to break the barrier between the original and the copy, they are in fact more likely to be used to enhance the power of the aura of the original moment of recording, via the consumerist practices of hi-fi.

The politics of sampling

I will finish by addressing the questions of realism and history in contemporary sampled pop. I want to suggest that there are really three strands of digital sampling in pop production, which roughly correspond to received cultural studies categories of realism (I would prefer the term naturalism myself, but the two seem to have become synonymous), modernism and postmodernism.

First, there is the 'hidden' sampling involved in using a machine such as a Linn drum to reproduce 'real' drum sounds, or in the process of using a Fairlight or Synclavier to steal a sound. This use of sampled sounds is motivated largely by economics rather than aesthetics – getting 'good' sounds and the 'right' performance from a machine is cheaper and easier than hiring musicians. In this kind of sampling the object is transparency, since the producer is using the technology to achieve a realist effect (the imitation of a 'real' performance) without calling attention to the mediating role of production technology. And this use of sampling is indeed so pervasive that we no longer notice it. Most of the songs we hear on the radio today use computerised and sampling devices at some point.

A second kind of sampling is more explicit. Some producers have created records and remixes that celebrate playfulness, sometimes through a kind of baroque over-indulgence. Trevor Horn (ABC, Frankie Goes To Hollywood,

Sample and hold: pop music in the digital age of production

Malcolm McLaren), Arthur Baker (Afrika Bambaataa, Cyndi Lauper, Ne
Order), Bill Lasswell (Material, Sly & Robbie), Daniel Miller (Depec.
Mode) and Rick Rubin (The Beastie Boys, The Cult) come immediately
mind as producers who straddle a line between pop realism and t
sometimes self-conscious exposure of their own craft.

The 1980s development of a mass market for extended 12″ remixes
pop songs is central here. Samplers are often used on remixes because th
can store a few bars of music as well as individual sounds. They can th
be used to manipulate, extend and/or condense the *structure* of a song,
well as its texture, arrangement and timbre. It is because this practice
seems to deconstruct the original text (the 7″ single) that record produc
Arthur Baker was once named 'Rock Critic Of The Year'.

This second layer of producers and musicians remain for me the mo
interesting group working with the new technologies, purely by virtue
the fact that their aesthetic radicalism takes place in what we once used
call the 'mainstream' – the charts. Listen to Arthur Baker turn m-o-r
Fleetwood Mac into modernist avant-gardists (on his remix of 'Big
and what you hear is a steadfast refusal to settle for the pleasures of pc
formula offered in the original. But the point here is that this aesthet.
isn't postmodern at all – it is modernist, with a dance beat. It is Theod
Adorno mistreating Fleetwood Mac, not Walter Benjamin celebrating then
(Furthermore, the remix market is saturated with *auteur*-theories focusin
on the producer-as-author.)

Finally there are those DJs, musicians and engineers, some of ther
associated with dance music and hip-hop, and others with punk and its afte:
math, who have made an aesthetic out of sampling ... and in some case
a *politics* out of stealing. M/A/R/R/S, Cold Cut, Steinski and Mantronix ar
in the former category. For this school of sampling, 'stealing' segments
other records is a part of the meaning of the 'new' text. The music press hav
dubbed this The Age Of Plunder, and the *New Musical Express* in particula
has tried to make a case for this aesthetic as the Next Big Thing. Punk
lagists, my second sub-category, include Cabaret Voltaire, Big Audi
Dynamite and the Justified Ancients of Mu Mu.

The problem here, for theorists of the postmodern condition, is this: first
many of these producers appear to be working with fairly traditional notion
of creativity and authorship – M/A/R/R/S – typically for pop – followe
up their 'postmodern' hit with a series of intra-band disputes designed t
establish who was *really* the 'creative' force behind their music. Second
and more devastating, is the argument that the Age of Plunder is in fact on
in which pop *recuperates* its history, rather than denying it. This
of interpretation is evident in the numerous instances in which digita

ontagists and scratchers claim to be educating the pop audience about its istory, as Tim Simenon suggests: 'Take James Brown, all of his records e being reissued. Kids of 18, 19 wouldn't have heard of him if it wasn't r hip hop.'[7] Arguments about authenticity, authorship and the aura in ontemporary pop are clearly very complex, and I don't claim to have even mpled the whole truth here. But it is clear, in my view, that the ostmodern and Benjaminite positions cited by Wollen are much too simple, cause they are (typically) too abstract. In the first place, it is clear that the leasure of consuming pop auras has not disappeared in the age of its mass roduction. If the aura is now produced on a mass scale, this has not led to s demystification. Indeed, I have noted that attempts to expose the arketing of the star aura in pop (some of them initiated by entrepreneurs nformed by political and social theories such as post-structuralism[8]), iled precisely because the discourses of authorship remain dominant ... nd because large sections of the pop audience refuse to consume self-onsciously. Pop fans generally appear to want their stars clad in demin, ather and spandex, not ironic quotation marks.

The fact the post-punk pop's effort to make the past contemporary might ast as easily be viewed as a new interest in its *history* is a further problem. ust as serious, it seems to me, are the continuing concern with creativity nformed via a Romantic aesthetic, the dominance of 'realist' and dance-riented uses of sampling technology, and the naturalisation of the technology' that the postmoderns make so much of.

Pop might be eating itself, but the old ideologies and aesthetics are still n the menu. That, in my view, is indisputable. The fundamental questions or the postmodern theorists are these: First, do we need a postmodern heory of society/aesthetic in order to understand postmodern cultural orms? And, second, what is the status of the developing postmodern esthetic? Is it, in Raymond Williams's terms, an emerging condition that vill perhaps rise to aesthetic dominance? Or is it in fact an aspect of conomic, historical and technological developments in pop that need to e understood in the context of the continuing dominance of realism, modernism ... and Romanticism?

In the essay I referred to in my opening comments, Peter Wollen con-idently states: 'Clearly, post-modernist forms ... demand a post-modernist aesthetic.' He goes on: 'The old critical apparatus has tended, in practice, to lead either to an exaggerated cultural pessimism or to a polemical over-enthusiasm' (Wollen, 1986: 169). And yet the fact that so-called postmodern theory reproduces *exactly* that banal polarity (albeit sometimes as parody) suggests that this body of work has no privileged hold on postmodern cultural developments. In my view the reason for this is very simple: by

Sample and hold: pop music in the digital age of production

conflating postmodernism as *theory* and as *condition*, the former fin
itself with a vested interest in promoting the latter, if not morally and/
politically, then as a cultural form of far greater significance than t
evidence often suggests. It is for this reason that we need to probe beyo
the ritual incantation of pastiche.

Notes

My thanks to Joe Gore for many suggestive and helpful comments on this essa

1   As I write, in March 1988, the US National Bureau of Standards has just rul
     againt record company proposals to include 'copy code' (an electronic syste
     for preventing home taping) on CDs.
2   'Beat generator', *New Musical Express*, 27 February 1988.
3   'Bytes and pieces', *New Musical Express*, 14 November 1987.
4   Random Notes, *Rolling Stone*, 24 March 1988.
5   'The wilder side of Depeche Mode', *Keyboard*, October 1986.
6   Interview, *Calendar Magazine* (San Francisco), 1 March 1988.
7   'Beat generator', *New Musical Express*, 27 February 1988.
8   I am thinking of the anarcho-situationist politics of Malcolm McLaren ar
     Jamie Reid (The Sex Pistols, Bow Wow Wow), and the playful pos
     structuralism of Green Gartside (Scritti Politti) and Paul Morley (Frankie Go
     To Hollywood, Art of Noise, Propaganda).

References

Baird, J. (1988), 'The neo-analogue revival hits NAMM', *Musician*, No. 114, Apri
Frith, S. (1985), 'Art versus technology: the strange case of pop', *Media, Cultu
     & Society*, Vol. 8, No. 3, July.
Frith, S. (1987), 'Copyright and the music business', *Popular Music*, Vol. 7/1.
Gore, J. & Goodwin, A. (1987), 'Your time is gonna come: talking about Le
     Zeppelin', *ONETWOTHREEFOUR: A Rock and Roll Quarterly*, No. 4, Winte
Grossberg, L. (1987), Paper to Conference on 'Popular Music: Research Trends an
     Applications', San José State University, May.
Mowitt, J. (1987), 'The sound of music in the era of electronic reproducibility', i
     Richard Leppert & Susan McClary (eds.), *Music and Society*, CUP.
Pattison, R. (1987), *The Triumph of Vulgarity: Rock Music In The Mirror c
     Romanticism*, OUP.
Pond, S. (1988), 'The song remains the same', *Rolling Stone*, 24 March.
Stratton, J. (1983), 'Capitalism and Romantic ideology in the record business'
     Popular Music, No. 3.
Wollen, P. (1986), 'Ways of thinking about music video (and postmodernism)'
     Critical Quarterly, Vol. 28, Nos. 1 & 2.

[11]

'Caught in a whirlpool of aching sound': the production of dance music in Britain in the 1920s*

by MARK HUSTWITT

In the years between 1910 and 1930 there occurred a number of changes in the forms of popular music enjoyed in Britain, in the ways this music was produced and disseminated, and in its use for pleasure and profit. In this article I am concerned with mapping together themes which have hitherto been investigated in isolation; I focus on the relation of musical forms to their users, bandleaders, musicians, dancers, 'jazz fans', record companies, etc., rather than on any single aspect of popular music. I investigate the way in which the importation of new forms of music and dance from the USA, the social disruptions of the First World War and the more general trends in British society and its economy coalesce to re-orientate musical pleasures during the 1920s. I begin by examining changes in music and dance immediately before and during the First World War.

Cakewalks, ragtime and war

After about 1909, many people in Britain, of all classes, became acquainted with forms of music and dance which came from the USA. The cakewalk had begun the move towards using the body more expressively when it was introduced in the late 1890s but it was the ragtime-based boston and the animal-based movements of dances such as the turkey trot, the bunny hug and the grizzly bear which accented this trend in the years before 1914. Ragtime consolidared itself in Britain following the visit of the US vaudeville act, the Original American Ragtime Octet in September 1912. In 1913 there were over seventy-five ragtime revues running in Britain, the first, *Hullo Ragtime*, being seen by some 400,000 people, and the music hall was also using the style (compare, for example, Marie Lloyd's 'The Piccadilly Trot', recorded November 1912, with Arthur Pryor's recordings of the period). In 1911 the *Dancing Times* published details of the boston, the most popular of the ragtime dances, and in 1913/14 the 'thé tango'

* This article is part of a larger study of the history of popular music in Britain since the 1890s, at present still in progress. I would like to thank Howard H. Davis, Simon Frith, Alison Lawes and Richard Middleton for their help on editing drafts.

8   *Mark Hustwitt*

became increasingly popular with many classes; 'dansants' visited Britain from the USA. Despite this significant encroachment, dancing before the war was still treated as 'low' and 'taboo' by respectable working-class people.

The First World War was a time of widespread change in the social, economic and moral life of Britain and this had important effects upon dancing and the music that came with it. The growth of military spending meant increased wages for all, a trend which lasted until 1921, and spending on entertainment increased greatly. Dance halls, gramophone records and sheet music sales boomed. Women replaced men in the workplace and were momentarily loosened from the economic and social ties of patriarchy; social and sexual mores relaxed considerably. Styles of dress and hairstyles became simpler, in part as a reaction to the new working conditions women entered, and in part as a response to clothing privations. The relaxed sexual mores of the war applied even more to the large transient population of soldiers. These men were constantly under threat of death, which encouraged hedonism on leave. The changes in the social fabric were held in check during the war by the military rule of the time, but when this was relaxed after 1918, the disruptions escalated. Liberalisation was given a further boost by the disproportion of women to men in the fifteen-to-thirty age group.

The working classes responded to these changes no less than the middle and upper classes. Working-class women shortened their skirts, bobbed their hair and regularly attended dance halls. Whilst the upper and middle classes frequented restaurant and hotel dance floors, the lower middle classes were catered for by the Palais de Danse, the numbers of which increased significantly between 1918 and 1920. The Hammersmith Palais de Danse opened on 28 November 1919, charging 3/6d and 5/- admission, and not serving alcoholic drinks. Its owners opened a similar Palais in Birmingham in 1920, charging 5/- and 7/6d, held dances at skating rinks, and ran nightclubs. The young manual workers were not left out; they crammed into the local 'barn' as Roberts calls it – well-maintained dance halls charging 6d a head (1/- on Saturdays) up to six nights a week (Roberts 1973, p. 232). Dance schools had begun before 1914 but the war boosted their business. In February 1922 the *Daily Mail* reported that 'some hundreds of dance schools have reduced the shortage of dancing men. For every man who danced two years ago, eight or nine dance now. Freak steps . . . have gone out, and easy straightforward steps are the rule' (quoted in Rust 1969, p. 89).

The gramophone (and later the wireless) allowed people to practise dancing at home, as well as to throw small dance parties in parlours.

The production of dance music in Britain in the 1920s   9

Young folk have the opportunity to practise at home to music supplied, via the gramophone, by first class bands. Up to date and up to tempo, these records have killed the shyness that used to overtake the infrequent dancer on entering a ballroom. This country is following the continental lead, where everybody dances.

('New Dance Records', The Gramophone, June 1923, p. 40)

. . . without the secret encouragement and private opportunity that a gramophone offers, dancing to-day would be almost wholly confined to the aged . . . Besides bringing the acquisition of the art of dancing within the reach of all, the gramophone has made it a domestic habit . . .

(Compton 1923, p. 32)

As the new forms of dancing were taken up by increasing numbers of people, and as gramophones appeared in a growing number of homes, the music associated with the new dances was heard by a growing audience. 'Jazz' was the latest arrival – but people's perceptions of 'jazz' when it first arrived in Britain were in general quite confused, and it is these confusions I want to consider next.

Nights in the jazz jungle

During the war years, practically all dance bands followed a formal method of syncopating their music, with the whole band playing the syncopated melody together, alternating between verse and chorus, and repeating a limited number of themes throughout the piece. The foxtrots and quicksteps introduced during the war tended to conform to the strict tempo of these ragtime bands (the Savoy Quartet being the most famous during the period to 1919).* Between 1916 and 1920, a number of bands arrived in Britain from the USA and interrupted this formalism by playing in what I will call a 'novelty' style. This was a form of musical presentation and performance which involved the use of musical and visual gimmickry. It employed whistles and funny hats, teddy bears attached to cymbals, saucepans used as drums, loud volume, the swinging of instruments and claims by the musicians not to be able to read music. It was these bands which introduced the word

---

* The band played at Murray's Club in London before the war, moving to the Savoy Hotel Restaurant in 1915. It consisted of banjo, banjo/vocal, piano and drums, the banjos plucking the tune, with the piano (seldom audible) playing mainly treble accompaniment, while the drummer beat military time and punctuated this with drumrolls, cymbals, woodblocks and whistles. The group's records compare badly with those of the Original Dixieland Jazz Band of 1917, both in sound quality and musically, and if the Savoy Quartet are representative of British dance bands of the period (and they were very popular, having seven 'hits' between 1917 and 1919), then it is not surprising that the Original Dixieland Jazz Band were so outrageous and successful.

10   *Mark Hustwitt*

'jazz' to British audiences and created in people's minds, at the same time, the idea of what a 'jazz band' should sound like, *must* sound like. These bands were at their most popular in the years 1916 to 1919, before being replaced in their influence upon British dance music in 1920 by the lusher arrangements of Paul Whiteman, Isham Jones, Jean Goldkette and the Benson Orchestra. Along with these bands, a number of exhibition dancers, such as Irene Castle, and variety artists, such as Elsie Janis, played an important part in setting the meanings and usage of 'jazz' during the war years.

'Jazz' was thought to refer to a specific dance, though both Castle and Janis spoke against this view.

On one point I am definite, there is no such dance as the 'jazz' and anyone who tells you there is is wrong . . . the nigger bands at home [in the USA] 'jazz' a tune, that is to say, they slur the notes, they syncopate . . . and each instrument puts in a lot of little fancy bits of its own . . . I have not come across a 'jazz' band in England, and I doubt if there is one. (Irene Castle, November 1918, quoted in Pearsall 1976, p. 56)

Castle finds it difficult to put into words exactly what it is the 'nigger bands'* do, but is certain that it is not what bands playing in Britain at the time were doing. Elsie Janis also had problems convincing the English that 'jazz' was not a dance, but her music was itself not very 'jazzy'. In 1918 she appeared in the revue, *Hullo America*, singing 'When I Take My Jazz Band To the Fatherland'; both this and her song 'The Darktown Strutters' Ball' (subtitled 'A Jazz Melody') were more ragtime than jazz. Her singing may have helped add the word 'jazz' to the British audience's vocabulary, but it did not itself introduce any jazz elements.† It was the 'novelty' bands which provided the musical introduction to jazz elements, in particular, to polyrhythm and solo improvisation.

There had been some movement of entertainers between Britain and the USA before the war, but many more Americans came to Britain between 1916 and 1920 than before. They followed the US troops across the Atlantic or were attracted by the hectic European night life of

---

* The use of the word 'nigger' here in such a throwaway manner shows just how great the gap was between white entertainers and blacks, both in the USA and Britain. Another example is that of Fred Elizalde's 'jazz suite' composed in 1927 which he called *Heart Of a Nigger*, though this was changed to *Heart Of a Coon* for its first performance (see p. 25 below).

† Janis's 'Darktown Strutters' Ball' is basically a ragtime piece with some clarinet improvisations, on which she affects a southern accent not evident on her other records, perhaps to give it an authentic 'dixie' sound (cf. her 'Florrie Was a Flapper' and 'I Want a Dancing Man'). She ends the song with 'when they play the jelly-roll blues', which must have added to the confusion of terms current at the time. On the whole her songs either follow the ballad style of the time or are ragtime based.

The production of dance music in Britain in the 1920s 11

these years. Many of these bands have been written about elsewhere (McCarthy 1971; Rust 1972; Pearsall 1976), and I will concentrate on the best documented and, it seems, most significant band of the period, the Original Dixieland Jazz Band (henceforth ODJB). The ODJB opened in Britain on 7 April 1919 in the revue *Joy Bells*, after creating storms of controversy in New York. The star of *Joy Bells*, music hall comedian George Robey, objected to their 'jungle' music and had them dropped after only one night. They then appeared at a number of London nightclubs and, for two weeks over Easter, at the London Palladium. They continued to appear regularly in London throughout the summer and on 29 November they were the band which, together with Billy Arnold's Novelty Jazz Band, opened the Hammersmith Palais de Danse. They remained resident there for nine months and returned to the USA in July 1920.

Their music was unlike any heard in Britain before (for recordings see the discography). Its instrumentation was different – cornet, trombone, clarinet (playing violin parts), with a piano and drums providing backing – and they featured improvised solos, even if within the context of a 'novelty' performance, which included 'farmyard hookum'.* The band's song titles added to the confusion of terms: 'Livery Stable *Blues*', 'Tiger *Rag*', 'Dixie *Jazz* One-Step'. Nevertheless it was within the context of 'novelty' bands and this proliferation of tags for their music that both the word 'jazz' and its musical elements were introduced to Britain. In 1919, then, the key to playing 'jazz' seemed to be excess; bands played very loudly, acted 'wild' on stage (duelling with violin bows, etc.), and added a variety of objects to the normal drum kit: tubular bells, gongs, frying pans, zinc baths, jugs, saucepans, motor horns and tin cans.

Like jazz, the blues was mistaken for a dance when blues records first became available in Britain in 1923. Harry Melvill wrote of 'the blues' that it

possess[es] undoubtedly an interesting, albeit a monotonous new rhythm. I have not yet seen it danced on Broadway, but I fancy it is not yet there, or

---

* This style had become popular, according to Schuller, with the song 'Farmyard Caprice', in which 'the musicians were required to imitate literally every farmyard animal' (1968, p. 179), though it probably dates back to the minstrel shows of the nineteenth century. Bands as diverse as the ODJB and Paul Whiteman's Orchestra can be heard producing such noises, and this, to a certain extent, reveals the tenuousness of the divide between 'novelty' and Whitemanesque 'symphonic syncopation' during the early twenties. (For Whiteman examples, see 'Whispering' and 'Rhapsody in Blue', reissued on *Paul Whiteman Vol. 1*, listed in the discography.) This style was combined with music hall comedy in some British dance music (e.g. Jack Payne's 'My Brother Makes the Noises for the Music' and 'Fire!Fire!Fire!', reissued on *Jack Payne with his BBC Dance Orchestra*).

12   *Mark Hustwitt*

elsewhere, what Broadway would call 'standardized'. The majority of those whom I have seen dancing it 'on this side', appear to imagine that it is a species of 'slow motion' fox-trot . . . [I have] several times attentively watched Miss Nora Bayes singing her *Yes, We Have No Bananas Blues* (HMV B 1720). The suggestion then conveyed to me by her feet was that of a tango . . .

(Melvill 1924, pp. 154–5)

It is apparent that British performers and audiences did not understand blues records, and unlike jazz, they lacked anyone willing or able to explain them.

A further confusion of what 'jazz' meant came from its use by the working-class street bands of the industrial towns of South Wales and the North. These bands followed the traditions of the so-called Waffen Fuffen or Tommy Talker bands which used mainly home-made instruments, but they adopted the name 'jazz band' during the 1920s, continuing to play in their usual manner on a variety of kazoo instruments.

Jazz, dancing and dance music were often seen in the immediate post-war period as symptomatic of social decay. In 1919 *The Times* reported a speech by a Canon Drummond in which, attacking jazz dance and nightclubs, he set out the 'respectable' view of these new phenomena:

it seemed to him to be a most degrading condition for any part of society to get into to encourage a dance so low, so demoralizing and of such low origin – the dance of low niggers in America – with every conceivable crude instrument, not to make music but to make noise. It was one symptom of a very grave disease which was infecting the country . . .

('Jazz Dancing: A Canon's Denunciation',
The Times, 15 March 1919, p. 7)

He went on to urge that 'civil fathers be on the alert to do what they could so far as the law permitted' to prevent jazz dancing and jazz clubs from opening. Leyton Urban District Council took his advice and in letting their municipal hall for dancing prohibited the one-step and jazz. At the same time as churchmen attacked the moral implications of dancing to jazz, the medical profession worried over the effects of such violent exercise on the body, particularly the shifting of organs, damage to the legs and a general shattering of nerves and loss of youthfulness. A Walsall School Medical Officer reported that 'children of all ages now seem unable to keep their feet still' (Rust 1969, p. 90).

Many of the attacks on jazz dance and music reflect existing biases. In some sections of British society there was strong resentment of the USA's financial gains from the war, of their successful social, cultural and sporting interventions and, by implication, of all things American. There was also blunt racism, as Canon Drummond's comments

The production of dance music in Britain in the 1920s   13

illustrate. The *Daily Mail* attacked the charleston as 'reminiscent of negro orgies' and blacks were consistently referred to in terms of their 'jungle' and 'primitive' nature. If jazz was mentioned at all in the early twenties by music critics it was seen as a vacuous commercial music, which had momentarily caught the distracted mood of people who would, if better musically educated, choose the classics instead.

Even those defending dance music could find nothing permanent in it:

Every month new and more exciting dance tunes are produced, which, as they weary us, we discard for newer and still more exciting ones. For it is notorious that jazz tunes, admirable as they are, do soon become a burden . . .

(Caskett 1923, p. 21)

These musical effusions are ephemeral – that is their whole essence; they are the very 'mayflies' of music. Their appeal is largely humorous and, like the best of jokes, loses interest with repetition. Hence there is an enormous output of new dance records . . .

('New Dance Records', *The Gramophone*, June 1923, p. 40)

No defence against the charges of emptiness or worthlessness is being offered here; the momentary pleasure of a record was its *raison d'être*, and it fitted its purpose remarkably well. In this, dance music was in direct contrast to the classics, whose pleasures developed over time. Jack Hylton's 1926 article, 'The British touch', begins by agreeing that the war-time dance music was 'an unholy row' and goes on to defend his own dance music in terms of its popularity. In *Melody Maker* (1926) he wrote: 'The public wants it and will not let it go. Surely that is the great and only test. Music . . . is at the mercy of the law of supply and demand, and if there is no demand, then syncopation dies away unmourned' (quoted in Pearsall 1976, p. 57).

'To move with perfect smoothness'

Throughout the twenties a number of informal conferences of dance teachers took place in an attempt both to restrain some of the more 'freakish' aspects of ballroom dancing and to standardise dancing under formal headings: waltz, foxtrot, quickstep, tango, etc. This led to the linking of specific musical tempos with specific formal dance steps. The first such conference was held in May 1920 and was called by Philip Richardson, editor of *Dancing Times*. In the following year, a number of meetings formulated the *correct* ways of dancing the steps mentioned above, and meetings continued throughout the twenties. In 1924, the Imperial Society of Teachers of Dancing, which had been founded in 1904, set up a section specifically concerned with ballroom

14   *Mark Hustwitt*

dancing, with the aim of continuing the process of standardisation. This standardising – which did continue, in the face of newly introduced forms of 'jazz dance' such as the charleston (1925) and the black bottom (1926) – was in part made possible by changes in the music which dance bands played, for after 1920 the organisation of the bands altered from the small units of the war years, to orchestras playing 'symphonic syncopation'.

The standardisation of music and dance also meant a codification of pleasure, of dancing as a sensual activity. The frenzy of the war-time dances had required a mutual understanding of the partner's possible movements, a cooperative improvisation, which brought the dancers together mentally and physically as well as socially. The continual changing of partners of pre-war years was abandoned as permanent partnerships became an increasingly necessary part of dancing. Standardisation of dance-steps did not alter this tendency towards close partnership but did change its direction: improvisation in dance was replaced by the need to go through the motions smoothly and together. This change of emphasis was not altogether unwelcome to many dancers themselves, who had found the tempo of 'novelty' bands difficult to follow, the dance-steps and ever-changing trends too hard to keep up with.

There are many ways to control activity and during the twenties a number were effectively used to formalise dancing. Some of the more outrageous forms were simply banned, as the charleston was both by London hotels and by the Hammersmith Palais de Danse. Others were strongly disapproved of, or ignored by the dance teachers and professional exhibitors, or stifled by the managers of the theatres in which they were danced. Dance teachers and exhibitors took the lead in showing people how dances should be done, and a small number of them were established as authorities during the early twenties – people like Philip Richardson, Santos Casini, Victor Silvester and Josephine Bradley. They set the correct tempos for dancing, and in 1928 Silvester formed a band of his own, to play the correct music. One final way in which dancing was standardised was in organised competitions: dancers followed their teachers' instructions before those same teachers acting as judges. Such competitions appeared around 1922, and in 1928, in one competition alone, 20,000 people took part in 288 local heats for prize money of £5,000 given by Columbia records.

One effect of these developments was an increasing similarity of dancing styles between social classes. Before the turn of the century, while the forms of dance may have been the same, the standards governing the practice of these dances varied from class to class. The twenties saw these divisions collapse: 'all classes now enjoyed the

The production of dance music in Britain in the 1920s 15

same dances and the same rhythms' (Rust 1969, p. 93). Everyone danced the new dances according to a single accepted standard, which was set by a few individual professionals. The class positions of the dancing public might determine the surroundings in which dancing occurred, but not the forms it took nor the standards it sought to attain.

A distinctly new syncopated rhythm

It is clear that there were a number of different social contexts in which dancing took place during the period of the First World War and the early twenties. They varied from small private parties in working-, middle- and upper-class homes to large society balls, from social venues such as hotels and nightclubs to more public performances in revue and palais de danse; 'the demand for live entertainment was tremendous and musicians would be booked to appear at anything from twenty-first birthday parties through weddings and firms' dinners to large private and public dances' (Lynn 1975, p. 32).

The boom in the number of dancers led to an equal boom in the demand for musicians to play for them. Many people who had received some classical training, had played in a military band, or had simply played at Edwardian musical evenings, now took up playing dance music professionally. Jack Payne's autobiography explains that most of the bands which played these dances and parties were *ad hoc* combinations, formed only for that particular 'gig' (his word). Payne began his career after leaving the Air Force. Finding no other work suitable to his talents, he began playing the piano in a trio around the Midlands in 1919, briefly turned promoter at the beginning of 1920, and then moved to London. He played numerous 'gigs' at society parties and took short residencies at hotels around the country, forming bands for each occasion as necessary. At that time, musicians went to Archer St in London to find work: 'daily between the hours of 12 and 2 you used to see five or six hundred out-of-work musicians and variety folk there to meet agents and pick up whatever booking may be going' (Payne 1947, p. 124).

The dance bands which played at these gigs cannot easily be placed in simple categories. Those playing for society venues such as the Savoy Hotel or at balls kept careful tempo and a polite profile; in terms of jazz they were unadventurous and it is not difficult to see why, for the stakes – regular, profitable employment – were high. Those which did experiment with melody or rhythm in the years directly following the war tended to find work in the *public* sphere – for example, the ODJB played mostly at nightclubs and at the Hammersmith Palais during their visit. But the bandleaders who became famous in the

16   *Mark Hustwitt*

1920s were not those who wished to experiment for the sake of abstract principles such as 'jazz'. It must not be forgotten that the bandleaders were entrepreneurs, first and foremost. Only during the late twenties did musicians begin to go against the wishes of dancers in their arranging and playing, and only then did a notion of jazz as art develop.

British bands had not excelled in their imitation of the novelty bands, and after the ODJB left Britain in July 1920, a different form of dance music came to replace it. This music followed the style set out by Paul Whiteman and his Orchestra, and by bands such as the Benson Orchestra, Jean Goldkette, and Isham Jones. Whiteman was very popular during the twenties: his first record, 'Wang, Wang Blues', sold 457,000 copies world wide just in 1920, while his 'Whispering'/'Japanese Sandman' disc sold over one million copies in Britain; he had nine 'hits' in 1921 alone. He is a central figure in the twenties because of his championship of 'symphonic syncopation', a form which became the main influence upon British dance bands. This differed from the music of the novelty bands in that it was carefully arranged (originally by Whiteman's pianist, Ferde Grofe, later by others) rather than the parts emerging haphazardly between musicians as they practised. It was conceived as a whole by the arranger, who also set out the soloists' parts, preparing their 'improvisations' for them. This gave a unity to a piece which novelty bands lacked, and although his early recordings (mentioned above) did include many 'novelty' elements, his work (especially his use of strings) soon moved closer to light orchestral music. This move towards light music was followed in Britain by the Savoy Orpheans, Jack Hylton and Jack Payne's BBC Orchestra. The lush arrangements, steady tempo and smooth solos were preferred by audiences dancing in the high society hotels, restaurants and nightclubs, and, after an influential Whiteman performance at the Aeolian Hall in January 1925, the Savoy Havana Band and the Savoy Orpheans combined to put on a concert of 'symphonic syncopation' at the Queens Hall. It was after Whiteman's band began to feature 'hot' soloists, such as Bix Beiderbecke, that British bands began to allow their own soloists to play 'hotter'.

Whiteman is atypical of dance bandleaders of the time only in the extent of his fame and his control of the popular media; most leaders in Britain followed his methods. He exploited his fame by forming numerous bands around the USA which performed using his name, but with which he had little direct contact, and in this he was followed by British bandleaders such as Jack Hylton, Jack Payne and Henry Hall. He was only one of a number of people responsible for changing the novelty jazz of the war years into the light orchestral dance music

The production of dance music in Britain in the 1920s   17

of the twenties, but his entrepreneurship made him visible and influential. Jack Payne saw him during a visit to Britain in 1923 and was impressed by his presentation:

> Here I thought was a real show band. Whiteman didn't just play; he presented his band as a stage entertainment. I have never forgotten the deep impression which that difference made on me. I decided that as soon as ever I had the chance I would feature *my* band just that way. The formula . . . seemed to me so exactly right, and I studied the reaction of the dancers, they too, welcomed the innovation. (Payne 1947, p. 125)

Aspiring bandleaders saw as their most important task getting a 'shop-window' engagement, a residency at one of the large hotels, clubs or restaurants. From here, other forms of media (recording, radio, theatre) which brought national popularity were accessible. Such a 'shop-window' did not give this access automatically, however; both Hylton and Payne had a number of early recordings rejected by their recording companies, and Ambrose, after recording a few sides in 1924, did not record again until 1928.

One interesting shift during the early twenties, when the band-leaders who were to dominate the decade established themselves, was in the names of bands. Words like 'novelty', 'jazz' and 'Dixie' were dropped, the names of establishments – the 'Hotel Cecil', the 'Devonshire Restaurant' – or combinations of personality and establishment – 'Jack Hylton's Kit-Kat Club Band', 'Jack Payne and his BBC Dance Orchestra' – replaced them. Some names, such as 'Deauville Dance Band', were in fact covers for studio bands, to give the illusion of attachment to an opulent establishment.

At this time, an establishment did not hire a band but a bandleader, who, as 'Musical Director', then independently contracted the band members, drawing upon the pool of musicians available. Discographies reveal that such units were only stable in the short term and the changes gradually occurring over two or three years could lead to the replacement of a band's whole personnel. The relationship between musicians and leaders varied greatly: 'some bandleaders were fun to work for, some commanded respect, others were heartily loathed' (Colin 1977, p. 27). If any division between the bands of the period can be made, it is perhaps between those concerned with the 'art' of dance music, and those preoccupied with its financial aspects. The latter predominated during the early twenties.

The musicians' work consisted of playing for dancers every night, with little break, and for this they drew upon a large number of tunes to avoid repetition. They also had to contend with the rapid changes in popularity of different tunes and dances, though after 1926 the

18   *Mark Hustwitt*

latter changed little. Of the Savoy Orpheans' workload, 'Peppering'
wrote:

> One is told that 'three to five hundred new dance pieces are composed every
> week' and that every week 'thirty or forty new items are added to the repertory
> of the Band' and that the Orpheans, who at a conservative estimate carry from
> five hundred to a thousand current tunes in their heads, change their
> programme gradually but completely about every three months . . . (*The
> Gramophone*, July 1925, p. 85)

Most of these tunes were not particularly demanding of the musicians
but were designed to keep the dancers happy, and the major bands
followed closely the strategy of the US orchestras, holding to the tune
while soloists played in clearly predictable places. The tempo
remained clear and the music was easy on the ear, breaks in the
formalised flow being for momentary effect rather than innovation.
The banjo and drums held the rhythm, the brass and piano played the
melody, with solos being taken by trumpet, saxophones, clarinet or
violin. Before the introduction of 'hot' solos after 1927, the only
significant innovation was the switch from banjo to guitar. In the early
twenties, vocals were rare and often consisted of a brief chorus of four
lines. As the decade progressed, vocals were used more extensively,
but it was only at the end of the decade, with the advent of 'crooning',
that dance bands acquired members whose main job was singing. Such
lyrics as existed tended to be concerned with the pleasures of dancing
or with romance.

The electric wind

In the early twenties dance music was spread beyond its base in the
dance halls and hotels by a number of media. There were changes in
the way music was produced and disseminated and dance music
became a very successful form. The new organisation of production
existed outside the music hall and sheet music publishing, which had
been dominant before the war, though it did not exclude the use of
these media. They were supplanted as the major source of income and
work by the dance halls, the nightclubs, revue and recording. The
gramophone had, by 1921, become a mass medium capable of
providing artists with an audience of hundreds of thousands, and
audiences with an almost instantaneous account of new tastes and
pleasures. Sheet music, too, despite a decline in sales, was important
in changing people's home music from Victorian and music hall
ballads to dance tunes. Such publishers as Lawrence Wright and
Chappell dominate this period, taking large advertisements in the

The production of dance music in Britain in the 1920s 19

trade and national press. In addition to piano scores, these publishers offered popular tunes of the day arranged in a number of ways, for a trio, for small or large orchestras. This meant that not only could everybody hear the same arrangement on record (and later on radio) but local dance bands could also play the same tune in the same way as the famous bands of the time.

Dance music was further promoted by the addition to the gramophone trade press of journals such as *The Gramophone* and *Melody Maker*. *The Gramophone* was founded in 1923 by Compton MacKenzie, aided financially by Walter Yeomans, head of the HMV education department, which had been set up in 1919 'to propagate the educational use of the gramophone'. It carried a 'New Dance Records' column but was more concerned with the promotion of the gramophone as a means of musical education and with the expansion of the library of 'good' recorded music. More important for dance music was the founding in 1926 of *Melody Maker* (with aid from Lawrence Wright) and *Rhythm*. They provided a forum for the discussion of 'syncopated' music and began formulating a vocabulary of jazz criticism. They published transcriptions and articles by 'hot' musicians, such as Fred Elizalde and Lew Stone, and promoted competitions (to discover new talent) and concerts by bands such as Elizalde's (when commercial promoters were not interested). Their impact cannot be fully evaluated here but was considerable.*

After 1923, it was the wireless which was the most important medium through which dance music reached its mass audience – if a band could manage to broadcast, it was almost certain of a recording contract. The first broadcast of dance music was on 23 March 1923, and three days later, Marius B. Winter's band became the first professional group to be transmitted. In April, the Savoy Havana Band made its first broadcast and on 24 May the first outside broadcast by a band took place, by Ben Davis's Carlton Hotel Dance Band. In September 1923, the two Savoy Hotel groups, the Savoy Havana Band and the Savoy Orpheans, began their regular outside broadcasts. The main reason for picking the Savoy seems to have been location, since it was near the BBC's Savoy Hill studios. It may also have been because the Hotel was a favourite haunt of BBC personnel. The Savoy bands continued to dominate broadcasting until Sidney Firman organised the first BBC Dance Band in 1926. Their domination of the airwaves was paralleled

---

* The most important of the trade press were *The Phono Record*, *Talking Machine News*, and *The Sound Wave*, all of which included record reviews and articles on dance music. Complete sets of these, along with *Melody Maker*, are held at the National Newspaper Library at Colindale. *Rhythm* is held at the British Library, while *The Gramophone* is held at the British Institute of Recorded Sound.

by their domination of record sales during the early twenties, the Orpheans alone selling over five million records.

To begin with, the wireless audience was not large but it increased rapidly (see Table 1); throughout the twenties it continued to be more middle than working class. The amount of dance band music on the air fluctuated but after 1926 tended to be about eight hours a week, ten per cent or more of the total broadcasting output (Table 2). It was not broadcast on Sundays, and was confined to the afternoons and late evenings, usually after 10.30 pm. On Sundays, people often tuned to the continental stations, which were more liberal with their supply of the music. The popularity of broadcast dance music is difficult to judge, though in the 1927 *Daily Mail* ballot it came fourth, after 'Variety and Concert Party', 'Light Orchestral' and 'Military Band', but outstripping classical forms. It is certain that a large number of people listened to the programmes and that the bands which broadcast were highly influential. By 1929, the popularity gained from broadcasting by such bandleaders as Jack Payne (who led the BBC's house band from 1928 to 1932) enabled them to make a good income touring variety theatres too. By now, a regular rota of bands had installed themselves in the BBC's late night spot, and these bands dominated the late twenties and the thirties.

'Records were like magic on the stock exchange'

The years between 1924 and 1930 saw considerable changes in the gramophone industry, both in the methods of production and in the organisation of the supply of records. Throughout this period, however, it was dance bands which provided the major source of income for the record companies. The industry was initially dominated by two companies, the Gramophone Company, with its HMV and Zonophone imprints, and Columbia Graphophone, with its Columbia and Velvet Face labels. Both companies had been started by US companies but by the end of the war had seceded; both did well during the upturn in the British economy after 1924. Between 1924 and 1928, sales of records rose from 22 million to 50 million a year, while prices fell from their post-war level of 2/- to 1/6d and 1/3d, shops such as Woolworth's and Curry's selling budget records for as little as 6d. By 1928 it was estimated that there were about 2.5 million record players in Britain, almost as many as there were licensed wireless receivers.

Considerable technical changes occurred during this period which directly influenced the recording style of the dance bands and their vocalists.

Before 1924 all recordings used an acoustic method which, except for

The production of dance music in Britain in the 1920s 21

Table 1. *The number of radio licences bought, 1922–32*

Year	Number	% change from year to year
1922/3	125,000	+498.4%
1923/4	748,000	+80.5%
1924/5	1,350,000	+45.2%
1925/6	1,960,000	+15.8%
1926/7	2,270,000	+9.4%
1927/8	2,483,000	+9.9%
1928/9	2,730,000	+13.22%
1929/30	3,091,000	+17.9%
1930/1	3,647,000	+26.7%
1931/2	4,620,000	

Source: Statistical Abstract of the UK. No. 76 Cmd. 4233, Table 196, pp. 278–9

Table 2. *Amount of dance music broadcast during one week in October*

	1926	1927	1928	1929	1930
Total hours of broadcasting	62	77.35	80	78.55	78
Dance music as a % of total hours	6.62%	16.43%	11.56%	9.92%	11.48%

Sources: Briggs 1961, p. 390; 1966, p. 35

the increased refinement of its components, was essentially the same as that first used by Edison in 1877. The recording artists would be positioned in front of a single recording horn, and the more musicians there were, the closer they had to gather around the horn and the louder they had to play. The sound had to be carefully balanced in the studio before recording began, since the various sound levels of the musicians could not be adjusted after the 'take'. In the case of dance bands the more powerful instruments (saxophone, trombone, trumpet, cornet) were positioned furthest from the horn, while the softer instruments (violin, banjo, clarinet, piano) were placed nearer.

The major technological change in the 1920s was the development of electrical recording during the period 1920–4. Electrical recording, first used commercially in 1924, meant that the sound was picked up by a microphone rather than a diaphragm at the end of a long horn, and turned into electro-magnetic signals rather than mechanical movements. Because the process was electro-magnetic, the signal carried to the cutting needle could be boosted, removing the need to have musicians gathered around a single point. Low bass notes were picked up for the first time, singers no longer had to shout to be heard, bands could play less stridently.

22   *Mark Hustwitt*

Initially the record companies did not announce the new process, fearing for their catalogue of acoustic recordings, and it was not until Columbia's *Adeste Fideles*, using a choir of over a thousand, that it attracted public notice. The pages of the trade press were full of comment during 1925–6, and by about 1927 all recording used electrical methods, despite some initial criticism.

As the technology of record production changed, so too did the financial organisation of the record companies. During the middle years of the twenties, both the major record companies were well quoted on the Stock Exchange, issuing shares to raise capital for expansion and electrical experiments. There were also a number of smaller but equally successful companies, such as Crystalite, Vocalion and Duophone, and they too issued large numbers of shares. The profitability of the record industry and a general growth in share prices are two major reasons for the increase in Stock Exchange activity concerning the record industry (Tables 3 and 4). Share prices increased rapidly during 1928 (Tables 5 and 6), when at least seventeen new companies were formed to deal in some way in gramophones and records. These companies were of two main types: they either took over an already existing private company, leaving the original owners in control but with much enlarged capital, or they started from scratch, hoping to break into the market. In both cases the floatation of the company was intended to take advantage of the share boom.

A number of factors led to the general collapse of this burgeoning industry during 1929 and 1930. The growth had been dependent on the share boom of 1928 and on the growing demand for records, both of which ceased by the end of 1929. The general industrial decline of 1927–8 led to a collapse in the market for records, as did the popularity of wireless, the running costs of which were far lower than those of the gramophone. As Table 1 shows, the number of wireless licences increased at the same time as the gramophone industry declined. The end of the share boom in 1929 cut off the companies' major source of finance: most of their profits had gone to pay shareholders, meaning that their major source of income for expansion was share issues (they seem to have borrowed little from the banks). The new companies formed in 1928 could not survive the high initial capital costs and patent payments combined with adverse trading conditions and bad management. Many of them had been formed merely to cash in on the share boom.*

* For reports of creditors' meetings, see *The Times* 30 November 1929, p. 4 (Cliftophone Records, Ltd); 16 January 1930, p. 5 (British Brunswick, Ltd); 9 May 1930, p. 5 (Duophone and Unbreakable Record Co., Ltd); 15 May 1930, p. 6 (Symphony Gramophone and Radio Co., Ltd); and 15 August 1930, p. 9 (Duophone (Foreign) Ltd).

Table 3. Gramophone company profits in the 1920s (in £ sterling)

	The Gramophone Company	Columbia Graphophone	Barnett Samual (Decca after 1929)	Vocalion	Crystalite	Ducetto	Itonia	Selecta
1920	125,162	*	*	*	*	*	*	*
1921	−2,659	*	*	*	*	*	*	*
1922	166,555	*	*	*	*	*	*	*
1923	289,737	*	*	*	*	*	*	*
1924	316,375	76,367	40,540	*	*	*	*	*
1925	413,962	126,620	69,398	14,701	21,131	*	*	*
1926	500,611	150,825	56,535	8,276	22,159	*	*	*
1927	780,555	180,443	61,002	98,627	23,279	*	*	*
1928	1,132,414	491,305	61,002	95,437	88,883	37,348	9,852	*
1929	1,200,912	505,121	−89,683	27,310	57,148	14,639	8,803	12,450
1930	840,931	580,159	−83,354	−46,235	71,888	−18,211	−9,927	10,000
1931	160,893		−68,837	*	76,270	−2,782	*	*
1932	16,114 (EMI)			*	82,233	*	*	796

*Figures not given in sources.

Note: These figures are not necessarily commensurate between companies or over time, since different companies declare their profits under different headings (e.g. Unappropriated Profits, Trading Profits, Balance), and some companies change their accounting procedures (e.g. The Gramophone Company shifts from using Unappropriated Profits to Trading Profits). Given these problems of interpretation, this table can give only an indication of the companies' success.

Sources: The Times and The Economist, 1918–33.

24   Mark Hustwitt

Table 4. *Highest and lowest prices of Columbia Gramophone shares, 1925–8*

	1925	1926	1927	1928
Highest	$2^{9}/_{32}$	$2^{31}/_{32}$	$7^{11}/_{16}$	$16^{13}/_{32}$
Lowest	$1^{5}/_{8}$	$1^{15}/_{18}$	$2^{7}/_{8}$	$6^{7}/_{8}$

Source: *The Economist*, 15 September 1928, pp. 478–9

Table 5. *Changes in the price of the major gramophone companies' shares during 1928*

| | 1928 | | Beginning of 1928 | June 25 | July 27 | Aug. 9 |
	Lowest	Highest				
Columbia Graph., 10/ shs	$6^{13}/_{16}$	$18^{1}/_{8}$	$7^{7}/_{16}$	$12^{3}/_{8}$	13	$14^{5}/_{8}$
Gramophone, £1 shares	9	$14^{1}/_{32}$	$9^{5}/_{8}$	$10^{3}/_{4}$	$11^{3}/_{8}$	$12^{1}/_{16}$
Victor Talking, no par	$54^{1}/_{4}$	$105^{1}/_{4}$	54	$83^{1}/_{2}$	$95^{1}/_{4}$	$97^{1}/_{2}$
Vocalion, 10/ shs	$2^{5}/_{32}$	$4^{1}/_{8}$	$2^{5}/_{32}$	$2^{7}/_{8}$	$3^{1}/_{4}$	$3^{11}/_{16}$
Duophone, 10/ shs *	13/	$4^{1}/_{2}$	13/	$2^{15}/_{16}$	$2^{5}/_{8}$	$2^{5}/_{8}$

*Introduced March, 1928

Source: *The Economist*, 11 August 1928, p. 281

Table 6. *Changes in share prices of some minor gramophone companies during autumn 1928*

Company	Share	Price 31 Aug. 1928	Price 27 Sept. 1928	Rise or Fall
British Homophone	Ord. 5/	4/7½	6/6¼	+ 2/0¾
Dominion Gram. Records	{ 10% Pref. 10/	6/9	6/6	− /3
	{ Def. 1/	2/6	3/6¾	+ 1/0¾
Electramonic	{ 8% Pf. Ord 10/	5/10½	7/9	+ 1/11½
	{ Def. Ord. 1/	3/6	5/9	+ 2/3
Goodson Gram. Records	5/	7/9	10/4½	+ 2/7½
Gramo. Records	Def. 1/	1/7½	3/2¼	+ 1/6¾
Metropole Gram	Ord. 1/	6/1½	21/6	+15/4½
Selecta Gramophone	5/	6/6	7/10½	+ 1/4½
Worldecho Records	2/	10/	5/10½	− 4/1½
American-Dominion	{ Pref. 5/ paid	4/ discount	3/ dis	+ 1/
Unbreakable Records	{ Def. 1/	1/3	3/	+ 1/9

Source: *The Economist*, 29 September 1928, p. 564

The production of dance music in Britain in the 1920s   25

The result of the general collapse of 1929 to 1931 was a large number of mergers. The Gramophone Company and Columbia Graphophone merged in 1930 to form Electrical and Musical Industries, while Barnett Samual, floated as Decca in 1929, eventually merged with Duophone, Crystalate and Vocalion to form Decca Records. This duopoly was to dominate the British record industry until the 1950s.

'Jazz – what of the future?'

The dance bands which had established themselves by 1926 had set up a system into which all new forms of music and all new bands had to pass to reach a mass audience. The different media – radio, recording, sheet music and forms of live performance – had become inter-linked, so that access to any of these required penetration of the others, at the core of which was the hotel or nightclub residency. The justification the bandleaders used was that they were 'giving the public what it wants', and, during the latter years of the twenties, these bands moved to stereotyped rhythmic dance music or into forms of 'light orchestral' music; the work of Victor Silvester exemplifies the former, that of Jack Payne at the BBC the latter. The choice between bands increasingly became a choice in terms of personality, visual image and presentation rather than involving any musical difference. 'Jazz' ceased to be the meaning of the music, as is made clear by the career of Fred Elizalde.

Fred Elizalde, and his brother Manuel, arrived at Cambridge, ostensibly to study there, from Los Angeles, in the autumn of 1926. Fred had already led a band in the USA and soon formed one at Cambridge, the Quinquaginta Club Ramblers, which played the Footlights revue that year. After this he began contributing piano scores and technical articles to *Melody Maker* and recorded for Brunswick (May 1927) and HMV (June, July 1927). His bands always performed 'hotter' jazz than others of the time and, as he gained access to the various media of the day, this led to conflicts with both his audiences and the managers of those media. His 'jazz suite', *Heart Of A Nigger* (retitled *Heart Of A Coon* for performance), was, after its first performance (by Ambrose's band at the London Palladium), relegated to matinee performances only by the management. Late in 1927, he was asked by the Savoy Hotel to form a band to play there but was constantly at loggerheads with the dancers for playing long out-of-tempo introductions and refusing to play waltzes. The BBC, which was compelled by a contract with the Savoy to broadcast its bands, twice took him off the air due to listeners' complaints. After the first occasion, the Savoy management had Elizalde change his policy, but in

26   *Mark Hustwitt*

1929 he was systematically denied access to the media essential for reaching a mass audience: in the spring, the BBC ended his broadcasts, and in July, the Savoy did not renew his contract with them; he was already without a recording contract (and had recorded little anyway compared to other bands). He attempted to take his music to the variety stage, but his tour ended after he was booed off stage in Scotland. In 1933 he left Britain to study under Falla in Spain.

The radical nature of Elizalde's music (for examples, see *Jazz at the Savoy – the 20s* and *Jazz in Britain – the 20s*, listed in the discography) had attracted a small following, based around *Melody Maker* – he won its poll in 1928 and the journal sponsored a concert by him in 1929. But his work did not appeal to the mass audience or to those in control of the popularising media whose perseverance might have made his music better understood and appreciated. The nature of his music was set out in an article he wrote in 1929 (perhaps in response to a previous article by Edgar Jackson, writing as 'Needlepoint') in *The Gramophone*. Both Elizalde and Jackson saw 'hot' jazz as *art* and are insistent upon its separation from the novelty jazz of the war years. Elizalde stressed that improvisation was an important feature of jazz, and predicted that bands would change the structure of songs, moving from conventional verse/chorus forms to set pieces and preludes. The rhythm would change during the course of a piece: 'By this a fox-trot may develop into a blues, after which the band will turn it into a one-step, and finally perhaps the rhythm will change to that of a waltz' (Elizalde 1929, p. 393). Finally he saw developments in arrangement which would place melody second to rhythm. In a reply to Elizalde, Bert Ambrose criticised this view, arguing that, when a dance started, his dancers at the Mayfair Hotel took 'the best part of half a chorus to settle down to the new rhythm', and if this was then altered 'they are not going to enjoy being whisked into something they do not like'. Ambrose stressed that the dancers must be kept happy and his view – which can be taken as typical of bandleaders of the time, though they seldom seem to have needed to put it into print – was that 'the melody should take first place everytime. It can be trimmed with frills and exploited indefinitely, but it must never be crippled, and however it is played the dancers should never be allowed to lose sight of it' (Ambrose 1929, p. 435).

It is Elizalde who is the less patronising of the two, hoping that people will see the 'art' in his work, whereas Ambrose sees himself as guiding the dancers in their pleasures. Elizalde was not simply playing music to be listened to, but music which had to be worked at for it to be entertaining. In its context and its time, such music was jarring. Its home was in the concert hall and nightclub jam session rather than the

The production of dance music in Britain in the 1920s 27

dance-floor or variety stage. The divide between 'hot' jazz and the big dance bands already existed in the USA, and in Britain a few musicians discovered the work of black musicians and imitated it in late night 'jams'; but the dance bands maintained their hegemony over access to the mass audience well into the 1930s.

Certain elements, considered vital parts of jazz, remained while others did not. Improvisation became much more controlled as the twenties and thirties wore on; and rhythmic shifts were increasingly eradicated. The short themes, derived from black music, which had been the core of jazz in the early twenties were replaced by themes taken from British musical tradition, 'treated' by arrangers for British sensibilities. As the size of dance bands grew, the uncoordinated polyphony of the ODJB became difficult to reproduce without unwelcome dissonance. This increase in size, too, necessitated some form of central authority and direction, and thus musical choices passed out of the hands of the musicians into those of their leader. At the same time, record companies were changing their promotional policies, from a stress on songs to one on personalities: it was the 'personality' of a band which sold records, not the tunes that it played. This too set the bandleaders (and a few noted musicians and, later, vocalists) above musicians in general.

Conclusion

This article, looking at one historical moment, has begun to map out the complexity of the relations surrounding the production and dissemination of forms of popular music within modern capitalist societies, and the discreet ways in which the forms of production and dissemination codify forms of pleasure. Given the preliminary nature of this cartography, only tentative comments can be made by way of a conclusion.

Firstly, notions of a single or primary determining social or economic force cannot be applied to the forms of popular dance music during the 1920s, or, by implication, to other forms in other times. Changes in attitudes to sexuality allowed for the possibility of more sensual dance in the twenties, and this was contemporary with more uninhibited and sensuous music; but at the same time the change in dance was a sign of the change in sexuality and an impetus for further changes, and reactions to changes, in sexuality. The dances define a 'moment' in a changing formulation of sexuality which occurs during the early twenties, and this is contemporary with the 'moment' of novelty jazz, which is part of the changing formulation of dance music.

Equally, the period after 1922–3, when dancing becomes more

28   *Mark Hustwitt*

formalised and dance music more 'symphonic', should not be seen simply as a repression of 'liberties' won in the post-war years. The change was more subtle. The codes of pleasure in the immediate post-war period centred on strategies of abandonment and hedonism, while, as the twenties wore on, a different centre emerged: the emphasis was now on relaxation, smoothness and calmness, reflecting a more passive set of strategies.

The twenties also saw the maturing of the mass consumer culture which had begun to develop in the 1880s with mass-produced foods and drugs. During the twenties, the electrical industries extended the demand for their products across classes and throughout the regions (though the north of England lagged behind the south). Before the beginning of the First World War, the only mass media which had not depended upon the direct interaction of producer and consumer had been the print media (newspapers, novels, 'penny dreadfuls'). The music hall, the previous major form of mass entertainment, required people to turn up at specially built places to watch performers, live, and the scale of the immediate transmission of the product was therefore limited. The war improved both the demand for and the technology of three forms of media (gramophone, cinema, wireless) whose commodity form enabled a greater spatial, and in the case of the first two, temporal, distance between producer and consumer to occur. The results of this change in the relation between producer and consumer were hotly debated during the twenties and thirties by cultural critics such as Constant Lambert and Theodor Adorno, and developed into the 'mass cultural' view of media. Such debates cannot be commented on here, but it is worth noting that, in Britain, classical music was well served by both the gramophone and the wireless – its lack of mass popularity was a result of tastes formed *before* the advent of these new media. At the same time, these media gained their mass markets as new forms of music were becoming popular, and music and media are bound up with each other, if in complex ways. The new musical forms came to Britain first via the variety and music hall stage, were spread by radio and by gramophone companies, which in turn benefited from their popularity, and marketed them strongly. But 'hot' jazz did not gain the same popularity as other, more danceable, forms of jazz; nor were the records of black artists popular in Britain. Indeed, the popularity of *all* dance records proved to be highly elastic. When economic crises occurred, in 1921 and 1929, people stopped buying records and turned out to see the bands at local variety theatres instead.

Clearly, I have only been able here to sketch out the contours of the problem of the relations between the elements which make up

The production of dance music in Britain in the 1920s   29

'popular music' in Britain in the 1920s; more detailed investigation into the strategies of production and pleasure remains to be undertaken.

Bibliography

Ambrose, Bert, 1929. 'Come, come Mr. Elizalde', *The Gramophone*, March, p. 435

Baldwin, Brooke, 1981. 'The cakewalk: a study in stereotype and reality', *Journal of Social History*, 15:2, pp. 205–18

Beresford, Steve, 1981. 'The angelic squeaking of a dozen penny trumpets', *Collusion*, 1, p. 14

Bird, Elizabeth, 1976. 'Jazz bands of north east England: the evolution of a working class cultural activity', *Oral History*, 4:2, pp. 79–88

Bradley, Josephine, 1947. *Dancing Through Life* (London)

Briggs, Asa, 1961. *The Birth of Broadcasting* (London)
    1966. *The Golden Age of Wireless* (London)

Buckman, Peter, 1978. *Let's Dance: Social, Ballroom and Folk Dancing* (London)

Caskett, James, 1923. 'A note on some dance records', *The Gramophone*, April, p. 21

Carter, Elsom, 1923. 'The gramophone as a factor in the musical education of the amateur', *The Gramophone*, June, pp. 26–30

Casani, Santos, 1928. 'What shall we dance in 1929?' *The Gramophone*, December, pp. 297–8

Colin, Sid, 1977. *And the Bands Played On* (London)

Compton, Fay, 1923. 'The power of the needle', *The Gramophone*, June, p. 32

Daly, Kevin, 1980. 'Your marvelous invention: the early history of the gramophone', in *The Music Goes Round and Round*, ed. Peter Gammond and Raymond Horricks (London)

Elizalde, Fred, 1929. 'Jazz – what of the future?', *The Gramophone*, February, pp. 392–3

Erenberg, Lewis A., 1975. 'Everybody's doin' it: the pre-World War I dance craze, The Castles, and the modern American girl', *Feminist Studies* 3:1/2, pp. 155–70

Finkelstein, Sidney, 1948. *Jazz: A People's Music* (New York)

Frith, Simon, 1980. 'Music for pleasure', *Screen Education*, 34, pp. 51–61
    1981A. 'The making of the British record industry, 1920–1956', unpublished paper given at the Aspects of Popular Music workshop, University of Kent, March 1982
    1981B. '"Wholesome brightness and quiet leisure": the BBC, light entertainment and the pleasures of the hearth', unpublished paper

Gelatt, Roland, 1977. *The Fabulous Phonograph*, 2nd edn (London)

Graves, Robert, and Hodge, Alan, 1949. *The Long Week-End*, 2nd edn (London)

Hale, F. F. G., 1917. 'Trade in the Midlands', *The Phono Record*, February, p. 15

Hall, Henry, 1955. *Here's to the Next Time* (London)

Hylton, Jack, 1926. 'The British touch', *The Gramophone*, September, pp. 145–6

Jackson, Edgar ('Needlepoint'), 1928. 'What's wrong with our dance music?', *The Gramophone*, December, pp. 299–300

30   *Mark Hustwitt*

1929. 'Ambrose vs. Elizalde: which is right?', *The Gramophone*, April,
      pp. 485–6
Lewis, Edward, 1956. *No C.I.C.* (London)
Lowe, Leslie, 1975. *Directory of Popular Music, 1900–1965* (Droitwich, England)
Lynn, Vera, 1976. *Vocal Refrain* (London)
Mackerness, E. D. 1964. *A Social History of English Music* (London)
McCarthy, Albert, 1971. *The Dance Band Era* (London)
Melvill, Harry, 1924. 'Say it while dancing', *The Gramophone*, January,
      pp. 154–5
Moore, Jerrold Northrop, 1977. *A Matter of Records* (New York)
Murrells, Joseph, 1978. *The Book of Golden Discs*, 2nd edn (London)
Nye, Russel B., 1972. 'A word about Whiteman', *Popular Music and Society*, 1:4,
      pp. 231–41
Payne, Jack, 1947. *Signature Tune* (London)
Peacock, Alan, and Weir, Ronald, 1975. *The Composer in the Market Place*
      (London)
Pearsall, Ronald, 1973. *Edwardian Life and Leisure* (Newton Abbot)
      1975. *Edwardian Popular Music* (Newton Abbot)
      1976. *Popular Music in the 20s* (Newton Abbot)
Pegg, Mark, 1979. 'British radio broadcasting and its audience, 1918–1939',
      University of Oxford D.Phil. thesis
Read, Oliver, and Welch, Walter L., 1977. *From Tin Foil to Stereo*, 2nd edn
      (Indianapolis)
Rieger, Jon H. and Rublen, Brian, 1974. 'Whiteman as the Don Quixote of jazz',
      Popular Music and Society, 3:1, pp. 3–23
Roberts, Robert, 1973. *The Classic Slum* (Harmondsworth)
Robertson, Alec, 1969. 'The gramophone in education – the early days',
      Recorded Sound, 33, pp. 381–2
Rust, Brian, 1972. *The Dance Bands* (London)
      and Walker, E. S., 1973. *British Dance Bands (A Discography), 1912–1939*
      (London)
Rust, Francis, 1969. *Dance In Society* (London)
St. Johnson, R., 1906. *History of Dancing* (Canterbury)
Scannell, Paddy, 1981. 'Music for the multitude? The dilemmas of the BBC's
      music policy, 1923–1946', *Media, Culture and Society*, 3:3, pp. 243–60
Schuller, Gunther, 1968. *Early Jazz* (New York)
Stone, Christopher ('C.R.S.'), 1923. 'A Decca romance', *The Gramophone*,
      August, p. 56
Tanner, Peter, 1971. 'Stomping at the Savoy', *Jazz Monthly*, January, pp. 26–30
Walker, Edward S., 1969. 'Early English jazz, some case studies', *Jazz Journal*,
      September, p. 24

Discography

Boyes, Nora. 'Yes, We Have No Bananas Blues', HMV B 1720
Golden Age of British Dance Bands, The, World Records SM 321–7, SMF 328 (eight
      LPs)

The production of dance music in Britain in the 1920s   31

Janis, Elsie. 'Darktown Strutter's Ball', HMV 2–3329, NSA spool 5915*
    'Florrie Was a Flapper', HMV B488, NSA spool 6038
    'I Want a Dancing Man', HMV 2–3040, NSA spool 5724
Jazz at the Savoy – the 20s, Ace of Clubs ACL 1102
Jazz in Britain – the 20s, Parlophone PMC 7075
Lloyd, Marie. 'The Piccadilly Trot', Zonophone 16045e, reissued on *Playing the Halls*, World Records SH 350
Original Dixieland Jazz Band and the Louisiana Five, The, Fountain FJ101
Payne, Jack. *Jack Payne with his BBC Dance Orchestra*, World Records SH 143
Pryor, Arthur. *Too Much Mustard: Ragtime, Cakewalks and Stomps vol. 3: the Bands of Jim Europe and Arthur Pryor 1907–1919*, Saydisc SDL 221
Savoy Bands, The, World Records SH 165/6
Savoy Quartet, The. 'Everything Is Peaches Down in Georgia'/'The Jazz Band', HMV 1008, NSA spool 5724
    'I'm All Bound Round With the Mason Dixie Line'/'The Darktown Strutters Ball', HMV B911, NSA spool 6038
    'Oh Man You'd Hang Around'/We'll Have a Jubilee In My Old Kentucky Home', HMV 3577, NSA spool 6038
Whiteman, Paul. *Paul Whiteman vol. 1*, RCA 7954

* This refers to the British Institute of Recorded Sound's National Sound Archive tape spool numbers.

[12]

Spice World: Constructing Femininity the Popular Way

Dafna Lemish

Introduction

The Spice Girls—a British manufactured all-female pop group had an unprecedented success in the global popular music market of 1997. Their first single "Wannabe" was the biggest selling debut single ever and was number one in the charts of 32 countries (Dibbens). Their first disc (*Spice Girls*) sold over 50 million copies within 1 year. Pre-adolescent girls worldwide are admirers of the five "Spices": Emma ("baby spice"), Geri ("ginger or sexy spice"), Melanie B. ("scary spice"), Melanie C. ("sporty spice"), and Victoria ("posh spice"). The girls enthusiastically listen to the group's latest hit disc or tape, watch their video-clips on MTV, attend to every detail about them in the gossip columns of their magazines and newspapers, hang their posters above their beds, wear their T-shirts, watches and wrist bands, collect their memorabilia, bind their school books in Spice Girls wrapping paper, and talk about them among themselves (Lemish).

Through their image in music, print and visual texts, the Spice Girls construct a particular feminine space, representing models for adoration, inspiring young girls' fantasies, providing legitimization for various modes of rites of passage into the world of femininity. What then defines being a young female today, à la Spice Girls? What are the characteristics and signs of femininity they choose to portray? What range of gender relationships do they provide for young girls growing up in today's confusing world of "feminisms"? It is to these questions that the following analysis is devoted.

Female pop stars

Previous analyses of female pop stars are infrequent but revealing. The advent of MTV introduced a different variety of female images from familiar representational forms of the plastic arts or of Hollywood movies. In reviewing the development of female expression in MTV, Lewis ("Gender Politics and MTV") suggests that the '80s exposed young audiences to women performers through "female-addressed videos designed to speak to and resonate with female cultural experiences of adolescence and gender" (109). Madonna (with "Like a Virgin"), Cyndi Lauper (with "Girls Just Want to Have Fun"), and Tina Turner (with "What's Love Got to Do With It?") are the more pronounced among them. As Tapper and Black suggest, female musicians have been producing video-clips that differ on a number of dimensions from those of male performers, such as: musical genre, sexual appeal, objectification of women, presence of violence, opposition to authority.

Peterson, for example, argues that Cyndi Lauper's "Girls Just Want to Have Fun" marks girls' unique space as being related to bedroom culture, magazine consumption, clothing styles and the like, through resisting dominant culture. The interpretive themes offered by Peterson—which include the "danceability" of the song, its fun nature, the sense of freedom it offers, and its rebellious connotations— illustrate previous attempts to fuse liberal-feminist notions within young girls' popular music.

Madonna, a pre-teen idol, has received much academic attention, as a performer who bases her career on challenging conventional perceptions of femininity, combining seductiveness with independence, and articulating a desire to be desired (Fiske, Kaplan, Longhurst, Schwichtenberg). Fiske (*Understanding Popular Culture*) claims that Madonna provides an image of independence and resistance to the ideological binary opposition of virgin-whore which is an empowering force: "Madonna's popularity is a complexity of power and resistance, of meaning and counter meaning, of pleasure and struggle for control" (113). Her image serves as "a site of semiotic struggle between the forces of patriarchal control and feminine resistance, of capitalism and the subordinate, of the adult and the young" (97). However, as Kaplan suggests, Madonna's challenge to patriarchy still remains inherently constrained through her focus on the female appearance as being crucial to identity.

In a recent analysis, Dibben attempts to understand "how gendered subjectivity is constructed through the particular representational system of music" (332). Applying both semiotics and Adorno's critical theory, she examines the ways in which music encourages the consumer to embrace a particular subject position towards the ideologies of femininity in three pop songs. The first, "Ooh, Aah … Just a Little Bit" by Gina G., encourages a patriarchal construction of femininity, while the second, "Dress" by P. J. Harvey, encourages a critical view of such a construction. The third analysis focuses on "Say You'll Be There" by the Spice Girls, and suggests that the video does not privilege one perspective over the other and can therefore be interpreted as either reinforcing or challenging traditional representations of femininity. Her detailed analysis of the lyrics, music, and images in that video suggests that while the Spice Girls are posing for the male gaze, offering traditional images for masculine fantasy, they are at the same time also portrayed as autonomous and expressive proud young women. Choice of musical material, including rap for example, appropriates male meanings and signifies power and group identity. In conclusion, Dibben argues that the Spice Girls, in common with other popular texts, offer the power of evasion of discipline and control through exaggeration and fun, as well as the power of resistance by using the patriarchal constructions of femininity in oppositional meanings. Both, however, as she rightly states, are problematic in that they do not deny the dominant ideology but work within it and therefore reinforce and sustain it.

While the discussion so far has centered on mainstream popular music, it is worthwhile to note the possible contributions of analyses of female rockers and alternative music performers to the debate (Whiteley). In her analysis of the Riot Grrrl movement's version of "grrrl power", for example, Leonard suggests that it opened debate concerning girls' position as music creators and performers. Their music style, forms of performance and body display, as well as celebration of girl-talk and female friendship and networking, creates a special space for a rebellious female voice. Such an alternative, although marginal to popular genres, helps set the stage for some changes in the feminine musical discourse of mainstream pop as well.

Popular music at the end of the millennium thus featured a great diversity of complex and mixed messages about women and femininity in society (Cooper). Therefore the Spice Girls can be analyzed as a progression of female stardom in popular music from the famous personas of the '80s and '90s, inhabiting the feminine space already cultivated before them.

The texts

The discussion of the Spice Girls as a particular case of interest is based on an extensive study of popular texts, clearly provided or stimulated by well-oiled marketing strategies. These texts include: the songs of the group's two discs and their video-clips, MTV specials, the "official" Spice Girls videotape and book, the movie *Spice World*, various posters, memorabilia and Internet sites. In addition, all issues of the three major popular pre-teen and teen weekly magazines in Israel (about 150 issues) were investigated and all Spice Girls-related material was studied.

What follows is a thematic semiotic analysis of "the feminine" as it emerges from these Spice Girls' texts. It is painted in rather broad strokes, highlighting clear motives rather than providing a finely detailed examination of specific texts (such as Dibben).

A second study, reported elsewhere (Lemish), preceded this one and focused on pre-teen age girls' reception of the Spice Girls in Israel. Insights from the focus-group reception study assisted me in delineating certain themes and, at the same time, in highlighting the similarities and differences between the preferred scholar-readings of the texts and those of the intended audience.

Femininities

The five "Spices" suggest five different personality-types, and five different definitions of femininity.

1 Childish and cute, Emma is "baby spice." She wears her blond hair in pigtails, favors light cotton, pastel-colored short dresses with straps and sports a gold necklace with the word "Baby" on it. She often sucks a lollipop and presents a blue-eyed, smiling baby face to the camera.
2 Geri is the spicy ginger; she is the sexy exhibitionist. Her reddish hair and selection of tight bright clothes, such as corsets, garters and stockings, clearly portray a "slut"-like image, to which her provocative stares toward the camera provide the added touch of a come-on.
3 Melanie B., the only woman of color in the group, is the "wild" spontaneous one. "Scary Spice," as she is called, has the most untamed long curly dark hair which she wears as a mane to suit her tiger-skin-type clothes of tight slacks, bras which expose more than they obscure and large overcoats. Her pierced tongue adds to the image of the independent outspoken "rule breaker" who is capable of doing whatever is on her mind.
4 Melanie C. is "Sporty Spice." In her workout suits of slacks and exercise bras, her straight hair tied back in a modest ponytail and her plain cheerful face she is "the girl next door," who happens to have a thin muscled body and a genuine interest in sports, specifically soccer, and fitness.

5 Finally, Victoria, "Posh Spice," is the elegant sophisticated "snob." In her short, tight black dresses and high heels, her shoulder-length straight dark hair and her serious, unsmiling posture, she conveys remote coldness, heightened by stories of her aristocratic background.

All these varieties of femininity are offered as possible and legitimate modes, each with its own identifying characteristics of behavior, facial expressions, clothing, hairstyle and accessories. Appearances are closely related to presumptions about "essence." The contextual connection between a construct of the woman and a presentation of the woman remains the core question at issue. As Tzeelon suggested in her historical analysis of fashion and clothing, appearance code "is a dynamic site of struggle for control of the power to define selves and situations" (122). Throughout history clothes were a means of defining peoples' roles, status, and gender. They were used to differentiate between the respectable woman and the non-respectable one, between the married and the single female, between the high-class lady and lower-class person, and other social distinctions. The five unique choices of symbolic appearances by the Spices clearly mark individual diversity and variability of styles pertaining to the more general conception of femininity. They offer a freedom to choose from a series of appearance identities, which together constitute a fragmented definition of womanhood: A girl can be childish and cute like Emma, but she could also be wild and crazy like Melanie B. She can be provocative and sexy like Geri, but she could also be snobbish and elegant like Victoria. She can even be an athletic tomboy like Melanie C.

Part of the textual discourse is the girls' exploitation of their own stereotypes and their oppositional manipulation. Such, for example, is Emma's "naive" and melting smile at a policeman in an attempt to win him over and prevent the group from being punished for misconduct; Melanie B.'s purposeful attempt to break the rules of a chess game; or Victoria's over-serious facial expression as she talks to an imaginary audience member about her stylish dress (scenes from the movie). Be what you are, and take advantage of it, they suggest. Moreover, change is not really possible, once you have settled in your own mold. When the girls try humorously to take each other's roles through appearances they discover how uncomfortable they are and revert back to their exaggerated uni-dimensional "selves." People don't change, seems to be the message and it is reinforced by their own declarations: "We haven't changed as people—we've kept our original personalities" (Spice Girls 48).

"Girl Power"

One can choose to be any of the "girls" as long as one is conventionally attractive, as are all five Spices. However, their attractiveness seems to feed on their boundless energy (at times to the point of chaos), clear self-confidence and self-awareness, and their sense of control over their own behavior and appearance. "None of us are conventional beauties," declares sexy Geri (Spice Girls 67) "That's inspiring for girls because it shows you don't have to be gorgeous to be up there doing it!" These are not Barbie dolls, the exploited images of the "beauty myth" (Wolf). Rather, these are strong-willed independent personalities, as manifested by their slogan "Girl Power." In the opening pages of their official book (Spice Girls 7), pink and black letters explain:

Popular Music and Society, Vol. 26, No. 1   21

Girl power is when... You help a guy with his bag
You and your mates reply to wolf whistles by shouting 'get your arse out!'
You wear high heels and think on your feet
You know you can do it and nothing's going to stop you
You don't wait around for him to call
You stick with your mates and they stick with you
You're loud and proud even when you've broken out in spots
You believe in yourself and control your own life

"Girl Power," so it seems, refers to both physical and mental strength. Girls can help a guy with his bag, have painful tattoos as Geri, or do sit-ups like Melanie C. But it is also standing up for your rights and dignity and having control over your life. "Girl Power" is also about freedom of expression and inner peace, about standing up for one's opinions and beliefs. "I'll tell you what I want, what I really really want," say the words of their first record-breaking hit, "Wannabe." Control and independence seem to be crucial to the "Spice" construction. "It's looking at yourself in the mirror and saying, 'This is me ... I'm not going to be dominated by anyone, especially not men'" (Spice Girls 37). A free spirit, self-acceptance and self-fulfillment are crucial characteristics of "Girl Power."

The fear of being out of control, argues Wolf, is characteristic of contemporary women, since loss of control is understood to be inappropriate and severely punished if discovered. Being overweight (loss of control in regard to food) or promiscuous (loss of control in regard to sex), are illustrations of gender-related phenomena against which society typically imposes negative sanctions.

But "Girl Power" seems to go beyond the personal and private. In an MTV performance, the Spice Girls attributed to the late Princess Diana—to whom the song was dedicated—the notion of "Girl Power": the capacity to inspire and to help others. "My talent is giving every person I come into contact with that little bit of zest for life again," says Melanie B. (Spice Girls 45).

While these are clearly well-rehearsed facades put up by the singers, with little ideational depth behind the clichés, they are still intriguing as an overall message choice. A group of five "hot," energetic, and extremely successful young women, declare their independence, take control of their lives, and invite you, a nine- or ten-year-old girl growing up in a confusing world of indeterminate gender boundaries, to join in!

Indeed, "Girl Power" is actively interpreted by many of the girls as an expression of independence, strength, success, and sense of self-worth. "It means," explained one twelve-year-old in the reception study, "equality ... that girls are strong, each one in her own way." One fourteen-year-old suggested: "In the content of the Spice Girls, they are much more feminist. That's the way they are. They do a lot ... to declare that they don't belong to men ... in all their songs they say 'Girl Power,' which is what they are. Really!" (Lemish 153–54).

This inclusion of feminist discourse, albeit at the superficial cliché level—in an extremely successful image—is in and of itself an interesting phenomenon. Such incorporation of the "women's lib" referent systems, has been featured in various popular texts such as in television series and advertising campaigns (among them, the famous "You've come a long way, baby" for Virginia Slim cigarettes). These texts have been charged with turning the feminist spear against itself by reinforcing women's dependency on capitalistic patriarchal systems (Williamson).

The inclusion of audience tastes in cultural products is a well-recognized econo-mic strategy, as Fiske ("Cultural Economy of Fandom") argues. What is striking in the Spice Girls' example, is the inherent conflict between the message and the reality. As the movie cynically indicates, the Spice Girls are handled, programmed, and marketed by male agents who are in control of their industry as well as of the images it presents. In the movie, the man in control is a high-class, rich, and mature "father figure" who denies them any time off from work. This is very much an imitation of the successful American series of the '70s, *Charlie's Angels*, present-ing three young beauties as talented policewomen, who blindly follow the unques-tioned authority of a male superior, whom they have never even met. The Spices, as mischievous girls, disobey the male authority figure, spontaneously running away to do "what's in their heads." However, they are back just in time to fulfill their obligations as performers, teetering along the thin line between obedience and resistance.

The "Spice Girls" might as well be like the figures in Plato's cave for the young musical audience: Young fans who are oblivious to the reality outside, and to the hands that manipulate the puppets. There is no reality of control outside of the performers' existence; there is no awareness of those who wield power behind the scenes. The Spice Girls are out there "doing it!" (Lemish).

Sisterhood

Female bonding and a sense of sisterhood is a major thread in all Spice Girls public appearances. The over-emphasis of this theme seems to go beyond a reas-suring publicity strategy, suggesting that the group is well and thriving. The theme seems to draw from the political notion of "sisterhood," which constituted a major component in the ethos of the women's liberation movement of the '60s. A strong emphasis is placed on the importance of friendship, unity, togetherness and coop-eration from which members of the group draw personal strength. "We're about unity and solidarity between female friends," declares Geri (Spice Girls 34); "We really care about each other and want the best out of each other, so we all look after each other," says Melanie C. (Spice Girls 48). Moreover, men too have to accept this womanly trait: "If you wanna be my lover you gotta get with my friends, make it last forever, friendship never ends," say the lyrics of "Wannabe." "My friends are with me when you ain't been around," they sing in "Love Thing." The Spice Girls' notion of sisterhood thus challenges patriarchy in three complementary ways: first, as an alternative to the prevalent stereotype of intriguing competitive "bitchy" females, jealous of each other's success, particularly in relations with men; second, as a counter model to the dominant masculine "Loner" (the "Lone Ranger," James Bond, the "Marlboro Man," Easy Rider, and so many other Western cultural heroes); and, finally, in opposition to feminist "Sisterhood," the notion of "Brotherhood" is often associated with war ("Brothers in Arms"), or with criminal "gangs" (including those of sexual violence). Thus, togetherness, for women, creates a positive, constructive force. This theme was clearly evident in the fans' discussion of the group: "Each [Spice Girl] feels that it strengthens her a lot that she has such a group around her, that they are together and not alone," suggests a fourteen-year-old fan. "They are good friends. They support each other," argues a twelve-year-old. "That's what makes them special. Friendship

Popular Music and Society, Vol. 26, No. 1   23

and cooperation. It has nothing to do with singing. The singing came out of their cooperation," contributes another twelve-year-old (Lemish 160–62).

The Spice Girls' friendship is clearly framed as being that of an adolescent nature. Ample examples exist in the movie, newspapers and book photos, presenting the "Spices" in typical girls' bedroom scenes. They are sprawled on bed covers or stretched out on rugs, lightly caressing each other, having pillow fights, sharing secrets, trying on each other's clothes, gossiping about boys, examining their appearances, teasing each other, engaging in "compare and contrast" rituals, grooming one another. In one such scene in the movie, they are in their bathrobes as if at a sleepover, and in another scene they are out together in the dark menacing woods, searching for a good place to pee, as girls might do when camping out. This all-girl subculture is described by Wolf from an adult, heterosexual perspective, as a lost Eden of "a love at once so intimate and so charged.... In a way, there will be nothing as exciting as this love between girls ever again" (55). The Spice Girls' appeal thus incorporates central themes of young pre-teen girls' culture, legitimizing it, bestowing upon it their popularity and fame, claiming it as theirs and that of their fans. At the same time, however, many of the Spice Girls video-clips, present them roaming the streets, taking mischievous rides (e.g. running away in a boat, stealing a bus) and exploring urban spaces in the dark. Such provocative behaviors, often associated with adolescent boys, pose clear challenges to the traditional private–public space division associated with gender in general, and with adolescence in particular (McRobbie).

Promiscuity

The Spice Girls' conscious exhibition of sexuality continues to challenge the traditional slut–virgin binary division of femininity, and thus provides young girls with alternative images. While being sexy is often perceived as being watched and stared at, in the Spice Girls' case, it is also doing the watching and extravagantly manipulating the stares. Rather than being a source of shame, as is often the case for young developing teens, the Spice Girls' sexuality is a source of pride. "Come on and do it," they urge in "Do It": "Who cares what they say—Because the rules are for breaking." Their hints at nakedness—widely exposed cleavages, stomachs and legs, are offered in this context not as signifiers of availability, but rather of self-confidence and choice. While being out of line sexually is commonly associated with becoming "sluts" in society's eyes, in the Spice Girls' case, it is portrayed as blunt opposition. Rather than controlling their sexuality and desire as a key to maintaining a desired "virgin" image in tact, they choose to expose their sexual energies overtly, with pride. Control becomes a matter of displaying sexuality rather than hiding it. In a world where girls are internalizing conflicting messages—you need to look sexy to be noticed, to be worthwhile and appreciated, yet you must not act upon that sexiness lest you become the disrespected "slut"—this is a challenging alternative.

However, exaggeration of the codes of feminine appearance up to actual sexual display can be understood as forms of self-presentation (Lewis "Consumer"). As in the case of Madonna, sexual provocation could possibly also be read as a mockery of patriarchal constructions of the slut–virgin dichotomy, as well as a challenge to dominant definitions of femininity. Whether pre-adolescent girls are really aware of these supposed mockeries and challenges, or whether they are buying into a consumer ideology that defines female worth as tied closely to their sexual attractiveness and availability, is yet another question. Analysis of fans' discourse suggests the existence of an active struggle of interpretation. Some of the younger girls had a strong need to frame the Spice Girls as whores yet idols, as one nine-year-old confessed: "I care that she [Geri] is a whore. She is pretty, but ... I won't want to be a whore, but I would want to be Geri. But not a whore" (Lemish 158). The older girls, also torn between these dichotomous concepts of femininity, used two lines of arguments to resolve the tension. First, they separated the Spice Girls' personalities from their roles as performers, and second, they cast the appearance in marketing terms, as a way to attract audiences. Analysis of their talk suggests that the Spice Girls provide a site of struggle with the conflicting forces of conformation and resistance to traditional norms of gendered appearances.

Douglas's historical reconstruction of "growing up female with the mass media" recalls similar experiences with girls' groups in the early '60s:

> Girl group music acknowledged—even celebrated—our confusion and ambivalence. Some of us wanted to be good girls, and some of us wanted to be bad. But most of us wanted to get away with being both, and girl group music let us try on and act out a host of identities, from traditional, obedient girlfriend to brassy, independent rebel, and lots in between. (88)

The Spice Girls, apparently, provide it all in one group.

Curiously enough, there is an effort made in interviews and official publications, to emphasize that sexual appearances do not contradict the existence of mind and soul, as the popular stigma would tell us. "I've always been a deep thinker. But then again, I'm loud and spontaneous and a bit of a twat sometimes..." confesses Melanie B. (Spice Girls 20), and later on adds: "The strong will survive and the wise excel" (23). Wolf (215) recalls the common "Feminist or slut?" dichotomy in popular debate, whereas famous women—from anarchist Emma Goldman, to popular writer Erica Jong, to pop singer Madonna—have struggled to integrate both. For the Spice Girls, so it seems, passion and sexuality are not at war with rationality and dignity. In their relationships with men, they are clearly demanding respect and refusing to be taken for granted. "Stop right now, thank you very much, I need somebody with the human touch," they tell a lover in "Stop"; "I left you behind, boy you were a fool, to treat me that way," in "Saturday Night Divas," or "Who do you think you are?" in a song of the same title. They seem to offer what Wolf (220) apparently craves: role models of women with both living minds and living bodies, and furthermore, women who are making room for that possibility in the lives of other girls!

Motherhood

A common construction of femininity suggests that there are sexy girls and there are mothers, but one can't be both. Motherhood is asexual and unattractive. While this is not a central theme in the Spice Girls' image, it comes through very clearly in a scene in the movie, when the Spices fantasize about themselves in the future as mothers. They are all bloated, wearing unattractive clothes, their faces and hair in a state of neglect, their expressions portray tiredness and unhappiness, and they are surrounded by the clutter of baby products. Motherhood is not a cheerful prospect. Moreover, having babies is in opposition to sexual pleasure; it even constitutes punishment for it at times (Wolf 164). Such is the case of their

Popular Music and Society, Vol. 26, No. 1 25

movie friend of Asian origin, who was deserted by her boyfriend while heavily pregnant. Men can't be trusted, so it seems. Women who get pregnant are not sexual anymore and are thus deserted by their men.

A complementary relationship with motherhood is expressed through their song "Mama," devoted to their own mothers, and the video-clip that followed. While the lyrics talk about the realization that Mama "would become the friend I never had," the visuals present childhood pictures of the Spices, and camera cuts to their mothers placed within the audience. Sitting in an elevated circle amidst the young audience, the Spices relate their revelation as girl scouts counselors passing down a secret: "Back then I didn't know why, why you were misunderstood. So now I see through your eyes. All that you did was love." Motherhood is a state of unappreciated devotion and dedication. Here too it is also an asexual state, as expressed by Geri: "Personally I found it a bit weird to bring my mum to work with me. . . . But it was nice for them to get made up, have their hair done and feel glamorous. . ." (Spice Girls 43).

Contradictory struggles

It is acknowledged that sexuality for adolescent girls (at least in the U.S.A., and, as is reasonable to assume, in other parts of the world as well) is highly problematic and fraught with conflict. Girls are socialized to look like sex objects, but not to act upon it, to provoke, but not to feel desire. As a result, sexuality is rationalized and moralized by girls by linking it to love and to a desire to satisfy the wishes of the loved one, rather than as a natural part of their femininity (Durham; Wolf). Prevailing messages in teen magazines, a highly popular medium for pre-teenage girls, promote restrictive ideologies of femininity, glorify heterosexual romance as a central goal for girls, encourage male domination in relationships, and stress the importance of beautification through consumption (Peirce; McRobbie; Mazzarella). Further, as Durham suggests, the discourse missing from teen magazines is that which recognizes the validity of girls' sexual feelings and desires apart from masculine desire.

In contrast to these prevailing messages, the Spice Girls suggest an alternative model that challenges dominant definitions of femininity and masculinity. Much in line with Fiske's analysis of Madonna, the Spice Girls seem to be in control of their own image and the process of making it. They manipulate the traditional concept of the female "look" in three senses: in what they look like; how they look at the camera and others; and how others look at them. In contrast to Madonna, however, the Spice Girls are celebrating their femininity in a playful childish fun-filled way. The context of sexual exhibitions—their boundless energy, girl-like mannerisms, playful defiance of authority, outspokenness—all suggest sexuality as part of an independent self at peace with itself.

What emerged, however, as the most striking element in the analysis of the Spice Girls' images, was the constant presence of contradictions within the messages conveyed. Each of the themes highlighted above offer oppositional polysemic readings (Dibben; Fiske), each echoing major cultural struggles and confusions.

First is the notion of independence and "power" so strongly voiced by the group. They declare their independence from men, yet most of their songs center on heterosexual love, on longing for satisfying relationships with men. They defy masculine authority just enough to remind the audience that they bow to such authority in the first place. They have the power to make their own choices and be anything they want—just as long as they adhere to dominant notions of prettiness and sexiness. In this sense, as Dibben argues, "'Girl Power' is a myth which supports the subordination of females within patriarchal society: it offers the lie that 'Girl Power' constitutes liberating empowerment and thereby diverts any possibility of real resistance" (348).

Furthermore, the Spice Girls use compelling language to encourage girls to get out "there" and do "it"—yet, they never offer any suggestion of what kind of social space it is that is "there" and what "it" constitutes. The promise of freedom exists—but no purpose for that freedom: A freedom to be where? To do what? No particular future is offered, no portrayals of professional or personal alternatives except for the obvious choice the Spices have selected for themselves: the glamorous sphere of female stardom, a world nourished by the female "look." In many ways this ambiguous discourse represents a sense of real confusion to young admiring girls.

A second, yet related dominating theme is the one glorifying female bonding. In contrast to Madonna, the Spice Girls work together, as a united group. This can work in oppositional ways. On one hand, it deepens the inner contradictions: Girls can be independent, but in order to be successful they need to join forces; girls can be anything, but only the combination of all five forms of femininity together creates the "whole," the "feminine," the impossible burden of the "superwoman." When their friend in the movie is debating which one of the Spice Girls to choose as a "godparent" to replace the role of a godfather, she ends up needing all five. It takes all five Spices to replace the traditional role of one distinguished man. On the other hand, as Zeck argues, female bonding in popular culture could also be perceived as a marker of a double resistance against patriarchal-capitalism: A successful world of women free of men, and the dismissal of the myth of bourgeois individualism. This becomes even more tangled when we examine the Spice Girls' merchandising and product marketing: from "Impulse" body spray in five scents to chips commercials; from promotion of their own clothing styles to memorabilia and dolls. By addressing the feminine investment in fashion culture, and reinforcing consumption as promoting femininity, they clearly serve existing social hierarchies, the ones they are seemingly opposed to (Lewis "Consumer"; Wolf).

Another manifestation of this contradiction is expressed in their outspoken admiration of former conservative British Prime Minister, Margaret Thatcher, and the legendary Princess Di. These two choices—of all possible female women role models—are far from reinforcing a "rebel" image. On the contrary, they cater to conservative social trends, emphasizing women's limited choices framed by patriarchal society as either the "iron bitch" or the "melancholy victim." Aware of the possible negative connotation feminism may still conjure up in wide social circles, yet feeling the need for a new image, they themselves declare: "Feminism has become a dirty word. Girl Power is just a nineties way of saying it;" "Of course I am a feminist. But I could never burn my Wonderbra. I'm nothing without it!" (Spice Girls 49). Feminists—yet detaching themselves from the negative stigmas of bra-burning angry, ugly women. Feminists—but women who are "nothing" without their bras. The "bra", the symbol of second-wave feminism, has regained its status as a sex symbol. Even as feminists, girls are nothing without it. . . .

Popular Music and Society, Vol. 26, No. 1   27

Related to female bondedness is the disturbing contradictory theme of race, so subtle and unspoken, yet clearly visible and disturbing. The one woman of color—Melanie B., is cast in the role of the "wild one:" She is the one to break the rules, she is the one to expose large portions of her naked body, she is the one to wear animal skin, she is the one with the pierced tongue. The literature on the fascination of the white gaze with the black body suggests that framing Melanie B. of all the Spices as the untamed wild creature cannot be dismissed as coincidental (see, e.g., Morrison). The admiration of the sexual nature of the colored person combined with the fear of the "savage" puts Melanie B. at the forefront of such a critique. This might be particularly relevant since the reception study of the Spice Girls among pre-teen girls (Lemish 163) presents evidence of girls' perception of Melanie as a victim of sexual violence. "Taming the wild," so it seems from young girls' perspectives, is achieved through the ultimate form of male domination and control—rape. It is particularly interesting to note that the movie *Spice World*, the most recent of all texts analyzed, seems to make a special attempt to downplay this role in comparison to earlier texts: Melanie is often portrayed in big, baggy clothes, covered from head to toe, her unruly hair tied back in small restrictive curls. In many scenes she wears glasses and speaks in a calm pleasant tone. One is left to wonder what brought about this clear change, possibly a growing awareness of the racist connotations of the original image?

Finally there remains the double-edged sword of self-identity. While clearly the five Spices are willingly promoting shallow, uni-dimensional stereotypes of themselves (baby, sexy, scary, sporty, and posh), they are at the same time, conveying the impossibility of change. The one made attempt to take on each other's roles turned out to have horrendous consequences. The possibility of personality development is negated. Accepting oneself could be a comforting psychological need for developing girls. However, in this particular case it centers around "accepting" your personality traits, while the "look" remains in need of constant improvement, as the Spice Girls' clothing, hair styles, accessories and promoted products suggest. In this way the Spices continue to promote the everlasting frustration with the unsatisfactory feminine body (Wolf) yet narcoticize the need for personality or educational self-improvement.

In sum, I would argue that the Spice Girls can be read in oppositional ways—as independent feminists out there to prove their "Girl Power" to the world—but at the same time, as a disguised version of the conventional "truth claim" of the centrality of the "look" in female identity, above and beyond any other possible role. Furthermore, "Girl Power" as represented by the Spices is essentially a very narrowly defined sexual power.

The popularity of the Spice Girls indeed offers a rich site of cultural struggle for young girls, as the complementary reception study suggests (Lemish). Being a fan has long been recognized as an important part of identity development and marking, and in this case could be used to create the space to explore girls' lives at the end of the millennium. The Spices themselves declare this to be their role and mission: "We want young girls at school to relate to us, to be one of us. Kids can smell bullshit. We can be positive role models for young girls and women" (Spice Girls 57). The Spice Girls' marketing, as is often the case with other artists, is to establish themselves in such a way that their musical and visual image transcends specific genres or lifestyles. In the case of pre-teenage pop, the emphasis has always been on "fun, energy, glamour and dream material" (Negus 77). However, the extreme popularity of the group (and many new female groups inspired by them all over the world) may well reflect something beyond those conventions. It can be interpreted as an expression of the deep need of young girls for appropriate role models, representing their own inner struggles with their place in a changing world of gender definitions.

Works cited

Cooper, B. Lee. "Images of Women in Popular Song Lyrics: A Bibliography." *Popular Music and Society* 22 (1998): 79–89.

Dibben, Nicola. "Representations of Femininity in Popular Music." *Popular Music* 18 (1999): 331–55.

Durham, Meenakshi G. "Dilemmas of Desire: Representations of Adolescent Sexuality in Two Teen Magazines." *Youth and Society* 29 (1998): 369–89.

Douglas, Susan J. *Where the Girls Are: Growing Up Female With the Mass Media*. New York: Penguin Books, 1994.

Fiske, John. "Television: Polysemy and Popularity." *Critical Studies in Mass Communication* 3 (1986): 200–16.

——. *Understanding Popular Culture*. Boston: Unwin Hyman, 1989.

——. "The Cultural Economy of Fandom." *The Adoring Audiences*. Ed. Lisa Lewis. New York: Routledge, 1992. 36–49.

Kaplan, E. Ann. "Feminism/Oedipus/Postmodernism: The Case of MTV." *Turning It On: A Reader In Women and Media*. Ed. Helen Baehr, and Ann Gray. London: Arnold, 1996. 33–43.

Lemish, Dafna. "Spice Girls' Talk: A Case Study in the Development of Gendered Identity." *Millennium Girls: Today's Girls and Their Cultures*. Ed. Sherrie A. Inness. New York: Rowman & Littlefield, 1998. 145–67.

Leonard, Marion. "'Rebel Girl, You Are the Queen of My World': Feminism, 'Subculture' and Grrrl Power." *Sexing the Groove: Popular Music and Gender*. Ed. Sheila Whiteley. London: Routledge, 1997. 230–255.

Lewis, Lisa A. "Consumer Girl Culture: How Music Video Appeals to Girls." *Television and Women's Culture: The Politics of the Popular*. Ed. Mary Ellen Brown. Newsbury, CA: Sage, 1990. 89–101.

Lewis, Lisa A. *Gender Politics and MTV: Voicing the Differences*. Philadelphia, PA: Temple University Press, 1990.

Longhurst, Brian. *Popular Music and Scoeity*. London: Polity Press, 1995.

Mazzarella, Sharon R. "The 'Superbowl of All Dates': Teenage Girl Magazines and the Commodification of the Perfect Prom." *Growing Up Girls: Popular Culture and the Construction of Identity*. Ed. Sharon R. Mazzarella, and Norma Odom Pecora. New York: Peter Lang, 1999. 97–112.

McRobbie, Angela. "Shut Up and Dance: Youth Culture and Changing Modes of Femininity." *Cultural Studies* 7 (1993): 406–26.

Morrison, Ton, ed. *Birth of a Nation'hood: Gaze, Script, and Spectacle in the O. J. Simpson Case*. New York: Pantheon Books, 1997.

Negus, Keith. *Producing Pop: Culture and Conflict in the Popular Music Industry*. London: Arnold, 1992.

Negus, Keith. *Popular Music in Theory: An Introduction*. London: Polity Press, 1996.

Peirce, Kate. "A Feminist Theoretical Perspective on the Socialization of Teenage Girls Through *Seventeen* Magazine." *Sex Roles* 23 (1990): 491–500.

Peterson, Eric E. "Media Consumption and Girls Who Want to Have Fun." *Critical Studies in Mass Communication* 4 (1987): 37–50.

Schwichtenberg, Cathy, ed. *The Madonna Connection: Representational Politics, Subcultural Identities and Cultural Theory*. Boulder, Colorado: Westview Press, 1993.

Tapper, John, and Black, David S. "Musical Genre, 'Girl Culture,' and the Female Perform-
    ers: The Root of Variation Between Music Videos." *Women and Media: Content, Careers,
    and Criticism.* Ed. Cynthia M. Lont. New York: Wadsworth Publishing Company, 1995.
    331–46.
The Spice Girls. *Girl Power!* Secaucus, NJ: Carol Publishing Group, 1997.
Tseelon, Efrat. *The Masque of Femininity: The Presentation of Woman in Everyday Life.*
    London: Sage, 1995.
Whiteley, Sheila, ed. *Sexing the Groove: Popular Music and Gender.* London: Routledge,
    1997.
Williamson, Judith. *Decoding Advertisements: Ideology and Meaning in Advertising.* London:
    Marion Boyars, 1978.
Wolf, Naomi. *Promiscuities: The Secret Struggle of Womanhood.* New York: Random House,
    1997.
——. *The Beauty Myth.* New York: Doubleday, 1991.
Zeck, Shari. "'The Hero Takes a Fall': The Bangles and '80s Pop." *Women and Media: Content,
    Careers, and Criticism.* Ed. Cynthia M. Lont. Belmont, CA: Wadsworth Publishing
    Company, 1995. 349–56.

*Prof. Dafna Lemish is Chair of the Department of Communication at Tel Aviv University,
Israel. Her teaching and research interests focus on the role of media in children's lives, and
on media and gender.*

[13]

Modelling the Groove: Conceptual Structure and Popular Music

LAWRENCE M. ZBIKOWSKI

LET me start with a somewhat problematic assumption, which is that listeners know a good groove when they hear it. What is problematic about this assumption is not that it in any way misrepresents what can often be observed: a groove starts up and people stop whatever they are doing and begin to pay attention to the music; they either put their bodies in motion or adapt ongoing motion to follow the pull of the groove. No, what is problematic is the status of the knowledge behind these actions: what is it that listeners know when they know a good groove?

Perhaps the problem is that most listeners are not long on detailed declarative knowledge when it comes to music, and so it is difficult to gain access to what they know. But musicians are not much better where the groove is concerned. When asked what makes for a good groove musicians as often as not become vague, refer to things like 'feel', and summarize with the koan-like 'You know it when you hear it.'[1] But again, what is it that musicians know when they know a good groove?

Part of the difficulty with asking this question lies with the fact that a groove is most typically created by a small group of musicians working together, each contributing parts to the composite whole. On the production end of things, then, a groove involves knowledge shared between musicians. This aspect of the groove was given a compelling analysis by Ingrid Monson in her 1996 *Saying Something*. There, Monson described in detail the contributions of members of a typical jazz rhythm section to a musical groove and discussed the complex

Research time crucial for the preparation and completion of this article was provided by the Center for Advanced Study in the Behavioral Sciences (March 2002) and the National Humanities Center (2003–4); a fellowship at the latter was provided by the National Endowment for the Humanities. I am also indebted to students in my 2002 seminar on the analysis of popular music for their helpful discussions of topics central to this article.

[1] For instance, Charlie Persip explains a groove as follows: 'When you get into that groove, you ride right on down that groove with no strain and no pain – you can't lay back or go forward. That's why they call it a groove' (quoted in Paul F. Berliner, *Thinking in Jazz: The Infinite Art of Improvisation*, Chicago Studies in Ethnomusicology, Chicago, 1994, 349). My point is not that musicians or listeners are inarticulate about grooves, but that characterizing the knowledge behind their descriptions is not easy.

social interactions that mark small-group improvisation.[2] It is these social interactions that present both a barrier and an opportunity to those interested in exploring the knowledge behind grooves. The barrier is a consequence of the failure to develop a theory of music adequate to the highly dynamic domain of improvised music. As Monson noted,

> this essential interactive component of improvisation, with its emergent musical shapes and historical as well as socially constructive dimensions, has not been an object of theoretical inquiry. Structural relationships [which are typically the focus of music-theoretical inquiry] must, of course, be included within the discussion of how music communicates, but they do not operate independently of – and in fact are simultaneous with – the contextualizing and interactive aspects of sound.[3]

But there is an opportunity here as well: interactive modes of musical production suggest a thorough re-examination of what counts as knowledge about music. Rather than limiting ourselves to conventional music-theoretical constructs (and their representations), we need to think of musical knowledge as involving a network of information that includes assessments about bodily states or the possibilities for bodily motion, knowledge about the basis of musical interaction, and abstract concepts.

In what follows I want to explore a way to model the knowledge basic to producing and understanding musical grooves that can accommodate this more general perspective on cognitive organization. My approach takes as its point of departure work in cognitive anthropology which proposes that culture consists of knowledge. As Naomi Quinn and Dorothy Holland put it, culture is 'not a people's customs and artifacts and oral traditions, but what they must know in order to act as they do, make the things they make, and interpret their experience in the distinctive way they do'.[4] Quinn and Holland proposed that cultural knowledge is organized through ideational complexes that are widely shared by members of a society and that play a central role in their understanding of the world and their behaviour in it. In my own work, which focuses on the cognitive processes basic to understanding music, I call such complexes conceptual models. Conceptual models are relatively basic cognitive structures that act as guides for reasoning and inference; each model consists of concepts in specified

---

[2] See Ingrid Monson, *Saying Something: Jazz Improvisation and Interaction*, Chicago Studies in Ethnomusicology (Chicago, 1996), chapters 2 and 5. A typical jazz rhythm section consists of drums, bass and piano or similar 'comping' instrument; the term 'comping' derives either from 'accompaniment' or 'complement' (see *ibid.*, 43).

[3] *Ibid.*, 190.

[4] Naomi Quinn and Dorothy Holland, 'Culture and Cognition', *Cultural Models in Language and Thought*, ed. Holland and Quinn (Cambridge, 1987), 3–40 (p. 4).

relationships and pertains to a specific domain of knowledge.[5] I view such models as basic to more extended knowledge structures that allow members of a group or society to perform complex actions as well as to communicate with one another.[6]

To give a better sense of what a conceptual model involves, in the first section that follows I shall present a rudimentary conceptual model for musical rhythm. This will provide a framework for my discussion of grooves, as well as an introduction to the broader view of musical knowledge that I want to develop. Essential to this view – and to the conceptual model I shall sketch – is the idea that knowledge structures are part of an active process of understanding and creating music. Knowledge structures are used by listeners to guide their understanding of a musical work as it unfolds; knowledge structures – but not necessarily the same ones – are also used by musicians to guide the performance of a musical work.[7]

Once I have this general perspective on musical and rhythmic knowledge in place I shall turn to the more specific case of modelling the groove. In developing this model I shall adopt a strategy somewhat different from previous studies of the groove.[8] In those studies, 'groove' has been either related to or considered

[5] For my treatment of conceptual models, as well as a discussion of their antecedents, see Lawrence M. Zbikowski, *Conceptualizing Music: Cognitive Structure, Theory, and Analysis* (New York, 2002), chapter 3. The conceptual model, as I construe it, is related to knowledge structures proposed by a number of other researchers in cognitive science and is thus similar to the idealized cognitive model (George Lakoff, *Women, Fire, and Dangerous Things: What Categories Reveal About the Mind*, Chicago, 1987), cognitive domain (Ronald W. Langacker, *Foundations of Cognitive Grammar*, i: *Theoretical Prerequisites*, Stanford, 1987; ii: *Descriptive Application*, Stanford, 1992), frame (Marvin Minsky, 'A Framework for Representing Knowledge', *The Psychology of Computer Vision*, ed. Patrick Henry Winston, New York, 1975, 211–77; *idem*, *The Society of Mind*, New York, 1985) and mental model (Philip Nicholas Johnson-Laird, *Mental Models: Towards a Cognitive Science of Language, Inference, and Consciousness*, Cambridge, MA, 1983). (Structures such as these also informed Quinn and Holland's approach to what they came to call cultural models.) From the larger perspective that I develop, musical concepts are a result of processes of categorization, and relationships between musical concepts are derivative of the process of cross-domain mapping. Conceptual models are consequently the first level of organization for concepts.

[6] For a rewarding study of more extended knowledge structures see Edwin Hutchins, *Cognition in the Wild* (Cambridge, MA, 1995). There Hutchins describes in detail the coordinated knowledge that allows the navigation team of a large naval vessel to control the vessel's movements.

[7] For the sake of concision I shall speak as though listener and performer were two different individuals. It is clear that this is typically not the case: most performers are engaged in active listening to music, and in many cultural settings the dividing line between listeners (that is, members of the audience) and performers is either unclear or non-existent. I should also note that my use of the notion of a 'musical work' is not very heavily freighted, and is intended to apply to the broadest possible range of musical expression.

[8] See, in particular, Charles Keil, 'Motion and Feeling through Music', *Journal of Aesthetics and Art Criticism*, 24 (1966), 337–49; Berliner, *Thinking in Jazz*, chapter 13; Josef A. Prögler, 'Searching for Swing: Participatory Discrepancies in the Jazz Rhythm Section', *Ethnomusicology*, 39 (1995–6), 21–54; as well as Monson, *Saying Something*.

equivalent to 'swing', with both viewed as species of musical 'feel' that are produced by complex and continuously changing interactions among musicians. I focus on a construct derived from such interactions but considerably more stable: this is 'the groove' as it appears in soul, rhythm and blues, jazz fusion and various other popular genres. A groove of this sort is typically a large-scale, multi-layered pattern that involves both pitch and rhythmic materials, and whose repetitions form the basis for either a portion or all of a particular tune. Because such patterns change only gradually over the course of a performance (if they change at all), developing a model for them is a relatively tractable challenge, yet one that has implications for the study of the performance and reception of popular music as a whole.

Teasing apart the elements of a composite whole like a groove is often challenging. There are, however, instances when a performance begins not with the whole groove but with only a portion of it (and, in some cases, a subsidiary portion at that). In the second section that follows I explore one such example from a recording by Eric Clapton, and propose how this groove is modelled both by performers and by listeners. There will emerge from this analysis a somewhat changed view of rhythm in popular music and the part embodied knowledge plays in its construal, as well as a fuller sense of what is encompassed by the notion of modelling a groove. I then discuss briefly the opening moments of two further recordings – one by Miles Davis, the other by James Brown – as a way of refining my characterization of how grooves are modelled. What will emerge from these analyses (which focus both on specific musical grooves and on ways we can understand the groove) is a perspective on the socially constructive dimensions of music which offers ways to think about how both individuals and groups contribute to the creation of music.

Conceptual models and musical rhythm

A basic conceptual model for musical rhythm

As noted above, conceptual models are relatively basic cognitive structures that act as guides for reasoning and inference. The approach to cognition that they embody assumes that knowledge is, at least in part, organized into fairly small, coherent structures. If, once one of these structures is active, we are given a little bit of appropriate situational context we have available many likely inferences on what might happen next in a given situation.[9] To get a better sense of what knowledge structures involve, let us consider a very basic model that might help to guide our reasoning about musical rhythm. We can think of the model as

---

[9] Although I characterize conceptual models as 'relatively basic' and 'fairly small', this is only within the context of higher cognitive processes (which is where I prefer to focus). Were we to consider the whole of cognition it would be apparent that conceptual models are hardly basic, and are of a compass that is far from small. For further discussion see Zbikowski, *Conceptualizing Music*, chapters 3 and 5.

organized around four informal propositions.[10] These propositions make up an integrated, mutually reinforcing whole – that is, a conceptual model for musical rhythm:

P1 Rhythm concerns regularly occurring musical events.
P2 There is differentiation between rhythmic events.
P3 Rhythmic events are cyclic.
P4 There is a strong sense of embodiment associated with musical rhythm.

Before discussing how the model is used I should note three things. First, this model is not intended to represent a sophisticated account of musical rhythm – it is formulated with an eye to practicality rather than to music-theoretical rigour – and is shaped in certain respects by practices typical of Western music. Second, while the model is intended to be broadly applicable to a fairly wide range of music, there will nonetheless be certain types of music – unmeasured harpsichord preludes of the seventeenth century, for instance, or some of the incredibly dense and complex music written by Conlon Nancarrow – that will fall outside its purview. Third, even if we accepted this model as a viable cognitive construct it is doubtful whether those who rely on the model to guide their musical judgments could articulate any portion of it. That is, the model represents implicit rather than explicit knowledge.[11]

With these things in mind, let us consider how this model might be used as a guide for musical understanding. Confronted with a sample of putatively musical sound we would look for manifestations of regularity (P1) which were in some way differentiated (P2). Were the sound only minimally differentiated – a series of taps on a table top, for instance, or the steady drip of water from a tap – we might suspect it was not music, and look for other things to clarify the situation. Among these would be some measure of cyclicity (P3) – that is, a higher-order pattern of differentiation which would group subsidiary patterns of more locally differentiated events. Finally, something that is really rhythmic, according to this model, is something we can, at the very least, tap our toes to (P4).

The model, as presented above, offers one way to characterize the knowledge behind a listener's judgments about whether the sounds they hear are musically rhythmic. The model, principally through its final proposition, also raises a question: just how does embodied experience contribute to our cognitive lives? For many researchers, 'cognition' means 'what the brain does when it thinks'.

---

[10] As will become clear in what follows, I am not concerned here with formal propositions of the sort that are either true or false. My focus is instead on informal propositions that embody beliefs or knowledge. My assumption is that such informal propositions could be rendered as formal propositions (and would then be true or false for some situation), but such an exercise is beyond what I want to accomplish here.

[11] By 'implicit knowledge' I mean knowledge that is not articulated; 'explicit knowledge' is, consequently, knowledge that is articulated. As I construe them, both implicit and explicit knowledge are accessible to consciousness; implicit knowledge is thus not equivalent to unconscious knowledge.

Although brains are, quite obviously, situated in bodies, it is assumed that information accumulated by and within the body – that is, the results of the processes of perception and proprioception – is simply of a different order from the information that forms the basis of our thoughts.[12] While it is also assumed that there is some connection between perceptual information and thought, the nature of this connection is often unspecified. The idea that there is 'a strong sense of embodiment associated with musical rhythm' is consequently treated as a habit of thought rather than a statement about knowledge grounded in embodied experience. In contrast to this view, other researchers have worked from the position that perception and proprioception contribute significantly and directly to the substance of our thought.[13] One of the most fully elaborated theoretical proposals based on this position has been made by the cognitive psychologist Lawrence Barsalou, and in the following I shall outline his proposal as a way of providing a fuller account of the sort of knowledge listeners use to make sense of musical rhythm.

Conceptual models and embodied experience
Key to Barsalou's approach is the assumption that neural states associated with perceptions are recorded in the brain.[14] Brain maps of such neural activations can operate even in the absence of bottom-up sensory stimulation (as when we remember a particular perception). Barsalou calls the neural records of perceptions and their associated brain maps 'perceptual symbols', and shows how cognitive operations that make use of perceptual symbols can represent types and tokens, produce categorical inferences, combine the symbols to produce hierarchical propositions, and yield abstract concepts. It is through operations such as these that perceptual symbols, which are for the most part not accessible to our consciousness, provide the basis for the conscious images and concepts that occupy our thoughts.

The schematic nature of the neural records basic to perceptual symbols makes it possible for perceptual symbols to participate in cognitive structures of which they were not initially a part, but with which they share focal features. For instance, our conceptions of rhythm in general, and of musical rhythm in particular, are strongly informed by the manifold regularities basic to human experience – the regular cycles of our breathing, the alternation of our limbs in

---

[12] See, for instance, Daniel C. Dennett, 'The Nature of Images and the Introspective Trap', *Content and Consciousness* (London, 1969), 132–46; Jerry A. Fodor, *The Language of Thought* (Cambridge, MA, 1975); Allen Newell and Herbert A. Simon, *Human Problem Solving* (Englewood Cliffs, 1972); Zenon W. Pylyshyn, *Computation and Cognition: Toward a Foundation for Cognitive Science* (Cambridge, MA, 1984).

[13] See, for instance, Mark Johnson, *The Body in the Mind: The Bodily Basis of Meaning, Imagination, and Reason* (Chicago, 1987); Gerald M. Edelman, *Bright Air, Brilliant Fire: On the Matter of Mind* (New York, 1992); Antonio R. Damasio, *The Feeling of What Happens: Body and Emotion in the Making of Consciousness* (New York, 1999).

[14] The theory is presented in Lawrence W. Barsalou, 'Perceptual Symbol Systems' and 'Perceptions of Perceptual Symbols', *Behavioral and Brain Sciences*, 22 (1999), 577–609 and 637–60.

walking or the repeated actions that accompany our physical work. These regularities are, of course, specific to the modality of proprioception rather than audition. For such regularities to inform our understanding of musical rhythm the properties and relations common to physical experience and musical rhythm must be exploited, and used for more abstract concepts that inform our understanding of both.[15] Three such concepts are regularity, differentiation and cyclicity. Regularity is the periodic recurrence of some event; Colwyn Trevarthen has recently argued that our knowledge of such regularity comes first from proprioception during the first months of life, and is only subsequently applied to musical experience.[16] Differentiation involves simultaneous non-identical regularities, such as what occurs when different limbs are engaged in regular but independent motions. Cyclicity involves composite regularities made up of coordinated differentiated regularities; most forms of human locomotion (including infants' creeping and crawling) involve cyclicity. Although I have characterized each concept in terms of information that could be gleaned from proprioception, regularity, differentiation and cyclicity can also be heard in rhythmic music. Indeed, from the perspective of Barsalou's theory, perceptual symbols associated with both proprioception and audition contribute to these concepts.

The concepts of regularity, differentiation and cyclicity, framed in terms of perceptual symbol systems, thus offer a sort of meeting ground for embodied

---

[15] Connections between perceptual symbols and abstract concepts are discussed in Barsalou, 'Perceptual Symbol Systems'; *idem*, 'Abstraction as Dynamic Interpretation in Perceptual Symbol Systems', *Building Object Categories in Developmental Time*, ed. Lisa Gershkoff-Stowe and David H. Rakison (forthcoming); and *idem*, 'Abstraction in Perceptual Symbol Systems', *Philosophical Transactions of the Royal Society of London: Biological Sciences*, 358 (2003), 1177–87. Support for the idea that the musical conception of rhythm is abstracted from proprioceptive information comes from recent neuro-imaging data which shows that musicians do not directly access information about sensorimotor function in their cognition of rhythm. See Lawrence M. Parsons, 'Exploring the Functional Neuroanatomy of Music Performance, Perception, and Comprehension', *The Biological Foundations of Music*, ed. Robert J. Zatorre and Isabelle Peretz, Annals of the New York Academy of Sciences, 0077–8923/930 (New York, 2001), 211–31. A rather different approach that provides a sensorimotor account of rhythm while avoiding the issue of concepts entirely (thus offering an alternative to the view I present) can be found in Neil P. McAngus Todd, Donald J. O'Boyle and Christopher S. Lee, 'A Sensory-Motor Theory of Rhythm, Time Perception and Beat Induction', *Journal of New Music Research*, 28 (1999), 5–28.

[16] Trevarthen proposes that within the first weeks of life infants begin to develop a body-moving rhythmic and emotionally modulated system called the Intrinsic Motive Formation (IMF) system. The IMF coordinates and regulates movements and their prospective sensory control, and in the process creates an integrated hierarchy of motor rhythms with varying qualities of expression called the Intrinsic Motive Pulse (IMP). Trevarthen writes: 'Musicality, the active part of it at least, is the aurally appreciated expression of the activity of the IMF, with the IMP as its agent' (Colwyn Trevarthen, 'Musicality and the Intrinsic Motivic Pulse: Evidence from Human Psychobiology and Infant Communication', *Musicae scientae*, Special Issue, 1999–2000, 115–215 (p. 160)). See also Colwyn Trevarthen and Kenneth J. Aitken, 'Infant Intersubjectivity: Research, Theory, and Clinical Applications', *Journal of Child Psychology and Psychiatry and Allied Disciplines*, 42 (2001), 3–48.

knowledge and knowledge about music. Regularity, for example, is instantiated both by periodic motions of the body and by a succession of evenly spaced musical sounds. These concepts can also be specified for music and coordinated through an inferential structure for making judgments about music, such as the conceptual model for musical rhythm discussed above. The concept of regularity is specified through P1 of the model, differentiation through P2 and cyclicity through P3. Although this specification foregrounds musical knowledge, embodied knowledge is still part of the picture. This is suggested by P4: rhythmic music is something to which we can move. When musical events summon the concepts of regularity, differentiation and cyclicity (either singularly or jointly), knowledge about both music and bodily motion is activated. Such events will, in consequence, function as ready targets onto which bodily motions can be mapped.

There are, nonetheless, limitations on how mappings between bodily motion and musical events can be accomplished. It is a simple psychological and physical fact that we cannot tap our toes to just anything: if recurrent musical events occur at too great a temporal interval (if the beat is too slow) the rhythmic frame diminishes in salience; if the temporal interval is too small (if the beat is too fast) we will typically find some other way of organizing the events in order to create a meaningful rhythmic frame.[17] More specifically, research on temporal acuity and judgment has demonstrated a significance for periodicities in the 600–700 millisecond range. Using the crotchet as the unit of the beat this yields a range of ♩ = 85–100, and whenever possible we prefer to locate the beat in this range.

The approach to embodied knowledge I have sketched here, and the relationship of that knowledge to musical knowledge, offers one way of explaining the strong connection between bodily motion and rhythmic music noted by many writers. The concepts key to our understanding of rhythm – regularity, differentiation and cyclicity – draw on focal features of both our embodied and musical experience. It is thus natural to imagine music that correlates with some of our favourite bodily motions, and to imagine bodily motions that correlate with some of our favourite music.

Conceptual models, listening and performing

From the perspective of research in cognitive psychology, the notion of rhythm – although not necessarily musical rhythm – is basic to human experience. This is the first sense in which I invoked 'listeners' at the beginning of this article: except in rare cases of neuro-anatomical dysfunction, human beings are rhythmic beings. It should not be assumed, however, that everyone responds to a given work of music in the same way – cultural knowledge, including knowledge about how to map bodily motion onto physical sound, is also involved.

---

[17] For a review of the relevant literature and empirical data see Justin London, 'Cognitive Constraints on Metric Systems: Some Observations and Hypotheses', *Music Perception*, 19 (2002), 534–9.

This is the second sense of 'listeners' that it is well to keep in mind: being a member of a musical culture means knowing how to interact with the musics specific to that culture. When listeners respond to a groove, they are demonstrating a particular kind of cultural knowledge, characterized in part by the conceptual model I have outlined.

Real or imagined bodily motion is, of course, how most listeners respond to a groove. It is also a prerequisite for the musicians producing the groove. This is not to say that we should equate, in a simple way, the physical activities associated with producing music and responding to it: clearly there are differences, and these distinguish people who can make music from those who cannot. There is a similar and related difference between the knowledge used to guide these activities: the conceptual models used to produce a work of music are not the same as those used to guide listening to that same work. But they are in most cases related. This issue will be explored in more detail below, but its outlines can be glimpsed by considering how the provisional model for musical rhythm sketched above could be applied to the creation of a satisfying musical performance. The musician who undertakes this task must get orientated to the set of regularly occurring musical events that make up the piece in question (P1), clearly differentiate its constituent elements by various stratagems of performance (P2), be sure to project the larger framework for rhythmic organization (P3; this is something that is particularly important for various kinds of dance music), and keep the music rhythmically alive (P4). Of course, a skilled musician relies on more than these general directions to produce a compelling performance. Nonetheless, this outline suggests that the basic touchstones we use to organize our understanding of and interactions with musical rhythm also serve as guides for musical performance.

Summary

According to the perspective I have developed here, our knowledge about music is organized through conceptual models. These models are cognitive structures, but cognition is here understood to include, by way of perceptual symbol systems, information drawn from perception and proprioception. Concepts like regularity, differentiation and cyclicity, all central to our understanding of musical rhythm, are a common ground where embodied and musical knowledge meet. Because such concepts rely on experiences shared by all humans, they will be in evidence (in one form or another) in all human cultures. This is not to say, however, that all cultures will apply them to music in the same way; indeed, being a member of a musical culture means knowing how to apply these concepts to the musics specific to that culture. And these applications will not be uniform even for members of the same musical culture, in that the concepts will be specified in one way for listening, and in another way for performing.

With these thoughts in mind, let us now explore the conceptual model behind a specific musical groove, starting from the perspective of the musicians generating the groove.

Example 1. First statement of the groove for Eric Clapton's 'It All Depends' (incomplete).

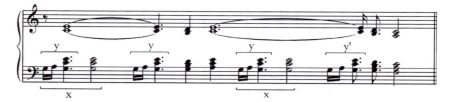

Modelling the groove

Eric Clapton, 'It All Depends'

'It All Depends' appeared on Eric Clapton's 1985 release *Behind the Sun*.[18] The tune, written by Clapton, is a moderate-tempo pop tune with something of a rhythm-and-blues flavour. The words for the song are occupied with an evaluation of a romantic relationship: is there something special between the singer and his beloved? 'It all depends on how you feel' – advice addressed predominantly to the beloved – is the answer provided by the chorus.

The recording begins with unaccompanied keyboards (synthesizers set up to sound a bit like inexpensive electronic organs, played by Chris Stainton and Peter Robinson) performing the music shown in Example 1. One thing notable about this music is the irregularity of the durations it presents. Were we to reckon these durations in terms of semiquavers, for instance, we would get the following pattern:

1 1 6 8 1 1 6 4 4 1 1 6 8 1 1 3 3 8

A common assumption among rhythmic theorists is that performers and listeners infer a regular beat (and thus a metre) when presented with such a pattern.[19] Indeed, given the importance of regularity to our conception of rhythm such an assumption seems fully warranted. And yet it need not be viewed as necessary in this particular case, in that more comprehensive regularities are evident within this passage. For instance, there are two statements of a large pattern (indicated with an 'x' on Example 1), which is four crotchets in duration and which comprises exactly the same pitch material both times. There are also four statements of a smaller pattern (three complete – 'y' – and one partial – 'y''), all of which are two crotchets in duration (except for y', which

---

[18] 'It All Depends' is not particularly noteworthy within Clapton's career; indeed, perhaps the most memorable song on *Behind the Sun* (Warner Bros. 9 25166-2) is 'Forever Man', which was the only tune on that release to get significant airplay.

[19] Fred Lerdahl and Ray Jackendoff, *A Generative Theory of Tonal Music* (Cambridge, MA, 1983), 18.

is truncated by a dotted quaver) and which have the same pitch material. And, as is evident from Example 1, the x and y patterns also overlap: each x begins with a y. These regularities suggest patterns typical of rhythmic music as characterized by the basic conceptual model outlined above. In line with P3 of that model (and to some extent supporting P1), the passage lays out two large cycles. Each begins with an x pattern, has a total duration of eight crotchets and, in its second half, has pitch material that contrasts with x. There are also four small cycles, resulting in the sort of differentiation of musical materials implied by P2. Each such cycle begins with a y pattern, has a duration of four crotchets and, in its latter half, involves pitch material which is sometimes almost exactly the same as y (something that happens when y co-occurs with x) and which is at other times different from y.

These various patterns suggest that, while a performer or listener might certainly infer a beat when hearing the music of Example 1, he or she would not have to do so in order to understand the passage as rhythmic, for the passage clearly sets out a multi-levelled rhythmic frame. The passage also provides an unambiguous tonal centre, which is projected both by the sustained pitches notated in the upper staff and by the statement of a C chord after each pair of semiquavers. Indeed, what we have here is a groove: a large-scale multi-layered pattern that involves both rhythmic and pitch materials. Although the notion of a groove that is not framed by a regular beat may seem counterintuitive, I would like to pursue it for a moment, both because of the lack of an explicit beat in Example 1 and because such a notion has interesting consequences for our understanding of grooves.

Were we to reflect, through musical notation, aspects of the rhythmic frame set out by this groove we might arrive at something like that given in the first portion of Example 2. There, the semiquaver figure is rendered as an upbeat, leading in each case to a tonic chord on the strong beat of the bar. This interpretation is supported by the entrances of the shaker (Phil Collins), guitar (Clapton) and bass (Donald 'Duck' Dunn), which are shown in the latter portion of the example. While the shaker, in semiquavers, lays out the ground for the various durations of the solo keyboard part (all of which can be understood as some multiple of a semiquaver), the guitar and especially the bass reinforce the sense that the tonic chords subsequent to the semiquavers should be heard as accented.

Although the time signature of Example 2 suggests the presence of a regular crotchet beat, the excerpt is remarkable for its studious avoidance of such a beat. Indeed, excepting the regular iterations of the shaker, the musicians articulate only beat 1 of the metre. The effect of the whole is remarkably like that of syncopation – note the agogic accents on the third quaver of the bar in bars 5, 7 and 8 and on the sixth quaver in bar 6, an emphasis Duck Dunn heightens by preceding each of these moments with silence – except that the regular metric cycle against which these emphases play is present only in its absence. What this suggests is an implicit quadruple metre, which is understood but never sounded by the musicians. There are thus two interacting rhythmic layers in the music of Example 2, each with a different function: an explicit layer, which projects

Example 2.   First and second statements of the groove for Eric Clapton's 'It All Depends'.

the essential materials of the groove (and which involves both pitch and rhythm); and an implicit layer, which serves as a frame of reference for the explicit layer and as something that is left unstated.[20]

---

[20] After hearing this example Joti Rockwell suggested that the recording was almost certainly done with a 'click track': that is, the musicians coordinated their performance by listening to a series of equally spaced clicks that were prerecorded on one track of the master recording. Once the musicians laid down their various parts the click track was switched off or erased. After listening to the recording with this in mind, I agree: I think it highly likely that the technique was used, for there is a rock-solid consistency to the rhythmic frame of 'It All Depends' that does not typically come about by chance. I do not, however, believe that making what is implicit explicit for the purposes of recording argues against the notion of an implicit frame for the groove, for two reasons. First, the click track is used simply to ensure the consistency of the final product – it is not an intrinsic part of the conception of the groove, and would not be used for live performance. Second, the click track is typically undifferentiated, whereas the implicit rhythm is differentiated. This latter point is taken up in more detail below.

Let me take these observations and incorporate them into a conceptual model that captures not only the interaction between these rhythmic layers, but also the larger organizational structure of the groove for 'It All Depends'. Again, the model is presented as a set of correlated propositions, but this time the perspective is that of the performing musicians.

G_1P_1 The rhythmic framework for the groove is a danceable quadruple metre, which is never stated as such.

G_1P_2 The main elements of the groove always line up on the downbeat, and are syncopated everywhere else.

G_1P_3 The bass anchors the basic syncopations of the groove, and all the other instruments align themselves with these.

G_1P_4 The materials of the groove are organized in two- and four-bar units; the groove starts again at the conclusion of the fourth bar.

G_1P_5 Textural elements (like the shaker) add dimension to the rhythmic layers of the groove, but do not directly participate in the groove's syncopations.

As was the case with the rudimentary conceptual model for rhythm, there is no expectation that the musicians who enact this groove would be able (or need) to render these propositions as explicit statements or formalize them in the way I have, nor do these propositions embody all of the knowledge necessary to play the groove. The model is instead intended to capture what is essential for performing this groove. For instance, consider what would happen were another musician to add a significant accent on the sixth quaver of bars 5, 7 and 8. Such an accent would not be in opposition to most of the propositions of the model, but it would conflict with G_1P_3. The result would not be wrong (in a simple way) but it would create a groove that was different from that heard on the recording. Note that the latter half of each bar of the groove (with the exception of bar 6) is relatively sparse; this provides an opening into which one of the musicians might insert a bit of fill. Clapton in fact does just this in bar 8, when his upward scoop signals the end of the groove pattern. Were the situation entertained above to transpire – another musician adding accents on the sixth quaver of bars 5, 7 and 8 – the opening in the last half of each bar would almost completely disappear, and the distinctiveness of Clapton's scoop would be lost.[21]

In a third iteration of the groove (the last before the vocals enter) a conga part (played by Ray Cooper) is added; the music is given in Example 3. Broadly speaking, this part conforms to G_1P_5 of the model: it is a textural element that does not directly participate in the syncopations basic to the groove (and is thus

---

[21] According to the conceptual model, the first pass through the groove with solo keyboards is also somewhat exceptional (in that there is no bass to anchor the basic syncopations). This would be in keeping with hearing this pass as introductory.

Example 3.   Third statement of the groove for Eric Clapton's 'It All Depends'.

similar to the shaker part). The conga part does, however, hint at the quadruple metre that is behind the groove by introducing agogic accents on beats 2 and 4. What is significant is that this is quadruple metre as it is usually performed in rock and roll: a four count with one kind of accent on beats 1 and 3 (the typical strong beats of quadruple metre) and another kind of accent – the 'backbeat' – on beats 2 and 4.

Conventional metric theory does not really have an adequate description for the differentiation of accents common in rock and roll: beats are either strong or weak.[22] An alternative, inspired in part by the distinction between explicit and implicit rhythmic layers drawn above, would be to construe a typical rock-and-roll quadruple metre as consisting of two levels of rhythmic activity: a primary level (with accents on beats 1 and 3) and a secondary level (with accents on beats 2 and 4). On the one hand, the secondary level is defined in relation to the primary level; whence the term 'backbeat', which designates a secondary kind of beat in relation to the main beats that are in 'front' of them.[23] On the other hand, the secondary level has a measure of independence, suggesting as it does a distinctive way to move the body (most often as some sort of reaction to the accents of the primary level). Extending this perspective to the groove of 'It All Depends', we could characterize the explicit layer of the groove as occupying a tertiary level: its rhythmic pattern is defined in relation to both the primary and the secondary levels of the implicit layer (remembering that the implicit layer is made partially explicit with the entrance of the conga part). Following the ideas about connections between embodied and musical knowledge developed above, each of these levels could function as a target onto which bodily motion could be mapped.[24]

Let me pause at this point and review features of the perspective on musical rhythm and metre developed in connection with my model for the groove of 'It All Depends'. First, the explicit rhythmic pattern of a groove may be framed in relation to an implicit pattern. This implicit pattern is knowledge shared by the musicians performing the groove, and its status is as something so familiar that it need never be stated. Second, the rhythmic structure of dance music may include distinct, and correlated, rhythmic levels. Such levels will be distinguished not solely by their place within a metric frame, but by association with distinctive timbres, registers, pitch collections, agogic accents or combinations of these things. Each level offers a target onto which we can map bodily motion.

---

[22] Recent metric theory enriches this picture by recognizing relative degrees of strength and weakness among beats: beat 3 of a quadruple metre is reckoned to be stronger than beats 2 and 4, but weaker than beat 1. However, this phenomenon is thought of as a consequence of interacting, hierarchically distinct cycles of strong and weak beats. (The classic study in this connection is Maury Yeston, *The Stratification of Musical Rhythm*, New Haven, 1976; see also Lerdahl and Jackendoff, *A Generative Theory of Tonal Music*, 18–21, and Harald Krebs, *Fantasy Pieces: Metrical Dissonance in the Music of Robert Schumann*, New York, 1999.) The differentiation between beats with which I am concerned – a differentiation common in dance music, including dances such as the sarabande, mazurka, hambo and Swedish polska – is not addressed by this approach to metre.

[23] This spatial metaphor is not, in my experience, worked out in discourse about rock-and-roll rhythm. That is, no one talks about 'frontbeats', or further spatializes their characterization of rhythmic relationships in ways distinct from those in which rhythm is generally characterized; for instance, musicians from a wide variety of backgrounds characterize musical events as 'on' or 'off' the beat, which I take to be a fundamentally spatial conception of beat location.

[24] Virgil Thomson, observing the prevalence of syncopation in early twentieth-century dance music, noted 'A silent accent is the strongest of all accents. It forces the body to replace it with a motion.' 'Jazz', *A Virgil Thomson Reader* (Boston, MA, 1981), 15–18 (p. 16). My thanks to Alex Ross for leading me to this quotation.

This motion may be real or imagined, and may involve only one portion of our body or one distinctive gesture (with another gesture or portion of the body assigned to another rhythmic level).

Having developed a conceptual model which could serve as the basis for producing a musical groove, let us now consider how this model might relate to one used for understanding that groove.

One groove, two models

As I have already suggested, we should not expect an audience's model of a groove to be the same as that of the musicians producing that groove; we should, however, expect there to be correlations between the two if we imagine them to be part of the same overall body of cultural knowledge. As a general rule, the audience's model will be more comprehensive and less specific – in other words, it will be quite a bit like the rudimentary conceptual model for rhythm we have already outlined. Figure 1 explores this through a diagram that places the two models in correspondence with one another. P1 from the basic model (which focuses on regularly occurring events) correlates with G_1P_2 and G_1P_3 of the model for 'It All Depends' (which pertain to the explicit layer of the groove). P2 (differentiation between events) correlates with interactions between the explicit and implicit layers (that is, G_1P_1, G_1P_2 and G_1P_3). P3 (cyclicity) correlates most directly with G_1P_4, although the propositions related to the explicit and implicit layers of the groove also have relevance for the cycles of rhythmic events assumed by P3. P4 (embodiment) correlates weakly with G_1P_1: on the one hand, both models have a place for embodied knowledge (in the case of the musicians' model this knowledge is represented by the notion that the quadruple metre basic to the groove should be danceable), but where this knowledge is front and centre in the basic model, it remains somewhat behind the scenes in the musicians' model.

As is evident from Figure 1, while there are connections between the two models it is not the case that the musicians' model is a straightforward expansion of the basic model; it is instead a specialization of the knowledge embodied in the basic model. The knowledge basic to P1, for instance, is manifested in two different propositions (G_1P_2 and G_1P_3), each of which is concerned with a different aspect of the explicit layer of the groove. These propositions, taken together with G_1P_1, also serve to represent the knowledge associated with P2. This seems to suggest that P1 and P2 from the basic model could be combined, yielding a proposition something like 'Rhythm concerns regularly occurring, differentiated musical events.' Nonetheless, while such a proposition certainly seems fundamental to the musicians' model, the concepts of regularity and differentiation (each associated with different proprioceptive information) are perhaps best kept distinct in the basic model for musical rhythm.

The connections between the two models seem clear. There remains, however, the question of how knowledge implicit in the musicians' model can be accommodated by the listener's model. Does it really make sense to say that a listener's expectation that musical rhythm is embodied will be satisfied by a

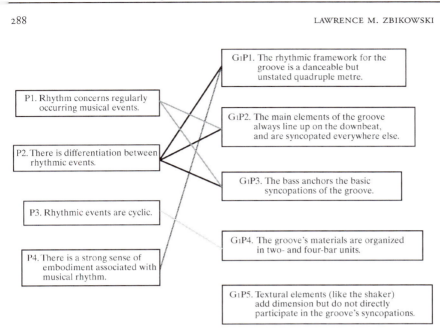

P1. Rhythm concerns regularly occurring musical events.

P2. There is differentiation between rhythmic events.

P3. Rhythmic events are cyclic.

P4. There is a strong sense of embodiment associated with musical rhythm.

G₁P1. The rhythmic framework for the groove is a danceable but unstated quadruple metre.

G₁P2. The main elements of the groove always line up on the downbeat, and are syncopated everywhere else.

G₁P3. The bass anchors the basic syncopations of the groove.

G₁P4. The groove's materials are organized in two- and four-bar units.

G₁P5. Textural elements (like the shaker) add dimension but do not directly participate in the groove's syncopations.

Figure 1. Correlation of the rudimentary model for musical rhythm and the model for the groove of 'It All Depends'.

rhythmic layer that is never stated? The answer lies in the limitations on human temporal perception that have been demonstrated by empirical research on temporal acuity and judgment.[25] Returning to the music of Example 2, we can note that there are only two evenly spaced series of musical events to be found there (and thus two possibilities for evenly spaced beats): the semiquavers of the shaker, and the combined attacks on the first beat of each bar. At the tempo taken in the recording, the semiquavers are spaced 170 milliseconds apart; at this speed the events occur simply too quickly to be processed individually, and will be heard not as beats but as subdivisions of the beat. At the other extreme, the first beats of each bar are spaced 2.73 seconds apart; these events occur too slowly to be understood as successive beats. The unstated crotchets of the implicit rhythmic layer, however, occur at intervals of 681 milliseconds, which is in perfect conformity with our preferred temporal interval for the beat. We are psychologically predisposed, then, to hear the constituent beats of the implicit layer of the groove for 'It All Depends'.

A psychological predisposition to hearing beats spaced at 681 millisecond intervals is not, however, quite the same thing as hearing a multi-levelled

[25] Justin London, 'Cognitive Constraints on Metric Systems: Some Observations and Hypotheses', *Music Perception*, 19 (2002), 529–50.

rhythmic pattern – remember that the full context for the groove assumes that beats 1 and 3 of the implicit layer are distinct from beats 2 and 4. Thus our predisposition must be combined with knowledge about what sort of metrical patterns are typical of popular music. We can reflect this stylistic knowledge by adding a proposition to the basic model for musical rhythm:

P5 Popular music and rock and roll involve a two-levelled quadruple metre.

This proposition then works together with the other four, yielding a model for musical rhythm in popular music (as distinct from the basic four-proposition model for musical rhythm).

Both the musicians' model and the listener's model for the groove thus combine embodied knowledge and conventional (or stylistic) knowledge, and this knowledge can be either explicit or implicit. Modelling the groove is not a simple matter of propositional knowledge, any more than it is an unthinking response to sonic stimuli. It is instead the result of a process where, as individual humans, we interact with what we hear as well as with the social and cultural context within which that hearing takes place.

Interactions with the groove

Even working within the limits I have set myself, the world of the groove is a rich and varied one. I consider only two further examples, with the expectation that the approach I have outlined could be applied to many more. The first, from a performance led by Miles Davis, demonstrates what happens when the features of the musician's model of the groove do not match those of the audience. The second example, from a performance led by James Brown, shows how a groove can engender a more highly specified dynamic frame, which in turn suggests a richer set of possibilities for mapping physical motion onto patterned sound.

Miles Davis, 'If I Were a Bell'
Miles Davis began his 1956 recording of Frank Loesser's 'If I Were a Bell' with eight finger snaps spaced about 625 milliseconds apart: a perfectly clear counting beat that sets up an indisputable metric frame.[26] But when Red Garland, playing piano, enters, he does so between the snaps, as shown in Example 4. Davis's snaps set out not the counting beat, but divisions of the counting beat. The result is what jazz musicians call a 'double-time feel', which involves playing twice the speed of the main metric frame but without speeding up the basic

[26] The personnel on the recording include Davis on trumpet, Red Garland on piano, Paul Chambers on bass, Philly Joe Jones on drums and John Coltrane on tenor saxophone. The recording session took place on 26 October 1956 in Hackensack, NJ, and appeared on *Relaxin' with Miles*. It has been re-released under the same name on CD as Prestige OJCCD-190-2. My thanks to Paul Steinbeck for bringing this performance to my attention.

Example 4.   Introduction to Miles Davis's version of 'If I Were a Bell'.

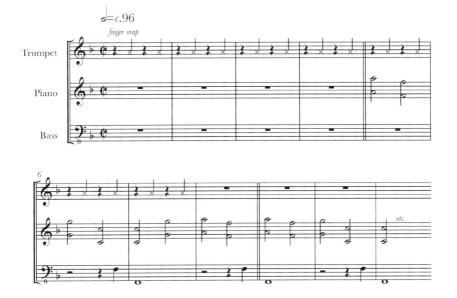

harmonic rhythm of the tune. The harmonic rhythm, as Garland's piano part suggests, is one main harmony per bar, and these are then grouped into two- and four-bar units (as Paul Chambers's bass part suggests, and the repetition of Garland's evocation of the Westminster chimes confirms).[27]

The model for the groove set up by Davis and his rhythm section is a straight-forward one, and can be characterized with just three propositions:

G_2P_1 The music has a double-time feel.
G_2P_2 The groove is organized into two- and four-bar units.
G_2P_3 There is one basic harmony per bar.[28]

While Davis's finger snaps, by themselves, almost certainly do not signify a double-time feel to most listeners, Garland's and Chambers's confident

[27] The Westminster chimes are more properly called the Westminster Quarters. For a discussion of the pitch successions basic to such chimes, see Daniel Harrison, 'Tolling Time', *Music Theory Online*, 6/4 (October 2000; <www.societymusictheory.org/mto/issues/mto.00.6.4/toc.6.4.html>).

[28] The notion that there is one basic harmony per bar fits not only with Garland's introduction, but also with the predominant harmonic pattern set out by Loesser in the original version of the tune. It should be noted, however, that in performance there is a harmonic change – sometimes subtle, sometimes more pronounced – in the second half of almost every bar, which is typical of the way such harmonic patterns are interpreted by the rhythm section.

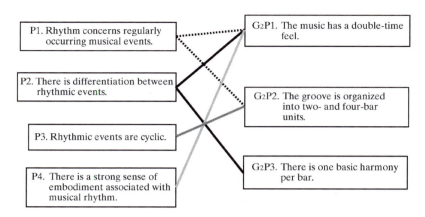

Figure 2.　Correlation of the rudimentary model for musical rhythm and the model for Miles Davis's version of 'If I Were a Bell'.

entrances, together with the musical pun of the introduction, suggest that the group had worked out the arrangement in advance and that Davis's finger snaps were understood as cues for the divisions of the beat.[29]

Setting aside, for the moment, the disruption caused by Garland's entrance we find that, once again, the musicians' model has a number of close relationships with the basic model for rhythm. Connections between the models are diagrammed in Figure 2. P1 from the basic model (regularly occurring events) correlates with G_2P1 and G_2P2 of the model for 'If I Were a Bell'; given the tempo, it is easier to hear the two- and four-bar units as contributing to an explicit sense of rhythm than it was in Clapton's 'It All Depends'. Similarly, P2 (differentiation between events) correlates with G_2P3 because, given the tempo, the harmonic changes occur at what would be a comparable minim level in many other tunes, and their contribution to the differentiation of materials is easily heard. P3 (cyclicity) correlates directly with G_2P2, and P4 (embodiment, perhaps activated by Davis's snaps) with G_2P1.

But let us return to the sense of disruption that makes the opening of this piece truly remarkable. The listener, of course, has no way of knowing how Davis's finger snaps are to be interpreted. Given the eight finger snaps, spaced at a temporal interval perfectly in keeping with our preferred level of the beat, the natural inclination is to take these as the beat. Garland's entrance forces a

[29] That Davis and the group had rehearsed this introduction is supported, indirectly, by Davis's comment to the engineer just prior to his finger snaps: 'I'll play it and tell you what it is later.' This suggests that Davis and the group knew quite well what the tune was, and how they were going to play it, but that this knowledge had not yet been shared with the technical staff on the recording. Davis also could have clarified the intent of his finger snaps by using a head nod or other gesture to signal the placement of the main beats relative to which his finger snaps were to be understood, but I am not aware of any evidence confirming that he did so.

double re-interpretation of the finger snaps: they are not only not the main counting beat, but they are divisions of the counting beat. I would not want to make too much of our preference to find the beat in the 600–700 millisecond range – after all, music can move at a variety of speeds – but I do find that accommodating both the main beats and Davis's divisions of those beats (once Garland has entered) gives a hurried feel to the music (the main beats and Davis's divisions occur about 312 milliseconds apart) which becomes attenuated once I move the metric framework completely to the main beats outlined by Garland's chimes.

Thus the disruption we feel when the metric frame is re-orientated by Garland's entrance can be attributed, at least in part, to our preference to locate the beat at what is the minim level in Davis's performance. Another factor, however, may be our expectation that metric cues given at the outset of a performance point to the counting beat, an expectation that seems to be of a different order from our preferred level for the beat. Once again, we could reflect this knowledge by adding a proposition to the basic conceptual model for rhythm, along the lines of:

P5′ One member of the group often counts in the others in live performance.

When we hear Davis's finger snaps, then, our default assumption is that he is setting out the basic beat for the performance, rather than the divisions of the beat that he actually indicates. That something like this is behind the jarring effect of Garland's entrance seems plausible: if we count double time from the point when the finger snaps start, the piano entrance is somewhat easier to assimilate, but we must still re-orientate the beat away from the finger snaps and onto the piano.

The opening of Davis's arrangement of 'If I Were a Bell' thus suggests that listeners bring a variety of knowledge to the understanding of grooves, including knowledge about performance practice. As my proposed expansion of the basic model for musical rhythm shows, listeners know (if only implicitly) that a groove is more than a large-scale, multi-layered pattern that involves both pitch and rhythmic materials; they know that it is also a consequence of a set of cultural practices that make music-making possible.

James Brown, 'Doing it to Death/Gonna Have a Funky Good Time'

There is nothing equivocal in the opening of James Brown's 'Doing it to Death', which he released under the name of Fred Wesley and the J. B.'s and which was also known by its opening line, 'Gonna Have a Funky Good Time'.[30] The recording starts with Brown's 'Hit it!', and in response the groove begins

---

[30] Fred Wesley, on trombone, directed James Brown's band during the early 1970s. 'Doing it to Death' was originally released in 1973, and has been re-released on *James Brown 40th Anniversary Collection*, Polydor CD 31543 3409-2, and on *Star Time*, Polydor 849 112-2. My thanks again to Paul Steinbeck, who not only brought this recording to my attention but also provided a transcription of the groove, upon which my transcription is based.

Example 5.   First two statements of the groove for James Brown's 'Doing it to Death/Gonna Have a Funky Good Time'.

immediately, stopping only when the recording comes to an end some five minutes later. And a powerful groove it is, an amalgam of drums, hand claps, bass and guitars, all framed around a near-constant pulse of $\bullet$. = 114.[31] The groove is built on the two-levelled quadruple metre which was basic to Clapton's 'It All Depends'. But in this case the quadruple metre subdivides by three, yielding the rolling 12/8 typical of the blues and blues-derived genres. (For the sake of simplicity I shall continue to refer to the main beats of the metric frame as if this were a straightforward quadruple metre.) As Example 5 shows, the bass drum, playing a steady $\bullet$ $\bullet$ pattern, anchors the groove, with the snare and hand claps providing the accents on beats 2 and 4. The bass guitar, for its part, contributes to the backbeat with agogic accents; indeed, without the context provided by the other instruments it would be very easy to hear the bass's long notes as setting out beats 1 and 3 rather than 2 and 4. Against this backdrop the second guitar uses two different strategies for grouping its attacks in the course of each bar. In the first half of the bar the guitar plays as though it were in 3/4 time, the three pairs of quavers and quaver rests equivalent to three crotchets. In the second half of the bar the guitar, putting itself in conformity with the other instruments, switches to 6/8 time. This strategy tends to destabilize the first half of the bar (with a grouping dissonance between the guitar and the other parts), and to stabilize the second half of the bar (when the groupings in all the parts agree with each other).[32]

---

[31] In his transcription Steinbeck notes that the tempo ranges between 112 and 116 beats per minute over the course of the recording – that is, ± 1.8%.

[32] Grouping dissonances of this sort are discussed in greater detail in Krebs, *Fantasy Pieces*.

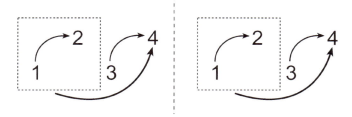

Figure 3.   Dynamic shape for the groove of James Brown's 'Doing it to Death/Gonna Have a Funky Good Time'.

This pattern of stability and instability is diagrammed in Figure 3. The two-levelled quadruple metre basic to the groove is represented through placing beats 1 and 3 and beats 2 and 4 at different heights on the page. The sense of moving toward beats 2 and 4 provided by the bass's figure is represented by arrows from beat 1 to beat 2, and from beat 3 to beat 4. Finally, the instability of the first half of the bar suggested by the second guitar's rhythmic pattern is represented with an arrow from the box that encloses beats 1 and 2 to beat 4, meant to suggest the culmination of the rhythmic pattern on the last main beat of each bar. The result is an end-accented structure typical of some Western African rhythms – indeed, Figure 3 shows a bar with a dynamic structure that is the mirror image of conventional quadruple metres in which beat 1 is the most accented and beat 4 the least accented.

As a consequence of all this rhythmic activity the groove for 'Doing it to Death' provides four possible targets for bodily motion, three of which are distinct from one another and one of which is comprehensive. The first two targets are those established by the two-levelled quadruple metre; the third is set up by the rhythmic pattern of the second guitar, which toggles between dividing the first half of the bar in three and the second half of the bar in two; the fourth (and comprehensive) target is created by the dynamic shape of each bar, which culminates in a strong arrival on beat 4. In short, the groove presents a number of possibilities for bodily motion as the combinations of these different patterns are realized. For instance, a dancer could move his hips with beats 1 and 3, his arms with beats 2 and 4, and gesture with his head in correspondence with the rhythmic pattern set up by the second guitar. Another dancer could move her feet with beats 1 and 3 but then move her whole body according to the dynamic pattern diagrammed in Figure 3. When the various ways a dancer could move his or her body are combined with the four targets for bodily motion set up by the groove the permutational possibilities are truly impressive, suggesting why, despite a lack of memorable lyrics or a striking melody, 'Doing it to Death' rose to million-seller status.

As was the case with the other grooves I have considered, that for James Brown's 'Doing it to Death' is a complex, multi-layered pattern that involves both pitch and rhythmic materials. And yet, because of the way these materials fit together and because they are repeated with little variation over 130 times in the course of the recording, the groove does not represent an intellectual challenge. Its complexity is instead one so common in our cognitive lives as to be thoroughly unremarkable: a complexity of perceptual and proprioceptual information, bodily motions (both potential and actualized), introspective states of awareness, thoughts and feelings that contribute to the texture of our conscious lives.[33] But it is precisely because our apprehension of rhythmic structure involves higher-order cognitive processes of the sort that regularly make sense of this complexity that grooves like that for 'Doing it to Death' seem so transparent. It is only when we pause to consider why grooves are so seductive, and their rhythmic compulsion so inevitable, that this complexity becomes apparent.

Conclusions

There is a tendency, especially among the literate, to regard knowledge as that which is or can be written down. Although this reflects the importance of language and systems of representation to human thought, an importance it would be foolish to deny, it leads to certain difficulties when one comes to the study of popular music. Not only is music as a whole a para-linguistic medium, but much – indeed, most – of popular music is part of an aural tradition of music-making which has little if any use for symbolic representation. If knowledge is indeed limited to that which is or can be written down, then much of popular music is beyond knowledge: to ask what a listener knows when he or she knows a groove is to entertain a question that can have no answer. But this seems silly, and extraordinarily limiting, as it places a vital part of contemporary life beyond inquiry. We instead need to entertain an expanded view of the nature of knowledge, a view that follows from construing knowledge as basic to the prospect of culture itself.

According to this view, the knowledge that is central to culture is organized through relatively basic cognitive structures that act as guides for reasoning and inference, structures that I call conceptual models. Conceptual models are used for both the understanding and the production of music. Important for all kinds of music, they come to special prominence when we consider how music of aural traditions manifests cultural knowledge. To the extent that someone is a member of a musical culture – whether that culture be so intensely local that it extends to only a small group of musicians and listeners, or so global that it encompasses an entire continent – he or she shares conceptual models with other members of that musical culture. Such sharing is never exact, but is part of a dynamic process through which culture is realized. The knowledge organized by

---

[33] On the complexity and efficacy of consciousness see Merlin Donald, *A Mind So Rare: The Evolution of Human Consciousness* (New York, 2001). On the relationship between feelings, emotions and consciousness, see Damasio, *The Feeling of What Happens*.

conceptual models is rarely propositional (although I have used a loose notion of 'proposition' to characterize the structure of the conceptual models I have discussed) and is built on information derived from perception and proprioception, as well as from cognitive structures more typically described as 'conceptual'. For a listener, knowing a groove means being able to summon conceptual models that can be used to guide behavioural or cognitive responses to the groove.

Among the models a listener might summon is a basic conceptual model for musical rhythm of the sort I described above. Such a model plucks out the salient features of a sequence of sounds that would allow them to be categorized as musically 'rhythmic' and provides a basis for response to these sounds: knowing that rhythm concerns regularly occurring musical events suggests the anticipation of such events; knowing that rhythmic events are differentiated suggests a heightened attention to the things that differentiate various elements of a specific sequence of events; knowing that rhythmic events are cyclic allows a response to a sequence of musical events that plays out over a larger time frame; and knowing that musical rhythm is associated with a strong sense of embodiment suggests that the most proper response to musical rhythm is to move. This is, of course, not all that is needed to make sense of a groove – the propositions I added to this basic model to accommodate aspects of Clapton's and Davis's grooves suggest that more is needed to make sense of many grooves – but it is knowledge of this sort, organized into coherent, holistic cognitive structures, that is essential to knowing a groove.

Conceptual models are used for understanding grooves, and they are also used for producing grooves. The models used by musicians may have a quite different structure from those of members of their audience, reflecting the intellectual and physical specificities of musical performance. The propositions of the models I described for Clapton's 'It All Depends' and Davis's 'If I Were a Bell' connect with the propositions for the basic model for musical rhythm, but reinterpret and reformulate these propositions in accordance with the demands of performance. In a somewhat similar fashion, my descriptions of how listeners and musicians model the groove fit with some but not all of the features of conventional theories of musical rhythm (which place more emphasis on a sounding beat as a basic unit of measurement for rhythmic understanding). More specifically, I have argued that listeners can make sense of a groove (as a large-scale, multi-layered pattern that involves both pitch and rhythmic materials) without reference to an explicit beat; an implicit knowledge of rhythmic frameworks (including but not limited to a knowledge of regular beat patterns) may help guide the process of making sense of a groove; and multiple patterns of accent, especially where these are correlated with the traditions of dance, can obtain within a rhythmic framework. This argument not only pushes the framework for understanding rhythm and metre beyond the sounding surface, but also makes a place for embodied knowledge within rhythmic theory. Our understanding of rhythm is shaped not only by our tendency to locate rhythmic periodicities within a somewhat limited range of temporal intervals, but also by our regard of rhythmic patterns as targets onto which we can map real or imagined bodily motion. A willingness to do such mappings adds dimensionality to the way we move with a groove, for, as we saw with the groove for Brown's 'Doing it to Death', a good groove offers a number of targets for bodily motion.

The conceptual models I have outlined are first approximations of the knowledge listeners use to make sense of grooves, and that musicians use to produce grooves. A fuller understanding of this knowledge will require more detailed models, a more elaborate account of the origins of conceptual models within perceptual symbol systems and the context within which they operate, and a more complete description of how conceptual models change over time. Nonetheless, this approach allows us to glimpse how we might confront the problem of modelling the groove, but now with groove understood as a phenomenon roughly equivalent to 'swing'. This sort of groove is rather more complex than the relatively straightforward patterns with which I have been concerned in the foregoing, for groove as a feel is a quicksilver thing as changeable as music itself. Even so, musicians must still have a conception of the basic framework which provides an opportunity for the creation of this sort of feel, a framework that includes knowledge about how rhythmic and pitch materials are organized and how members of a musical ensemble will realize this organization. They have to know how to model a groove.

What does someone know when they know a good groove? Quite a lot: they know what makes for musical rhythm, how the body might respond to rhythm, and the context within which large-scale, multi-layered patterns of pitch and rhythmic materials are produced. In short, they know music.

ABSTRACT

A musical groove is most typically created by a small group of musicians working together, each contributing parts to the whole. Characterizing the knowledge behind such interactive ventures has proved to be challenging. This article attempts to characterize the knowledge basic to grooves first by concentrating on 'the groove' as it is practised in soul, rhythm and blues, jazz fusion and various other popular genres, and second by focusing on cognitive knowledge structures called conceptual models. It is argued that musicians rely on such structures to produce grooves, and that listeners make use of similar structures to understand them. Grooves from the music of Eric Clapton, Miles Davis and James Brown are discussed, and conceptual models for each are developed.

Part III
Subjectivity, Ethnicity and Politics

[14]

LIKE A VIRGIN-MOTHER?: MATERIALISM AND MATERNALISM IN THE SONGS OF MADONNA

BARBARA BRADBY

Video killed the radio star?

I n the recent writing on music video and postmodernism, Madonna occupies a privileged place. Whether one believes that music television can be explained away as an advertising strategy at a period of falling record sales, or whether one sees it as the postmodern Utopia, Madonna stands out as the star who has most successfully built her career through the new medium. If music video is just a new form of the commodification of music, then Madonna is the successful product; on the other hand, who better than Madonna exemplifies the 'postmodern' strategy of 'ironic inauthenticity', where

> it doesn't matter what image one takes; take any image and live it for as long as you want or like. It is the construction of any image as absolutely real and totally ironic. One can deconstruct gender at the moment of celebrating it (and celebrate it precisely because one can deconstruct it). (Grossberg, 1988: 327–8)

Either way, it seems, the songs themselves have become less important as conveyors of meaning than have the visual images that accompany and sell them. Grossberg even goes so far as to say that 'in a paradoxical sense, music video has freed the music from the image', and uses Madonna as exemplification of this contention:

> For example, one likes Madonna – whose music always sounds the same, but whose images are constantly changing – if one believes that she does not take her images too seriously. (326)

What does this mean? Out of context, one might assume that Grossberg is appealing to the old rock aesthetic, which regards images as illusory and equates 'liking' a star or group with liking their music. But Grossberg must be aware that the phrase 'the music always sounds the same' resonates with parental and class opposition to rock and pop music, and it seems that for him too, the music has become at best incidental. Grossberg's 'rock'n'roll fan' in the era of MTV is for ever appropriating, celebrating and deconstructing images, styles, poses – the emphasis all the time on the visual, and the cross-references to film and to TV serials not to music.

But this freeing of the music from the image is indeed paradoxical. For, in one sense, it is a real economic fact, since songs endure in commodity form as *records*, whereas most music videos never even go on sale as individual commodities. Until 1990, for instance, the video of Madonna's 'Material Girl', had never been on sale, yet has been the subject of lengthy academic analyses (Brown and Fiske, 1987; Kaplan, 1987; Fiske, 1989). The *song*, however, as well as being a hit single in the US and UK in 1985, has always been available on the platinum-selling album, *Like a Virgin*. What is contentious in 'the freeing of the music from the image' is not, then, the independent existence of the song: it is the assumption that *the image is thereby freed from the music*. For while the existence of commercial radio and of the record industry proves that the songs have meaning in isolation from video images, it is impossible to imagine watching MTV for any length of time without a soundtrack. And since watching a video is inseparable as experience from listening to the song, the question arises as to what critics are doing in purporting to analyze video simply as *image*, in isolation from the song-text that is an integral part of it.

The problem with the claims made implicitly by both Grossberg and Kaplan, that Madonna can be 'read' without reference to her songs, goes beyond an economic argument. There is also a semiotic problem in attempting to read music video as a purely visual text. In this paper I hope to demonstrate that, despite their appearance of autonomy, such readings are ultimately *dependent* on the song-text to make sense of the visual images. I shall do this by comparing two analyses of 'Material Girl', the video (Brown and Fiske, 1987; Kaplan, 1987), with my own analysis of 'Material Girl', the song, which was written before I became aware of the video analyses.[1] While both Kaplan, and Brown and Fiske, do refer to the song in their analyses, both sets of authors treat the meaning of the song as static and self-evident. I shall argue that if one analyzes the song as narrative, and as itself a group performance between differently gendered voices, one can come to a better understanding of how Madonna is seen to achieve 'control' (over men, over images) in this video.

Images of material girls (1), the screen romance

Brown and Fiske are forthright in their assessment of 'Material Girl' as a feminist video:

> A fantasy that proposes an empowered heroine controlling the meanings of herself and her gender relations is an oppositional, resistive fantasy that has a political effectivity. (1987: 71)

Their argument in support of this claim has two parts and requires two kinds of 'intertextual' reading. The first part is a reading of the 'love story' of the video, in relation to conventional romantic narrative, a generic knowledge of which can be assumed in the viewer. The second requires more specific knowledge about the life and star persona of Marilyn Monroe, and is an analysis of the *spectacle* of the song/dance performance, which interrupts the flow of narrative in the video. In this way, the video rewrites nineteenth-century romance and twentieth-century sexuality for girls of the 1980s.

The 'love story' sketched in the video differs from conventional romantic narrative, according to Brown and Fiske, in that the process of 'feminisation' of the hero is achieved not through the lonely suffering of the heroine,[2] but while 'Madonna remains in a position of power throughout' (64):

> The narrative opens with the 'poor' hero and a producer watching some film rushes of Madonna; he insists that Madonna is perfect and nothing needs changing. She arrives at the studio with the rich hero, and the dressing room romance develops in parallel with her studio song-and-dance number. The 'poor' hero realizes that she is playing with and parodying her desire for wealth in the song and dumps the expensive present he has bought her into the trash can and instead gives her a simple bunch of daisies. At the end he buys a workman's truck and drives Madonna off in it. The final shot shows the two kissing as the rain beats on the truck windows. (64)

The 'feminising of the hero' is therefore achieved through the transition from rich suitor to 'poor' one, with money being used as a metaphor for (male) power. But Brown and Fiske go on to argue that ambiguity around whether or not Madonna believes that the second suitor is 'really' poor allows for two narrative 'readings'. In the first, the story is the conventional one of the triumph of love over money, *and therefore contradicts the overt message of the song*. In the second, the 'poor' suitor is really rich, but his interpretation of Madonna's *song* performance as masquerade prompts him also to masquerade as the 'sincere but poor' suitor. But then we are left wondering 'how Madonna "really" relates material wealth and true love' (65). This ambiguity of closure to the narrative is a further departure from romance conventions (64–5).

Kaplan's account of this video also turns on the ambiguity of the relationship between the 'love story' and the song performance which interrupts it, but diverges from the analysis of Brown and Fiske in two important ways. Firstly, she is concerned with the way in which the video disrupts the viewing conventions of classic Hollywood cinema. In the conventions of 'the musical', song performances are an interlude in the narrative, and subordinate to it; but in the Madonna video, the performance of the song rapidly takes over from the narrative, which is reduced to quick shots inserted into and around the song performance. So that while the video starts by foregrounding the way in which classic cinema equates the act of viewing with male desire for a woman on screen (Mulvey, 1975), this clear 'male' audience position is disoriented when the camera 'disappears' into the screen for the song performance, which takes place simply on a stage, with no audience position shown or implied.[3] This is a crucial difference from, for

THE SONGS OF MADONNA 75

instance, the original Marilyn Monroe performance of 'Diamonds are a Girl's Best Friend' where the cinema audience is aligned with the 'internal' male audience watching the show throughout.

As regards the content of the 'love story' and its relationship to the message of the song, Kaplan's analysis is simpler than Brown and Fiske's. She sees the Madonna of the 'love story' as the 'good girl', set up as object of desire and eventually 'won' by the sincere suitor (who Kaplan calls 'the Director'). But this Madonna is continually overtaken by the 'brash, gutsy "material girl"', who, for Kaplan, is the 'bad girl' (1987: 125). The blurring of the relationship between the framing narrative and the performance is therefore also the blurring of 'reality' and 'fiction', represented here by the polar opposites of 'good girl' and 'bad girl' (125).

Kaplan seems justified in concluding that this results in 'an ambiguous representation of the female image', which is part of a wider postmodernism in the video which involves 'the blurring of hitherto sacrosanct boundaries and polarities' (126). But is she justified in calling this a 'postmodern feminism'? In other words, does the blurring of two conventional representations of women result in one, unconventional one?

Brown and Fiske have, of course, argued that both representations depart from the conventional in crucial ways. As regards the 'good girl' of the romance narrative, their claim that 'Madonna remains in a position of power throughout' rests on the argument that she does not have to suffer in order to transform her hero, as do the heroines of literary narratives. But Kaplan's account reveals a weakness in this argument, since it is not directly the second suitor's witnessing of Madonna's stage performance that causes him to dump his expensive present, but his overhearing of Madonna's dressing-room phone conversation where she offers a friend a diamond necklace she has just been given. While being given diamond necklaces is not usually a cause for female suffering, it is easy to imagine that it could be, if this vignette were expanded into a full-length story about the life of a star. The video has already given us an indication that diamonds bring no pleasure to the already rich Madonna, leaving the way open for the 'bunch of daisies' approach to her heart.

There is also a further question as to the appropriateness of the intertextual comparison with *literary* romantic narrative, since the conventions invoked by the video are those of classic *screen* romances. While these have much in common with their literary counterparts, the gendered politics of *viewing* sets them apart, and makes it far harder to discern a female-oriented genre of films, than of novels (Mulvey, 1981). Kaplan's analysis of how this video knowingly, but not critically, invokes the positioning of the female star as object of the male gaze within film narrative, makes it difficult to sustain Brown and Fiske's straightforwardly feminist reading of this 'story'.

Images of material girls (2), the song and dance: Monroe and Madonna

Whether this representation of woman in the 'love story' (Kaplan's 'good girl') is itself subversive of older representations remains doubtful then.

Turning to the 'bad girl' Madonna of the song performance, both analyses here invoke the intertextual relationship to Marilyn Monroe, and specifically to her performance of 'Diamonds are a Girl's Best Friend' in the film *Gentlemen Prefer Blondes*. Brown and Fiske note the similarities between the dance routines in the two performances, but see certain differences which make Madonna's the more 'feminist' of the two. For them it is clear that Madonna is parodying Monroe, and is much more assertive. Monroe sings in part to a female chorus, while Madonna projects 'independent self-sufficiency'. Monroe's gestures are 'supplicatory', while Madonna's 'excessiveness contains elements of disdain for the men who admire her' (Brown and Fiske, 1987: 70). Kaplan is much more guarded in her assessment, emphasizing the 'postmodern' far more than the 'feminist' aspects. For her, 'we cannot tell whether the Monroe sequence is being commented upon, simply used, or ridiculed by exaggeration', despite the fact that Madonna's performance follows it closely (1987: 122).

As for the song itself, again the analyses invoke the relationship of similarity and difference from Monroe's song. For Kaplan, the meaning of both songs is self-evident and similar: the difference between them comes from the way in which they are inserted in the love narrative. Monroe's message in 'Diamonds are a Girl's Best Friend' is *consonant* with her aim of catching a rich man which she pursues single-mindedly throughout the film, *Gentlemen Prefer Blondes* (Kaplan, 1987: 125). By contrast, Madonna's song which, for Kaplan, simply 'deals with the girl . . . for whom love is reduced to money', is completely *discrepant* from the video narrative which, as we have already outlined, is about the triumph of true love over money (124).

Brown and Fiske quote some of the lyrics of the two songs, and again produce a clear, feminist reading of Kaplan's ambiguous 'bad girl'. For them, the songs are 'basically similar' in that both assert 'the right of the woman to use her body, the only asset granted her under patriarchy, for *her* interests, not those of men'. However, they argue, there are 'differences of tone' (1987: 69). But the authors do not explain how these differences relate to the texts of the two songs, let alone to the songs as musical performances. So, for instance, they argue that while Monroe is 'calculatedly looking after her own interests', Madonna '*enjoys* her power over men . . . Monroe shows none of the pleasure that Madonna does as she sings' (69). But it is surely possible to argue back to this that Madonna, too, shows calculated self-interest in her song, that Monroe also enjoys her power over men, and that there is more overt pleasure in Monroe's sensuous singing style than in Madonna's alienated techno-voice. The crucial question of Madonna's 'power over men' in this song remains unexplained.

The authors cite Madonna's 'control over language' in the puns in her song, which merge 'her financial demands . . . with her sexual pleasure and self-esteem' (70). But the pun in the title line of Monroe's song is not dissimilar in its working. Finally they argue that, by contrast with Monroe, Madonna 'does not use men to fill a lack in her life. Indeed all that she lacks is the *need* for men. . . . Men are there . . . to be objects of feminine pleasure

THE SONGS OF MADONNA 77

and subjects of feminine power' (70). But again, this is unsatisfactory in that, while one can agree with the authors on the impression they take from the song, the pleasure and the power remain unexplained as they arise in the text and its performance.

Now in Brown and Fiske's argument, this analysis of the similarities and differences between Madonna's and Monroe's song/dance routines comes *after* a generalized assessment of the way in which the video as a whole compares the two 'worlds' of Madonna, as star and as person, with the corresponding worlds of Monroe (68–9). Monroe's world as star is represented through Madonna's parody of the dance routine, but the world of Monroe the person is not represented at all. This 'real' world of Monroe, however, 'is there as a crucial intertextual gap from which Madonna's "real" world is to be read' (68–9). The video requires quite specific intertextual knowledge from its viewers, for instance of 'the history of Monroe as a powerful star and a powerless person', or of her 'suicide and powerlessness' (69). In this way, 'Monroe's absence of control over her "real" world and "star" world is significantly opposed to Madonna's control over both' (69).

However, it is not entirely clear how this interpretation of Madonna 'in control' versus the 'powerless' Monroe relates to the evidence from the video. There, the images that connote Monroe are glamorous, seductive, showbiz ones, so that one would have to mentally 'switch off' from the video to recall the side of Monroe that was vulnerable, pathetic, and ultimately suicidal. In any case, the kind of 'intertextual knowledge' invoked here by Brown and Fiske seems more appropriate to the wisdom of middle age rather than to the audience of teens and pre-teens to whom the video was principally addressed. While there was certainly a general awareness among this audience that Madonna was imitating Monroe's 'look', it does not follow that they would interpret this comparison in the way that Brown and Fiske do. One group of eleven-year-old girls, interviewed in 1986, for instance, saw Madonna's imitation of Monroe as part of her desire to become a great actress (O'Connell, 1986).[4] So that Brown and Fiske's interpretation of the comparison between the 'real' worlds of Monroe and Madonna is certainly not the only possible one, and particularly not for the younger audience.

Rather than assuming that the video works by calling up knowledges external to itself, we are on firmer ground if we analyze the external references made from within the video. Certainly, the visual reference to 'Diamonds are a Girl's Best Friend' is one of these. And Brown and Fiske's comparison of the lyrics of this song with those of 'Material Girl' is perhaps the closest they get to firm evidence for their thesis that the video shows Madonna's control through a comparison with Monroe's powerlessness. They argue, for instance, in relation to the songs, that:

> Monroe, as was appropriate to her period, is concerned with women's ability to provide for themselves within patriarchy. Madonna asserts women's power to use patriarchal values *against* men. (1987: 70)

But this is, of course, to take the surface message of Monroe's song very literally. A more detailed reading of 'Diamonds . . .' would surely show that the 'romantic' alternative, which the song continually discards in favour of the 'wealthy' one, is made to sound far too attractive for the surface message to be totally convincing. (One must remember that the 'continental' 'kiss on the hand' and the Frenchman 'glad to die for love' are what we as listeners are being asked to *reject*.) And there is an element of 'excess' in the way these messages are reconciled in the impassioned breathing of the names of famous diamond merchants, 'Tiffany's Cartier, etc.' Arguably, the song finds diamonds themselves *romantic*, which is a 'perversely feminine' mutation of the patriarchal worship of mammon.

However, even if one agrees with Brown and Fiske's interpretation of 'Diamonds . . .' as indicating Monroe's powerlessness within patriarchy, it is not clear that this can be part of the interpretation of the song 'Material Girl' by teenage audiences. For the songs were linked only by the *visual* reference in the video, and, as we have already noted, this would have been inaccessible to most teenagers. As *auditory* experiences, the two songs have absolutely nothing in common. Indeed, it is musical style that most clearly marks them as of their particular periods. It is paradoxical that despite the fact that the song 'Diamonds . . .' probably has much wider currency than the film whence it came, radio listeners or disco dancers would have no immediate reason to link 'Material Girl' with it, let alone see it as some kind of 'cover version'.

It is, indeed, extraordinary that Brown and Fiske make no reference to the music or *sound* of the song in their analysis. It is almost as if what we normally think of as 'the song' has become an unconscious background in their writing. Kaplan is more aware that she is dealing with only one aspect of a complex phenomenon, but she still tends to refer to the song itself as part of 'the soundtrack' of the video (1987: 124). It is perhaps ironic that, after all the painstaking visual analysis of differences between Madonna and Monroe, it is the music itself that signals the difference from the fifties visual image most clearly and immediately. This lack of any deference to a need to *sound* like Hollywood in the fifties surely also contributes to the impression of 'control' over the images that Madonna gives in this song, as well as to the feeling of the 'postmodern' collapse of history into the present.

The video interpretations we have looked at so far make strong claims about the 'postmodernity' and 'feminism' of Madonna's use of visual images. But the arguments to support the 'feminist' claim, in particular, seem weak. Kaplan falls back on traditional notions of the 'good girl' and 'bad girl', so that her argument can go no further than finding a radical, 'postmodern' ambiguity in the blurring of the line between them. The attempt by Brown and Fiske to show Madonna as a modern feminist is weak in its reliance on detailed comparisons with Monroe's life and work, which cannot be a large part of her mainstream appeal to teenagers.

More importantly for the argument of this paper, both sets of authors rely in part on an interpretation of the song lyrics in order to give meaning to the visual images. But only Brown and Fiske analyze the lyrics in any way, and their rather partial analysis, which is based on only two verses and does not take musical performance into account, has not turned up any really firm

THE SONGS OF MADONNA   79

evidence for their impression that Madonna is 'in control' in a way that Monroe was not. The next section therefore turns to an analysis of the song itself.

'And now they're after me': pronouns, gender and subjectivity in 'Material Girl'

Figure 1 transcribes the lyrics of 'Material Girl', as actually performed on the record, which differs considerably from the neat verses reproduced on the inner sleeve of the album *Like a Virgin*. In addition, I have indicated the parts sung by the different voices in the performance, as follows:

Madonna as solo singer	= ordinary typeface
Madonna as girl-group, or female chorus, i.e.,	
using her own voice as backing vocal	= *italics*
MADONNA + MALE CHORUS OF THREE BACKING VOCALISTS	= CAPITALS
Madonna's voice as interrupting response	= {lyrics}
prominent electronic echo effects	= lyrics

Madonna, 'Material Girl', discourse analysis

	Lyrics	Discourses	Pronouns
Intro.	(4 lines rhythm alone, then 4 lines with prominent melody in the bass)		
Verse 1	Some boys kiss me, some boys hug me	maternal/romance	– me
	I think they're OK	everyday	I – they
	If they don't give me proper credit	money/school	they – me
	I JUST WALK AWAY	everyday	I
Verse 2	They can beg and they can plead, but	romance	they
	They can't see the light, {That's right},	religious/everyday	they
	Cos the boy with the cold hard cash is	money/	
	ALWAYS MISTER RIGHT	romance	
Chorus 1	Cos we're *living in a material world*	material	we
	And I am a material girl	material	I
	You know that *we are living in a material world*	material	you, we
	And I am a material girl	material	I
Verse 3	Some boys romance, some boys slow dance	romance	
	That's all right with me	everyday	me
	If they can't raise my interest then I	money	they, I –
	HAVE TO LET THEM BE	everyday	– them
Verse 4	Some boys try and some boys lie but	teaching/maternal	
	I don't let them play, {No way},	maternal	I – them
	Only boys that save their pennies	maternal/money	
	MAKE MY RAINY DAY	everyday	
Chorus 2	Cos we're *living in a material world*	material	we
	And I am a material girl	material	I
	You know that *we are living in a material world*	material	you, we
	And I am a material girl	material	I
Chorus 3	Cos we're *living in a material world*	material	we
	And I am a material girl	material	I
	You know that *we are living in a material world*	material	you, we
	And I am a material girl	material	I

Lyrics	Discourses	Pronouns

Instrumental Break 1
(4 lines of bass theme from intro. + voice 'ah's ending in 'ouch')

	Lyrics	Discourses	Pronouns
Chorus 4	LI – VING IN A MA-TE-RI-AL WORLD <u>ma-te-ri-</u>	material	
	LI – VING IN A MA-TE-RI-AL WORLD <u>-al</u>	material	
	LI – VING IN A MA-TE-RI-AL WORLD <u>ma-te-ri-</u>	material	
	LI – VING IN A MA-TE-RI-AL WORLD <u>-a – al</u>	material	
Verse 5	Boys may come and boys may go and	everyday/romance	
	That's all right you see	everyday	you
	Experience has made me rich and	money/everyday	me
	NOW THEY'RE AFTER ME	everyday/romance	they – me
Chorus 5	Cos everybody's *living in a material world*	material	
	And I am a *material girl*	material	I
	You know that we are *living in a material world*	material	you, we
	And I am a *material girl*	material	I
Chorus 6	Cos we're *living in a material world*	material	we
	And I am a *material girl*	material	I
	You know that we are *living in a material world*	material	you, we
	And I am a *material girl*	material	I

Instrumental Break 2
(2 lines of bass theme from intro. + voice 'ah's, leading straight into)

	Lyrics	Discourses	Pronouns
Voice	<u>a material, a material,</u>		
	<u>a material, a material,</u>		
Chorus 7	LI – VING IN A MA-TE-RI-AL WORLD <u>world</u> <u>ma-te-ri-</u>	material	
	LI – VING IN A MA-TE-RI-AL WORLD <u>-al</u>	material	
	LI – VING IN A MA-TE-RI-AL WORLD <u>ma-te-ri-</u>	material	
	LI – VING IN A MA-TE-RI-AL WORLD <u>-a – al</u>	material	
Chorus 8	LI – VING IN A MA-TE-RI-AL WORLD <u>ma-te-ri-</u>	material	
	LI – VING IN A MA-TE-RI-AL WORLD <u>-al</u>	material	
[fade]	LI – VING IN A MA-TE-RI-AL WORLD <u>ma-te-ri-</u>	material	
	LI – VING IN A MA-TE-RI-AL WORLD <u>-a – al</u>	material	

The second column, entitled 'discourses', assigns each individual line to a particular discourse. In other words, language is here being used as a pop lyric, and, importantly, to construct a discourse of 'sexuality', but it is being

THE SONGS OF MADONNA   81

borrowed from other social contexts to which it is appropriate, for instance the language of borrowing and lending money, or 'money discourse', the language of a mother talking to her children, or 'maternal discourse', etc. The third column simply lists pronouns as they occur line by line, with subject-object sequences being written as e.g., 'I–them' and subjects of separate clauses as e.g., 'you, we'. If looking at the discourses tells us something about the content of each line, this then tells us about the structuring of the language around a subject position. Taking this pronoun column first, we can look at the way in which a subject position is established in the song by relating the first person pronoun to significant others. This relationship may be of two basic types: it may be a relationship of *control/dependence* (where the first person is either the subject, 'I', or the object, 'me'), or it may be a relationship of *independence*, where the subject, 'I', is independent of subject pronouns of different persons. Broadly speaking, this division corresponds to that between verses and chorus in the song. So that while we can identify a progression of 'control/dependence' sequences throughout the song verses, they are always followed by repetitions of the 'independent' I in the chorus.

Bearing this in mind, we can abstract the lines containing pronoun sequences from the song, forming a skeletal 'story':

Line	Sequence	Place in song
1. I think they're OK	I – they	verse 1, line 2
2. If they don't give me proper credit	They – me	verse 1, line 3
3. I have to let them be	I – them	verse 3, lines 3–4
4. I don't let them play	I – them	verse 4, line 2
5. Now they're after me	They – me	verse 5, line 4

This story is, of course, more a progression through discursive subject positionings than a conventional narrative. In sequence 1 ('I think they're OK'), 'I' expresses an ambivalent relationship to 'they' as another subject (albeit the subject of an object clause).[5] No real relationship of control is established. By contrast, in sequence 2 ('If they don't give me proper credit'), the first person, 'me', is *dependent* on the third person subject, 'they', for approval, even though this dependence is expressed conditionally, and in the form of a mild threat. This means that in this first relationship of control established in the song, the first person, which we hear and understand as female, is objectified as 'me' and dependent on the controlling third person, male, 'they'.

In sequence 3, 'I' asserts its subjectivity over 'them' as object, but in such a way that a relationship is still not established: 'I just let them be' implies that desire between 'I' and 'them' is a potential that is *foregone*. By contrast, sequence 4 ('I don't let them play'), implies, for the first time in the song, a relationship of *control* between 'I' and 'them', a relationship which we will discuss further below.

Sequence 5 ('And now they're after me'), looks at first like a return to the objectified dependence of the first person in verse 1. But here we see that to look at grammatical structure alone is not enough. The expression here maintains the first-person *control* of sequence 4, but converts it into the 'passive' control of *seduction*. 'And now' implies the end of the story, bringing the listener up to the present, and making it into a *consequence* of the foregoing: so that in 'they're after me', we understand not that 'me' is the passive victim of an aggressive pursuit, but that this first person *object* is in control of 'their' desire. This understanding seems to be reinforced by a secondary meaning of 'after' as 'following', in the sense of 'subordinate to'. In other words, if 'they are [coming] after me', then 'I come before them'. We will return to the sense of leadership and followers below, in looking at the relationship between singer and male chorus acted out in the final choruses of the song.

Fleshing out the pronoun 'story' a little, we notice that in verse 1, Madonna's rejection of male control leads to a defiant, but lonely, independence with the line, 'I just walk away'. The fact that the male chorus joins in on this line means that we also hear something like a mutual distancing: the boys too are walking away. And as the singer resumes her story with verse 2, 'they' is the only pronoun, i.e., the boys are the only subjects. She reaffirms her independent subjectivity in the first chorus, where her 'I' is positioned within the wider world of the subjects 'we' and 'you'. But this reorientation does nothing directly to change the relationship between 'I' and 'they'.

In verses 3 and 4, the independent 'I' somehow gains control and converts the subjects 'they' into dependent objects 'them' (at first tentatively in verse 3, where 'me' and 'they' also appear, then more definitely in verse 4). In this context, then, the repetitions of the independent 'I' in the choruses that follow appear as strengthening the control position of the 'I', rather than as expressions of aloneness.

This strong position, where the female 'I' has, as it were, both grammatical and social control over 'them', the boys, is modified in verse 5, with the reversion to the 'they-me' sequence grammatically, even if socially/sexually, female control is maintained via 'seduction'. But although the independent 'I' has disappeared from the verse, it is reaffirmed again in the choruses that follow the final verse (i.e., choruses 7 and 8). It seems that female control can be maintained only at the cost of the conventional 'splitting' of the female subject into 'me' and 'I'.

In performance, the 'me' of sequence 5 is also 'split' by the fact that this is a chorus line, so that the male chorus, too, sings, 'Now they're after me'. Are we then to understand this chorus as articulating a sort of homosexual undercurrent to the song, positioning itself here as object of the 'romantic' boys' pursuit? I think not since, in Madonna's case, this line has the meaning it does because it follows her singing of the line 'Experience has made me rich, and'; the male chorus do not sing this line, although they are the internal audience to Madonna singing it.

If we look back over the male chorus's part in the 'pronoun story', we see that there is another reference to 'them', in the chorus line of verse 3. While Madonna sings 'I have to let them be', the chorus sings simply 'Have to let

THE SONGS OF MADONNA   83

them be'. This means that the chorus does not come across here as foregoing it's *own* subjective desire for the 'boys', but rather as reinforcing Madonna's expression of foregone desire with a command, or piece of advice addressed to her. Such advice from a man to a woman conventionally implies desire on the part of the man. This message could be seen as reinforced by the male chorus's participation on the words 'Make my rainy day' at the end of verse 4, if heard as an invitation addressed to Madonna. So that by the time we get to the final pronoun sequence, the male chorus has already distanced itself from the 'romantic' boys, and indicated its desire for the female singer. I would suggest, then, that when this chorus sings 'Now they're after me', the meaning we hear in performance is that 'they', i.e., the 'romantic' boys, come after 'me' in the competition for the singer's favours.

Looking at the subject positions established by the use of pronouns has enabled us to see some of the discursive transformations at work in the song. But it leaves several ambiguities around the whole question of Madonna's 'control over men' in this song. Is this control to be reduced to the traditional position of seductress? We also need to discover what alternative is being offered to the 'romantic' male subject position in the song. Both these questions imply looking in more detail at the relations between Madonna and men that are *internal to the song performance*, i.e., at the relationship between Madonna and the male chorus in the song.

Materialism and maternalism: Madonna and the male chorus

We have looked briefly at the enunciation of a male subject position in the participation of the chorus in the final lines of each verse of the song. But the main contribution of the chorus occurs *after* the 'pronoun story' and the elaboration of subject positions have already finished. A return to Figure 1 will show that when the last pronouns have been sung there remains an instrumental break and two repetitions of the chorus. These choruses are the 'male' version of the chorus, which first appeared in chorus 4, and is itself a much simplified version of the 'female' version, chorus 1 and its repetitions.

This simplification is both at the level of lyrics and of music. Musically, the 'female' version is sung by Madonna as girl-group, using her own voice as backing harmony (see record credits). This backing voice harmonizes above Madonna's melody line, the effect being of two simultaneous melody lines being sung in harmony with each other. And at the level of words, this 'girl-group' version uses a complex array of pronouns, relating the independent subject 'I' as 'material girl' to a collective 'we' who 'are living in a material world' and an incorporative audience address to 'you' as recognizing this collectivity.

The 'male' version of the chorus is in fact a duet between the male chorus and Madonna's solo voice, augmented with echo-effect. In this duet, a clear sexual division of labour is followed: the men sing in a punctuated, rhythmic monotone, i.e., all on the same note, their voices effectively sounding like electronically produced sound. Madonna 'word-wraps' around the end of their lines, with a high-pitched, melodic, echoing sound, on the single world 'material'. The mechanical effect of the men's voices is reinforced by their simplification of the words of the chorus: all pronouns are omitted, as they simply repeat the words, 'living in a material world', themselves drawn from the 'female' version of the chorus.

As a rhythm, the male vocal part in this chorus is already familiar to us, since it is very close to the rhythm of the instrumental introduction to the song. This introductory theme is repeated in the instrumental breaks which immediately precede both occurrences of the male chorus (i.e., before choruses 4 and 7). The two are shown below diagramatically for comparison:[6]

Beats:	1	2	3		4	1	2	3		4
INTRODUCTION:	x		x		x	x	x	x	x		[x]
MALE CHORUS:	x		x	x	x	x	x	x		x	
	Li	–	–	–	VING	IN	A	MA-	TE- RI-	AL	– WORLD

While the male vocalists intone the *rhythm* of the instrumental introduction (repeated in the breaks), the lead singer's *melody*, which weaves around their rhythm, can also be traced to this instrumental. For instance, the two-line vocal introduction to chorus 7:

is a simple transformation of the closing phrase from the first line of the introduction:

And Madonna's repeated, melodic 'material', which 'word-wraps' with the male chorus's rhythm:

THE SONGS OF MADONNA   85

can be traced to the ending phrase of the second line of the introduction:

Now this musical structure, where solo singer sings melody around a rhythm sung by the chorus, is a classic one in rock music. It is common, for instance, in the 'doo-wop' vocal groups of the fifties and in the girl-groups of the sixties (Bradby, 1990). As a *sexual* division of labour, it is less common, given the single-sex tradition in rock and vocal group singing, but Charlie and Inez Foxx's 'Mockingbird' was a well-known sixties hit based on such a division between a male singer's 'rhythm' and a female singer's 'melody'. And the occasional use of a high falsetto by the 'melody' singer in male 'doo-wop' groups shows the implicit potential for this sexualization of vocal division.[7]

But to say that this vocal division of labour is a familiar structure does not explain what it means in the context of this song. To get at this, we must return to the analysis of discourses set out in column 2 of Figure 1. First of all, we may note that of the five verses, four of them (verses 1, 2, 3 and 5) are mainly mixtures of romance, money, and everyday discourses. Verse 4 differs, in including a substantial amount of what I have called 'maternal' discourse. In particular the central lines 'I don't let them play' and 'Only boys that save their pennies' seem taken straight from the domestic relations of the nursery. In other words, they are taken from what is possibly the only undisputed social space where females control males. And whether 'I don't let them play' is taken as the teacher's account of her maintenance of discipline over little boys or whether this is the little girl herself explaining her exclusion of antisocial boys from girls' games, both seem to derive from the right of mothers to socialize their sons.

The last two lines of verse 4, 'Only boys that save their pennies/Make my rainy day', are a clever wordplay on various everyday sayings, most obviously, 'Make my day', and 'Save it for a rainy day' (itself probably best-known as the second line of Perry Como's 'Catch a Falling Star'), but probably also including 'Look after the pennies and the pounds will look after themselves' for English speakers within the sterling area. Analyzing these lines in more detail, we may note that teaching children to save pennies (in piggy-banks, etc.) is an important function of mothers, if their children are to be successful. However, in this nursery context of early training, 'saving pennies' evokes its opposite, 'spending a penny', which the little boy may think of as like 'making rain'. In this sense, potty training is about learning to 'save pennies', or the ability to control the activity of 'spending a penny'. The lines, 'Only boys that save their pennies/Make my rainy day' can therefore be taken as expressing the mother's approval of the boy who has learnt to pee in the appropriate situation. The preceding line, 'I don't let them play' then acquires an additional meaning of not letting the boys play around with their 'pennies', the coins colloquially known as 'pees'.

The materialism of the girl, then, depends on a discursive relation to maternalism. The step into maternal discourse in verse 4 is what allows Madonna to establish control over her male chorus, a control already manifested in the 'I-them' pronoun sequence that occurs in these lines. This maternal mode positions the 'boys' of the song as *little* boys, playing with and saving pennies, unlike the 'boys' of the other verses, where the financial allusions are all to the adult, *men's* world of banking ('credit', 'hard cash', 'interest'). Of course in the adult context of finance and romance, set by the rest of the song, Madonna's not letting the boys play with their 'pennies', but save them for her, acquires an adult, sexual meaning.

This maternal discourse is what provides the way out of the financial/ sexual dependency of the first verse, the only alternative to which is a defiant independence ('I just walk away'), and leads to the financial/sexual control of the last verse. The mechanical-sounding 'male' version of the chorus, then, which does not occur until after verse 4, represents the acting out, or musical performance of this relationship of control. It is the relation between mother and little boy that structures our understanding of the way the voices are divided in chorus 4. This chorus leads into verse 5, and the final, rather ambiguous pronoun sequence, 'And now they're after me' sung by both lead singer and male chorus. The discursive context has returned to the adult world of experience and riches ('Experience has made me rich'). But the power and control maintained from the maternal context are what allows the song to achieve its meaning of female control over men from within a conventional positioning of the female as object.

The participation of the men in this final pronoun sequence positions them as objects too, in a relation of control, we have suggested, over the romantic 'boys' as subjects. But if we now look at the difference between the singing parts of Madonna and of the male chorus *after* this final pronoun sequence, there is a crucial difference of meaning in performance. Madonna returns firmly to the position of 'independent subject' in the two 'female' choruses that follow, and to a position of 'freedom' in her melodic weaving around the final, male 'mechanical' choruses. The male chorus, however, *act out the part of objects* in their rendering of the 'material world' without subjects, in the final choruses. This seems to bear out the 'leader/followers' interpretation of 'And now they're after me', since the male chorus here perform musically the part of followers to Madonna's 'lead'.

The male chorus have therefore moved from the position of subjects, in the first chorus line of the song [verse 1, line 4], to that of objects in the closing 'material' choruses. And from the point of view of the female subject, there has been a double transformation: of 'romantic' boys into 'material' ones, and of powerful banking men into controllable little boys. It is almost as if Madonna recognizes that in the world of sexual fantasy, women are structured as objects of male desire, but that in the material world, both

THE SONGS OF MADONNA   87

men and women are objects: if women are to change the structure of sexual desire, they must get men on to the material terrain.

Visual/musical/verbal meaning and the Virgin-Mother

It is time to go back and consider how these narrative meanings of the song relate to the video analyses that we looked at in the first part of this paper. There, much hinged on the idea that the song, and its accompanying dance routine in the video, *contradicted* the message of the 'framing' love story. This contradiction could be put in sexual terms, the 'bad girl' of the song at odds with the 'good girl' of the love story; or it could be put in terms of money, the Madonna of the song preferring money to romance, the Madonna of the love story acting out the opposite.

The first thing the song analysis shows very clearly is that these contradictions are *already present in the song*, inasmuch as they are ultimately about female activity/passivity in relation to men and sexual desire. The 'bad girl' is the active 'I' of verse 4, controlling the boys, while the 'good girl' corresponds to the passive objectification of the 'me' in the opening and closing verses. But since we hear these transformations as a *narrative*, we understand that Madonna *rejects* the passivity and dependence of the opening position and moves to a position of active control. This move is discursively linked to a rejection of 'romance' as traditionally posed for women. And if verse 5 does return the lead singer to passivity, the difference is that in the intervening sequences she has shown that she *can* take control, and this feeling of control shapes the way we hear the ending of the song.

Rather than seeing 'the song' as a simple component making up the more complex whole of 'the video', we could just as well argue, then, that both 'stories' in the video are necessary to illustrate the contradictory positions presented in the song. The opening 'framing' of the video only follows the opening of the song in presenting and apparently rejecting an unsatisfactory 'romantic' positioning of women as passive. And the closure to this romantic story in the video, where Madonna accepts the 'poor' suitor, contains ambiguities similar to those in the final verse of the song, with its positioning of women as 'passive but in control'. The other video 'story', then, the song and dance routine, corresponds to the intervening 'control' sequences in the song, and to their acting out in the final choruses. A major difference between the two structures, if seen as narrative, though, is the way in which the video closes with the 'happy ending' of the love story, whereas the song continues on after the end of its love story ('And now they're after me'), acting out female control and male ojectification in the final choruses.

'The song' as it figures visually in the video, then, is simply a one-dimensional *representation* of the song itself. Analyses of the video that take this representation as exhausting the meaning of the song ignore the fact that *hearing* the song is part of 'seeing' the video. In Kaplan's analysis, for instance, the song simply 'deals with the girl for whom love is reduced to money', and the video builds its meaning by juxtaposing this simple unit of meaning with its 'opposite', the girl for whom love is more important than money. But the more detailed analysis of the song presented here suggests that it is only subsidiarily concerned with this traditional opposition between women's need for money and need for love. More important is the opposition between women's positioning as dependent objects in both spheres, and a position of female independence and control over both men and money.

This takes us closer to the reading of the video by Brown and Fiske, but their analysis, too, now appears as a one-sided over-simplification of the song's meaning. Madonna is not 'in a position of power throughout', but instead works towards a position of control. The song starts from the generalized condition where women are *not* in control, either of men or of money. It does not particularly imply that this is the position of women forty years ago, but starts from the perspective of any frustrated teenage girl today. More importantly, Madonna's position of control is achieved not by a kind of voluntarism, but through linguistically and musically working towards an engagement with men that is based on an empirical situation where women and girls do use controlling language towards members of the opposite sex.

If this uncovering of 'maternal' discourse is the other major insight provided by the present song analysis, questions remain about what kind of sexuality is being constituted in the song. Except in verse 4, we have not discussed the language of sexual innuendo in the song. The innuendo occurs on the third lines of verses 2, 3, 4, and 5, but is everywhere rather deeply buried, perhaps more so because the surface 'financial' meaning of these lines is anyway strikingly playful in the song's context of heterosexual romance. And to bring this sexual innuendo up to the surface involves a rather 'heavy' reading of the song. If it is *sexual* experience that has made the singer rich in verse 5, if the boy of verse 2 has more than cash that is cold and hard, then the singer's position seems to be that of the economically successful prostitute, albeit taking pleasure in her career (the boys must 'raise her [sexual] interest').

While undoubtedly some listeners did 'hear' this meaning,[8] it seems too serious for the generally playful mood of the song, and rather more than Kaplan probably intended with her 'bad girl' epithet. It also has difficulty in explaining the reversal implied in 'and now they're after me'. Does this then mean that the 'material girl', having made her money through prostitution, can now afford to give it up? That instead of pursuing rich clients, rich men now pursue her for marriage? If it does, then the 'prostitute' interpretation is not maintained, but becomes a means to its opposite, going straight in marriage.

The language of verse 4 also raises difficulties for this interpretation if, for consistency, 'sexual' meanings are prioritized here too. For the sexual meaning of 'I don't let them play' is 'I don't give them sexual access' (i.e., the boys that 'try' and 'lie'); if this is taken together with the subsequent lines about the 'boys that save their pennies', and giving 'pennies' a 'sexual' meaning as the plural of penis, then the verse becomes more a demand for

THE SONGS OF MADONNA 89

sexual fidelity from the boys, perhaps even sexually repressive. And here we reach an interesting point in the analysis. For if we take the 'financial' meaning of this verse as the surface, uppermost one, then there is perhaps an implication of prostitution in 'Only boys that save their pennies/Make my rainy day'. But the underlying, 'sexual' meaning of this verse carries the *opposite* implication, of *virginity and sexual restraint*.

This reminds us that if, as Brown and Fiske state, 'her body is the only asset granted to a woman under patriarchy', women have evolved different ways of using it, one of the most powerful being as the asset of 'virginity'. The video promotion was only one of the contexts in which the song 'Material Girl' was consumed and, as argued above, a relatively ephemeral one. The song is more lasting as the 'title' track (i.e., the first track on the first side) of the album, *Like a Virgin*. This substitution of 'Material Girl' in the place where 'should' have been the song 'Like a Virgin' could be seen as a 'postmodern' ironic distancing, a deliberate confusion of traditional categories. But the involvement of a negative, 'virginal' sexuality in the construction of female 'strength' in 'Material Girl' implies that more straightforwardly meaningful connections can be drawn. In the remainder of this paper I shall argue that there is a sense in which this album contains a *materialization of the story of the Virgin Mary*.

This is no more than a thread of meaning running across some of the principal songs, but it involves a different sort of intertexuality from those raised in the video analyses. From this point of view, 'Material Girl', the first song on the album, derives its meaning from the difference between the material girl presented and the immateriality of the Virgin Mary. And we should note that the Virgin defied material laws not in her girlhood, but in her *motherhood*, which was brought about by spiritual, not bodily, sexual, contact. The second song on the album, 'Angel', immediately evokes the biblical 'Annunciation' in portraying a dialogue between a girl and an 'angel'. Unlike the biblical meeting, however, where the discourse is all the (male) angel's revealing the truth of Mary's virginal body to her, in the song 'Angel', the discourse is a woman's addressing the man as 'angel'. In this concrete reversal of the biblical situation, she playfully reveals the truth about this man ('Ooh, you're an angel in disguise I can see it in your eyes').[9] And once again, this position of female discursive strength draws heavily on everyday 'maternal' language. The man/angel is addressed as 'baby' and with the 'ooh' of 'baby talk'. The woman looks into the man's eyes as the mother does into the baby's.

'Angel' is followed by the true title track of the album, 'Like a Virgin'. This song's explicit comparison between the singer and 'a virgin' invokes the feelings of the virgin, just after she has been 'touched for the very first time'. In the album context, we can hear this song as a reflection on the girl's meeting with the 'angel', addressing him with praise ('You're so fine') and thanks ('Didn't know how lost I was/Until I found you'). It therefore takes the same structural place in the narrative as does the 'Magnificat', which in the biblical story is Mary's humble hymn of praise/thanks to the Lord, after her meeting with the angel and impregnation by 'the holy spirit'.

The language of 'Like a Virgin' starts off as rather vaguely religious,[10] evoking biblical ideas of being lost in 'the wilderness' and of being 'incomplete', and implying the need for wholeness and renewal, which is brought by 'you' ('Like a virgin touched for the very first time/You made me feel shiny and new'). Undoubtedly the song, and hence the album, here appeals to the widespread cultural ideal of virginity as the highest state for women. But as Fiske and others have noted, this is virginity recognized only in the moment of its loss — another 'ironic distancing', perhaps, of self from the archetype invoked.

If the subsequent lines, much repeated, evoking the union of two bodies, are heard simply as about sexual union, then this 'ironic' interpretation can perhaps be upheld. But once again we find that this 'sexual' meaning is constructed out of discourse whose literal use is in another context, that of a mother addressing her baby. So the repeated 'With your heartbeat next to mine' becomes at the end of the song:

> Ooh baby,
> Can't you hear my heartbeat
> For the very first time?

This might be the pregnant woman talking to the baby she feels move inside her for the first time (again famous from the biblical 'the babe leapt in her womb' applied actually to Mary's elderly cousin Elizabeth when the two pregnant women meet and exchange experiences), or an address to the baby whom the mother holds against her body in the first moments after birth. In either case, since the baby cannot speak, we have an excellent primary source for the one-sided 'dialogue' so typical of pop song, where the feelings or response of the other must be imagined. The singer can hear 'your', i.e., her 'baby's' heartbeat, but has to pose an unanswered question as to whether he is conscious of hearing hers.

The way in which this song overlays the metaphor of the virgin in her moment of bodily 'knowledge' with that of the baby in its first moment of independent bodily life is clever, and seems to work through the imagined voice of the mother. Rather than simply seeing the postmodern blurring/juxtaposition of virginity and sexuality in the song, we can see also a 'sexual' reworking of the linking of virginity and motherhood in the Christian tradition. This 'sexuality' is achieved both by recognizing and performing the material and bodily aspects of this link, and by superimposing an implied sexual 'difference' on to it.

If the language of the maternal body in 'Like a Virgin' is only a very underlying theme, it is made more explicit in the song that closes this side of the album, 'Love Don't Live Here Anymore'. The first verse of this starts 'When you lived inside of me', an image of maternal fullness which is then contrasted with the emptiness of the present, 'Just a vacancy, Love don't live here anymore . . . Just emptiness and memories . . . You went away, Found another home'. The grief of the mother for the child who has left home is a well-known metaphor in pop music for grief over the loss of a lover (and satirized in the Beatles' 'She's Leaving Home'). But here the 'home' that has been left is specifically the woman's body, a metaphor that while being 'sexual' can hardly avoid also being 'maternal'.

If this song brings us to a point in the story of the 'material girl' where her body experiences emptiness and loss after giving birth, two songs on the second side of the album evoke the discourse of a mother towards a growing child. 'Dress You Up' uses language taken from the desire of mother for child expressed through clothing while 'Shoo Bee Doo' is musically and verbally a lullaby, addressed to 'baby' ('Shoo bee doo bee doo baby, Come to me baby, Pretty darling, don't say maybe').

The use of maternal discourse is very common in expressions of 'love' in popular music (Bradby and Torode, 1984; Bradby, 1990), and so no claim is implied here about the uniqueness of these songs. What is interesting is the way in which these images of maternal loss and love occur in the context of an album entitled *Like a Virgin* and of the sense of a materialization of the biblical story that runs through 'Angel' and 'Like a Virgin'. Returning to the song, 'Material Girl', in a sense the principal song on the album, and the one which has probably had the most lasting impact in its association with Madonna, this analysis of the album context does confirm the previous reading of what is involved in the construction of female sexual control in that song. This control is achieved by the complex combination of two traditional positions of power for women, virginity and motherhood. But in Madonna's song, instead of being held out as a materially contradictory ideal for women as in the figure of Mary, the Virgin-Mother, both positions are sexualized. Virginity is here not a lack of sexuality, but is about the ability to say 'no' sexually to men, without which sexual choice and control for women are meaningless concepts. Motherhood is not a position of long-suffering passivity, but is about an active discourse of control over men positioned as 'boys'.

Although these meanings have been taken from the words and music of the song, there is no doubt that Madonna's use of visual images helps to saturate the songs with 'sexuality'. The traditional location of 'sexuality' in the female body and its representation are used by her to emphasize that the power she is claiming for women is a sexual power. But these meanings cannot be arrived at through analyzing the visual images of the video in isolation from the song. The images of women presented there – the spoilt film star, the sincere sweetheart – are not only traditional images but also consciously presented as such. If there is an 'ironic distancing' from these images, it results not so much from their juxtaposition with each other, as from their conjunction with the verbal-musical messages of the song.

It is perhaps paradoxical that after all the controversy surrounding Madonna's visual images of active female sexuality, it is the message of sexual non-availability that comes across as the novel ingredient from the song analysis. And the novelty of this message should not be underestimated. If rock music expressed the fantasies of the movement towards 'sexual liberation' in the sixties, these were inescapably masculine. The terms set for women's freedom from sexual repression were the masculine ones of the always available 'easy lay'. Rock itself did not always condemn these easy women, often turning them into objects of worship ('Sweet Little Sixteen', 'Carrie Ann', or The Kinks' 'my sister always did'); but in the real world, availability to men tended to earn women the label 'slag' (Cowie and Lees, 1981). And even when rock music went through a 'feminized' period, as with the later Beatles music (Frith and McRobbie, 1978: 13–14), the feminizing effect is felt through the impact of a message like 'All you need is love' on a *male* audience. For the women at the 'love-in' the message was the same as ever: 'All you need is love' still preaches availability for the fulfilment of male sexual fantasies.

In this discursive context there can be no freedom for a woman in actively seeking sex so that, paradoxically, the beginnings of sexual liberation come with learning to say 'no'. The feminist movement of course asserted this right, both generally, and very specifically, in the anti-rape campaigns with their slogan 'No means no'. And as a sexual movement, feminism can be seen as a reaction to the negative effects for women of the previous decade of sexual 'liberation'. Now that pregnancy had ceased to be the overriding sanction on female sexual 'activity', these effects could be conceptualized more in terms of the lack of freedom in the passive notion of female sexual availability. But feminist versions of sexuality foundered on their easy assimilability to the other male sexual stereotype of women as 'drags' (Cowie and Lees, 1981). For women of Madonna's generation, to be a 'feminist' already had connotations of being sexually unattractive and anti-men.

One of the achievements of women in the eighties was surely to reclaim a pleasure in appearances and the body which is 'feminine', but which is quite unlike either fifties 'glamour' or sixties cute 'sexiness'. This dissimilarity is not because eighties women 'do not need men', as Brown and Fiske said of the 'material girl' in contrasting her with her fifties counterpart. On the contrary, men are an essential part of the audience, and heterosexual play is welcomed as fun. The difference comes from the rewriting of the sexual subtext of female 'availability', to one which includes non-availability as a real and stated option. The eighties ideal of the 'streetwise girl' – a notion both applied to and enacted by Madonna in her films – seems to contain both a knowledgeable pleasure in appearances and a stance of sexual non-availability based on a rejection of the intimidatory powers of 'the street' over girls. The contrast is clear if one compares this with traditional terms for (restricting) women's presence on the street, such as the sexually available 'street walker' (McRobbie and Garber, 1976; Cowie and Lees, 1981). If Madonna has made the ability to say 'no' to men not only something that girls can take seriously for themselves but also something they can find sexually attractive, then we can surely argue that this is an interesting advance not only on women's first encounter with 'sexual liberation' in the sixties, but also on seventies feminism.

Madonna's use of the script of 'virginity' works both by its similarity and its difference from the traditional one. The same can be said of her use of the language of 'motherhood'. While the traditional notion of loving tenderness is certainly there in the songs on the album that address 'baby', they are

THE SONGS OF MADONNA 93

dominated, if only as songs of that period in time, by the image of the 'material girl'. And as argued in this paper, 'Material Girl' uses maternal language as a language of control, positioning men as 'boys'. Socially, this involves a recognition that mothers' role as socializers of small children necessitates their having power over them. Feminists have probably been happier with consensual models of mother-child relations, equating power and conflict with a model of male parenting which was to be rejected, and being frightened by the psychoanalysts' label of 'bad mother'. Again, Madonna can make some claim to being 'postfeminist' in her willingness to take on the language of power.

Finally, Madonna's rewriting of the script of the distinguishing symbol of Catholicism, the story of the Virgin-Mother, 'the' Madonna, is a fascinating subversion of the ongoing dominance of 'Western' culture by Protestantism.[11] As Marina Warner put it at the end of her book on the Virgin Mary, 'a goddess is better than no goddess at all, as in the sombre-suited world of the Protestant religion' (1978: 338). As she also pointed out, women today can choose to be neither virgins nor mothers, an option quite publicly pursued by the real-life Madonna. Without reverting to the traditional constrictions that virginity and motherhood placed on women's lives, it seems important not to give up the *strength* of these positions, at any rate until alternative sources of strength are available to women. What Madonna's work in *Like a Virgin* shows is that these strengths are available and can be appropriated at the level of discourse. As discourse they can be reworked and put into new contexts and uses. Visual meaning certainly enters in here. How could it not, when one considers the whole history of the Madonna as a silent visual representation? At the same time, the argument of this paper has been that Madonna's visual representations do not exist in a vacuum, but in relation to specific verbal texts, the lyrics of her songs in their musical arrangements. In sexualizing the Virgin, Madonna has also allowed her to speak.

Notes

1 This paper was first given at a conference of the UK branch of the International Association for the Study of Popular Music, held in Oxford in December 1987. The present version is substantially rewritten in order to incorporate the contributions of Kaplan and of Brown and Fiske.

2 In Fiske's updating of the Brown and Fiske analysis (Fiske, 1989: 115–32), he makes reference to Radway's work on romance reading, where she argues the importance of this process of feminization of the hero for women readers of Harlequin fiction (Radway, 1984).

3 Kaplan does acknowledge that television screenings of this video regularly *cut* this sequence, so foregrounding the song/dance sequence even further, and making the references to the 'love story' even more confused and disconnected than in the complete version that Kaplan reviews.

4 In O'Connell's interview with eleven-year-old girls in Dublin, the topic of Monroe came up in the context of Madonna's marriage to Sean Penn. One girl, Helen, argues that: 'She thought he was great because he was an actor and she

wants to be an actress. She said she didn't want to be any old film star, you know.' Another girl, Rhoda, carries on from this with the information that Madonna 'is dying to be like Marilyn Monroe'. Helen then disagrees, saying that in an interview Madonna 'said she was sick of people saying that she wanted to be Marilyn Monroe', but when Rhoda sticks to her point, Helen qualifies hers, arguing that 'she said she wanted to be like her in the Material Girl video, but . . . that was just for the video, that was just for the song' (O'Connell, 1986: 36–7). I have analyzed other aspects of this interview/conversation elsewhere (Bradby, 1991).

5 Thinking someone is 'OK' can, in everyday talk, mean *either* that one approves of them quite strongly, *or* that they are rather mediocre, the difference being indicated through voice intonation. In this case, the falling intonation in the melody on 'K' inclines one towards the second interpretation.

6 Of course, the rhythm of the male chorus here is very similar also to the lead singer's rhythm on the identical words in the 'female' version of the chorus:

Beats:	1	2	3		4		1	2		3			4	
FEMALE CHORUS:									x	x	x	x	x	x
									You	know	that	we	are	
												Cos	we	are
	x			x	x x x	x	x x x							x
	li – – – ving in a ma te- ri- al world													And

But here the syncopated anticipation of the beat on 'world' and the generally looser singing style mean that, despite the verbal connection, the 'female' chorus *sounds* quite different from the male chorus's mathematically exact and 'on-beat' incantation. By contrast, the opening introduction and instrumental breaks, even though they possess melody, are rhythmically exact and *on* the beat, and therefore sound like the male chorus.

7 Well-known instances of this use of falsetto by a male lead singer, who sings the melody while his backing group keep the rhythm, can be heard in The Tokens' 'The Lion Sleeps Tonight', or in Maurice Williams and the Zodiacs' 'Stay'. Other examples are in The Mystics' 'Hushabye' and in the coda to The Five Satins' 'In the Still of the Nite'. All of these songs are in some sense *lullabies*, and the falsetto voice is very clearly 'imitating' that of the mother. Clyde McPhatter uses a more or less prominent falsetto on many of his lead parts. Hank Ballard uses falsetto 'tweaks' at the beginning and end of phrases. With the transition to rock'n'roll, the preference seems to have been for a high male voice rather than actual falsetto. Compare, for instance, Frankie Lymon and the Teenagers' 'Why Do Fools Fall in Love'.

8 I have discussed this interpretation, as well as ones that contest it, in Bradby (1991).

9 There are many instances on this album of 'intertextual' references to other pop lyrics. Here there is an obvious allusion to Elvis Presley's 'You're the Devil in Disguise' ('You look like an angel, Walk like an angel, Talk like an angel, But I got wise, You're the devil in disguise').

10 Fiske has an interesting analysis of 'Like a Virgin' in which he looks at the 'semiotic excess of puns' created through the intertwining of four discourses: religious love, sexual love, romantic love, and the discourse of 'street-wisdom' (1989: 108–9)

11 Williamson's contention that Madonna and the mythology of her success ('being special' plus 'hard work') are symptoms of the Protestantism of Anglo-American culture seems to me to be a very partial reading indeed (1985: 47).

References

Bradby, B. (1990) 'Do-talk and don't-talk: the division of the subject in girl-group music', in Frith and Goodwin (1990).

Bradby, B. (1991) 'Freedom, feeling and dancing: Madonna's songs traverse girls' talk', *Onetwothreefour: a Rock and Roll Quarterly* No. 10.

Bradby, B. and Torode, B. (1984) 'Pity Peggy Sue', *Popular Music* 4.

Brown M. E. and Fiske, J. (1987) 'Romancing the rock: romance and representation in popular music videos', *Onetwothreefour: a Rock and Roll Quarterly* No. 5.

Cowie, C. and Lees, S. (1981) 'Slags or drags', *Feminist Review* No. 9, Autumn.

Fiske, J. (1989) *Reading the Popular* Boston: Unwin Hyman.

Frith, S. and McRobbie, A. (1978) 'Rock and sexuality', *Screen Education* 29, Winter 1978/9.

Frith, S. and Goodwin, A. (1990) editors, *On Record: Rock Pop and the Written Word* New York: Pantheon; London: Routledge.

Grossberg, L. (1988) 'You (still) have to fight for your right to party: music television as billboards of post-modern difference', *Popular Music* Vol. 7, No. 3.

Hall, S. and Jefferson, T. (1976) editors, *Resistance Through Rituals* London: Hutchinson.

Kaplan, E. A. (1987) *Rocking Around the Clock: Music Television, Postmodernism and Consumer Culture* London: Methuen.

McRobbie, A. and Garber, J. (1976) 'Girls and subcultures', in Hall and Jefferson (1976).

Mulvey, L. (1975) 'Visual pleasure and narrative cinema', *Screen* Vol. 16, No. 3.

Mulvey, L. (1981) 'Afterthoughts on visual pleasure and narrative cinema' *Framework*, 15–16.

O'Connell, M. (1987) 'Ordinary girls unpack Madonna's extraordinary gloss', (Interview transcript), Dept. of Sociology, Trinity College, Dublin.

Radway, J. (1984) *Reading the Romance: Feminism and the Representation of Women in Popular Culture* Chapel Hill: University of North Carolina Press.

Warner, M. (1978) *Alone of All Her Sex: the Myth and the Cult of the Virgin Mary* London: Quartet.

Williamson, J. (1985) 'The making of a material girl', *New Socialist* October.

Acknowledgement

The following titles are quoted by permission of Warner Chappell Music Ltd: 'Angel' (Madonna/Bray; 'Like a Virgin' (Kelly/Steinberg); 'Material Girl' (Brown/Raus); 'Love Don't Live Here Anymore (Niles Gregory); 'Shoo-Bee-Doo'.

[15]

"That Ill, Tight Sound": Telepresence and Biopolitics in Post-Timbaland Rap Production

DALE CHAPMAN

Abstract
This article investigates the music created by current rap and R&B producers such as Timbaland and Pharrell Williams in order to understand how their works evoke certain constructions of sonic space. The opaque, spare, two-dimensional qualities of the virtual spaces assembled by these artists serve as a useful window onto broader cultural forces, such as the peculiar short circuit of space and temporality that Paul Virilio evokes in his concept of "telepresence." The author argues that the sonic construction of telepresence allows contemporary black music to comment upon the notion of "biopolitics," the reduction of the political to the horizon of the body.

In "Up Jumps da Meme," Sasha Frere-Jones traces the near ubiquitous presence of the "Timbaland sound" in the contemporary soundscape. This title signifies upon the title of the 1997 Timbaland hit "Up Jumps Da Boogie," and it alludes to the almost viral quality of a good musical idea, the way that an instantly recognizable riff or texture can spread from one song to another, quickly saturating the cultural field, until it comes to define something of the texture of its time.[1] As Timbaland, Virginia-based producer Tim Mosley has made a seismic impact on popular music since the late 1990s, redefining several aspects of musical production in R&B and hip-hop. In the years after he initially established himself with songs like Aaliyah's "One in a Million" and "Are You That Somebody?," his stylistic approach was copied so frequently that he and his longtime collaborator, Missy "Misdemeanor" Elliott, came to assume a defensive posture in their songs, lashing out at the "beat-biters" who would emulate the nervously syncopated "boom-tee-boom" patterns underlying their hits.[2]

The Timbaland sound has asserted itself as one of the crucial memes in our moment, somehow condensing several amorphous elements of contemporary culture into a tactile, densely charged immediacy. Mosley is part of a wave of artists

I am grateful to Christopher Schiff and Charles Nero, who have provided helpful suggestions in the early stages of this article's preparation. I would also like to thank Amy Frishkey, Cristian Amigo, and Loren Kajikawa for our ongoing discussions about hip-hop, production, and digital sampling.

[1] Sasha Frere-Jones, "Up Jumps Da Meme," *The Village Voice*, 12–18 April 2000, http://www.villagevoice.com/music/0015,frere-jones,13988,22.html. The title of my article derives from Mosley's description of his own production sound in an interview with Frere-Jones. See Sasha Frere-Jones, "These Beats Work: Timbaland," *The Wire*, December 1998, http://www.thewire.co.uk/archive/interviews/timbaland.html.

[2] See Simon Reynolds, *Bring the Noise: 20 Years of Writing About Hip Rock and Hip Hop* (London: Faber and Faber, 2007), 227. On the opening track of his album *Tim's Bio*, Mosley uses the phrase "boom-tee-boom" as shorthand for the heavily syncopated bass, snare, and hi-hat patterns he programs on so many of his productions. See Timbaland, *Tim's Bio: From the Motion Picture "Life from da Bassment,"* Blackground Entertainment 92813-2, 1998.

for whom *Wired* magazine has coined the term "superproducers," which aptly expresses something of the expansive, almost hegemonic quality of certain contemporary production sounds.[3] Alongside Mosley, other artists, such as Pharrell Williams, Swizz Beatz, and Scott Storch, have established a new degree of visibility for the rap producer, earning star billings virtually equal in prominence to the artists that they produce. In this respect, their situation recalls figures such as Phil Spector, or Kenneth Gamble and Leon Huff, producers whose innovative sounds garnered them a degree of celebrity. At the same time, though, the prominence of rap's superproducers also reflects the central role of musical style in late capitalist culture, in the way that it adheres to the logic of branding: the artist who calls on the services of a Timbaland assumes that he will provide a readily identifiable sound, one inseparable from questions of marketing and promotion strategy.[4]

For this reason, these figures engage in fierce contestation over the originality and derivation of their musical visions, staking vigorous claims to their ownership of the minutiae of rhythmic and timbral vocabulary. An artist who can come up with a new beat, or a new way of reconfiguring an old beat, can establish a musical platform that resonates throughout popular culture and transcends the normative boundaries of genre and style, linking a particular groove to a producer's name, no matter whose vocals are floating over the top.

In spite of the substantive differences between the current generation of producers, both in their stylistic approaches and in their personal antagonisms, their music shares a few basic features. Commenting upon his early works, Frere-Jones noted that Mosley's sound tended to draw upon everything except the straightforward sampling and looping of breakbeats from 1970s funk and soul recordings, the approach that characterized most hip-hop produced between the late 1980s and the mid-1990s.[5] In his wake, other producers have adopted this approach, replacing the old, unbroken sequences of breakbeats with drum samples used in isolation—a short snare hit, a hi-hat click, a bass drum kick—or with the sonic palette of drum machines such as the Roland TR-808, a staple in earlier genres such as electro, techno, and Miami bass. In particular, southern "krunk" producers such as Lil' Jon or Al Kapone have drawn extensively upon the Miami bass sound, with its stripped-down emphasis upon percussion, its singular combination of powerful bass, and the almost sterile precision of its trebly features. Many figures, such as Swizz Beatz, replaced the old samples of soulful 1970s chord progressions or funk vamps with harmonic textures created directly on synthesizers, often evoking a "dirty"

---

[3] Robert Levine and Bill Werde, "Superproducers," *Wired*, October 2003, http://www.wired.com/wired/archive/11.10/producers_pr.html.

[4] In an interview with pitchforkmedia.com about her collaboration with Mosley on her recent album, *Volta*, Björk spoke about his fairly blunt way of approaching the project. Her description of their initial meeting made him seem as if he saw himself as a design consultant brought in to achieve a specific stylistic effect for marketing purposes: "The first time I met him, he was like, 'So what do you wanna do? You wanna do something weird? Or something like a hit?' And I'm like, 'How can you say that?' I could never work like that—sort of decide what it is before you even start." Björk, quoted in Amy Phillips, "Björk Announces Tour Dates, Talks Timbaland Collab," *Pitchfork*, 19 March 2007, http://www.pitchforkmedia.com/article/news/41776-bjork-announces-tour-dates-talks-timbaland-collab.

[5] Frere-Jones, "These Beats Work: Timbaland."

sensibility constructed from the brittle, enervating sounds of Casio keyboards or cheap 8-bit technology.[6] These features of contemporary mainstream hip-hop production have lent it a texture and sense of sonic space that is fundamentally different from that of early 1990s hip-hop, with its evocation of the warmth of 1970s live music, and its frequent inclusion of the grit, crackle, and reverb of ribbon-microphone recordings and vinyl samples.

A pervasive move among hip-hop critics, or rock critics who review hip-hop, is to celebrate its sonic innovations while decrying the misogyny, celebration of materialism, and glorification of violence in its verbal content.[7] The problem, we are told, is that rappers and R&B singers pursue a regressive vision of social possibility that has not kept pace with the formal inventiveness of their own lyrical flow or the musical experimentation of their producers' textures and grooves. This critique can be patronizing, insofar as it ignores the less blatant and more insidious pervasiveness of misogyny, materialism, and narcissism in popular culture as a whole. Those who offer this position usually fail to note their complicity in a long-standing tradition of critics (often white) speaking from a position of assumed superiority about the supposed moral shortcomings of African American music. Moreover, we should dismiss this critique for a more fundamental reason. The dichotomy that many critics set up between mainstream rap's "regressive" verbal content and its "progressive" music is a false dichotomy, a dualism that fails to acknowledge the vital role that music plays in making the words compelling.

Music establishes the ontological conditions through which a song's words can be understood as *more* than words, underwriting and making tangible its claims to truth. From this perspective, we can and must take a more complex view of the role that rap production plays in rendering corporeal the vision of society that emerges from rap, narratives about rap, and representations of rap. In the case of post-Timbaland rap and R&B production, the beats and textures of this music do not contradict the lyrical worldview of mainstream rap in any straightforward way. Rather, they render audible dimensions of this worldview inaccessible to verbal language alone. In so doing, they demonstrate the extent to which the bleak perspective of mainstream rap serves not as a lamentable remainder of outmoded attitudes, but rather as a crucial canary in the coal mine, a warning about what might come to pass.

This study will begin with a close analysis of several tracks from different moments in the last decade and a half of rap, hip-hop, and R&B. My approach will focus less upon the lyrical content or rhetorical delivery of the rapping and singing, and more upon what the immediacy of the songs' vamps, the specific densities of their textures, can tell us about the kind of context in which such songs might become legible. In particular, I would like to demonstrate that the decisions these producers make at the level of the groove are crucial, for they foreground the ways in which certain kinds of broad, large-scale social developments might make themselves felt: the collapse of the public sphere; the radical change wrought by the collapsing of

---

[6] For discussions of these artists' work, see Reynolds, *Bring the Noise*, 226–30; 362–64.

[7] See, for example, Simon Reynolds's account of his reaction to Dr. Dre's *The Chronic*, in which he finds himself torn in an "aesthetics-vs-ethics dilemma" (*Bring the Noise*, 168).

physical space in quotidian experience; and the reduction of human possibility to the immediate confines of the body.

My account of this post-Timbaland moment in contemporary rap production will proceed by way of a discussion of Paul Virilio's concept of "telepresence," the radical realignment of social relations catalyzed by the widespread use of contemporary communication technologies.[8] The notion of telepresence invites us to think about the ramifications of a world in which the privatized virtual space of electronic communication comes to replace the face-to-face interactions that have historically constituted the public sphere. I will describe the ways in which telepresence might serve as a useful analogy for a production aesthetic that, in its evocation of a two-dimensional sonic environment, reinforces the retreat of R&B and rap lyrics from the domain of public interaction to a virtual non-place of private enjoyment.

Finally, I will demonstrate that this account of musical telepresence contributes to our understanding of Paul Gilroy's claims about the implications of contemporary "biopolitics" for black public culture, that is, a politics concerned with the regulation and control of the body. For Gilroy, the reduced political horizon of the black subject finds itself reflected and reinforced by a cultural sensibility that would sever the black body from broader romantic, civic, or political aspirations.[9] Whereas Gilroy's critique centers around the lyrics of contemporary rap and R&B, post-Timbaland music production provides evidence that this sensibility also makes its presence felt at the level of the groove.

The aesthetics of rap production are closely bound up with the stylistic dimensions of hip-hop culture as a whole. In her influential study *Black Noise: Rap Music and Black Culture in Contemporary America*, Tricia Rose, drawing upon terminology formulated by filmmaker Arthur Jafa, cites rap production as one of several interrelated stylistic practices that are bound together by a hip-hop aesthetic of "flow" and "rupture." For Rose, the rhyming vocalizations of rap, the DJ's manipulation of the sound system, the breakdancer's jerky choreography and the guerrilla murals of graffiti art are all infused by this same set of aural and visual strategies. In the same way that rappers and breakdancers build their rhymes or moves by alternating between gestures of lucid flow and stark cuts or interruptions, DJs and producers build their soundscapes around funk or rock beats that alternate between seamless arcs of continuity and the sudden breaks that cut against them. They reinforce and extend these rhythmic gestures with practices such as scratching, in which the DJ manipulates the records on the turntables, breaking the flow of the music on the source recordings.[10]

---

[8] Paul Virilio, *Open Sky*, trans. Julie Rose (London: Verso, 1997).

[9] Paul Gilroy, *The Black Atlantic: Modernity and Double Consciousness* (Cambridge, Mass.: Harvard University Press, 1993); and Gilroy, *Against Race: Imagining Political Culture Beyond the Color Line* (Cambridge, Mass.: Harvard University Press, 2000).

[10] Tricia Rose, *Black Noise: Rap Music and Black Culture in Contemporary America* (Middletown, Conn.: Wesleyan University Press, 1994), 21–61. Because of its centrality to contemporary American (and global) popular culture, hip-hop has become a vital topic of research in recent years, with studies

That Ill, Tight Sound

Rose conceives of this ubiquitous aesthetic of flow and rupture as the response of hip-hop's creators to the social conditions in which they lived. The visual and aural style of breakdancing, rapping, and DJing, with its normalization of unpre-dictability, might have served as a coping mechanism, a means of adapting to the structural violence wrought by deindustrialization and urban renewal in the South Bronx neighborhoods where the elements of hip-hop style initially took form. Rose also asserts that in hip-hop production, producers' early use—or "misuse"—of turntables as musical instruments, reflects this strategy of adapting to prevailing socioeconomic conditions in that they "make do" with the available resources, coaxing their "makeshift" devices to do things they were never made to do. By this reckoning, turntables, digital samplers, sound systems, and hip-hop's other technological appropriations primarily reflect the material situation in which this culture comes into being:

> Worked out on the rusting urban core as a playground, hip hop transforms stray techno-logical parts intended for cultural and industrial trash heaps into sources of pleasure and power.... In hip hop, these abandoned parts, people, and social institutions were welded and then spliced together, not only as sources of survival but as sources of pleasure.[11]

However, if the creators of hip-hop do use their materials "against themselves," turning the detritus of postindustrialism into a critique of itself, there is a danger in ascribing too much of this phenomenon to socioeconomic determinism. Joseph Schloss, citing the commentary of hip-hop pioneer Prince Paul, notes that DJs and producers gravitated towards the equipment of rap production—turntables, drum machines, digital samplers—largely because of their aesthetic appeal, their ability to generate previously unknown sonic possibilities. To advance a strictly socioeconomic explanation for what were mostly artistic choices is to provide an inadequate account of the creativity behind hip-hop's galvanizing sonic impact.[12]

If the material conditions in which hip-hop took shape do not predetermine its aesthetic in any straightforward way, there nevertheless remains an important social dimension to the sound of hip-hop and R&B, as with all musical genres. Aesthetically pleasing musical decisions are compelling because they resonate with our most fundamental, unspoken assumptions about the moment we live in. Turntablism and its successor, digital sampling, have allowed producers to use fragments of prerecorded sound in ways that signify upon intuitions about memory, cultural knowledge, and subjectivity that are peculiar to their time and place. The more recent shift in production style in contemporary black popular music that I address

---

emerging from a range of disciplines. For a more extensive discussion of rap and hip-hop culture, see Jeffrey Chang, *Can't Stop Won't Stop: A History of the Hip-Hop Generation* (New York: St. Martin's Press, 2005); David Toop, *Rap Attack #3: African Rap to Global Hip Hop*, 3rd edn. (London: Serpent's Tail, 2000); Cheryl L. Keyes, *Rap Music and Street Consciousness* (Urbana: University of Illinois Press, 2004); Adam Krims, *Rap Music and the Poetics of Identity* (Cambridge: Cambridge University Press, 2000); Imani Perry, *Prophets of the Hood: Politics and Poetics in Hip Hop* (Durham, N.C.: Duke University Press, 2004); Tony Mitchell, ed., *Global Noise: Rap and Hip-Hop Outside the U.S.A.* (Middletown, Conn.: Wesleyan University Press, 2001).

[11] Rose, *Black Noise*, 22.

[12] Joseph Schloss, *Making Beats: The Art of Sample-Based Hip Hop* (Middletown, Conn.: Wesleyan University Press, 2004), 26–29.

here, what I am referring to as a "post-Timbaland" sound, has come to feel just as intuitive to current listeners, because of its own unusual and powerful access to post-millennial sensibilities.

The process of building loops from digital sampling has been the focus of much of the existing scholarly literature on hip-hop production.[13] In the early 1980s, producer Marley Marl famously stumbled upon the process of sampling breakbeats, the sections in rock, funk, and soul tunes in which a drum "break" is isolated from the rest of the surrounding musical texture.[14] The process ensured that the producer would be able to draw upon the suppleness of the drummer's sound, the intricacy of timing and accent specific to live, acoustic drumming. Moreover, the sampling of breakbeats also captured the grittiness of hiss and crackle, a grittiness derived from the noise produced through sampling vinyl recordings, and from the different sound quality of the original recordings, which often used ribbon microphones or other technologies specific to their time.

In "Making Old Machines Speak: Images of Technology in Recent Music," Joseph Auner reminds us of the ways that these audible traces of old technologies signify upon our culture's relation to memory and nostalgia.[15] If the looping of samples tends to emphasize the artifice of a song's construction, the ragged stitches holding it together, it also maintains a connection to the sense of acoustic space generated in the source recordings. The live drumming on 1960s and 1970s soul recordings frequently uses copious amounts of reverb, evoking a sense of spatiality within the sound world of the recording, and some element of this was brought into the music that sampled it.[16] Beyond this, though, the use of twenty-year-old samples, the characteristic tunes of an earlier era, allows hip-hop producers to signify upon a different kind of space and distance, the long perspective of passing time. Moreover, the materiality of these recorded samples, their saturation with buzz and crackle, intensified their demarcation of a distance between past and present.

Auner's argument on behalf of the British trip-hop textures of Portishead holds true, I believe, for American hardcore rap production as well. Adrian Utley's use (in his Portishead instrumental backdrops) of the crackle of vinyl, the boom and hiss of earlier recording technologies, the tinny, "AM radio" quality in his processing of Beth Gibbons's vocals—all of this tends to encourage a fetishistic privileging

[13] For example, see Schloss, *Making Beats*; Rose, *Black Noise*, 62–97; and Robert Walser, "Rhythm, Rhyme, and Rhetoric in the Music of Public Enemy," *Ethnomusicology* 39/2 (Spring–Summer 1995), 193–217. For a discussion of looping and sampling in the context of electronic dance music culture, see Simon Reynolds, "Digital Psychedelia," in *Generation Ecstasy: Into the World of Techno and Rave Culture*, 40–55 (New York: Routledge, 1999). For a useful documentary providing an overview of rap production, see Ray Stewart, dir., *The Beat Kings: The History of Hip Hop*, Nature Sounds, 2006.

[14] Rose, *Black Noise*, 79.

[15] Joseph Auner, "Making Old Machines Speak: Images of Technology in Recent Music," *Echo: a music-centered journal* 2/2 (Fall 2000), http://www.echo.ucla.edu/volume2-issue2/auner/aunerframe.html.

[16] Examples of this sense of space embedded in samples are in Obie Trice's "Cry Now," which samples a boomy segment from "Blind Man" by the Bobby Blue Band (*Cry Now*, Interscope INTR-11785-1, 2006); and the astounding track "Holla," in which Wu-Tang associate Ghostface Killah simply lets the Delfonics' recording "La La Means I Love You" run underneath his verses for the duration of the song (*The Pretty Toney Album*, Def Jam B0002169-02, 2004). In each case, much of the song's emotional power derives from the reverberant space imported from the old song into the new one.

That Ill, Tight Sound

of old technology, and perhaps the absent, bygone worlds to which that alludes. Portishead is a white production team supporting a white torch singer, singing introspective songs focusing upon personal anxiety, regret, and disillusionment, and, as a consequence, Utley's gritty production here winds up channeling this fetishism of the past through the lens of individual loss.

The same formal lens, though, placed in the hands of hardcore rap producers such as the RZA (Robert Diggs) on the Wu-Tang Clan's *Enter the Wu-Tang (36 Chambers)* can be used to signify upon an entirely different set of social meanings. In contrast to the warm, soulful samples that Utley puts to work in Portishead's recordings, the RZA saturates the atmosphere of *Enter the Wu-Tang* with samples of martial-arts B-movie soundtracks and gritty, subterranean breakbeats, alluding to an urban context of social antagonism and street menace.[17] Where Utley's sound is preoccupied with interiority, the RZA's sound channels its emotional energy outward, training its eyes (or ears) upon public space.

Sean Combs's production team, which programmed the underlying textures for Notorious B.I.G.'s influential album *Ready to Die*, also harness sampling technology in a way that focuses upon the public resonances of these older musical references, particularly their evocation of history, nostalgia, and the anxieties of social change.[18] On "Things Done Changed," Biggie Smalls ruminates upon the swift dissolution of public spaces in black neighborhoods, rapping,

> Damn, what happened to the summertime cookouts?
> Everytime I turn around, a nigga gettin' took out

Here, Small's opening track functions as an establishing shot, an epic backdrop for the more personal narratives of street jeopardy and sexual misadventure to follow. Smalls's producers take the long historical view on this track, building up a dense, lush layering using samples from such songs as the Main Ingredient's "Summer Breeze," upbeat soul songs gesturing towards an earlier, more hopeful moment in African American social experience. There is a tremendous historical and emotional distance separating the tone of these sampled songs from that of the bleak scenarios depicted in Smalls's lyrics, an aching distance of wrenching change and reduced horizons. Here, the brooding unison strings that Smalls incorporates over the later verses further reinforces this sense of distance. The epic tone that Smalls sets in this track serves as an implicit conscience, an awareness of other moral possibilities that permeates the album and watches over the amoral violence wrought by his protagonist on tracks such as the ultraviolent "Gimme the Loot" and the sexually omnivorous "Friend of Mine." The distance between past and present in "Things Done Changed" alludes to, while never making explicit, the structural violence wrought by postindustrialism within black communities, the rapid atrophying of civic potential within inner-city regions eviscerated by the flight of stable industrial employment and other kinds of social investment.

The looping of digital samples served as the dominant production style in hip-hop from the late 1980s through the mid-1990s. It was pervasive across stylistic

---

[17] Wu-Tang Clan, *Enter the Wu-Tang (36 Chambers)*, Loud 66336-2, 1993.
[18] Notorious B.I.G., *Ready to Die*, Bad Boy 73000, 1994.

boundaries, as a common formal denominator in music ranging from the sonic bombast of Public Enemy and N.W.A., through the whimsical jazz references of Native Tongue crews, to the gritty realism of early 1990s hardcore rap. Loop-based production presided over a period encompassing economic recession, the intensification of the "war on drugs," and heightened tensions in the wake of the beating of Rodney King. In this context, the tactile materiality of looped samples allowed many rap tracks to evoke an atmosphere consistent with Chuck D's description of rap as "black people's CNN": that is, their invocation of the "real," of a reality beyond the surface of the song, underwrote the street narratives of rappers as diverse as Ice Cube, Biggie Smalls, Nas, and Tupac Shakur.

The latter, more prosperous half of the decade of the 1990s witnessed a sea change in black musical aesthetics, catalyzed by changes in the immediacy of musical grooves, their constituent textures. Mosley is probably the most instrumental figure in this sonic shift. His production credits include artists ranging from Missy Elliott and Ginuwine to Justin Timberlake and Nelly Furtado, and he developed his sound in a studio based in Virginia Beach, an area with a history of innovative production in hip-hop. Teddy Riley developed the "New Jack Swing" style there in the late 1980s, and the area later gave rise to the Neptunes, a production duo consisting of Pharrell Williams and Chad Hugo, named for their mutual fascination with water and sea.[19] The Neptunes have extended and added to the aesthetic Timbaland developed in the late 1990s, with an overtly "tech-y," futuristic sound that, like Mosley's, makes use of an elaborate process of beat construction that builds its hooks from "scratch."[20]

If songs such as Notorious B.I.G.'s "Things Done Changed" proceed by way of a rich, densely assembled sonic atmosphere, building up "strata" of memory by means of sampled loops, Timbaland's production on Aaliyah's 1997 hit "Are You That Somebody?" reflects a radically different approach.[21] Here, Mosley constructs a beat whose most striking feature is its "start-stop" quality, its alternation of skittish, syncopated beats with moments of dead space. In this vamp, everything from the staccato chord progressions to Aaliyah's vocal phrasing subordinates itself to the rhythm, a rhythm whose complexity betrays no trace of live acoustic space. The silence between beats is total: Mosley applies no reverb, no sonic filler, nothing to interfere with the sense of two-dimensional flatness that this groove evokes.[22]

---

[19] Roni Sarig, *Third Coast: OutKast, Timbaland, & How Hip-Hop Became a Southern Thing* (Cambridge, Mass.: Da Capo Press, 2007), 148–53.

[20] In an interview with *Sound on Sound* magazine, the Neptunes' engineer, Norman Coleman, notes the extent to which the Neptunes' companion project, N*E*R*D, depends upon a mix of hip-hop and rock production techniques. Williams might lay down a live groove on drum kit, which Coleman would subsequently cut into 16-bar loops. He further notes that much of their production attempts to combine the speed of digital recording with the "values" of analog recording, with its ostensible "warmth." This attentiveness to the specific resonances of drum sounds, and of sound in general, makes itself apparent in such tracks as the Neptunes-produced "Grindin'" by Clipse, which combines the starkly minimal framework of post-Timbaland aesthetics with a markedly "live" drum sound. See Dan Daley, "Recording the Neptunes," *Sound on Sound*, July 2005.

[21] Aaliyah, "Are You That Somebody?" on Various Artists, *Dr. Doolittle*, Atlantic/WEA 83113-1, 1998.

[22] Frere-Jones describes this beat as follows: "And his masterpiece, Aaliyah's 'Are You That Somebody?', is full of holes, literally—big half-second pauses between beats and voices that make the music

That Ill, Tight Sound **163**

Mosley's approach to production, also evident on tracks such as his tabla-funk Missy Elliott hit, "Get Ur Freak On" or his recent work for Justin Timberlake on songs such as "My Love," also eschew the conventional means of creating sonic "fullness," such as reverb, pan, delay, echo, or other effects that might construct a mental image of sonic space.[23] They do not entirely avoid sampling: "Are You That Somebody?" makes particularly clever use of a giggling baby as a rhythmic device, and both the Aaliyah hit and "My Love," recorded ten years afterward, draw upon a peculiar beatboxing sound Mosley obtains by jiggling his cheeks. However, these are not complete, unbroken loops, building textures out of four- to eight-bar segments, but instead consist of sonic fragments, building blocks isolated from their immediate musical contexts. Mosley is famously mute on the subject of his influences. In other artists' work, though, this strategy of sampling makes use of the potential, in devices such as the Akai MPC series of samplers, for breaking larger samples into "regions," shorter segments often consisting of little more than a kick drum or snare sound from the original breakbeat.[24] The fragmentation of sounds allows Mosley to harness the punctuating, percussive dimension of sounds without bringing along too much of their additional baggage: their evocation of sonic ambience, the gritty materiality of their source as vinyl samples, the historical connections and allusions they forge as part of longer, recognizable phrases.

One should be careful here, because samples inevitably do point outside themselves as simulacra of earlier recorded events. Timbaland is famously catholic in his musical references, building his sound through some unusual sources. However, samples in Timbaland's work usually take on an instrumental role, subordinating their referentiality to their sonic impact as discrete rhythmic and textural events. The baby's giggle in "Are You That Somebody?" is certainly evocative, but in the context of the Aaliyah groove, it is largely part of the polyrhythmic construction.

Even in those instances in which Mosley does use evocative melodies, timbres, or rhythmic patterns to gesture towards particular cultural references, he presents them in such a way that they rarely evoke the same meanings as similar gestures derived from sampled "live" sound sources. In "Get Ur Freak On," he superimposes a tinny orientalist riff, seemingly generated by some kind of Japanese shamisen or koto synthesizer preset, over the top of an intricate tabla groove. In a context in which a producer had sampled these sounds from live performance, they would be inseparably linked to the ambience of the rooms in which they were performed, lending the music a sense (however illusory) of being grounded in a physical location. However, within the meticulously spare, reverbless sonic environment of

---

sound like it's being shot out of a cannon over and over. Timbaland's tracks have the unique distinction of stopping and starting more often than any other pop music" (Frere-Jones, "These Beats Work").

[23] See Missy Elliott, "Get Ur Freak On," *Miss E: . . . So Addictive*, Elektra 62643-2, 2002; and Justin Timberlake, "My Love," *Sexyback*, Jive 82876-87068-2, 2006.

[24] For a discussion of sample regions on the Akai MPC series, see *Akai MPC 1000 Music Production Center, Version 2.0, Operator's Manual*, 59–60, http://www.mpcsounds.com/download_akai_mpc_manual.php. Mosley denies that his work was influenced by jungle or drum 'n' bass, but many observers believe that this British dance music genre, which constructs elaborate polyrhythms from fragmented breakbeat samples, must have had an impact on him as he created his own distinctive style. See Reynolds, *Bring the Noise*, 227–28.

Mosley's production, such references sound oddly abstracted, cut off from their broader resonances with the concrete dimensions of historical time and place.

Mosley builds up beats largely from scratch, generating all of the polyrhythmic intricacy of funk, yet mostly eschewing the things that ordinarily happen between the beats: sonic decay, reverberation, the ghostly traces of the past. In live music, such events occurring "between the beats" tend to bear witness to the forces producing the music, the bodily labor of the performers themselves. Their inclusion in sampled grooves not only participates in the music's citation of cultural referents but also suggests the possibility of its connection to a concrete time and place. The Mosley breakbeat, on the other hand, effaces such concrete connections, remaining as a minimal trace, alluding only in the most abstract fashion to the material circumstances in which other funk grooves have been created.

If Timbaland is cryptic about who has influenced him, many cite the impact of Miami "bass music," or "Miami bass," both in his music and throughout the entire panoply of contemporary southern rap. Critic Roni Sarig locates the music's origins in the electro-funk of the 1980s, in tracks such as Afrika Bambaataa's "Planet Rock." In their attempt to evoke the futuristic artifice of Kraftwerk, Bambaataa and the Soul Sonic Force used the Roland TR-808, a drum machine that Roland had stopped making because its drum samples were wholly unconvincing in their imitation of live drumming. It was precisely this anti-realism, this peculiarly tinny and sterile ambience of the 808's beats, that underwrote the aesthetic of electro, foregrounding a cybernetic funk entirely distinct from the sounds created by turntablist DJs in hip-hop's earliest years. With Marley Marl's introduction of sampled breakbeats as a new basis for hip-hop production, New York largely abandoned electro, but in Miami, figures such as erstwhile telephone technician James McCauley or DJ Pretty Tony wedded the 808-based beats of electro to the resonant bass that local sound-system DJs had brought out in their party sets.[25]

It is worth noting the peculiar association of the sterile, immaculately "clean" beats of Miami bass with the explicit, often misogynistic lyrics of the "booty music" that spread throughout the Miami scene after the release of 2 Live Crew's 1987 album *Move Something*.[26] Because of their emphasis upon the rigid eighth-note groupings allowed by the device's sequencer, TR-808 beats often sound unfunky upon first hearing. That these antiseptic grooves could support such raunchily specific rap verses would seem like a contradiction in terms. However, the 808 textures of bass music do map out alongside the sexual lyrics of booty music in one important respect. The disembodiment at the core of bass music production, its heavy dependence upon the obviously synthetic sound of the drum machine, suggests a spatial two-dimensionality, a "foreground" of groove that thwarts our ability to envision live musicians in the "background" responsible for the performance. Such an aspatial, two-dimensional production serves as an appealing aural analogue to bass music's emphatically sexual lyrics, which refuse all emotional commitments beyond the immediate here and now of the dance floor or of the sexual act.

---

[25] Sarig, *Third Coast*, 13–15.
[26] Ibid., 20.

That Ill, Tight Sound   **165**

If my discussion thus far has focused upon the *sparseness* of production styles such as that of Timbaland, or that found in Miami bass, one final example here illuminates how even "fuller" musical textures might still evoke a more "flat," two-dimensional quality of sonic space. On his production for the 2006 hit "What You Know" by rapper T.I., Atlanta producer DJ Toomp centers the track around a repeated four-measure harmonic progression, played using an especially obnoxious synthesizer sound.[27] He programs each note in the bass line to continue straight through to the end of each beat, with utterly no decay in the sound, or any space between the beats. Only the crisp percussion sounds of the 808 in any way punctuate this unrelenting *tenuto* texture. Praising the track in his review of T.I.'s album *King* for the All Music Guide, Andy Kellman describes it as follows:

> The slow victory lap that is "What You Know" is T.I.'s greatest track yet, a Toomp production with high and low synthesizer notes—all of which sound like severely pitched-down synthetic horn lines—drawn out to the point where they're practically bleeding into one another; T.I. similarly extends his syllables ("Just keep it very cooool, or we will bury yooou") for maximum looming effect.[28]

Here, the unbroken, sustained texture of Toomp's production serves as the complementary opposite of the starkly minimal beats on songs such as "Are You That Somebody?" Toomp creates a sonic wall of radical *opacity*, a flat plane of unrelenting sound that denies depth, perspective, relief, with just as much insistence as the dead space and staccato beats of Aaliyah's hit.

Many scholars have noted this pervasiveness of a two-dimensionality elsewhere in contemporary aesthetics, an emphasis of shallow surface over spatial or temporal depth. Most famously, Frederic Jameson established more than two decades ago that postmodern aesthetics had largely abandoned the constructions of interior depth in earlier artwork in favor of a celebration of depthless surface, a laconic flatness severed from the dialectical turbulence of the grand narrative.[29] One of the more disturbing dimensions of this flatness is its erasure of any notion of the spectral, of ghostly traces, of some remainder that might complicate the integrity of the images we consume, of the sounds we absorb. Avery Gordon in her *Ghostly Matters: Haunting and the Sociological Imagination* frames these ideas through the concept of "hypervisibility," that condition of postmodern culture in which everything is understood as eminently accessible, offering itself to our gaze, evacuated of its historical tensions or antagonisms:

> Hypervisibility is a kind of obscenity of accuracy that abolishes the distinctions between "permission and prohibition, presence and absence." No shadows, no ghosts. In a culture seemingly ruled by technologies of hypervisibility, we are led to believe not only that everything can be seen, but also that everything is available and accessible for our consumption.

---

[27] T.I., "What You Know," *King*, Atlantic/WEA 12278, 2005.

[28] Andy Kellman, review of *King* by T.I., *Allmusic*, http://allmusic.com.

[29] Here I have in mind his well-known comparison of Vincent Van Gogh's *A Pair of Boots*, with its frenzied brushstrokes, its unsettled texture, and Andy Warhol's *Diamond Dust Shoes*, with its bland, uninflected representation of ballet shoes, its validation of surface over depth. See Frederic Jameson, *Postmodernism: Or, the Cultural Logic of Late Capitalism* (Durham, N.C.: Duke University Press, 1991), 6–8.

In a culture seemingly ruled by technologies of hypervisibility, we are led to believe that neither repression nor the return of the repressed, in the form of either improperly buried bodies or countervailing systems of value or difference, occurs with any meaningful result.[30]

Hypervisibility (or, we might add, its aural counterpart, hyperaudibility) brooks no alternatives to total media saturation or uninflected, dead space. Every webpage can theoretically occupy the same flat plane as any other, can find its physical distance from the viewer radically truncated by search engines and hypertext links. Similarly, "reality" television and YouTube allow us an unseemly proximity to the private ruminations and unsolicited intimacies of total strangers.[31] In this way, our media-constituted reality comes to resemble the depressing contours of pornography, a filmic genre, Slavoj Žižek reminds us, that hides nothing, and thereby negates its own capacity for establishing the "minimal distance" that lends weight to representation, that fleeting, elusive element that exceeds the immediate grasp of representation.[32]

However, the quality of aspatial "flatness" that characterizes many of the production styles of early twenty-first-century mainstream rap and R&B comments upon an even more ominous dimension of contemporary reality, one frequently invoked by Virilio. One of his chief contributions to theoretical critique is his assessment of the cultural ramifications of instantaneous electronic communication. In *Open Sky*, he demonstrates how real-time electronic communication transforms the journey, the movement from one place to another that used to necessitate a physical displacement beginning with a departure, moving through a journey, to arrive at a destination. If new modes of transportation invented in the nineteenth and twentieth century had modified the journey, reducing its necessary delay, the development of real-time electronic communication in the late twentieth century eliminates departure, creating the situation of a "generalized arrival" where "everything arrives without having to leave," the distance separating two points on a map reduced to an abstraction, easily neutralized by the opening of a channel between two nodes in a network.[33]

Virilio uses the concept of "telepresence" to designate this specific relation to the world brought into being by the possibility of real-time electronic communication and action. Telepresence, the ability to meet at a distance, results in a peculiar short-circuiting of conventional space and time, where electromagnetic communication radically collapses the distance separating subject from object, and eradicates the historical situatedness of the present, that of an event anchored in a concrete "here and now" bound to the past and to the future. Telepresence isolates the present in time and place, situating it within a "no-place," an "atopia" separate from our spatial-temporal coordinates.[34]

---

[30] Avery F. Gordon, *Ghostly Matters: Haunting and the Sociological Imagination* (Minneapolis: University of Minnesota Press, 1997), 16.

[31] Here I am citing Thomas de Zengotita's notion of "unseemly access" in his *Mediated: How The Media Shapes Your World and the Way You Live in It* (New York: Bloomsbury, 2005), 227–29.

[32] Slavoj Žižek, "Is It Possible to Traverse the Fantasy in Cyberspace?" in *The Žižek Reader*, ed. Elizabeth Wright and Edmond Wright (Oxford: Blackwell Publishers, 1999), 111–12.

[33] Virilio, *Open Sky*, 15–16.

[34] Ibid., 10–11.

That Ill, Tight Sound   167

For Virilio, this short circuit imposed by the temporal-spatial disconnect of telepresence presents us with a number of troubling considerations. On a broader scale, Virilio argues that a "tyranny of real time" has wrought structural violence at a socioeconomic level, as the speed of exchange permitted by the instantaneous transfer of electronic information has facilitated the automation of tasks formerly executed by workers (and, one might add, has facilitated the practice of outsourcing, in which local labor is made redundant by easier and less expensive modes of global capital flow). On a more regional scale, though, Virilio also decries the way in which telepresence, with its isolation of the event from the material context of physical space, has resulted in an inversion of "near" and "distant," with calamitous repercussions for social ties and communities:

> The paradoxes of acceleration are indeed numerous and disconcerting, in particular, the foremost among them: getting closer to the "distant" takes you away proportionally from the "near"—the friend, the relative, the neighbour—thus making strangers, if not actual enemies, of all who are close at hand, whether they be family, workmates, or neighbourhood acquaintances.[35]

What Thomas de Zengotita describes as our "unseemly access," our ability to truncate the distance between ourselves and even the most remote images or sounds, comes at a price: we must ignore all that lurks behind, or comes between us and the information we summon forth.[36] The opacity of the flattened, severed image obscures our view, preventing us from understanding the material difficulties of what it represents, the way in which it stands in for the immediacy of human contact.

Some of the positive ramifications of the emergent information technology complicate any straightforward account of telepresence as an inherently negative social development. For example, in a study commissioned by the MacArthur Foundation titled *Confronting the Challenges of Participatory Culture: Media Challenges for the 21st Century*, a group of new media scholars led by Henry Jenkins presents an assessment of emergent communications technology that centers around the idea of "participatory cultures." Participatory cultures harness the social potential of contemporary interactive technologies, using what is frequently real-time communication to build communities that exceed the boundaries of the networks they emerge from. Such technologies as networked gaming, weblogs, video upload sites such as YouTube, or networking sites such as MySpace or Facebook allow new, previously unimagined possibilities for civic and political engagement, artistic expression, and other kinds of communal interaction.[37]

At the same time, though, Jenkins and his co-authors acknowledge some of the pitfalls and dangers associated with these new avenues for community. The "digital divide," the gap between those with both material and social access to these participatory cultures, and those without, may actually function to exacerbate

---

[35] Ibid., 20.

[36] De Zengotita, *Mediated*, 227–29.

[37] Henry Jenkins et al., *Confronting the Challenges of Participatory Culture: Media Challenges for the 21st Century* (Chicago: MacArthur Foundation, 2006), 8–11, http://www.digitallearning.macfound.org.

existing socioeconomic divisions.[38] This digital divide operates in tandem with the "inversion of near and distant" that Virilio identifies within the phenomenon of telepresence, the marginalization of those who fall between the nodes of the network. Moreover, in the same way that participatory cultures have allowed the development of unprecedented possibilities for community building and interaction, they also have given rise to new, unprecedented ethical challenges. Those with unrestricted access to the instantaneous, widespread distribution of their ideas and thoughts may not feel the same social constraints that they do in an environment of local, face-to-face interaction and social ties.[39] In this sense, the "no-place" of electronic communication involves an unstable and highly ambiguous, if not contradictory, set of social assumptions: media that creates new distances as it eradicates old ones; untrammeled communication via channels that also flatten the contours of social "depth," those cues that have historically allowed us nuanced interactions and served as constraints upon those interactions.

Against this backdrop, then, the "two-dimensionality" that I have been attempting to locate in contemporary rap production bears a larger ethical dimension. The dead air surrounding Timbaland's stark percussion, the unyielding sonic proximity of DJ Toomp's production on "What You Know," these textures emulate the no-place of Virilio's telepresence, the collapsed, ahistorical abstraction that has come to replace the ordinary dynamics of physical and temporal distance and proximity. In their impenetrable immediacy, their subordination of external reference to the internal dynamics of the groove, these sound worlds capture something of the radical redefinition of public space implicit in the widespread use of technologies of telepresence. In this way, they perform a crucial function: they bring to the ear's attention a dimension of contemporary experience that, by definition, negates absence, eschews permanence, and resides nowhere.

The spatial topography, or perhaps *anti*-spatial topography, that I am attempting to identify in southern production styles raises some crucial issues about the relationship between race, the body, and technology.[40] One of the most powerful dimensions of the music's appeal derives from its establishment of an aesthetic that challenges conventional notions of the "human," a category that has historically been denied to African-diasporic peoples, and one that has become increasingly problematic in light of postmodern interpretations of subjectivity. This aesthetic challenge to Eurocentric conceptions of the human, though, functions in concert with the music's aesthetic realization of telepresence, and as a consequence we will need to consider precisely how the new modes of subjectivity represented

---

[38] Ibid., 13–14.

[39] Ibid., 17.

[40] It is worth speculating on how such an aspatial musical topography could come to characterize a specifically *regional* style. It is possible that the flattening of musical space in post-Timbaland rap might signify upon the distinct forms of urbanism found in the fast-growing cities of the South. For a discussion of constructions of "Southernness" in the music of Atlanta-based groups such as OutKast and Goodie MoB, see Adam Krims, *Rap Music and the Poetics of Identity*, 123–51.

in this music relate to the broader social questions raised by the concept of telepresence.

In "'Feenin': Posthuman Voices in Contemporary Black Popular Music," Alexander Weheliye positions black popular music in relation to the category of the "posthuman," the cybernetic, hybrid construction of subjectivity explored by N. Katherine Hayles.[41] In *How We Became Posthuman*, Hayles's strategy is to demonstrate how a new category of the "posthuman" has come to displace the classical liberal construction of the "human," that is, a subject with discrete boundaries, internal consistency, and unconditional agency. This posthuman, by contrast, assumes no fixed boundaries between human beings and the intelligent machines they operate, with prosthetic technologies extending and fundamentally conditioning "human" subjectivity.[42]

Weheliye argues that Hayles's racially unmarked construction of the posthuman is predicated upon a Eurocentric notion of the human, one that takes for granted a universal, undifferentiated model of post-Enlightenment subjectivity. For Weheliye, these assumptions fail to account for the contested and problematic relation of subjectivity to African-diasporic culture, given that those descended from slavery have never easily acquired unconditional access to full humanity. In this context, he asserts, it makes more sense to understand the specifically black posthuman in the terms set by Kodwo Eshun, who conceives of a posthumanism that has emerged from a conception of the *sub*human, for the most part bypassing any unproblematic embrace of the white liberal subjectivity implicit in the term "human."[43]

The black posthuman envisioned by Weheliye and Eshun challenges those narratives of black progress that might seek to measure progress in the terms of Eurocentric liberal subjectivity. Against a portrayal of black music that would decry the loss of the human, Weheliye posits a posthuman subject utterly at home in an environment of fragmentation and mediation, where the human stands in a complex relation to technology, the virtual, the machinic. The black posthuman presents a complex imbrication of the body within the virtual, where "because . . . black cultural practices do not have the illusion of disembodiment, they stage *the body* of information and technology as opposed to the lack thereof."[44]

As I have argued, the "virtuality" of post-Timbaland rap production emerges from its evocation of a sonic no-place, where the dancing body resides as a starkly minimal, mechanical trace of the more "human" breakbeats that earlier rap production would sample from 1960s or 1970s soul. As such, it presents itself as an especially likely home for the type of posthuman subject that Weheliye invokes. Indeed, he specifically identifies the "hypersoul" of contemporary R&B as a locus for the posthuman, a site where the virtual and the concrete, body and soul, are caught up in intricate and paradoxical relationships. In particular, Weheliye focuses

---

[41] Alexander G. Weheliye, "'Feenin': Posthuman Voices in Contemporary Black Popular Music," *Social Text* 71 (Summer 2002): 21–47.

[42] N. Katherine Hayles, *How We Became Posthuman: Virtual Bodies in Cybernetics, Literature, and Informatics* (Chicago: University of Chicago Press, 1999), 2–4.

[43] Weheliye, "'Feenin'," 28–29.

[44] Ibid., 39.

on the innovative use of musical technologies such as the vocoder in black music, which allows a contradictory virtualization of the embodied voice, in order to understand how such technologies underscore the intricate processes of mediation described in the lyrics. In the songs of Timbaland, Ginuwine, Missy Elliott, Destiny's Child, Aaliyah, and others, the cell phone, the chat room, and the pager figure as tools through which the concrete dimensions of desire can be negotiated in the virtual no-place of electronic communication.[45]

For Weheliye, one of the consequences of this profound immersion of the desiring subject within a machinic information network is that subjectivity becomes radically transformed by this encounter, with human desire beginning to take on the characteristics of the technologies it utilizes. In the same moment, though, the body does not disappear, but is amplified via the technological medium. Citing Jodeci's song "Feenin'," in which this vocoder-filtered word (implying "fiend," or drug fiend) is used to imply a desire that resembles drug addiction, Weheliye notes the extent to which "feenin'" indexes an almost total erasure of humanistic elements from the song's expression of bodily desire. Desire here is not the province of spiritual longing or of romantic love, and yet it remains fundamentally embodied, with the "body" here understood as an extension of the technologies that possess it. Here, the song's protagonist ceases to be a "human" subject in any conventional sense, and is instead reconstituted as material desire, borne out of neurochemical addiction and channeled through the electronic medium of digital sound.[46]

If the black posthuman subject feels so at home in the "hypersoul" of contemporary R&B, this is because post-Timbaland production styles have provided us with sonic textures that resonate so powerfully with the eclipse of the human implicit in songs like "Feenin'." The "two-dimensionality" of the post-Timbaland sound, with its frustration of interiority or emotional depth, speaks to the historical contingency of the human that Weheliye addresses in his discussion. However, the constructions of black subjectivity cited by Weheliye must also be understood within a larger context. My discussion of telepresence above foregrounds the unsettling political and ethical implications of a phenomenon that upends and rearranges ordinary concepts of near and far, substituting virtual presence for physical presence. As a model of subjectivity that resides within virtual space, the black posthuman of hypersoul is inseparable from these considerations. Moreover, the inescapable presence of the body within the collapsed space of post-Timbaland "musical telepresence" requires that we consider the ways that this music might offer us a window on more wide-ranging conversations about the political and juridical status of the body.

In *The Black Atlantic* and *Against Race*, Paul Gilroy devotes considerable attention to the ways that African-diasporic musics comment upon the politics of the black body.[47] His critique of contemporary R&B and hip-hop reads its distinctive gender politics, with its preoccupation with bodies, as a microcosm of larger transformations within the black public sphere. In *The Black Atlantic*, he argues that music

---

[45] Ibid., 33.
[46] Weheliye, "'Feenin',"" 38–39.
[47] See Gilroy, *The Black Atlantic*, 72–110; and Gilroy, *Against Race*, 177–206.

That Ill, Tight Sound   **171**

registers the dimension of race relations through its articulation of sexual or gender relations between its songs' protagonists:

> Gender is the modality in which race is lived. An amplified and exaggerated masculinity has become the boastful centerpiece of a culture of compensation that self-consciously salves the misery of the disempowered and subordinated. This masculinity and its relational feminine counterpart become special symbols of the difference that race makes. They are lived and naturalized in the distinct patterns of family life on which the reproduction of the racial identities supposedly relies.[48]

By this reckoning, of course, the hypersexualized lyrics of a song such as Missy Elliott's "Pussy Don't Fail Me Now" dramatize the extent to which the invocation of romance in current R&B has receded to the contours of the body.[49] For Gilroy, this replacement of an idealized romance with an unsentimental sexual candor always involves an erosion of the human, of those dimensions of human interactions that "go beyond" the immediate gratification of desire. Writ large, this erosion of romantic possibility translates into an erosion of the very possibility of political community, of emancipation.[50]

Gilroy argues that the rise of an increasingly explicit sexuality in rap, alongside its ongoing celebration of violence, maps out along a broader terrain demarcated by the concept of "biopolitics."[51] As Giorgio Agamben outlines in *Homo Sacer: Sovereign Power and Bare Life*, biopolitics is the term that Michel Foucault gives to a politics that centers around the control, administration, and management of the simple, living body. In the context of Foucault's late research, the idea of biopolitics informed two primary avenues of inquiry: on the one hand, those techniques of state power that allow the state to corral, administer, and discipline the individual body, and on the other hand, those "technologies of the self" that enable the subject to police his or her own identity and connection to external power.[52]

---

[48] Gilroy, *The Black Atlantic*, 85. For an account of Marvin Gaye's music that centers on this interplay between racial and sexual politics, see Mark Anthony Neal, *What the Music Said: Black Popular Music and Black Public Culture* (New York: Routledge, 1999), 61–72.

[49] Missy Elliott, "Pussy Don't Fail Me Now," *Under Construction*, Elektra 62813-2, 2002. In this song, Elliott's protagonist sees her sexual performance as the only thing that will save her relationship.

> Pussy don't fail me now
> I gotta turn this nigga out
> So he don't want nobody else
> But me and only me
> Pussy don't fail me now
> I gotta turn this nigga out
> So he don't want nobody else
> But me and only me

[50] See Gilroy, *Against Race*, 195.

[51] Ibid., 184.

[52] See Giorgio Agamben, *Homo Sacer: Sovereign Power and Bare Life*, trans. Daniel Heller-Roazen (Stanford: Stanford University Press, 1998), 3–6. In addition to Agamben's discussion of biopolitics, which focuses upon its relevance to our understanding of state power, Michael Hardt and Antonio Negri have also contributed to our understanding of how biopower functions within the context of global neoliberalism. See Michael Hardt and Antonio Negri, *Empire* (Cambridge, Mass.: Harvard University Press, 2000); see also Hardt and Negri, *Multitude: War and Democracy in the Age of*

Agamben's interest in biopolitics centers around the relationship between the biopolitical body and the power of the state. This relationship finds its extreme endpoint in the "state of exception," the situation in which civil discourses and social relations of ordinary life are suspended.[53] In the state of exception, the broader political proclivities of the human are stripped away and the body is left naked before state power, no longer protected by the due process or the rule of law.[54] We might imagine that an absolute point of demarcation separates those domains of the state where the rule of law is in force, on the one hand, from those under the state of exception, on the other. However, Agamben notes that in the present era, the state of exception in contemporary Western societies has come to coexist with the quotidian application of law, creating a zone of indistinction between the state's application of juridical authority and its simultaneous application of unrestrained force.[55]

In many respects, this peculiar situation of suspension describes the conditions that have faced many African American communities during the rise of the postindustrial state. In instances such as the 1985 bombing of the MOVE collective in Philadelphia or the indiscriminate police raids of "Operation Hammer" in Los Angeles in the late 1980s, the police forces in large metropolitan centers have frequently applied a broad-scale, disproportionate use of force that blurs the lines between law enforcement and low-intensity combat. The unrestrained brutality involved in such incidents as the assault of Haitian New Yorker Abner Louima by New York police in 1997 indicates how black men continue to be subject to a selective application of the rule of law. At the same time, we need to be cognizant that there can be no straightforward celebration of the "rule of law" in an era that has witnessed the introduction of many wholly legal mechanisms that have intensified the draconian "war on drugs" and that have brought about the current unprecedented rates of black male incarceration.

The biopolitical consists of a reduction of the boundaries of the subject to its body, and for this reason, Gilroy sees it as having an immense explanatory power for understanding the shrinking confines of the black public sphere, the reduced horizons of intimate love, and the precariousness of the black body before the law in postindustrial society. These three social developments are intricately wedded to one another:

> [T]he vernacular forms that were once called "street culture" are in the process of deserting the streets. They are no longer seen primarily as a privileged space for the elaboration of cultural authenticity but rather as the location of conflict, violence, crime, and social pathology.... The vital unfolding of racialized culture is now more likely to be imagined in discrete private, semi-private, and private-public settings that can be found, like the

---

Empire (New York: Penguin Press, 2004). For a useful account of the relationship between these two formulations of biopower, see Leeom Medovio, "Global Society Must Be Defended: Biopolitics Without Boundaries," *Social Text* 25/2 (Summer 2007): 53–79.

[53] This "state of exception" is more commonly referred to as the "state of emergency."

[54] Agamben, *Homo Sacer*, 84–85.

[55] Ibid., 38.

That Ill, Tight Sound   **173**

basketball court, between the axes established respectively by the intimacies of the bedroom and the fortified mobile enclosure of a sports utility vehicle.[56]

For Gilroy, the retreat of the R&B song's horizons from black public spaces to the privacy of the domestic sphere is concomitant with a similar imagining of what transpires within the domestic sphere itself. If, as Gilroy asserts, the family often serves in R&B songs as the only acceptable remaining site for the envisioning of social change, it can find its own boundaries further curtailed to the vicissitudes of sexual pleasure, to the gratification of the desiring body. In this way, even the most intimate depictions of sexuality in R&B link back to the biopolitics of the state of exception, insofar as they, too, envision a black body that is stripped of everything beyond its capacity for pleasure or suffering.

As I have discussed above, the flat, uninflected sonic space of post-Timbaland rap and R&B provides an agreeable home for the posthuman black subject described by Weheliye. However, this hospitality comes at a cost, for this aesthetic of anti-humanism, this refusal of interior depth or emotional transcendence, also unwittingly colludes with a biopolitics in which the socially engaged black subject of the public sphere is reduced to the confines of a desiring, suffering body. As Virilio argues with respect to telepresence, virtuality fundamentally reorders the relationship between near and distant, bringing together private nodes of communication in the same moment that it severs its ties from the local and the public. It intensifies the hold of biopolitics through its erasure of the context that gives bodies historical weight and political relevance. We must be wary of a posthuman that is so eager to celebrate virtual space that it neglects the accelerating deterioration of concrete space and the bodies that occupy it.

In this account of the music of Timbaland, the Neptunes, and bass music, I hope I have demonstrated that the "purely musical" constructions of rap and R&B production, with their powerful depictions of sonic space, are capable of signifying upon the larger environment in which they are situated. My discussion might seem to present an unduly bleak conception of what this music represents. However, my analysis of its capacity for signifying upon the experience of telepresence and biopolitics, is not intended as some kind of indictment of its ostensibly "regressive" qualities. Rather, I hope to have demonstrated this music's singular *prescience*, its powerful insights into the nature of social and spatial relations in the early twenty-first century. Lawrence Kramer has argued that music itself is a form of criticism, a criticism that has access to modes of commentary that are unavailable to language or visual representation.[57] Contemporary black music has done much to demonstrate the validity of this statement, and it is therefore crucial that we attend to what is "said" in its nonverbal mutations and transformations.

[56] Gilroy, *Against Race*, 189.
[57] Lawrence Kramer, "Music and Critical Inquiry: Three Variations on the *Ruins of Athens*," *Critical Inquiry* 32/1 (Autumn 2005): 76.

References

Agamben, Giorgio. *Homo Sacer: Soverign Power and Bare Life*, trans. Daniel Heller-Roazen. Stanford: Stanford University Press, 1998.

Akai MPC 1000 Music Production Center, Version 2.0, Operator's Manual. http://www.mpcsounds.com/download_akai_mpc_manual.php.

Auner, Joseph. "Making Old Machines Speak: Images of Technology in Recent Music." *Echo: a music-centered journal* 2/2 (Fall 2000). http://www.echo.ucla.edu/volume2-issue2/auner/aunerframe.html.

Chang, Jeffrey. *Can't Stop Won't Stop: A History of the Hip-Hop Generation*. New York: St. Martin's Press, 2005.

Daley, Dan. "Recording the Neptunes." *Sound on Sound*, July 2005.

De Zengotita, Thomas. *Mediated: How The Media Shapes Your World and the Way You Live in It*. New York: Bloomsbury, 2005.

Frere-Jones, Sasha. "These Beats Work: Timbaland." *The Wire*, December 1998. http://www.thewire.co.uk/archive/interviews/timbaland.html.

———. "Up Jumps Da Meme." *The Village Voice*, 12–18 April 2000. http://www.villagevoice.com/music/0015,frere-jones,13988,22.html.

Gordon, Avery F. *Ghostly Matters: Haunting and the Historical Imagination*. Minneapolis: University of Minnesota Press, 1997.

Gilroy, Paul. *The Black Atlantic: Modernity and Double Consciousness*. Cambridge, Mass.: Harvard University Press, 1993.

———. *Against Race: Imagining Political Culture Beyond the Color Line*. Cambridge, Mass.: Harvard University Press, 2000.

Hardt, Michael, and Antonio Negri. *Empire*. Cambridge, Mass.: Harvard University Press, 2000.

———. *Multitude: War and Democracy in the Age of Empire*. New York: Penguin Books, 2004.

Hayles, N. Katherine. *How We Became Posthuman: Virtual Bodies in Cybernetics, Literature, and Informatics*. Chicago: University of Chicago Press, 1999.

Jameson, Frederic. *Postmodernism: Or, the Cultural Logic of Late Capitalism*. Durham, N.C.: Duke University Press, 1991.

Jenkins, Henry, et al. *Confronting the Challenges of Participatory Culture: Media Challenges for the 21st Century*. Chicago: MacArthur Foundation, 2006. http://www.digitallearning.macfound.org.

Kellman, Andy. Review of *King* by T.I. *All Music Guide*. http://allmusic.com.

Keyes, Cheryl L. *Rap Music and Street Consciousness*. Urbana: University of Illinois Press, 2000.

Kramer, Lawrence. "Music and Critical Inquiry: Three Variations on the *Ruins of Athens*," *Critical Inquiry* 32/1 (Autumn 2005): 61–76.

Krims, Adam. *Rap Music and the Poetics of Identity*. Cambridge: Cambridge University Press, 2000.

Levine, Robert, and Bill Werde. "Superproducers." *Wired*, October 2003. http://www.wired.com/wired/archive/11.10/producers_pr.html.

Medovio, Leeom. "Global Society Must Be Defended: Biopolitics Without Boundaries." *Social Text* 25/2 (Summer 2007): 53–79.

Mitchell, Tony, ed. *Global Noise: Rap and Hip-Hop Outside the U.S.A.* Middletown, Conn.: Wesleyan University Press, 2001.

Neal, Mark Anthony. *What the Music Said: Black Popular Music and Black Popular Culture.* New York: Routledge, 1999.

Perry, Imani. *Prophets of the Hood: Politics and Poetics in Hip Hop.* Durham, N.C.: Duke University Press, 2004.

Phillips, Amy. "Björk Announces Tour Dates, Talks Timbaland Collab." *Pitchfork,* 19 March 2007. http://www.pitchforkmedia.com/article/news/41776-bjork-announces-tour-dates-talks-timbaland-collab.

Reynolds, Simon. *Bring the Noise: 20 Years of Writing About Hip Rock and Hip Hop.* London: Faber and Faber, 2007.

———. *Generation Ecstasy: Into the World of Techno and Rave Culture.* New York: Routledge, 1999.

Rose, Tricia. *Black Noise: Rap Music and Black Culture in Contemporary America.* Middletown, Conn.: Wesleyan University Press, 1994.

Sarig, Roni. *Third Coast: OutKast, Timbaland, & How Hip-Hop Became a Southern Thing.* Cambridge, Mass.: Da Capo Press, 2007.

Schloss, Joseph. *Making Beats: The Art of Sample-Based Hip Hop.* Middletown, Conn.: Wesleyan University Press, 2004.

Toop, David. *Rap Attack #3: African Rap to Global Hip Hop.* 3rd edn. London: Serpent's Tail, 2000.

Virilio, Paul. *Open Sky,* trans. Julie Rose. London: Verso, 1997.

Walser, Robert. "Rhythm, Rhyme, and Rhetoric in the Music of Public Enemy." *Ethnomusicology* 39/2 (Spring–Summer 1995): 193–217.

Weheliye, Alexander G. "'Feenin': Posthuman Voices in Contemporary Black Culture." *Social Text* 20/2 (Summer 2002): 21–47.

Žižek, Slavoj. "The Fantasy in Cyberspace." In *The Žižek Reader,* ed. Elizabeth Wright and Edmond Wright, 102–24. Oxford: Blackwell Publishers, 1999.

Filmography and Discography

Elliott, Missy. *Miss E: . . . So Addictive.* Elektra 62643-2, 2001.

———. *Under Construction.* Elektra 62813-2, 2002.

Killah, Ghostface. *The Pretty Toney Album.* Def Jam B0002169-02, 2004.

Notorious B.I.G. *Ready to Die.* Bad Boy 73000, 1994.

Stewart, Ray, dir. *The Beat Kings: The History of Hip Hop.* Nature Sounds, 2006.

T.I. *King.* Atlantic/WEA 12278, 2006.

Timbaland. *Tim's Bio: From the Motion Picture "Life from da Bassment."* Blackground Entertainment 92813-2, 1998.

Timberlake, Justin. *Sexyback.* Jive 82876-87068-2, 2006.

Trice, Obie. *Cry Now.* Interscope INTR-11785-1, 2006.

Various Artists. *Dr. Doolittle: The Album.* Atlantic/WEA 83113-1, 1998.

Wu-Tang Clan. *Enter the Wu-Tang (36 Chambers).* Loud 66336-2, 1993.

[16]

Sex, Pulp and critique

ERIC F. CLARKE AND NICOLA DIBBEN

In an article entitled 'Sexist Pulp ads attacked', the *Independent on Sunday* (*IoS*) reported public reaction to the posters advertising Pulp's new album *This is Hardcore* (posters had been defaced with the words 'this is sexist'), and described the advertisements as part of a turn away from political correctness towards a new 'anything goes' realism (Kelly and Clay 1998). The poster shows the naked upper torso of a woman face down on a red leather cushion, in an awkward and ambivalent posture, with lipsticked, half-open mouth. Emblazoned across the centre of the image (which is a reproduction of the album cover) are the words 'This is Hardcore' in pink capitals. A leader in the paper on the same day, under the heading 'This is violent. This is offensive', interprets the image as a demeaning, sexist and violent representation of women and as an offence to the record-buying public. The leader asserts that 'Just to sell a few songs, it shows a woman violated', and concludes with the words: 'To ban it [the poster] now would only generate more publicity for Pulp. So the only advice we have is for anyone thinking of buying the album. Don't bother.' (*IoS* Leader, 1998, p. 4)

Whether or not the image is really as demeaning as the *IoS* suggests (a matter to which we return), there are two possible interpretations of the newspaper's advice. Either the *IoS* assumes that the album is completely compromised by its offensive advertising, utterly discrediting any critical meaning or value that the music might have; or it assumes an identity between the advertising and album in which the music is as violent and offensive as the poster. In this second case, a fundamental issue is raised: how is it possible to attribute social content (in this case qualities such as 'violence against women', or 'offensiveness') to music? Furthermore, how might music be identified as having either a critical or an affirmative stance towards any such content? This paper is an attempt to show, for the specific case of 'This is Hardcore', that the music does indeed have a critical quality, albeit of a rather uncomfortable kind, and that the *IoS*'s verdict on both the album and the poster is superficial and hasty. Although arguably many of the tracks on the album deal with related issues using methods similar to those discussed below, for the purposes of this paper we focus solely on the title track of the album. We start with the question: Is the track about the same subject matter as the poster, and if so how?

An obvious place to start is with the words: the opening line of the track ('You are hardcore. You make me hard.') is unambivalent in its declaration that this is a track about a male experience of sex. In terms of content, the text contains few indications of a critical attitude to its subject matter – except perhaps for the lines 'It's what men in stained raincoats pay for' and 'I've seen the storyline played out

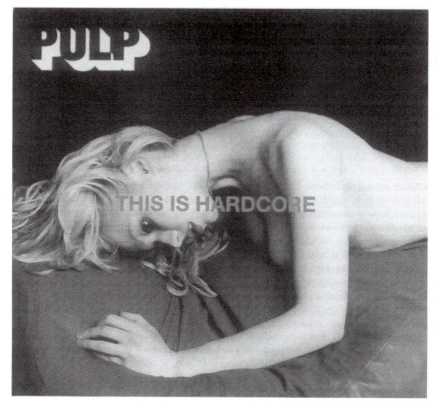

Figure 1. Reproduction of the album cover and poster advertisement for the album This is Hardcore.

so many times before', both of which convey a disengaged cynicism about the sex industry. The track turns out to be concerned with a man's experience of a complex mixture of sexual fantasy and reality. There is no doubt that a sexual act is described, but that direct experience is interlaced with the protagonist's fantasy about himself as both director and sex 'star' in his own imagined film ('I wanna make a movie, so let's star in it together'; 'Don't make a move 'til I say, "Action"'). The relationship between fantasy and reality is presented in a complex manner in that statements that clearly have the quality of fantasy (such as those above) are directly juxtaposed with others which relate to the reality of the scene being enacted (such as 'Leave your make-up on, and I'll leave on the light'). The control implicit in the protagonist's role as 'director and star' in his movie fantasy, and the self-conscious choreography or arrangement of 'Leave your make-up on, and I'll leave on the light' make it clear that the woman with whom this sex is going on is both a real sexual partner and the vehicle for a fantasy. Fantasy is a pretence that makes up for the inadequacies of reality.

While the process of describing the textual content of the track is relatively transparent, it is less clear how, or even whether, we can do something analogous with the music. Theories of musical meaning have been dominated by an intramusical approach: an example is Leonard Meyer's theory which considers musical meaning (embodied meaning) to arise out of the patterns of implication and realisation set up within musical structures (Meyer 1973). However, whatever the merits of looking at intramusical meaning, an approach of that kind is quite incapable (by definition) of addressing the relationship of music to an explicitly extramusical subject matter – in this case attitudes towards sex. The issue is how sounds can have social content. By contrast with an intramusical approach to musical content, the analysis presented here conceives of musical material as socially sedimented: musical materials are socially constituted since they are always the product of socialised human behaviour, and carry with them their historical situation. More specifically, musical materials have a 'history of use', one consequence of which is that sounds are heard as cultural references and associations. For example, the use of bell sounds in a whole variety of music is historically associated with religious worship or solemn occasions. Quite apart from this direct association, however, the 'history of use' of musical materials is also always bound up with their compositional function: for example, the last movement of Haydn's string quartet op. 76 no. 5 starts with a repeated perfect cadence and plays with the consequences of this apparently incongruous beginning, based on the premise that this conventionalised history of use will make an immediate impact on listeners. The advantage of this approach to musical meaning is that it does away with the crude distinction between intramusical and extramusical meaning: sounds always have a compositional function *and* are part of a social situation. The bell sounds have a function in their particular musical contexts at the same time as having wider reference, and the cadences in Haydn have a social character just as much as a musical function.

As may already be apparent, the approach taken here draws upon two different precursors: semiotic theory, of the kind used by Philip Tagg, and critical theory, of the kind represented by Theodor Adorno. Tagg has argued that musical materials have social and cultural meanings by virtue of their associations with prevailing cultural 'topics': in his analysis of the Kojak theme tune, for instance, he points out that the sound of horns and their characteristic large interval leaps have a long-standing association with hunting and alert/alarm calls (post horns, fanfares) (Tagg 1979). The materials and their association signify an aggressive, active, predatory masculinity – the image of Kojak, the detective. Adorno's approach has certain similarities, but engages far more directly with the issue of ideology and mass culture: in essence it is based upon the principle that critique is to be found in the immanent properties of the musical material, regarded as socially sedimented (Adorno 1984). When the material is used as if its properties and possibilities are natural and unproblematic, it simply affirms the musical and social *status quo*. Affirmation is not only an acceptance of musical conventions, but is also complicitous with the social situation that those materials embody. By contrast, when the material questions the conventions from which it has sprung, it has a critical perspective. Beethoven's use of disrupted and unsettling juxtapositions in a late quartet is critical in that it throws into question the compositional conventions of sonata form and the chamber music genre, just as music which uses deliberately historically or culturally distanced materials has the potential to be critical (such as Mahler's exploration of the grotesque in juxtapositions between music of the street and music of the concert hall). This is critique directed at musical processes and therefore at the social situation within which they arise and are heard. Two approaches to critique can be identified: one which can be called immanent, illustrated by the Beethoven example above; the other which operates by means of stylistic reference and juxtaposition, represented by Mahler's approach. Immanence and reference both have the capacity to be either critical or affirmative.

Our approach here, therefore, will be to identify the compositional character and cultural associations of musical materials and to use these to consider the ideological allegiances – complicit or critical – of the music of 'This is Hardcore'. The approach has some similarities to Philip Tagg's 'inter-objective comparison' in which the meanings or associations of musical materials are established on the basis of shared characteristics with previous instances. For example, the meanings of masculinity and predation attributed to the horn motif in the Kojak theme mentioned above are demonstrated by citing other examples of similar materials which also occur in similar semantic contexts (Tagg 1979, 1992). Although we use a similar principle in the analysis which follows, we make no attempt to provide an exhaustive account of the meanings of materials in terms of their parallel occurrences. To do this systematically would require a large number of secondary illustrative examples. Alternatively, support for these interpretations could derive from empirical investigation of listeners' perceptions of musical meanings. Since the main aim of this paper is to consider critique and collusion in the music of 'This is Hardcore', rather than to make a methdological point, we have presented these interpretations without always arguing the case for them, on the basis of a shared cultural context.

The Music

Figure 2 is a graphic overview of the track which provides a context for the more detailed comments which follow. Although the track starts with a strophic structure, it turns out to have a more through-composed and continuously developing form. In a fairly obvious and simple way this parallels the sexual act that is the subject matter of the song. After a listless and rather weary start, there is a continuous heightening of energy and drive through an increasing textural density, harmonic rhythm and movement of the bass line. The song reaches a climax at the words 'I can't believe it took me this long', and then dies away into a looser ensemble with a more mobile harmony and sustained string sound. This section in turn generates its own momentum which is suddenly dissipated when, at the return of the words 'This is Hardcore', the original texture and instrumentation becomes more audible again (it is present in the background throughout most of the track) as the strings of the previous section fade and pitch-bend downwards to leave just the kit and brass section of the opening. This is a detumescent gesture of futility: the protagonist's fantasy peels away to reveal the shabby reality that underpins the whole track leaving it back where it started.

Just as the text is obviously and directly about sex, so too is the music – but in this case by virtue of its stylistic references. The big, slow, foregrounded drum sound and more distant brass/big band sound in a very reverberant acoustic suggest a club or strip joint setting by virtue of their association with a style of orchestration (big band), a rhythmic/harmonic style (cabaret/jazz

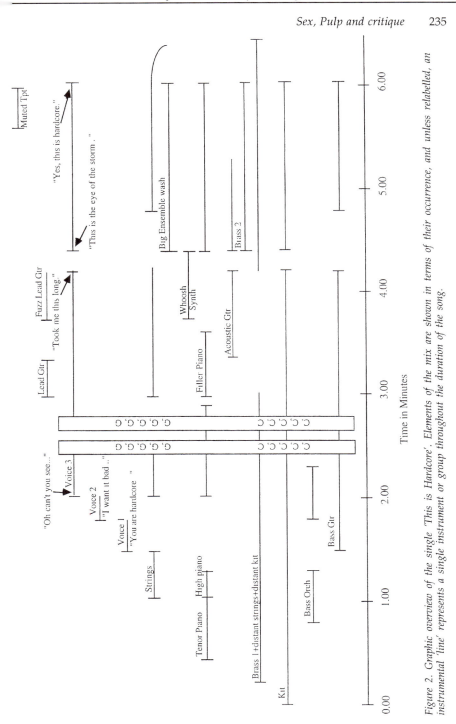

Figure 2. Graphic overview of the single 'This is Hardcore'. Elements of the mix are shown in terms of their occurrence, and unless relabelled, an instrumental 'line' represents a single instrument or group throughout the duration of the song.

236   *Eric Clarke and Nicola Dibben*

Example 1.

Example 2.

Example 3.

Example 4.

influenced tonal harmony – Em9, and a repeated pattern of syncopation (see Example 1)), and space (reverberation suggesting a large, empty interior). A dramatic, chromatically descending bass which energises it is the music of big cabaret/show numbers – a kind of 'Shirley Bassey' sound (Example 2). A high register piano riff with a little clichéd 'blue' note (Example 3) is cocktail bar piano in contrast to the circling tenor register piano monody which precedes it (Example 4). The association of all these materials is of various locations linked with sexual encounters of one sort or another: singles bars, strip joints, night clubs and cabarets. But how are we encouraged to 'hear' these locations? The reverberation and lack of background sounds suggest an empty hall, and the placement in the mix (middle distance) suggests a kind of remoteness and disengagement. Equally, the slow tempo (76 beats per minute) indicates a weary lack of interest while the circling piano melody is contained, futile. The voice, when it enters has a thin filtered quality as if over a tannoy or poor-quality sound system. The effect is distant, listless, empty, hollow, and the overall character of this opening section as a whole is of a run-down, worn-out glamour.

Already in the introduction the track presents musical materials which reference a number of different styles and associations, and it is this referencing of other styles which is an important way in which the track works both to present a subject matter (sex) and a subject position (ambivalent). It is unnecessary, and not our purpose, to present a systematic or complete analysis of the track in these terms; rather we will focus on a smaller number of examples which illustrate the argument.

Sex, Pulp and critique   237

Example 5.

A recurrent theme in the musical references is the relationship between antasy and reality. Just as the ending of the whole track reveals an underlying shabby emptiness, so also other sections present by turns a glamorous and a seedy image of sex. The section that rises to the song's climax features an increasingly prominent lead guitar played through a fuzz box in a 'cock-rock' style, with its associations of a hard, aggressive male sexuality. The section following the climax begins in a more reflective manner, but soon acquires more epic and overblown qualities as successive layers of instrumentation are engaged (bass, an increasingly prominent and melodic string section, and a free-wheeling, muted jazz trumpet (see Figure 2)). This is fantasy-film music and the sense of excess that these materials generate increasingly suggests that the music shouldn't be taken at face value – particularly since it coincides with the most cynical and world-weary passage in the lyrics: 'It's what men in stained raincoats pay for. . . This is the end of the line. I've seen the storyline played out so many times before.'

In every case, although the increasing energy and excitement of the section engages and draws the listener in, the discontinuities of style and their self-conscious treatment alienate and disengage the listener. The concern with reference as a technique is so all pervading that even Pulp themselves become an object for the method: at the end of the only strophic section of the track a rhythmically emphatic repetition of unharmonised Cs and then Gs (Example 5) punctuates the structure and at the same time functions as Pulp's own signature: exactly the same gesture was used in their equally controversial single 'Sorted for e's & wizz' (Example 6). Nothing is authentic: anything can be used in this game of references, and it is this that gives the whole track its distanced quality. At no point is the listener allowed to feel engaged: the music is 'presented' in the same way that the image is 'presented' with its declaration that 'This is Hardcore'.

Drawing together all the above, the track elicits an uncomfortable mixture

Example 6.

of complicity with, and critique of, a prurient attitude to sex. A variety of factor
draw the listener in. First, the track consists of materials which are stylisticall
familiar and it is this familiarity which gives them their allure. Second, there i
a captivating quality to the sensual pleasure afforded the listener by the technic
excellence and gloss of the production techniques. Third, there is a change i
the placing of materials in the mix from distant, at the beginning of the track
to an increasingly close and full treatment, as if the music is coming forwar
to meet and engage the listener. Fourth, the first person voice of the text, an
the placement of the singer in the foreground of the mix, creates an illusion c
interiority, or of access to an individual psyche, encouraging identification wit
the singer-protagonist on the part of the listener.[1] By contrast with these tech
niques of engagement, other factors distance or alienate the listener: for example
the disruption caused by the juxtaposition of diverse styles and genres, the us
of 'excess' as a technique of parody (overly glossy production techniques, th
musically redundant cock-rock guitar solo) and the direct signification of alien
ation and distance through such means as place in the mix, treatment of th
vocals (e.g. tannoy-like filtering of the voice at the start) and the sudden collaps
of the musical texture (just after the climax, and again at the end). This i
critique carried out with complicitous materials whose power derives from thei
ability to involve the listener in their manifest content while simultaneousl
inviting (or obliging) the listener to take up a critical perspective.

The album's concern with film as a theme, and the imbalance betweer
fantasy and reality, has a personal resonance with Pulp's (particularly Jarvi
Cocker's) experience of fame, as well as with their direct experience of film
production and consumption (Pulp were engaged in a number of film project
at the time of making the album):

All of my life I've been an observer, not only of films and TV, but of life, and then as
soon as you get that form of public acceptance, then you are somebody else's show.
You're actually part of the action on the screen. . . That's why there's a bit of an obsession
with it [film/TV] on the record. It's comparing what it was like as a spectator and what
it's like being part of the action, and that's always going to be a bit of a disappointment.
(Cocker 1998a)

Pornography, and films, are employed here as the most dramatic examples of a
more general disparity between the intensity of imagined experience and the
disappointment of its realisation.

In the light of this consideration of the music we can reconsider the image
which was the starting point for the press and public reaction to the album.
Although superficially the image has many of the properties of a pornographic
photograph (a glossily produced photo of a naked blonde with a gold chain on
a red leather bed or couch, in a submissive posture), there are three elements
which undermine the identification that a conventional image might elicit: first,
the words 'This is Hardcore', right across the centre like a censor's stamp create
a distance which tells the viewer to regard this as an object – a specimen.
Second, the glossy production which reeks of pornographic magazine, is heightened through digitisation and the treatment of colour such that the photographic
image is given an unreal, distant quality. And third, the woman looks either
dead or made of plastic which problematises her otherwise conventionally
attractive appearance. All three of these properties can be regarded as offensive
(in the way that the *IoS* interprets them), but equally they can be seen as

preventing the kind of collusion that might go with a more conventional image. Just as the music pulls the listener in the directions of both complicity and critique, so also the viewer is caught between experiencing the image as pornography on the one hand and as alienating and problematic on the other. Indeed, in responding to criticism of the advertising in the *IoS*, Jarvis Cocker pointed out that this was precisely the conception of the album cover and advertising, and of the theme of the album itself:

...the idea with that picture was that, intially, it would be attractive: you'd look at the picture and realise it's a semi-clad woman. But then her look is vacant, it almost looks as if she could be dead, or a dummy. So it was supposed to be something that would draw you in and then kind of repel you a bit. That was *on purpose*. (Cocker 1998B)

It was more like a bit of the theme of the record. . .be attracted to something and repulsed by it at the same time. (Cocker 1998c)

Engagement, resistance and critique

This analysis of the track 'This is Hardcore' and its advertising poster has tried to show that there is a far more integral relationship between the title track and poster image than the *IoS*'s assertion (that 'Just to sell a few songs, it shows a woman violated') would suggest. Both display a similarly disturbing ambivalence towards their subject matter – a mixture of collusion and critique. This is not a sign of confusion or incoherence, but rather a deliberate tactic in which critique of a particular ideology (constructions of sex and gender) takes place with, and within, the forms of that ideology (its images and music). In order to experience the critique it is necessary to be familiar with, to be a part of the culture of and in some sense therefore to identify with, the conventions of those very phenomena against which the critique is directed – in this case hardcore pornography. To recoil immediately in horror at such an identification, as the *IoS* does, is to adopt a superficial moral righteousness which never engages with the problem. The irony is that the representation, which is the target of their moral outrage, is itself part of a critique whose purpose is to expose that aspect of patriarchal constructions of sexuality which is at an extreme in the hardcore sex industry. Because the *IoS* sees only the demeaning aspects of complicity in the poster, it also writes off the album. The newspaper can bask in its own self-righteousness while simultaneously accepting advertising (the recent Citroen Xsara advertisement, for example) which, with no critical intent whatsoever, exploits and promotes an image of women which is consistent with the social construction of sexuality at which 'This is Hardcore' is critically aimed:

I think being blatant and hardcore is more honest than putting a model next to something and having everybody buy it. (Cocker 1998c)

Because the *IoS* is not prepared to enter into the collusion at all, it never realises the critique, and its attention is turned away from the real issue – changing the social situation in which women are demeaned – towards an easier target – the suppression of a particular representation of a woman.

And yet the situation is not so clearcut. If the images *can* be interpreted as demeaning and sexist then their critical function is compromised, and if in reality most people see and hear the material as offensively salacious then critique becomes no more than a theoretical possibility. The whole approach that

240   *Eric Clarke and Nicola Dibben*

'This is Hardcore' represents – critique that entails an element of complicity – is a dangerous strategy: The balance between the two subject positions can easily collapse, and the 'defence' that an offensive representation is intended ironically or critically can be used to cynical and exploitative ends. In the words of one Pulp fan:

...even if you computer generate it, write distancing slogans over it, or dress it up in irony, a pornographic image of a degraded woman is always a pornographic image of a degraded woman.[2]

The advertisers who created the publicity for 'This is Hardcore' no doubt realised that they could appeal both to people's lascivious interest in the image, and perhaps its more critical audience.

The compromised critique which 'This is Hardcore' offers, and the danger that it can be exploited to cynical ends, is one reason for trying to consider a different critical stance. The strength of negative critique (of the kind espoused by the Frankfurt School) is its refusal to have any part in an ideology to which it is resolutely opposed. Adornian critique works by a negation of the material forms of ideology. Its weakness is that it risks removing itself entirely from the very sphere within which it aims to exert its influence. It is this as much as anything that led to allegations of a high cultural elitism against the followers of the Frankfurt School. If the remoteness that the Frankfurt School represents is to be avoided, there seems no alternative but to engage with the forms of the dominant ideology and to 'get one's hands dirty', with all the compromises that this entails. By contrast, the strength of the type of critique illustrated by 'This is Hardcore' is its capacity to draw in listeners such that they experience not only the critique of an ideology but are also forced to acknowledge their own involvement in it. Critique involves the recognition of oneself as implicated in the problem: it may have to be uncomfortable if it is really to engage its audience.

Acknowledgements

This research was carried out while Nicola Dibben was supported by a British Academy Postdoctoral Fellowship. The authors are grateful to Island Records for permission to reproduce the image from the album cover 'This is Hardcore'.

Copyright acknowledgements

Endnotes

1. This is discussed in relation to popular music by Terry Bloomfield (1993).

2. Letter of the Week, *Melody Maker*, 27 June 1988, p. 2.

References

Adorno, T.W. 1984. *Aesthetic Theory*, ed. G. Adorno and R. Tiedemann, trans. C. Lenhardt (London)
Bloomfield, T. 1993. 'Resisting songs: negative dialectics in pop', *Popular Music*, 12(1), pp. 13–31
Cocker, J. 1998A. 'Deconstructing Jarvis', Interview in *Ray Gun*, Issue 55
      1998B. 'Festival guide: Sheffield of dreams', *Melody Maker*, 27 June, p. 33
      1998C. Interview in *America Online*
Kelly, A., and Clay, A. 1998. 'Sexist Pulp ads attacked', *Independent on Sunday*, 19 April, p. 19
Leader Article. 1998. 'This is violent. This is offensive', *Independent on Sunday*, 19 April, p. 4
Meyer, L.B. 1973. *Explaining Music* (Chicago)
Tagg, P. 1979. 'Kojak, 50 seconds of television music. Towards the analysis of affect in popular music', in *Studies from the Department of Musicology, Göteborg*, 2
      1992. 'Towards a sign typology of music', in *Secondo Convegno Europeo di Analisi Musicale*, ed. R. Dalmonte and M. Baroni (Trento)

Discography

Pulp, 'This is hardcore', *This is Hardcore*. Island. 524 486–2. 1998
Pulp, 'Sorted for e's & wizz', *Different Class*. Island. 524 165–2. 1995

[17]

Pop and the Nation-State: towards a theorisation

MARTIN CLOONAN

Recent years have seen two noticeable trends in Popular Music Studies. These have been on the one hand a series of works which have tried to document the 'local' music scene and, on the other, accounts of processes of globalisation.[1] While not uninterested in the intermediate Nation-State level, both trends have tended to regard it as an area of increasingly less importance. To state the matter more boldly, both trends have underplayed the continually important role of the Nation-State.

At one level there seems to be a common-sense consensus about the importance of the Nation-State in all political matters,[2] but there has been no coherent account of the way in which Nation-States deal with, and influence, popular music. These processes are outlined in the first, and main, part of this paper. The second part suggests models which might be used to describe the relationship between popular music and the Nation-State. The conclusion outlines the importance of these observations.

First it is necessary to say something about the role of the state. This has, of course, been the subject of intense political debate. In recent years three models of the state have tended to come to the fore: pluralist, élitist and Marxist (Marsh and Stoker, 1995). For my purposes it is sufficient to note that the Nation-State is a body which claims sole jurisdiction over a given territory and the right to implement particular policies within that territory. In order to legitimise its rule the Nation-State may use certain cultural artefacts and will seek to exercise both cultural and political hegemony. Underpinning the state will be, in Weber's famous dictum, the monopoly of legitimate violence over a given territory. However, for my purpose it is enough to note that this monopoly acts as the ultimate guarantor of the policies which will be focused upon here.

At this point it is useful to note how the Nation-State has been underplayed in Popular Music studies in recent years. For example, Simon Frith (1993, p. 23) has argued that the local and global are now so intertwined that 'the national level no longer matters when every household has access to the global media flow'. Although Frith talks here of the national level rather than of the Nation-State, the implication is that the Nation-State is of diminishing importance in an increasingly global world of communications. Ross Harley makes a similar point when he argues that:

National boundaries matter little in the contemporary music world, where a Detroit producer may have more in common with a London-based DJ or a Belgian remixer than anybody in his or her immediate geographic environs. (1993, p. 225)

But while it is obviously possible that people in one location might share musical influences with those thousands of miles away, rather than in their immedi ate environs, they are likely to be subject to different constraints upon how they can indulge those tastes. As will become apparent, the main constraints may be the particular Nation-State which they inhabit. The object of this paper is to argue against the sorts of views expressed by Frith and Harley and to highlight the con tinually important role of the Nation-State in popular music.

Before continuing it is necessary to note that often the local and the nationa are discussed as being the same thing – especially with regard to such places Luxembourg, Finland or New Zealand.[3] But by local here is meant the sub-Nation State level. In other words, local relates to music scenes in regions, cities and so on Musics and musicians which relate to the Nation-State level will be referred to as 'domestic' rather than 'local'. The global begins at a level higher than the Nation-State.

It also needs to be acknowledged that Nation-States often respond to processes at the global level. I do not wish to argue that processes of globalisation are not important, as they obviously are. What is often more important for popular music is the way in which Nation-States vary in their responses to both globalisation *and* popular music. The relative autonomy of many Nation-States also needs some acknowledgement. Overall this paper aims to re-situate the Nation-State as a focus for popular music studies. In order to do this, it is necessary to highlight some of the roles Nation-States can play.

Part one: unsound effects?

There are a number of generalisations that one can make about the role of Nation-States in popular music. Here the most important areas will be outlined, although the list will not be exhaustive. This part concentrates upon various aspects of Nation-State policy and how they impact upon popular music. In particular it examines policies around broadcasting, censorship, the law and culture. It also suggests that the Nation-State is of continuing, and possibly increasing, importance in the politics of identity.

Broadcasting

Within broadcasting, it is undoubtedly true to say that, at least in the West, the Nation-State has retreated from some of its traditional roles in recent years. Deregulation has swept across Europe and, although Malm and Wallis (1992, p. 217) have suggested that this phase might have peaked already, the growth in satellite television stations suggests that the process is by no means over. There has also been debate over how far – if at all – Nation-States can prevent broadcasts they disapprove of from coming across their borders. The internet is the starkest example of this.

Nevertheless, the Nation-States cannot simply relinquish their roles as controllers of broadcasting. As Malm and Wallis (ibid, p. 252) have noted, airwaves are finite resources which need regulating. Nation-States remain the prime source of such regulation, as even transnational agreements rely on Nation-States to police them. Moreover, few Nation-States have decided that they would rather not have a state broadcasting service. Even the United States, which has *not* got a state-run roadcasting service, still seeks to control the output of the commercial stations via ne Federal Communications Commission (FCC).

With regard to the provision of broadcasting services, debate has generally entred upon what mixture of public and private provision is appropriate and few dvocate *total* deregulation. In this debate popular music has seldom featured as he major focus of attention, but Nation-States *do* have to take policy decisions about popular music and broadcasting.

For example, in February 1994 the Iranian government banned all non-Iranian music from its airwaves (*Guardian* 14 February 1994) and in July 1996 it was reported that Afghanistan was about to make a similar move (*Guardian* 16 July 996). Censorship is dealt with in greater detail below, but at one level debates about censorship are concerned with what might be the appropriate sort of music o allow on a Nation-State's airwaves.

It is Nation-States which determine the ratio between private and commercial broadcasting within their borders. In 1996 this took a somewhat bizarre turn in Britain when the band Status Quo took out a court case against the state broadcasting company, the BBC, for the failure of its Radio 1 station to play their single 'Fun, Fun, Fun'. The court action failed, but what was at stake in the case was the role that a publicly owned broadcasting station should play. The debate was partly one about how a public service should be fulfilled. For Status Quo and their lawyers the role of Radio 1 was to play the most popular records. As 'Fun, Fun, Fun' had entered the charts it should, they held, have been played on the nation's most popular radio station. In their defence Radio 1 claimed that their job was to promote new music, not just simply to reflect the charts. The judge accepted Radio 1's arguments and dismissed those of Status Quo. The band faced a £50,000 bill for costs and were told by the judge: 'Maybe Radio 1 don't like your records – they don't have to' (*NME* 13 July 1996).

This case was not of only parochial interest for Radio 1. As a radio station which is under public-ownership and part of a state broadcasting service, Radio 1 nevertheless plays a very important *international* role. For example, its role in promoting 'Britpop' has been widely recognised.[4] The implication of this is that had important changes *not* taken place at Radio 1, then its audience – and implicitly the international audience – would have been fed a daily diet of Status Quo and Phil Collins rather than of Blur and Oasis. Instead Radio 1 chose to stress its cultural worth. It committed itself to up and coming bands and to live music. This helped to differentiate it further from the commercial stations which are more chart-based and play a much narrower range of music.

Looking beyond the narrow confines of Britain, perhaps the most interesting debates on broadcasting and pop have concerned the desirability or otherwise of imposing quotas to ensure the presence of domestic music on the airwaves. Putting aside the problems of defining exactly what music counts as belonging to which Nation-State,[5] there can be little doubt about the importance of such quotas, especially for those musicians working within smaller, less powerful, Nation-States.

In terms of New Zealand, Pickering and Shuker (1993, p. 21) have gone so far as to suggest that the issue of quotas is *the* most important issue for Nation-States facing a large amount of imported music. Pointing out that often the only way that New Zealand artists could get airplay was to leave the country (Shuker and Pickering 1994, p. 274),[6] they have argued that quotas are necessary for New Zealand music (as they define it[7]) to survive. The French government has also taken the decision to back quotas (Laing 1992, p. 135; Sage 1996) which have again been implemented in Australia and Canada (Grenier 1993; Turner 1993) with, argue Shuker and Pickering (1994, p. 270), beneficial results for domestic musicians.

But the quota debate is one which goes well beyond Western Nation-States. Tanzania, Israel and Jamaica are amongst those Nation-States which have also used quotas (ibid, p. 277). Malm and Wallis (1992, p. 98) note that Kenya implemented quotas in 1980 and 1988, and they credit Radio Tanzania's 100 per cent quota the 1970s onwards with helping Tanzanian music survive (ibid, p. 122). They also note that the use of quotas was successful in raising the amount of domestic popular music that was played in Trinidad and Jamaica (ibid, p. 254). The overall impact of quotas may be ambiguous, but they are certainly an example of the continuing importance of the Nation-State in popular music. In instances such as that of Radio 1, Nation-State broadcasting policies might have an international importance; in others, such as Tanzania, the impact might be primarily domestic. But all show the continuing importance of Nation-State policies.

Radio broadcasting has been concentrated upon here as it is still arguably the most important promoter of popular music.[8] Nevertheless, it is obviously the case that the advent of video and, in particular, of MTV, has had an important impact on popular music. But here too the Nation-State has intervened. At least one state has sought to counter the influence of MTV. In Turkey in 1994 Kral TV ousted MTV as the most popular music television. Kral TV was broadcast in Turkish and was set up following a ban on MTV using Turkey's terrestrial stations. The Turkish government feared that if MTV was beamed into Turkey, then Kurdish broadcasts might follow (*Guardian* 24 August 1994).

Meanwhile in Sweden, Malm and Wallis (1992, p. 168) note that a decision to produce a weekly Swedish-only pop video show, Listan, on the state-run Swedish TV, had an important impact on domestic musicians. So MTV has not had it all its own way. Some Nation-States have been standing *in* its way.

Thus it is necessary to be more cautious about the impact of MTV than some have been. It *might* be pioneering global tastes, but its impact is still mediated by the Nation-State. More recently MTV itself has recognised the need to reflect national and regional youth cultures, as well as seeking to be global. Meanwhile, it is important to remember that satellite is still a minority pursuit in Western Europe, while in remote parts of Africa even radio signals are hard to pick up. It is thus a little premature, to say the least, to start talking of anything like a transglobal culture, especially in terms of broadcasting pop.

Censorship

The issue of censorship is clearly closely aligned to that of broadcasting and general control of the media. There is a long history of records and videos being banned from the airwaves within various Nation-States for various reasons and it seems unlikely that this process will end, as the decision by Radio 1 to ban The Prodigy's 'Smack My Bitch Up' in 1997 shows. But censorship takes place at various levels and under various Nation-State regulations and statutes. What is defined as being 'obscene' varies from Nation-State to Nation-State. Some constitutional edicts may change the entire nature of the censorship debate. For example, the First Amendment in the American Constitution which guarantees the right to free speech can be invoked in a way which is impossible in other Nation-States. Laws on censorip – and the ability and willingness of Nation-States to implement those laws – ve an important impact on the type of pop which is permissible within Nation-ate boundaries.

Perhaps most important of all is the fact that Nation-States are still concerned ith controlling immigration. Border control has been used to regulate the type of pular music – particularly live popular music – that enters a Nation-State. For ample, Michael Jackson was banned from performing in South Korea in 1993 cause his flamboyant stage show was thought to be unsuitable at a time when e government was bringing in an austerity package (*Daily Post* 14 August 1993). on Maiden found themselves banned from Chile in 1992 (*NME* 1 August 1992) ter the Catholic Church had described them as Satanists, and they were banned so from the Lebanon in 1995 (*Observer* 24 September 1995). This followed a spate teenage suicides after which the police raided record shops and seized various ck records. The Interior Ministry then decided to ban heavy metal groups from uring the country (ibid).

Steve Jones (1993) has documented how immigration control was used in the nited States as an effective part of cultural policy. By restricting the amount of reign bands that could play, the Americans effectively adopted a protectionist olicy on behalf of domestic musicians. Elsewhere more overt censorship has con-nued. In New Zealand in 1992 there were attempts by the police to prevent Ice T om playing in Auckland (Sluka 1994, p. 62) and an unsuccessful attempt to pros-cute the track 'Cop Killer' under the country's Indecent Publications Act. In 1997 crackdown on heavy metal fans in Egypt by SSI, the State security service, was ported (di Giovanni 1997) and it was also disclosed that Britain's internal security rvice, MI5, had kept tabs on musicians such as John Lennon, Crass, The Sex Pistols nd UB40 (Norton-Taylor 1997).

Even when allowed to perform, some artists have had their acts censored. In 995 when Roxette played Beijing they were forbidden from including the lines 'I ee you comb your hair/I like the way you undress now' from their hit 'How Do ou Do!'. The words 'rock-n-roll' were also vetoed (*Guardian*, 21 February 1995). ack in the West, censorship in Germany has involved such things as the song Helmut Kohl', which the band Die Artze were forbidden to play live (Denselow 989, p. 273), and banning records by Kiss and Cancer (*NME* 10 November 1990). n 1996 the two members of the French rap band Nique Ta Mére (NTM – Fuck Your Aother) were jailed for three months and banned from performing for six months fter a private prosecution was brought against them for their 'Je Nique Le Police' I Fuck the Police) which advocated pissing 'on the brainless police machine' (*NME* 3 November 1996). The band later appealed and remained out of jail. Although he prosecution was private, it is the Nation-State which regulates censorship and he conditions under which such actions take place.

While censorship of pop has occurred in a number of democratic capitalist Nation-States, it was also widespread in more undemocratic capitalist Nation-States uch as South Africa, Turkey (Stokes 1992, p. 215) and Argentina. In the latter case he military dictatorship which ruled the country often took drastic steps to sup-ress Rock Nacional gigs which took place between 1977 and 1983. Tactics used ere included using tear-gas on fans; rounding them up; and 'advising' halls not to ook such gigs (Vila 1992, p. 214).

But it is the Nation-States of the former Communist bloc which perhaps show the most overt forms of state censorship. Sabrina Ramet's book *Rockin' The State*

(1994), documents a number of forms of censorship in the former eastern blc
Apart from banning records and performances by Western performers, the
Nation-States sought to control domestic musicians. Often this was done by issuir
licences for live performances and only allowing those with such licences to be ab
to perform. Such a system was used, for example, in Czechoslovakia.[9]

Ramet's book also documents that in Bulgaria the band Signal were banne
from performing in 1982 because they caused 'excessive excitement' (Ramet 1994
p. 7). The Bulgarian live scene was also hampered in 1987 when a 9 p.m. curfe
was placed on under 19-year olds (Ashley 1994, p. 151).

In the German Democratic Republic in 1975 there was a purge of
musicians including the Leipzig band the Klaus Renft Combo, who were forced
disband because their continued existence was thought to be a threat to the workir
class (Leitner 1994, p. 30). Censorship of songs often occurred on the basis of or
word or phrase such as 'assembly line' (Wicke 1992, p. 84).

In Hungary the band the Spions were forced to disband in the 1970s (Kür
1994, p. 77), and a survey of Budapest pop musicians carried out in 1986 found tha
all the musicians questioned had suffered some sort of censorship during the
careers (Szemere 1992, pp. 96–7). One result of such censorship was a plethora c
songs with double-meanings (ibid, p. 97). In Poland in 1983 the pro-Solidarity ban
Prefect were banned from performing in the larger cities (Kan and Hayes 1994, p
51).

Recorded music also suffered. For example, in the Soviet Union only pro
fessional bands singing in Russian were recorded (Survilla 1994, p. 227). In additio
there were bans on records by such artists as The Who, The Sex Pistols and Kis
(*Index on Censorship* No.6, 1985). However, according to Ramet (1994b, p. 7), onl
Albania was successful in instituting a total ban on foreign popular music.

Anna Szemere (1992, p. 96) argues that overall the debate in Eastern Europ
was more often over whether a song should be recorded at all, rather than, as i
more often the case in the West, a battle over something that is already available i
the market place. But it is obviously the case that the regimes of Eastern Europ
had a profound effect on popular music there. Censorship was almost routinel
applied. As Peter Wicke has noted (Garofalo 1992, p. 10), one effect of this was t
make popular music 'Political' in Eastern Europe in a way that was inconceivabl
in the West.

The bans referred to immediately above come from a past era in Easter
Europe, but at a minimum they show the censorial *potential* of the Nation-State
Even if various media are now able to flout international boundaries, control anc
regulation of *live* music is likely to remain the domain of the Nation-State. More
over, it is too often assumed that the de-regulation of broadcasting is here to stay
but it is at least *possible* that this will *not* be the case. The logic of globalisation i
that of capitalism and the history of capitalism is that for every era of liberalisatior
of trade, there is another one of closed borders and protectionism.

In sum, censorship – in one form or another – by Nation-States seems bound tc
continue. But this is only one area where the state is still required to be a policeman

Law and Copyright

A Nation-State's legal system will impact upon its popular music. For example,
Malm and Wallis (1992, p. 29) have noted that laws set parameters to music business

tivities, which suggests that the Nation-State has a continuing impact via its legal system on the treatment of cultural artefacts such as popular music. An example is ow raves in Britain have suffered greatly since the 1994 Criminal Justice Act, sections of which were aimed specifically at outlawing certain types of rave.

Paul Rutten (1993, p. 43) suggests that a government's most important role ith regard to popular music is in the regulation of economic and cultural processes nd that copyright is a key area here. He has pointed out that lack of sufficient opyright laws will, and has, hit the amount of investment that has been made in he former Soviet bloc (ibid, p. 44). The problem is even more exaggerated in the hird World (Sreberny-Mohammedi 1991, p. 10; Laing 1992, p. 132). Copyright is so hard to enforce in Nation-States which have traditions of music being seen as collective – as opposed to individual – expression (Malm and Wallis 1992, p. 29).

For example, Japan has no tradition of claiming rights (Harker 1995, p. 43) nd its current copyright legislation dates back to only 1971. Music recorded before his time can be sold without royalties being paid. In May 1996 the EU filed an fficial complaint to the World Trade Organisation about the slow rate of reform of apanese copyright legislation (*Reuters* 30 May 1996).

It is clearly much harder for smaller Nation-States to enforce copyright Harker 1995, p. 68) and some national organisations are simply not able to. Thus ob Marley was unable to enforce copyright within Jamaica and had to rely upon he American BMI organisation to do so for him (Malm and Wallis 1992, p. 56). In 983 Kenya introduced a new copyright law, but this apparently had little effect as he state was unable to enforce it (ibid, p. 89).

Copyright is one area that the music business is particularly concerned about n the late 1990s as potential profits are denied in Nation-States which cannot, or vill not, either prevent the manufacture of pirate CDs and tapes, or introduce copyight legislation which suits the major entertainment industries. Thus in February 995 PolyGram attacked the EU for not protecting its markets from imported Chinese-manufactured CDs as that the United States had done (*Guardian* 22 February 995). In July 1996 the International Federation of Phonogram Industry (IFPI) called or joint European and American action against Chinese and Bulgarian pirate CDs Reuters 12 July 1996). Bulgaria was the centre of much industry anger, with Rick Dobis, President of Polygram Continental Europe, accusing its pirates of 'open theft' Wroe 1996).

Meanwhile the issue of Chinese CD manufacturing plants took centre stage in ong-running trade talks between the United States and China. China is seen as the next big market for the international music business, but that business is wary of the lack of copyright there (Long 1995; Spencer 1996). However, China has made some moves towards recognising Western concepts of copyright by, for example, allowing IFPI agents to work within its borders (Harker 1995, pp. 44–5).

In the West, Dave Laing (1992, p. 134) has pointed out that while EC laws on copyright have been harmonised to some extent, the copyright collecting agencies are still organised on *national*, Nation-State lines. He argues that these are likely to stay so because:

1. Most campaigners on copyright issues are concerned with the music of their own countries.

2. British music is regarded within the EC as part of an Anglo-Saxon onslaught which is driving French and German music off the airwaves.

Thus again the Nation-State retains importance even when there are inte national agreements in place. Although copyright is in the process of being harmo ised in the West, many parts of the rest of the world have trouble enforcing an copyright laws. The willingness and/or capability of Nation-States to take on th task is of crucial importance to investment decisions of foreign firms. In many way copyright sees Nation-States acting in the interests of international capital, but relative autonomy of the state in deciding how, or even whether, to police copyrigh shows that the Nation-State is of continued importance within the business of popu lar music.

Cultural policy

Cultural policy is often a matter of how much Nation-States wish to intervene i the market. Certainly a number have felt the need to promote domestic cultura goods. For example, Australia has a national Music Day (Breen 1993, p. 76), th Sandanista government in Nicaragua saw music as something of a national asse (Denselow 1989, p. 164) and Britain launched a National Music Day which ha taken place from 1992 onwards – albeit with marginal impact. It should also b noted that various national awards and competitions can also affect the amoun and type of popular music produced within a Nation-State.

Many Nation-States, such as Britain, have had a tradition of conservative cul tural policies which have favoured the so-called high arts over the low. Fo example, in Britain government funding for the arts goes to art forms which 85 pe cent of the population never go to and only 3 per cent of the population visit regu larly (*Guardian* 9 February 1994). In this respect it is important to note, as Annabelle Sreberny-Mohammedi (1991, p. 135) does, that a Nation-State's cultural policies ca *define* culture within its borders. If pop is not defined as culture it is unlikely to state help. Indeed, Roy Shuker (1994, p. 71) has suggested that debates about cul tural policy are part of the battle over the very meaning of pop. Britain is just on place where pop has been regarded as the domain of the market rather than of the state, although Simon Frith (1993, p. 14) has noted how pop in Britain has benefitted from a great deal of indirect support such as Radio 1. But such indirect support has often proved inadequate.

In Britain in 1994 the Main Music Agenda was set up to represent the range and diversity of British music and to protest about the fact that: 'from the current debate we might conclude that not much is going on except for symphony orches tras and London opera companies' (*Guardian* 20 January 1994). This protest had little impact but by 1998 the new Labour government announced that a new com mittee was to be set up by the Department of Culture, Media and Sport to examine issues of concern to the music industry (*Guardian* 7 January 1998). Again the Nation-State was seeking to influence the fate of popular music.

This had previously been apparent in other Nation-States with cultural poli cies that had been designed to stimulate domestic music-making. For example, in Holland 15 per cent of a levy which was raised on blank tapes went to Dutch music and the Dutch Rock Federation obtained arts grants from central government from 1975 onwards (Rutten 1993, pp. 39, 48). Levies on blank tapes remain an area where the Nation-State can raise revenue for developing domestic talent. Often moves to develop such talent are attempts to prevent the home country from being swamped by mainly American culture (Bennett *et al.* 1993, p. 10; Breen 1993; Straw 1993).

Nation-States have obviously varied greatly in their cultural policies and how they have responded to international conditions. Some have set out to use music to build the nation,[10] while others have almost ignored culture altogether and had no policy as such. In the former Soviet states the other side of the censorship coin was that some regimes tried to promote certain types of popular music, as is also shown by Ramet (1994, p. 7).[11] Although Keith Negus (1993, p. 311) has argued that, in the age of the multi-national corporations, it is hard to associate any cultural artefact purely with one Nation-State, it seems clear that Nation-States have to adopt some attitude towards musicians who come from their particular patch and attach importance to this. Here policy becomes vital.

It is also important to acknowledge that Nation-State policies outside the cultural can also impact on popular music. To again cite British examples, the decline of art schools, which produced many musicians in the 1960s, and the decline of the college live circuit in the wake of increasing student poverty, can also be seen as having important effects on up-and-coming bands.

Taxation policy is also important. This has had various effects on pop. For example, in New Zealand records were taxed but books were not on the grounds that the former were *not* culture (Shuker 1994, p. 55). In 1996 Michael Jackson said that he would not be playing any more gigs in Germany because of high taxes in the country (*Reuters* 8 May 1996). Political situations in a Nation-State can also affect the output of popular music. Here Edward Larkey (1992, p. 175) notes that Austria was too affluent to engender an active punk scene, while Tony Mitchell (1992, p. 195) argues that the onset of punk in Poland can be seen as commencing with the introduction of martial law in 1983. Thus various Nation-State policies continually impact upon popular music.

Identity

It is important to note that nationalism is the most successful ideology ever.[12] As Anthony Smith (1991, p. vii) has noted, it is the most enduring identity myth in the world. The desire to build and rebuild Nation-States continues unabated, as recent events in Eastern Europe continue to show. It is often argued that it is increasingly hard to locate a particular musical form within a particular nation, but historically music has often played an important role in constructing national identity. Generally it has been classical and folk music that have been used in such constructions, but it is also often claimed that pop has the capacity to say something about the particular Nation-State from which it allegedly sprung.

As I have argued elsewhere (Cloonan 1997), it is interesting to note again how the term 'Britpop' came to prominence in Britain from 1994 onwards. At one level this was just a marketing term or an attempt by a journalist to create a scene which did not actually exist. Nevertheless, the debate around 'Britpop' shows how popular music is still used as a means to identify Nation-States. In the case of 'Brit-pop' the nation seemed to be represented by white, male, heterosexual artists working in the pop–rock idiom. Often it was claimed that certain acts represented the British nation or Nation-State in some way or another. Numerous examples could be quoted and the following give a taste of them.

A 1992 *Sunday Times* article claimed that:

a study of The Smiths, XTC, The Jam, Madness, Magazine or many other 'English' pop group could tell us a great deal about the national landscape in the last 20 years. (Taylor 1992)

There have been other claims about how pop reflects Englishness.[13] Suede'
first album was described as 'an instant English classic, all decaying council block
and weird sex' (Spencer 1993). Morrisey was described as having an 'English view
of the world' (Evans 1994, p. 6) and his *Vauxhall and I* album was said to have th
spirituality of 'a dirty British dawn and a savage British dusk' (ibid, p. 11). Hi
previous band, The Smiths, have also been linked with a particular type of English
ness (Stringer 1992).

At one point it was almost impossible to pick up an article on Blur withou
the word 'English' leaping out. Thus they were said to have songs 'boasting a very
Englishness' (Hibbert 1995), to make 'quintessential, modern English pop' (Shelley
1995, p. 12) and, in particular, to have an 'Orton-esque Englishness' (ibid, p. 15).[14]

It also seems impossible, in Britain at least, to read about U2 without them
being described as Irish, or, more particularly, to read about The Manic Street Pre
achers without the fact that they are Welsh being mentioned. Somehow it seems to
matter to the writers and readers of these articles that those artists come from par
ticular Nations or Nation-States. Following on from this are claims that these artists
can tell us something about the countries from which they come.[15] In the case o
'Brit- pop', the bands who attracted this epithet were all *English*, implying
while Welsh and Scots acts might be able to speak on behalf of their nations they
did not articulate what it meant to belong to a larger Nation-State. (The situation
in Northern Ireland is subsumed in its political situation. It is suffice to note here
that Northern Irish bands were not included by the press as being within Britpop's
ambit.)

By December 1995 it was alleged that 'Britpop' was dead (Sweeting 1995). But
this was not to prevent some politicians from trying to use 'Britpop' for political
purposes. In March 1996 the former Secretary of State for Wales, erstwhile chal-
lenger for the leadership of the Conservative party and leading New Right thinker,
John Redwood, made a somewhat farcical attempt to appropriate Britpop for his
Euro-sceptic cause. He claimed that, amongst other things, the band the Lightning
Seeds showed the English that they had a distinct culture (Redwood 1996). Again
an ill-defined, but apparently close, relationship between pop and the nation was
proposed.

There have been numerous other examples of this outside Britain. Sabrina
Ramet has shown a similar pattern in the former Yugoslavia where punk rock and
the nation were equated (Ramet 1992, p. 103). It is also a sobering thought to see
how pop was used in the wars in that country. One report described the music
cassettes produced by Serbs and Croats which eulogised their respective nations
and, unsurprisingly, vilified their opponents. This was described as a 'war of music'
(Lukovic 1993, p. 9). The symbolic height of the link between pop music and the
war was the marriage of the 'Queen of turbo folk', Ceac, to the alleged Serbian war
criminal, Commander Arkan, in February 1995 (*Guardian* 20 February 1995).

In somewhat less traumatic circumstances, in Australia the trade unions have
called for intervention in the pop industry in order to help forge national identity
(Breen 1993, p. 70). In France supporters of the quota system said that it helped to
preserve national identity (Sage 1996). In Germany Hans Giessen (1995, p. 124) has
argued that pop texts provide the best means for showing the rise of Nazi sentiment
in the 1990s, partly because there were no other sources available. In Austria Larkey
(1992, p. 187) has argued that support for Austropop is part of a struggle over what
parts of the international market will be used to delineate cultural and national

lentity, and in December 1995 a battle for the soul of Irish music was reported
MacRory 1995).

Further examples of the continued importance of the Nation-State as a source
f identity can be seen in the Eurovision song contest. At one level this contest is
ne height of kitsch, but it has also caused international incidents. In 1995 Norway
won the contest, but the Swedish judges awarded the Norwegian entry no points.
1 Sweden the Norwegian victory was followed by xenophobic coverage in parts
f the Swedish press. Eventually this led to an apology from the Swedish ambassa-
or to Norway (Culf 1996). Again popular music was held to be bound up with
ational identity and lack of respect for this caused a minor diplomatic incident.

In 1996 the Euro '96 football tournament took place. In Britain this resulted in
. minor row after Beethoven's 'Ode to Joy' was chosen by the BBC to go along with
ts coverage of the tournament. Education Secretary Gillian Shepherd and Con-
ervative Party chairman Brian Malwhinney criticised the use of music by a German
ather than British composer (*Observer* 2 June 1996). Meanwhile in Germany the
national ZDF television station chose Oasis' 'Look Back In Anger' to go with its
overage because, in the words of a spokesman, 'we wanted to find a suitable theme
hat was especially British' (*NME* 16 June 1996). A number of songs were recorded
o tie in with the tournament and England's went to the top of the domestic charts.
Again the link between popular music and national identity was shown, albeit
somewhat crudely.

Simon Frith (1996, pp. 110–111) has rightly argued that identity is not so much
an object as a process and that it is imposed from the outside rather than coming
from the inside (ibid, p. 122). In the case of pop it is clear that some commentators
have sought to *impose* national identities upon popular musicians, while others have
suggested that such musicians have an important role to play in defining national
identity.

At a minimum it seems that popular music has a continuing role to play in
constructing national identity. At one level this is mere marketing or scene-making,
but at another popular musicians have been said to encapsulate something about
the nation. Nation-States need to foster allegiances and pop has been one of the
sites where such allegiances have been sought and articulated.

To sum up the argument thus far: it has been shown that the Nation-State is
of continuing importance in popular music. Two levels of this – policy and identity – have been suggested. At one level this is something of a tautology. But, as
noted in the introduction, the Nation-State has been somewhat underplayed in
Popular Music Studies recently. Having redressed the balance a little, I now want
to lay out some ideal types of Nation-State-popular music relationships.

Part two: a framework of relationships

It is apparent that there are three types of Nation-State-popular music relationship
which I shall call authoritarian, benign and promotional.

The authoritarian. Such Nation-States might most usefully be exemplified by
those of the former Soviet bloc. In these Nation-States there was generally strict
control of recording, a licensing system for live musicians and strict control of
imports. Authoritarian regimes are sensitive to *all* cultural artefacts.

In some ways authoritarian states might be seen as something from the past,
but Nation-States such as Algeria, China, Egypt, Iran and Afghanistan still strictly

control cultural artefacts. Whether such control can be maintained in the futur
might be a moot point, but in the immediate future a decline in *attempts* to contrc
seems unlikely. In all the celebrations that followed the collapse of Communism i
Eastern Europe, the fact that free, uncensorial Nation-States would follow seemec
to be almost taken for granted. But events such as the rise of Islam in Nation-State
such as Algeria and Afghanistan and the war in the former Yugoslavia suggest tha
censorial Nation-States are just as likely.

The benign state. Britain might be seen as the paradigmatic example of this
Benign Nation-States control live music, but generally leave popular music to th
market, indirect subsidies not withstanding. They have censorship and broadcast
ing laws, but tend to regard the state's role as being to referee between competing
business interests rather than controlling or promoting popular music. Popula
music is not high on the cultural agendas of such Nation-States. They will react
events in the popular music field, such as raves and 'obscene' records, but are
generally content to let the music industry go about its daily business uninterruptec
and to reap the taxes that industry success brings.

Promotional. In such Nation-States popular music is regarded as something o.
a national asset. Nation-States in this category are likely to be concerned abou
being dominated by Anglo-American music and will try to devise policies, such
radio quotas and promotion of domestic music, to combat this. Examples of thesε
sorts of states would include, at various times, Canada, France and Holland.

It should be noted that there is some overlap between these ideal Nation-State
types. Most especially authoritarian states will also often be promotional.
(1994, p. 9) gives examples of states which assisted various types of domestic music
in order to combat Anglo-American music.

One unifying factor with regard to Nation-States is that they often react to
events at the global level, but they differ in that some have tried to be pro-active.
Perhaps the best Nation-States as far as popular musicians are concerned are promotional ones, but there are lots of problems with this proposal.[16]

Conclusion: bringing it all home

One reason why the continuing importance of the Nation-State in popular music
should be acknowledged is that fans, musicians, academics and other grassroots
supporters of popular music can often feel powerless in the face of globalisation
and multi-national corporations, but Nation-States retain the potential for intervention. The Nation-State has always acted somewhat ambiguously in its role as
protector of culture and different parts of capital, but many Nation-States retain the
power to intervene in the global market and to help local musicians reach a wider
audience than they otherwise would. The results may be contradictory but it is hard
to see what other mechanisms to promote domestic talent might be available, other
than *major* changes of heart from the major record companies. The important point
to bear in mind is, as Pickering and Shuker (1993, p. 21) have noted, that the desire
to express allegiance to domestic products and artists is not *necessarily* a reactionary
one. To admit that some forms of popular music need Nation-State assistance can
be to defy the market rather than to promote xenophobia.

It was noted earlier that the role of Radio 1 in promoting Britpop has now
been recognised. This followed structural changes within this publicly owned
national radio station. In other words, a semi-autonomous part of a Nation-State's

broadcasting network helped to promote music that was held in some way to represent certain characteristics of that Nation-State. The rise of 'Britpop' was tied into the broadcasting policies of a particular Nation-State, but its impact was international.

In examples such as this the Nation-State can step in to help some forms of popular music in a way that the market may not. It might even be the case that it is the Nation-State, rather than the market, which is the guarantor of diversity in pop. British radio is one example of this. Deregulation has tended to bring more of the same, such as a proliferation in oldies and MOR stations, rather than diversity.[17] In this case Radio 1 has shown that the Nation-State, rather than the market, can be the most successful provider of diversity. Although less regulated systems, such as those within the United States, have led to more stations, it is arguable that none of these stations covers the breadth of popular music that Radio 1 does. Rather, they cater for niche markets. Meanwhile Nation-States' subsidies for the arts have also helped to encourage diversity, such as those distributed via the Arts Councils in Britain and the National Endowment for The Arts in the United States.

Malm and Wallis (1992, p. 256) have rightly argued that the main point is to get the widest possible range of musical activity. It is doubtful that this can be achieved without some input from Nation-States. Nation-States vary enormously in the amount of power they have, but they remain vitally important in the areas of policy and identification. It is still the case that the location and regulatory strength of one's Nation-State will determine in large part the popular music environment one lives in. The point is that fans, academics and musicians should be trying to get as much input as possible into Nation-State policies, however contradictory some of the results might be.

This paper has suggested that far from being of little importance, the Nation-State continues to be of major importance in pop. I agree with Annabelle Sreberny-Mohammedi (1991, p. 135) that:

> we require a third-term between the two terms of 'global' and 'local', that recognizes the separate level of 'state' structures and national policy-making.

This paper has attempted to interpret the role of the Nation-State in popular music. The point remains, as Marx would tell us, to change it.

Endnotes

1. For the 'local' see Cohen (1991a, 1991b, 1995), Frith (1995) and Street (1995). For globalisation see Bennett *et al.* (1993, pp. 10–12; 21–24), Longhurst (1995, pp. 49–53), Negus (1993) and Robertson (1992). But also note that Cohen (1991b, p. 343) says that pop is getting more both more international *and* more local at the *same time*.

2. See, for example, *Political Studies* (1994).

3. This can cause some confusion. For example, Mitchell's 1996 book *Popular Music and Local Identity* deals with music in four Nation-States. But his section on New Zealand includes discussion of the 'Dunedin sound' – a local sound associated with the sub-national level. For this reason I prefer to use the term 'domestic' music for national music and 'local' for *sub-national*. See also Regev (1992).

4. See, for example, Spencer (1996).

5. As far as popular music is concerned there seems to be a consensus that national music is generally a form of Anglo-American music which has been given a particular local twist. This idea comes from Simon Frith and is noted by Malm and Wallis (1992, p. 212).

6. It is interesting to note that while New Zealand academics are interested in ending a situation where domestic musicians have to leave the *country* to get a market, Cohen (1991b) has noted that in Britain supporters of Liverpool's

206   *Martin Cloonan*

music scene have been concerned to prevent local musicians from leaving the *city*.

7. See Shuker and Pickering (1994, p. 272).

8. There is evidence from Britain to back up this claim as a March 1990 survey found that more people bought records after hearing them on the radio than through any other medium (*NME* 31 March 1990).

9. See Mitchell (1992) for more on censorship in Czechoslovakia.

10. As, for example, in Tanzania under the regime of Nyerere (Malm and Wallis 1992, p. 114).

11. See also Wicke and Shepherd (1993).

12. See Smith (1991, p. vii) and Pryke (1993, p. 3).

13. See Fisher (1993) and Sinker (1987).

14. The references here are to England, which is a nation but *not* a Nation-State. It is, however, the dominant nation within the Nation-State of Britain, the Nation-State which gave its name to 'Britpop'.

15. This is actually nothing new. For example, Laing (1972) made an attempt to outline types of Englishness in pop.

16. See Malm and Wallis (1992, pp. 188–189) for some of the pros and cons of subsidies.

17. See Barnard (1989).

References

Ashley, S. 1994. 'The Bulgarian rock scene under communism', in *Rockin' The State*, ed. Ramet, S.P. (Oxford), pp. 141–63

Barnard, S. 1989. *On The Radio* (Milton Keynes)

Bennett, T., Frith, S., Grossberg, L., Shepherd, J. and Turner, G. (eds) 1993. *Rock and Popular Music* (London)

Breen, M. 1993. 'Making music local' in *Rock and Popular Music*, eds Bennett, T., Frith, S., Grossberg, L., Shepherd, J. and Turner, G. (London), pp. 66–82

Cloonan, M. 1997. 'State of the nation: "Englishness", pop and politics in the mid-1990's', *Popular Music and Society*, 21, 2 (Summer), pp. 47–70

Cohen, S. 1991a. *Rock Culture in Liverpool* (Oxford)

1991b. 'Popular music and urban regeneration: the music industries on Merseyside', *Cultural Studies*, 5, 3, pp. 332–46

1995. 'Localizing sound', in *Popular Music: Style and Identity*, eds Straw, W. Johnson, S., Sullivan, R. and Friedlander, P. (Montreal), pp. 61–8

Culf, A. 1996. 'Nulpoints no more', *Guardian*, 18 May, p. 26

Denselow, R. 1989. *When The Music's Over* (London)

di Giovanni, J. 1997. 'A deadly divide', *Guardian*, 4 October, Magazine, pp. 20–4

Evans, J. 1994. 'The object of love', *Guardian*, 26 February, Magazine, pp. 6–11

Frith, S. 1991. 'Anglo-America and its discontents', *Cultural Studies*, 5, 3, pp. 263–9

1993. 'Popular music and the local state', in *Rock and Popular Music*, eds Bennett, T., Frith, S., Grossberg, L., Shepherd, J. and Turner, G. (London), pp. 14–24

1996. 'Music and identity', in *Cultural Identity*, eds Hall, S. and du Gay, P. (London), pp. 108–27

Garofalo, R. (ed.) 1992. *Rockin' The Boat* (Boston)

Giessen, H.W. 1995. 'The new German Nazism: pop song texts as indicators', *Popular Music and Society*, 19, 1, pp. 107–32

Grenier, L. 1993. 'Policing French-Language music on Canadian radio: the twilight of the popular record era?', in *Rock and Popular Music*, eds Bennett, T., Frith, S., Grossberg, L., Shepherd, J. and Turner, G. (London), pp. 119–41

Harley, R. 1993. 'Beat the System', in *Rock and Popular Music*, eds Bennett, T., Frith, S., Grossberg, L., Shepherd, J. and Turner, G. (London), pp. 210–30

Harker, D. 1995. 'It's a jungle sometimes: the music industry, the crisis and the state', unpublished article

Hibbert, T. 1995. 'Toony boppers', *Mail on Sunday*, 30 April, Night & Day Section, p. 32

Jones, S. 1993. 'Who fought the law? The American music industry and the global popular music market' in *Rock and Popular Music*, eds Bennett, T., Frith, S., Grossberg, L., Shepherd, J. and Turner, G. (London), pp. 83–95

Kan, A. and Hayes, N. 1994. 'Big beat in Poland', in *Rockin' The State*, ed. Ramet, S.P. (Oxford), pp. 41–53

Kürti, L. 1994. 'How can I be a human being? Culture, youth and music in Hungary', in *Rockin' The State*, ed. Ramet, S.P. (Oxford), pp. 73–102

Laing, D. 1972. 'Roll over Lonnie (Tell George Formby the news)', in *Rock File*, ed. Gillett, C. (London), pp. 45–51

1992. ' "Sadness", Scorpions and single markets: national and transnational trends in European popular music', *Popular Music*, 11, 2, pp. 127–40

Larkey, E. 1992. 'Austropop: popular music and national identity in Austria', *Popular Music*, 11, 2, pp. 151–85

Leitner, O. 1994. 'Rock music in the GDR: an epitaph', in *Rockin' The State*, ed. Ramet, S.P. (Oxford), pp. 17–40

Long, S. 1995. 'America readies for war over bootleg Beatles', *Guardian*, 28 January, p. 23

Longhurst, B. 1995. *Popular Music and Society* (Cambridge)

Lukovic, P. 1993. 'Guns 'n' cassettes', *Guardian*, 1 April, Part Two, pp. 8–9

MacRory, A. 1995. 'The uncivil war for the soul of Irish music', *Guardian*, 15 December, Part Two, pp. 8–9

Malm, K. and Wallis, R. 1992. *Media Policy and Music Activity* (London)

Marsh, G. and Stoker, G. (eds) 1995. *Theory and Methods in Political Science* (Basingstoke)

Mitchell, T. 1992. 'Mixing pop and politics: rock music in Czechoslovakia before and after the velvet revolution', *Popular Music*, 11, 2, pp. 187–203

1996. *Popular Music and Local Identity* (London)

Negus, K. 1993. 'Global harmonies and local discords: transnational policies and practices in the European recording industry', *European Journal of Communication*, vol .8, pp. 295–316

Norton-Taylor, R. 1997. 'Rank and file in cold war paranoia', *Guardian*, 26 August, p. 4

Pickering, M. and Shuker, R. 1993. 'Radio gaga: popular music and the quota debate in New Zealand', *New Zealand Sociology*, 8, 1, May, pp. 21–59

Political Studies. 1994. Special Issue, 'Contemporary Crisis of the Nation State?'

Pryke, S. 1993. *Nationalism as Culturalism: A critique* (Newcastle)

Ramet, S.P. 1992. *Balkan Babel* (Oxford)

(ed.) 1994a. *Rockin' The State* (Oxford)

1994b. 'Rock: the music of revolution (and political conformity)', in *Rockin' The State*, ed. Ramet, S.P. (Oxford), pp. 1–14

Redwood, J. 1996. 'There's always England', *Guardian*, 23 March, p. 13

Regev, M. 1992. 'Israeli rock, or a study of the politics of "local authenticity"', *Popular Music*, 11, 1, pp. 1–14

Robertson, R. 1992. *Globalization: Social Theory and Global Culture* (London)

Rutten, P. 1993. 'Popular music policy: a contested area: the Dutch experience' in *Rock and Popular Music*, eds Bennett, T., Frith, S., Grossberg, L., Shepherd, J. and Turner, G. (London), pp. 37–51

Sage, A. 1996. 'Gallic pop silences Brits in funless France', *Observer*, 18 February, p. 27

Shelley, J. 1995. 'Pop art', *Guardian*, 12 August , Weekend Section, pp. 12–16

Shuker, R. 1994. *Understanding Popular Music* (London)

Sinker, M. 1988. 'Look back in anguish', *NME*, 2 January, pp. 14–16

Sluka, J. 1994. 'Censorship and the politics of rock', *Sites*, 29 (Spring), pp. 45–70

Smith, A. D. 1991. *National Identity* (London)

Spencer, N. 1993. 'Men in suits take the fun out of rock 'n' roll', *Observer*, 26 December, Arts Section, p. 12

1996. 'Britpop's morning glory', *Observer*, 30 June, p. 15

Sreberny-Mohammedi, A. 1991. 'The global and the local in international communications' in *Mass Media and Society*, eds Curran, J. and Gurevitch, M. (London), pp. 118–38

Stokes, M. 1992. 'Islam, the Turkish state and arabesk', *Popular Music*, 11, 2, pp. 213–27

Straw, W. 1993. 'The English Canadian recording industry since 1970', in *Rock and Popular Music*, eds Bennett, T., Frith, S., Grossberg, L., Shepherd, J. and Turner, G. (London), pp. 52–65

Street, J. 1995. '(Dis)located? rhetoric, politics, meaning and the locality', in *Popular Music: Style and Identity*, eds Straw, W. Johnson, S., Sullivan, R. and Friedlander, P. (Montreal), pp. 255–64

Stringer, J. 1992. 'The Smiths: repressed (but remarkably dressed)', *Popular Music*, 11, 1, pp. 15–26

Survilla, M.P. 1994. 'Rock music in Belarus' in *Rockin' The State*, ed. Ramet, S.P. (Oxford), pp. 219–41

Sweeting, A. 1995. 'Pop goes the Britpop', *Guardian*, 8 December, Part Two, p. 11

Szemere, A. 1992. 'The politics of marginality: a rock musical subculture in socialist Hungary in the early 1980s', in *Rockin' The Boat*, ed. Garofalo, R. (Boston), pp. 93–114

Taylor, D.J. 1992. 'Heavens knows he's miserable now . . .', *Sunday Times*, 14 June

Turner, G. 1993. 'Who killed the radio star? The death of teen radio in Australia' in *Rock and Popular Music*, eds Bennett, T., Frith, S., Grossberg, L., Shepherd, J. and Turner, G. (London), pp. 142–55

Vila, P. 1992. 'Rock nacional and dictatorship in Argentina' in *Rockin' The Boat*, ed. Garofalo, R. (Boston), pp. 209–29

Wicke, P. 1992. 'The times they are a-changin'', in *Rockin' The Boat*, ed. Garofalo, R. (Boston), pp. 81–92

Wicke, P. and Shepherd, J. 1993. 'The cabaret is dead: rock culture as state enterprise – The political organization of rock in East Germany', in *Rock and Popular Music*, eds Bennett, T., Frith, S., Grossberg, L., Shepherd, J. and Turner, G. (London), pp. 25–36

Wroe, M. 1996. 'Slav pirates milk music market', *Observer*, 4 August, p. 8

[18]

'Believe'? Vocoders, digitalised female identity and camp

KAY DICKINSON

In the two or so years since Cher's 'Believe' rather unexpectedly became the number one selling British single of 1998, the vocoder effect – which arguably snagged the track such widespread popularity – grew into one of the safest, maybe laziest, means of guaranteeing chart success. Since then, vocoder-wielding tracks such as Eiffel 65's 'Blue (Da Ba Dee)' and Sonique's 'It Feels So Good' have held fast at the slippery British number one spot for longer than the now-standard one week, despite their artists' relative obscurity. Even chart mainstays such as Madonna ('Music'), Victoria Beckham (with the help of True Steppers and Dane Bowers) ('Out of Your Mind'), Steps ('Summer of Love') and Kylie Minogue (the back-ups in 'Spinning Around') turned to this strange, automated-sounding gimmick which also proved to be a favourite with the poppier UK garage outfits (you can hear it on hits such as Lonyo/Comme Ci Comme Ca's 'Summer of Love', for example).

As this article progresses, I want to examine how and why the popularity of this timbral modifier ballooned in the subsequent years, and to think through the new ideas it has bounced with it around the representational practices of the voice, of computer-made music, of femininity and of homosexuality. More specifically, I shall be homing in on the recent appropriation of the vocoder by female artists. I hope to demonstrate that, although it has traditionally been the preserve of certain more avant garde male performers, from 1998 until the present, women working within the genre of pop have joined their throng, creating some fascinating and potentially empowering new meanings for the vocoder. However, before focusing on these more recent applications, it seems apt to cast around in the vocoder's more than sixty-year history to see how it has been handled and what it has meant to its listeners.

The vocoder's history and meanings

The vocoder was invented in Germany in 1939 as a means of disguising military voice transmissions. Etymologically, the word is an abbreviation of 'voice coder' and so intentionally bears the connotations of 'coding' human expression, of delivering it in cyphers. Like so many military technologies, the vocoder eventually found its way into the music industry and has been manufactured and marketed by companies such as Korg, Roland, E.M.S. and Moog.

At that time, it was a piece of analogue equipment which worked by superimposing a ghost of a chosen – usually vocal – signal over an instrumental line, most often a keyboard or guitar track. A vocoder will divide the vocal source signal (which gets called the 'modulator') into various frequency bands which can then be used to process a 'carrier' signal – the keyboard or guitar track – and render it more sonically complex. The result is an overlap where the instrument takes on the timbre and articulation of the vocals – including the coherence of the lyrics – whilst superimposing some of its own texture and a more emphatic sense of its tempered pitch, and thus its melodic priorities. The polyphonic capacities of the keyboard also allow the user to translate the modulator line into a chord, giving the impression of a chorus to a single voice. With the intervention into voice recording of the keyboard (and, on digital models, an on-screen keyboard), it becomes very easy to imprint 'real notes' onto vocal lines. As glissandi and more 'human', momentarily out-of-tune 'misses' are obscured, pitch changes become decidedly jolty and 'robotic' – perhaps the vocoder's most recognisable signature and signifier.

Unsurprisingly, then, early pop interest in the vocoder came from (mainly male) musicians with heavy investments in types of futurism, artists such as Kraftwerk, Stevie Wonder, Devo, Jean-Michel Jarre, Cabaret Voltaire and Laurie Anderson. Later, the vocoder became a stalwart technology of early electro and has, since then, infused contemporary hip hop and the work of more retro-tinged dance acts such as Daft Punk and Air.

Perhaps in response to this rising curiosity about a device that had, since the mid-1980s, seemed almost obsolete, on 26 September 1998 the Prosoniq Orange Vocoder plug-in for VST, a Cubase variant, was launched. Consequently, a realtime vocoder audio plug-in was available for the DAW (digital audio workstation) which has pretty much become the dance music industry standard because of its long-standing versatility and power. Patches included within the program offered such voices as 'rotating robot', a knowing nod towards the android analogies which have grown up around the vocoder. More than any other factor, the arrival of this particular piece of software at the end of 1998 helped open the flood-gates for the slew of vocoder-laden tracks which followed in the wake of the mainstream success of 'Believe'.

However, the very noticeable vocoder-style vocal lurch to be found in 'Believe' emerged between these developments: in the digital era, but before the more easy-to-use vocoder software hit the market. Mark Taylor (the song's remixer) devised an interim mix 'n' match solution after initially experimenting with a Korg VC10 vocoder. He describes the process:

I played around with the vocals and realised that the vocoder effect could work, but not with the Korg; the results just weren't clear enough. So instead, I used a Digitech Talker, a reasonably new piece of kit that looks like an old guitar foot pedal, which I suspect is what it was originally designed for. You plug your mic straight into it, and it gives you a vocoder-like effect, but with clarity; it almost sounds like you've got the original voice coming out the other end. I used a tone from the Nord Rack as a carrier signal and sequenced the notes the Nord was playing from Cubase to follow Cher's vocal melody. That gave the vocals that 'stepped' quality that you can hear prominently throughout the track; but only when I shifted the Nord's notes back a bit. For some reason, if you track the vocal melody exactly, with the same notes and timing, you hardly get any audible vocoded effect. But I was messing about with the Nord melody sequence in Cubase and shifted all the notes back a fraction with respect to the vocal. Then you really started to hear it, although even then it was a bit hit-and-miss. I had to experiment with the timing of each of the notes in the Nord melody sequence to get the best effect. (Uncited quotation offered by Lynn Fuston of 3D Audio Inc. in response to my chat-room plea)

This sucking of the human voice backwards into the less nuanced scale types of the computer's tone bank gives it a certain cyborg feel common to earlier vocoders. What happens, then, when these two concepts (human and android) overrun each other? What can it mean to mangle the specific ideas that each has come to stand for?

Sooner or later during these exercises, the manipulated human voice bangs into some deeply rooted beliefs about expressiveness within popular music, beliefs which so often grow out of how we constitute 'the human body' at any given time. The vocoder's thumb-print for the most part spans the zone of timbre, of vocal texture (the area of the guttural and the nasal, to give just two examples) where pop is arguably at its most corporeal. As it rubs up against all these other timbral indexes, the vocoder must necessarily negotiate its place within the 'palpable humanity' so central not only to pop's appeal, but also often to its worth/worthiness. Through a semantic ripple effect, the vocoder's sound then carries along certain questions about music's position *vis-à-vis* technology and the bodily self, where one starts and the other stops, or whether distinctions of this order are, in fact, unhelpful.[1]

Technology, authenticity, the voice and corporeality

Evidently, there are conventions and conditions controlling what 'real' talent and 'real' music are at any given time. As Leach points out:

> Markers for authenticity in rock are the presence of a talented individual or small group formed organically from 'naturally' knowing one another, driven to write songs as the only outlet for their (personal) emotions and (political) views, who forge the music and play it themselves, typically in the standard musical arrangement of two different guitars, lead and bass, with optional keyboard, obligatory drums and a vocalist who might also be a guitarist, and is usually the songwriter unless (as is possible) she is only a woman. The fundamental White masculinity of these groups is epitomised in their organic unity and the way the group channels its identity through one singer who forms the expression of a group-originated song. Such a band should progress naturally as artists (rather than being an industry confection and being told what to do) and would be able to perform live (rather than requiring the artifice of technology or the commercialisation of recording). (Leach 2001, pp. 146–7)

These comforting and involving fantasies about value and meaningful expression have been and continue to be outrageously selective in their recourse to technology, labour and self-hood. Guitars and microphones – to pick the easiest examples – are somehow less intrusive in their mediation of artistic expression than other equipment, such as the vocoder.[2] Evidently, the capacity for you to *be* the music (and for the music to be you) filters through these hand-picked technologies. In turn, these are governed by certain dominant power groupings which lord over the likes of genre division and access to equipment, and which are marshalled according to categories such as class, 'race', and, the two I want to concentrate on here, gender and sexuality. By the same token, one's sense of truth and truth to one's identity inevitably incorporate gender position and how life is experienced according to one's access to power.

The convention of loading the notion of artistic authenticity onto the human voice weighs heavily upon what the sound of the vocoder means.[3] For many listeners, specific musical practices (including a capitalisation on certain timbres) can seem to make flesh the Romantic chimera of unfettered, pure expression. In particular, certain vocal conceits are cherished as exceptionally direct conduits to the core of the self, to some sort of emotive truth, with Bob Dylan's scratchiness or James

Brown's grunts winning more of these types of prizes than the smooth, non-grating and physically less aligned vocal offerings of the likes of ABBA.

While the strategic manufacture and manipulation of these notions of authenticity have long been an upheld truth-claim within academia, this philosophy cannot undermine these transmissions' ability to strike chords within their audiences by plucking certain accultured emotional strings. The expulsion of feeling through the voice, through visceral bodily vibrations, consequently bears the potential to trigger sentient responses within the listener too, responses which vary from elation to the threat of harm. The issue we need to focus on here is not the tactility *per se*, but how its meanings and consequences reverberate through equivocating networks of power. The involvement of the body – also a fluctuating cultural factor – means that all the attendant politics from which it is woven and which it attracts cannot be erased from the sphere of popular music and discourse. That notions of the body might simultaneously wander amidst debates over mechanisation not only begs discussions of the 'standardisation' of leisure and culture, but also of pain and harm, of inclusion and exclusion as they are translated by these political arenas into concepts of the self.

Evidently, vocoder tracks vividly highlight the inextricable bond between subjectivity and mechanisation. They propose a dichotomy between the vocoded voice and the more 'organic' one, which then crumbles under closer inspection, most obviously because both are presented as exuding from the same human source-point. Cher's voice in 'Believe' does not strike us as coming totally from within; nor, though, should any recorded voice which has inevitably been minced through various pieces of machinery before we hear it, including those which turn it into and back out of zeros and ones, adding and subtracting along the way. And that is just the technological side of things. For the most part, however, non-professional discourses surrounding the recorded voice treat it as extremely close reproduction rather than rendition or a representation. Yet in vocoder tracks, the vitality and creativity inherent in the technologies in use stand centre stage, pontificating on questions of authenticity and immediacy. Almost incidentally this becomes an onslaught on a certain economically powerful, supposedly more 'real', yet often restrictive system of agency.[4] As McClary says of Laurie Anderson's vocoder work: 'The closer we get to the source, the more distant becomes the imagined ideal of unmediated presence and authenticity' (McClary 1991, p. 137). The key question here is not: where is Laurie Anderson, but, if this is one Laurie Anderson, what can she mean?

That said, singularity and autonomy evidently loom large in performers' personae and in their selling power – the fall-out from confounding these certain accepted standards of truthful performance often infects them with derision or worse. Many of the current vocoder tracks are shrugged off as meaningless gimmickry because they spring from that lowlier, more seemingly ersatz genre, pop (more of which later) – a reaction which shows some particularly destructive snobbery in action. Taking the issue of pop further, it also becomes difficult to by-pass entrenched systems of expertise and *work* as they reside within not only authenticity, but also artistic polish and effortlessness (or perhaps lack thereof) within respectable and respected music. The vocoder, after all, is often seen as a sparkly bauble which distracts us from a lack of talent hiding 'underneath'. The degree of individual star labour undertaken within pop is frequently considered to be lesser than that of, say, rock, especially if musicians do not write their own material,

annot cut it live, have to have their pitch digitally corrected, and so on. Although he vocoder outwardly fits this bill (it is read as being done to, rather than done by, the artist's voice), the flagrant embrace of technological opacity we hear in its mechanised obviousness opens up further, perhaps more fascinating, questions circing some tenuous notions of single-handed musical genius.

However, the issue here is not so much the need for an acceptance of mediation's place within creativity, but the urgency of discerning how power is henceforth distributed to those seen performing with these technologies, those working with them – on stage and behind the scenes – and those consuming them. What bodies are being represented sonically and visually? What work is being done by them or for them? What technologies are countenanced within the musical canons and the economies of the music industry? And how do political movements (such as those grouped as feminism) that are eager to shed particular types of subordination sit within these matrices? This last issue seems all the more current because, for the first time in its history, the vocoder is now much more readily conjoined with if not the female voice, then at least the 'feminised' one.[5] Apart from Laurie Anderson's experiments,[6] this marks a distinct shift in the device's application and this must surely echo through what the vocoder, women's voices and men's rights to technology come to mean here. With this in mind, the role of recording technologies in the construction of female musical corporeality and feminist reactions to it cannot go unexplored.

As Downey, Dumit and Williams argue: 'In problematizing the body and foregrounding the politics and pleasures of sexualization, feminist studies have articulated just who and what is reproduced (And by what sorts of technologies) when a "human subject" is recognized.' (Downey *et al.* 1995, p. 345) For these three (and many other theorists besides), the selection processes involved in the multiple technological ways and means of representation trail down from and up to specific conglomerations of power. Which types of technological mastery garner prestige and which do not (knowing one's way around Cubase ranking significantly higher than being able to work a 'domestic' or sweat shop tool like a sewing machine) are telling here. Music technologies, then, also moonlight as systems of both control and empowerment; in the instance of the vocoder, this discursive formation constitutes women, as I am hoping to argue, in a peculiarly polysemic manner.

Women's musical participation, as Green (1997) points out, has traditionally short-circuited around core technology and this would include our decreased access to revered pop musical instruments like the guitar and certain computer software. Green argues that, for many female music stars – many more than men – the *body* is their instrument, a condition which helps promote the age-old rooting of women in the 'natural' and the anti-technological. Yet the vocoder effect, however it is produced (and even by whom), impairs the 'naturalism' of the female voice not by ignoring it, but by creating the illusion of rummaging around inside it with an inorganic probe, confusing its listener as to its origin, its interior and its surface. At this point, oppositions of inside or outside, organic or inorganic, whole or dispersed, haze over, and their ability to hold court in so facile and divisive a manner waivers considerably.

These concerns have circled pop for an indefinitely lengthy period, although with a different flight pattern each time. Pop, maybe more than other genres, has seen many skirmishes over artifice's actual meaning and worth, but, although pop has economic clout here, its ideas often go unheard in the bustle to cynically cash in without admitting any actual faith in the genre's politics. It is not uncommon to hear sentiments along the lines of: 'It is only pop and the vocoder is just another means of pulling a wool spun of talentlessness over the eyes of the gullible'. What pop might have to say is less easily locked out, though, when its 'underhand' means of deflection are dabbled with by musicians of consensus-approved singing ability such as Sonique. When artists who are not currently seen to need to augment their skills so desperately and who cannot so easily be accused of hiding behind gim-micks turn to these self-proclamatory tools, they use their power to instigate a much prouder acknowledgement of computer co-enterprise.

Similarly, writers such as Celia Lury (1998) – here talking more broadly about prosthetics – are eager not to predict this as a disintegration of the self or even a loss of control and instead chart it as the growth of a more possessive individualism. This concept of the prosthesis undoubtedly has a lengthy string of historical precur-sors within our everyday lives and our means of expressiveness, being preceded by such accoutrements as guns, guitars, spectacles and tooth fillings. For Lury, 'through the adoption of prostheses, the previously naturally or socially fixed or determined aspects of self-identity are increasingly brought within the remit of choice or, better, selection' (Lury 1998, p. 19). The use of prosthetics in this sense – and this would include women singing with vocoders – is maybe most profitably thought of not as a replacement for something lacking, but as a booster added on to enhance one's capabilities. This may be somewhat utopian given both the prices involved in choosing to purchase such implements, and the music industry's hold over its artists' creativity and its meanings in the first place. However, if things like vocoders are more actively thought of as tools rather than shields or parasites, women's attitudes towards them might prove distinctly less defensive. Speaking more broadly, perhaps the most salient point to remember here is that the fluctu-ation between performances of the self and technologies is of seismic proportions. With the ground shifting so dangerously, whole sections of society are at risk of being dragged into chasms from which it is enormously difficult to climb out. The extent to which pop cultural devices such as the vocoder might act as ropes for women in this plight is what I intend to investigate next.

Deliberately coupling with machines: female musicians and cyber ident-ity

In edging towards a discussion of the positions for women within music technol-ogy, it might prove fruitful to head off into the realm of theory most commonly labelled cyber-feminism. Although often divergent in their thinking, key exponents such as Braidotti (n.d.), Haraway (1991), Wakeford and Squires (1995) and Plant (1997) are linked through their fascination with constructions of self-hood on boundary-lines and with the potential for new technological interactions to effect female control and power. Whilst cyber-theorists rarely analyse music-making software, many of their observations about the wearing away of some of the harsher distinctions between the emotional/human and the mechanical/inorganic seem equally applicable to readings of the vocoder. Inevitably, some of these writers' approaches are more hopeful than others (Plant, for example, delights in cyberspace as almost inherently empowering for women), and some are more perturbed by economic disability. Braidotti is perhaps the most cautious:

Thus, while the computer technology seems to promise a world beyond gender differences, the gender gap grows wider. All the talk of a brand new telematic world masks the ever-increasing polarisation of resources and means, in which women are the main losers. There is strong indication therefore that the shifting of conventional boundaries between the sexes and the proliferation of all kinds of differences through the new technologies will not be nearly as liberating as the cyber-artists and internet addicts would want us to believe . . . The alleged triumph of high-technologies is not matched by a leap of the human imagination to create new images and representations. Quite the contrary, what I notice is the repetition of very old themes and cliches, under the appearance of 'new' technological advances. (Braidotti n.d.)

The question that now arises is whether certain uses of the vocoder sympathise with a reactionary or an empowering configuration of femininity. Before answering this, however, it seems more pressing to delineate the vocoder's specific cyber-potential.

The vocoder's popularity may well lie in the symbolic bridge it is seen to form between the vacillating perceptions of the human and the machine (or, more specifically, the digitising, encoding machine). It can also be interpreted as a bond holding the two close when either concept becomes too flighty and abstract to be related to the other. Obviously, though, anything which draws attention to border-lines might also help elucidate old-guard distinctions which have been drawn up in the past. However, that said, simple dualisms do not sit well within the contemporary vocoder's timbral output and, although these circumstances might not necessarily inspire drastic re-negotiation, it does formulate a very different relationship between the organic and the inorganic in comparison to the textures of other dance musics.

As elsewhere in the history of music, the (usually female) voice often serves as an emblem for pure human physicality within dance genres (this is particularly true of house and garage), while variations with more of an investment in stark automation (such as techno) purposefully eschew vocal lines. Returning to my key example, 'Believe', on the other hand, maintains many of the instrumental qualities of these genres, but plots out its vocal aesthetic differently. Its instrumental timbres, which have very little grounding in 'traditional'/non-computer generated instrumentation, evoke the trancier end of techno. Shorter sci-fi stabs meet surging upward flourishes which also link 'Believe' stylistically to disco and Hi-NRG, associating the track with certain gay subcultural histories, a point that I discuss later. However, unlike most dance musics, 'Believe' is also very song-like with an alternating rather than a terraced structure. The vocals are uncharacteristically high in the mix – as they would be in a pop track – making 'Believe' an obviously presentable and popular hybrid of technologies and genres. In more than one sense, then, it dwells on borderlines. Following dance music conventions (which often seep back and forth between other genres), Cher's vocals are frequently double tracked or looped to create an echo effect. This evokes a sense of the multiplicity and incoherence of the self through the voice, but in ways which most pop fans are comfortable with. Interestingly, the vocoder effect only tinges the odd phrase during the verses and does not pervade the chorus at all until the fade out, where it then colours everything Cher sings. Here Cher phases in and out of traditional notions of vocal 'reproduction' and deliberately obvious track manipulation. Unlike the use of the more sustained vocoder heard in, say, Kraftwerk's music, Cher's employment of it teeters between what is currently constituted as the organic and the inorganic, rather than heralding some bold and pure technological futurism.

Likewise, in the lyrics to 'Believe', Cher draws on love, strength and the pain of loss – supposedly visceral emotions – without pushing them away from her technological self. Here we return to the impossibility of distancing so-called manipulated artifice from the present understanding of pain. 'Do you believe in life after love?' encapsulates what are considered to be exclusively 'human' and concepts (most obviously 'believing' and 'loving'). In this sense, the song exemplifies the argument that damage and pleasure, although frequently shunted into the realms of the exclusively 'authentic' and corporeal, are necessarily techno-logically delineated – in music and elsewhere – but none the less emotionally felt because of this.

Cher's assumed identity also encompasses many of these ideas about the body and technology and, as she cannot help but be illustrative of her gender, this becomes a feminist concern. It develops into an even more urgent one when the politics of her plastic surgery face up to the greater debates surrounding the representation, production and perception of women. The stakes are again raised because Cher's 'Believe', unlike more self-effacingly created dance tracks, follows the rules of pop stardom. The song is solidly 'Cher' and, although Cher is not solidly organic or singular as a site of production, she is still a star persona, a firm identity to which much of the song's meaning can be attributed, however speculatively. This 'Cher', though, now seems as much assembled as grown. She looks almost as though she has donned a smooth carapace with wrinkles and ambiguous edges airbrushed out. This sharp, surgically altered Cher, so different from the hair-flicking 1960s version resplendent in tactile, organic suede and sheep-skin, assumes a much more droid-like set of signifiers. As a side-line, surely this could also be understood as a partial departure from the sadly more typical female rationale for having cosmetic surgery: to become more 'ordinary', to not stand out (Davis 1995). If this is the case, then it could be argued that Cher's more flagrant and odd transmogrifications may well deserve more sustained attention from feminist theorists because of their very flirtation with the *plastic* (rather than so rigidly and exclusively cosmetic) realms of non-essential surgery.

However, there are definitely less ambiguous or potentially destructive aspects of Cher to pin feminist dreams on. As I have suggested, within her contemporary, more visually and vocally machinic incarnation, she has not lost her coherence. She perpetuates a very firm sense of self and, whilst she mutates from time to time (as all good technology does), she is engineered according to principles which equate with notions of autonomous choice. This seems largely possible because of her position within the genre of pop (so often seen as a disempowering space). In pop's forms of stardom and fandom, the desire for iconic presences is practically inescapable, opening up certain fortuitously haphazard opportunities for assuming strength through solidity. Granted, there have been many attempts to shoot Cher's potency from under her by dismissing her as a freak. However, although the impetus behind this (most notably the cosmetic surgery) may make her anathema to many strains of feminism, it cannot dispel everything she means within representational politics: she is too popular and too much a part of discourse to ignore. That she is a woman (however 'she' is constituted) raises questions not only about where machines and humans stop and start, but also about how this inevitable conjunction might lessen or enhance female power. This model of a woman's use of a vocoder strongly prompts us to think through some newer possibilities for women's profitable social mobility through music (and beyond) which might

…clude a construction of a femininity which wields much more automated power
within its conception of female selfhood.

Women, vocoders, power and agency

Admittedly, several men have featured on vocoder singles, most notably
Gianfranco Randone of Eiffel 65 with 'Blue (Da Ba Dee)'. However, it is telling that
the band's album is called *Europop* in reverence to a musical style not usually associated with heterosexual masculinity. During this post-'Believe' period, no long-
standing male artists of the stature of Madonna (no Bryan Adamses or George
Michaels) have used the device, nor even have the more 'feminised' male performers such as the contemporary boy bands. While a vocoder frequently pops up
on the chartier UK garage tracks (featuring mainly on the female vocal sections),
the femininity of that genre should also be taken into account. Garage has rapidly
developed into a romance music,[7] a dance genre which appeals to women more
than many other club musics. Garage clubs are often spaces where women appear
fairly powerful (albeit in very traditionally feminine ways) and where machismo
from men seems more out of place than at, say, drum and bass events. So, whilst
men have maybe not left the arena altogether, they are definitely having to share
this space that was once more exclusive, looking on as its geography is changed by
the newly arrived immigrants.

With women's increasing centrality within contemporary vocoder use established, it now remains to be seen whether this can actually benefit a feminist politics
of representation. Certainly, as I have argued, women are usually held to be more
instinctive and pre-technological, further away from harnessing the powers of
machinery (musically and elsewhere) than men, so performers such as Cher can
help by putting spanners in these works. Many people are not familiar with the
word 'vocoder', but they know what it is and often refer to it by terms like 'that
Cher noise'. This attributes mastery to a woman, even if she was not part of that
particular production process, and here the benefits of solid pop stardom become
evident. Even if the vocal manoeuvre was not negotiated by 'the real Cher', she
does become a metaphor for what women could possibly achieve with more pres-
tigious forms of technology.

There is also something potentially liberating, as I have suggested, about Cher
pointing out the computer mediation of her voice. Cultural studies has long
applauded women who engage in gender parody of a visual order – such as
Madonna and Annie Lennox – but, in some ways, this can lessen the worth of the
work they do within their careers as musicians. A vocoder intervenes at an unavoidable level of *musical* expression – it uses the medium as the message – encouraging
the listener to think of these women as professionals within music practice. Interestingly, the voice is a sphere where a lot of female artists with complex philosophies
about masquerade maintain a particularly staid paradigm: that soul or hip hop
stylisations are representative of a supposedly more honest form of communication,
that African–American musical form is somehow more 'authentic' (Annie Lennox
and Lil Kim, for example, work in these ways).

However it is carried out, though, a ludic attitude towards gender is not necessarily a feminist endeavour in its own right. In pointing out the performative side
of femininity, a rationale should perhaps be delivered and women's political motiv-
ations often clash. By lending herself to workout videos and cosmetic surgery, Cher

has toyed with what are enormously problematic issues for many feminists. Armed with much persuasive empirical data, writers such as Chapkis (1986), Bartky (1990) and Wolf (1991) have defined most cosmetic surgery as fragments of the larger web of capitalist, patriarchal oppression. There is definitely an amount of consternation surrounding Cher, asking whether she throws herself under the scalpel in a subversive or a reactionary manner – in ways which undo or reaffirm certain restrictive notions of female beauty. Certainly Bordo (who discusses Madonna, but with equal applicability to Cher) is enormously critical of most interpretations of body modification as 'postmodern play', arguing that there needs to be a greater acknowledgement of how cosmetic surgery reinforces limiting and age-old ideas of beauty and Otherness. She stresses that, 'This abstract, unsituated, disembodied freedom . . . celebrates itself only through the effacement of the material praxis of people's lives, the normalizing power of cultural images, and the sadly continuing social realities of dominance and subordination' (Bordo 1993, p. 289). So, whilst Cher herself as a triumphantly active and sexual older woman, at what cost does she do so? She does not necessarily look good for her age – through some very expensive surgical decisions, she simply does not look her age at all. These are mixed messages indeed and they may well have economically debilitating repercussions which both fall into and help maintain the standard and often insurmountable contradictions implicit in upholding femininity. Kathy Davis, in perhaps the most sensitive investigation of cosmetic surgery, offers an alternative analytical framework – one which is more forgiving of women's struggle for agency using the limited tools offered up by patriarchal structures:

[the issue] is situated on the razor's edge between a feminist critique of the cosmetic surgery craze (along with the ideologies of feminine inferiority which sustain it) and an equally feminist desire to treat women as agents who negotiate their bodies and their lives within the cultural and structural constraints of a gendered social order . . . Cosmetic surgery [and here I would also wish to input vocoder use – KD] can be an informed choice, but it is always made in a context of limited options and circumstances which are not of the individual's own making. (Davis 1995, pp. 5–13)

Yet it may seem all too easy for someone as powerful as Cher to benefit from or subvert the rules which govern the choices women can make about their bodies. This insurgency is perhaps the beauty of the Cher persona, but also maybe its most frustratingly inimitable quality as concerns 'ordinary' women leading 'ordinary' lives.

With all these arguments at the front of our minds, perhaps what Cher represents is less muddling a point of identification for a certain type of man than it is for women. This is something I shall be tackling later, but first I want to continue with an exploration of the extent to which 'Cher' might come across, in certain instances, as male. One perhaps vital part of her track's inception marks this out: 'Believe' was produced by two men, Mark Taylor and Brian Rawling, and Cher did not write it either. Can this factor cut short the power I have already ascribed to vocoded female articulacy? Are Taylor and Rawling just other types of surgeon moulding 'Cher' into something which cannot help but represent masculine dominance and the male resuscitation of a waning female singing career? Or is there still a lot to be said for the fact that pop's systems of stardom place the *female* Cher at the song's helm? As Bradby (1993B) points out, within dance music, the female vocalist is usually in a more transient position; she is often 'featured' rather than a secure member of any outfit. Within these practices, and sampling in particular, it

·ould not seem untoward to derive extremely disempowering readings from male ·roducers chopping chunks out of women's performance.

But Cher is something different from that. As I have argued, Cher-as-not-man the acknowledged presence here – as whole as any form of representation will ·llow. Her fetishisation has encased her in a kind of armour – she has been 'technol- gised' as it were – and the end result works more in her favour. On the topic of ·etishism, (heterosexual) male attraction to an android or digitised woman – from ·1etropolis' robot to Lara Croft – need not simultaneously speak ill of feminism ·mply because it might pander to the tastes of an often drearily predictable type ·f straight man. Similarly, although male production and responsibility are a glar- ·1g issue here, they may well not be able to outshine what Cher has to offer the ·e-negotiation of women's musical presences. This is fundamentally a matter of ·eflecting attention away from the replicative and the productive and focusing ·nstead on representation. Although not entirely omnipotent or emancipating, the ·ortunately misconceived citation of Cher as source point here does offer us food ·or thought and inspiration. This is a temporary fast-track to the advantages of ·ppearing technologically adept within music production, of assuming the implied ·wnership which accidentally springs from some of the systems of pop iconogra- ·hy. If this seems like playing dirty, then the rules by which the rest of the industry ·perate (particularly as regards the exploitation of female artists) need to be taken ·nto account.

With these kinds of cards laid on the table, it is hardly surprising that female ·isteners might find this rather an uneasy alliance – one similarly sullied by Cher's ·osition within the politics and economics of body modification. Having potentially ·ut myself off at the pass here, I now want to draw on extra troops who have been ·ager to accrue something beneficial from Cher's presence: gay men.[8] To do this, I ·ieed to search out, more specifically, the position of camp within cyber-theory.

Gay men, camp, cyber theory and the politics of popular culture

·For quite some time now, gender's relation to (digital) technology has occupied ·academics and, within this and of particular interest here, there have been various forays into the possible inter-plays between embodiment and disembodiment that they manifest. The favourite topic of discussion here, without a doubt, has been the ·chat room and how it might or might not confound standard strictures of gender or sexuality. However, the dynamics of chat rooms have much to do with one's limited access to any given subject's appearance or voice – quite the reverse of how the vocoder functions. As yet, there seems little work on what happens when the links between the audio-visually perceived body, gender and sexual identity are not eroded, when large portions of the product are passed off as non-digitally reproduced. The cyborg we see and hear and how it relates to sexuality, or, in this instance, to camp, has not really provoked much interest, despite definite parallels in each's complication of the 'natural' and the 'normal'. Cher, a recognised icon within gay male culture, in some senses draws the two together, although she is preceded by a definite history of technologies manifesting certain homosexual sensi- bilities. While the camp markers of fussiness and snippy asides can be witnessed in the representation of automated entities (HAL in *2001: A Space Odyssey*, KIT in *Knight Rider* and *Star Wars'* C3PO, for example), these technologies are often thought not to be fluffy and gorgeous enough to be camp. There might also be an

assumption that the sex-less droid is automatically pumped out as heterosexual k
default, or that sexuality is not an issue (although aesthetic alignment most certain
has to be). Camp, after all, is not a sexual practice.

To focus this argument, it would, again, be wise to home in on Cher's use
the vocoder as perhaps the first exception to a practice which was, at the tim
still, for the most part, heterosexualised:[9] Laurie Anderson may question normativ
gendering but she is less interested in sexuality, and UK garage (unlike its America
forerunner) does present a decidedly straight front. Unlike these musicians, Che
fits snuggly into the diva role so beloved of various gay cultures. More specificall
she maintains the lone, rather monumental fronting of a dance track in the wa
that, say, Gloria Gaynor or Ultra Nate have done. Lyrically, 'Believe' also invoke
a theme familiar to gay dance classics: the triumph and liberation of the dowr
trodden or unloved. This song is a bittersweet declaration of strength after a brea
up and, by saying 'maybe I'm too good for you', Cher conjures up certain
to the vocabularies of gay pride.

One of camp's more pervasive projects is a certain delight in the inauthentic
in things which are obviously pretending to be what they are not and which migh
to some degree, speak of the difficulties of existing within an ill-fitting publi
facade – something which evidently concerns 'Believe'. The track also volunteers
reliable amount of resolution: although it accords with contemporary notions of th
ersatz, it is nonetheless touching and expressive and it achieves this withou
resorting wholly to certain restrictive concepts of authenticity which are implicitl
grounded in straightness. Cher's affront to and dismissal of fraudulence's bad repu
tation shines forth from her position as an 'impostor' within a dance scene she i
too mainstream and too old to be truly welcomed into. She is usurping a culture o
pleasure which would ordinarily deny her access, and her jubilance, despite no
belonging, loops back into camp and certain strategies of queer everyday life.

Hand in hand with this enjoyment of the unconvincing comes a partiality for
things which are maybe out of date, which have fallen by the wayside, and this
again, shows support for the neglected underdog. This maps conveniently onto
vocoder use once more: its timbre seems reedy and more a 1970s or 1980s evocation
of robotry than a newly contemporary effect. Like Cher herself, it has hardly been
a recent 'latest thing' – what all the kids are clamouring to associate themselves
with. It is now a deliberately vintage sound and the fact that it was once the height
of modernity lends it a certain charm.

Having given some indication of how 'Believe' rests upon camp, I now feel
that finding out how camp might simultaneously offer a leg up to the song's female
listeners (straight or otherwise) would be worthwhile. Firstly, as I have suggested,
'Believe' may have had to jostle particularly hard for political attention because it
is a product of a more derided genre. Not so in the mainstream of queer musical
aesthetics where pop, along with other genres which 'Believe' also looks to (such
as disco, the torch song and US garage) is one of *the* most politicised musical forms.
Essentially camp disregards standard modes of readership and gives its objects
subversive qualities without worrying about whether they are 'authentic' or written
into them 'in the first place'. Camp, then, might point out an even broader spectrum
of strategies for all manner of (maybe even straight) people who are drawn to this
music because they feel out of place within representation yet still have the need
to forge their identities through these types of cultural produce.

That said, this is a difficult operation and it is important not to aspire to kidnap camp from its valuable position within queer history – it must be observed *in situ* rather than stolen. As Andy Medhurst (Medhurst and Munt 1997) argues, camp has long been a shared pleasure within gay communities, a way of coping within a culture which marginalises you, and a means of recognising the like-minded within societies which, to one extent or another, outlaw homosexual practices. As such, it is not the most suitable bandwagon for straights to climb on just for the fun of it, not least because such an action would undermine a minority's sense of power through cultural ownership. Camp may seem to make light, but that does not mean it is to be taken lightly. Yet, having said this, camp has always basked in the limelight offered by (unfortunately) implicitly heterosexual institutions ranging from prime-time television scheduling to chart music. In many ways, this makes camp a shared cultural language – although some readers are habitually more fluent in it than others.

With these provisos heeded, camp can undoubtedly prove inspirational in its survivalist hints. It proposes an incredibly thoughtful model of how to consume a popular culture which does not necessarily purport to speak for certain marginalised social groups – and these might also include female musicians and female fans. As yet there are precious few other strategies for actually falling in love with the mainstream and keeping one's political convictions intact. By pushing current (largely straight male) standards of pop, perfection, fakery and behind-the-scenes mechanisation in unusual directions, a vocoder, like other camp objects, might complicate staid notions of reality, the body, femininity and female capability. Even if all the other uses of vocoders have not been as knowingly camp as Cher's (not that intentionality has ever been a prerequisite), camp can motivate how they are listened to and how they might seem empowering to women. Although none of this reading 'too deeply' and warping of musical meaning is likely to break down all the repressive structures of the music industry, it can definitely contribute to more egalitarian hegemonic shifts within pop's role in identity construction. Camp has always been about making do within the mainstream, twisting it, adoring aspects of it regardless, wobbling its more restrictive given meanings – something which this reading of the vocoder undoubtedly does too. Most of all, camp is about appropriation and a *usage* of popular culture which might not accord with the masculinist status quo, despite any notion of 'original intent' or authorship. If everything is not as might be desired within music production, then a certain type of consumption provides solace and stimulus in the meantime.

These are greedy, opportunist readings both in the way they pick up on camp for further ulterior motives and in their possible lack of 'obviousness' to the everyday listener. Surely, though, there is important work to be done in expanding the deliberately quasi-implausible, especially in areas of popular music where the manufacture of representations connives all too frequently to undermine the value of female performance. A control of meaning by way of rhetorical grasping and grabbing admittedly seems more precarious considering the inevitable sabotage to be expected from the various discouraging and destructive forces at work in music production and consumption. However, when theorising the 'mere fripperies' of chart music culture it is surely still vital not to give up hope and to try and build something fortifying out of debris left by these male struggles for technological dominance. For the moment, then, strategies like camp seem not only profitable in the short term, but also more than capable of being adapted to accord with historical and technological change.

346 *Kay Dickinson*

Acknowledgements

I would like to thank two Andrews – Clare and Medhurst – for donating thei. respective expertise in plug-ins and grammatical elegance.

Endnotes

1. Here a parallel arises with the case of Stephen Hawking whose now somewhat crude artificial speech device has become synonymous with him – in fact in many representational instances he might not be recognisable without it.
2. Here it might be worth invoking the long-running feud between ELO and Queen over the use of synthesizers – another technology which frequently reeks of both inauthenticity and femininity. Queen's denigration of the synthesizer and love of the electric guitar might help explain the band's loyal heterosexual male fan base, despite the unabashedly camp antics of lead singer Freddie Mercury.
3. My present emphasis on production and recording's role in the cultural wrangles about authenticity is not intended to undermine the more popular academic topic of live performance and authenticity. I simply wish to help expand such debates into even more spheres of music-making and listening.
4. This hegemonic position is continually and hotly debated, for example, when bands such as the Spice Girls are criticised for miming. The investment in this type of agency was enforced when Milli Vanilli were stripped of their Grammys for not singing their 'own' material.
5. This becomes evident when referring back to the list of vocoder tracks and their artists with which I started this article.
6. Arguably Anderson is less interested in the feminine potential of the vocoder. Although she is definitely using the device to start up a debate on gender, she uses it to deepen her voice through polyphony, to make sound more androgynous, as well as more android. Her work is perhaps more about the freedom to reject gender or to present an *unheimlich* grouping of simultaneous gender-scrambling musical selves.
7. Craig David's enormous success with a line of address which seems evocative almost of courtly love is representative of this.
8. In talking about queerness for the rest of this paper I wish to concentrate, for the most part, on gay men's, rather than gay women's, interest in camp. This is not to say that camp is exclusively the domain of gay men, but rather than there seems to be more of a tendency for lesbians to involve themselves in the music of other lesbians (or at least deliciously 'crypto' female performers) rather than dwell on the output of more evidently straight musicians such as Cher (Bradby 1993A).
9. Since then, Steps, Madonna, Victoria Beckham and Kylie Minogue (all of whom have substantial gay followings) have helped to 'queer' the vocoder.

References

Bartky, S. 1990. *Femininity and Domination: Studies in the Phenomenology of Oppression* (London)

Bordo, S. 1993. '"Material Girl": the effacements of postmodern culture', in *The Madonna Connection*, ed. C. Schwichtenberg (Bolder, CO)

Bradby, B. 1993A. 'Lesbians and popular music: does it matter who is singing?', in *Outwrite: Lesbianism and Popular Culture*, ed. G. Griffin (London)

1993B. 'Sampling sexuality: gender, technology and the body in dance music', *Popular Music*, 12/2, pp. 155–73

Braidotti, R. [n.d.] 'Cyberfeminism with a difference', http://www.let.ruu.nl/womens_studies/rosi/cyberfem.htm

Chapkis, W. 1986. *Beauty Secrets* (London)

Davis, K. 1995. *Reshaping the Female Body: The Dilemma of Cosmetic Surgery* (London)

Gray, C. (ed.) 1995. *The Cyborg Reader* (London)

Green, L. 1997. *Music, Gender, Education* (Cambridge)

Haraway, D. 1991. *Simians, Cyborgs and Women: The Reinvention of Labour* (London)

Leach, E. 2001. 'Vicars of "Wannabe": authenticity and the Spice Girls', *Popular Music*, 20/2, pp. 143–67

Lury, C. 1998. *Prosthetic Culture: Photography, Memory and Identity* (London and New York)

'Believe' 347

AcClary, S. 1991. *Feminine Endings: Music, Gender and Sexuality* (Minnesota)
Aedhurst, A., and Munt, S. 1997. *Lesbian and Gay Studies: A Critical Introduction* (London)
Plant, S. 1997. *Zeros and Ones* (London)
Volf, N. 1991. *The Beauty Myth: How Images of Beauty are Used Against Women* (New York)
vww.harmony-central.com/software/Mac/Articles/Orange_Vocoder/

rword

ould be safe to say that, since this article was originally written (more than ten years the vocoder effect has proven itself a mainstay of pop production. What is more, it has welcomed into other genres. R&B luminaries like Mary J. Blige (on "The One") have ly used it and it is a ubiquitous presence on hip hop albums, such as Kanye West's *808s Heartbreak*, where the jolting, manipulated vocals cleverly underscore personal grief and ation.

the meantime, what has also become abundantly clear is that an effects pedal almost inly did not bring the world "Believe"'s vocoder treatment. Unsurprisingly, the song's ucers had hoped to throw imitators off the scent of the new technique they had created safe-guard its exclusivity. In fact, this sound and the thousands of other replicants that followed in its wake were spawned by Auto-Tune, a plug-in or stand-alone implement arily designed to imperceptibly smooth out pitch inaccuracies via similar principles to original vocoder.

hile the error remains within my original essay, the revelation of Auto-Tune usage builds ad of steam for various of my arguments. If this technology was initially designed to oticeably remedy vocal flaws (like corrective cosmetic surgery might a bodily feature), applying Auto-Tune to warp the voice, to render its artificiality conspicuous, to foreground machinic interference that is central to musical labour and output is a stark reversal of o-Tune's inventors' intentions. Yet it can still mask weaknesses, although more by hiding n in the light. In these ways, Auto-Tune resurrects the entrenched disagreements about enticity that surface in the article. Auto-Tune exists to cushion those accused of lacking nt or of not having worked hard enough to legitimately deserve musical success. Disputes r merit come to a head with Jay-Z's famous "D.O.A (Death of Auto-Tune)" where the os of "keeping it real" challenges the inorganic ways in which this technology strives for unearned) perfection or distorts raw, "human" expression. All in all, the same debates ut skill, aptitude, capacity, intervention and worth are alive and well, rendered even more plex, in how Auto-Tune supplies a vocoder effect.

[19]

Music and Canadian Nationhood Post 9/11: An Analysis of *Music Without Borders: Live*

Susan Fast
McMaster University

and

Karen Pegley
Queen's University

> [Cultural memory] is a field of contested meanings in which [people] interact with cultural elements to produce concepts of the nation, particularly in events of trauma, where both the structures and the fractures of a culture are exposed. (Sturken 2–3)

The terrorist attacks of September 11, 2001, were followed by innumerable artistic outpourings: music, film, and literature were among the many cultural expressions that raised funds for victim relief and helped us come to terms psychically with a previously unthinkable event. Within the United States, a series of benefit concerts were quickly organized; through these events, the structures of a culture were evident (the richness of Western popular music) as were the fractures (the vulnerability of musicians live from undisclosed locations for fear of further attacks). On September 21, 10 days after the attacks, the first mass-mediated benefit concert, *America: A Tribute to Heroes*, aired on stations both within the United States and internationally. On the weekend of October 20–21, more concerts ensued in the United States: *The Concert for New York City* (New York), *United We Stand* (Washington DC), and *Country Freedom Concert* (Nashville) brought together millions of viewers in an attempt to raise funds, bind together again a wounded—and still bleeding—American community.

That same weekend, on the other side of the 49th parallel, millions of Canadians were watching *Music Without Borders: Live*, a benefit concert held in Toronto, Ontario. Unlike the earlier concerts that raised money for American victims of the 9/11 terrorist attacks, this concert was held as a benefit for Afghani refugees. This concert, then, marked a distinct change of focus relative to the previous events. While this shift may have been surprising for some Americans who had just witnessed the most destructive terrorist attacks against their own on US soil, it was not atypical for many Canadians who have long been enveloped in the narrative of Canada as the international peacekeeper, the hero of the underdog, and the provider of basic human needs. and who would argue against this compassionate rationale in the face of the Afghani refugees' overwhelming need in October of 2001? As MuchMusic VJ Namugenyi Kiwanuka explained at the concert: "Historically, Canada has been known as a country that reaches out to other nations in times of need and tonight we continue that legacy."

Indeed, that night, audience members were presented with a host of "Canadian legacies" and nationalistic narratives; some of these, including the peacekeeping legacy, were explicit while others were perilously implicit, quietly reinforced, and simply uncontested. In this paper, we unravel some of these unchallenged narratives and explore how this event served to raise funds for a displaced people half a world away while reinforcing hegemonic power relations right here at home. This concert, we hope to show, was a powerful opportunity to shape Canadians' cultural memory of themselves, of Americans, and of the world at large, offering a precious moment to produce—and reproduce—concepts of the Canadian nation.

Eva Mackey begins her book on cultural politics and national identity in Canada with an image that serves to distinguish Canadian national identity from that of Americans. She discusses a postcard on which a Canadian mounted police officer is shaking hands with a native chief, both dressed in traditional costume.

> The caption reads, "Here indeed are the symbols of Canada's glorious past. A Mountie, resplendent in his famed scarlet, greets Chief Sitting Eagle, one of Canada's most colorful Indians ... .' The image of the Mountie and the 'Indian Chief' places a representative of the state and a representative of minority culture— coloniser and colonized—in a friendly, peaceful and collaborative pose. Aboriginal people and the state are represented as if they are equal: as if the Mountie did not have the force of the crown and the military behind him, shoring up his power. This image of collaborative cultural contact could be contrasted with a quintessential American frontier image: cowboys chasing and killing 'Indians.' In the American images, the cowboys are presented as rugged *individuals*. In contrast, the Mounties in the Canadian image are symbols and representatives of the kind of benevolent *state*—the

state that supposedly treated, and still treats, its minorities more compassionately than the USA (1–2).

Mackey calls this the "Mountie myth," which she says "utilises the idea of Canada's tolerance and justice towards its minorities to create national identity" (2). This idea has assumed the status of governmental policy through the concept of "multiculturalism," which advocates that different ethnic groups living within Canada maintain their cultural heritage and traditions, as opposed to the "melting pot" of the US. As Mackey argues, however, the danger with this policy is that "multiculturalism implicitly constructs the idea of a core English-Canadian [white] culture, and . . . other cultures become 'multicultural' in relation to that unmarked, yet dominant, Anglo-Canadian core culture" (2).

This narrative of Canadian national identity is directly relevant to *Music Without Borders: Live*. This concert was held at the Air Canada Centre and aired simultaneously on the Canadian Broadcasting Corporation (CBC) and MuchMusic, Canada's first and today most pervasive music television station in the country (Table 1). Six artists performed at the concert; these were described by reviewer Kieran Grant as the "[the] Canadian A-list [of] musical talent" and included Alanis Morissette, Bruce Cockburn, Our Lady Peace, The Tragically Hip, the Barenaked Ladies, and Choclair (1). Below is a more detailed description of the entire concert as it appeared on television that night.

The unproblematic homogeneity of this "A-list" of Canadian talent is not only telling but deeply concerning: all but one of the headlining musical artists—Choclair—are white, and all but the African-Canadian rapper Choclair are associated with rock, or the related singer-songwriter tradition. With few exceptions, both these musical genres have historically been defined and perpetuated by white, middle class performers. In fact, the artists might have all been white had Choclair not joined in at the last moment (his involvement was not announced in the initial publicity for the event); he, in fact, had to *ask* to join the group, as opposed to being invited (Cantin 1).

Furthermore, all the artists were English-speaking Canadians (and all from Ontario, one of the more affluent Canadian provinces). This is enormously significant in a country that continually struggles with issues of national identity related to the two "official" cultures, French and English; Quebecois culture was found in two brief and marginal moments of the event, neither of them "musical." The first was during Prime

Table 1. Order of Events: *Music Without Borders: Live* (televised version)

1. Prime Minister Jean Chrétien—message to "the nation."
2. Voice-over with visuals introduces artists
3. Comedian Rick Mercer and VJ George Stroumboulopoulos introduce event
4. Our Lady Peace, Live ("Naveed," "Whatever," "Starseed," "Life," "Right Behind You," "Superman's Dead")
5. Our Lady Peace interrupted: Backstage with George Stroumboulopoulos who introduces:
6. CBC Reporter Don Murray, reporting from Afghani refugee camp
7. Backstage interview: Rick Mercer with Greg Lyndon (a lawyer just returned from Afghanistan)
8. Alanis Morissette introduces Bruce Cockburn from the stage
9. Bruce Cockburn "Justice," "Lovers in a Dangerous Time" (with Paige)
10. VJ Namugenyi Kiwanuka, from audience, introduces:
11. CBC reporter Suhana Meharchand reporting on the history of Canadian giving
12. Kiwanuka and Meharchand in audience
13. Mercer interviews Cockburn backstage
14. VJ Bradford Howe with French VJ backstage
15. Vince Carter introduces:
16. Choclair ("Let's Ride")
17. Kiwanuka backstage interview with Vince Carter
18. Stroumboulopoulos in audience introduces Steven Paige and Gord Downie
19. Paige and Downie introduce Morissette from the stage
20. Alanis Morissette ("What I Really Want," "A Man," "I am Your Nuclear Bomb?," "Sister Blister," "You Live You Learn")
21. Mercer interviews Afghani journalist (this may have been pre-taped; she is not present at the ACC)
22. Stroumboulopoulos backstage plea to viewers to donate
23. Howe and Harland Williams introduce Jason Priestly
24. Priestly introduces Barenaked Ladies from the stage
25. Barenaked Ladies ("Pinch Me," rap sequence, "Falling For the First Time," "One Week," "Call and Answer," "If I Had A $1,000,000")
26. Stroumboulopoulos backstage interview with Choclair
27. CBC news anchor Peter Mansbridge introduces The Tragically Hip from the stage
28. Tragically Hip ("Grace Too," "My Music at Work," "Super-Capacity to Love," "Poets")
29. Mercer backstage interview with Morissette (interrupts Hip performance)
30. Stroumboulopoulos backstage interview with Paige
31. CBC news report on refugees
32. Mercer and Stroumboulopoulos backstage with Mansbridge
33. Back to Hip performance ("Bobcaygeon" (midstream) "Courage," "Fully Completely," "Ahead By a Century")
34. Mercer and Stroumboulopoulos come on stage and end evening intro finale
35. Finale

Minister Jean Chrétien's videotaped introduction to the event, part of which he delivered in English and part in French (more on this below), and the second was when Anne-Marie, a VJ from MuchMusic's French-language sister station in Quebec, MusiquePlus, appeared with a

Pop Music and Easy Listening   *363*

MuchMusic VJ to encourage Quebec viewers to donate, addressing them in French. Interestingly, in a country where both English and French are official languages, it appeared that Anne-Marie addressed only those whose first language is French, returning to English when she addressed what is framed as the "main" (or "core") audience. This includes the MuchMusic VJ Bradford Howe, who clearly knows little or no French, and, in fact, jokes self-deprecatingly that he "couldn't have said it better" himself after Anne-Marie finishes speaking French. Quebec, and French-Canadians in general (there are communities of French-speaking Canadians in regions of the country other than Quebec), are marginalized in this moment, treated as an "other" to the "core" white, English-speaking majority of Canadians. In an event during which the notion of "Canada" and Canadian identity was invoked and celebrated over and over again, this marginalization of French-Canadian culture—not to mention other ethnic minorities—is deeply problematic. The white, Anglo-Canadian culture seemed to stand in for Canadian-ness in general; in fact, MuchMusic VJ George Stroumboulopoulos, co-host of the event, introduced the list of artists playing the concert as "the finest collection of music this country has to offer." Clearly, there was no self-consciousness about how "the finest Canadian musicians" happen to be predominantly white, rock-oriented, from Central Canada, and English-speaking.

One can argue that the concert was "hastily put together," without much time to think about the politics of representation, but it is just such scenarios that tend to replicate hegemonic ideas, and there are choices being made in such circumstances, whether conscious or not. "The power to choose who is included in the category of national music," Inbal Perelson has suggested, "becomes a way to socially define the nation" (cited in Duffett 6). If Canada prides itself as a "multicultural" nation, why were all the musicians initially asked to participate white and English-Canadian? Where were the representatives from other ethnic minorities in this concert? Why were genres of music other than rock under-represented? In part, the answer may be that one of the guiding principles of benefit concerts is that to generate the most money, the biggest commercial artists should play their biggest hits; that way, the greatest number of people will be enticed to go to the event, or to watch on television, and to donate.[1] But this argument, too, leaves us with a problematic reality: according to this narrative, Canada's most commercially successful artists are white, usually male English-Canadians, who make rock or rock-related music. But, where were the international best-selling women artists Celine Dion or Shania Twain? and doesn't Sarah McLaughlin qualify for Canada's "A-list"? Clearly, these artists must be acknowledged when compiling a list of Canada's most successful musicians internationally Commenting on Quebec artists, Mark Duffett notes that they "fail to draw outside their province," which, he argues, is a reason that they were not included in an event called the Great Canadian Party, organized to celebrate Canadian nationalism on Canada Day (July 1), 1992 (Duffett 6). One must wonder, too, why in a country supposedly so devoted to the concept of multiculturalism, these particular white, male, rock-based stars would invited (Morissette initiated the idea of a benefit concert and was a participant from the outset). Why would not the diverse population of Canada be drawn to a concert that celebrates the variety of musics being created and performed in this country, as opposed to "mainstream" acts? Herein lies one of the contradictions and dangers of Canadian self-identity: while many support Canada's multicultural policy, they often overlook the complex ways in which hegemonic privilege underpins our cultural articulations, so that, as Homi Bhabha has observed, "the universalism that paradoxically permits diversity masks ethnocentric norms, values and interests" (208).

The issue of ethnic, not to say gender, representation becomes further complicated when one considers the running order of the concert, as well as the time allotted to each artist. Both authors attended this concert, and this insider privilege provided us with information we did not expect, including the difference between the chronological appearance of the artists in the live concert and the televised line up that appeared on CBC and MuchMusic. Altering the artist line-up before airtime was possible because, despite the concert's title, the televised program was only partially "live": many of the artists were pre-recorded and reordered for the televised event. No indication was given in the televised broadcast that some of the performances being shown were pre-taped, so it would be reasonable to assume that viewers thought all the acts were live. Concert order, of course, assigns or reaffirms notions of celebrity and cultural capital. Bruce Springsteen, for instance, opened *America: A Tribute to Heroes*, and the *Concert for New York City* began with David Bowie. Clearly, these two superstars added weight to the beginning moments of these shows. Those who were at the Air Canada Centre for the *Borders* concert saw Choclair perform first for fifteen minutes, Bruce Cockburn followed with a half-hour set, and then The Barenaked Ladies, Our Lady Peace, Alanis Morissette, and finally, The Tragically Hip performed a 40-minute set each. Choclair's short performance began at 6:00 p.m., with only a fraction of the audience yet in attendance. When the program went to air at 9:00 p.m., however, rockers Our Lady Peace appeared first—live—followed by pre-taped broadcasts of the more marginalized performers Cockburn (with only two songs—he is older, not as "sexy" as the younger rock artists and much more overtly "political"), and Choclair (with one song), then complete sets by Morissette, The Barenaked Ladies, and finally The Hip. The narrative established here was the importance of the white male rock band both to begin the concert and to end it. Not even the international best-selling artist and co-organizer Morissette, the only woman on the bill, could undo that power.

A similar entrenchment of gender and racial hegemony characterized the finale. The song chosen for the finale was fellow-Canadian Neil Young's "Rockin' in the Free World," one of the few songs that night that could be construed to have any kind of overtly "political" message (more on this below). Again, this is a "rock" song, by a white rock artist. The verses were sung by pairs of artists: Gord Downie and Alanis Morissette, Steven Paige and Tyler Stewart from The Barenaked Ladies, and Bruce Cockburn and Raine Maida, lead singer for the group Our Lady Peace. In between each verse, guitar solos were played by Bruce Cockburn and Hip guitarist Bobby Baker. The choice of genre excluded the one non-white artist, Choclair. He stood behind a line-up of electric guitars, an instrument that plays little role in rap, and did not contribute a verse of the song but rather joined in on the chorus only. He seemed decidedly out of place in this rockist environment.

Not only were The Tragically Hip the only band to appear in the final position in both the live and televised event, but they were only one of three performers who were introduced by non-musician celebrities that evening (the others were introduced by fellow musicians performing at the event, which lends them less "special" than having the outsiders give introductions). Television star, and Canadian, Jason Priestly gave a cursory introduction to The Barenaked Ladies. Vince Carter of the Toronto Raptors, the city's professional basketball team, introduced Choclair. Carter's presence here was significant, for he had become one of the most recognizable sports figures in Canada. Still, one might question how his introduction was received, for two reasons: first, it could be read as a sort of ghettoization of African Canadians and African Americans, the performance having been inserted early in the show (or live, if one were at the venue) after which it was possible to move onto the "important music." His appearing first in the live show did not carry the same weight here as it might have in other circumstances, because most of the crowd had not yet assembled. His status could be likened to that of an opening act, which often does not warrant the presence of most of the audience, let alone their attention. Second, while Carter was a basketball star living in Canada, he was not a Canadian citizen He remained an American who simply worked in Canada, an outsider who could (and did) go back to his home country when his contract expired. One wonders then, whether having rap "validated" by the only American-born celebrity, and the only black celebrity to appear on stage that night, reinforced for some viewers the connection between rap, blackness, and the United States, and, because of its ghettoized presentation, a conflation of the musical, racial, and national "other".

Contrast this with the introduction of The Hip by CBC nightly news anchor Peter Mansbridge, perhaps the most recognizable media personality in Canada and associated unmistakably with Canadian national identity because he works for the country's national public broadcaster. His familiarity and connection with the government-supported public network gave his introduction of The Hip significant institutional weight. Most importantly, he introduced The Hip as "Canada's band" and pointed out that "for the past 15 years they have been the greatest musical chroniclers of our time." The Hip's connection to things Canadian had been alluded to earlier by MuchMusic VJ George Stroumboulopoulos, when at the beginning of the event he mentioned that The Hip were "the band that opened this venue," i.e., The Air Canada Centre. Air Canada is "Canada's airline," a heavily government-subsidized institution that exists to unite the vast geographic expanse of the country, much like the CBC. But how did The Hip get to be "Canada's band?" Can we imagine a parallel for the United States or the United Kingdom? Who might be called "America's band" or "England's band?" The notion seems absurd, perhaps in part, because the music industries in these countries are enormous, but surely also because the diversity is recognized to be much too great for any one artist to somehow represent the nation: one can imagine the issues that would arise concerning, especially, racial politics, if a white rock band that is heavily indebted to the blues, as The Hip is, were to be crowned "America's band." Why then in a country with an official policy of multiculturalism, is this white, all male rock band that is heavily indebted to the blues (an American musical genre) considered "Canada's band," and not only by Peter Mansbridge?

The story of The Hip is a long and intricate one, an analysis of which would include an examination of rock privilege within Canadian music history narratives, governmental endorsement, and corporate (particularly beer) sponsorship at concerts, especially national Canada Day celebrations.[2] But it is worth considering that in both this concert and on other occasions, the band has expressed disappointment with Canadians (Wayne Gretzky, to cite just one example) who have crossed the border to take advantage of the larger American market (Duffett 8). This narrative of not selling out to the United States is echoed throughout Canadian celebrity discourses. The paradox is this: while many are proud when a Canadian is recognized south of the border, success within the American market often results in the loss of Canadian markers and renders these icons "less Canadian" to their fans at home. Because The Hip has not been able to "clear customs" and become a major player in the US market, they are proudly perceived by many Canadians as "one of us."

This does not mean that the band willingly buys into a construction of a unified Canadian identity: during these national celebrations lead singer Gord Downie has been known to use what Mark Duffett calls his "demented genius persona" to critique the entire nationalist project (8). Through this persona, in fact, Downie frequently speaks a biting cynicism, arguably giving voice to what many fans might want to say but dare not. At the *Borders* concert, Downie sarcastically welcomed the conflict in Afghanistan and undercut the tone of the humanitarian agenda by opening the set with the following directive to the audience: "Put your hands in your pockets. You people at home, dig out your wallets. Go into mummy's purse, bring out her wallet. It's a new war. It's a new war, what are you waiting for?" This cynicism, of course, was directed at George Bush's statement that his post 9/11 "war on terrorism" marked a "new war." "Canada's band," less connected to American purse strings relative to many other Canadians who have penetrated the American market (such as fellow performer Morissette), simultaneously raised money for humanitarian aid while sucker-punching the American-led military initiative.

But there are certainly difficulties in locating The Hip as "representative" of Canada: it perpetuates the notion that important events and ideas come out of central Canada. Peter Hodgins writes that "[there is a] Central Canadian perception that the important events in Canadian history all take place in the Toronto-Ottawa-Montreal-Quebec nexus. All other events are of merely 'regional' interest."[3] Regardless of whether those from other regions in Canada have contested this idea vigorously in recent years and won some ground in how they are represented—federal politics is a good place to look for signs of this change—a band from central Canada can still be uncritically claimed as "Canada's band." We might also point to Mansbridge's characterization of The Hip as a "band," as opposed to a "group," a far more neutral term: rock "bands" are linked with the idea of fraternity—they are almost exclusively a male domain, and, although rock bands generate complex and diverse social meanings, an important way in which they have been characterized is as a forum in which males can "bond" with each other. Mansbridge seems to play up this aspect of the male rock band in his introduction, which includes the comment that a little known fact about the band is that they are good golfers. In other words, they not only work together but play together. Mansbridge also makes himself an "insider" to Hip culture when he reveals this little known fact about the band. The notion of The Hip as "Canada's band," then, serves to perpetuate a masculinist, white, English-speaking, central Canadian idea of what the country is about.

The Hip's cynical take on Bush and American foreign policy was facilitated by the fact that, with the exception of Vince Carter, this was an event that included "Canadians" exclusively. (We put "Canadian" in quotes because some of the artists, such as Morissette, while born in Canada, have made their careers, and their homes, in the United States). This unified space, perhaps not surprisingly, became a site where Canadian involvement in the "new war" was examined. More importantly, it provided an opportunity to reflect on—or, more accurately, highlight preferred narratives of—Canada's international role to unify Canadian identity. Ian Angus argues that within modern nation-states there exist three steps to forging national identity, and it could be argued that all three were present that evening. First, the institution of a nation necessitates that the inside must be distinguished from an outside; second, there must be an accumulation of symbolic markers that provide the content of a national identity (the rhetoric of a nation); and finally, there must be a national actor or a people who act on behalf of a national identity (20). We have already explored the third step to some degree— The Hip were among Canada's "national actors" during the concert. In terms of first and second steps, Canadians were differentiated from Americans by organizing an event that construed not only Americans but *primarily* the Afghan people to be the "victims" of the 9/11 terrorist attacks; in fact, on only one occasion were the American victims acknowledged. Unlike any of the American benefit concerts, in which the *only* victims were unquestionably construed as Americans, *Music Without Borders: Live* was billed as a humanitarian benefit concert for Afghani refugees, who were fleeing their country in response to the "American" bombing, which was, of course, being carried out in direct response to

9/11. This agenda was made explicit from the very outset of the program, when a voice-over announced that "to benefit the United nations donor alert appeal Canadian musicians are rallying together to raise money in the wake of September 11." Later in the program, MuchMusic VJ and co-host of the program George Stroumboulopoulos again linked the attacks of 9/11 with the humanitarian agenda of the concert. In a plea for people to donate money, he argued that "the world changed on September 11 and we all wondered what we can do—well, now you know" [i.e., donate money to this cause]. The concert began with a federal endorsement in the form of a videotaped welcome by Canadian Prime Minister Jean Chrétien. "My fellow Canadians," he said, "I cannot be with you tonight but I want to express my full support for what you are doing, because you are showing the world that Canada is a friend of the Afghan people and that *in this struggle against terrorism, we are on the side of the victims, on the side of justice and human dignity*" (emphasis added). This is an extremely bold anti-American statement—Chrétien suggests that the only victims of the attacks are non-Americans ("we are on the side of *the* victims," who are identified throughout the concert as Afghanis) and implies an "other" that is somehow *not* on the side of justice and human dignity.

This is part of the "rhetoric of a nation" to which Angus refers. It is at the core of a powerful Canadian identity narrative, one that is fleshed out over the course of the concert. Canada is a country that "reaches out" to others in need beyond its borders, and this is often accomplished by the Canadian military in a "peacekeeping" role; these priorities are seen as rendering Canadians superior to Americans. In fact, an anti-American stance is often part of the rhetoric associated with Canada's perception of itself as peacekeeper and aid giver. As Peter Hodgins argues, "It seeks to reaffirm the Canadian faith in 'soft power'—persuasion, dialogue, compromise and negotiation—as a more efficient means of ensuring peace, harmony and prosperity as opposed to uncivilized America's use of violence and to suggest that [this] is somehow a Canadian invention."[4] These three interrelated ideas with respect to Canada's place in the world are linked to the Canadian identity marker of "tolerance" within our borders, interrogated by Eva Mackey above. This narrative was established during the concert using strategies that can be divided into three categories (again, interrelated): (1) Canada as the humane nation; (2) Canadians as having an "all-seeing" perspective on world issues; and (3) Canada as the country that attends to the world's urgent needs. Anti-American rhetoric permeates all of these categories, but there were also examples of the latter that stand alone.

Canada, as the humane nation, was first articulated by comedian and co-host of the event, Rick Mercer, who said in his introduction of the event "tonight Canada is sending out a message of hope to the people of Afghanistan." This theme was furthered by Raine Maida, front man for the band Our Lady Peace, who, in introducing one of the band's songs, said to the crowd, "I don't know about you guys but I'm damn proud to be Canadian tonight. This next song is about compassion, understanding, it's about treating people the way you'd like to be treated. It's a song called 'Life.'" These sentiments conflate the notion of Canada as a humane nation with patriotic sentiments concerning this national characteristic. Interestingly, overt patriotism such as this is generally frowned upon by Canadians, because it is perceived to be an American trait, and is often spoken of as part of American "jingoism."[5]

This celebration of Canadian patriotism is articulated again later in the event by Canadian comedian Harland Williams in an exchange with MuchMusic VJ Bradford Howe:

> Williams: Canada's a great country, best country in the world, right? (cheers from the crowd)
> Howe: Canadians really help out when they need to, don't they?
> Williams: Canadians—We've always been generous and this is a chance to give a little something to people who need it ….

In a humorous rap by Barenaked Ladies' singer Steven Paige, Canada was portrayed as being "about" helping out; but more than this, it distinguished Canada from Afghanistan as a privileged country that does not need to ask for outside help. This was accomplished not only through the words "we don't" [need outside help] but in the way that Paige set these words off, outside the normal flow of the rap; it is a blunt, unadorned statement about the remarkable richness enjoyed by a "first world" nation—paused over, but not for long, before the focus shifted back to how we help out. In an ironic twist back to the fact that most Canadians do not need help to be fed, Paige ended the rap by referring directly to his own size—not only do we not need help being fed, we're so well fed that we're overweight.

> Oh I like to support a real good deal
> and I think the folks of Afghanistan deserve a meal
> and that's why we're here, we're gonna help them out
> cause that, folks, that is what Canada's about

we like to help out the people of the world, yes indeed
we like to help people cause we know they gotta feed,
they gotta do what they do, we gotta hope that they would do it back
for us if we had the same problem ourselves .... .
We don't.
So we're glad to help out
I want to give everyone here a shout out
From St. John's to Vancouver Island
I hope this show leaves all of you smilin'
And dialin' on the phone and tryin to get in some money
Just because United Nations ain't funny
Kofi Anan is the guy who's in charge
My name is Steve and man am I large!

The narrative of an "all-seeing" Canadian perspective and the freedom to challenge dominant discourses were first set forth in an interview between Choclair and MuchMusic VJ George Stroumboulopoulos. Choclair begins:

> We have to feel for all the victims of September 11, but we also gotta feel for all the victims around the world. Artists from Canada, one thing they [i.e., outsiders] kind of see us as is, not necessarily anti-American but we kind of have this little leaning point .... . We get a different point of view ... right now in the States you're getting ... to see what's going on CNN ... and also you get to see ... American pride building back up but over here we get to see an overall view of everything going on.

"That's right," injected the VJ, "and I think when events first happened a lot of people ... naturally their inclination was to go and watch the American news media but everybody came home, because there was an observation level, an ability that happens with Canadian news .... ." Not only are Canadians simply distinguished from Americans in terms of their ability to view world politics from a broader perspective in this discourse, but this is put forward as something that makes Canadians superior to Americans: "we" might initially think that their cable news is the best source for information, but when "we" gather our wits about us, we return to our own news outlets, which will give us a more balanced view.

In a later interview segment with Canadian actress Sonja Smits, this idea that Canadians have a broad view of the world was articulated through her invocation, also inextricably wrapped up with Canadian identity, of multiculturalism: "It's a small world, and we're all composed of people who come from all over the world and one of the reasons we're here is because of hardship in our original countries ... As Canadians we have a unique opportunity because _our background gives us a really clear idea of world issues_" (emphasis added). One wonders, however, how a white, English-speaking Canadian, born, raised, and currently living in central Canada, can include herself within the multicultural "dispossessed" seeking refuge in Canada; or, for that matter, how it is that _she_ has been chosen to speak on behalf of Canadians on this topic.

We were also told during this concert that Canada is the country that attends to the world's urgent needs, and, on occasion, even cleans up the messes left by the United States. A report by CBC news correspondent Suhana Meharchand consists of historical video footage edited into a montage; the clips illustrate various instances in which Canadians have "reached out" to various peoples of the world who were in crisis. Meharchand's voice-over begins:

> In famine, and floods, earthquakes, and hurricanes, disasters made by misfortunes and by man, Canadians have always been there ... It's a Canadian tradition of helping and caring that reaches out across time and around the world. Canadians in small towns and big cities respond when they see communities in need, no matter where that need is. [Footage of people donating food and clothing] That spirit of giving is part of what makes us Canadians.

Meharchand is engaging here in what Stuart Hall characterizes as the desire to emphasize "continuity, tradition and timelessness" in national discourses, or in what Hobswam and Ranger characterize as "the invention of tradition" (cited in Hall 294). The identification of Canada with "peacekeeping" missions and humanitarian aid is not "timeless," but has its beginning point in 1956, when the term "peacekeeper" came into use. Here and elsewhere in the discourse around Canadian national identity, however, it is as if the Canadian peacekeeper has always existed.[6] Furthermore, while humanitarian aid and peacekeeping is in principle admirable—there is, certainly, much to be admired in the ways in which Canadians have engaged in these kinds of activities—it also, as Peter

Hodgins has pointed out, does significant ideological work.[7] One gets a sense of the kind of ideological work it does by consulting Canada's official foreign policy document. There, the goals of international assistance are to

> connec[t] the Canadian economy to some of the world's fastest growing markets—the markets of the developing world. And, in the long-run, development cooperation can help lift developing countries out of poverty. This means that it contributes to a stronger global economy in which Canadians, and other peoples, can grow and prosper. International Assistance also contributes to global security by tackling many key threats to human security, such as the abuse of human rights, disease, environmental degradation, population growth and the widening gap between rich and poor. Finally, it is one of the clearest international expressions of Canadian values and culture—of Canadians' desire to help the less fortunate and of their strong sense of social justice—and an effective means of sharing these values with the rest of the world.[8]

Here, humanitarian aid is directly linked to Canada's fiscal interests—something that would probably appall most Canadians—as well as to Canadian security. Particularly interesting, though, is the final idea articulated here, that through these acts Canadians "share" their values with others "less fortunate," perhaps indicating that these less fortunate do not hold these values already. The document, which perhaps reflects in part the general public's feelings about the benefits of international aid, has something of the "white man's burden" of colonial discourse about it; again, as Peter Hodgins points out, a cynic might view this "combination of economic and 'civilizing' motives for humanitarian aid as dangerously close to the arguments that justified the nineteenth-century colonialism."[9]

This is the frightening theory, and the practice has, at times, been even more destructive. Sherene Razack describes modern peacekeeping as a color line with civilized white nations on one side and uncivilized Third World nations on the other (10). In these remote nations where evil breeds—"the axis of evil"—we send our unsuspecting troops. We subsequently learn of their heroism, but we hear precious little about the atrocities our military commits abroad. Exceptions, of course, include the highly publicized Somalia Affair, although the Canadian Commission of Inquiry established to investigate the unthinkable violence against Somali citizens was halted before it could fully investigate the crimes. The final report, typically, blamed poor leadership and trauma-tized peacekeepers overwhelmed by the savagery they witnessed. The traumatized peacekeeper turning violent, Razack argues, has become a powerful Canadian icon used to explain our otherwise inexcusable behav-ior (10). Once all the reports were submitted, Canadians, in the face of extreme evil, were shown repeatedly to be themselves the victims, too naïve and soft to handle "absolute evil." We then fall once again into our "illusion of benevolence," requiring, the next time we engage in our peacekeeping missions, a new cast of "grateful natives" (10). Enter 9/11 and the Afghani refugees.

Alongside these pro-Canadian images were direct anti-American sentiments. In a report by CBC correspondent Don Murray showing devastating footage of the refugee camps on the outskirts of Afghanistan, including a baby who had gone blind from infection because of the dust, Murray states:

> Refugee after refugee told us, and one even wrote it on this piece of paper that the American air drops of food at the beginning of this campaign were a dubious farce; the soldiers of the Northern Alliance scooped up all the food .... When the Americans started bombing more people fled from the Taliban sector just 20 kilo-metres away.

A central part of this report focused on the American responsibility for the Afghani's situation. Canada's contribution to both peacekeeping and fixing these mistakes was communicated both implicitly and explicitly over the evening.

The most explicit anti-Americanism was evident in the concert's finale when all artists, CBC reporters, and VJs congregated on stage. As mentioned previously, the song chosen for this finale was Neil Young's "Rockin' in the Free World," released in 1989 on his album *Freedom*. The lyrics to the song are decidedly anti-American. Young conjures up several powerful images, beginning in the first lines of the song with his reference to the "red, white and blue" of the American flag. This not only situates the song in the United States, so that there can be no mistake about the critique that follows, but he also cleverly references that most powerful of symbols meant to inspire national pride and patriotism, the flag. He juxtaposes this with images of homelessness, of a drug-addicted young girl who dumps her child in a garbage can, of people who think "we'd be better off dead." Interspersed are phrases and ideas taken from George Bush senior's policy statements twisted to reflect what Young considers to be their true consequences:

> We got a thousand points of light
> For the homeless man
> We got a kinder, gentler,
> Machine gun hand

There are, of course, many ways in which lyrics can be construed, depending upon the context within which they are consumed and Young's lyrics are no exception. A reviewer in *Q Magazine*, for instance, commented that "Rockin' In The Free World" bitterly contrasts the American dream with the all-too-prevalent reality, first as a plaintive acoustic strum to ironic cheers and, then, to close the album, as a gloves-off statement of intent (1) and the *All Music Guide* characterized the song as "... one of Young's great anthems ... a song that went a long way toward restoring his political reputation ... by taking on hopelessness with a sense of moral outrage and explicitly condemning President Bush's domestic policy" (1). There is something particularly relevant about these lyrics to the general sentiments expressed in the *Music Without Borders* concert: they are concerned primarily with the suffering of those who have little or nothing, even though Young's lyrics are about Americans and not refugees in the strict sense of the word. It is also possible, of course, that the key element of the song on that evening, as is so often the case, was the chorus, which consists only of the line "Keep on Rockin' in the Free World." This might have been intended to point to and give thanks for the privilege of living in a democracy or of the power of popular music to effect change. Given the ragged performance of the verses (everyone except Steve Paige was reading from lyric sheets on the floor, and many had trouble getting through their verse at all), many in the crowd who did not already know the song well probably did not pick up on the anti-American elements of the song. Nevertheless, there must certainly have been those who did know the song well (including the artists who chose it) and who knew the powerful critique of the American government contained in the lyrics; sung by outsiders—Canadians as opposed to Americans—the song becomes for those who know it a scathing anti-American anthem.

It is significant that *Music Without Borders: Live* was broadcast not only on MuchMusic but also on the government-funded CBC.

According to the CBC's official website, the mandate of the company is to "tel[l] Canadian stories reflecting the reality and diversity of our country" and to "buil[d] bridges among Canadians, between regions and the two linguistic communities of Canada" (1). Nothing of the sort exists in the United States; National Public Radio, for example, is privately owned and financed through individual donor contributions, as are public television stations. Canada is often distinguished from the United States by the greater role that government plays in its citizen's lives. As Eva Mackey argues, "state intervention in economic, social, political and cultural life [increased after World War II], as Canada experienced a huge expansion in the public-enterprise and public-service economy. State intervention was itself to become one of the chief characteristics of Canada as a nation" (53). The CBC's broadcast of the *Music Without Borders* concert turned it into a state-sanctioned event, guaranteed to reach the widest possible audience, because the CBC broadcasts to even the remotest areas of Canada, where many private broadcasters do not. Unlike the *Concert For New York City*, which through its broadcast on VH1 targeted a specific demographic, i.e., a younger audience that is drawn to rock music, the concern that this kind of music might alienate some of its older listening public did not deter the CBC from broadcasting the event. A public broadcaster needs to worry less about what the economic ramifications of such audience alienation might be. Furthermore, there must have been a notion by those in power at the CBC that such an event would be— or should be—of considerable interest and importance to Canadians as a whole, as opposed to a single, targeted demographic.

The concert's relaxed and unpretentious energy was carefully constructed for the television-viewing audience: VJs, news reporters, and some of the celebrities made introductions from within the audience's space, surrounded by the crowd. Comedian Harlind Williams and VJ Bradford Howe, for example, conducted their exchange about Canadian charity toward others from within the audience, as did CBC reporter Suhana Meharchand and VJ Namugenyi Kiwanuka. The television audience was also granted backstage access to this event, because almost all of the interviews with musicians and others were conducted there, *during the concert*. The camera regularly cut away from performances to capture an interview that took place backstage; during these moments, it was possible to hear the live musical performance continuing on in the background. Even the headlining performance of the evening, that of The Tragically Hip, was interrupted for a full seven minutes of interviews.

This form—the backstage access and the celebrities mingling with the crowd—was not unique to this concert but is derived from a particular approach to making television developed at MuchMusic's parent station, Toronto-based City TV. As Karen Pegley has argued elsewhere, "[While] MTV makes a clear separation between the preparation and dissemination of information .... . Much[Music] collapses front and back regions," making fluid the boundaries that normally exist between audience and spectator, areas in front of the camera and those traditionally "behind the scenes," and between polished script and improvisation. The effect of this is a "demystification" of the process of television, as well as the people who make it and appear on it, i.e., our celebrities (155). Pegley argues alongside Miller and other scholars of Canadian television that this is part of the reluctance of Canadians to worship celebrity: Canadians have never been very comfortable elevating our popular celebrities, and the CBC, in particular, has repeatedly refused to create a star system to compete with the United States. We might also note in this respect that none of the performances at *Music Without Borders* are differentiated in terms of stage settings or lighting, parts of the production of live events that can create hierarchy among performers: everyone is bathed in the same light, and occupy the same area of the stage, unlike the *Concert for New York City*, where different performers were differently situated with respect to lighting choices and where on the stage area they were situated. To cite just three examples, Celine Dion performed "God Bless America" at the end of *America: A Tribute to Heroes* bathed in white background light as if to convey her angelic status. Similarly, David Bowie was the only performer in the *Concert For New York City* to have white light used throughout his performance—a kind of lighting effect that similarly suggested an otherworldly status; Melissa Etheridge later in that show gave her performance from the side of the stage—a wing, actually—which situated her in a less-prominent, less-powerful position in relation to those who performed at center stage (The Who, David Bowie, Paul McCartney). By prerecording acts and inserting them later in the televised event while the stagehands moved, dismantled, and set up band equipment, all of the acts in the *Borders* concert could appear as equals on the same stage (although, as previously noted, some lacked an audience). Furthermore, conducting interviews within the audience's space or cutting away to interviews during live performances minimized celebrity status. This was unlike the American concerts: celebrities in the *Tribute* concert were aired from undisclosed locations in fear of further attacks thus heightening their collective power, and in the *Concert for New York City*, with few exceptions the celebrities appeared only on stage, separated from the audience members. That celebrities were stripped of their status and deemed "unspecial" in the *Borders* concert suggested that we as Canadians are "all in this together." The performance of our nationality was, in that moment, very "un-American."

This concert is illustrative of a particular Canadian dynamic relative to the United States and Afghanistan: if the attacks had happened in another country (including Canada itself), it is entirely likely that what was embedded within this concert—the narratives, the perspectives, the legacies—would have been markedly different. Had there been no Afghani refugees and this were a concert to raise money for American victims, what might have this concert looked or sounded like? Who would have performed? How would we have positioned ourselves in relation to the United States, the sole victims of a horrible attack?

What is striking is the way in which the predominant "narrative of the nation, as it is told and retold" (Hall 293) was so much in the forefront of this concert. Perhaps this is because the concert was situated not simply as a nationalistic event, but as such, an event constructed *in response to* the way in which Americans were handling the attacks; eking out a national identity distinctive from that of the United States seemed to be the primary task of the evening. Representing a *unified* Canadian national identity at this time of crisis—the fantasy that, Stuart Hall remarks, constitutes difference as unity in constructing national identity—was crucially important and carefully negotiated (297). Hegemonic values were reinforced very subtly, but pay no attention: Canadians were flooded with overwhelming images of a loving, peacekeeping, generous, and artistically talented nation-state, where motives need not—*should* not—be questioned. We applauded enthusiastically, filling the Air Canada Centre with our boisterous sound while a red and white maple leaf flag hung quietly, gently, almost imperceptibly—far above us.

Notes

1. See, for example, the case that Bob Geldof made for this strategy when organizing Live Aid in 1985; cited in Susan Fast (2006).

2. For a discussion of beer sponsorship of live concert events in Canada, see Duffett.

3. See Hodgins. We thank the author for sharing excerpts from his book manuscript with us prior to its publication.

4. Hodgins, forthcoming.

5. For further discussion of this, see Mackey.

6. The history of Canadian peacekeeping missions is outlined as part of the Canadian foreign policy document; the section on peacekeeping begins:

> The eruption of conflict in the Middle East, specifically between Egypt and Israel, prompted Lester B. Pearson, then Canadian secretary of state for external affairs and later prime minister of Canada, to propose the deployment of an international peace force under the UN flag.
> It was through this particular, successful intervention that Canada began to be associated with peace-keeping missions. Prior to this, Canadian military forces took part in combat missions during World Wars I and II, and in Korea; the moniker of "peace keeper" is therefore relatively recent.

7. Personal correspondence with the authors.

8. See the Canadian Foreign policy document. "International Aid" receives a section unto itself, as does "Peace Keeping."

9. We thank Peter Hodgins for pointing us to Canada's foreign policy statement and for suggesting this interpretation of it.

Works Cited

All Music Guide. Review <http://www.allmusic.com/cg/amg.dll?p=amg&sql=A2v8 o1vkjzzxa>.

Angus, Ian. *A Border Within: National Identity, Cultural Plurality, and Wilderness.* Montreal and Kingston: McGill-Queen's UP, 1997.

Bhabha, Homi. "The Third Space. Interview with Homi Bhabha." *Identity, Community, Culture, Difference.* Ed. Jonathan Rutherford. London: Lawrence Wishart, 1990.

Cantin, Paul. "Alanis, The Hip Headline Concert for Afghan Refugees." *JAM!* Mon. 22 Oct. 2001 <http://www.canoe.ca/JamConcertsL2Q/music withoutborders-can.html>.

CBC. Official Website <http://cbc.radio-canada.ca/htmen/fast_facts.htm>.

Duffett, Mark. "Going Down Like A Song: National Identity, Global Commerce and the Great Canadian Party." *Popular Music* 19.1 (2000). 1–11.

Fast, Susan. "Popular Music Performance and Cultural Memory. Queen: Live Aid, Wembley Stadium, July 13, 1985." *Performance and Popular Music. History, Place, and Time.* Ed. Ian Inglis. London: Ashgate P, 2006. 138–54.

Grant, Kieren. "The Music of Love." *Toronto Sun.* Mon. 22 Oct. 2001 <http:// www.canoe.ca/JamConcertsL2Q/musicwithoutborders-sun.html>.

Hall, Stuart. "The Question of Cultural Identity." *Modernity and its Futures.* Eds. Stuart Hall, David Held, and Tony McGrew. Cambridge: Polity P, 1992. 273–325.

Hodgins, Peter. *The Canadian Dream: The Heritage Minutes and the Nostalgia for Myth and Memory in Contemporary Canada.* Vancouver: U of British Columbia P, forthcoming.

Mackey, Eva. *The House of Difference: Cultural Politics and National Identity in Canada.* Toronto: U of Toronto P, 2002.

Miller, Mary Jane. *Turn Up the Contrast: CBC Television Drama Since 1952.* Vancouver: U of British Columbia P, 1987.

Pegley, Karen. "An Analysis of the Construction of National, Gendered and Racial Identities on MuchMusic (Canada) and MTV (U.S.)." Dissertation, York U, 1999.

Q Magazine. Dec. 2000 <http://www.q4music.com/nav?page=q4music.review. redirect&fixture_review=117284&resource=117284&fixture_artist=144662>.

Razack, Sherene H. *Dark Threats and White Knights: The Somalia Affair, Peacekeeping, and the New Imperialism.* Toronto: U of Toronto P, 2004.

Sturken, Marita. *Tangled Memories: The Vietnam War, the AIDS Epidemic, and the Politics of Remembering.* Berkeley: U of California P, 1997.

[20]

BLACK POP SONGWRITING 1963–1966: AN ANALYSIS OF U.S. TOP FORTY HITS BY COOKE, MAYFIELD, STEVENSON, ROBINSON, AND HOLLAND-DOZIER-HOLLAND

JON FITZGERALD

Black songwriter-performers such as Fats Domino, Little Richard, and Chuck Berry achieved success on the U.S. pop charts[1] as leading contributors to the development of 1950s rock and roll. Rock and roll's impact had waned by the late 1950s, however, and white songwriter-producers dominated the creation of U.S. pop hits. Many of the successful songwriters from this period have been referred to as "Brill Building" composers—so named after a building (located at 1619 Broadway in New York) that first housed music publishers during the Great Depression. Successful writers and writing teams (e.g., Don Kirsher/Al Nevins, Jerry Leiber/Mike Stoller, Doc Pomas/Mort Shuman, Carole King/Gerry Goffin, Barry Mann/Cynthia Weil, and Phil Spector) created material for a wide range of artists (including male and female soloists, duos, and girl groups). They typically functioned as producers as well as songwriters,

---

1. *Billboard* began publishing a weekly U.S. national pop chart in 1940. The first *Billboard* "Top 100" chart was published in 1955, and the "Hot 100" chart (typically used as the music industry's primary source for singles chart data) commenced in 1958. This article draws on Whitburn's (1987) summary of *Billboard* chart information. Hesbacher et al. (1975a, 1975b) examine the procedures involved in compiling pop chart information; although they identify some shortcomings, they describe the *Billboard* charts as "a vast data source that both historians and social scientists should continue to use" (1975a, 14).

JON FITZGERALD is associate professor of music theory and history in the contemporary music program at Southern Cross University. His doctoral thesis examined the development of popular songwriting in the early 1960s, and he has published numerous articles and book chapters on aspects of popular music theory and history. He is also an experienced composer-performer and has toured in Australia, Europe, southeast Asia, and South Korea.

and some went on to form influential record companies such as Aldor (Kirshner/Nevins), Redbird (Leiber/Stoller), and Philles (Spector/Sill).[2]

Betrock (1982, 38) describes the Brill Building sound as emanating "from the stretch along Broadway between 49th and 53rd streets." He also provides a sense of the frenetic activity of the New York pop scene: "You could write a song there, or make the rounds of publishers with one until someone bought it. Then you could go to another floor and get a quick arrangement, . . . get some copies run off, . . . book an hour at one of the demo studios, . . . round up some musicians and singers, . . . and finally cut a demo of the song" (39).

The dominance of writer-producers meant that black performers of the day (like their white counterparts) depended largely on these professional writers to supply them with potential pop-chart hits.[3] For example, Leiber/Stoller provided material for the Coasters and the Drifters, Goffin/King created hits for the Drifters, Shirelles, Cookies, and Little Eva, while Mann/Weil's artist roster included the Drifters and Crystals.

The first sign of a new "crossover" breakthrough into the pop charts for black songwriters came in the late 1950s, in the form of hits by Sam Cooke and Curtis Mayfield. Described by Reed (2003, 89–90) as "the first widely-celebrated professional gospel singer to seek a secular career," Cooke achieved a number-one U.S. Top Forty hit in 1957 with "You Send Me." By 1963, he had a total of eighteen Top Forty entries (many self-penned). Mayfield's first U.S Top Forty hit was "For Your Precious Love" (written for Jerry Butler in 1958). He followed this up with a series of hits for artists such as Jerry Butler, the Impressions, and Major Lance.

During the early 1960s, black songwriters associated with the Motown label joined Cooke and Mayfield on the pop charts. The Motown Record Corporation (together with Jobete Music Publishing Company) was created by Berry Gordy in 1959. Gordy had previously operated an unsuccessful jazz record shop (from 1953 to 1955), eventually receiving some financial rewards by writing songs for Jackie Wilson. Gordy was convinced by William "Smokey" Robinson (whom he met in 1957) that "the way to really make it was to stop leasing records to others and to begin marketing and merchandising their music themselves" (Robinson, cited in George 1985, 27).

Motown released its first song in mid-1959, and by 1961, the company had produced a number-one R&B hit (and number-two pop hit) with "Shop Around," written by Robinson and performed by the Miracles. With an increasing roster of performing artists, an established core of spe-

2. Shaw (1992) provides an overview of Brill Building artists and record companies.
3. At this time, writer-performers were a rarity. Exceptions included Roy Orbison and Del Shannon.

:ialist session players, and talented and ambitious young writer-producers, the company soon achieved considerable pop-chart success, ultimately becoming "the largest independent label and the largest black-
owned business in America of the 1960s" (Kooijman 2006, 123). Smokey
Robinson and the team of Brian Holland, Lamont Dozier, and Eddie
Holland (Holland-Dozier-Holland, hereafter referred to as H-D-H) were
Motown's main songwriters, and they monopolized the production of
pop hit songs for the company. A&R director William Stevenson also
(co)wrote a number of early hits for the label.

By 1963, then, black songwriters were achieving unprecedented pop-
chart success.[4] Table 1 lists the number of U.S. Top Forty hits by the most
successful black pop songwriters of 1963–1966.[5] It demonstrates that
Motown's impressive chart achievements coincided with Curtis
Mayfield's most prolific period as a pop writer while simultaneously
overlapping with the final phase of Sam Cooke's career.

It might be expected that the successful black songwriters listed in
Table 1 brought some new elements into the pop "mainstream," and various writers have indeed attempted to describe the distinctive nature of
the new black pop music. McEwen and Miller (1992, 279), for example,
speak of the "gospel-pop fusion" of Berry Gordy's early songs and suggest that H-D-H "exploited gospelish vocal gestures in a pop context"
(281). Heilbut (1985, 76) argues that "Motown soul is equally shot
through with [gospel] quartet influences," while McEwen (1992, 76) col-
orfully describes Sam Cooke's pop music as "the place where soul and
feeling of gospel meets the finger-snapping, ascot-wearing ambience of
supper club pop."

These types of generalized assessments provide some sense of the new
black pop music, but any attempt to define the specific musical and lyrical characteristics of the crossover songs needs to be grounded in a
detailed examination of the repertoire. I aim here to contribute to the literature surrounding black pop songwriting by (a) documenting the

---

4. Brackett (2005, 75–76) rightly draws attention to the "fluid" nature of music industry
categories, commenting that "the music categories of 'popular,' 'R&B,' and 'country' each
encompass genre labels that emerge in other media contexts, all of which are in a perpetu-
al state of transformation." Nevertheless, Table 1 signals the beginnings of unprecedented
exposure for black pop songs. Jerry Wexler describes Motown's achievements, for example,
as "something you would have to say on paper was impossible. They took black music and
beamed it directly to the white American teenager" (Guralnick 1991, 2).

5. Table 1 includes all black songwriters with eight or more U.S. Top Forty hits 1963–1966.
Influential black songwriters James Brown and Norman Whitfield had both begun to
achieve some pop-chart success during the period under consideration, but their most prolific and influential period came later. (Brown, for example, had thirty-four Top Forty hits
between 1967 and 1974 [Whitburn, 1987].)

100   BMR Journa

Table 1. U.S. Top Forty hits by the most successful black songwriters, 1963–196
(Whitburn 1987)

	1963	1964	1965	1966	Total
Holland-Dozier-Holland	7	8	8	12	35
Robinson	5	5	9	4	23
Mayfield	5	6	4	1	16
Stevenson	2	2	3	2	9
Cooke	1	3	4	0	8

results of musical and textual analysis of all of the songs from Table 1 and
by (b) drawing on these results to reflect on the trajectory and significance of the early 1960s crossover phenomenon. The present work
reflects my belief that musical and textual analysis can play an important
role in providing data to inform historians and theorists as they attempt
to formulate a comprehensive account of the development of popular
music. As Keightley (1991, 5) suggests: "[T]heoretical overviews and textual instantations are necessary and ongoing parts of the study of popular culture. They are complementary, not opposite; one approach should
not dominate to the detriment of the other."

Brief Biographies of Cooke, Mayfield, Robinson, H-D-H, and Stevenson

Sam Cooke (1935–1964) was born in Chicago and began singing gospel
music from age nine, first with the Singing Children and subsequently
with the Highway QCs. He joined the Soul Stirrers in 1950 and recorded
for Specialty Records. In 1956, he began to record secular songs. "You
Send Me" (1957) was the first in a lengthy series of pop hits. Cooke
formed his own record label (Sar), which rereleased gospel-influenced
R&B hits, and he joined RCA as a solo artist in 1960, negotiating a new
contract that afforded him considerable artistic control. He recorded his
own songs, as well as songs by other writers, until his death in 1964.
Several of his songs continued to appear on the pop charts in 1965.

Curtis Mayfield (1942–1999), also born in Chicago, sang with his
cousins in the Northern Jubilees (which included Jerry Butler, for whom
Mayfield wrote many of his early songs). Mayfield's strongest early
musical influence was gospel, but by the mid-1950s, he was also listening
to R&B and rock and roll. He became especially interested in the music of
the Coasters. Mayfield formed the Impressions in 1957 with Butler, who
subsequently left to pursue a solo career (with Mayfield as guitarist and
songwriter). Mayfield continued to write and perform with the

mpressions and also supplied pop songs for solo artists such as Major
Lance and Gene Chandler. He formed his own independent record company (Curtom Records) in 1969.

Born in Detroit, Smokey Robinson (b. 1940) studied saxophone from an
early age and sang in a church choir. He formed a high school group (the
Matadors) that included Ronnie White, Bobby Rogers, Warren Moore,
and Robinson's future wife, Claudette Rogers. They performed original
songs, mostly written by Robinson. At his audition for Gordy in 1957,
Robinson told him that he had already written over one hundred songs.
Gordy offered Robinson advice about songwriting and suggested that the
Matadors change their name to the Miracles. Between 1959 and 1975, the
Miracles had forty-six U.S. Top 100 songs (mostly written and produced
by Robinson). Robinson also wrote numerous songs for other Motown
performers, including the Temptations, Mary Wells, and Marvin Gaye.

Another Detroit native, Eddie Holland (b. 1939) joined Berry Gordy's
publishing company as a singer. He tended to imitate the vocal style of
Jackie Wilson and achieved some minor success on both the R&B and pop
charts. A nervous and reluctant performer, he decided that he was better
suited to studio work.[6] After observing the financial rewards his brother
Brian was obtaining from songwriting, he asked him if they could work
together. When Brian Holland (b. 1941) was sixteen, he met Gordy, who
encouraged him to compose melodies to lyrics. Holland became involved
with studio production by writing and producing songs for Motown's
first girl group, the Marvelettes, and worked with a number of partners,
including William Stevenson, Robert Bateman, Freddie Gorman, and
Lamont Dozier.

Also from Detroit, Lamont Dozier (b. 1941) first recorded at age fifteen
with the Romeos. He moved to New York and worked outside of the
music industry until his return to Detroit in 1958. As Lamont Anthony, he
recorded for Motown and began to write songs with Brian Holland. In
1962, Brian Holland, Eddie Holland, and Lamont Dozier began to work
as a songwriting/production team, and by 1963, they were achieving
substantial success. They worked together at Motown until 1968 and
composed a large number of pop hits for many of Motown's most successful groups, such as the Supremes and Four Tops.

William Stevenson began recording R&B and gospel music in the mid-
1950s and tried to obtain support from Detroit businessmen, doctors, and
lawyers for a black record company. George (1985, 37) observes that these
people "weren't interested in entering what they saw as the hustling,

6. George (1985, 40) describes Holland as a "dull" and "frightened" performer, whose
decision to abandon performing was influenced by a "rough experience before the Apollo
Theatre's notoriously demanding audience."

unsavory world of black show business." Berry Gordy knew o
Stevenson's support for black music and offered him the position as A&I
director at Motown. Stevenson encouraged the use of jazz musicians fo
Motown sessions and also wrote and produced a number of hits for the
company.

Top Forty Hits by Cooke, Mayfield, Robinson, H-D-H, and Stevenson: 1963–1966

Tables 2–6 list the U.S. Top Forty hits by Cooke, Mayfield, Robinson, H
D-H, and Stevenson between 1963 and 1966. Eleven songs performed by
Cooke reached the Top Forty between 1963 and 1965. He wrote seven o
these (see Table 2). In addition, the Animals (one of the British blues
bands that followed the Beatles' 1964 "invasion" of the U.S. charts
achieved a hit in 1965 with a cover of Cooke's "Bring It on Home to Me."
Mayfield achieved consistent chart success during the years 1963 to 1965
and wrote an even balance of songs for his own group (the Impressions)
and for other performers (all male soloists).

Robinson functioned both as writer-performer (as lead singer of the
Miracles) and professional songwriter, supplying songs for other
Motown artists. Apart from composing several songs for Mary Wells, he
wrote mainly for male performers, establishing a particularly productive
partnership with the Temptations and Marvin Gaye. Although several
members of the Miracles regularly received credit as cowriters with
Robinson, Robinson was seemingly the primary creative force within the
various writing partnerships.[7] He usually bore total responsibility for
lyrics and major responsibility for the musical elements, receiving only
occasional assistance with aspects such as the creation of melodies and
guitar riffs. Consequently, the songs involving Robinson as both sole and
joint writer are considered collectively.

H-D-H functioned exclusively as professional songwriters and composed songs for a large number of Motown performers, both male and
female. They wrote primarily for groups—especially the Supremes, Four
Tops, and Martha and the Vandellas.

William Stevenson cowrote and produced eight songs for a variety of
Motown performers. Mitch Ryder and the Detroit Wheels, for example,
covered "Devil with a Blue Dress On"—originally written for Motown
performer Shorty Long.

7. In his autobiography, Robinson (1989, 169) explains, "For years I'd tried to supplement
the Miracles' income by having them help me compose. If they worked a writing session
with me—whether I used their ideas or not—I put their names on the tunes and, consequently, they enjoyed extra earnings."

Table 2. U.S. Top Forty hits by Sam Cook, 1963–1966 (Whitburn 1987)

Year	Performer	Song Title
1963	Cooke	Another Saturday Night
1964	Cooke	Good News
	Cooke	Good Times
	Cooke	Cousin of Mine
1965	Cooke	Shake
	Cooke	A Change Is Gonna Come
	Animals	Bring It on Home to Me
	Cooke	Sugar Dumpling
1966	—	—

Table 3. U.S. Top Forty Hits by Curtis Mayfield, 1963–1966 (Whitburn 1987)

Year	Performer	Song Title
1963	Jan Bradley	Mama Didn't Lie
	Major Lance	The Monkey Time
	Impressions	It's All Right
	Major Lance	Hey Little Girl
	Jerry Butler	Need to Belong
1964	Major Lance	Um, Um, Um, Um, Um, Um
	Impressions	Talking about My Baby
	Impressions	I'm So Proud
	Impressions	Keep on Pushing
	Impressions	You Must Believe Me
	Major Lance	Rhythm
1965	Impressions	People Get Ready
	Major Lance	Come See
	Impressions	Woman's Got Soul
	Gene Chandler	Nothing Can Stop Me
1966	Impressions	You've Been Cheatin'

Song Analysis

Lyrics

An overview of the lyric content of the songs analyzed here shows that lyrics relating to aspects of relationships are in a clear majority (see Table 7).[8] Cooke, Mayfield, Robinson, and Stevenson favor either positive or ambivalent sentiments, while H-D-H's songs deal much more frequently with negative sentiments. Faithfulness is a topic of common concern to all

---

8. Recordings of all songs from Table 2 to 6 were analyzed and data entered in a database.

Table 4. U.S. Top Forty hits by Smokey Robinson, 1963–1966. Cowriters: (B) J. Bradford, (M) W. Moore, (Mi) Miracles, (R) R. Rogers, (T) M. Tarplin, (W) R. White (Whitburn 1987)

Year	Performer	Song Title
1963	Miracles (Mi)	You've Really Got a Hold on Me
	Mary Wells	Laughing Boy
	Miracles	A Love She Can Count On
	Mary Wells (B)	Your Old Standby
	Mary Wells	What's Easy for Two Is So Hard for One
1964	Temptations (R)	The Way You Do the Things You Do
	Mary Wells	My Guy
	Temptations	I'll Be in Trouble
	Miracles (T)	I Like It Like That
	Miracles (R, M)	That's What Love Is Made Of
1965	Temptations (W)	My Girl
	Marvin Gaye (M, T)	I'll Be Doggone
	Miracles (M)	Ooo Baby Baby
	Temptations (M)	It's Growing
	Miracles (M,T)	The Tracks of My Tears
	Temptations (M)	Since I Lost My Baby
	Marvin Gaye (M, R, T)	Ain't That Peculiar
	Miracles (M, T, W)	My Girl Has Gone
	Temptations (M, R)	My Baby
1966	Miracles (M, R, T)	Going to a Go-Go
	Marvelettes	Don't Mess with Bill
	Marvin Gaye (M, R, T, W)	One More Heartache
	Temptations	Get Ready

Various authors (e.g., Hennion 1983, 163; Moore 1993, 32) have stressed the importance of considering the sound recording as musical text. Recordings were original 1960s versions of the songs obtained from a variety of sources (including specialist retail outlets, radio stations, private collections, and the sound recording archives at Bowling Green State University). Recent CD compilations were avoided, since record companies tend to remaster (even remix) the originals. Original transcriptions were used to facilitate some of the analytical calculations entered in to the database. Sheet music (if available) was avoided since it usually differs significantly from the recorded version of the song. As Nettl (1983, 48) has noted, "circumscribing, defining, or enumerating the content of a music is indeed difficult," and music analysts have suggested a wide range of possible parameters that may provide a broad analysis of musical texts. In the present study, I grouped parameters into six common areas: lyrics, melody, rhythm, harmony, form, and production. A comparable amount of analytical data was sought within each area.

Table 5. U.S. Top Forty Hits by Holland-Dozier-Holland, 1963–1966 (Whitburn 1987)

Year	Performer	Song Title
1963	Martha and the Vandellas	Come and Get These Memories
	Martha and the Vandellas	Heat Wave
	Miracles	Mickey's Monkey
	Mary Wells	You Lost the Sweetest Boy
	Marvin Gaye	Can I Get a Witness
	Martha and the Vandellas	Quicksand
	Supremes	When the Lovelight Starts Shining through His Eyes
1964	Miracles	I Gotta Dance to Keep from Cryin'
	Marvin Gaye	You're a Wonderful One
	Supremes	Where Did Our Love Go
	Four Tops	Baby I Need Your Lovin'
	Supremes	Baby Love
	Marvin Gaye	Baby Don't You Do It
	Supremes	Come See about Me
	Marvin Gaye	How Sweet It Is to Be Loved by You
1965	Supremes	Stop in the Name of Love
	Martha and the Vandellas	Nowhere to Run
	Supremes	Back in My Arms Again
	Four Tops	I Can't Help Myself
	Four Tops	It's the Same Old Song
	Supremes	Nothing but Heartaches
	Supremes	I Hear a Symphony
	Four Tops	Something about You
1966	Supremes	My World Is Empty Without You
	Four Tops	Shake Me, Wake Me (When It's Over)
	Isley Brothers	This Old Heart of Mine (Is Weak for You)
	Supremes	Love Is Like an Itching in My Heart
	Jr. Walker and the All Stars	(I'm a) Roadrunner
	Supremes	You Can't Hurry Love
	Jr. Walker and the All Stars	How Sweet It Is to Be Loved by You

Table 5, cont.

Four Tops	Reach Out I'll Be There
Supremes	You Keep Me Hangin' On
Martha and the Vandellas	I'm Ready for Love
Miracles	(Come Round Here) I'm the One You Need
Four Tops	Standing in the Shadows of Love

writers, but H-D-H more often address the anguish associated with relationship difficulties or the ending of a relationship. Many song titles (e.g., "Where Did Our Love Go," "You Lost the Sweetest Boy," "Standing in the Shadows of Love") signal this type of lyric content. Such lyrics are designed provide a powerful "feeling" of the song's emotional content, as in this example from "Standing in the Shadows of Love," recorded by the Four Tops: "I want to run, but there's nowhere to go. Because heartache will follow me I know. . . . Standing in the shadows of love. I'm getting ready for the heartaches to come."

The songs by H-D-H also frequently portray a state of dependence on a relationship (often despite indifference or unkindness displayed by a partner). Sentiments of this type are expressed by both males and females. Typical lyrics include the following:

- "Baby love, my baby love, I need you, oh how I need you. But all you do is treat me bad, break my heart and leave me sad." ("Baby Love"—Supremes)
- "Some say it's a sign of weakness for a man to beg. Then weak I'd rather be, if it means having you to keep." ("Baby I Need Your Lovin'"—Four Tops)
- "Set me free why don't you babe. Get out' my life why don't you babe. 'Cause you don't really need me, you just keep me hangin' on." ("You Keep Me Hangin' On"— Supremes)

Mayfield refers explicitly to dancing in five of his sixteen songs ("Come See," "The Monkey Time," "Hey Little Girl," "Rhythm," "It's All Right"). These songs mention popular dances of the day (or those that the song hopes to establish in the dance repertoire) and frequently suggest dance movements. Typical lyrics include:

- "Do the Monkey yeah. Do the Monkey yeah. A-twist them hips, let your backbone slip." ("The Monkey Time"—Major Lance)
- "Come now not later, see the Mashed Potato yeah. My feet go berserk as I do the New York Jerk." ("Come See"—Major Lance)

Table 6. U.S. Top Forty hits by William Stevenson, 1963–1966. Cowriters: (G) M. Gaye, (P) C. Paul, (H) I. Hunter, (W) N. Whitfield, (M) S. Moy, (L) F. Long (Whitburn 1987)

Year	Performer	Song Title
1963	Marvin Gaye (G,P)	Hitch Hike
	Marvin Gaye (G,W)	Pride and Joy
1964	Martha and the Vandellas (G,H)	Dancing in the Street
	Martha and the Vandellas	Wild One
1965	Four Tops (H)	Ask the Lonely
	Marvelettes (H)	I'll Keep Holding On
	Martha and the Vandellas (H,P)	You've Been in Love Too Long
1966	Martha and the Vandellas (M)	My Baby Loves Me
	Mitch Ryder and the Detroit Wheels (L)	Devil With a Blue Dress On

Social comment is rare within the song field. Those by Mayfield involve symbolic, quasi-spiritual lyrics such as "Look-a look-a look-a yonder, what's that I see? A great big stone wall stands there ahead of me. But I've got my pride and I'll move the wall aside. Keep on pushin'," from "Keep on Pushin'," recorded by the Impressions. Cooke's "A Change Is Gonna Come" (which entered the Top Forty after his death) uses a similar, quasi-spiritual tone to evoke a sense of the "world-weary" spirit and express a hope for better times: "It's been too hard living but I'm afraid to die, 'cause I don't know what's up there beyond the sky. It's been a long along time coming but I know a change gonna come, oh yes it will."

Although all writers use poetic devices to some extent, Robinson's lyrics are by far the richest and most carefully crafted in this regard, and he regularly creates distinctive and memorable images. A favored technique is the chain of parallel statements, usually involving a device such as simile or metaphor, as in the following example from "The Way You Do the Things You Do," recorded by the Temptations: "You got a smile so bright you know you could've been a candle. I'm holding you so tight you know you could've been a handle. The way you swept me off my feet, you know you could've been a broom. The way you smell so sweet, you know you could've been some perfume." A similar technique involves contrasting, paradoxical images or statements, as in the following examples:

Table 7. *Lyric content (percentages indicate the proportion of songs by each writer that contain the given element)*

	Cooke %	Mayfield %	Robinson %	H-D-H %	Stevenson %
Relationships					
Overall	71	68	96	97	87
General tone					
positive	43	37	48	38	62
ambivalent	14	6	26	9	12
negative	14	25	22	50	12
Specific topics					
beginning	0	0	0	9	0
ending	14	12	22	38	12
faithfulness	29	19	26	21	0
dependence	0	6	13	29	0
yearning for love	0	6	22	24	0
marriage	0	0	4	0	0
advice	0	12	0	9	0
Activities					
Dancing	14	31	9	6	12
Social comment					
Overall	0	12	0	6	0

Table 7, cont.

	Cooke %	Mayfield %	Robinson %	H-D-H %	Stevenson %
Poetic devices					
Overall	29	31	78	42	25
Simile	29	12	35	15	12
Metaphor	0	19	17	18	0
Alliteration	0	0	13	6	0
Parallel statements	0	6	30	3	0
Paradox	0	0	26	0	0
Direct address					
Overall	29	31	61	79	25
Vernacular					
Overall	100	94	100	97	100

- "I've got sunshine on a cloudy day. When it's cold outside I've got the month of May." ("My Girl"—Temptations)
- "I don't like you but I love you, seems that I'm always thinking of you. Though you treat me badly I love you madly. . . . I don't want you but I need you, don't want to kiss you but I need to." ("You've Really Got a Hold On Me"—Miracles)

Robinson sometimes displays an almost playful approach to lyric creation, using unusual or extensive rhyming passages, as in the following example from "Since I Lost My Baby," recorded by the Temptations: "Next time I'll be kinder. Won't you please help me find her? Someone just remind her of the love she left behind her—'till I find her I'll be tryin' to. Every day I'm more inclined to find her."

H-D-H frequently use short, repeated lyric statements, particularly in choruses. These chorus hooks (e.g., "Baby I Need Your Lovin'," "How Sweet It Is to Be Loved by You," "Nowhere to Run") normally combine a few memorable catchwords, together with a short repeated melodic idea.

While Mayfield's songs are mostly narrative, songs by H-D-H are mostly personal direct-address style. Robinson uses a fairly even balance between the two approaches. Both Cooke and Stevenson favor the narrative style and largely avoid direct address.

Melody

Table 8 provides an overview of the melodic content of the songs. Mayfield uses a more extended vocal range than the other songwriters, regularly using, for example, the male falsetto register for melodic climaxes (e.g., "It's All Right," "I'm So Proud," "Keep on Pushing"). He also demonstrates a marked preference for major pentatonic melodies, using the scale in nine out of ten songs. This scale is also regularly used by Cooke, Robinson, and H-D-H, particularly for melody hooks.

The major hexatonic scale is also used regularly (especially by Cooke), but complete major scales are extremely rare. Robinson makes the most use of the mixolydian mode, while Stevenson regularly creates blues-influenced melodies, using the flattened third scale degree extensively within major keys (and alternating it with the major third), as well as featuring the flattened seventh in prominent locations. H-D-H's melodies also include regular blues inflections.

All of these songwriters show a liking for melodies with flat overall contours (i.e., those that do not rise appreciably in pitch for chorus statements or bridge sections). Mayfield and Cooke make extensive use of arch contours for verse melodies, while the Motown writers clearly favor flat or irregular verse contours. Many of their melodies involve the exten-

itzgerald • Black Pop Songwriting 1963–1966   111

Table 8. Melodic content

	Cooke %	Mayfield %	Robinson %	H-D-H %	Stevenson %
Vocal range					
Less than octave	14	0	35	29	25
Octave to tenth	71	44	43	56	50
Greater than tenth	14	56	22	15	25
Mode type					
Major pentatonic	29	87	43	38	0
Major hexatonic	43	25	30	26	12
Major (ionian)	14	0	9	3	12
Minor pentatonic	0	0	9	9	0
Mixolydian	0	0	22	12	12
Blues inflections	14	12	4	32	75
Aeolian	0	0	0	9	0
Disjunctive intervals within phrases					
0–5	57	25	52	56	62
6–10	14	25	22	29	37
Greater than 10	29	50	26	15	0

Table 8, cont.

	Cooke %	Mayfield %	Robinson %	H-D-H %	Stevenson %
Overall contour					
Rising	0	37	26	24	0
Falling	14	12	13	26	12
Flat	71	37	52	35	62
Verse contour					
Arch	43	56	26	12	37
Rising	14	6	0	9	0
Falling	0	0	9	15	0
Flat/irregular	29	37	61	56	62
Melodic riffs					
Overall	14	6	17	12	0

ive reiteration of short melodic statements based on a small range of
pitches.

H-D-H's songs often contrast simple, repetitive chorus melodies with
longer, more complex verse melodies (e.g., "Baby I Need Your Lovin',"
"Standing in the Shadows of Love"), while melodic ornamentation is a
feature of many of the pop crossover melodies. Although specific ornamentation may result from the input of the singer rather than the songwriter, the songwriters were usually closely involved in the production
process and therefore can be said to have endorsed the ornamentation
present on the recordings. In addition, Mayfield and Robinson incorporate ornamentation when performing their own songs, indicating the
inherent nature of this element to the crossover hits.

Rhythm

As indicated in Table 9, which provides an overview of the rhythmic
content of the songs analyzed here, the largest proportion of songs fall
within the range 120–139 beats per minute (bpm), although Robinson
demonstrates a preference for slower tempi (more than half of his songs
are less than 120 bpm), while H-D-H regularly use fast tempi (one-third
of their songs are over 160 bpm).

All writers, apart from Cooke, use straight eighth-note subdivisions
more than triplet eighth-note subdivisions (shuffle). But while Mayfield
clearly prefers the former, Robinson uses an almost even balance of the
two. There is, however, clear evidence that Robinson's songs moved
away from a shuffle feel and toward the straight eighth-note feel over
time. The songs of 1963 and 1964 are predominantly shuffles (eight of ten
songs), whereas those of 1965 and 1966 mostly use straight eighth-note
subdivisions (ten of thirteen songs). A similar trend is evident in the
songs by H-D-H. Ten of the fifteen songs from 1963 and 1964 employ
shuffles, but fifteen of the twenty songs from 1965 and 1966 have a
straight eighth-note feel.

The Motown songs normally incorporate a heavy emphasis on beats
two and four (backbeat). A large number of instruments (e.g., snare, tambourine, handclaps or finger snaps, brass, and guitars) combine to provide the backbeat emphasis, with guitar parts often displaying a distinctive heavy staccato downpick and a metallic tone. Repeated syncopated
rhythmic motives also feature prominently in the songs by all writers
except Cooke. Both Mayfield and Robinson make extensive use of the
dotted quarter note followed by eighth note (in both shuffle and straight-
eighth feels). This motive appears in approximately one in three songs
(see Table 10).

Table 9. *Rhythmic content*

	Cooke %	Mayfield %	Robinson %	H-D-H %	Stevenson %
Tempo (beat per min.)					
Less than 100	29	19	17	0	0
100–119	0	12	35	15	37
120–139	14	62	30	50	50
140–159	29	6	9	3	12
160 plus	29	0	9	32	0
Beat subdivision					
Shuffle/triplet eighth	57	31	48	38	25
Straight eighth	43	62	52	53	75
Sixteenth	0	0	0	6	0
Changing subdivision	0	6	0	3	0
Specific features					
Heavy four in bar	0	0	0	15	0
Use of triplets	0	0	4	0	25
Distinct harmonic rhythm	29	68	61	62	62
Sectional rhythm changes	0	44	26	38	25
Riffs					
Overall	0	56	52	68	50
Rhythmic-chordal	0	50	48	47	50

Table 10. Songs by Curtis Mayfield and Smokey Robinson featuring the dotted-quarter eighth-note motive (S = shuffle)

Mayfield	Year	Robinson	Year
It's All Right (S)	1963	I Like It Like That (S)	1964
Need to Belong	1963	It's Growing	1965
Talking about My Baby	1964	The Tracks of My Tears	1965
You Must Believe Me	1964	Since I Lost My Baby	1965
Woman's Got Soul (S)	1965	My Girl Has Gone	1965
You've Been Cheatin'	1963	Going to a Go-Go	1966
		Get Ready	1966

On most occasions, the dotted quarter–eighth-note rhythm is associated with one or more repetitive chord progressions and is used as part of rhythmic-chordal riffs—which often act as a structural framework supporting the melodic and lyric development (see "Form/Structure"). Table 10 indicates that while Mayfield employs this technique as early as 1963, Robinson uses it most frequently after 1965.

Songs by H-D-H incorporate a wide variety of repeated rhythmic motives and rhythmic-chordal riffs and use a number of different patterns (see Table 11).[9] Like Robinson, H-D-H make increasing use of these devices over time. By 1966, their songs include several complex syncopated patterns.

All writers except Cooke regularly create distinct harmonic rhythms by attaching syncopated rhythms to chord changes. This often occurs in association with short repeated chord cycles, but they also apply syncopated rhythms to longer chord sequences. Mayfield and H-D-H often associate significant rhythmic changes with sectional changes and/or begin and end riffs at sectional points within songs, providing further evidence of their sensitivity to the rhythmic aspects of song composition. An example of this process occurs in the H-D-H song "When the Lovelight Starts Shining through His Eyes," in which the verse's even eighth-note rhythmic riff contrasts markedly with the chorus's shuffle feel.

Many of the vocal melodies by Mayfield, Robinson, and H-D-H were performed with rhythmic flexibility typical of much African-American popular music. Singers regularly placed notes on either side of the beat and began phrases at different points in the bar, helping to create a sense of rhythmic freedom.

9. This table previously appeared in Fitzgerald (1995a, 6).

Harmony

Table 12 provides an overview of the harmonic content of the songs. The harmonic language used by Cooke and Mayfield is extremely simple. Almost two in three songs use diatonic harmony exclusively, while the remaining songs involve only common secondary-dominant progressions or occasional borrowed or unusual chords. Robinson uses borrowed chords in one in six songs and chord colorations in almost half of

Table 11. Rhythmic motives employed by H-D-H (S = shuffle)

Rhythmic pattern	Song title	Year
♩ ♪♩	Heat Wave (S)	1963
	You Lost the Sweetest Boy (S)	1963
	Quicksand (S)	1963
	Shake Me, Wake Me (When It's Over)	1963
♩ ♪♩♩ ♩♩	Mickey's Monkey	1963
	When the Lovelight Starts Shining through His Eyes	1963
	I Gotta Dance to Keep from Cryin' (S)	1964
	Baby Don't You Do It	1964
♩ ♫ ♫	Come See about Me	1964
	Nowhere to Run	1965
	Back in My Arms Again	1965
	Nothing but Heartaches	1965
	Something about You	1965
	Love Is Like an Itching in My Heart	1966
	Standing in the Shadows of Love	1966
♩ ♪ ♪♫ ♫♪	My World Is Empty without You	1966
♫ ♫ ♫♫	You Can't Hurry Love	1966
♫ ♫ ♫♫	You Keep Me Hangin' On	1966
♫ ♫ ♫♫	I'm Ready for Love	1966

Table 12. Harmonic content

	Cooke %	Mayfield %	Robinson %	H-D-H %	Stevenson %
General					
Exclusively diatonic	57	62	39	44	37
Predominantly diatonic	43	37	57	12	50
Complex	0	0	4	44	12
Special features					
Blues based	14	0	9	6	37
Repeated short chord cycle	43	87	61	71	50
Common diatonic progressions					
(I) ii V I	0	12	9	12	12
(I) IV V I	14	6	13	3	0
I ii	14	25	22	0	25
I IV	14	44	39	35	25
I vi	0	12	17	0	0
I vii ii V	14	12	0	0	0
Extended step bass	0	56	4	32	0

Table 12, cont.

	Cooke %	Mayfield %	Robinson %	H-D-H %	Stevenson %
Secondary dominant progressions					
Overall	43	25	35	26	37
II7 V	14	19	17	6	25
III7 vi	14	6	4	6	25
Extended cycle	14	0	9	0	0
Mixolydian progressions					
Overall	14	0	13	18	25
Borrowed/unusual chords					
Overall	0	6	17	41	12
Chord colorations					
Overall	28	19	48	29	37
Major/minor 6	0	12	9	6	0
Major 7	0	0	22	18	25
Dominant 9/11	14	12	4	3	0
Diminished	14	0	4	3	0

his songs. Almost half of the H-D-H songs are exclusively diatonic, but the remaining songs incorporate a variety of harmonic features (e.g., borrowed chords, modulation between song sections, ambiguity of key center)——representing an increased level of harmonic complexity compared with the songs by the other writers. The songs by Mayfield and H-D-H are notable for their use of extended step bass progressions (see Table 13).

The other diatonic chord progression strongly favored by all writers (apart from Cooke) is the I–IV progression. In many cases, this progression forms part of a repetitive rhythmic-chordal riff (see Table 14), rather than being used to harmonize melodic movement. When used as part of the I–IV riff, the IV chord acts as an embellishment (double appogiatura) of the I chord, and the rhythmic elements of the riff often take aural prominence.

Table 13. Extended step chord sequences in songs by Mayfield (M) and H-D-H

Ascending patterns	Song	Year
I ii iii	Woman's Got Soul (M)	1965
I ii iii IV	Nothing Can Stop Me (M)	1966
	You've Been Cheating (M)	1966
ii iii IV	Come See about Me (H-D-H)	1964
	I'm So Proud (M)	1964
	Rhythm (M)	1965
ii iii IV V	Come and Get These Memories (H-D-H)	1963
	Heatwave (H-D-H)	1963
	Woman's Got Soul (M)	1965
	I Can't Help Myself (HDH)	1965
iii IV V	The Monkey Time (M)	1963
	You Lost the Sweetest Boy (H-D-H)	1963
Descending patterns		
i VII VI	Standing in the Shadows of Love (H-D-H)	1966
vi V IV	How Sweet It Is to Be Loved by You (H-D-H)	1964
	Stop in the Name of Love (H-D-H)	1965
IV iii ii	Need to Belong (M)	1963
	Baby Love (H-D-H)	1964
IV iii ii I	You Must Believe Me (M)	1964
chord/bass descent	(I'm a) Roadrunner (H-D-H)	1966
	(Come Round Here) I'm the One You Need (H-D-H)	1966

Table 14. Songs with rhythmic-chordal riffs involving the I–IV progression

Composer	Song	Year
Mayfield	Need to Belong	1963
	Talking about My Baby	1964
	You Must Believe Me	1964
	Come See	1965
	Woman's Got Soul	1965
	Nothing Can Stop Me	1965
Robinson	The Way You Do the Things You Do	1964
	I'll Be in Trouble	1964
	I Like It Like That	1964
	That's What Love Is Made Of	1964
	My Girl	1965
	It's Growing	1965
	The Tracks of My Tears	1965
	My Girl Has Gone	1965
H-D-H	Heatwave	1963
	Mickey's Monkey	1963
	You Lost the Sweetest Boy	1963
	Baby I Need Your Lovin'	1964
	Baby Don't You Do It	1965
	Come See about Me	1965
	Back in My Arms Again	1965
	Nothing but Heartaches	1965

Rhythmic-chordal riffs involving other chord sequences also occur with some frequency. Mayfield, for example, uses the I–ii sequence for riffs in several songs ("You've Been Cheatin'," "The Monkey Time," "Hey Little Girl"), while H-D-H incorporate a wide variety of riff chord sequences. Table 15 provides some examples of some other H-D-H chord sequences.

Sometimes H-D-H make very small adjustments to chord sequences,[10] thereby creating variety within an otherwise highly repetitive framework. "You Lost the Sweetest Boy," for example, reverses the I–IV progression of the verse to make a IV–I progression in the chorus (while maintaining the same rhythmic riff). "Baby Don't You Do It" attaches the rhythm outlined in Table 11 to three alternative chord sequences.

Repeated short chord cycles are also frequently used in songs without notable rhythmic-chordal riffs. This is especially true of the H-D-H songs

10. It is highly likely that the Motown session players also made regular contributions in this area as well (see "Production").

Table 15. Other riff chord sequences used by H-D-H

Chord sequence	Song	Year
ii V	Reach Out	1966
I IV V	Standing in the Shadows of Love	1966
I v IV I	Nowhere to Run	1965
	Something about You	1965
(I) bVII IV I	Baby Don't You Do It	1964
	Something about You	1965
	You Keep Me Hangin' On (verse section, in C)	1966
(I) v bVII bVI	You Keep Me Hangin' On (chorus section, in A)	1966

(e.g., "You Can't Hurry Love," "Where Did Our Love Go," "I Hear a Symphony," "This Old Heart of Mine"). Chord cycles are often longer when they are not attached to rhythmic riffs. For example, "You Can't Hurry Love" repeats a I–IV–I–iii–vi–IV–V pattern, while "This Old Heart of Mine" cycles I–iii–IV–iii–ii–V).

Form/Structure

Table 16 provides an overview of the form of the songs. The songs by Cooke and Mayfield are very short (between two and two-and-a-half minutes), while Robinson and H-D-H prefer slightly longer durations. The verse-chorus form (with or without bridge) is preferred by all writers, although Stevenson and Robinson use the AABA form regularly. H-D-H's extensive output is notable for the complete avoidance of the AABA form.

Irregular patterns of verses and choruses occur frequently within both Robinson's (one in four songs) and H-D-H's songs (almost one in two songs). H-D-H's "Heat Wave" provides an example of this practice. After proceeding twice through a predictable verse-prehook-chorus sequence, the song continues with two more verse-prehook sections without the chorus, which seems to begin but then fails to continue as anticipated. Some songs, such as "You Can't Hurry Love," introduce previously unheard melodic material over an already established verse or chorus chord progression.

A contributing factor to these more irregular, fluid forms is the presence of riffs that often play an important role in song structure. Although all writers (apart from Cooke) use riffs extensively, H-D-H use them most often (in four in five songs). In addition, as discussed under "Rhythm"

Table 16. Structural content

	Cooke %	Mayfield %	Robinson %	H-D-H %	Stevenson %
Duration					
2 min.–2 min. 30 sec.	86	62	0	18	37
2 min 31 sec.–3 min.	14	37	91	82	37
3 min. 01 sec.–3 min. 3 sec.	0	0	9	0	12
greater than 3 min. 30 sec.	0	0	0	0	12
General form type					
Verse-chorus	57	31	35	74	62
Verse-chorus-bridge	14	19	30	12	12
AABA	14	37	26	0	0
AAA	14	12	9	12	12
Irregular	0	0	0	3	12
Special features					
Irregularity	0	12	26	44	25
Prominent pre-hook	0	6	9	21	0
Chorus first	29	19	9	21	37
Step modulation	0	0	13	6	0

Fitzgerald • Black Pop Songwriting 1963–1966   123

Table 16, cont.

	Cooke %	Mayfield %	Robinson %	H-D-H %	Stevenson %
Riffs					
Overall	14	62	61	79	50
Melodic	14	6	17	12	0
Rhythmic-chordal	0	50	48	47	50
Rhythmic	0	12	9	26	0
Instrumental solo					
Overall	43	31	48	53	12
Guitar	14	6	0	3	0
Keyboard	0	0	4	3	0
Brass	0	19	9	6	0
Saxophone	14	0	39	41	12
Strings	14	6	9	6	0

and "Harmony," they use the greatest variety of both rhythmic and chordal patterns in the creation of riffs. It is not surprising, then, that these writers should also be most aware of the structural possibilities of riffs. They regularly use both rhythmic-chordal riffs and general rhythmic changes as structural elements within songs.

The presence or absence of a riff helps differentiate between verse and chorus in some of H-D-H's songs (e.g., "Love Is Like an Itching in My Heart"). At other times (e.g., "Nothing but Heartaches"), two or more different riffs provide verse-chorus contrast. Occasionally, the riff-based structure does not coincide exactly with the lyric/melodic division of verse and chorus but serves instead to provide an element of surprise (e.g., "Come See about Me"). In "Baby Don't You Do It," neither lyrics nor melody provide any clear differentiation between verse and chorus, and so the rhythmic motif and changing chord sequence assume primary importance in defining song sections.

This manipulation of riffs, in combination with regular general rhythmic changes between song sections, allows the writers to create variety within a compositional style that typically involves numerous repetitive elements (e.g., riffs, chord cycles, short recurring lyric and melodic hooks), as well as a relentless and emphatic backbeat.

Another recurring formal element in the songs of H-D-H in particular (and to a lesser extent in the songs of Robinson and Mayfield) is the short, repeated chorus statement. As already noted, this type of chorus consists of a few memorable catchwords, allied to a short and easily recognizable melody. The writers use repetition to reinforce the lyric statement and establish the melody in the listener's mind. Table 17 lists the songs containing this type of chorus, demonstrating H-D-H's particular preference for short statements.

In addition to the songs listed in Table 17, several other H-D-H songs use slightly different techniques to approximate this effect. Both "Heatwave" and "Quicksand" (recorded by Martha and the Vandellas) use repeated hook statements by backing voices, to which the lead voice adds further melodic and lyric ideas. "Nothing but Heartaches" involves a repeated hook followed by further melodic development. Backing vocals are also regularly used to create call-response patterns that play an important role in the black pop crossover songs (see the Production section).

Production

Because Mayfield, Robinson, H-D-H, and Stevenson were writer-producers, studio production can be seen as an integral part of their song cre-

Table 17. Songs by Curtis Mayfield, Smokey Robinson, and H-D-H with short chorus hooks

Composer	Song	Year
Mayfield	Mama Didn't Lie	1963
	It's All Right	1963
	Um, Um, Um, Um, Um, Um	1964
Robinson	I Like It Like That	1964
	Ooo Baby Baby	1965
	Ain't That Peculiar	1965
	Going to a Go-Go	1966
	Don't Mess with Bill	1966
	Get Ready	
H-D-H	Mickey's Monkey	1963
	You Lost the Sweetest Boy	1963
	Can I Get a Witness	1963
	You're a Wonderful One	1964
	Baby I Need Your Lovin'	1964
	Baby Don't You Do It	1964
	Come See about Me	1964
	How Sweet It Is to Be Loved by You	1964
	Stop in the Name of Love	1965
	Nowhere to Run	1965
	Back in My Arms Again	1965
	My World Is Empty without You	1966
	Shake Me, Wake Me	1966
	Love Is Like an Itching in My Heart	1966
	I'm Ready for Love	1966
	Standing in the Shadows of Love	1966

ation process. Mayfield uses brass instruments in most songs (87%) and favors them for instrumental solo sections. They also use saxophone (57% of songs) and strings (37%) regularly. Robinson uses a similar mixture of brass (83%), saxophone (57%), and strings (35%) but prefers saxophones for solo sections. H-D-H also prefer saxophones for solo sections (41% of songs compared with 6% featuring brass) and use them more extensively overall (79%). Brass instruments are present in 65% of H-D-H's songs and strings in 24%. The baritone saxophone is often used on repeated bass patterns, providing the bass register with a distinctive sonority. As well as piano, both Robinson and H-D-H regularly use the electronic organ and vibraphone in their songs, although the placement of these sounds in the final mix makes it at times difficult to be certain of their presence in a particular song and therefore to quantify their use reliably. Similarly, handclaps, finger snaps, and tambourines regularly augment the standard drum-kit sounds.

The Motown productions often used a large rhythm section and a regular core of specialist session musicians. Keyboard player Earl Van Dyke describes the situation as follows:

> In most rhythm sections, you might have four or five players, but at Motown we usually had nine or ten, and sometimes as many as a dozen. That's why it was so powerful. You might have three guitars, two keyboards, two or three percussionists, two drums, and even two basses on one tune. We were also much tighter and much more precise than any other rhythm section around. When Robert [White, the guitar player] and I played parts in unison, we played so close and tight that a lot of times they would stop the session and say, "I can't hear the piano," or "I can't hear the guitar," because they couldn't separate us. (quoted in Slutsky 1993, 93)

In addition, the Motown rhythm section often used distinctive instrumental voicings. As Van Dyke observes: "With so many people playing chords, we all had to be very conscious of the registers we played in. . . . [T]he guitarists used to divide up the neck so that one guy would play up high, one would be in the middle, and the third guy would be down low. We'd do the same thing with the keyboards. The section sounded like one big chord voicing" (100).

As well as using large instrumental forces, H-D-H songs sometimes make particular use of dramatically contrasting instrumental textures, with sparsely orchestrated sections alternating with tutti sections. This technique is especially evident in some of their later songs for the Four Tops, such as "Reach Out" and "Standing in the Shadows of Love."

Backing vocals are present in most songs by all writers, apart from Cooke (see Table 18). Mayfield uses male voices almost exclusively, Stevenson's and H-D-H's songs most often feature female backing vocals, and Robinson's songs employ a mixture of voice types. Together with using traditional triadic backing harmonies, all writers also make extensive use of unison/octave parts. These parts often double the lead melody (e.g., "I Can't Help Myself" [H-D-H], "Come See" [Mayfield]). Sometimes the backing voices deviate slightly from the lead melody, while still supporting the lyric hook (e.g., "How Sweet It Is to Be Loved by You" [H-D-H]).

Call-response—contrapuntal patterns between lead and backing vocals—are used extensively and take a variety of forms. Backing vocals sometimes echo the lead voice, a technique favored by Robinson in particular (e.g., "I Like It Like That," "The Way You Do the Things You Do").

Table 18. Backing vocals

	Cooke %	Mayfield %	Robinson %	H-D-H %	Stevenson %
Overall occurence	43	87	100	98	100
Parts					
Male	29	75	43	24	0
Female	0	6	26	65	75
Mixed	14	6	30	9	25
Main intervals					
Unison/octave	14	75	52	88	62
Triads/chords	29	62	87	38	100
Main styles					
Harmony	29	56	52	32	12
Sustained	0	0	30	29	50
Contrapuntal/echo	14	50	91	79	75
Melody doubling	0	75	30	71	12

Sometimes backing voices complete a lyric-melodic statement initiated by the lead voice, as in H-D-H's "Come See about Me," which proceeds as follows:

> *Lead voice*:   "Smiles have all turned"
> *Backing voices*: "to tears"

On other occasions, the backing voices sing the main lyric-melodic hook, to which the lead voice adds new material (e.g., "Heat Wave").

Given the dominant position of Motown songwriters within the black pop crossover domain, it is important to consider the distinctive aspects of the Motown studio production process. This process saw the song-writer-producers collaborate with a team of specialist session players, such as Earl Van Dyke (keyboards), James Jamerson (bass), Benny Benjamin (drums), and Robert White (guitar). Session musicians were on call for recordings with a wide range of Motown performers, and session bands developed a tightness of sound more commonly found among members of long-established groups.

The session players (often following minimal directions) would create grooves that could often become the building blocks for songs. Earl Van Dyke recalls that H-D-H would "come in with about five chords and a feel" (George 1985, 115). Riffs and feels drew on the extensive musical knowledge and experience of the session players (most of whom were skilled jazz musicians), and many Motown songs exhibit bass, drum, and keyboard parts that are highly complex and innovative for the pop main-stream at the time.[11] As well as providing a solid foundation for the songs, these parts help to provide points of interest within the repetitive frame-work of Motown songs. Dozier (1992) has acknowledged the importance of the contributions from the session players, observing that "a lot of the ideas wouldn't have been possible without the Funk Brothers" and that after players had filled out a basic idea given by the producers, his reaction was often "Hey, did I write that?" Since elements such as rhythmic-chordal riffs (normally involving several or all of the main instruments of the rhythm section) play such an important part in the song, the session players clearly contributed significantly to the creation of many Motown songs.

In addition to the creative input provided by the session players, Motown's songwriters were assisted by a range of innovative ideas relat-

---

11. For example, James Jamerson's contributions have been transcribed, discussed, and analyzed by Allan Slustky (1989). There is some dispute about "who did what and where" (Cunningham 1996, 75) in terms of certain Motown sessions. For example, famous Los Angeles–based session bassist Carole Kaye claims to have played bass on some of Motown's biggest hits (e.g.)"Reach Out, I'll Be There," "Baby Love," "My Guy" [74]).

ing to sound engineering (George 1985, 112–114). For example, Motown was one of the first studios to use "punch-ins," to run guitars and bass directly into the console, and to employ limiters and equalizers. In addition, small car radios were used to assess the quality of the sound that listeners were likely to hear.

Summary and Discussion

Rhythmic elements play a prominent role in many of the black pop crossover songs. These elements include heavily reinforced backbeats (in the Motown songs in particular), dance tempi between 120 and 139 bpm, syncopated rhythms attached to chord changes, and repeated rhythmic-chordal and rhythmic riffs—which often help define the song's structure. Sam Cooke's songs tend to incorporate more on-beat vocal delivery and rarely use rhythmic riffs or syncopated harmonic rhythms. At the other extreme are H-D-H's songs, which are permeated with structural riffs built from a wide variety of rhythmic motifs and harmonic sequences. In between these extremes are the songs by Curtis Mayfield and the other Motown writers. While incorporating all of the rhythmic elements mentioned, they use a smaller number of rhythmic and harmonic patterns and less of the complex riff structures associated with the songs of H-D-H.

It is not surprising that rhythmic elements should take prominence in black pop crossover music. The significance of rhythm within various African-American musical styles has been stressed by many authors (e.g., Shaw 1970, 180; Crawford 1977, 555; Maultsby 1990, 192–193). James Brown asserted that "Black music's basically rhythmic, it's all about Africa and dancing" (Hall 1976, 38). As already noted, however, in the early 1960s, black pop performers mostly recorded songs written and produced by white writer-producers, and the songs by these writers, although they often incorporate certain stylistic elements associated with African-American traditions, rarely reflect intimate involvement with these traditions. A focus on the subtleties of rhythm is especially lacking. In contrast, Motown, the dominant new force in black pop crossover music, supplied its performers with songs written and produced by black writer-producers who had extensive first-hand experience of black musical traditions (gospel in particular) and offered writers the opportunity to adapt aspects of these traditions to the pop mainstream. Therefore, it is not surprising that rhythmic elements were afforded a significant role in these new crossover songs.

There are, of course, many other stylistic elements common to African-

American songwriting traditions.[12] Melodic elements include the flattened third and seventh scale degrees (associated with the blues in particular), pentatonic scales, improvisation, melodic embellishment, pitch variation, melisma, varied and expressive (sometimes "raw") vocal tone, riffs, and other repetitive elements. These elements are present in varying degrees in the songs analyzed here. Melodies regularly involve pentatonic scales, melisma, and repetition (although the latter is much less evident in Sam Cooke's songs, which tend to consist of longer, more developed phrases rather than short repeated motifs). Melodic embellishment occurs frequently but varies in extent according to the particular performing artist. For example, Marvin Gaye and Levi Stubbs (lead singer of the Four Tops) use a great deal more embellishment than Diana Ross (lead singer of the Supremes).

It is impossible to determine the extent of free vocal improvisation within the crossover hits examined in this study, but one can surmise that it was limited. Compared with the often free and expressive improvisatory vocal of many blues songs and late 1960s soul songs, the vocals are often fairly constrained and only quasi-improvisatory. They regularly feature repetition of a particular embellishment, suggesting writer-producer direction rather than spontaneous improvisation. Lamont Dozier (1992) remembers, "We were meticulous about the delivery of a song." However, even H-D-H were prepared to adjust this meticulous approach at times. For example, Dozier (1992) acknowledges that when working with Marvin Gaye, "We let him do what he felt."

It is also impossible to determine the extent of writer-producer input into vocal timbre, but considering the light, sweet tone of writer-performers Cooke, Mayfield, and Robinson, as well as performing artists such as Diana Ross, it seems clear that this style of vocal tone was generally preferred by black pop crossover writer-producers (and pop audiences) to more raw, soulful timbres. Of all the writers, H-D-H show the greatest affinity for soulful timbres. For example, their songs for Levi Stubbs showcase freer, gospel-influenced vocals.

Melodic contour is notably lacking in discussions of African-American popular music, but this study indicates that the presence of flat or irreg-

---

12. These elements have been discussed by numerous writers. This present discussion of African-American melodic, harmonic, and formal elements draws in particular on the work of Middleton (1993, 1983), Maultsby (1979, 1983, 1990, 1992), Crawford (1977), Williams-Jones (1975), and Wilson (1974). There are also many elements that relate to aspects of performance rather than songwriting, but they are beyond the scope of this study. It should be noted, however, that a clear distinction cannot always be made. For example, the Motown writer-producers clearly had input into aspects of vocal delivery for particular performers. It should also be noted that various elements that assume prominence in African-American musical traditions are rarely exclusive to these traditions (see, e.g., Tagg 1989).

ılar verse contours (and relative absence of arch contours) is a notable
feature of the new 1960s crossover hit song. The only writer to use the
arch contour extensively is Sam Cooke. All other writers tend to write
repetitive, short melodic phrases, often combined with repeated rhythmic and harmonic patterns.

Attention has already been drawn in the literature to the presence of
various harmonic elements within many African-American musical traditions. These include twelve-bar blues patterns, "static" dominant seventh chords (those used for their sound quality rather than functioning as
V chords), and short repeated sequences (which often form part of repetitive grooves). These elements are also present in the black pop crossover
songs of 1963–1966. In particular, short chord sequences play a prominent
role in the songs of all writers. These sequences, often attached to riffs,
provide chord movement without drawing attention to the actual progression itself and provide further evidence that the black pop crossover
songwriters were more concerned with the overall groove than functional tonality. Similarly, the IV chord in these songs normally acts as an
embellishment of the I chord, rather than supporting a strong melodic
movement. Cooke alone regularly uses more ballad-style extended
"functional" chord sequences.

Interestingly, none of the black pop crossover writers make much use
of the most pervasive African-American harmonic formula, the twelve-
bar blues progression. Of all the songs analyzed in this study, only eight
examples provide a literal (or nearly literal) version of this chord
sequence, and of all the performers of songs discussed here, Marvin Gaye
is the only artist regularly associated with the twelve-bar blues.

There is an additional harmonic element—extended step chord progression—that regularly recurs within the black pop crossover songs but
has not normally featured in discussions of African-American popular
music. Although Moore (1993, 51) has asserted that, in rock music,
"Stepwise moves are normally highly limited," and that "there are clear
grounds for arguing that there is a *single harmonic* language for
rock/pop/soul" (1992, 81), my analysis indicates that step chord movement is in fact an important aspect of the harmonic language employed
within black pop crossover hits (especially those by Mayfield and
H-D-H).

Aspects of song form associated with African-American musical traditions include the (normally twelve-bar) blues sequence, "musematic"
repetition,[13] and call-response structures. While the twelve-bar structure,

---

13. Middleton (1990, 269) uses the term *musematic* to describe repetition of short musical
cells (as in the case of riffs), in contrast to repetition of longer phrases, which he labels *discursive*.

as already noted, rarely appears in the black pop crossover songs, the other two elements play an extremely important role. Mayfield and the Motown songwriters often use musematic repetition (in the form of riffs) as a structural element, while H-D-H demonstrate a particular awareness of the structural possibilities of riffs, using them to help create variety in an otherwise highly repetitive framework, as well as to provide a foundation on which more free-flowing, irregular song forms can be constructed.

Call-response dialogue between lead and backing vocals is also an integral part of Motown songs. Contrapuntal interplay between these parts is a feature of (on average) four in five Motown songs (as opposed to one in two Mayfield songs and one in seven Cooke songs). Lyrics and melodies are often divided between lead and backing voices.

When considered as a whole, the pattern of musical characteristics identified in the songs analyzed confirms that, of the various African-American musical traditions, gospel music had the most profound influence on the creation of the new black pop crossover sound. Maultsby (1990, 202) stresses the importance of the gospel tradition, which, "for more than eighty years . . . has preserved and transmitted the aesthetic concepts fundamental to music-making in Africa and African-derived cultures." Gospel music typically played an integral role in the development of the musical sensibilities of black musicians. Dozier (1992), for example, notes of the Motown writers and performers, "We were all from the gospel church."

It is not surprising, then, that gospel elements found a place in pop songs by black songwriters. These elements have been the subject of considerable research and, in some cases, debate. Crawford (1977) quotes from sworn court witness statements by gospel practitioners, publishers, and others attempting to define the musical and lyrical elements of gospel. Gospel is described as "a vehicle to entertainment and to spirituality" and is said to differ from hymns because "it deals with the ordinary human emotions" (555). Other elements include "characteristic form of verse . . . and chorus. . . . The tempo of these gospel songs is usually fast as opposed to a slower tempo for the traditional hymns. The rhythm, the rhythmic element of these gospel songs is almost a predominant one." Syncopation is "a very characteristic idiom" while flattened notes are said to give the music "an effect that you will find very much in blues songs" (555).

Other writers identified additional musical characteristics common to gospel, such as the use of call-response, melismatic melodies, varied and expressive vocal tone, vocal dexterity, melodic variation, embellishment and improvisation, repetition, percussive playing techniques, handclap-ing and foot tapping, and the importance of instruments such as piano nd tambourine.[14] Boyer (1992, 285) identifies the vamp as a "short musial phrase of two, four, or eight measures that is repeated over and over" nd describes it as "the most important stylistic element in contemporary gospel." Some of these features are also common to a range of African-American musical styles, and their existence in the black pop crossover songs has already been discussed. However, many of the most prominent eatures of the pop crossover hits analyzed in this study are quite specifically related to the gospel tradition.

Looking first at musical form, one can clearly see gospel elements. Boyer (1992, 280) discusses the predominance of verse-chorus forms in the gospel repertoire (with the addition of an occasional repeated refrain AAA form) and describes the different melodic styles normally applied to these song sections. The verse "with its complex melodic line" is contrasted to the chorus, which consists of "a genuine sing-along refrain that the marginally sophisticated gospel ear can pick up after one hearing." This scheme is ideally suited to the call-response between preacher/soloist (singing the verse) and congregation (singing the chorus). These verse-chorus forms dominate the black pop crossover songs and are increasingly evident in the songs by Mayfield, Robinson, and H-D-H. The song forms used by the latter writers occur in exactly the type of profile identified by Boyer, with verse-chorus forms dominating, an occasional AAA form, and the absence of AABA forms. In addition, many black pop crossover songs use the type of short, sing-along chorus identified by Boyer as typical of the gospel song. H-D-H are again at the forefront of this stylistic development within the popular mainstream, writing by far the greatest number of songs of this type. A large number of their songs also feature contrasting verse and chorus melodies similar to those described by Boyer.

Complementing the gospel nature of many of those songs featuring "sing-along" choruses are lyrics that consist of a few memorable catchwords. These are designed to be repeated extensively and serve, like their gospel counterparts, both to offer entertainment and to deal with normal human emotions. H-D-H lyrics, in particular, often sound like a secularized gospel plea or statement of joy (e.g., "Baby I Need Your Lovin'," "How Sweet It Is to Be Loved by You").[15] The use of backing voices to

14. The most comprehensive overview of gospel practice is Reagon's (1992) *We'll Understand It Better By and By*, in which a number of gospel scholars discuss aspects of gospel history and musical style. Maultsby's (1992) article on the impact of gospel in the secular arena is particularly informative, as is Boyer's (1992) detailed analysis of the music of Roberta Martin. Other useful sources of information on gospel music include Hillsman (1990), Heilbut (1985), Broughton (1985), and Williams-Jones (1975).

15. Southern (1984, 29) observes the "advisory or moralizing" nature of Motown songs.

reinforce important lyric/melodic licks also helps create a sense of communal, congregational involvement. This technique is applied most frequently by Mayfield and H-D-H, both for short choruses and key word within verses. At times, the backing vocals deviate slightly from the lead melody—singing notes of different pitch and/or rhythmic duration to create the effect of congregational singing.

Scale choices in the black crossover melodies also have much in common with the spiritual and gospel repertoire. Maultsby's (1975, 328–332) analysis of the scale types present in one hundred spirituals reveals the predominance of major hexatonic and major pentatonic scales and the virtual absence of minor pentatonic and mixolydian scales. Boyer's (1992, 275–286) analysis of gospel songs by Roberta Martin reveals the prevalence of ionian and major pentatonic scales and a similar avoidance of minor pentatonic and mixolydian scales, although he notes that "any great folk singer, especially a gospel singer, will alternately brighten or darken a third or a seventh" (280). The songs of the black pop crossover writers demonstrate a similar profile of scale usage,[16] with a clear predominance of major pentatonic and major hexatonic scales and limited use of minor pentatonics and mixolydian scales. Blues inflections are most often employed by H-D-H and Stevenson.

The importance of riffs in the music of Mayfield and the Motown writers bears direct comparison with the importance of the vamp in gospel music. In addition, the Motown songs in particular regularly use instruments and other sounds (such as the tambourine, piano, and handclaps or finger snaps) with specific gospel associations. Maultsby (1992, 31) notes the important contributions made by Roberta Martin and Ray Charles in elevating the function of the piano in gospel and gospel-derived music "from that of background for vocals" to an integral part of the performance. The Motown songwriters, ably assisted by session pianists such as Earl Van Dyke, continued this process.

Conclusion

Analysis of the black pop crossover songs demonstrates that Curtis Mayfield and the Motown writers injected numerous gospel elements into the mainstream charts. This article supports Reed's (2003, 111) assertion that "the ascendancy of Curtis Mayfield" was a "potent example of

---

Maultsby (1983, 55) notes, however, that specific social comment is rare in songs by black writers prior to the era of soul (1965–1969).

16. The only dissimilarity relates to the greater presence of complete major scales in the gospel songs of Martin (see Boyer 1992, 280).

the re-churchification of black secular sound" and demonstrates that the Motown writers (especially H-D-H, the most successful and gospel-oriented of all the writers) continued this process to the point that gospel-infused music became one of the dominant sounds of the early 1960s pop mainstream. Although gospel-influenced music had previously crossed over from the sacred to secular domain (through artists such as Ray Charles and Little Richard), the extent of that crossover had been limited. The new composers showed beyond doubt that black songwriters could achieve substantial pop-chart success by adapting the musical language of gospel to create gospel-nuanced pop hits.

This article also supports the idea that Sam Cooke is a transitional figure in terms of the movement of gospel into the pop mainstream. Cooke's crossover success undoubtedly represented a major breakthrough for black musicians. However, he tended to write what Guralnick (1991, 37) describes as "lightweight but durable pop material" for mainstream audiences. And, as shown here, his U.S. Top Forty hits between 1963 and 1966 are minimally imbued with the musical language of gospel. Reed (2003, 105) argues that in the late 1950s (when Cooke's crossover success began), black artists like Cooke and the Platters deliberately avoided "textual nuances that might conjure up the image of spirit possession" in order to "convey an image of sophistication and conformity to mainstream norms." Shaw (1970, 85) suggests that Cooke's restraint was effective in that it "moved soul singers to strive for something beyond surface values, beyond the vocal exhibitionism of gospel possession."

Not all of the songs by Mayfield and the Motown writers display obvious links to gospel tradition. Many early Motown songs in particular (e.g., Robinson's "My Guy," "You've Really Got a Hold on Me") incorporate teen-romance lyrics, shuffle rhythms, arch melodic contours and functional harmony—elements more readily associated with the songs by the 1960s Brill Building writer-producers than gospel traditions (Fitzgerald 1995b). Even H-D-H first entered the U.S. Top Forty charts in 1963 with a typical girl-group pop song ("Come and Get These Memories"). Neither is the so-called Motown sound a completely consistent entity. For example, H-D-H increasingly prefer declamatory, rhythmic melodies, allied to anguished lyrics, whereas Robinson's output is notable for sweet melodies and happy, positive lyrics. Robinson is also rightly regarded as one of the most poetic pop lyricists of all time;[17] his songs use devices such as simile, metaphor, and parallel or paradoxical statements to create distinctive and evocative images. Motown perform-

---

17. Legend has it that Bob Dylan once referred to Robinson as America's "greatest living poet."

ers often used a mixture of material from both H-D-H and Robinson (and other writers) and in so doing built song repertoires with a considerable amount of textual and musical variety.

The new crossover music is clearly characterized overall by a demonstrable shift in focus toward specific gospel techniques, rhythmic elements, and rhythm-based structures. Few white songwriters of the day used rhythm as a central element or in a structural way (Fitzgerald, 1996); in fact, they typically treated rhythm as an element of relatively minor importance.[18] The black songwriters discussed in this article should therefore be considered significant innovators in the history of popular songwriting, and their songs can be seen to have pointed the way to the rhythmic intensity of late 1960s–early 1970s black music by songwriters such as James Brown and Norman Whitfield.[19] Maintaining and extending their pop chart success during the height of the British Invasion,[20] while many of the previously dominant white writer-producers struggled to compete with bands that wrote their own songs,[21] black songwriters were able to establish a presence as prominent members of a new generation of 1960s pop songwriters.

18. Leading Brill Building songwriter Jeff Barry has described the songwriting process (with partner Ellie Greenwich) as follows: "[B]asically there were three parts to the song—the words, the melody that the words were hung on, and the chord bed" (cited in Smith 1990, 144). Rhythm does not rate a mention in his account.

19. James Brown had already created rhythmically oriented pop songs, such as "I Got You (I Feel Good)" (1965), and his subsequent series of hits maintained this rhythmic focus. Norman Whitfield moved Motown toward the rhythmic funk of songs such as "Papa Was a Rollin' Stone" (recording by the Temptations in 1972).

20. The British Invasion is commonly seen to have begun in 1964 with the Beatles' assault on the U.S. pop charts—and continuing with the success of other British bands such as the Kinks and Rolling Stones.

21. For example, Goffin/King's U.S. Top Forty hits numbered eight (1963), four (1964), one (1965), and two (1966). See Fitzgerald (1997) for additional chart analysis demonstrating the declining chart success of leading Brill Building writers.

DISCOGRAPHY

Animals. Bring it on home to me. MGM 13339 (1965).
Bradley, Jan. Mama didn't lie. Chess 1845 (1963).
Brown, James. I got you (I feel good). King 6015 (1965).
Butler, Jerry. Need to belong. Vee-Jay 567 (1963).
Chandler, Gene. Nothing can stop me. Constellation 149 (1965).
Cooke, Sam. A change is gonna come. RCA 8486 (1965).
———. Another Saturday night. RCA 8164 (1963).
———. Cousin of mine. RCA 8426 (1964).
———. Good news. RCA 8229 (1964).
———. Good times. RCA 8368 (1964).
———. Shake. RCA 8486 (1965).
———. Sugar dumpling. RCA 8631 (1965).
Four Tops. Ask the lonely. Motown 1073 (1965).
———. Baby I need your lovin'. Motown 1062 (1964).
———. I can't help myself. Motown 1076 (1965).
———. It's the same old song. Motown 1081 (1965).
———. Reach out I'll be there. Motown 1098 (1966).
———. Shake me, wake me (when it's over). Motown 1090 (1966).
———. Something about you. Motown 1084 (1965).
———. Standing in the shadows of love. Motown 1102 (1966).
Gaye, Marvin. Ain't that peculiar. Tamla 54122 (1965).
———. Baby don't you do it. Tamla 54122 (1965).
———. Can I get a witness. Tamla 54087 (1963).
———. Hitch hike. Tamla 54075 (1963).
———. How sweet it is to be loved by you. Tamla 54107 (1964).
———. I'll be doggone. Tamla 54112 (1964).
———. One more heartache. Tamla 54129 (1966).
———. Pride and joy. Tamla 54079 (1963).
———. You're a wonderful one. Tamla 54093 (1964).
Impressions. I'm so proud. ABC-Paramount 10544 (1964).
———. It's all right. ABC-Paramount 10487 (1963).
———. Keep on pushing. ABC-Paramount 10554 (1964).
———. People get ready. ABC-Paramount 10622 (1965).
———. Talking about my baby. ABC-Paramount 10511 (1964).
———. You must believe me. ABC-Paramount 10581 (1964).
———. You've been cheatin'. ABC-Paramount 10750 (1966).
———. Woman's got soul. ABC-Paramount 10647 (1965).
Isley Brothers. This old heart of mine (is weak for you). Tamla 54128 (1966).
Junior Walker and the All Stars. How sweet it is to be loved by you. Soul 35024 (1966).
———. (I'm a) roadrunner. Soul 35015 (1966).
Lance, Major. Come see. Okeh 7216 (1965).
———. Hey little girl. Okeh 7181 (1963).
———. Rhythm. Okeh 7203 (1964).
———. The monkey time. Okeh 7175 (1963).
———. Um, um, um, um, um, um. Okeh 7187 (1964).
Martha and the Vandellas. Come and get these memories. Gordy 7014 (1963).
———. Dancing in the street. Gordy (1964).
———. Heat wave. Gordy 7022 (1963).
———. I'm ready for love. Gordy 7056 (1966).

————. My baby loves me. Gordy 7048 (1966).

————. Nowhere to run. Gordy 7039 (1965).

————. Quicksand. Gordy 7025 (1963).

————. Wild one. Gordy 7036 (1964).

————. You've been in love too long. Gordy 7045 (1965).

Marvelettes. Don't mess with Bill. Tamla 54126 (1966).

————. I'll keep holding on. Tamla 54116 (1965).

Miracles. A love she can count on. Tamla 54078 (1963).

————. (Come round here) I'm the one you need. Tamla 54140 (1966).

————. Going to a go-go. Tamla 54127 (1966).

————. I gotta dance to keep from cryin'. Tamla 54089 (1964).

————. I like it like that. Tamla 54098 (1964).

————. Mickey's monkey. Tamla 54083 (1963).

————. My girl has gone. Tamla 54123 (1965).

————. Ooo baby baby. Tamla 54113 (1965).

————. That's what love is made of. Tamla 54102 (1964).

————. The tracks of my tears. Tamla 54118 (1965).

————. You've really got a hold on me. Tamla 54073 (1963).

Mitch Ryder and the Detroit Wheels. Devil with a blue dress on. New Voice 817 (1966).

Supremes. Back in my arms again. Motown 1075 (1965).

————. Baby love. Motown 1066 (1964).

————. Come see about me. Motown 1068 (1964).

————. I hear a symphony. Motown 1083 (1965).

————. Love is like an itching in my heart. Motown 1094 (1966).

————. My world is empty wihtout you. Motown 1089 (1966).

————. Nothing but heartaches. Motown 1080 (1965).

————. Stop in the name of love. Motown 1074 (1965).

————. When the lovelight starts shining through his eyes. Motown 1051 (1963).

————. Where did our love go. Motown 1060 (1964).

————. You can't hurry love. Motown 1097 (1966).

————. You keep me hangin' on. Motown 1101 (1966).

Temptations. Get ready. Gordy 7049 (1966).

————. I'll be in trouble. Gordy 7032 (1964).

————. It's growing. Gordy 7040 (1965).

————. My baby. Gordy 7047 (1965).

————. My girl. Gordy 7038 (1965).

————. Papa was a rollin' stone. Gordy 7121 (1972).

————. Since I lost my baby. Gordy 7043 (1965).

————. The way you do the things you do. Gordy 7028 (1964).

Wells, Mary. Laughing boy. Motown 1039 (1963).

————. My guy. Motown 1056 (1964).

————. You lost the sweetest boy. Motown 1048 (1963).

————. Your old standby. Motown 1047 (1963).

————. What's easy for two is so hard for one. Motown 1048 (1963).

REFERENCES

Betrock, Alan. 1982. *Girl groups: The story of a sound.* New York: Delilah.

Boyer, Horace. 1992. Roberta Martin: Innovator of modern gospel music. In *We'll understand it better by and by: Pioneering African American gospel composers,* edited by Bernice Reagon, 275–286. Washington, D.C.: Smithsonian Institution.

Brackett, David. 2005. Questions of genre in black popular music. *Black Music Research Journal* 25, no. 1/2: 73–92.

Broughton, Viv. 1985. *Black gospel: An illustrated history of the gospel sound.* New York: Blandford.

Crawford, Dan. 1977. Gospel songs in court: from rural music to urban industry in the 1950s. *Journal of Popular Culture* 11, no. 3: 551–567.

Cunningham, Mark. 1996. *Good vibrations: A history of record producers.* London: Sanctuary Publishing.

Dozier, Lamont. 1992. Telephone interview with the author, October 22.

Fitzgerald, Jon. 1995a. Motown crossover hits 1963–66 and the creative process. *Popular Music* 14, no. 1: 1–11.

———. 1995b. When the Brill Building met Lennon-McCartney: Continuity and change in the early evolution of the mainstream pop song. *Popular Music and Society* 19, no. 1:59–78.

———. 1996. Popular songwriting 1963–1966: Stylistic comparisons and trends within the U.S. Top Forty. Ph.D. diss., Southern Cross University.

———. 1997. Songwriters in the U.S. Top Forty 1963–1966. *Popular Music and Society* 21, no. 4: 85–110.

George, Nelson. 1985. *Where did our love go?* New York: St. Martin's Press.

Guralnick, Peter. 1991. *Sweet soul music: Rhythm and blues and the southern dream of freedom.* London: Penguin.

Hall, Dan. 1976. Back an' proud. *Black Music* 3, no. 35: 35–38.

Heilbut, Anthony. 1985. *The gospel sound: Good news and bad times.* New York: Limelight.

Hesbacher, Peter, Robert Downing, and David G. Berger. 1975a. Sound recording popularity charts: A useful tool for music research. I. Why and how they are compiled. *Popular Music and Society* 4, no. 1: 3–18.

———. 1975b. Sound recording popularity charts: A useful tool for music research. II. Some recommendations for change." *Popular Music and Society* 4, no. 2: 86–99.

Hennion, Antoine. 1983. The production of success: an anti-musicology of the pop song. *Popular Music* 3: 159–193.

Hillsman , Joan. 1990. *Gospel music: An African-American art form.* Washington, D.C.: Middle Atlantic.

Keightley, Keir. 1991. The history of exegesis of pop: Reading "All Summer Long." Master's thesis, McGill University.

Kooijman, Jaap. 2006. Michael Jackson: Motown 25. In *Performance and popular music: History, place and time,* edited by Ian Inglis, 119–127. Burlington, Vt.: Ashgate.

Marsh, Dave. 1989. *The heart of rock and soul.* New York: Penguin.

Maultsby, Portia. 1975. Afro-American religious music: 1619–1861: Part I—Historical development; Part II—Computer analysis of one hundred spirituals. Ph.D. diss., University of Wisconsin–Madison.

———. 1979. Influences and retentions of West African musical concepts in U.S. black music. *Western Journal of Black Studies* 3, no. 3: 197–215.

———. 1983. Soul music: Its sociological and political significance in American popular culture. *Journal of Popular Culture* 17, no. 2: 51–60.

————. 1990. Africanism in African-American music. In *Africanisms in American culture*, edited by Joseph Holloway, 185–210. Bloomington: Indiana University Press.

————. 1992. The impact of gospel music on the secular music industry. In *We'll understand it better by and by: Pioneering African American gospel composers*, edited by Bernice Reagon, 19–33. Washington, D.C.: Smithsonian Institution.

McEwen, Joe. 1992. Sam Cooke. In *The Rolling Stone illustrated history of rock and roll*, edited by Anthony DeCurtis, James Hencke, and Holly George-Warren. 135–138. New York: Random House.

McEwen, Joe, and Jim Miller. 1992. Motown. In *The Rolling Stone illustrated history of rock and roll*, edited by Anthony DeCurtis, James Hencke, and Holly George-Warren, 277–292. New York: Random House.

Middleton, Richard. 1983. Play it again, Sam: Some notes on the productivity of repetition in popular music. *Popular Music* 3: 241–261.

————. 1990. *Studying popular music*. Buckingham, Great Britain: Open University Press.

————. 1993. Popular music analysis and musicology: Bridging the gap. *Popular Music* 12, no. 2: 177–190.

Moore, Alan. 1992. Patterns of harmony. *Popular Music* 11, no. 1: 73–106.

————. 1993. *Rock, the primary text: Developing a musicology of rock*. Buckingham, Great Britain: Open University Press.

Nettl, Bruno. 1983. *The study of ethnomusicology: Twenty-nine issues and concepts*. Urbana: University of Illinois Press.

Phinney, Kevin. 2005. *Souled America: How black music transformed white culture*. New York: Billboard Press.

Reagon, Bernice, ed. 1992. *We'll understand it better by and by: Pioneering African American gospel composers*. Washington, D.C.: Smithsonian Institution.

Reed, Teresa. 2003. *The holy profane: Religion in black popular music*. Lexington: University of Kentucky Press.

Robinson, Smokey, with David Ritz. 1989. *Smokey: Inside my life*. London: Headline.

Shaw, Arnold. 1970. *The world of soul: Black America's contribution to the pop music scene*. New York: Cowles.

Shaw, Greg. 1992. Brill Building pop. In *The Rolling Stone illustrated history of rock and roll*, edited by Anthony DeCurtis, James Hencke, and Holly George-Warren. New York: Random House.

Slutsky, Allan [Dr Licks, pseud.]. 1989. *Standing in the shadows of Motown: The life and music of legendary bassist James Jamerson*. Wynnewood Pa : Dr. Licks Publishing.

————. 1993. Motown: the history of a hit-making sound and the keyboardists who made it happen. *Keyboard* May: 84–104.

Smith, Joe. 1990. *Off the record: An oral history of popular music*. London: Pan.

Southern, Eileen. 1984. Soul: A historical reconstruction of continuity and change in black popular music. *Black Perspective in Music* 12, no. 1: 28–43.

Tagg, Philip. 1989. Open letter: Black music, Afro-American music and European music. *Popular Music* 8, no. 3: 285–299.

Whitburn, Joel. 1987. *The Billboard book of Top 40 hits*. New York: American Photographic Books.

Williams-Jones, P. 1975. Afro-American gospel music: A crystallization of the black aesthetic. *Ethnomusicology* 19: 373–385.

Wilson, Olly. 1974. The significance of the relationship between Afro-American music and West African music. *Black Perspective in Music* 2 (Spring): 3–21.

[21]

"A Fifth of Beethoven": Disco, Classical Music, and the Politics of Inclusion

KEN McLEOD

After the social and political turmoil of the 1960s and early 1970s, North America was fertile ground for an escapist, nonthreatening music that could transcend geographical, racial, gender, and class boundaries. Various authors have lauded disco and the disco era for having "obsolesced isolation" and for creating a "magical dance floor" that included a mélange of gays, straights, business executives, working-class heroes, whites, blacks, and Latinos, all boogying to a disco beat.[1] Though baby boomers were by far the largest market, disco appealed to a wide range of age groups and was often the music of choice at many cross-generational gatherings such as weddings and bar mitzvahs.[2]

Disco pluralism was, at least in part, related to the politics of gay inclusion (personified in the Village People) that intimated that we are all the same underneath and that gay men and women, though repressed from acknowledging their sexual orientation in a straight-dominated society, exist in all walks of life. For the gay community, as for many others, disco united people with diverse experiences on the dance floor, participating in a shared experience of the body.[3] In the collectivity of the dance floor, dance and dance culture manifest a politics of community, typically as a means by which individuals bind together in order to empower themselves. As such, disco clubs and dance floors operated as sites of relatively pluralistic cultural diversity, a diversity that, at least initially, was reflected in the large variety of musical styles and approaches that were incorporated in the disco phenomenon. Unlike

Ken McLeod is an assistant professor of music and coordinator of music history at Belmont University in Nashville. His research focuses on the study of gendered narratives of national identity in eighteenth-century English theatre music and various sociopolitical aspects of popular music.

overtly American popular music genres such as jazz, swing, or rock 'n' roll, the roots of disco are much more tangled, crossing many national and cultural borders and including a broad range of musical influences from salsa to rock, calypso to R&B. In the words of critic Abe Peck, disco enabled African American artists to "conquer the pop charts in a way they never did even during the height of rhythm and blues."[4] European artists and producers such as Giorgio Morodor, Alex Cerrone, ABBA, and the Bee Gees also had a heavy impact on the North American disco scene, and the rage for disco engulfed South America and Australia as well as Europe and North America.

Despite its broad appeal, disco was not a monolithic construct. In the early 1970s several distinct subsets of the genre appealed to different aesthetic sensibilities. "Gay disco," for example, was typically characterized by the emotionally affecting music of artists such as Barry White or Donna Summer, while "straight disco" was more likely to be more influenced by the aggressive percussion of funk artists such as George Clinton. As the popularity of disco increased, it moved from its funk-oriented origins in underground clubs and private parties into a more upscale, sophisticated sound associated with the smooth consonances of Philadelphia soul and the heavily produced orchestral music of Eurodisco producers such as Alec Costandinos and Alex Cerrone. The success of the 1977 movie *Saturday Night Fever* brought disco firmly into the realm of the mainstream commercial marketplace. It is estimated that by 1979 disco generated approximately $4 to $8 billion and accounted for between 20 and 40 percent of *Billboard*'s chart action, and that there were some 20,000 disco clubs.[5] In the years following the unparalleled success of *Saturday Night Fever*, disco, which had originated in marginalized, working-class, gay, and African American communities, came to be connected to elite circles. In the words of one critic, disco became "the height of effete snobbery" and "the ultimate in mindless narcissism."[6] Disco's initial pluralistic inclusion eventually degenerated into a world of exclusion and elitism.

The reasons behind disco's initial capacity for inclusion were situated in many of the stylistic techniques of the music itself. The heavy reliance on new studio technology allowed for relatively simple production formulas (involving 125–160 beat-per-minute synthesizer/drum machine rhythm tracks, massive 4/4 kick-drum effects, tape loops, sequences, and interchangeable rhythm patterns). Such technology and formulaic production manifest a relatively mobile sonic space dissociated from questions of national or cultural identity, and thus enabled a wide variety of artists to adapt their music to the disco style.[7] Many recording artists who were not primarily working in disco, from the Rolling Stones ("Miss You") and Rod Stewart ("Do Ya Think I'm Sexy") to Blondie ("Heart of Glass"), adapted their sound to the disco style. To a large degree, though it was never a completely unified or singular style, disco resulted in a global, Esperanto-like music that would be shared by, and marketed to, the world. Nonetheless, in the face of such compelling images of universal participation and pluralistic inclusion, the popularity of disco could not be sustained for long. Growing institutionalization by major record labels eventually resulted in increasingly hierarchal approaches to the genre as manifest in exclusionary club entrance policies.

One of the most interesting and extreme examples of disco's capacity for musical inclusion arose in the mid- to late 1970s with a profusion of disco-classical music fusions. Works such as Walter Murphy's "A Fifth of Beethoven," David Shire's "Night on Disco Mountain," and revivals of Wendy Carlos's *Switched on Bach* and *Brandenburg* recordings became instant commercial radio and dance hits. K-Tel records initiated their popular "Hooked on Classics" series of recordings that combined classical music with elements of disco and pop music. This trend spawned a number of disco-classical albums such as *Klassiks Go Disko*, featuring "A Sixth of Tchaikovsky" and "Brahms's Disco Dance No. 5," and *Saturday Night Fiedler*, an album of disco arrangements by the Boston Pops. In a slightly different vein, the Electric Light Orchestra, while not appropriating actual classical melodies, merged the two genres in their classically inflected disco-pop songs that featured the heavy use of orchestral arrangements, such as "Strange Magic" and "Don't Bring Me Down." To a greater degree than any previous popular music form with the possible exception of film music, disco exposed classical music to the masses in the commercial marketplace.

Saturday Night Fever

Perhaps the most prominent and influential example of the cross-pollination of disco and classical music was introduced in 1977 with the mega-hit movie and soundtrack album *Saturday Night Fever*. Originally released as a double LP, it was the biggest selling album of all time until Michael Jackson's *Thriller*.[8] The soundtrack won the 1978 Grammy Award for Album of the Year and changed the face of pop music in leading the disco craze of the later 1970s. It featured a plethora of chart-topping disco anthems; indeed, six of the album's seventeen tracks became number one singles in the United States while ten achieved hit single status in both the United States and the United Kingdom.[9] Songs such as the Bee Gees' "Stayin' Alive," "Night Fever," "More than a Woman," "How Deep Is Your Love," "You Should Be Dancin'" and "Jive Talkin'," as well as Yvonne Ellman's "If I Can't Have You," and the Trammps' "Disco Inferno" all became well-known disco standards. Significantly, the only track on the album to achieve Billboard number one status not to have been written by the Bee Gees was Walter Murphy's arrangement of Beethoven's Symphony No. 5 in C Minor, entitled "A Fifth of Beethoven."

This work is often regarded as a novelty tune and has remained infamous as a perennial favorite on "worst ever" song lists.[10] "A Fifth of Beethoven" is easily the highest profile instance of disco appropriation of classical music. Originally released by Walter Murphy & The Big Apple Band, it had originally topped the charts in late 1976 before being included in the *Saturday Night Fever* soundtrack the following year. The soundtrack also featured another instrumental disco-classical interpretation, David Shire's "Night on Disco Mountain," an adaptation of Mussorgsky's orchestral tone poem "Night on Bald Mountain." The presence of two clearly identifiable disco-classical works on one of the best-selling records of all time helped to forge a connection between classical music and disco.

The *Saturday Night Fever* soundtrack album itself manifests an ideology of disco inclusiveness. The recording pays tribute to the influence of both calypso and salsa on disco in Ralph MacDonald's "Calypso Breakdown" and in David Shire's "Salsation." Funk and R&B influences are also present with Kool and the Gang's "Open Sesame" and M.F.S.B.'s "K-Jee." Indeed, the featured artists, the Bee Gees, a group of white Australian-British pop stars who relied heavily on R&B, themselves embody a cosmopolitan plurality of musical influences and styles.

The movie *Saturday Night Fever* also exploits the idea of disco inclusivity. Inspired by an article by Nik Cohn published in *New York* magazine, the movie attempts to explore society's barriers to inclusion, be they economic, social, or ethnic.[11] The hero, Tony Manero, comes from a stereotypical Italian working-class family from Brooklyn and aspires to the wealth and success he sees in the sophisticated world of upper Manhattan. He and his friends are blatantly racist and sexist and throughout the movie commit several acts of violence against rival ethnic gangs and women. Tony's attempt to achieve satisfaction and success through winning the disco dance contest is thwarted by his realization that a Puerto Rican couple, although losers in the competition, were actually the better dancers.

The use of disco-inflected classical music in the film represents the economic and social success to which Tony and his friends ultimately aspire. The disco milieu represents one form of illusion—the illusion of power in the outside "real" world that Tony imagines he will gain through his dancing prowess on the magical dance floor. Another form of illusion is represented by Stephanie, the dance partner of Tony's dreams. When Tony sees Stephanie, an unrefined social climber who seeks the sophisticated high-class world of upper Manhattan, he realizes that his working-class disco lifestyle fails to offer him all he desires. Like Manhattan, success, and wealth, Stephanie fascinates and attracts him.

Similarly, classical music represents an exotic world of sophistication, elitism, and wealth which, especially when merged with a homogeneous disco beat, becomes an enticing symbol of the unattainable, illusory, and artificial nature of Tony's dreams. Whereas classical music represents the illusory dreams of attaining success, wealth, and love, disco music bridges both Tony's real-life Brooklyn and his dream world of Stephanie and Manhattan as an element common to both lifestyles. In the film, disco thus functions as the medium that can bridge wide economic and social gaps.

Murphy's "A Fifth of Beethoven" is the first piece of music that Tony and his friends hear upon their initial arrival at the 2001 Oddyssey [*sic*] disco club, which forms the central backdrop in the movie. To the background accompaniment of disco-Beethoven, Tony enters the club as a king might enter his court and is mobbed by throngs of friends and admirers wishing to pay him homage.[12] The near universal esteem in which Beethoven and his C-minor Symphony are held is here transferred to Tony and his friends, and serves to reflect Tony's status as the new hero of the dance floor. To some extent he is represented as the new heir to the cultural prestige of classical music. The seemingly contradictory and almost synthetically forced fusion of classical music and disco underlines the artificiality of his entrance and of the world into which he has crossed. It is likely no accident that the famous "fate" motive, heard here near the beginning of the movie, functions as a foreshadowing of the dramatic events that will soon unfold within this world.

The other disco-classical number in *Saturday Night Fever* is David Shire's "Night on Disco Mountain." This number occurs as an instrumental accompaniment to a dramatic bridge scene early in the movie where Tony and his friends jokingly pretend to jump off the Verrazano-Narrows Bridge. This scene foreshadows a later scene in which Bobby, Tony's troubled friend, has a nervous breakdown and in fact does tragically fall to his death from the bridge. By contrast, the initial scene is one that mocks the importance and seriousness of life as Tony and his gang cavort on the bridge. The use of "Night on Disco Mountain" similarly mocks the seriousness of classical music; the faked suicides are symbolized by the "fake" classical music. In this manner the value of goals such as wealth and status, symbolized by classical music, are directly called into question when contrasted with life and death issues.

"A Fifth of Beethoven"

"A Fifth of Beethoven" raises several related problems such as the location of the "author" (Beethoven or Murphy) and the ideology of the borrowing of Beethoven's cultural prestige, ostensibly for commercial purposes. Perhaps most interesting, however, is the question of the cultural recontextualization of one of the world's most well-known pieces of classical music. How does Murphy's musical adaptation alter the reception and meaning of the so-called fate motive, and how does his disco version contravene traditional musicological readings of the "heroic" and "aggressive" nature of Beethoven's work?

Murphy was a student of both classical and jazz piano. He enrolled as a composer in the Manhattan School of Music and wrote arrangements for Doc Severinsen and the *Tonight Show* orchestra before graduating in 1971. In the midst of a successful career writing advertising jingles for Woolworth's and Revlon and creating soundtracks for several television shows (*The Big Blue Marble*, *The Savage Bees*, and *The Night They Took Miss Beautiful*), Murphy turned to rock recordings. He was particularly drawn to those involving classical themes such as the Toys' hit "A Lover's Concerto" of 1965 and Apollo 100's best-selling "Joy" of 1972. Regarding his inspiration for and conception of "A Fifth of Beethoven" Murphy claims:

> I had this crazy idea to take symphonic music and combine it with a contemporary rhythm. Nobody had done it in a while, and nobody had done it in this particular way. It was an experiment—taking an instrumental that was about as far from pop music as you could get, and making a hit single out of it. . . . I wrote the song, arranged it, played most of the parts; it was basically my own doing.[13]

It is notable that Murphy, in this explanation of the work's creation, gives no credit to Beethoven. Rather, he appears to go out of his way to take sole credit for the work. To claim that he "wrote the song" seems, at best, an oversight of Beethoven's undeniable influence on the piece. Nonetheless, in claiming sole authorship in this manner, Murphy eschews whatever reflected prestige might be had through claiming collaboration with Beethoven's ideas. The statement also, of course, serves to further remove any "high" art associations from the work.[14]

Beethoven's Fifth Symphony is typically hailed as one of the world's greatest musical masterpieces, a universal statement on the triumph of the human condition and endures, to quote Joseph Kerman quoting Carl Dahlhaus, as "that paradigmatic 'musical work of art' for their time and ours."[15] Given its years of accrued cultural prestige and constant critical reinforcement, its status as a work of "important" music has been consistently compounded such that it ostensibly stands as emblematic of classical music and "high art" pretensions in general.

Outside of the world of classical music, the universal musical message of Beethoven's Fifth Symphony has been largely negated by the lofty prestige of its imagined cultural status. Murphy's disco adaptation, however, serves to diffuse many of the musical techniques that have been traditionally credited with establishing the symphony's exclusivity and prestige, and attempts to create a more inclusive, less hierarchical musical statement. Perhaps the most overt instance of this process is found in the title "A Fifth of Beethoven." This title inverts the word order of the commonly used title of the original and references the slang term for a measurement of hard liquor. The inversion of word order here inverts the status of the two versions of the work, implying that this disco-classical fusion is "drunken Beethoven," and thus serves to undermine the exclusivity of the original.

In comparing their scores, the most obvious difference between the two works is the 4/4 time signature in Murphy's adaptation in contrast to Beethoven's use of 2/4. The use of 4/4 exploits the traditional meter of modern popular dance music and immediately brings this work into the realm of contemporary social experience. 4/4 is used throughout the number with the exception of two brief appearances of 2/4 at measures 16 and 25. These measures somewhat awkwardly punctuate the end of phrases, disturbing the regularity of the 4/4 dance pulse, and thus provide a slightly alienating reminder of Beethoven's original meter.

Murphy begins his adaptation with an exact quote of the famous four-note major third "fate motive" and of the opening five bars of the original work (see Example 1). The ambiguity inherent in Beethoven's novel opening has often been noted. The rhythm is relatively undefined due to the presence of the interruptive fermatas. In addition, the section lacks a clear harmonic underpinning, as the orchestra is limited to playing in octave unisons, in itself immediately imparting a nonhierarchical setting. Perhaps most important, however, is the tonal ambiguity of the "fate motive," which appears to suggest E-flat major rather than C minor. As E. T. A. Hoffman commented, "[T]he key is not well-defined; the listener presumes E flat major."[16] Indeed, it is not until the following phrase that C minor is established as the key at all.

The ambiguity of Beethoven's opening is a feature which Murphy, in deciding to offer the motive in a relatively unaltered form, exploits in its entirety. Such openness provides precisely the platform for inclusion that was so central to disco ideology. Its ambiguity is noninvasive, nonthreatening, and nonexclusionary. Of course, the near universal famil-

Example 1. Walter Murphy, "A Fifth of Beethoven," mm. 1–5

iarity with the "fate motive" would have made the piece immediately identifiable to dancers and listeners alike and underlined the audacity of such a significant cultural appropriation. It is likely no accident that one of the most famous pieces of classical music, certainly the most famous four notes in classical music, was the original target for a disco cross-pollination and the only instance of such an appropriation—in any genre of pop-rock music—reaching number one on the U.S. charts.

Scott Burnham has recently described the following heroic scenario upon listening to the opening of Beethoven's Fifth.

> The listener is irrevocably drawn into Beethoven's drama with this opening that is more a direct command than an exhortation. This is to construe the opening not only as an expression of the self but as a challenge to the self, a combination that of course constitutes the characteristic force of a command: the invasive expression of a will.[17]

Of course such a commanding invasion of the will carried a far different message in the context of the dance floor than in the concert hall. The message, though perhaps still willful, is a decidedly antiheroic encouragement to get up and boogie in the face of both Beethoven's will and that of cultural elitism. As Walter Hughes has aptly observed, "[T]he beat [of disco songs] brooks no denial, but moves us, controls us, deprives us of our will. Dancing becomes a form of submission to this overmastering beat."[18] Thus we are subjected not to the cerebral will of an individual or individuals, but rather to a powerful instinctive urge for bodily expression.

Murphy's work refers largely only to the first theme area of the first movement of Beethoven's symphony. The adaptation as a whole employs a large ternary *dal segno* form, A A B B A, with closing. The repeated A section represents a fairly comprehensive adaptation of the first fifty-five bars of Beethoven's work. Following the quotation of the opening motive, Murphy's orchestration uses the traditional string-dominated symphony orchestra, which plays a conflated quotation of Beethoven's material juxtaposed against a modern disco combo of electric bass, acoustic snare drum, hi-hat, kick drum, and clavinet playing newly composed syncopated dance material. Murphy sets up a disco-funk groove in the bass and drums based on the rhythmic motive shown in Example 2.

This bass rhythm and instrumental combo underlies almost the entire piece, unifying and blurring the distinction between sections A and B and typifying the inclusive homogeneity that marked the disco style. Murphy, perhaps invoking his classical piano background, employs the sound of a clavinet, which sounds very much like an electric harpsichord. Employing a modern imitation of an archaic instrument (particularly when in fact no keyboard instrument of any kind is called for by Beethoven) serves

Disco, Classical Music, and the Politics of Inclusion   355

Example 2. Murphy, "A Fifth of Beethoven," bass groove

as a metaphor of the artificiality of the updated arrangement as a whole. Indeed the use of inauthentic or "artificial" instruments in general serves to undercut the "natural" or conventional voice of the original work.

Mimicking the French horn bridge to Beethoven's second theme area, Murphy employs a C–E-flat alternation in sustained whole notes, which heralds the arrival of the B section rather than a fully developed second theme. Murphy predictably shuns the movement's sonata form and substitutes a newly composed section that remains in C minor throughout; thus Murphy negates the traditional tonal and thematic hierarchy of the original form by avoiding Beethoven's second theme modulation to the relative major. The B section continues the underlying disco groove as initiated in the A section, but largely drops the orchestral quotation. Aside from orchestral interjections of the "fate motive" that, almost mockingly, punctuate the end of phrases, the B section bears little resemblance to Beethoven's work. Instead, the listener is presented with a contrast of style and mood as the drama and tension of Beethoven's heroic opening theme area gives away to an ebullient keyboard solo over a syncopated disco-funk bass and drum groove, supplemented by periodic gratings from a guiro that inscribes a sense of exotic foreignness on the arrangement. As such there is no sense of subordination between the two themes or sections and they function more or less as equals.

Functioning like a loose development, the B section is mainly constructed of a series of repeated two-bar phrases, each of which contains a gradual accretion of melodies and texture. An initial two-measure bass and drum module is augmented by a keyboard solo, another repeated module of two measures. This combination, in turn, is supplemented by the overlay of a string section playing a sustained pedal. This building of material is again reflective of inclusion at work in this piece as, unlike Beethoven's development that fragments the opening motive down to a single note, instruments and melodies do not drop out or become negated. They merely become subsumed in a larger collective.

To some extent the B section, in its reliance on a pop instrumentation, lack of modulation, static harmonies, solo breaks, repetitive two- and four-bar phrasing, and absence of Beethovenian orchestral material, subverts whatever dramatic tension was built into the A section. As Scott Burnham has suggested, Beethoven's modification of periodic and harmonic structure in his Fifth Symphony ensures that any sense of "leisure is revoked [and that] there is no safe projection of the future."[19] The B section of Murphy's version restores that sense of leisure and voids the question of the future by transforming the Fifth into apparently frivolous dance music intended to be enjoyed in the moment.

Following a final repetition of the A section, the entire piece concludes with a five-measure closing shown in Example 3. The closing reverts to quoting Beethoven's original work, and there is a similar four fold reiteration of dominant to tonic cadences. As in the original, this extended cadential combination would appear to remove any doubt as to the centrality of C minor. Murphy, however, abruptly reinjects a state of tonal and rhythmic ambiguity with a striking *sforzando* unresolved German augmented sixth harmony that lasts an entire measure.

Further inscribing a sense of ambiguity, the piece ends with a restatement of the opening motive, the final note of which continues onto the second half of the initial downbeat of the final bar. Unlike Beethoven, who forcefully concludes on the downbeat of a perfect authentic cadence, Murphy, having paid homage to the force of Beethoven's signature dominant-tonic reiterations, dissipates the violence and absoluteness of this ending by refraining from any traditional cadence formula and by causing the rhythmic accent to spill out of its traditional mold and into the offbeat. In Murphy's adaptation we arrive back at the beginning without, it seems, having made any significant progression or achieved any particular goal. The listener is certainly left without any transcendent modulation from minor to major that is a significant feature of Beethoven's symphony, and is likewise denied a powerful final cadence. If nothing else, this pluralistic blending of classical and disco styles effectively diffuses something of the force and single-mindedness of Beethoven's drive to the concluding cadence.

Beethoven's symphony is typically associated with notions of monumentality, heroism, fate, and relentless transcendence of the will. Burnham writes: "Working with the manipulation of the temporal experience of periodic phrasing to sustain a feeling of presence is Beethoven's monumentalization of harmony: there is an accretion of mass in momentum, and what might be merely impetuous becomes inexorable."[20] Murphy ultimately provides a more mundane yet more humanly identifiable work that seeks and finds its acceptance in the need to succumb to

Example 3. Murphy, "A Fifth of Beethoven," closing

common human desires, such as dancing, rather than superhumanly transcending them.

"Night on Disco Mountain"

The other disco-classical work included in *Saturday Night Fever* is David Shire's "Night on Disco Mountain," an adaptation of Mussorgsky's tone poem "Night on Bald Mountain." Though it was not as commercially successful as "A Fifth of Beethoven," "Night on Disco Mountain" provides a valuable and interesting take on disco-classical fusion. The work employs many of the same techniques found in "A Fifth of Beethoven" such as the use of 4/4, a steady disco dance beat, and modification of Mussorgsky's original material.[21] However, unlike "A Fifth of Beethoven," this adaptation was recorded specifically for the movie in 1977, antedating Murphy's work by at least a year; it would seem, as such, an unlikely work to be subjected to disco adaptation and is perhaps most notable for its exotic and strange mixture of instruments, sounds, and recording effects.

The most well-known version of Mussorgsky's "Night on Bald Mountain" is Rimsky-Korsakov's arrangement. His orchestration exploits a variety of instruments, such as bells, harp, tuba, cymbals, and tam tam, which along with Mussorgsky's ominous and brooding harmonies produced a work of characteristic Russian orientalism. Mussorgsky's tone poem, originally titled called "St. John's Night on the Bald Mountain," contains a programmatic element that he described in a letter:

> "St. John's Night on the Bald Mountain" . . . So far as my memory doesn't deceive me, the witches used to gather on this mountain, gossip, play tricks and await their chief—Satan. On his arrival they, i.e. the witches, formed a circle round the throne on which he sat, in the form of a kid, and sang his praise. When Satan was worked up into sufficient passion by the witches' praises, he gave the command for the Sabbath, in which he chose for himself the witches who caught his fancy. —So this is what I've done. At the head of my score I've put its content: 1. Assembly of the witches, their talk and gossip; 2. Satan's journey; 3. Obscene praise of Satan; and 4. Sabbath . . . The form and character of my work are both *Russian and original.* Its general tone is hot-blooded and disordered [emphasis added].[22]

The "hot-blooded" and demonic nature of this authorial description helps to account for Shire's decision to choose this particular work. Mussorgsky's exhilarating harmonic progressions and the swirling string arrangement helps to paint the forbidding nighttime scene in which Tony and his friends perilously cavort on the Verrazano-Narrows Bridge,

which stands in for the mountain, with the frigid turbulent water of the
New York Harbor far below; the rambunctious gathering of Tony's gang
on the bridge suggests the gathering of witches in Mussorgsky's work.

Shire's adaptation, based only on the thematic material from the first
of Mussorgsky's programmatic sections, underlines and heightens the
fantastic nature of the original and injects a variety of even more incongruous musical effects and instruments. To the already rich romantic orchestration Shire adds a wah-wah electric guitar solo, synthesized bells,
a constantly throbbing electric bass, hi-hat, snare drum, and a variety of
exotic bongos and percussion instruments. To this unusual instrumentation various studio sound effects are added, including pitch bending and
stereo phase-shifting, which further add to the atmosphere of eerie un-
familiarity. To cap off this unruly mix of effects and instruments, toward
the end of the number Shire introduces an otherworldly synthesized
chorus singing a homophonic melody, thus evoking a quasi-religious
choral atmosphere. Shire's arrangement capitalizes on the exhilaration
of Mussorgsky's original but adds another layer of grotesque ambient
sounds to further heighten the atmosphere of chaos and alienation. This
seemingly confused mélange of sounds, of course, mirrors the mix of
disco and classical music which overrides the adaptation. Perhaps even
more important, this mixture can be viewed as another reflection of
the pluralistic dance floor in that it presents a diverse blend of musical
sounds crossing traditional aural boundaries. It incorporates timbres
from a classical orchestra but also uses elements more typically associated
with "lowbrow" rock such as electric guitars, drums, and synthesizers.
The arrangement combines a sacrilegious demonic program, reinforced
by the profanity of the bodily experience of disco, with the religious connotations of bells and a heavenly choir. Finally it juxtaposes the familiar
timbres of a traditional Western classical orchestra with an international
and futuristic potpourri of sounds and percussion instruments. The result
suggests the ancient Greek theory of *discordia concors*, a harmony born of
a union of opposites. In this manner disco music and its practitioners are
collectively portrayed not as an exotic alien Other but as a celebration
of the multivalent exotic Self. Like the witches that congregate to sow
disorder in the darkness of Mussorgsky's work, disco dancers gather
in the darkness of clubs to brew their own particular bodily brand of
nonhierarchical, nonexclusionary chaos.[23]

Conclusion: Disco-Classical Crossover

The reasons behind disco's fascination with classical music are numerous.
The centrality of the notion of inclusion to the ideology of disco coupled
with the compositional and studio production formulas of disco encouraged a wide range of stylistic appropriations. To some degree classical

music represented the perfect fodder for disco as many of its qualities such as structural complexity and cultural prestige were natural targets for simplification, reduction, and transmission to a mass audience. The transformation of seemingly stolid and arcane classical music into fashionable dance music represented a notable feat of homogenization.

Though inclusiveness was apparently central to the ideology of disco and an indisputable element in its marketing to the public, a central contradiction in the disco phenomenon resulted from the increasing erosion of this pluralistic ideal. Though the initial expressions and impetus of disco came from independent labels and producers, such as TK records (KC and the Sunshine Band) or Casablanca (Donna Summer and the Village People), by the late 1970s, following the massive success of *Saturday Night Fever,* disco had become thoroughly homogenized and heterosexualized. Its marketing, controlled by a limited number of faceless corporations, such as Warner, Polygram, and Elektra-Asylum, directly attempted to "universalize" or homogenize the product, which had the opposite effect on an already widely popular phenomenon and effectively removed any local or regional stylistic variants from the genre.[24]

Ironically, the inclusive façade of disco was also maintained in the face of increasingly exclusionary club entrance policies, fiercely competitive dance contests, and an image of wealth and high fashion. Disco and its participants—record companies and venues alike—were concerned with creating an artificial fantasy lifestyle that briefly glittered like the strobe lights on the dance floor, then quickly burned out. As Jim Curtis points out, "Artificiality—conscious deliberate artificiality—was the order of the day not just in music, but also the setting in which one heard the music, and the costumes which one wore."[25] Thus disco finds equivalence with classical music, which, at its heart, also thrives on the notion of the consciously artificial. As in a discotheque, classical music is often enjoyed and appreciated in escapist settings by wealthy, well-dressed devotees. This parallel can be extended to similarities between classical and disco compositional style. Like much classical dance music, disco relies on rigid structural symmetry and formulaic rules of composition. As such, formal classical dances, such as the minuet or sarabande, are stylized and highly choreographed in much the same manner as disco formalized many dance steps and dances such as the Bus Stop or L.A. Hustle. Indeed, disco often invoked classical music through its incorporation of complex orchestral arrangements and elaborately virtuosic vocalizations as epitomized by Donna Summer or Diana Ross. Disco was heavily produced and presented a hedonistic, sartorial image similar to that sometimes promoted in classical music circles. Paired by their similar sonic and visual projections of wealth, leisure, and excess, disco and classical music often were a comfortable match.

To some degree, the high level of musical organization and complexity exhibited by classical music may have inspired disco hybrids. As Hugh Mooney has commented, disco "was precisely arranged; the very antithesis of improvised, literally disorderly . . . rock."[26] Thus, at least to some extent, disco's appropriation of classical music may be seen as an ironically sympathetic reaction to the perceived disorder of rock music. To be sure, such fusions, as implied even by the tongue-in-cheek title "A Fifth of Beethoven," were done with a sense of playful irony, as humorous subversions of privilege rather than as overtly political or antagonistic statements on pluralism.

In keeping with Bourdieu's notion of the creation of a taste hierarchy, Simon Frith has commented that consumers of "Low culture . . . (such as dance club cultures) which are organized around exclusiveness . . . have a richer experience of their particular pleasure than 'ordinary' or 'passive' consumers."[27] This is to say that fans of disco, and other analogous forms of stereotypically "low" culture, replicate the same hierarchies of exclusion as fans of "high" cultural music. In this manner disco challenged the notion that hierarchical superiority was the exclusive property of classical music.

Disco, of course, was not the only popular musical genre to experiment with classical music. Progressive rock artists such as Emerson, Lake and Palmer and Procol Harum also experimented with mixing classical music with rock tunes.[28] Robert Walser, among others, has illustrated the influence of "classical" instrumental music on heavy metal such as Eddie Van Halen and Ritchie Blackmore.[29] Crossovers have also emerged from the influence of minimalism on rock composers and vice versa.[30]

As typified by "A Fifth of Beethoven" and "Night on Disco Mountain," disco appropriated instrumental classical music that, notwithstanding Mussorgsky's original program for "A Night on Bald Mountain," lacked a specific articulated message. Disco's appropriation of classical works made little or no attempt at authenticity or historical accuracy. Indeed, the reverse was true: disco artists often removed classical music's traditional hierarchical values and claim to cultural and intellectual privilege. Nonetheless, the excessive and hedonistic nature of classical music was regarded as a metaphor of disco's own excessive and decadent nature.[31]

Disco, especially in its fusions with historical works of classical music, epitomized a late-1970s postmodern lifestyle. The mixing of disco's futuristic utopian dream with classical music's arcane cultural cachet echoes the postmodern condition as described by Lawrence Grossberg: "We have been thrown into a maelstrom of constant change, apparently under no-one's control and without direction. Both the past and future have collapsed into the present, and our lives are organized without any appeal to the place of the present within a historical continuum."[32]

As manifested in "A Fifth of Beethoven" and "Night on Disco Mountain," disco futurism was marked by a heavy reliance on technology, including synthesizers and a variety of electronic studio recording effects and techniques. Futurism was also evident in many of the most popular discotheque names and themes, such as 2001 Oddyssey and Xenon. Futurism in these nightclubs, and many others, was highlighted by the use of space age and postnuclear interior designs and furnishings, phantasmagoric high-tech lighting effects, and atmospheric smoke machines. Such technological trappings were representative of an ideal future and of a glittering space age prosperity as represented by the magic dance floor. This otherworldly atmosphere combined with classical and other historical forms of music to distort temporal existence, creating a sense that linear history and time—and the concomitant traditional notions of musical and social hierarchical order—were out of sync.

Ultimately, the question of how inclusive disco actually *was* depended upon who was asked. Of course, in addition to other external trappings of exclusivity associated with the disco lifestyle, other politics were at work in disco—the objectifying male gaze and manifestations of power enacted in some dances, for example. Nonetheless, to a large degree disco was a celebration of openness. It represented the literal bodily empowerment of a generation and a challenge to the dominant structures of the past, symbolically represented by classical music. Disco-classical fusions such as "A Fifth of Beethoven" and "Night on Disco Mountain" stood as an uncommon, and ultimately short-lived, experiment in pluralistic musical expression.

The emergence of disco, driven as it was by various marginalized communities, directly questioned the white male hegemony that had previously typified and sustained the rock music tradition. The resulting backlash, as manifest in the "Disco sucks" campaign, was fast and furious. The fall of "A Fifth of Beethoven," from a number one *Billboard* hit in 1976 to a perennial favorite on the "worst ever" song lists testifies to the lasting impact of this reaction. Perhaps no other work has, however inadvertently, single-handedly challenged the hegemony of both rock and classical music. Its subsequent categorization as an object of ridicule was the price it ultimately paid. And as with rock, classical music also reacted against such fusions.

Disco's appropriations of classical music remain a contradictory practice. The nature of disco's image, lifestyle, and lavish production values ironically perpetuated something of the elitist sonic manifestations of wealth and power associated with classical music. However, Murphy's "A Fifth of Beethoven" and David Shire's "Night on Disco Mountain" provided models of musical inclusion. In these works, Murphy and Shire consciously problematized the terms of classical music and actively negated many of its hierarchical musical techniques. The unlikely blending of the seemingly incongruous musical styles of classical and disco resulted, if only for a fleeting moment in history, in a harmony of

362   McLeod

opposites in which neither style could claim dominance, privilege, or status. Indeed, such fusions transgressed established cultural and social boundaries and hierarchies and drew on a world of musical diversity that reflected the inclusivity and plurality of the dance floor.

NOTES

1. Jim Curtis, *Rock Eras: Interpretations of Music and Society, 1954–1984* (Bowling Green, Ohio: Bowling Green State University Popular Press, 1987), 301. For related discussions of the club and dance floor operating as magical sites for the dissolution of class, race, and sexual differences, see Brian Currid, "'We Are Family': House Music and Queer Performativity," in *Cruising the Performative: Interventions into the Representation of Ethnicity, Nationality, and Sexuality,* ed. Sue-Ellen Case, Philip Brett, and Susan Leigh Foster (Bloomington: Indiana University Press, 1995), 184; and Simon Reynolds, *Blissed Out: The Raptures of Rock* (London: Serpents Tail, 1990), 154.

2. In part, a proliferation of nonalcoholic teen discos and "all age" dances helped to bridge this generation gap.

3. This ideology, though it originally fulfilled an important function, has largely fallen by the wayside. Today many gay men refuse to be stereotyped as such, and resist homogeneous identification as "gay men" in favor of asserting their unique individuality. For more on the ideology of the community of the dance floor, see Tom Smucker, "Disco," in *The Rolling Stone Illustrated History of Rock & Roll,* ed. Anthony DeCurtis and James Henke (New York: Random House, 1992), 562.

4. Abe Peck, "Disco! Disco! Disco! Four Critics Address the Musical Question," *In These Times,* June 6–12, 1979, 20. Also quoted in Reebee Garofalo, *Rockin' Out: Popular Music in the USA* (Upper Saddle River, N.J.: Prentice-Hall, 2002), 252.

5. Garofalo, *Rockin' Out,* 288.

6. Don McLeese, "Anatomy of an Anti-Disco Riot," *In These Times,* Aug. 29–Sept. 4, 1979, 23.

7. For a more complete description of the conventions of disco recording, see Curtis, *Rock Eras,* 302–3.

8. By 1992 estimated sales were 25 million copies. See Joel Whitburn, *The Billboard Top Pop Albums, 1955–1992* (Menomonee Falls, Wis.: Record Research, 1993).

9. John Tobler, liner notes to CD rerelease of *Saturday Night Fever,* PolyGram International 800068, [1977] 1995.

10. A 1979 *New York Daily News* poll, for example, rated "A Fifth of Beethoven" the twenty-fifth worst-ever song while a similar poll conducted in 1997 by WFMU radio in New Jersey rated it as high as number 11.

11. Nik Cohn, "Tribal Rights of the New Saturday Night," *New York,* June 7, 1976. (Cohn famously admitted later that he fabricated the article.)

12. Tony's white suit, which became a staple costume of disco, also lends a sense of religious purity to his presence. The image of a new messiah seems equally applicable to that of the king of the dance floor.

13. Walter Murphy, quoted in Gary Theroux and Bob Gilbert, *The Top Ten* (New York: Simon and Schuster, 1982), 247.

14. That Murphy claims personal credit for a work that heavily relies on the work of another composer has, of course, many precedents in classical music. Though scholars regularly question Handel's "borrowings," for example, few would question his genius in recontextualizing the work of other composers or question his claim to authorship.

15. Joseph Kerman, "Taking the Fifth," in *Write All These Down: Essays on Music* (Berkeley: University of California Press, 1994), 207.

Disco, Classical Music, and the Politics of Inclusion 363

16. David Charlton, ed., *E. T. A. Hoffman's Musical Writings* (Cambridge: Cambridge University Press, 1989), 239.

17. Scott Burnham, *Beethoven as Hero* (Princeton, N.J.: Princeton University Press, 1995), 32.

18. Walter Hughes, "In the Empire of the Beat: Discipline and Disco," in *Microphone Fiends: Youth Music and Youth Culture*, ed. Andrew Ross and Tricia Rose (New York: Routledge, 1994), 149.

19. Burnham, *Beethoven as Hero*, 38.

20. Ibid., 39.

21. Of course, though the work is properly credited to Mussorgsky, the likely source of Shire's adaptation would have been Rimsky-Korsakov's well-known orchestration of 1886. Shire's adaptation of an already adapted work serves to blur further the composer's authority in this work and hence perhaps allows more room for Shire's manipulations of the musical material.

22. Mussorgsky to Vladimir Nikolsky (July 12/25, 1867), quoted in Gerald Abraham's foreword to *Night on the Bare Mountain by Modest P. Mussorgsky* (London: Eulenberg, 1900), iii–iv.

23. In *Saturday Night Fever*, however, "A Night on Disco Mountain" is used to create an ominous atmosphere around the group of Italian American men who congregate on the bridge and who demonstrate sexist and racist attitudes.

24. Currid discusses this phenomenon in relationship to house music in "We Are Family," 174.

25. Curtis, *Rock Eras*, 300.

26. Hugh Mooney, "Disco: A Music for the 1980s?" *Popular Music and Society* 7, no. 2 (1980): 84–94.

27. Simon Frith, *Performing Rites* (Cambridge: Harvard University Press, 1996), 9.

28. For an informative look at the incorporation of classical music style in progressive rock, see John Covach, "Progressive Rock, 'Close to the Edge,' and the Boundaries of Style," in *Understanding Rock: Essays in Musical Analysis*, ed. John Covach and Graeme Boone (Oxford: Oxford University Press, 1997), 3–31.

29. See Robert Walser, "Eruptions: Heavy Metal Appropriations of Classical Virtuosity," *Popular Music* 11, no. 3 (Oct. 1992): 263–308. Classical operatic vocal influences are found in the work of pop/rock artists such as Queen, Nina Hagen, Klaus Nomi, and Annie Lennox. Formal operatic conventions have also been employed by The Who, The Kinks, and others in the creation of "rock opera." Still other artists who are usually associated with rock or pop music have crossed over to experimenting with conventional operatic and vocal art music styles. Paul McCartney's *Standing Stone* and *Liverpool Oratorio*, David Byrne's *The Forest*, and Stewart Copeland's minimalist opera *Holy Blood and Crescent Moon* are examples of serious operatic art pieces that, at most, exhibit only residual rock influences. For an account of these works, see Dennis Polkow, "Rock Meets Classical," *Musical America: The Journal of Classical Music* 112, no. 1 (Jan. 1992): 16–21.

30. Terry Riley, Steve Reich, and Philip Glass commonly play venues previously only inhabited by rock stars, and the common fascination with minimalism has even spawned crossover collaborations such as Philip Glass's *Songs from Liquid Days* (CBJ FM39564, 1986), in which he collaborates with David Byrne, Paul Simon, Suzanne Vega, and Linda Ronstadt among others.

31. In being considered an exotic, effeminate, and often extravagant art form, classical music was linked with disco in its "openness," and hence it appealed to the gay community.

32. Lawrence Grossberg, "'I'd Rather Feel Bad than Not Feel Anything at All': Rock and Roll, Pleasure and Power," *Enclitic* 8 (1984): 95–112.

[22]

"The Digital Won't Let Me Go": Constructions of the Virtual and the Real in Gorillaz' "Clint Eastwood"[1]

John Richardson
University of Jyväskylä, Finland

The Brit awards have, since their inception, been regarded as one of the most reliable barometers of the *Zeitgeist* in the UK popular music scene. Witnessed by millions, popular music awards ceremonies such as this have turned into increasingly lavish spectacles, which punctuate the musical year and thereby function as temporal markers of sorts, illuminating personal histories and charting changes in culturally mediated identities. The opening moments of these events serve a crucial framing function, priming the audience for what is to come and providing terms of reference that will instruct and inform interpretations of the ensuing performance. So it was at the opening of the 2002 Brit Awards in London's Earls Court Arena.

The houselights were lowered and an aerial tracking shot surveyed the venue before homing in on a darkened stage. Kick-drum simulations of a heartbeat triggered the illumination of four towering screens. The silhouetted image of 2D, the aptly named animated frontman of "virtual band" Gorillaz, emerged out of the primal matter of television static in a manner resembling a key scene in the classic suspense film *Poltergeist*. Three additional figures materialized on separate screens before the muscular arms of animated hip-hop henchman Russel smashed out the four-beat snare-drum introduction to the hit song "Clint Eastwood."[2]

I had the good fortune to attend this event. I mention this not to imbue my account with the empirical authority of ethnographic work. This was, above all, a mass media event witnessed by millions on national television, all of whom would have access to the core material I am utilizing in this discussion. Nor do I claim that my presence afforded privileged access to the Benjaminian "aura" of live performance. After all, the band themselves were physically absent (unlike Kylie, Dido, Sting and others), replaced by animated caricatures of the "real musicians." Indeed, the poor quality of "live" sound in the venue, frequent disjunctions in narrative flow (edited out of the television coverage), and over articulations of social hierarchy,[3] all served to accentuate the socio-culturally constructed nature of the event and to undermine any sense of authentic or unmediated communion between artists and audience. It was in this context, of an event already replete with unintentional alienation effects and the potential for deconstructive gesture, that Gorillaz took the stage, towering over the standing audience and countering the gazes of the privileged many, seated in expansive restricted areas of the venue, with their own blank stares.

This extraordinary spectacle, reported to have cost more than £170,000, came at the zenith of a period of high exposure for the band ("Gorillaz Planning"). The music press in both Britain and the United States had embraced Gorillaz, seeming to take inordinate pleasure in joining them in their satirical mixed media games by interviewing cartoon character surrogate band members rather than the "real musicians." Their flash-media-encumbered Web site http://www.gorillaz.com took more than 500,000 hits a month in 2001, this site serving as the primary publicity vehicle for the group in lieu of more conventional celebrity appearances (Garrat). Add to this platinum record sales on both sides of the Atlantic, sales of video games, and other merchandize including a lucrative contract with Playstation, a feature-length animated film and related concept album scheduled for release in 2004, and negotiations with the Cartoon Network for airings of the band's promotional videos, and the scale of the band's burgeoning influence begins to take shape.

All of this at a time when "manufactured pop" acts were riding high in the UK hit parade, when reality TV shows filled the channels, and when the language of spin, simulation, and makeover was reaching into all areas of the popular imagination from politics to play. The calculated irony of Gorillaz' Brit Awards performance was that some of the key architects of manufactured pop were watching from the audience as animated caricatures of the acts they created paraded cockily before them with vacant eyes and mocking smirks.

To perceive critical intent in Gorillaz' ostensibly shallow and unapologetically juvenile multimedia art is not to impose the falsifying lens of cultural theory on intellectually naïve pop artefacts. Interviews and other promotional paraphernalia tell of the band's wish to resist commodification pop by refusing access to the real (the real musicians) while exaggerating traits conventionally associated with pop stardom (the spectacle of performance). For UK audiences in particular, this critical message is inseparable from the star persona of Blur frontman Damon Albarn, who is widely known to be the musical founder of Gorillaz, whose voice is instantly recognizable as the same as that of his animated counterpart 2D, and whose highly publicized criticism of manufactured pop acts has been the subject of much debate in the UK music press. In a rare personal interview on the band, Albarn comments:

> We—I mean they—are a complete reaction to what is going on in the charts at the moment.[…] Everything is so manufactured these days […]. Gorillaz are different. They may only appear in cartoon form but, believe me, they are larger than life. (Duerden)

The most obvious index of this reaction is in the apparent withdrawal of the "real band" from public life, which stands in stark contrast to the fly-on-the-wall perspective on the pop industry, and the "real people" who populate it, offered by reality TV shows like Pop Idol and its North American offspring American Idol. It is highly significant, however, that even Gorillaz offer audiences restricted access to the "real band."

Albarn's critique of the cult of personality in pop is unambiguously stated also in the title of Gorillaz' DVD, *Phase One: Celebrity Take Down* (henceforth *POCTD*). Hinging on the notion of the virtual as a conduit for parodic artistic expression, the subversive intent of the band's evasive strategies was predestined to be compromised by the singer's iconic status within British popular culture (more on this in the next section). The project nevertheless represents an earnest attempt to eschew the usual trappings of pop industry that is evocative of a variety of musical and visual precursors.

Noteworthy antecedents include bands featuring cartoon characters, such as the Beatles of Yellow Submarine, the Archies, and Josie and the Pussycats; Cyborgs, such as Kraftwerk and Devo; fictional bands, such as the Monkees and *Sgt Pepper's Lonely Hearts Club Band*; spoofs, such as Spinal Tap and the Rutles; and bands in which the identity of the musicians is withheld, such as the Residents and Handsome Boy Modeling School (brainchild of Gorillaz producer Dan "The Automator" Nakamura). In the North American context, "bubblegum pop" of the 1960s and 1970s, as represented by bands like the Bugaloos and the Banana

Splits, is also a salient point of reference. More significant than all th
above, however, is the current fascination with Japanese *anime* or *mang*
cartoons across the technologically advanced world. This influence can b
attributed in part to the pervasiveness of gaming culture (such as Gamebo;
and Playstation), to the rapid influx in Europe and North America o
Japanese cartoon series (including *Pokemon, Digimon,* and *Sailo.*
Moon), and to the growing popularity of feature-length animated movie
produced for adult consumption (e.g., *Legend of the Overfiend* and *Ani*
matrix). Such imagery has unsurprisingly found its way to the visua
representations employed in recent pop, including extracts of erotic *anime*
in performances on Madonna's *Drowned World Tour*, a concept album
sorts by the Flaming Lips based on a fictitious *anime* heroine namec
Yoshimi (*Yoshimi Battles the Pink Robots*), a feature-length *anime* "house
musical" by French dance outfit Daft Punk (*Interstella 5555*), and a growing
number of music videos, including Björk's "Hyperballad" and "I Miss
You." Common to all of the above is a fascination with technology
expressed both visually and in sound, an interest in "lo-fi" sound textures
juxtaposed with more contemporary sounds, a postpunk, deconstructive
sensibility, and an engagement with aspects of disposable youth culture
("bubble gum pop") that resists notions of good taste and flaunts commercial
intent. More specifically, some form of parodic coding would seem to be
implied, which in its rejection of transparent discourse resembles camp
expression.

    Such performances are best explained with reference to theories of
the virtual to have emerged in postmodern theory. Of particular relevance
is Baudrillard's now notorious concept of the simulacrum: a ubiquitous
virtual reality that masks the absence of epistemological depth or substance in contemporary experience. Baudrillard is renowned for his
pessimism, but other theorists, including Hutcheon (*A Theory*; *The*
Politics), see the self-conscious move toward artifice in postmodern
representations as having the potential to serve a potent critical function.
While it has been suggested that the average pop listener might not
possess sufficient reserves of Bourdieu's "cultural capital" to decode
putative critical messages (e.g., Auner, para. 32), a growing number of
scholars take for granted the presence of critical voices either within or at
the margins of the pop mainstream (e.g., Brackett; Hawkins, *Settling*;
McClary; Walser; Whiteley, *Women*).

    Parody is a particularly salient resource in recent pop, which per-
mits the effortless combination of "serious" and more playful strategies.

his underlying binarism of experimental intent and mainstream
iessages is expressed in the comments of Gorillaz co-founder, cartoonist
amie Hewlett (creator of *Tank Girl*). According to Hewlett, "delivery of
iisinformation is as valid as the delivery of information" (qtd. in
OCTD). And from Albarn: "[t]he people who work on Gorillaz are
iere because they love the idea of experimenting in the mainstream"
qtd. in Baltin). Given Albarn's celebrity status, it is of course moot
vhether he could experiment anywhere *but* in the mainstream. Never-
ieless, the intentions encapsulated in this statement reveal a wish to
dentify his approach with a classic postmodernist strategy that privileges
he illocutionary force of artistic utterances over "content."[4] In such
:ircumstances, commercial ends are no longer seen as precluding artistic
vorth. Indeed, this aspect of Gorillaz' "message" is almost wholly con-
ingent on the exploitation of existing codes saturated with an explicit
:ommercial agenda.

This agenda is mediated both in the band's music and concomitant
visual representations in parodically marked "virtual realities" that
operate on several embedded levels. The remainder of this article is
concerned with elucidating meanings thus produced in a specific Gorillaz
song: "Clint Eastwood" (*Geep*). Drawing on methods from cultural and
media studies in combination with textual approaches from popular
music studies, this article combines hermeneutic and empirical work
with a view to providing a model for research of this kind. Although
this article is not exclusively musicological, I have thought it instructive
to supplement discussions of musical sounds with graphic representations
of salient features. It is hoped that these figures will lead both the musically trained and untrained toward a closer engagement with significant
details of the musical text, which should encourage a greater appreciation
of the cultural work done in this medium in relation to other relevant
discourses.

Virtual Band Gorillaz and Its Authorial Double

Given the apparent human predilection to look and listen for authorial
points of identification in music, it is unsurprising that some of the strongest
criticism of Gorillaz has targeted the perceived human progenitors of the
band more than their virtual creation. For audiences and critics, it would
seem, the authorial re-construction of the "real band" in large part conditions
perceptions of its animated counterpart. To the extent that the real band too is
a construction, a highly mediated version of reality produced for public

consumption, the idea of an authorial "virtual band" that is a shadow or doub! of its animated counterpart easily emerges. Albarn characterizes his role in th band in precisely these terms:

> I want to make another Blur record, but then again, whether you'< ever be able to see Blur again—whether I'll be prepared to step of the shadows [...]. I don't know, because I like it in th< shadows. It's so much more fun to see stuff from the side of th< stage, so to speak. [...] I could be in the audience with Gorillaz (Baltin)

This is no mere metaphor. In "live performances," Albarn and hi< musical collaborators assumed the form of shadows moving behind opaque screen, thereby deflecting attention from the animated images anc in so doing arguably subverting some of their more subversive intentions. A shadowy presence is a presence nonetheless, which in this case points directly to a prominent figure on the British musical landscape, whose solo escapades have received substantial coverage in the UK music press. Music journalists and Blur aficionados alike have understood Albarn's animated adventures as one in a series of side-projects by the former Britpop star, including collaborative work with Malian musicians and the composer Michael Nyman. Much of this music has been well received. Enthusiasm seems to have waned, however, when it came to Gorillaz' "live performances." In the shadowgraph concerts referred to above, widespread dissatisfaction among critics and reports of unrest in audiences have been documented (Bliss; Naylor; Sullivan), which could be inter- preted as evidence of the power of conventional modes of representation over the popular imagination, or of a simple breakdown in communication between the band and its target audience(s).

Gorillaz' shadowy double extends beyond these performances to numerous discursive texts, including interviews and a variety of apocry- phal and more authoritative inside stories on the "real band." Notably, audiences are permitted more explicit glimpses of Albarn and Hewlett in a mock interview included on the DVD and photographic material packaged with it. In these images, the two men parade bandages and bruises telling of their latest violent run-in with their animated progeny. Such cameo appearances resemble walk-on performances by Hitchcock, Lynch, and others in their work in film and television and underline the license granted to the *auteur* to play with reality—to insert into the diegetic

ame characters we know are not "actors," thereby creating a kind of
uthorial signature while simultaneously bringing into sight the artifice
nat is his or her creation. Undoubtedly such strategies work against any
retense of anonymity in the reception of the band, encouraging more than
estabilizing the attribution of agency to these "key players," arguably at
ne expense of even less-visible collaborative "agents." A self-reflective
wist is added, however, by the acknowledgment that all is not right in
jorillaz' diegetic world. These are wounded and therefore "distanced"
uthors. They are not, however, Barthesian *dead* authors. Far from it: their
gency is never seriously challenged.

The inclusion of the band-behind-the-band is not restricted to these
mages. Several critics have commented on resemblances between the
nimated characters and members of the "real band," which arguably
oregrounds further the creative roles of authors *in absentia* Albarn and
Iewlett (at the expense of the full creative cast). Albarn clearly resembles
zonked out, postpunk pretty-boy 2D in both physical appearance and body
anguage, and the chiseled features of bass player Murdoc could easily be
mistaken for those of the more diminutive Hewlett. The ethnicity of these
two characters, moreover, reinforces the associations. In contrast, virtual
drummer Russel embodies the hip-hop connection, while the techno-
Orientalism that is so central to the band's aesthetic is anthropomorphized
in guitarist Noodle.

An enigmatic line on the DVD sleeve artwork states "[a]n ego is a
dangerous thing to feed." This tallies with the band's explicitly stated
anticelebrity agenda. But why include even parodic representations of the
band's founders in Gorillaz merchandize if some notion of stable and
transparent personal identity overseeing and informing reception is not
germane to the project? Why do the two men speak in even self-deprecating
terms of their creative roles in interviews (*POCTM*) if an authorial
presence is not desired? These performances suggest that the band must
on some level engage with the music industry on its terms ("real,"
"human" terms) if they are to achieve their goals, or it might simply
intimate that the artistic egos of the two men have developed an appetite.
Albarn's apparent dilemma brings to mind earlier attempts to escape the
trappings of celebrity, such as John Lydon's PIL, in which the erstwhile
Sex Pistols star jettisoned his band, stage name, and widely recognized
musical style in favor of dub-influenced deconstructive pop that prefigures
Gorillaz' music. Such ventures represent a wish to circumvent and
challenge the hype encountered when working in the context of an iconic

band, while simultaneously benefiting from the exposure afforded b
celebrity status thus gained. The ascription of authorship in such cases i
undoubtedly more complex than in bands in which none of the musician
started out being stars. Indeed, the evidence encountered here and in othe
cases suggests that claims of authorial anonymity and democrati
collaboration allied to such anticommercial projects are rarely reflecte
directly in reception. The politics of representation between perceivee
primary and secondary creative roles is also a crucial matter fo
consideration. I will return to both of these questions below, but a
this stage let it suffice to flag up a discrepancy between the apparen
"replaceability" of Gorillaz collaborators (everyone from rap performer:
to studio engineers) and the more elevated positions occupied by the
primary *auteurs*, particularly Albarn.

It is possible, of course, for a subsection of Gorillaz' audience tc
suspend disbelief by taking the band's audiovisual messages at face value.
Fans can go online, "meet" the fantasy characters and, in a limited sense,
communicate with them; join the fansite (http://www.fans.gorillaz.com)
and add a virtual identity to a list of fans whose identities are similarly
veiled behind cartoon characters of their own making. This is unquestionably a part of what Gorillaz are about, especially for those who are unable
or unwilling to look beyond the enticing "bubblegum" imagery of the
animations, the catchy melodies and infectious beats of the songs, and the
faux-naïf surrealism of the lyrics.[5] But, for the vast majority of pop
consumers, *another* virtual band exists that the creative forces behind
the representations, despite strenuous efforts, exert less control over. It is
appropriate, therefore, to talk of two virtual bands, the animated band and
its authorial double, the duplicity of which makes special demands on
audiences and critics. This underlying doubleness permeates all communicative layers of Gorillaz' artistic "messages," not least of which is the
musical text, to which I shall now turn.

Temporality and the Virtual World of Music Production

The recorded popular song is almost invariably made up of its
own "virtual realities" that to varying degrees support or disrupt notions
of emotional and performative realism as encoded within its narrative
make-up. Although the idea of narrative content in pop is most easily
associated with its linear tendencies, as represented by Middleton's
discursive repetition (267–93), some notion of temporal organization,
implying a form of narrative coding, can be recognized also in horizontal

erms. In multitrack recordings, the virtual reality is constructed of discretely recorded parts coalescing in a single time-bound performance. This impression is supported by various means, not least of which are production techniques that mimic the sonic effects of spatial proximity, distance, size, as well as the physical characteristics of the performance space, all of which anchor the illusion of a simultaneous unfolding performance conducted by real musicians located within an integrated performance area (see Moylan 173–210 and Jones). In recent years, new forms of music are being made that suggest the emergence of revised notions of performative space and time or which extend or play with listeners' expectations in these regards. In popular as in experimental genres, first analog then digital technologies have been employed as tools that can assist the creative artist to break down dominant naturalistic assumptions and thereby deflect attention toward the mediating roles of people such as the performers, the producer, and the DJ. Significantly, this mediation gives rise to new temporalities, in which the musical text is no longer seen as a static object but as an encapsulated process that becomes the subject of multiple transformations in the various stages of production and performance. It is clear that this temporal coding has ideological implications, although the temptation to jump to premature conclusions concerning the democratic significance of such strategies will here be resisted.

The hit song "Clint Eastwood" (*Geep*) belongs to a new generation of recordings that could not have come into existence without the assistance of digital recording technology. Just as the onset of analog multitrack recording left an indelible watermark in the music of the late sixties and seventies (Chanan 143–50), production techniques distinctive to digital media have since their inception informed the musical end products that populate today's music charts (e.g., Dickinson; Goodwin; Hawkins, "Joy"). This does not imply a technologically determinist view of musical change. Human actions and interventions invariably come into play, whether in the production and development of new technologies or in uses made of existing ones (Middleton; Sterne 338). These practices are, moreover, bound up with the ethos and attitudes of individuals acting in particular times and places. Thus, allusions to technologies associated with a particular musical style or genre (the use of taped echo in dub reggae) invoke broader cultural formations and practices (those of the Caribbean diaspora, in the UK context, and related subcultural groups) that shed light on both individual motivation (Damon Albarn's choice of this musical style) and the more general

cultural significance of the music (connotations of hedonistic escape ar
subcultural opposition).

Technology is very much implicated in the temporal encoding o
Gorillaz' artistic messages. To understand better where the band cam
from musically, let us briefly consider Damon Albarn's background
Albarn rose to celebrity status as lead singer of the band Blur, whos
music is often associated with the suburban southeast of England. In th
mid-1990s, this band and Manchester-based Oasis, who fostered a mor
overtly working-class image, developed a rivalry that helped propel bot
bands to the forefront of the Britpop movement. As the names suggest
Britpop was concerned with the search for a quantifiably British musica
identity in response to the Acid House movement of the late 1980s and the
growing influence of North American grunge bands of the early 1990s.
The movement extolled a return to the songwriterly values and traditional
rock arrangements of the 1960s and 1970s. As Scott has noted, these
tendencies never led to a complete musical regression or to stylistic
isolationism. Moreover, for Albarn these musical influences ran parallel
with an early interest in psychedelia and plasticity (including the influence
of David Bowie and Kurt Weill) that would become more prominent still
later in his career, as would an emerging eclecticism, involving the
incorporation of elements from styles like grunge ("Song 2" from *Blur*),
dub reggae ("Death of a Party" and "Theme from Retro," from *Blur*),
gospel ("Tender" from *13*), and electronic dance music (much of *13*). This
growing eclecticism facilitated access to the highly lucrative North American
market, as evidenced by the chart success of "Song 2," the "whoo hoo"
hook of which is now heard at countless sports events in the United States.
Gorillaz offered Albarn an opportunity to push this eclecticism further,
essentially starting with a clean slate. Moreover, the Britpop star's
relatively unknown status in North America might be viewed as an
advantage in this cultural milieu in light of Blur's more parochial stylistic
baggage.

Arguably, it is to "production techniques" that we should turn
in order more fully to appreciate the significance of the musical sea
change. While there is some evidence of the incorporation of production techniques resembling those employed by Gorillaz on recent Blur
albums, such as *13* and *Think Tank*, in most songs the band retains the
sonic identity of a rock band whose dominant mode of expression is
embedded within traditional song arrangements and form. The greater
part of their music, also on these albums, was recorded in traditional

ashion, albeit with the help of digital recording software such as Pro
Tools, with a core performance of a pre-existing song embellished with
overdubs in the studio. Gorillaz' *Geep*, in contrast, was composed and
recorded in a more fragmented way, involving the manipulation of
materials on a computer screen rather than in the rehearsal room prior
to recording. Producer Jason Cox recalls the production and composi-
ion process as follows:

> I think the reason why we worked in a different way is because
> we've got this whole *Logic* [Logic Audio software] thing going on,
> so instead of working in a linear world where you're using tape,
> you've got a hell of a lot more flexibility. [...] It just gives you a
> chance to experiment, basically chuck a whole load of paint at the
> canvas and see what sticks, and weed out all the drips of paint that
> you don't want! (qtd. in Inglis)

This approach would permit greater flexibility when recording but would
also lead to some unexpected musical repercussions. Indeed, the "copy
and paste" mentality associated widely with work in digital media
(Théberge 229) became so deeply ingrained that in this case musicians
and producers alike had difficulty distinguishing the tracks they were
working on from one another.[6]

Focusing on the single mix of "Clint Eastwood," the confluence
of technologies and musical practices in the song might be charted as
follows:

1. In light of the producers' comments concerning the recording
   process, it is not surprising to find a high degree of apparent
   interchangeability between musical parts within and between
   tracks. Sounds are very similar across album tracks and similar
   musical materials are found in several songs. There results a partial
   corrosion of narrative flow, due to the interpolation of events
   apparently only loosely bound up with the surrounding musical
   milieu, and of the idea of the song as a unique and self-contained
   whole.

2. This interchangeability extends to the concept of "remix," whose
   genealogy here has as much to do with the influence of dub reggae,
   mediated by late 1970s to 1980s UK punk, as to the influence of
   recent dance styles (more on this below). While in a limited sense, the

Geep version of "Clint Eastwood" could be regarded as the primary
text, listeners with an interest in UK garage have tended to prefer Ed
Case's two-step "refix," while the "Phil Life Cypher version" has
received more exposure in clubs and radio programming where
reggae and related styles (such as drum'n'bass and jungle) predom-
inate (*G Sides*).

3. A structural analysis of the different musical parts in "Clint
Eastwood" reveals the concrete impact of an aesthetic of "copy
and paste" attributable, in part, to the use of music editing software. When working in the "arrange window" of software
packages such as *Logic*, structural relationships that may not be
immediately apparent to the listener can easily be recognized on
the computer screen, such as rhythmic layering that does not conform neatly to the discursive structure of the song. This can be seen
in Figure 1, the spatial layout of which resembles the appearance
of windows in music production software. Particularly salient is
the part labeled "psychedelic string synth," which cuts across the
underlying structure of the backing track (measure 67), and slices
again through one of the song's main macrostructural blocks
(measure 83) before eventually dovetailing with the underlying
discursive structure (measure 93). But by this time Albarn's lead
vocal and melodica are willfully disregarding the song's macrostructure precipitating a gradual slide into the relative incoherence
of the song's dub section, in which the simulated analog technology of tape delay takes over from its digital counterpart in the
looping of the synthesizer part.

4. The most immediate sense in which technologies are implicated in
the music of "Clint Eastwood," however, is in the choice of sounds.
When compared to Albarn's earlier music, a new esthetic of sound
pervades here, which focuses on microlevel transformations and
interpolations rather than stable sonic forms embedded within an
overarching discursive macrostructure. In "Clint Eastwood," sounds
distinctive to recent digital technology include bass subnotes (see
Figure 1), the harmonizer applied to sections of Albarn's lead vocal,
and a variety of effects including reverse reverb (measures 14 and 49–
56), filtering, and panning effects (prominent in the coda and dub
sections: after measure 67). Many of these effects are extensively
employed in recent dance genres but as indicated above much of this
track makes conspicuous reference to the analog sound world of

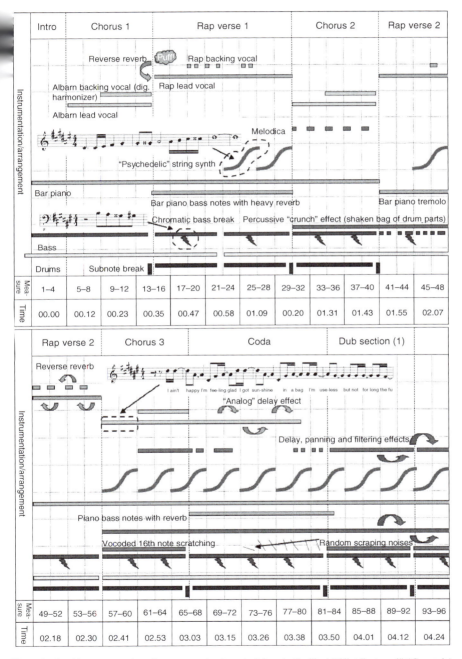

Figure 1: Graphic representation of arrangement and musical form in Gorillaz' "Clint Eastwood" (*Geep* mix).

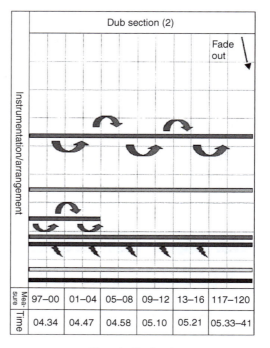

Figure 1: Continued.

1970s and 1980s dub reggae at the same time as it is more transpar-
ently marked as belonging to the era of digital recording. This
juxtaposition between parallel sonic worlds encoded as "contemporary" and "historical" is central to the semiotic workings of the song.

"Clint Eastwood" is characterized therefore by its general piecemeal
feel and by the principle of interchangeability that finds its expression on
several interlocking levels. Given this significant shift away from the
more tightly circumscribed sonic landscapes of Britpop toward an eclectic
approach to materials incorporating influences from reggae, hip-hop,
punk, dub, and dance styles, it is understandable that critics of Albarn's
earlier musical output have responded more favorably to Gorillaz. The
cross-market potential of the band is, moreover, maximized in the diverse
audiences catered to in the various remixes of "Clint Eastwood," just as it is
in the band's parodic cartoon imagery incorporating influences from *anime*,
western, and suspense genres, not to mention appropriations of hip-hop's
ubiquitous culture of graffiti and textual appropriation. The crossover appeal

f Gorillaz would not be possible were it not for the band's penchant for
arody, which allows multiple encodings of musical and visual texts permit-
ng both mainstream and experimental interpretations. This opens the music
p to different generations of listeners, who recognize in the musical text
echnologies that sound like their own.

patiality and the Virtual World of Music Production

"Virtual realities" are created also in terms of spatial representations
f the musicians in the mix, which intersect in significant ways with
ttendant visual representations. In most recorded music, live performance
s simulated to some degree (Jones). The recent emphasis on DJing and
emix in club culture challenges these conventions to some extent, but even
n hip-hop, rap, and dance genres the live encounter between performers and
udience is still largely upheld as ideal. The music of Gorillaz largely
adheres to the conventions, although there is evidence of a deconstructive
sensibility in the combinations of music and visual materials in the performances discussed here.

In the Brit Awards performance of "Clint Eastwood," each of the
animated musicians is projected onto a separate screen. (In the *POCTD*
recording, the viewer is permitted to choose between "virtual" or "real"
performative spaces.) As might be expected, the position of the projected
figures approximates the spatial locations of the sounds associated with
them in the mix (see Figure 2). The lead singer and rapper occupy
positions "close" to the listener (little reverb has been added and the
onset of reflections is long); both are panned to center.[7] Backing singers
(including Albarn's harmonized backing vocal) are panned slightly to the
left, approximating the conventional positions of performers on the stage.
Conventional positions are occupied also by other instruments: bass
sounds fill the center area along with bassier percussion sounds, including
a crunching sound produced by shaking a bag full of metallic drum parts
(Inglis); the piano is located right of center with an ethereal synthesizer
characteristically floating in a large area slightly to the left and in the
distance. A haunting melodica similarly occupies a large area in the
distance and initially it is panned to the left. Special effects, such as
scratching, are panned hard left and right. As the song progresses,
however, the virtual fingers of the producer enter the equation as panning
pandemonium is unleashed. Here, playfulness in postproduction replaces
sensory realism as the decentering influence of the DJ/producer is felt, and
scratching, piano and melodica parts all go walkabout swinging alternately

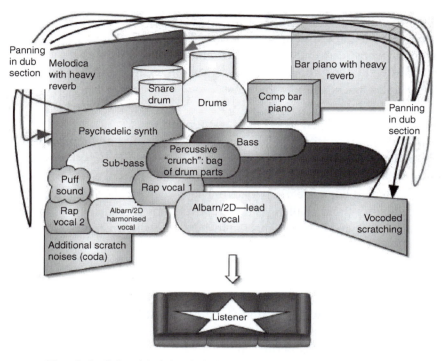

Figure 2: Implied spatial relations in Gorillaz' "Clint Eastwood" (*Geep* mix, stereo).

hard to the right and left (see arrowed lines on Figure 2). The resulting disorientation has its historical roots in roots reggae and can be related to conventions of psychedelic coding in the lyrics and music (more on this below).[8]

The disruption of virtual locations enumerated above combines with the obvious artifice of the visual pseudo-performance to draw attention to the constructedness of notions of spatial location in this particular song and by extension more generally in pop. The mirroring of these conventions in the visuals reveals the arbitrary nature of realist performance conventions. The band's cartoon characters are initially unable to break out of their individual projection screens (their "cages," as referred to in the lyrics), whose frames indicate the rigidity of recording conventions, although in the dub section of the song this is precisely what happens in musical terms. Visible tension between the "virtual performance" of Albarn and his fellow musicians and the "real perfor-mance" of the rappers further amplifies the growing sense of incongruity, although, as suggested earlier, this raises problems of authorship and ownership: which musicians are the real creative force behind the band

and which the "hired help"? The physical absence of Albarn and his team would seem to imply a different relationship to the audience than that of the rappers, who are required to "sweat it out" on stage and whose performances are ultimately deemed replaceable. While the division of labor between primary and secondary creative forces in this performance would appear to have clear political implications, a counterpoint of messages at the connotative level makes unequivocal interpretations injudicious. Rapper Del Tha Funky Homosapien, as his name suggests, is a real person and not one of the Gorillaz, who despite their resemblance to human beings are not cast as "human" but as animated and, in name if not appearance, *animal*. This juxtaposition, aside from serving a significant rhetorical function—emphasizing the difference between "real" and "virtual" performers—can be interpreted as an ironic and potentially destabilizing inversion of racial stereotypes.[9] Returning to the rhetorical force of this gesture, the simultaneous presence of human beings and cartoon figures might intimate—together with the line between anonymity and authorship that is self-consciously crossed by *auteurs* Albarn and Hewlett in their cameo appearances—that notions of "the virtual" and "the real" in this context are best viewed as strategic constructs at the service of a specific artistic agenda rather than natural categories. The Real in this context is therefore best viewed as a symbolic construct that dances in dialectical equilibrium with representations encoded as "imaginary" or "phantasmagorical." Each is a symptom of the other.

Gazing Gorillaz and Bass Pleasures: Virtual Worlds within Worlds in the Narrative of "Clint Eastwood"

A fourth and final sense in which "Clint Eastwood" invokes "virtual realities" is through the creation of embedded narrative worlds in the combination of media employed in the song. There is no direct reference to the actor Clint Eastwood in the music or lyrics of the song that bears his name. Instead, interview material suggests that the choice of the title was justified by the song's general "Western feel" (Inglis). The actor's name was nevertheless incorporated, and the following discussion shows that its inclusion serves as a significant "hermeneutic window" opening expansive vistas onto several discursive fields.

Regarding the star persona of Eastwood, characters in the actor's early career occupied complex ethical positions that defied Euro-American stereotypes of heroism as association exclusively with the category "good" (Dyer, *Stars* 49).[10] Dyer has discussed conventional male strategies designed

to deflect or invert the gaze, which include looking away as if disinterested
the viewer, glancing upwards as if engaging in spiritual communion, an
confronting the viewer by staring back at the camera ("Don't Look" 61–63
Eastwood's performances are characterized by precisely such strategies c
evasion and inversion and by an icy detachment that is understood b
characters in his films and viewers alike as self-empowering. Because c
the independence of his characters vis-à-vis collective forms of power, thi
aspect of his identity can easily be interpreted as "oppositional" or "
establishment" (Carlson 11). Since the violence meted out by him i
generally at the expense of callous and dehumanized adversaries who ar
every bit as tough as the hero himself, viewers who identify with the star'
perceived oppositional attributes tend not to mind (Dyer, *Stars* 49).

Eastwood is known for many roles, including maverick cop Dirt
Harry, but made his name and a star persona that would carry acros
numerous roles in Sergio Leone's spaghetti Westerns (Dyer, *Stars* 49–50)
These films, which were strongly influenced by Akira Kurosawa'
Samurai epics, now enjoy cult status. Although seldom commented
in the popular literature, the East Asian genealogy of the spaghetti Westerns is particularly salient to the present discussion. The highly stylizec
portrayal of violence that characterizes both Eastwood's Westerns anc
their cinematic antecedents has much in common with the violence tha
permeates Gorillaz' animated representations. Significantly, the two have
common genealogical ties. Representations in the Japanese *anime* tradition, which are knowingly invoked in Hewlett's cartoon characters, repeatedly allude to heroic Samurai culture. Superimpose on this the toughness
of UK punk and the stylized violence of hip-hop subculture, and an
aesthetic confluence begins to take shape. The very nature of these
representations, as crystallized also in the techno-Orientalist character
Noodle (who resembles many an *anime* heroine), points to a form of
"globalization" that resists definition as exclusively "Euro-American."
Rather, it is bound up with more fluid patterns of production, dispersion,
and reception that characterize the deployment of mass media in the
postindustrial contemporary world. At the same time, Gorillaz' representations offer the possibility of identification with a grittier heroism than
that of the traditional romantic hero in the West, the highly stylized nature
of which leaves open the possibility of nonmainstream interpretations. The
confluence of these two streams, therefore—the East Asian artistic
sensibility of Gorillaz' visual style and references to cinema's best-
known tough guy—should not be seen as "accidental." Both are

ɔmologous with the affected naivety of the music, with all of its parodic ɪvocations of disposable youth culture.

The ethos of the spaghetti westerns is reinforced in the Brit awards ɪerformance in the Eastwood-like appearance of bass guitarist Murdoc, ʰho wears a crucifix that brings to mind Boot Hill-style graveyards, and in ɪnger 2D's John Lydon-like vacant stare. Both the promotional video and ɪe graphics of the single reinforce this impression in different ways, with ɪe archetypal graveyard location of Westerns playing a notable role in the ideo and the hands of a cartoon audience doubling as cacti on the prairie n the sleeve artwork of the CD single. The stony-faced detachment of the ɪartoon characters, which draws on codes of the masculine recognizable ɪom Eastwood's movies as well as from punk and so-called cock-rock, is ɪasily transferred to the unseen human band members. The reference to ɪastwood, therefore, brings into play intertexts of global politics; but also, ɪnd not insignificantly, constructions of masculinity.

As noted above, the actor is not directly alluded to in the lyrics but ɪe is in the music. Albarn's melodica and a stereotypical detuned bar ɪiano—referred to by the producers as a "cheesy upright" (Inglis)—are ɪoth evocative of Westerns in general and Ennio Morricone's spaghetti ɪWestern soundtracks in particular. The melodica is timbrally close to the ɪarmonica heard in the soundtrack to these films, while the tremolo effect ɪf the upright piano in the rap sections is reminiscent of the piano styles ɪeard in Western bar scenes. In addition, the expansive reverb on several ɪnstruments in the dub section, although liable to be approximated in the ɪeal world only in canyons with very high walls, is conventionally asso-ciated with wide-open spaces such as the desolate landscapes seen in ɪGorillaz' video and CD artwork. The semiotic modus operandi here is ɪthat of synecdoche, the extraction, and relocation of the musical signifiers ɪsufficing, in collaboration with the title and visual spectacle, to resurrect something of the mood and ethos of the original cinematic experience.

But the allusion to Eastwood goes further than this. Reggae toaster Clint Eastwood, whose fame coincided with the early punk period, is an obvious point of reference. Affinities between the punk movement and reggae are well documented in research on subcultures. Albarn was strongly influenced by punk, as evidenced in his indolent vocal style and general laddish demeanor, and a parallel interest in reggae is more than apparent in the music and production of this song. It should be noted that the sound world of dub reggae was a conscious point of reference during the making of the album, sections of which were recorded in

Jamaica (Inglis). All of this begs the question, why Clint Eastwood The appeal of the star in oppositional subcultures cannot be reduced to single overarching explanation, but one could view the actor's iconi presence as representing an uncompromising, partially self-ironic respons to social injustice and a reaction to inaccessible or unappealing main stream models of masculinity. References to Eastwood are consonant wit the hip-hop sensibility implied in the rap sections of the song in tander with the scratching that punctuates its rhythmic texture, which connot a streetwise hardness that is double-edged, recognizable as camped-u posturing from one vantage point and testosterone-fueled defiance another.

As we have seen, the music draws from a palette of influences. The prominent bass line recalls both the rootsy stomp of Robbie Shakespear and the postpunk drive of Jah Wobble. This sound, produced not on a bas guitar but a moog synthesizer, is bolstered half way through the firs section by subnotes, indicating an affinity with contemporary urban style including drum'n'bass and UK garage. This textural adjustment, whict brings into play the subwoofers and bass boost buttons on contemporary hi-fi systems, invites identifications across generations and cultural groups. Reggae permeates the sonic identity of the song more deeply still: Augustus Pablo's trademark use of the melodica is unashamedly signified on, while the production techniques of the dub section recall the ideals of mixing guru Lee "Scratch" Perry. But the sounds of reggae are mediated through a form of double coding that employs the character-istic slow tempo and upbeat chop of reggae (implied in the second upbeat), while seasoning this with syncopated sixteenth-note scratching produced not with turntables but digital vocoder software. Ambiguities between reggae toasting and its descendent rap are similarly exploited, and the faster, more rhythmically dynamic phrasings of contemporary dance styles infect in turn virtually every instrument in the mix: from the lead vocal in the first rap section, to the scratching hands of the DJ/producer, and, finally, to the melodica solo in the dub section. This dialogical exchange between musical parts provides the main rhythmic impetus of the song and encodes its musical textures as unmistakably contemporary while evoking past musical worlds.

Melodically, the sections sung by Albarn are characterized by a lazy aeolian/pentatonic oscillation between the tonic and the dominant in the first two measures, giving a nondirectional, aimless feel, the dysphoric charge of which is heightened by passing aeolian thirds (see Ex. 1).

Gorillaz' "Clint Eastwood" 21

I ain't happy I'm fee-ling glad I got sun-shine in a bag I'm use-less but not for long the fu-

-ture is co-ming on, is co- ming on is co-ming on is co-ming on

Ex. 1: A notational approximation of Albarn/2D's lead vocals in "Clint Eastwood".

The melody sinks lethargically down to the subdominant in the third bar and the lower tonic in the fourth. The final step incorporates a minor third descent, which brings a sense of disillusionment or submission. Finally, the melody rests on the simple alternation of the aeolian seventh degree and the tonic, coinciding with the echoing line "it's coming on, it's coming on." The apathy of the singer is reinforced in his slurred articulation and references in the lyrics to his own uselessness; a situation we are told will change in the not-so-distant future. The line "sunshine in a bag," the main hook of the song, is ambiguous: it could refer to something the character has done—this song, for example, if an author-centered reading is privileged—which will eventually pull him out of his malaise, or it could imply the prospect of drug-induced bliss.

Interpretations of the lyrics are likely for many listeners to be conditioned by concomitant musical coding. The fairground organ-like, chromatically rising synthesizer line is particularly significant in this regard. Add to this, the disorientation brought about in the dub section as the discursive structure of the song disintegrates while conventions of performative realism are knowingly undermined and a clear set of cultural references is mobilized. The strategies employed here resemble those discussed by Whiteley in her work on Jimi Hendrix: "upward" musical movement, nondirectional, or "floating," movement, "blurred," unclear or distorted timbres, and chromaticism are all conventional markers of the psychedelic ("Progressive Rock" 236, 249–50). In this case, the hallucinatory effects of marijuana are implied through the association with dub reggae, although the reference to "sunshine" could be understood to refer to Californian Sunshine, a form of LSD or "acid" widely available in the 1980s, which was often sold in small plastic bags. In the context of pop/rock subculture, these allusions would seem to serve a fairly conventional function, working against the taken-for-granted structures of "square" or "uncool" mainstream culture while endorsing an escapist, undeniably masculinized notion of freedom. Significantly, however, this tendency is countered by another, more dynamic force. Albarn's world-weary, possibly drug-induced, disengagement contrasts sharply with rap singer Del Tha Funky Homosapien's more pro-active stance. Within the overall world-within-a-world of the song, then, two virtual spaces vie with another. When release comes, it is engendered by means of musical and linguistic initiatives located in the rap sections of the song. It is the combative and highly energized world of rap (Del Tha Funky Homosapien: "finally someone let me out of my cage"), therefore, which eventually provides the required antidote to Albarn's lyrically languid choruses (Albarn: "I'm useless, but not for long, the future is coming on"). The release of energy is substantial and has the impact of a genie let out of its bottle (images in the music video support this interpretation). In the lyrics as well, animate and inanimate forces are unleashed or "let out of their cage" as the song progresses, a line that is anticipated by an eerie reverse reverb culminating in an ambiguous "puff" sound. The musical catalyst for this change is rhythm, located, by the rapper, "under each snare."

Afterthoughts

What sense can be made of Gorillaz' multimedia performances? Is this a playful deployment of Derridean deferral, where semiotic slippage brought about by listeners' inability to locate the band, makes a mockery of the very act of representation, thus foregrounding spectacle and pleasures of the lower register? Perhaps, this deployment has a critical edge, with the partial withdrawal of the "real band" from the public eye allowing audiences to re-examine their relationship to acts that employ more conventional modes of representation, and to recognize their own alienated condition as propagated by a nonbenign and dehumanizing music industry. When viewed in the light, the larger-than-life projected characters of the band and the unseen forces that guide them raise similar questions to those brought up in avant-garde music and theater.[11]

Similar issues have been addressed also in recent cinema. At the end of a key scene in *The Truman Show*, the creator of a fictional reality TV series warns its hero not to step outside of the simulacrum he has lived in since birth: "there's no more truth out there," he observes, "than there is in the world I created for you." This quotation, with its obvious Baudrillardian echoes, is paraphrased in a comment of Hewlett's: "Gorillaz may not be real but they are no less so than the caricatures that are Marilyn Manson and Eminem" (Duerden). It is possible, however,

o ignore or overlook the parodic side of Gorillaz, in which case the
*runching rhythms and towering figures of the virtual musicians might
esemble more than they disarm existing modes of representation.

Unsurprisingly, long-time Blur adversary Noel Gallagher is
nconvinced. In a recent interview he has commented:

> "Is there a bandwagon passing? Park it outside my house." He'll
> be in a heavy metal band next year when it's fashionable […].
> [I]t's fitting that he ended up a cartoon. He always was a cartoon.
> (qtd. in Odell 100)

Here, Gallagher seems to recognize both Albarn's troubling complicity with the culture industry and the apparent futility of his idealistic
attempts to step outside of its symbolic apparatus. But by placing *himself*
on the outside the Oasis singer does little more than to revert unreflectively
to stereotypes of authenticity as the exclusive property of the rebellious
male rock star. Returning to Albarn, there can be no doubt that in this
project he has taken a disconcerting step toward the lucrative youth market
on the one hand and the postcountercultural hedonism of dance on the
other. His new audiovisual environment, created using the nonlinear,
object-oriented logic of Logic Audio and a semi-anonymous wealth of
collaborative talent is infuriatingly flexible, apparently impossible to pin
down to a fixed ideological agenda, preoccupied with production techniques
and presentation rather than the serious business of writing and performing
songs. In the space between the flickering of the animated figures and a
booming synthetic bass, however, an agenda of sorts can be recognized
and this agenda is closely bound up with the technological keystones of
the music.

"The digital won't let me go," Albarn sings in the refrain of the
song "Tomorrow Comes Today" (*Geep*), which brings to mind Adorno's
controversial comments regarding the impact of industrial technology on
African-American music. In his view, genres such as jazz and blues were
so saturated with the rhetoric of oppression, as conveyed most obviously
in their repetitive form, that even the most politically reactionary song
became an unintentional affirmation of technocratic servitude. He was not
willing to concede that transforming the material conditions of oppression
musically might lead to a form of emancipation. In Gorillaz' music, like
the blues, the source of greatest anxiety in pop might also be
the source of listeners' greatest pleasure. A powerful subtext in the

words, music, and visual representations of their songs points to the alienation of a technologically savvy, postapocalyptic "lost generation" embracing a life of pointless pleasure and streetwise skepticism Technology is inextricably bound up with the band's musical world well. While the music of "Clint Eastwood" makes nostalgic reference to the analog technology of punk era dub reggae, the song would not have turned out the way it did had it not been produced in a contemporary digital setting incorporating an array of current styles. This is conveyed both in the choice of sounds and in the structural properties of the music. It results in a form of temporal stratification between "historical" and "contemporary" styles that leads to the partial rebuttal of narratives of technological progress, but, more importantly, it enables the tracking of personal and collective changes among diverse audience groups. The power of Gorillaz' music, however, can be explained only when all of this cross-referencing is inscribed within the context of a carefully crafted and deceptively simple pop song, which in no small measure is attributable to the handiwork of Albarn. The *auteur* in the age of digital pop may well be mortally wounded, as evidenced by Albarn's disheveled appearance, but he certainly does not seem willing to lie down and die.

This is decidedly not, however, a 1960s-style singer-songwriter *auteur*. If the running call of that generation was Timothy Leary's catch phrase "turn on, tune in, drop out," a reversal of these sentiments might be indicated by 2D's final act of the Brit Awards performance. In a gesture as self-empowering yet evasive as man-without-a-name Damon Albarn's reluctance to take center-stage in this project, his animated double approaches the camera with haughty indifference at the end of the Brit Awards performance to extinguish his own image. This measured response to his own "overexposure" may find a parallel in pop consumers' growing skepticism toward the overexposure of manufactured pop acts as indicated by the plummeting sales recent music industry figures have recorded. Perhaps, the critics are right and pop has no need for soapboxes, as each generation critiques itself in music and music sales.

Acknowledgments

I am greatly indebted to Stan Hawkins, who attended Gorillaz' Brit awards performance with me and gave invaluable feedback on several versions of this article. I also thank Sheila Whiteley, Anne Sivuoja-Gunaratnam, and two anonymous peer reviewers.

Notes

1. This research was supported by the Academy of Finland.

2. For a journalistic account of this event, see Richardson ("Is that the Sound").

3. Music industry representatives and pop artists seated high above the dance floor were served champagne and gourmet food throughout the evening. Complementary tickets were distributed to a small number of students, who inhabited the dance floor and had no access to the greater part of the venue.

4. The idea of the illocutionary act as emphasizing the performative is indebted to J. L. Austin's theory of speech acts, imported to musicology by Kramer.

5. My ten-year-old daughter is a case in point. She has no desire to interpret Gorillaz as anything other than a cartoon band.

6. The following quotation illustrates this point: "At the beginning loads of songs merged into each other [...]. Say if we had four tunes, all those four tunes would be made up of all the same bits ... We'd keep swapping bits round, and whatever it sounded best in, we'd leave it in that song and take it out of the other song [...]. The confusing thing was the names changing all the way through. We would have our name for a song, Damon would have his [...], and we'd be sitting there for ages having to listen to all the songs again to find out what he was calling it!" (Cox qtd. in Inglis)

7. This applies to the Dolby Digital surround sound recording as well, where the surround sound channels are used predominantly for ambient sound.

8. Panning conventions have been notably discussed by Tagg, whose interpretation of Abba's "Fernando" points to the ideological significance of situating the Western European lead vocalist center-front in the mix while "ethnic" quena flutes are located at the periphery (97).

9. For a detailed discussion of the racial implications of the use of the word "gorilla" and its homophone "guerrilla" in hip-hop culture, see Potter (76–79). Originally conceived of as a racist slur on African-Americans, the term has been knowingly "Signified on" by rappers, who invest it with positive connotations of streetwise toughness and exoticism. The appropriation by Albarn and his collaborators of the hip-hop usage betokens a wish to partake of these

subversive qualities and seems apt in light of the band's dehumanized visual representations.

10. For more on the gaze in popular and television music, see e.g., Dibben (102), Hawkins (*Settling* 184), and Richardson ("Laura and Twin Peaks").

11. Including that of Laurie Anderson and Philip Glass. On Glass, see Richardson (*Singing Archaeology*) and McClary (139–45).

Works Cited

Auner, Joseph. "Making Old Machines Speak: Images of Technology in Recent Music." *Echo* 2.2 (2000): 32 pars. 13 Feb. 2004 <http://www.humnet. ucla.edu/echo>.

Baltin, Steve. "Albarn Going Ape Over Gorillaz: Blur Frontman Prefers Animated Life 'in the Shadows.'" *Rolling Stone* 25 July 2001. 24 Jan. 2004 <http://www.rollingstone.com/>.

Baudrillard, Jean. *Simulations.* Trans. Paul Foss, Paul Patton, and Philip Beitchman. New York: Semiotext(e), 1983.

Bliss, Karen. "Rocky Start to Gorillaz Tour: Tight Quarters Prevent Crowd from Enjoying Music/Animation Project." *Rolling Stone* 25 Feb. 2002. 24 Jan. 2004 <http://www.rollingstone.com/>.

Brackett, David. *Interpreting Popular Music.* Cambridge: Cambridge UP, 1995.

Carlson, Michael. *Clint Eastwood.* Harpendon: Cox & Wyman, 2002.

Chanan, Michael. *Repeated Takes: A Short History of Recording and Its Effects on Music.* London: Verso, 1995.

Dibben, Nicola. "Pulp, Pornography and Spectatorship: Subject Matter and Subject Position in Pulp's This is Hardcore." *Journal of the Royal Musicological Association* 126 (2001): 83–106.

Dickinson, Kay. "'Believe'? Vocoders, Digitalised Female Identity and Camp." *Popular Music* 20.3 (2001): 333–47.

Duerden, Nick. "Gorillaz in Our Midst." *The Observer* 11 March 2001. 24 Jan. 2004 <http://www.guardian.co.uk/arts/>.

Dyer, Richard. "Don't Look Now: The Instabilities of the Male Pin-Up." *Screen* 23.3–4 (1982): 61–73.

———. *Stars.* London: BFI, 1998.

Journal of Popular Music Studies 17.1 (2005): 1-29.

Garrat, Sheryl. "Hey, hey, we're the Gorillaz. The Observer Profile: Damon Albarn." *The Observer* 7 Sept. 2001. 24 Jan. 2004 <http://www.guardian.co.uk/arts/>.

Goodwin, Andrew. "Sample and Hold: Pop Music in the Digital Age of Reproduction." *On Record: Rock Pop and the Written Word*. Ed. Simon Frith and Andrew Goodwin. New York: Pantheon, 1990. 258–73.

"Gorillaz Planning Giant Video Performance for Brits." Editorial. 1 Aug. 2002. 24 Jan. 2004 <http://www.musicgoeson.com>.

Hawkins, Stan. "Joy in Repetition: Structures, Idiolects, and Concepts of Repetition in Club Music." *Studia Musicologica Norvegica* 27 (2001): 553–78.

———. *Settling the Pop Score: Pop Texts and Identity Politics*. Aldershot: Ashgate, 2002.

Hutcheon, Linda. *A Theory of Parody: The Teachings of Twentieth-Century Art Forms*. London: Routledge, 1985.

———. *The Politics of Postmodernism*. London: Routledge, 1989.

Inglis, Sam. "Tom Girling and Jason Cox: Recording Gorillaz's Clint Eastwood." *Sound on Sound* Sept. 2001. 20 May 2002 <http://www.sospubs.co.uk/>.

Jones, Steve. "A Sense of Space: Virtual Reality, Authenticity, and the Aural." *Critical Studies in Mass Communication* 10 (1993): 238–52.

Kramer, Lawrence. *Music as Cultural Practice: 1800–1900*. Berkeley: U of California P, 1990.

McClary, Susan. *Conventional Wisdom: The Content of Musical Form*. Berkeley: U of California P, 2000.

Middleton, Richard. *Studying Popular Music*. Milton Keynes: Open UP, 1990.

Moylan, William. *The Art of Recording: Understanding and Crafting the Mix*. Woburn: Focal P, 2002.

Naylor, Tony. "Gorillaz: Manchester Academy." *NME*. Undated. 24 Jan. 2004 <http://www.nme.com/>.

Odell, Michael. "The Oasis Interview." *Q magazine*. May 2002: 92–100.

Potter, Russel A. *Spectacular Vernaculars: Hip-Hop and the Politics of Representation*. Albany: SUNY P, 1995.

Richardson, John. *Singing Archaeology: Philip Glass's Akhnaten*. Hanover: Wesleyan UP, 1999.

————. "Is that the Sound of Pop Eating Itself?" *Times Higher Education Supplement* 27 June 2003: 16–17.

————. "Laura and Twin Peaks: Postmodern Parody and the Musical Reconstruction of the Absent Femme Fatale." *The Cinema of David Lynch: American Dreams, Nightmare Visions*. Ed. Annette Davison and Erica Sheen. London: Wallflower P, 2004. 77–92.

Scott, Derek. "(What's the Copy) The Beatles and Oasis." *Beatlestudies 3*. Ed. Yrjö Heinonen et al. Jyväskylä, Finland: Dept. of Music Res. Rept., 2001. 201–11.

Sterne, Jonathan. *The Audible Past: Cultural Origins of Sound Reproduction*. Durham: Duke UP, 2003.

Sullivan, Caroline. "Damon Albarn Monkeys Around." *The Guardian* 24 Mar. 2001. 24 Jan. 2004 <http://www.guardian.co.uk/arts/>.

Tagg, Philip. "Analysing Popular Music: Theory, Method, and Practice." *Reading Pop: Approaches to Textual Analysis in Popular Music*. Ed. Richard Middleton. Oxford: Oxford UP, 2000. 71–103.

Théberge, Paul. *Any Sound You Can Imagine: Making Music/Consuming Technology*. Hanover: Wesleyan UP, 1997.

Walser, Robert. *Running with the Devil: Power, Gender and Madness in Heavy Metal Music*. Hanover: Wesleyan UP, 1993.

Whiteley, Sheila. "Progressive Rock and Psychedelic Coding in the Work of Jimi Hendrix." *Reading Pop: Approaches to Textual Analysis in Popular Music*. Ed. Richard Middleton. Oxford: Oxford UP, 2000. 235–61.

————. *Women and Popular Music: Sexuality, Identity and Subjectivity*. London: Routledge, 2000.

Discography

Blur. *Blur*. EMI (724385556227), 1997.

Blur. *13*. EMI (4991292), 1999.

Blur. *Think Tank*. Virgin (B0000931OG), 2003.

Gorillaz. *Geep*. EMI (33748), 2001.

Gorillaz. *Clint Eastwood*. EMI (879050), 2001.

Gorillaz. *G Sides*. EMI (11967), 2001.

Flaming Lips. *Yoshimi Battles the Pink Robots*. Warner (48141), 2002.

Videography and Filmography

Animatrix. Dir. Peter Chung et al. DVD. Warner, 2003.

Drowned World Tour. Madonna. Dir. Hamish Hamilton. DVD. Warner, 2001.

Interstella 5555: The 5tory of a 5ecret 5tar 5ystem. Daft Punk and Leiji Matsumoto. DVD. EMI, 2001.

Legend of the Overfiend. Dir. Hideki Takayama. Film. Central Park Media, 1994.

Phase One: Celebrity Take Down. Gorillaz. DVD. EMI, 2002.

Poltergeist. Dir. Tobe Hooper and Steven Spielberg. Film. MGM, 1982.

The Truman Show. Dir. Peter Weir. Film. Paramount, 1998.

[23]

Navigating the "Channel": Recent Scholarship on African-American Popular Music

David Sanjek

William Barlow. 1999. *Voice Over: The Making of Black Radio*. Philadelphia: Temple University Press, 334 pp. (paperback), $22.95.

Ellis Cashmore. 1997. *The Black Culture Industry*. New York/London: Routledge, 203 pp. (paperback), $22.99.

Mark Anthony Neal. 1999. *What the Music Said: Black Popular Music and Black Public Culture*. New York/London: Routledge, 198 pp. (paperback), $19.99.

Suzanne E. Smith. 2000. *Dancing in the Streets: Motown and the Cultural Politics of Detroit*. Cambridge, MA: Harvard University Press, 320 pp. (paperback), $24.95.

Brian Ward. 1998. *Just My Soul Responding: Rhythm and Blues, Black Consciousness, and Race Relations*. Berkeley: University of California Press, 600 pp. (paperback, $24.95.

Craig Werner. 1999. *A Change Is Gonna Come: Music, Race, and the Soul of America*. New York: Plume Books, 430 pp. (paperback), $19.95.

In the parlance of doo-wop performers, there is a phenomenon known as the "channel." Literally, it describes "the bridge, or middle-eight section in a 32-bar song, usually coming around two-thirds of the way through the lyric" (Ward, 64). For singers, the channel offers the opportunity to break free from a song's predetermined text and affix upon its performance their own unique signature. This form of individuality amounts to a number of choices, including the recitation of a dramatic monologue (the "spoken" bridge) or a wide range of modifications of timbre, harmony, and rhythm. Typical of these alterations and one of the most exciting occurs when the various vocal parts switch their accustomed sequence; you can hear this in the Channels' 1956 "The Closer You Are," in which a three-part harmony lead vocal is placed in front of a bass and tenor accompaniment.

To use an athletic analogy, the channel is equivalent to that section of figure skating or gymnastics competitions when the athlete has completed the prescribed moves for

168

the judges and now has the liberty to show off his or her tricks of the trade Appropriately, the audiences at, say, the Apollo responded, year after year, to unique handling of the channel with the requisite cacophony of applause and approval.

To step back from the subject of African-American popular music performance traditions to the scholarship about them, we can see the accumulation of a body of knowledge that, like the channel, offers an opportunity for inspiration as much as for enervation on the part of analysts. More often than not, the approach to the field takes on the conceptual equivalent of the requisite set pieces that constitute most musical performances. In countless books and articles, we encounter the standard tropes of strategic moments, recordings, and musicians as well as shopworn angles of attack that rehash the accumulated common wisdom about the subject. These works collectively propose a of theoretical, narrative, and musicological "greatest hits," and one searches earnestly, often to no avail, for the degree to which the individual scholar, historian, or journalist has stepped beyond these tropes and occupied the channel with a fresh approach to the subject.

Furthermore, for a long time, not only has there not been any appreciable addition to that body of tropes about African-American popular music, particularly the material performed and recorded from the 1940s to the 1970s, but the handful of volumes on the subject have been neither critiqued nor subjected to revision. We find ourselves, therefore, at the moment when the middle-eight occurs, waiting to see how much the results will be either a rehash of time-worn tropes or the rejuvenation of a subject that has taken on a lackluster air.

The recent publication of six volumes that endeavor, with relative degrees of success, to occupy this conceptual channel and augment these tropes is cause for tempered enthusiasm. For the most part, most of the noteworthy recent scholarship on African-American popular music has concerned itself with either jazz or hip hop. While box sets have proliferated and singles once available only to the most ardent fan have been made widely available, there appears to be a lack of interest in other dimensions of the black popular musical past.

This historic amnesia has been particularly disconcerting as the technological practice of digital sampling in hip hop composition has allowed for the commercial rejuvenation of back catalog—a position epitomized by Greg Tate's (1992: p. 130) admonition that hip hop specifically is a form of "ancestor worship"—but the effort necessary to reinhabit the original production and reception of this material seems to be lacking. Past recordings are valued more often than not for the degree to which they can be ransacked rather than revered, appropriated rather than rearticulated.

169

Paul Gilroy lamented that digital sampling too often "makes the past available in the here and now but only subserviently. History is conscripted into the sacrifice of the present" (1997: p. 87). In the end, Gilroy feared, we risk reverting to the smug posture of the *retro neuvo*, and the result is a form of composition and performance that "[does] not play with the gap between then and now but rather uses it to assert a spurious continuity that adds legitimacy and gravity to the contemporary" (1997: p. 111).

Whatever one might criticize of the recent work by Ellis Cashmore, Mark Anthony Neal, Craig Werner, William Barlow, Brian Ward, and Suzanne Smith, none of the six volumes they have published unashamedly basks in the pool of predetermined facts and assumptions about black popular music. Collectively, their writings constitute a long overdue rearticulation of a potent cultural tradition yet, individually, they both come to terms with as well as thoughtlessly recapitulate some of the knee-jerk tropes that preceded their studies. Before examining each of these publications in turn, I want to outline some of the most crucial and contested parameters of the tropes at work in scholarship about African-American popular music. I will conclude by suggesting some of the potential avenues of investigation that these six sensitive analysts have failed to exhaust. There are plenty of strategies for occupying the channel, and these six ways of engaging in the field leave ample room for subsequent research.

It is easy to forget but necessary to emphasize that the narrative record of African-American popular music is neither unitary nor unidimensional. As Keith Jenkins asserted:

> Bear in mind that "history" is really "histories," for at this point we ought to stop thinking of history as though it were a simple and rather obvious thing and recognize that there is a multiplicity of types of history whose only common feature is that their ostensible object of inquiry is "the past." (1991: p. 3)

That being said, to date two opposing paradigms govern the existing account of African-American popular music, and they in turn embody a set of contrasting assumptions not only about race but also about nationhood. In *The Death of Rhythm and Blues* (1988), Nelson George categorized them as the assimilationist model embodied by Booker T. Washington as opposed to the self-sufficient, racially exclusive model illustrated by W.E.B. Du Bois. George elaborated on this antithetical body of strategies by delineating individuals and music business entities who sought to become part of the corporate and creative mainstream as opposed to those who pursued a racially defined and economically self-supporting vision. His use of this paradigm was itself the reflection of two groundbreaking works: LeRoi Jones's *Blues People* (1963) and Albert Murray's *Stomping the Blues* (1976).

170

Jones laid the groundwork for the racially driven analysis of African-Amer
can musical expression; he asserted, "Negro music is *always* radical in the cor
text of formal American culture" (1963: p. 235). It is the embodiment of
attitude or stance "concomitant with what seems to me to be the peculiar socia
cultural, economic, and emotional experience of a black man in America" (p
235); while that experience is not homogeneous or devoid of friction—Jones
particularly sensitive to the ravages of class conflict in our society—without i
influence, music is aesthetically arid as well as devoid of any social or ideologic;
utility (pp. 147–148).

Murray, on the other hand, conceived of the nation as an incontestabl
mulatto sphere, wherein the divisions between races matter less than the vigor
ous expression of a more universal human spirit. While he did not deny that th
racial origins of African-American music reinforce certain forms of creative ac
tivity over others, he nonetheless defined blues—the core of his aesthetic a
well as social vision—as a form of affirmation in the face of adversity conduce
by means of the sophisticated deployment of idiomatic forms of expression. Ii
the end, "[Blues] are not a matter of having the blues and giving direct persona
release to the raw emotion brought on by suffering. It is a matter of masterin;
the elements of craft required by the idiom" (1976: p. 126). While neither the
possession nor the management of craft is race-neutral, it nonetheless absorb
any variety of influences and never is defined wholly by virtue of skin color
craft, for Murray, amounted to a heroic activity that permits one to engage ir
"rituals of elegant endeavor and perseverance in unfavorable circumstances"
(p. 250).

Although both Jones and Murray have been incontestably influential, the
bulk of the major works on African-American popular music for the period
between 1940 and 1970—Nelson George being a notable exception—are inclined more to Murray's than to Jones's position. For example, in *Sweet Sou*
Music: Rhythm and Blues and the Southern Dream of Freedom, Peter Guralnick (1986)
argued (as his subtitle would indicate) that the activities of racially mixed groups
of creators in the studios of Memphis, Muscle Shoals, and Nashville embodied
an egalitarian proposition that "a truly democratic arena open to anyone as
much on the basis of desire as technique, as much on the basis of gut instinct as
careful calculation" could exist if not prosper for as long as American society
itself supported, however waveringly, the ideological assumptions such a proposition illustrates (p. 15).

Barney Hoskyns (1987, 1998) pursued a similar agenda but with an even
less overtly ideological point of view than Guralnick's; for Hoskyns, the fact that
blacks and whites could work together musically or that country and rhythm
and blues interfused commercially acknowledges how "protean and elastic"
American national culture can be (p. 2).

171

The principal histories of the period and form embody more often than not
an even less overt social agenda. Rather than seeing in the record of a commercial form of entertainment the nation's fractured core writ large, they focus on
the collision between corporate entities, as typified by Charlie Gillett's analogy
of David and Goliath in *The Sound of the City: The Rise of Rock and Roll* (1970,
1992), to distinguish between the retrograde major record labels and the more
adventurous, risk-taking independents. Arnold Shaw's *Honkers and Shouters: The
Golden Years of Rhythm and Blues* (1978) added to this dramatic narrative arc a
command of detail about the business affairs of the record industry—Shaw was
participant—as well as a respect for the words and deeds of his subjects, illustrated by the plentiful incorporation of oral history testimony.

Other works in the field—including John Broven's volumes on New Orleans and the bayou-drawn subgenre of "swamp pop" (1974, 1983), Robert
Gordon's chronicle of the more obscure denizens of Memphis (1995), Rickey
Vincent's exhaustive chronicle of funk, and Robert Pruter's duo of analyses on
the doo-wop and soul scenes of Chicago (1991, 1998)—add to the mix an attention to the influence of the unique characteristics of geography upon cultural
production.

However, it must be admitted that much of the scholarship, academic and
otherwise, on African-American popular music remains driven by personalities
and observes the subject through a fascination with the activities of a handful of
individuals. This has been most notable in the proliferation of works on the
most successful enterprise in the field, Motown Records, and its charismatic
entrepreneur, Berry Gordy. In addition to Gordy's expansive yet ultimately un-
satisfying autobiography *To Be Loved* (1994), Motown has been valorized in a
number of ways: as the "ultimate myth of black capitalism" (George, 1985: p.
201); as the crystallization of "a black public and a black public taste that was
taken seriously as an expression of a general aesthetic among a broad class of
Americans" (Early, 1995: p. 4); as a business built on the conviction that paying
lip service to familial camaraderie could outweigh an inevitable corporate and
social hierarchy; as an application of Fordist principles of industrial production
to the creation of popular music; and, most often, in contradistinction to Stax
Records, an enterprise pledged to an assimilationist model that perceived the
"Sound of Young America" (the company's slogan) as one that progressively
eroded the evidence of inner-city realities while it elevated the appeal of mainstream appetites.

So appealing has been the mythology attached to Motown that—except
for Rob Bowman's 1997 history of Stax Records, *Soulsville U.S.A.*, and Charlie
Gillett's chronicle of Atlantic Records, *Making Tracks* (1974)—no other extended
chronicle of a label devoted to African-American popular music has been published. The absence of such work has meant that our knowledge about and

172

understanding of the commodification of African-American popular music
mains driven by the most unproductive assumptions: For example, corpora
control, whether in the hands of white or black executives, routinely exti:
guishes artistic individualism and, furthermore, any deliberate expression
racially charged material is impossible (or at least irreparably compromised
the marketplace). In the end, for all the rich and rewarding material these wor.
contain, we find ourselves crippled by a set of potent but puerile metapho
about an ongoing conflict between the forces of assimilation or cooptation, a
thenticity or artificiality, corporatism or entrepreneurialism. Our ideas abo
African-American popular music remain no more integrated than the socie
from which it emerged.

Ellis Cashmore's *The Black Culture Industry* (1997) endeavors to amend th
conundrum by attending to the manner in which Cashmore believes th
commodification of African-American culture, regardless of the racial owne
ship of those commodities, invariably serves to uphold inhibiting, destructiv
relationships and perpetuate cultural myths. As Cashmore states, "The
significant value of black culture may be in providing whites with proof of th
end of racism while keeping the racial hierarchy essentially intact" (p. 2); fur
thermore, "Black people have served as a kind of mirror to whites, but not on
that gives a true image; more like a warped, polished surface that provides
distorted representation" (p. 178).

In Cashmore's view, African-American popular music inhabits a kind o
conceptual funhouse wherein social transformation succumbs to solipsistic en
tertainment and the images cast by the walls deface the abject circumstances o
the black experience by transforming trauma into tomfoolery. Very little abou
culture is redemptive or even instructive in this view for, time and again, it:
forms of expression assuage our appetites but ignore our consciences. This leav
black entertainers, should they wish to appeal to a mass, racially diverse audience, inevitably attached to their "Sambo" legacy, accommodating themselve:
to the demands of the masses only by extinguishing within themselves any
evidence of the complex humanity their social experience creates. This truncated existence is further compromised by the exigencies created by the system
of cultural production.

Cashmore posits that the historical necessity of relying upon mass-market
streams of manufacture and distribution ideologically enables the evisceration
of the substance, certainly the humanity, of African-American culture. He writes,
"the experience of blues was an embryo of the whole black culture industry:
authentic, original and loaded with virtuosity; yet exploitable and ultimately
dependent on white culture for its production, dissemination and its recognition as a legitimate cultural product" (1997: p. 39). Syncretism of diverse cul-

173

ral phenomena always amounts to sacrifice. Virtually all the efforts on the
rt of African-American entrepreneurs to provide the means for their peers to
rform succumb to some form of annihilating accommodation. As Cashmore
ys of Berry Gordy, he merely gave "Young America" what it wanted: "not
arrantable human beings, perhaps, but performing marionettes. . . . Wonder-
l to watch and listen to, but somehow inhuman" (p. 112).

As the title of Cashmore's work indicates, the analysis is permeated by the
sumptions and ideologies of the Frankfurt School. On the positive side, this
ort-circuits any ill-considered encomiums to the unblemished benefits of cross-
ver. On the negative side, it holds out few if any possibilities for forms of ex-
ression that are not doomed to succumb to the stain of racism. For that matter,
hat we get from Cashmore is not so much the bitter yet invigorating influence
f the Frankfurt School's refusal to presume that popular culture possesses some
nique opportunity for ideological redemption but a dilution of its elaborate
ssessment of the complexities of commodification. Adorno Lite, one might call
, for little in Cashmore's volume indicates a detailed understanding of how the
nusic industry functions other than as the structural equivalent of a racist soci-
ty. More often than not, Cashmore depicts its operation in such a way that
reative autonomy is time and again throttled by corporate prohibitions.

The historical record admittedly forces one to concede that prohibitions far
nore often outweigh the encouragement of social critique, let alone cultural
ransgression, but Cashmore undercuts if not eviscerates this argument by re-
eated errors of fact or assertions unhinged from some form of cogent argu-
nent. In particular, he fails to indicate any developed understanding of the
ayers of organization and management that govern the recording enterprise,
he manner in which a variety of individuals act as intermediaries in the creation of the final product.

Take, for example, his analysis of the production of blues recordings:

[It] was strictly a passive affair. The choice of numbers, takes, accompaniment and indeed all the major decisions that conventionally rest
with production engineers were made by the musicians themselves.
One hesitates before hailing blues as a "true" original: a musical form
that was plucked whole from its natural environment and consumed
without modification. Yet it does appear to be a cultural product that
found its way into people's homes plain and unvarnished. (Cashmore,
1997: p. 46)

The assumption that blues music was produced by means of a "hands-
off" policy flies in the face not only of the body of scouts (like the noted H. C.

174

Speir) who acted as initial gatekeepers for the record labels in search of tale
but also of the fact that they required the artists they solicited to perform
specific number of purportedly "original" compositions before they would re
ommend them to the main office. Furthermore, the work by the early arti:
and repertoire (A&R) staff (like Ralph Peer and Frank Walker) is left out of t!
equation, as is the way their choice of repertoire created the body of a blu
tradition as much, and in some cases more so, than the very artists they
corded. Finally, the fact that blues musicians had to contend with the tempor
restrictions of the recording process as opposed to the free-wheeling enviro
ment of the road house or juke joint makes the blues anything but "plain ar
unvarnished."

This failure to comprehend the complex variety of factors that contribu:
to the commodification of popular music, African-American and otherwise, o
curs elsewhere in *The Black Culture Industry,* as does the failure to accord with th
historical record, as when Cashmore incorrectly asserts that, during the 194(
and more or less until the advent of rock and roll, the six major record corpora
tions (Capitol, Columbia, Decca, Mercury, MGM, and RCA) totally ignored ra
cial markets, not only black but rural Southern whites (1997: p. 42). Try tellin
that to the Ink Spots or Merle Travis, to name but two. Or when he asserts tha
"not for sixty years after [black theater tycoon Charles] Hicks' death in 190
was a black entrepreneur able to wrest control of a sector of the black cultur
industry large enough to rival white-owned corporations." This statement flie
in the face of the gospel music publishing market, which was controlled b
African-Americans, most notably Sallie Martin of Chicago.

Cashmore's evaluation of entrepreneurialism itself is confusing, for with
out attending to the prohibitions under which these individuals operated, h
categorically dismisses their activities, calling Bobby Robinson a "commercia
failure" and even more dubiously dubbing Don Robey, owner of Duke/Peacock
a "smalltime wheeler-dealer" (1997: pp. 82–83). To reduce Robey's career to a
mere summary of his purported attack of Little Richard and then add nothin;
about his number of hit records, club ownership, management company, or
publishing operation is a selective enterprise, to say the least.[1]

At the start of his book, Cashmore astutely asserts that the existence of an
"unbroken continuum" of cultural forms throughout the history of African-
American popular music is a "myth" that results from a "melodramatic construction of black culture and one which does no justice to its intricacies or
indeed hiatuses" (1997: p. 2). Sad to say, in the end his work amounts to a form
of ideological melodrama whereby those very individuals whose forms of cultural expression he wishes to valorize are routinely transformed into oppressed
and inadequate subjects of a trumped-up system. Cashmore makes little of his

175

-portunity to occupy the critical or historical channel and ends up singing a
-ed song.

Mark Anthony Neal also ascribes to racism the inhibiting force it has played
American society and culture, yet *What the Music Said: Black Popular Music and
-ack Public Culture* (1999) provides a more balanced and factually grounded
:count of its subject. As the work's subtitle indicates, Neal concerns himself
ith the manner in which commercial enterprise reflects as well as influences
.e daily life of African-Americans: the way the cliché "music is the soundtrack
: our lives" possesses a theoretical application. For Neal, music not only acts as
ne of the principal bulwarks against repression but also gives shape to and
rovides a record for the acts of transgression against the antagonisms perpetu-
.ed by the powers that be. He writes, "the black popular music tradition has
ften contained the core narratives of these efforts to create and maintain con-
:pts of community that embody a wide range of sensibilities, formations and
urposes" (1999: p. x).

The latter portion of that assertion illustrates one of the most valuable
ynamics of Neal's perspective: the fact that he does not essentialize the black
ommunity into a homogeneous mass. The forms resistance takes are as mani-
old as the forms of music that give expression to it. Music acts across the space
f time and place as a way of reminding members of the black public how others
.ave confronted and, in some cases, surmounted repression. Neal posits:

> [T]he black popular music tradition has served as a primary vehicle
> for communally derived critiques of the African American experi-
> ence, and that the quality and breadth of such critiques are wholly
> related to the quality of life in the black public sphere. (1999: p. xi)

Music forms one of the crucial elements of those spaces in the lives of
African-Americans, one that affords "safety, sustenance, and subversion" and
incorporates what James C. Scott deemed "hidden transcripts"—bodies of information and emotion that constitute crucial lessons formative to racial and individual survival (Neal, 1999: p. 2).

Neal acknowledges that the material contained in those transcripts is by
no means devoid of dubious characteristics, engaging at times in little more
than the "commodification of black dysfunction" or the rendering of complex
social realities into encomiums to the life of the emotions alone (p. 10). At the
same time, he does not shun the engagement in consumer culture by African-
Americans, as does Cashmore, although he recognizes "the tumultuous marriage between black cultural production and mass consumerism—one in which
black agency is largely subsumed by market interests" (p. 17). He therefore

176

focuses on what is expressed in and what can be transformed through the co:
modities we purchase.

Furthermore, Neal understands that, through the collective acquisiti
and rearticulation of commodities, we produce communities of desire and p
tentially encourage a collective dedication to social transformation. This c
occur even when the manufacture and distribution of those commodities is o
of the hands of African-Americans, as is often the case. Unlike Cashmore, N
stresses the productive irony "that white record label owners, who may or ma:
not have been sympathetic to the crises within the black community, help
cilitate black music's role in providing spaces of recovery and political agen
because of their economic aspirations" (1999: p. 45).

One of the most rewarding threads to Neal's analysis is the way he appli
these ideas to the live recording. Such artifacts permit the "aural reproductic
of community," much like the Chitlin' Circuit (where a number of them we:
made) permitted the "the reconstruction of community and the recovery
cultural memory" (pp. 31, 33). Hearing James Brown at the Apollo or Lo
Donaldson at New Jersey's Cadillac Club reinforces the transformative potenti
of those instances of collective understanding and common experience that hav
permitted the often fragmented black community to achieve transitory cohe:
ence. Neal further amplifies these ideas when discussing the late Julian "Car
nonball" Adderley's live recordings with their interpolated spoken introduc
tions. Tunes such as "Walk Tall," "Mercy Mercy Mercy," and "City Preacher
illustrate and embellish "black music's role in communal catharsis and pride
and underscore that, even in the seemingly inhibiting and solipsistic practice
listening to a recording in the privacy of one's home, an "aural community c
resistance" can be invoked (pp. 79–80).

One might add that Neal's references to both Donaldson and Adderley
both mainstream artists but both often left out of the record of black
music, indicate the substantial and thoughtful character of his choice of ex
amples. This is not simply a matter of electing in a fan-like manner to includ
lesser-known performers but a more crucial issue of widening the canon an
making its participants more representative and inclusive.

At the same time, although Neal indicates ways that mass-market com·
modities can serve progressive social movements and notes that cultural mate·
rials, which seem intrinsically devoted to pleasure, can simultaneously have
polemic edge, there is an inferred causality to his argument. By this, I mean tha
believing popular culture to be prominent among the influences upon social
activism is one thing, demonstrating quantitatively or even through first-person testimony that the presumed form of metamorphosis actually occurred is

177

uite another. Neal is far from alone in following this line of argument, as popular music studies (and other discourses connected to the analysis of the mass media) engage in such extrapolation time and again. The question remains, to what degree are such conclusions more a confirmation of the investigator's preconceptions than an illustration of a close-to-the-ground analysis of the community under examination? Admittedly, Neal does not engage in an essentialization of the black public sphere; in fact, he routinely recognizes its complexity and the fissures that often split the community into disconnected entities. But one must keep in mind that assuming a linear connection between consumption and ideologically driven behavior is not an unproblematic matter.

How, for example, does one account for the socially excluded, often ostracized behavior of a subcommunity that a friend of mine (born in Chattanooga, Tennessee, who came of age in the late 1960s and early 1970s) refers to as the "nippies," a conflation of Negro and hippy? This constituency was attracted by the work of a distinct body of individuals, most notably Jimi Hendrix and Sly Stone, which exemplified the mulatto strain of American culture celebrated by Albert Murray (although Murray might blanch at the analogy). Others in the black community at best ignored and at worst despised both artists for their mixing of genres and avoidance of race-specific identities, and they ostracized the nippies as a result. Examining this kind of conflict and form of identification would give more experiential credence and narrative texture to the kind of ungrounded conclusions Neal sometimes makes. However, by and large, *What the Music Said* is a worthy and illuminating addition to the scholarship on the subject. Its unveiling of certain of the "hidden transcripts" within African-American culture gives a shape and a direction to mass culture that other studies lack or ignore.

In *A Change Is Gonna Come: Music, Race, and the Soul of America,* Craig Werner (1999) tries to give a deliberate and decidedly ideological shape and direction to American musical culture. As the double-edged noun in the title indicates, Werner is concerned with both that subgenre of popular music that we call "soul" and the national affective consciousness. Furthermore, he says that the former is connected to—in fact, might be said to calibrate—the latter. Werner asserts that his study is not solely a matter of musical or even cultural analysis but, "my attempt to help renew a process of racial healing" (p. xi). Music affords him a means to talk about broader issues for, he states, "my underlying intention is to suggest useful ways of thinking about the problems that keep America from realizing its own democratic ideals" (p. xii).

In that sense, popular music functions for Werner in a virtually homeopathic manner, assuaging the fractiousness of our multicultural society and instilling within us the energy that permits persistence in the face of adversity.

178

This position possesses antecedents. In his acknowledgments, Werner indicat
the vital role rock critic Dave Marsh has played in his thinking, particula:
Marsh's 1989 volume *The Heart of Rock and Soul: The 1001 Greatest Singles Ev*
Made. Werner says of it, "more than anything else I have read, [it] taught
how to hear" (p. 354). Marsh shares with Werner a conviction that songs (n
albums) generate the greatest American popular music as well as form the foc
of the affective allegiances audiences locate in individual compositions. The tw
authors share as well a sense that African-American popular music, particularl
rhythm and blues, forms the bedrock of rock and roll, reflecting the uneasy b
inevitable social synthesis of the races in an aesthetic mode. Most of all, the
both are driven by a belief that American popular music styles in general, an
R&B and rock and roll in particular, uniquely combine energies that elicit rebe
lion and reconciliation. Marsh writes:

> If rebelling—against musical limitations and broadcasting restrictions,
> emotional repression and the color line, middlebrow good taste and
> bohemian snobbery, working-class defeatism and folk-radical false
> optimism—gave birth to rock and roll, what kept the music alive was
> its resilient ability to reconcile its own contradictions, to find some
> stratum of peace and ease among the clamor. . . . Most writers imply
> that when rock isn't rebelling, it's engaged in some form of personal
> or social capitulation—selling out its own best interests. But the real
> sell-out is limiting rock's import to statements of rebellion. The yearn-
> ing to belong, to fit in, to *start* making sense, has all along been a part
> of the music's tradition. (1999: pp. xxiii–xxiv)

Werner in turn makes sense of the history of American popular music
since the World War II as driven by those energies in the African-American
tradition that refuse "to simplify reality or devalue emotion" (p. xiii). He labels
those energies "impulses" and locates them generically in the repertoires of blues,
gospel, and jazz. The first, he associates with the ability to accommodate the evil
in life; the second, with the courage to conquer adversity; and the third, with
the inescapable impulse toward cultural and social innovation. It should be added
that, while Werner locates these impulses in the African-American experience,
he does not argue that they are altogether racially defined. Instead, they act as
generative energies, impelling the activities of American civilization.

Admittedly, the descriptions of these terms are vague, more a matter of
attitude or agency than of the music itself, yet they constitute the conceptual
architecture for Werner's study. The fact that they often lack the kind of social,
cultural, or aesthetic specificity that helps explain the complex patterns of American and African-American culture makes *A Change Is Gonna Come* a frustrating
volume. For example, although it seems more than plausible to assert that the
blues incorporate a philosophy about life, to label that perspective "mostly about
finding the energy to keep moving" (1999: p. 71) reduces a rich body of atti-

179

Jes and aptitudes to mere emotional persistence, a kind of ideological stiff per lip. Admittedly, Werner states, "all forms of storytelling oversimplify the tterns, but music simplifies less than most" (p. xi). Less, perhaps, but when fined on the basis of generative impulses, too simple for my tastes.

On the other hand, Werner's narrative focus is more deliberately drawn. 1e music he celebrates has a notable consistency. It embodies a kind of social 1lift with a beat that supports a populist view of cultural production whereby dividual works function best when they assist in radical forms of transforma- >n. This is illustrated by his characterization of southern soul:

> Like gospel, Southern Soul spoke to the burdens of life and the need to reach for something higher. The rough edges reflect something fundamental about life in a place where the rednecks and the children of the ghetto shared enough of a common culture to challenge everything they'd been taught about race. (1999: p. 78)

The language Werner chooses does not descend to the allegorical, but at mes one feels that he favors an individual performer, group, genre, song, or lbum because it provides him with a musical example that confirms an ideo- >gical paradigm. And that paradigm seems to require a positive, forward-look- ng perspective above all else.

For example, Werner faults punk rock (mistakenly, I believe) for being 1egative: "Judging by their continued reliance on juvenile gestures designed to nfuriate the middle class, most punks didn't care" (1999: p. 222). Apparently, music must act as a force for social cohesion; Werner shares with Marsh the)elief that "Within our society, there's an essential cultural need (or anyway, desire) for a unitary, memorable musical motif (Marsh, 1989: p. xiv). One can 1rgue that such a desire for unity could be oppressive, denying certain points of view and ways of life (such as punk, it would seem) for not contributing to the :ause. It should be stressed, however, that Marsh (unlike Werner) admits many >f the best popular songs stand out because "so much concentrated energy be- comes focused on them" and "the dialogue they create just never burns out" (March, 1989: p. xiv). It's not so much that Werner seems disinclined to engage in dialogue, but he appears to be drawn by a narrow range of topics, the more ideologically progressive the better. Despite his favorable quotation from James Baldwin that too many people narrowly assume that "happy songs are happy and sad songs are sad" (1999: p. 26), one gets the feeling Werner is drawn to exhortation rather than jeremiad—more Curtis Mayfield and less Sex Pistols.

It is this narrowness of focus and the predictable nature of Werner's choices that make *A Change Is Gonna Come* a rudimentary rather than a radical reading of the history of African-American popular music and its offshoots. Also, while I

180

might grant his assumption that both John Fogerty and Bruce Springsteen body the blues impulse (I can't buy that the former is the "patron saint of gar bands"), the attention given to those who are acolytes of Werner's trinity impulses rather than the progenitors of them makes the book more an ove selective historical text than the embodiment of its subtitle: *Music, Race, and Soul of America.*

The belief that the healing forces of music demand not only a predete mined affective frame of mind but also a prescribed range of musical for limits rather than expands my sense of the national soul. It should include t Velvet Underground as well as Frankie Beverley's *Maze*. If the impulses Werr celebrates refrain from simplifying reality or devaluing emotion, his espousal them comes across as narrow in example and restrictive in the kind of emotio they promote. Even if he argues that "the spirit doesn't check IDs" (1999: xiii), Werner's notion of community comes across as a club with a demandi doorman.

Certain subjects are so germane to the investigation of African- popular music that the absence of extensive scholarship about them is a positi scandal. For years, one of these omissions has been the radio DJ, both tho black employees of white-owned stations and those white individuals who a pealed to racially mixed audiences and whose promotion of African-Americe popular music helped increase its audience on a national, and eventually globe scale. Nelson George stressed their importance and influence in *The Death Rhythm and Blues* (1988): first, by comparing their sophisticated and creative of language to the black oral tradition and, second, by arguing that their entre preneurial activities established a precedent for the consolidation of African American economic and social power in a white-dominated industry.

George argued:

> [I]f you consider these deejays as entrepreneurs, and not merely as employees, then in the midst of this integration (but not assimila-tion) it is clear the era produced a wealth of [Booker T.] Washingto-nian figures. They benefited from the power to entertain, and from the exploitation of black music, and were crucial to its growth. (1988: pp. 56–57)

Those in the music industry, particularly fellow African-Americans, un derstood the power these individuals personified and took opportunities to ben efit from it as well as reward the deejays monetarily—the dreaded payola—a their economic clout certainly did not come from their station salaries. In addi tion to George's groundbreaking volume, earlier works by Arnold Passmar

181

971), Louis Cantor (1992), and parts of Gene Fowler and Bill Crawford's study *rder Radio* (1987) constitute the only studies of this crucial subject.

William Barlow's *Voice Over: The Making of Black Radio* (1999) is the first bstantial treatment of the subject. A long-time DJ himself and the author of veral noteworthy works on African-American music, Barlow also acted as ie of the principal interviewers and researchers for the 1996 Peabody Award-inning series "Black Radio: Telling It Like It Is," which was broadcast on Na-onal Public Radio. His volume benefits from some of this oral history material id amounts to the smoothest and most readable kind of cultural history.

Chronologically linear in its telling, Barlow's work reinforces some of the oncepts developed in Neal's work, for he characterizes the medium of radio as a major force in constructing and sustaining an African American public sphere. has been the coming-together site for issues and concerns of black culture: inguage, music, politics, fashion, gossip, race relations, personality and com-iunity are all part of the mix" (p. xi). More specifically, Barlow sculpts the rolific anecdotal information contained in *Voice Over* through a master meta-hor: the notion of "racial ventriloquy," coined by Mel Watkins in his study of lack comedy, *On the Real Side: Laughing, Lying, and Signifying* (1994).

Watkins used the term to articulate the kind of acoustic impersonation hat occurred either when black DJs spoke with an overly "white" inflection so .s to accord with the industry's on-air standards of behavior, or when white DJs "blackened" their speech. Barlow infers a Bahktinian edge to such activity, quot-ng the Russian theorist's observation that any "word in language is half some-one else's" (1999: p. 1) and asserting, therefore, that our speech becomes our own only when we use it deliberately to reinforce our expressive intentions. However, such theoretical discourse informs *Voice Over* implicitly rather than explicitly, the bulk of the volume being narrative-driven.

Barlow contextualizes radio practices in earlier traditions that began in the minstrel show and then transferred themselves to the T.O.B.A. (Theater Own-ers' Booking Association—*aka* Tough on Black Asses) circuit. In the case of the former, radio was influenced by the likes of Dan Emmett, the Wolfman Jack of his day; in the case of the latter, the majority of white station owners not only required the same rigid adherence to racial stereotypes as the T.O.B.A. manage-ment but also permitted the suspension of such shuckin' and jivin' only to the degree that DJs spoke in "whiter than white" tones.

These analogies aside, what is compelling about Barlow's accumulation of information is both the early date at which black performers and DJs began to

182

appear on the airwaves and the amount of autonomy some were able to atta
The first black-owned radio venture (Harlem Broadcasting) hit the
1929, and the first show dedicated to "negro journalism" was aired in 1927
Pittsburgh's WGBS. The undisputed patriarch of black radio, Jack Cooper
Chicago, who broadcast from the mid-1920s to the 1950s, admittedly typifi
the Caucasian-sounding announcer; but the amount and variety of progra
ming he developed is staggering, from *Amos-n-Andy*-like serials to sports cove
age to religious shows and even a program, "Search for Missing Persons, th
helped relocate family members lost in the Northern migration (Barlow, 19
p. 50).

Barlow also provides rich detail about the integration-focused progra
ming developed during World War II and the post-War years before blacklisti
bowdlerized the airwaves. Finally, he summarizes the conclusions of two fas
nating and groundbreaking reports in the industry publication *Sponsor* in 19
and 1952: The first, "The Forgotten 15,000,000," amounted to "the first time
major trade publication on the business side of the industry had devoted atte
tion to this new broadcast phenomenon, proving an in-depth look at black
peal radio in the context of the newly emerging, consumer-oriented 'Neg
Market'" (Barlow, 1999: p. 125). Coming nearly 20 years before the Columb
Records-financed *Harvard Report*, which sought to describe and quantify th
African-American market for recordings, these articles provide a fascinating (an
heretofore little-known) instance of the marketplace acknowledging the cor
sumer power of black people at a time when few businesspersons were willin
even to accede to their social integration.

The many portraits Barlow incorporates into *Voice Over* of the DJs, bot
black and white, who populated the market are compelling, although the amour
of material he has to cover rarely allows for the kind of scintillating detail tha
Robert Gordon incorporated in his chapter on Dewey Phillips (the white DJ i
Memphis who helped Elvis Presley break into the market) in his deftly wr
It Came From Memphis (1995).[2]

One wishes Barlow had more opportunity to convey a sense of how thes
DJs commanded the airwaves through the force of untrammeled personality
particularly today when the newly affirmed laws of duopoly allow radio con
glomerates more and more control. That aside, *Voice Over* is a crucial addition t
the history of the mass media and public consumption of popular music.

At 600 pages, Brian Ward's *Just My Soul Responding: Rhythm and Blues, Blac
Consciousness, and Race Relations* (1998) is certainly one of the most substantia
studies of African-American popular music. The work of an English scholar,
examines rhythm and blues released between the 1940s and the 1970s in order

183

ɔ "illuminate changes in mass black consciousness during the peak years of ivil rights and black power activities" (p. 2). It also endeavors to reinterpret many of the conventional wisdoms about the history of rhythm and blues by etting it firmly within the context of changes in American race relations during his period" (Ward, 1998: p. 2).

Throughout the book Ward balances his focus between the tumultuous ight for racial equality and the alleviation of the anxieties attendant to life in America by producing and consuming popular music. While he never espouses a monolithic connection between culture and politics, Ward does contend:

> [C]hanges in black musical style and mass consumer preferences of-
> fer a useful insight into the changing sense of self, community and
> destiny among those blacks who rarely left the sorts of evidence, or
> undertook the sorts of activities, to which historians are genuinely
> most responsive. (1998: p. 4)

The changes in musical style Ward delineates also bear witness to the dissension within the music's community of origin; even in material that does not explicitly bear the mark of overt ideology, the changes offer evidence of a body of assumptions and allegiances crucial to the conduct of black daily life. Ward's work is therefore "guided by the belief that the popular cultures of oppressed groups usually contain within them—explicitly or implicitly—a critique of the system by which those groups are oppressed, and thus actually constitute a mode of psychological resistance to their predicament" (1998: p. 4).

Considered in the context of preexistent material, Ward's approach to African-American popular music is not significantly different in scope or attitude than the other authors reviewed here. However, his analysis stands out by virtue of its exhaustive documentation of these ideas and because of his careful (although never hesitant or mealy-mouthed) point of view. Ward states at the outset that three assumptions guide his work:

> [First,] the social or political meanings of any given piece or style of
> commercially produced popular music are located at the intersection
> of a number of different, sometimes antithetical, musical, economic,
> legal, racial, gender, class, generational and other forces.

> [Second,] black consumers have never been passive in their con-
> sumption.

> [And third,] in America there exists a conventionally recognized
> spectrum of musical techniques and devices which range from nomi-
> nally "white" to nominally "black" poles. (1998: pp. 4–5)

184

As a result, unlike Cashmore, Ward does not demonize entities of production or essentialize the body of consumers; both sets of individuals possess complex, and at times incompatible, motives and desires. He also shares with Alber
Murray a sense that the United States is "incontestably mulatto"; but that doe
not deter him from examining material that is, in its own right, driven either b
Afro-centric or by integrationist motives. At the same time, these motives ar
shown to be embodied in a definite set of actions and assumptions, for War
does not engage in the kind of leaps of argument that occasionally mar Neal'
study.

Finally, Ward refuses to accept any conclusions predicated on the belie
that music—and all forms of popular culture, for that matter—cannot brir
about some appreciable degree of social or ideological transformation but, in
stead, merely reinforce the hegemony of external domination. Consumption
and of itself affects, in some definite although not always quantifiable fashion
the status quo; they also serve the transformation of society.

Although Ward blazes no new conceptual paths, he approaches the subject with an admirable focus and grasp of detail, weaving together discographic
information, political machinations, and social assignations between various
factions of the black community. Ward's value to popular music studies can be
ascribed to his balanced perspective and the sense that he never lets ideology
come before empirical fact. This perspective has its liabilities, a point I will return to shortly, but its virtues are altogether evident, particularly in the context
of the frequent arguments over what is and is not "authentic" black music. Such
hair-splitting has bedeviled the study of African-American specifically and American popular music in general, and Ward avoids its infection by attending to
what people *bought* regardless, of whether it legitimized some prescribed notion
of what "black" music might be.

Take, for example, the period of the late 1950s and early 1960s and the
ascendance of what Ward dubs "black pop," epitomized by the successful recordings of Sam Cooke, Jackie Wilson, and Roy Hamilton. Some commentators
have denigrated these works as sterile efforts to command white audiences by
steering clear of the emotional complexity of earlier black music and replacing it
with an idealistic realm of adolescent emotion and ersatz romanticism. By contrast, Ward stresses not only how these recordings were rooted in the ballad
tradition of earlier performers—the Platters, Bull Moose Jackson and Sonny Til,
and the Orioles, to name but a few—but also how their appeal to "black audiences of all ages, classes, sexes and locations in the 1950s suggests that [they]
articulated ideas and emotions which were always present, but often latent,
obscured and under-commemorated elsewhere in male black popular culture"
(1998: p. 89).

185

This material is further linked to the fascination with harmony rather than rhythm and timbre—the predominant forces of African-American music—articulated by countless doo-wop ensembles of the 1950s. Many of these performers engaged in what Ward calls "reverse crossover," covering material from the "white" pop mainstream and giving it an articulation resonant with African-American vocalizing (1998: p. 139). Ward adds that, while these recordings may not have mined the "terrifying seams of despair near the heart of the blues," they avoided some of the "raging misogyny and sexual anxieties" that course through much African-American music (p. 88).

Another useful dimension of Ward's study is his even-handed analysis of the support by black artists of the Civil Rights struggles of the 1960s. Other commentators have addressed this matter with a broad brush, inferring that there was widespread approval of and active involvement in these movements by popular musicians. But Ward counters that argument deftly:

> [T]he claims that rhythm and blues provided some sort of explicit running commentary on the movement, with the men and women of soul emerging as notable participants, even leaders, tacticians and philosophers of the black struggle, have usually depended more on partisan assertion than hard evidence. (1998: p. 290)

He adds that these assumptions frequently result from a logocentric scrutiny of lyrics (as often occurs in Craig Werner's work), driven by the presumption that any inference of ideological fervor amounts to a statement of personal conviction. Far from the case, many artists had as little attraction to the call for black insurgency as their audiences. In fact, the people who routinely gave their time, money, and physical presence to political causes often were associated with jazz, folk, and Hollywood rather than rhythm and blues—as is illustrated by the consistent support of Lena Horne, Diahann Carroll, Dick Gregory, Sammy Davis, Jr., and most notably Harry Belafonte, who bankrolled SNCC, gave 20% of his income to the cause, and acted as one of the executors of the Martin Luther King, Jr., estate.

Some participants in the struggle from outside the rhythm and blues community came as a surprise, like blind jazz singer Al Hibbler, who braved Bull Connor's nightsticks, dogs, and fire hoses during the 1963 Birmingham campaign: "Though I'm blind, I can see injustice here," he announced (Ward, 1998: p. 297). In addition, some of the more consistent entertainers at political benefits came from the "black pop" contingent, most notably Jackie Wilson and Roy Hamilton.

Ward notes that a variety of factors acted against more widespread activism, writing:

186

The configuration of economic and managerial power within the recording and broadcasting industries of the early-to-mid-1960s consistently worked against the likelihood that rhythm and blues would
become a major source of artistic comment on American racism, or
of public support for black insurgency. (1998: p. 326)

However, a number of figures from that world did feel that their succe:
financial and social, added to the general amelioration of social injustice by
lustrating the possibility that African-Americans could ascribe to the Americ:
dream, even if such sentiments could be argued to illustrate nothing more th:
knee-jerk accommodation to the status quo. For some, Ward concludes, "rhyth
and blues did what black popular culture has always done best; it promoted a:
sustained the black pride, identity and self-respect upon which the Moveme:
and its leaders were ultimately dependent" (1998: p. 336).

Conversely, the balanced nature of Ward's assessment of this complex i
sue illustrates some of his study's blind spots. He seems, by intellectual an
perhaps personal inclination, less persuaded by and less drawn to the argt
ments associated with nationalist claims for racial self-sufficiency and separ:
tion from the social mainstream. It is not so much that he chides or derides th
activism of a Ron Karenga as that, as he observes less widespread support for i:
principles, he downplays its influence on the African-American community as
whole.

Additionally, Ward spends less time on recordings that possess a more over
ideological focus and (it can be argued) had more direct influence on the think
ing of the black (and white) public—such as Marvin Gaye's "What's Goin' On
and Sly Stone's "There's a Riot Going On"—than he does more overtly popula
works of the "black pop" contingent. He also perceives little of ideological sub
stance in the "blaxploitation" film cycle and focuses largely on its social cliché.
and sexual stereotypes.

Furthermore, Ward perceives disco—a phenomenon that admittedly ar
rives at the end of his historical narrative— as a "banal and vacuous caricatui
of black music's more corporeal and sensual drives," one whose gender stereotypes cause it to "hold its own in the sexism and objectification sweepstakes"
(1998: p. 426).

On the whole, Ward's balanced perspective serves him better when he is
discussing earlier history, where his adjustment of shopworn perspectives causes
us to see the subject anew. At other times, one can apply to Ward his own
assessment of the sexual politics illustrated by the mid-1970s female-driven black
soul, which thrust before the public the aggression of women's sexuality as a

187

esponse to the male braggadocio of the "Jody" cycle: "[T]here remains a sense hat the net result of fighting fire with fire may just have been that more people got burned" (Ward, 1998: p. 385).

Sometimes, Ward's own fingers seem a little charred; but, on the whole, *Just My Soul Responding* is a substantial, revelatory, and indispensable addition to popular music scholarship in general and the study of African-American popular music in particular.

The last work I want to examine here, Suzanne E. Smith's *Dancing in the Streets: Motown and the Cultural Politics of Detroit* (2000), addresses what one might think would be an exhausted subject: Berry Gordy's musical empire. Admittedly, the majority of scholarship on this subject has advanced a limited and limiting set of metaphors: the label as the cultural equivalent of the auto assembly line; as the embodiment of Gordy's Booker T. Washingtonian, middle-class uplift; and as the devolutionary narrative of a culturally affiliated "family," in which dedication to a set of common ideals succumbs to dysfunction. Commentator after commentator has struggled with the ideological thrust of the enterprise: Was it overtly political, covertly so, or capable of critique only when Gordy overlooked the radical disposition of his more self-motivated stars (for example, Marvin Gaye's "What's Goin' On" or Stevie Wonder's post-*Innervisions* career)? Even the issue of who these songs addressed has been a matter for contention: When Gordy designated his label the "Sound of Young America," was it a multicultural vision he espoused, or a bottom-line-directed wooing of the white middle class?

A number of compelling responses have been made to these questions and others; but, until Smith's study, the research has had an oddly and unnecessarily dislocated quality. Rather than addressing the broad environment inhabited by "Young America," Smith returns us to the primary cultural, social, racial, and political location of Gordy's endeavor: Detroit.

The reinterpretation of the Motown legacy embodied by *Dancing in the Streets* is a well-written, broadly researched, and eminently readable demonstration of "how a focus on Detroit presents a sharper picture of Motown's cultural, political, and historical contributions throughout the civil rights era" (Smith, 2000: p. 8). Smith dismisses the intractable argument over whether Motown's music was a diversion from social realities or a confrontation with them by acknowledging, "Music, particularly music created in Detroit's black community during the 1960s, could rarely, if ever, transcend the politically and racially charged environment in which it was produced"; inevitably, she argues, "music in Detroit's black community constituted daily life rather than acted as a diversion from it" (2000: p. 2).

188

To illuminate how daily life in Detroit could be transformed, and perhaps transcended, Smith examines how cultural politics were conducted o a grassroots level by Gordy, his associates, and many others in the Motor City To that end, she draws on Raymond Williams's notion of a "cultural formation" This is the idea that an environment can simultaneously constitute a set of in digenous artistic forms and also provide a particularized social location. Giver this notion, Smith can examine how the cultural workers at "Hitsville, U.S.A. produced material that "can be understood in political terms regardless of whethe or not the company or its artists perceived it as such" (2000: p. 11).

As others have, Smith dissects how Gordy's vision of an enlightened black capitalism both impacted and was impacted by the Civil Rights Movement as well as by the more incendiary episodes of the 1960s. Therefore, she argues, the records he released were more than simply a musically proficient and economi- cally successful soundtrack to the era: "The company and its sound were ac- tive—though sometimes reluctant—agents in the politics of its time" (2000: p. 20).

Smith's re-situation of Motown in the daily life of Detroit is augmented by her detailed and deliberate illustration of the activities of other individuals— members of the church, politicians, union activists, fellow members of the mu- sic industry, and other cultural workers—and the ways they contributed to the cultural, political, and social dynamics of the city. Earlier commentators rou- tinely assessed the label as if it existed in a social sphere divorced from its fellow citizens, except as they acted as consumers of its products. As a result, the lyrics sung by Motown artists have been addressed as illustrations of broad themes and tendencies throughout the nation during the 1960s without integrating the very local and far from parochial issues faced by the black citizens of Detroit.

In contrast, Smith establishes fascinating parallels between popular music and public protest, as in the activities of the Freedom Now Party, whose *Now!* magazine often featured Motown artists; the local political collectives, the De- troit Council on Human Rights, and the Northern Negro Leadership Council, which split over the collision between calls for integration and calls for segrega- tion; and the many union organizations, most specifically the radical auto workers union DRUM, which argued in the *Inner City Voice* that "the black working class would be the vanguard of the revolutionary struggle in this country" (Smith, 2000: p. 221). All of these groups, and others, espoused the belief that forms of cultural expression were not separate from ideological agitation but served as vehicles for the communication of and debate over political messages. There- fore, the way that Motown's legacy has been read as a form of cultural politics— both covertly and overtly enunciated—bears analogies to the activities of other local contemporary groups and individuals who failed to separate the two spheres as antithetical entities.

189

Developing these analogies also permits us to unpack the complex mo-
ives that drove Gordy's empire. For example, let's return to the earlier argument that Motown embodied the Fordist principles of the automobile assembly
ine. The fact that Gordy articulated a set of mainstream business practices, ab-
orbed them, and rearticulated their principles to his own purposes reinforces
now his self-help imperative was both mainstream and revolutionary. At the
ame time, if we examine the heated legal battles over royalties and recognition
hat arose between the executive and the writing/production team of Holland-
Dozier-Holland, we see the cultural equivalent of DRUM's responses to the au-
omobile industry.

As Smith asserts:

> Producing and marketing the cultural work of the black community
> in a city economically dominated by the automobile industry, which
> excluded African Americans from controlling the means of produc-
> tion and profited from their labor, was an inherently political act.
> (2000: p. 97)

Smith's work helps us understand how multifaceted such political acts can
be. Obviously (as in the case of the Holland-Dozier-Holland conflict), one can
profit from the labor of others even while giving them the platform to carry out
their desires. Time and again, Smith's groundbreaking study undermines the
frequent practice of referring to the label's activities and Gordy's business practices as *sui generis* behavior, either lauding the executive as an innovator or
castigating him as a race traitor. His behavior, and that of all the members of the
Motown "family," is as conflicted and confounding as the city in which it took
root. Motown's products may have transcended their geographical origins, but
they remain distinctly and irrevocably bound up in the Motor City's history.

As I said at the beginning of this article, for all the strengths of these six
works, the field of black popular music is far from exhausted; in fact, it remains
underexamined and undertheorized. Our understanding of the canon of black
popular music during the period from 1944 and 1955—an arc defined by the
start of the post-War independent labels and the ascendance of rock and roll—
is the most insubstantial. This period is one of the most vital and revelatory of
the entire twentieth century, yet, for the most part, the main point made about
it is the previously mentioned antagonism between independent entrepreneurs
and the major record labels. We need to know more about the internal workings of both and stop lambasting the majors for their erroneously assumed lack
of interest in racially defined culture.

Another field ripe for exploration is the emerging influence of regionally
defined musical centers; for example, Seattle and the coastal towns of Texas

190

were centers of rich and influential modes of creation. In addition, our under
standing of the influences of gospel music on black harmonies should be supple
mented by the vocal stylings of groups like the Ink Spots and the Delta Rhythm
Boys, who gave a unique coloration to the mainstream repertoire. Likewise, our
comprehension of gender and its role in black popular music has been narrow
The post-War period boasts an ample body of successful women performers, bu
where are the studies of Dinah Washington, Esther Phillips, and Ella Johnson
Some women have been used as negative examples—such as the frequent slam
of the classical boogie stylings of Hazel Scott and Hadda Brooks—but no on
seems to attend to what these women actually played or why it was so popular

As these brief examples indicate, the field is wide open. I hope this sudden
proliferation of studies augers an even more bountiful set of works to come
rather than another cessation of interest in the rich tradition of African-Ameri
can popular music. Our souls have much more to respond to, for this music
continues to speak to us in complex and often confounding ways.

WORKS CITED

- Bowman, Rob. 1997. *Soulsville U.S.A.: The Story of Stax Records*. New York: Schirmer Books.

- Broven, John. 1974. *Walking to New Orleans*. Bexhill-on-Sea, UK: Blues Unlimited.

- ———. 1983. *South to Louisiana: The Music of the Cajun Bayous*. Gretna, LA: Pelican.

- Cantor, Louis. 1992. *Wheelin' on Beale*. New York: Pharos Books.

- Early, Gerald. 1995. *One Nation Under a Groove: Motown and American Culture*. New York: Ecco Press.

- Fowler, Gene, and Bill Crawford. 1987. *Border Radio*. Austin: Texas Monthly Press.

- George, Nelson. 1984. *Where Did Our Love Go? The Rise and Fall of the Motown Sound*. New York: William Morrow.

- ———. 1988. *The Death of Rhythm and Blues*. New York: Pantheon.

- Gillett, Charlie. 1974. *Making Tracks: Atlantic Records and the Growth of a Multi-Billion Dollar Industry*. New York: Dutton.

- ———. 1992. *The Sound of the City: The Rise of Rock and Roll*. New York: DaCapo Press.

191

Gilroy, Paul. 1997. "'After the Love Has Gone': Bio-Politics and Ethno-Poetics in the Black Public Sphere," in *Back to Reality? Social Experience and Cultural Politics*, edited by Angela McRobbie, 83–115. Manchester, UK: Manchester University Press.

Gordon, Robert. 1995. *It Came from Memphis.* Boston: Faber & Faber.

Gordy, Berry. 1994. *To Be Loved: The Music, the Magic, and the Memories of Motown—An Autobiography.* New York: Warner Books.

Guralnick, Peter. 1986. *Sweet Soul Music: Rhythm and Blues and the Southern Dream of Freedom.* New York: Harper & Row.

Hoskyns, Barney. 1997. *Say It One Time for the Brokenhearted: Country Soul in the American South.* London: Bloomsbury.

Jenkins, Keith. 1991. *Rethinking History.* New York: Routledge.

Jones, LeRoi. 1963. *Blues People: Negro Music in White America.* New York: William Morrow.

Marsh, Dave. 1989. *The Heart of Rock and Soul. The 1001 Greatest Singles Ever Made.* New York: Plume.

Murray, Albert. 1976. *Stomping the Blues.* New York: McGraw Hill.

Passman, Arnold. 1971. *The Deejays.* New York: Macmillan.

Pruter, Robert. 1991. *Chicago Soul.* Urbana: University of Illinois Press.

———. 1998. *Chicago Doo Wop.* Urbana: University of Illinois Press.

Sanjek, David. 1997. "One Size Does Not Fit All: The Precarious Position of the African American Entrepreneur in the Post WWII American Music Industry." *American Music* 15(Winter): 55–74.

Shaw, Arnold. 1978. *Honkers and Shouters: The Golden Years of Rhythm and Blues.* New York: Collier Books.

Tate, Greg. 1992. *Flyboy in the Buttermilk: Essays on Contemporary America.* New York: Simon & Schuster.

Vincent, Rickey. 1996. *Funk: The Music, the People, and the Rhythm of the One.* New York: St. Martin's.

Watkins, Mel. 1994. *On the Real Side: Laughing, Lying, and Signifying.* New York: Simon & Schuster.

END NOTES

1. I engaged the subject of the African-American entrepreneur in the music industry during the second half of the century in "One Size Does Not Fit All"

192

(Sanjek, 1997). There I wrote:

> [M]y principal goal in this essay is to address a specific and
> underreported portion of the broad spectrum of the American music
> industry, the African American entrepreneurs and their activities in
> the post-WWII era. Too often, and yet with a great deal of empirical
> credence, the dominant narrative of the history of American popular
> music depicts a racially charged terrain wherein virtually all power
> lies in the hands of white businessmen who prey upon and gain their
> prosperity at the expense of African Americans. The attendant dis-
> course of scale routinely places African Americans, and other mi-
> norities, in the subordinate position, ill-equipped even to conceive of
> themselves as eventually rising to the status of a "David" and there-
> fore forever trapped as yet another victim of a corporate "Goliath."

2. A consummate iconoclast, Phillips was an acoustic anomaly, not only for th
   kind of music he played (a rich brew of rural blues and raucous rock an
   roll) but for way he twisted and reconfigured language. The commercial
   available CD of Phillips's broadcasts remains an ear-opening experience, fc
   time has not erased their out and out weirdness.

[24]

Prince as Queer Poststructuralist

Robert Walser

"I'm not a woman. I'm not a man. I am something that you'll never understand." So sings Prince.[1] But why? What pleasures are made possible by his particular version of androgyny?

"In order to resist organ-machines, the body without organs presents its smooth, slippery, opaque, taut surface as a barrier.... In order to resist using words composed of articulated phonetic units, it utters only gasps and cries that are sheer unarticulated blocks of sound" (Deleuze and Guattari 9). So say Deleuze and Guattari. But why? What pleasures are made possible by their particular version of—philosophy?

I want to assert that these sets of statements and questions are not only relatable but already related. I should admit at the outset that I write as one who has in the past regarded the "materialist psychiatry" of Deleuze and Guattari as difficult and irrelevant at best, simply difficult and annoying most of the time. Yet I have lately found their work, especially their book *Anti-Oedipus*, useful in helping me to understand certain aspects of Prince's music-making and the world in which the cultural work Prince does is possible and successful. I am not arguing that Prince and Deleuze would recognize each other's projects as similar (although they might). Still, it is not accidental, I think, that they deploy precisely the same language of desire: flows, melting, delirium, machines—terms which inhabit the central critical vocabulary of *Anti-Oedipus* and recur in Prince's lyrics throughout his career. I will argue that these bodies of work deal with comparable concerns, however vastly different their institutional, biographical, and discursive locations. My main point is that they can "interilluminate" each other, to use Bakhtin's term.

To begin with, let me point out that Prince's only successful movie, *Purple Rain*, was clearly a story about one kind of de-Oedipalization, the struggle over the social reproduction of patriarchy (although no other

80 Popular Music and Society

critic, to my knowledge, has commented on this). Quasi-autobiographical, the film chronicles the rise to stardom of "The Kid," whos relationships with his father and with several women—his mother, hi new girlfriend Apollonia, his bandmates Wendy and Lisa—propel th narrative. The most dramatic moments of the film are scenes of c abuse: first we see the Kid's father committing it, and soon after, the Ki himself manifests the same sort of violent behavior. The horror the Ki feels upon realizing that he is reproducing his father's abuse of leads to anguished visions of following his father's footsteps all the way to suicide. The movie is built around the Kid's crucial struggle with the violent impulses he has long hated in his father, but which he comes tc realize are inside him as well: the Kid's deepest fear is that he wil become a patriarch. The movie's narrative closure depends upon the Kic confronting his own patriarchal tendencies and resolving them through collaboration with the female members of his band. This final cooperative effort produces the song "Purple Rain" and saves the Kid's career.

In a different sort of collaborative effort, a paper delivered in 1989 which remains unpublished, Susan McClary and I argued that through his visual and verbal imagery, as well as in his music itself, Prince regularly challenges dominant patriarchal models by producing new ways of experiencing gender and eroticism.[2] We noted the controversies which periodically erupt around Prince, especially the actual censorship of the *Lovesexy* album cover, and adduced that Prince is perceived as threatening not because he is sexually explicit, but because his work often stands in stark contrast to conventional representations of "the masculine" and "the feminine" (see Fig. 1). In songs such as "Kiss," "If I Was Your Girlfriend," Little Red Corvette," and "When Doves Cry," modes of eroticism that are usually associated with women are celebrated and even envied, rather than controlled and trivialized, which are more common impulses in popular as well as classical music. In songs like "Strange Relationship," Prince reflects on the contradictions built into dominant narratives about gender and erotic relationships. In what we saw as more problematic songs, such as "U Got the Look" and "Darling Nikki," Prince sometimes resisted, sometimes succumbed to patriarchal structures of pleasure.

What interests me now is the possibility of developing a more complex and adequate description of Prince's politics of pleasure by juxtaposing with it some recent theoretical work. I will begin with Fred

Prince as Queer Poststructuralist 81

Fig. 1.

Pfeil's intriguing characterization of postmodernism as, in Raymond Williams's phrase, a "structure of feeling," rather than either a progressive artistic movement or a reactionary one. Pfeil attempts to account for the pleasures enabled by a fairly narrow group of post-modern artists, among whom he places centrally Laurie Anderson and the *Talking Heads*. He links this postmodernism to the historical experiences of its primary audience, which he asserts is made up of white, middle-class, college-educated managerial types, aged 18 to 40-

82 Popular Music and Society

something. These are the people, Pfeil says, who have lived through
histories such that this art makes sense of their experience. He ground
this distinctive experience largely in the post-War American family
arguing that this group of people experienced comparatively les
paternal authority and are less hailed (as Althusser uses the word) by it
He uses the term "de-Oedipalization" to refer to this experience of an
increasingly strong pre-Oedipal period and a subsequently lessened
loyalty to the rigid social codes associated with patriarchy. New
strategies result: "The alternatives, in short, are to disperse ourselves
across the codes or take enormous, well-nigh paranoid precautions
against them: Laurie Anderson invites us to 'Let X = X'; David Byrne
warns us to watch out for animals ('They're laughing at us') and 'Air' "
(Pfeil 385).

Pfeil's insistence that postmodernism is linked to the historical
experiences of particular audiences is important. Yet I agree with those
who might find his emphasis on the family too restricting, who would
point to other sorts of changes that are likewise driven primarily by the
dynamics of capitalism. Even if we are most interested in gender, even if
we are using Oedipalization as a trope for certain processes of social
formation and regulation, we must be willing to look beyond the family.
Indeed, I take one of the main arguments of Judith Butler's *Gender
Trouble* to be that a genealogical critique of identity categories requires
understanding them as effects "of institutions, practices, and discourses
with multiple and diffuse points of origin" (ix). Thus, while I respect the
specificity of Pfeil's argument, I would like to see his idea of postmodernism as a structure of feeling, largely grounded in experiences of
de-Oedipalization, extended to other audiences and discourses.

For a host of factors, from feminist activism and criticism to the Viet
Nam War, have helped to foreground the constructedness and contra-
dictoriness of gender identities and relations in the past two decades.
Indeed, popular musicians often present ingenious and public
negotiations of identity in the course of their work as rhetoricians of
desire. Since issues of gender and sexuality are central to Prince's work,
and since we know that his music and images have been found
extremely attractive or repellent by millions of people, we might find in
these texts and responses evidence for a more broadly based structure of
feeling similar to the one described by Pfeil—similarly postmodern, with
similar potential for de-Oedipalized performances.

Prince as Queer Poststructuralist 83

This brings us back to the "body without organs." Gilles Deleuze nd Félix Guattari have emerged as preeminent theorists of how apitalism structures desire, unhinging it from previous formations and earticulating it ever more efficiently. They argue that desire is not the esult of a lack of something, but that it is itself productive, and thus it must be coded and territorialized "by society," or, as I would prefer to say, "within societies." Deleuze and Guattari have been criticized, properly I would say, for using an essentialist concept of desire, which or them exists prior to all representation, outside of all codes.[3] This is eminiscent of the way that many people think about music, which does not exist outside codes, but which certainly *feels* like it does, perhaps more than anything else. An essentialist concept of desire enables Deleuze and Guattari to valorize the liberation of desire from its social restrictions and channelings while avoiding certain aspects of the question of how societies create the contexts within which desires become possible and compelling (just as Romantic and Modernist artists appeared to struggle to escape the very social "context" that allowed their work to be imaginable and meaningful).

What I find useful in the work of Deleuze and Guattari is their insistence on the importance of the politics of pleasure. Social change, they argue, depends on changing desires as much or more than changing minds. This is what I see as the strength and the weakness of not only Deleuze and Guattari, but also Prince. All tend to eschew ideological battles, all seem to neglect the crucial work of building critical consciousness in favor of liberating the body. All participate in, but do not explicitly acknowledge or valorize, discursive struggle. Deleuze and Guattari appeal to the radical potential of what they call the "body without organs," a theorization apparently designed to avoid evoking the humanistic notion of the subject. The body without organs refers to the experience of schizophrenics who come to understand their bodies as undifferentiated masses, unarticulated by the social apparatus of differentiation. Thus the body without organs is the body that resists hegemonic coding, the body that is detached and able to be transformed. This schizophrenic refusal of social schemes of differentiation is not purely a utopian possibility, they admit, since real schizophrenics are not ideal models in every respect; yet it remains for them the best hope for working through to other modes of desire and relation.

84　Popular Music and Society

If Deleuze and Guattari are difficult to understand, it is partiall; because the resources they choose to deploy towards their reformulatio of desire are drawn from psychiatry. Prince, on the other hand, is ofter all too clear, because he typically uses signs and constructions that coded as "feminine" as resources for recoding masculinity and sexuality This kind of move in the politics of culture can be regarded problematic. For example, the culmination of Theresa de Lauretis' essay "The Technology of Gender" is a critique of what she sees as the philosophical upward trivialization of women. Deleuze, Derrida, Lyotard, and Foucault are criticized in these terms: "only by denying sexual difference (and gender) as components of subjectivity in real women, and hence by denying the history of women's political oppression and resistance, as well as the epistemological contribution of feminism to the redefinition of subjectivity and sociality, can the philosophers see in 'women' the privileged repository of 'the future of mankind' " (de Lauretis 24).

It is true that deconstructing gender boundaries and liberating desire do not automatically lead to better lives for real men and women. Michael Jackson is the perfect example of this: though he himself has seemingly slipped the moorings of sexual (and racial) identity, his songs and videos are filled with misogyny, gynophobia, and rape fantasies.[4] But Prince, unlike the philosophers mentioned above, is often very interested in addressing women, and he doesn't so much use "woman" as a trope as perform through his music and his body a whole range of possible fusions and transformations of conventional gendered signs. His recodings of desire thus fall within the boundaries of "queer" performance.[5] His dissatisfaction with an economy of desire regulated by the assumptions of patriarchy and homophobia is evident in the possibilities he explores, the desires he arouses, and the anxieties he inflames. In his music, the makeup of his band, and his presentations of himself, Prince blurs the binary distinctions that are central to the social organization of concepts of race and sexual orientation, and in many of his songs he has constructed fantastic spaces—sometimes labeled "Uptown" or "Paisley Park"—from which such categories and the intolerance that sustains them are banished.

Prince seems less interested in reifying women—positively or negatively—than in disarticulating the gendered signs that bind desire in patriarchal—not just gendered—channels. He invites men to imagine

Prince as Queer Poststructuralist 85

ifferent modes of eroticism and relations, and invites women to nagine men who could imagine such things. Most important, though, e invites everyone to be interpellated into structures of desire that are ot territorialized by rigid patriarchal distinctions. Like Deleuze and juattari, he is after a sort of body without organs that can escape)edipal structures. He is much more intelligible than they because he is ble to enact recodings of desire through music and images rather than aving to critique them through language.

I want to turn now to the example of two videos, the first made by 'rince to accompany his song "Kiss," the second a remake of the same ong by Art of Noise featuring Tom Jones. I want to compare them as a le-Oedipalizing, de-territorializing statement by Prince, and a re-erritorializing recoupment by Jones. This is not to suggest that the Jones video *had* to happen; indeed, it is a pretty unlikely document. But the lialogue suggested by the videos reveals some of the stakes at risk on he field of struggle we call "popular culture."⁶

On MTV, Prince's video was sometimes introduced by a brief clip from one of his rare interviews. "The music we make is an alternative," he tells us coyly. "And if someone wants to go along for that ride—then: cool." For Prince, "Kiss" is yet another articulation of desire that appears to transcend social categories, including gender and perhaps even sex, in the tradition of "When Doves Cry" and "If I Was Your Girlfriend." For Tom Jones, the song is yet another articulation of male lust, in the tradition of—well, lots of culture. The visual differences are startling: Prince's lithe, flighty body is replaced by Jones's centered posturing. Prince uses the sort of mirrored doubling and vaginal imagery one often sees in recent women's art; Jones keeps his feet planted, cocks his hat and smirks. Prince dances through a space of free play, interacting differently with two women. Jones operates in a fantastic context inhabited by no one but himself; no women are present, just their signs—high heels, lips, lipsticks, the bottom halves of Playboy bunnies, headless women astride bucking horses. In Prince's video, he and a female dancer both wear high heels and move in ways that blur the sorts of fixed images of gender Jones reinscribes. Jones is supported by an array of phallic symbols which assist his stabilization of gender— lipsticks (again), scissors, trumpets, and least subtle of all, screws, shown actually screwing. There is only one typical phallic sign in Prince's version, the guitar being played by Wendy, and even that is the

86 Popular Music and Society

least phallic of all possible electric guitars, a hollow-body that look
more like an acoustic guitar than the flashy electrics played by most roc
and funk musicians.

Tom Jones changes a few words for his version: where Prince
warned that "women, not girls," rule his world, Jones says "women an
girls," transforming Prince's preference for maturity into a boast o
indiscriminate lust. But the most striking difference between the tw
performances is their voices. Prince uses an androgynous falsetto
trembling with desire and vulnerability. Jones recasts the song in
manly voice of the aging hipster, centered and posturing, just like
dancing. Only twice in his version does Prince use a conventionally male
vocal sound, for an interpellated "yeah" that is visually attributed to the
female dancer. Prince looks askance at this, acknowledging the gender
anxieties he is arousing (rather like Aerosmith later did, in their song
"Dude Looks Like a Lady'"). For Tom Jones, there are no anxieties,
because he is performing a version of masculinity that requires, and
works towards, secure sexual dominance. Prince, on the other hand, even
appears to lose control of his voice at the end, as he breaks into screams.
As in songs like "International Lover," "Darling Nikki," "The Beautiful
Ones," and "Delirious," he enacts his own loss of control, the dissolution
of his centered subjectivity in the face of desire.

Other aspects of Prince's music serve to flesh out the mode of desire
articulated by "Kiss." The song is grounded on a 12-bar blues progression, yet Prince slows down the rate of harmonic change by half
relative to the rhythmic structure, producing a kind of suspended
animation akin to an erotic trance. Long-term coherence is guaranteed
by the blues progression, yet awareness is suspended in a present non-
teleological moment. In the foreground, complementing his quivering
voice, Prince places teasing guitar licks that emphasize what I call the
"funk tritone," the minor third and the major sixth. He thus creates what
Deleuze and Guattari call a "plateau," a term they derive from Gregory
Bateson's comments on the libidinal economy of Bali. As Brian
Massumi summarizes this notion, a plateau is "a pitch of intensity that is
not automatically dissipated in a climax leading to a state of rest. The
heightening of energies is sustained long enough to leave a kind of
afterimage of its dynamism that can be reactivated or injected into other
activities, creating a fabric of intensive states between which any
number of connecting routes could exist."[8]

Prince as Queer Poststructuralist   87

To debate whether such a politics of desire is as important as theoretical deconstructions of gendered ideologies or representations is ultimately as futile as debating whether or not postmodernism is a good thing. There are many modes and arenas of intervention, and Prince's great strength is that he is an imaginative and consummately skilled decoder and recoder of desire. If he seems to lack the social relevance of self-consciously "political" artists, it is because he is a rhetorician who deals with aspects of social intercourse that seem—perhaps *must* seem—most private and natural. To engage, disrupt, and rearticulate these affective investments can be as consequential as any more overt struggle over signification or ideology. As evidence for this assertion I would point not only to de-Oedipalization and other changes in the realm of gender, sexuality, and the family, but also to phenomena such as what Cornel West has called the "African-Americanization" of white youth, which, I would argue, has proceeded along similar lines—through style, dance, and recodings of desire (84).

Prince continues to work at evading territorialization. From "I Would Die 4 U" to "Sign '⊕' the Times," Prince has played with various signs and their potential to signify outside of language. One album was not even given a title in words; it is designated by a symbol. But in June of 1993 he went further by announcing that he had legally changed his name to that symbol (see Fig. 2). A combination of male and female gender signs that retains the morphology of the female sign, this device has been used ornamentally or emblematically by Prince for some time. Yet to claim it as his name presents problems. When I asked his press agent how to pronounce it, she replied, "There is no pronunciation. You have to explain it or figure something out."[9] Just as Deleuze and Guattari claim that the body without organs resists "using words composed of articulated phonetic units," Prince's name foils the pretentions of language to universality. He is not erasing difference, but rather merging signs to figure a space that is not yet territorialized.

One might argue that if Deleuze and Guattari are the theory, Prince is the practice. Yet we might also see things the other way around, if we believe that intellectual work has "practical" consequences, and if we recognize that Prince is a fully articulate theorist of gender and desire who works primarily in discourses other than language. What is certain is that both bodies of work dance around rationality, teasing it, reminding it that it is not master of all it surveys. While I retain

88 Popular Music and Society

Fig. 2.

reservations about the theorization of desire presented in *Anti-Oedipus*, Prince has helped me to understand its value. In fact, I can almost imagine Deleuze and Guattari saying: "The philosophy we produce is an alternative. And if someone wants to go along for that ride—then: cool."

Notes

[1]Prince, "I Would Die for U," *Purple Rain* (Warner Brothers, 1984). A version of this paper was presented as "Sex and the De-Oedipalized Guitar Player" at the Feminist Theory and Music II conference at the Eastman School of Music, 17-20 June 1993.

[2]Robert Walser and Susan McClary, "Prince and His Revolution: Liberatory Models of Gender and Eroticism in Music," International Association for the Study of Popular Music, International Conference at the Centre d'ethnologie française, Musée des arts et traditions populaires, Paris,

Prince as Queer Poststructuralist 89

rance, 17-20 July 1989. I am drawing on some of the arguments and analysis resented in that paper, and I thank Susan for graciously permitting this.

[3]See, for example, Steven Best and Douglas Kellner, *Postmodern Theory: Critical Interrogations* (New York: Guilford, 1991) 76-110.

[4]See, for example, the videos for "The Way You Make Me Feel," Thriller," and "Dirty Diana."

[5]For a lucid and insightful introduction to issues of queer theory and community, see Lisa Duggan, "Making It Perfectly Queer," *Socialist Review* 2.1 (Jan.-Mar. 1992): 11-31.

[6]See Stuart Hall, "Notes On Deconstructing 'The Popular,'" in *People's History and Socialist Theory*, ed. Raphael Samuel (London: Routledge and Kegan Paul, 1981) 227-40.

[7]For a discussion of gender representations in heavy metal, see chapter four of my *Running with the Devil: Power, Gender, and Madness in Heavy Metal Music* (Hanover, NH: Weslyan/University Press of New England, 1993).

[8]Brian Massumi, *A User's Guide to* Capitalism and Schizophrenia Cambridge, MA: MIT, 1992) 7. See also Gilles Deleuze and Felix Guattari, *A Thousand Plateaus: Capitalism and Schizophrenia* (Minneapolis: U of Minnesota P, 1987).

[9]Phone conversation with a contact person in the office of Prince's press agent, 16 June 1993. The name change was announced on 7 June, Prince's birthday.

Works Cited

Butler, Judith. *Gender Trouble: Feminism and the Subversion of Identity*. New York: Routledge, 1990. ix.

de Lauretis, Teresa. *Technologies of Gender: Essays on Theory, Film, and Fiction.* Bloomington: Indiana UP, 1987. 24.

Deleuze, Gilles, and Félix Guattari. *Anti-Oedipus: Capitalism and Schizophrenia.* Minneapolis: U of Minnesota P, 1983. 9.

Pfeil, Fred. "Postmodernism as a 'Structure of Feeling.'" *Marxism and the Interpretation of Culture*. Ed. Cary Nelson and Lawrence Grossberg. Urbana: U of Illinois P, 1988. 381-403.

West, Cornel. *Race Matters*. Boston: Beacon, 1993. 84.

Robert Walser, Assistant Professor of Musicology, UCLA.